# The Sword of

# Scandinavia

**Ronald L Tarnstrom**

*Trogen Books*

Published by Trogen Books
Lindsborg, Kansas U.S.A.

Printed in the United States of America by
Bookmasters, Inc., Mansfield, Ohio

Library of Congress Catalog Number 94-090244

ISBN 0-922037-13-2

# CONTENTS

# PREFACE

As the Scandinavian nations have only reluctantly participated in modern wars, most current studies have neglected their armed forces. Yet not only did troops from all Scandinavian countries participate in the Second World War, in previous centuries they were the most feared fighters in Europe. Sweden, because of her size and bountiful natural resources, has always been the dominant realm. Her Vikings are less well-known than their western brethren, for they chose to invade the great river systems of Russia. Slow to organize as a nation due to civil war between their two major factions, the Swedes began to dominate the Baltic once they had that settled. However, a fondness for war by some of their kings, and a terrible protracted struggle with their perennial foes, the Russians, left the Swedes weary of war. Their isolated position on the frigid flank of Europe permitted their subsequent practical abdication from European affairs. The advent of a world-viewing German dictator in the mid-20th Century convinced them of their error. They spent the war desperately building their armed forces with every available weapon and successfully countering every German attempt to create a Swedish satellite by increasing their forces sufficiently to convince Germany that an invasion was not worthwhile. Having learned her lesson, during the postwar East-West confrontation, Sweden has maintained strong armed forces employing some of the most advanced weapons in the world. Although continuing her neutral stance, Sweden is clearly in the Western camp.

Denmark was the chief rival to Swedish ambitions. Early absorbtion of the advanced cultures discovered by her Vikings during their raids on western Europe permitted assumption of Nordic leadership by the denizens of Copenhagen. She maintained her stranglehold on the entrance to the Baltic, often cooperating with the Russians and West Europeans in foiling Swedish designs on the all-important straits. British fleets finally broke Danish power early in the 19th Century. The German Confederation reduced her to a minor European power during the struggle for the basal penisular provinces of Schleswig and Holstein at mid-century. With resources too small to create effective defenses, the Danes elected to rely upon the good will of her neighbors and retain but minimum forces. Her suffering at the hands of her neighbor during the Second World War led Denmark to join NATO postwar.

As a nation deprived of natural resources, Norway has had great difficulty in establishing and maintaining a national identity. At first under the sway of Denmark, then Sweden, she realized the futility of creating armed forces sufficient to defend her long coastline. However, vacillation in the face of invasion left her valiant troops exposed to suffering at the hands of the well-equipped Nazi armed forces. Norwegian soldiers, sailors and airmen fought throughout the length of the country but, despite Western aid, fell to the invader. Close association with the Western powers during the war led to Norway joining NATO postwar in cooperative defense.

Conventionally, Finland is not considered a part of Scandinavia. The Finns spring from a different racial stock who to this day esteem tribal over national identification. Nevertheless, their geographic position, sandwiched between the Teutons and Slavs, involved them in Scandinavian affairs from early times. Swedish Vikings settled the shores of the Gulf of Finland and pushed inland. The two races developed a close affinity. However, the less organized Finns remained subjugated by their neighbors. Large numbers of them were organized into homogeneous regiments in the Swedish Army and participated in the Thirty Years War. The disastrous outcome of the military adventures of Swedish King Charles XII initiated Russian encroachment that resulted in the reduction of Finland to a Russian province early in the 19th Century. Independence was regained a century later, but after only twenty years was again threatened by the European crisis. Defiantly, the Finns fought, and surprisingly prevailed against the Russian juggernaut for a time. The far-sightedness of Field Marshal Mannerheim restrained Finnish operations when the war resumed. Finnish troops never advanced into indisputable Soviet territory. The lack of support by Sweden left Finns with much resentment towards their former friends. They were also prohibited by the Soviet Union from joining any Western alliances following the war.

Even Iceland has experienced some conflict. Largely left alone after Viking times, her position astride weather approaches to Europe assumed importance in the new air age. Iceland's importance was augmented by her position along the convoy routes to the White Sea. She suffered through the benevolent occupation by Allied forces during the war. Three decades later, she got into a shoving match with Great Britain over fishing rights.

## ACKNOWLEDGMENTS

In preparing this book, a great deal of assistance was received from several individuals. The tangled organization and armament of the Swedish tank forces was sorted out by members of the Svensk PansarHistorisk Forening. Captain Per-Ake Kronbladh patiently answered numerous questions about weapons while Colonel Hans Nilsson, retired commander of the Swedish armored division, supplied much information about organizational development. Lennart Andersson provided much information about the Swedish Air Force even before he published his excellent books on the subject. Similar help with the Finnish air forces was given by Martti Kuivalainen, while the folks at the Panssarimuseo assisted in detailing the Finnish tank forces. Knut Erik Hagen overwhelmed us with a flood of information about the Norwegian armed forces. From the Flyvevabnets Historiske Samling came information and photographs of Danish aircraft. Detailed ship lists of the Swedish Navy were provided by Lars Ericson at the Krigsarkivet and of the Danish Navy by the Orlogsmuseet.

The color plates were created by Michael Swanson, who also provided much technical assistance. Cover art was developed by Jay Richardson.

*To My Parents*

*Kenneth and Viola Tarnstrom*


*who early instilled in me*

*a sense of history*

*They dwell in a hidden land,*

*the retreat of wolves,*

*wind-swept headlands,*

*terrible fen-defiles,*

*where the mountain-stream rushes down*

*under the mists of the headlands,*

*a flood under the earth.*

**Beowulf of the Geats**

# ᴄhule

Small bands of humans, venturing northward through western Europe for the first time around 10,000 B.C., encountered cold and wet weather as they pursued herds of animals through the forests. As they pushed on against biting cold winds, vegetation grew denser, and streams more common. Something strange loomed ahead. A huge mass of glimmering ice covered the whole earth, groaning and snapping as if alive. They had reached the end of their world.

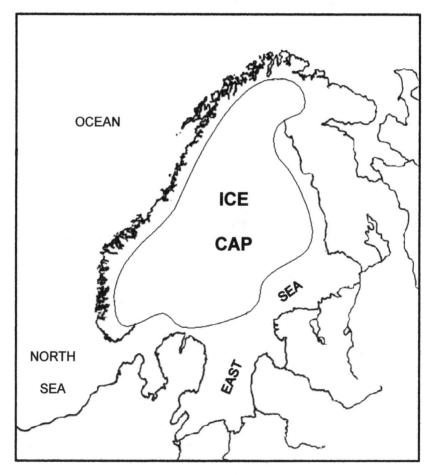

Scandinavia in 10,000 B.C.

1

Apparently caused by snowfall too abundant to melt during the brief northern summers, the huge glacier had slowly grown to cover all of present day Scandinavia, and parts of the British Isles. Yet, humans found good hunting along the margins of the glacier. Reindeer, their principal source of food, hides and bone tools, were easily trapped against the towering tongues of ice. Lush vegetation, well nourished by glacial melt water, provided nuts and berries during the summer hunting season. Utilizing crude tools fashioned from stones, they processed the meat and hides thus acquired, and provided rudimentary shelter for their families as they moved from place to place according to the season and food supply. Those who stayed on through the harsh winters sheltered in caves, but many of the nomads went south during the cold months. As the climate fluctuated, large migrations took place. Some tribes moved as far south as the Mediterranean, then returned to the north when the climate improved. Tribes that remained in the north could do little more than subsist from year to year, but waves of new peoples from Africa periodically brought cultural advances with them. Tools and hunting techniques improved. Yet, no permanent settlements appeared.[1]

Around 7000 B.C., the climate moderated and the ice cap melted away. The humans that moved back to the shores of the northern seas were a race of tall, fair, blue-eyed people that came to be known as Teutons. From the center of Teutonic tribal activity, at the base of the Cimbric Peninsula and on the neighboring islands, their culture spread into the southern part of the Scandinavian peninsula and along its western coast, where the climate was moderated by the Gulf Stream. That remarkable ocean current warmed even the North Cape area sufficiently to allow humans to hunt there after traversing the Arctic coast from the White Sea.

Men along the Tigris and Euphrates Rivers of Mesopotamia learned to cultivate cereals and domesticate animals around 5000 B.C.. This new agricultural way of life required permanent settlements, creating the Sumerian civilization. A millennium later, the first European community appeared near the modern Greek city of Volos. The new practice spread slowly across Europe, through the valley of the Danube, and along the north coast of the Mediterranean Sea. By 3000 B.C., the farming culture reached Scandinavia, men burning clearings into the forests to plant crops, then moving on in a few years when the soil became depleted. Liberated from the need to remain near the sea to fish, Teutons built their communities inland, where they were more secure from piratical incursions by sea rovers. The stability conferred by the development of agriculture allowed some workers to specialize in tasks other than food gathering. Quarries in southern Skåne and northern Jutland yielded flint. From it, tools and weapons were manufactured on Sjaelland (Zealand). These flints came into much demand throughout northern Europe. From 2500 B.C., Teutons from the mouth of the Elbe River settled in the southern parts of the Scandinavian peninsula and along the south coast of the East Sea. Then they pushed southward up the German rivers, building communities on the divides and intermingling with the Danubian civilization in the loess-filled valleys to produce the tribes of Central Europe.[2]

The climate of northern Europe approached the warmth of the Mediterranean littoral about 2000 B.C. Scandinavians were able to wear knee-length sleeveless coats, round leather caps, and leather sandals in imitation of their more southerly brethren. Nomadic warriors from central Asia encroached on northern Europe about the same time, entering Teutonic territory from the south and southeast. Herdsmen, they introduced the breeding of draft horses. Having had contact with the advanced copper workers of southwestern Asia and the

Mycenaeans of Greece, they were accustomed to metal weapons. Copper deposits were unknown in Europe at this time, but the newcomers, called "Battleaxe people" from their distinctive weapon, were ignorant of flint-working. They soon employed the conquered Teutonic craftsmen in making flint weapons patterned after their original copper ones. Taking the production of the Teutonic quarries, they traded the popular flint to northern Scandinavians for furs. The furs, along with highly prized northern amber, were traded to the Mycenaeans for copper and other metals. However, copper was too soft for most practical uses until about 2000 B.C., when Mesopotamian smelters began hardening it with tin to produce an alloy, bronze. The new technique quickly spread to Europe, where manufacturing centers developed near tin deposits in Spain, Italy, Brittany and Cornwall.[3]

*The Bronze Age* - 1500-500 B.C.

The auspicious Bronze Age reached Scandinavia about 1500 B.C., persisting for a millennium. European bronze production became centered in Bohemia, where tin was mined to combine with Hungarian copper. However, the new metal was expensive, generally limiting its use in Scandinavia to weapons and ornaments for the wealthy, who began importing bronze bars and casting their own objects. The Scandinavian Bronze Age flourished around the Cimbric peninsula, which possessed abundant amber. The northern Teutons on the Scandinavian peninsula remained largely in the Stone Age, although those around Lake Mälaren prospered from trade through the German rivers to the south. The more settled life style led to social development as well. Neighborhood communities, called *bygd*s, were formed. The power of their chieftains increased, especially around Lake Mälaren and along the Ocean coast.

Europe now possessed a network of trade routes, which did much to unify its culture. Northern Teutons, the Inguaeones, had long plied the nurturing inland waterways and coastal waters, using dugout tree trunks and animal hides stretched over rough frameworks. Daring seafarers from the Mediterranean reached the Cimbric peninsula midway through the 6th Century. These advanced Carthaginians astounded the backward Inguaeones with their beaked galleys, which the northerners soon emulated to cross the North Sea to Britain.

**Inguaeone War Boat**
400 B.C., 20 men

Utilizing their curved ends to beach the boats nightly, merchants greatly increased trading activities. Some crews also engaged in various nefarious expeditions. Although without sail power, the new vessels established nautical capabilities that would explode into violent piratical forays a millennium later. However, the increased commercial intercourse also brought into conflict the four main related European tribes - Teutons of North Europe, the Dorians invading Greece, Illyrians in northern Italy, and the Celts of Central Europe. The Teutons occupied the basin of the Elbe River, together with the adjacent coasts of the North and East Seas. Some lived on the Cimbric peninsula and the nearby islands. They were surrounded on the continent by Celtic tribes. The two peoples often intermarried, to produce tribes like the Belgae. Around 500 B.C., a particularly bitter winter was followed by a cold summer which melted

3

little of the heavy snow that had accumulated on upland plateaus of Scandinavia. The following years were even worse, causing glaciers to form. Was a new ice age beginning? Living conditions deteriorated, the northern regions becoming uninhabitable. Even around the seas, livestock had to be sheltered and grain required indoor threshing. Celts and Teutons exchanged their warm-weather attire for long trousers. The easy living of the Bronze Age was over.[4]

## The Iron Age - 500 B.C.-800 A.D.

Succor again came from Sumer. Rusty nodules had been found to produce a hard gray metal when melted with limestone to remove impurities. The Hittites of Asia Minor capitalized on the new discovery around 1275 B.C., building numerous foundries that produced weapons superior to those of their rivals. Southern Europe had learned the technique by 900 B.C. The Celts adopted North Italian helmets, iron weapons and chariots, then began expanding from their base on the upper Danube. Throughout the 4th-3rd Centuries B.C., they moved both east and west, overrunning Gaul, Spain and Italy, then crossing Macedonia into Asia Minor. Light two-wheeled chariots, copied from the Etruscans, gave them a mobility in battle they had lacked with their former heavy four-wheeled cargo vehicles. Their attacks were preceded by showers of javelins and arrows. The foot soldiers then advanced with long swords, accompanied by cavalry and chariot charges. These advanced tactics, later adopted by the Romans, gave them command of Central Europe, cutting off the Teutons from the Mediterranean.

The northerners now had to deal with Celtic middlemen, greatly increasing prices and impoverishing the tribes. Yet, the Celts never reached Scandinavia. By the 2nd Century B.C., the Teutons were already beginning to push them westward. Iron made the difference. It was found all over Europe, particularly in the cold peat bogs of the north. Individual farmers could smelt their own, using charcoal made from the nearby forests. Even in Finnmark, iron tools finally displaced stone. As the poor could afford iron, the class structure of Teutonic society changed, the powerful rural landholders being replaced by villagers. The first *runes* were scratched onto magical stones. Soon they would develop into a written language.

The Cimbrians left their namesake peninsula during the 2nd Century B.C. and wandered along the Danube for years, clashing with the Celts living on both banks of the river. Led by Boiorix, they traversed Gaul, but were thrown back by the Belgae in 103 B.C. Crossing the Alps, they penetrated as far south as the Po River before a Roman army annihilated them near Vercellae in 101 B.C., killing King Boiorix and ending the first Barbarian invasion of Italy.

A century later, at the beginning of the Christian Era, a Roman fleet reconnoitered the peninsula now designated Jutland in recognition of the Jutes, who had acquired the former Cimbrian hegemony. Advancing into the valley of the Danube, and conquering Gaul during the 1st Century B.C., the Romans broke Celtic power. Teutonic tribes took the opportunity to expand southward. The Burgundians left their home island of Burgendaland (Bornholm) and occupied northern Germany between the Elbe and the Vistula. Lombards and Vandals moved farther inland, driving the Celtic Boii out of Bohemia. In western Europe, the Teutons (called Germani by the Romans) forced the Celtic Helvetii away from their Main River territories and back upon the Alps. The Romans established a defensive cordon of military camps on the Danube and the Rhine, delimiting the newly enlarged Teutonic territory.

The Rhine became the most important link with Rome, although Teutonic tribes pushed up the valleys of the Elbe, Oder and Vistula to reach the Roman roads carrying traders to the Mediterranean and Asia Minor. With the Celtic middlemen gone, merchandise resumed flowing to the north, down the Elbe to Jutland and along the Vistula to the East Sea. Scandinavians again grew wealthy, trading furs, skins, walrus ivory, food and slaves to the southern merchants for silks, spices, wines, weapons, ornaments and utensils.

By 100 A.D., the Suiones around Lake Mälaren had become the dominant northern tribe. Although many Goths remained in Götaland (around Lake Vättern to the south) and on the island of Gotland, much of this rival tribe had crossed to Pomerania. After a century of fighting through southeastern Europe, they spread as far as Scythia. While contemporary Scandinavians remained a loose confederation of independent tribes, the Suiones (their Roman name) became a disciplined society under the rule of chieftains with absolute power. Calling themselves the Svear, and their country Sverige, they possessed a strong fleet of boats with which they traded and raided around the East Sea. Their armed men, on land and sea, carried short swords and small round shields. Avoiding battle while raiding, the Vikings were fierce fighters when cornered. In battle, they formed a *svinfylking*, a wedge shaped formation with picked young warriors at the point. Few could stand against the fearsome charge of this assembly.[5]

With its success, the Roman Empire produced its own destruction. Rotted by prosperity, the disciplined state failed to maintain its military and political integrity. When Europe's Barbarians were uprooted by Asia's Huns in the middle of the 4th Century, Rome was unable to stop them from encroaching upon her territory. Attila's horsemen swept into Scythia, starting terrified Goths fleeing from the lower reaches of the Dneiper River. The Ostrogoths of Ermanaric, east of that major trade route, remained largely in place, submitting to subjugation. West of the river, the Visigoths streamed into central Europe to seek protection in Roman arms. Half a million people were on the move, swarming over the long frontiers of the Empire.

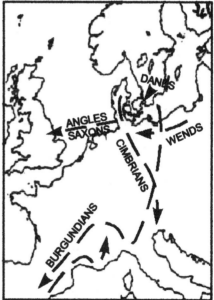

Burgundians and Vandals crossed the Alps in 405, but were driven back and passed through Gaul to Spain. After Alaric's Visigoths traversed the Adriatic coast to sack Rome in 410, they went on to drive the Vandals into North Africa. Gunnar the Burgundian retired with his people to the district of eastern Gaul that has borne their name ever since. Thus, Scandinavians took up residence far from their origins. The Vandals formed a civilization north of the Sahara Desert that completely altered the Mediterranean balance of power. Their ruthlessness lent their name to acts of wanton destruction ever since. On the other hand, the Burgundians established a cultured state at the foot of the Alps.

Known to the ancients as Thule, Scandinavia also felt the tumult of the Great Migrations. From Jutland, the Celtic Angles set out in their long boats along the coast of the North Sea and reached Britain in 450. They were followed by many Terutonic Jutes and Saxons. Pressured by the events in Asia, more Teutonic tribes crowded westward, causing constant turmoil. Scandinavian farmers were forced to abandon their ravaged farmsteads for fortified camps. Much conflict between the Svear and Goths caused families to move into the Lake Mjösa region and Ocean coast of the western peninsula. The Norse kept in touch with their Anglo-Saxon relatives in Angleland (England), developing a large maritime commerce as far south as the Flemish and French coasts. Others moved south. The Danes crossed to the islands at the mouth of the East Sea, driving the Herules out of Jutland.

However, Slavic tribes were also being displaced by the Hunnish incursion. The Wends moved west from Pomerania along the coast of the East Sea as the Angles and Saxons migrated to Britain. When they occupied the mouth of the Elbe, Scandinavia was cut off from the rest of the Teutons. This event insulated the northerners from most of the devastation occurring in Europe. The isolation allowed independent social and technical development that would soon make Scandinavians the scourge of Europe.

During the second millennium B.C., groups of Scandinavian families had banded together in *bygd*s to cooperate in hunting common territories bounded by natural features such as mountains, lakes or forests. To resolve conflicts between *bygd*s, a democratic meeting called a *thing* was organized.

They also began to support military districts, referred to as *herred*s, that protected groups of adjacent *bygd*s from pirates. The capacity of the individual peasants to smelt their own iron for hunting, building and defensive tools caused the *bygd*s to disintegrate during the Iron Age. The Great Migrations of the 5th Century renewed communal cooperation. Many strongholds were built throughout Scandinavia, to which the peasants could repair when danger threatened. The fortresses were supervised by *jarl*s, who were mainly landless aristocrats. Most of the land was owned, or worked, by free peasants called *karl*s, a term also used for craftsmen, peddlers and soldiers of varying financial status. Scandinavian industry also required the labor of slaves, known as *thrall*s.

Much of the goods plundered in Europe during the Barbarian migrations found its way to Scandinavia, enriching the ruling classes. The most distinguished *karl*s organized permanent military forces and had authority over specific territories. Great chieftains in western Norway derived their wealth from the large maritime trade that developed during the 5th-6th Centuries.

**Norse War Boat**
5-700 A.D., 20 men

The advent of the iron axe facilitated cutting ships timbers from the abundant forests. Norse boats had developed into light, yet strong, vessels suited to coastal navigation. Stem and stern were gracefully curved to elevated points above the clinker-built hull. Although most were still rowed, simple square sails on a single stubby mast had appeared by the 6th Century, permitting longer voyages and encouraging the crossing of open water..

With their many ships, the Norse traded furs and other products to the Frisians and Franks for glass objects, metals and cloth. There was also extensive trade with England. Ships followed the Frisian coast to the base of the Jutland peninsula, worked up river, and portaged to the first major port to develop in

6

the north - Hedeby. From there, they sailed north through the Danish straits to their destinations. The Norsemen adopted the short Saxon sword and heavy lance they saw in use by the Franks they encountered.

As aristocratic families outgrew their constituencies, the younger *jarls* began raising bands of *karls* for trading and raiding. Their enthusiastic reports led others on piratical expeditions to relieve the wealthy burghers of Denmark and the East Sea coast of their wares. Thus, the patterns that would result in the Viking Age were established.

There was a leadership role to settle on the eastern side of the peninsula. For many years, the Goths, and their cousins the Geats, had been fighting with the Svear for dominance in the lake region. In an effort to conquer their antagonists during the 6th Century, the Svear probed the forests of Götaland, but were surprised in camp by the Geats under King Hygelac. Driven back to their home in Uppland, with the body of slain King Ongentheow, the Svear rallied under King Athils and eventually prevailed. Hygelac was killed by the Franks in a battle of 520 A.D., and the Gothic kingdom disintegrated. The Svear extended their hegemony over all of Sweden north of Skåne by the 11th Century, also gaining much influence in eastern Norway. Driving back the Lapps, both the Norse and the Svear expanded northward to exploit the furs, timber, walrus ivory and iron found in abundance.

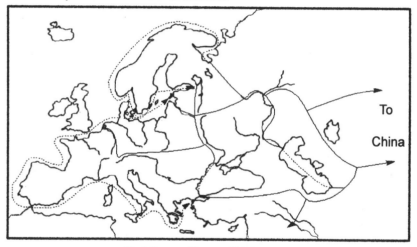

Trade Routes of Europe - 10th Cent. A.D.

By 750, the runic Norse tongue had become differentiated from the Germanic language and the Anglo-Saxon of England. The new division into Norse, Svear and Danish territories served to evolve separate languages for them by the time the second Christian millennium began. Old Norse has survived, virtually unchanged to the present day, only in Iceland. Thus, although the Scandinavian peoples were still quite similar, their paths began to diverge. The Danes consolidated their position at the convergence of the trade routes between western Europe and Russia. Norsemen began exploratory voyages to the Faroes and Iceland early in the 9th Century. The Svear and Gotlanders colonized the eastern shores of the East Sea during the 7th-8th Centuries, where they founded two trading centers. Grobin, in present-day Latvia, controlled the trade along the Vistula. At the mouth of the Oder River, Wollin became the largest town in Europe by 1000 A.D.[6]

7

# THE AGE OF THE VIKINGS

Commercial activity in Scandinavia continued unabated while the rest of Europe was being ravaged by migrating Barbarians. Hedeby, on Jutland, remained the major northern port, but other small trading towns developed, usually near a royal capital. Kaupang, on the wealthy west shore of the Vikin (later Oslofjord), exported valued soapstones to Hedeby, and acted as a transshipment point for northern vessels carrying furs, skins, walrus ivory and walrus ropes. Bergen and Trondheim also flourished near kingly thrones where the topography leveled sufficiently to produce rich agricultural land. However, none of the Norse villages grew into major mercantile centers like those near Uppsala, seat of the kings of the Svear, which became important to medieval trade.

**Viking Knorr**
**600-1100 A.D., 12 men**

Merchant vessels had now developed into full-fledged sailing ships. Clinker-built hulls were faired into sharp vertical cutwaters at stem and stern. The boats were usually rowed, but a small square sail was set on a short mast when sailing before the wind. The cargo was stored on the floorboards in the middle of the boat while a few rowing thwarts were provided at either end for the small crew. Several types of trading craft were used, but the *knorr* was common.

From the 5th Century, Helgö, on an island in Lake Mälaren, had enriched the royal treasuries, producing rope and bronze jewelry as well as collecting the raw materials of the north. Toward the end of the 8th Century, it was eclipsed by the nearby town of Birka, which developed trade throughout northern Europe, Russia and England. Craftsmen used local ore to manufacture iron implements, and produced ornaments from metal and glass imported from continental Europe. The main wealth of its 1000 inhabitants, however, came from the fur trade. Merchant ships arrived in summer to carry the winter's catch to Hedeby and to the Eastern Caliphate of the Arab Empire, passing through the Svear colonies on the eastern shore of the East Sea. [7]

Most of Europe was in chaos in the aftermath of the Great Migrations. Strong, organized military forces did not exist. Scandinavia had largely escaped the devastation. Indeed, Norse freebooters found rich pickings among the defenseless inhabitants of a Europe in the throes of the Dark Ages. When they returned with tales of wealth and adventure, a veritable explosion of activity resulted. Scandinavia had too many people on too little land. The disinherited younger sons of the landholders sought other gainful pursuits.

## Voyages of the Western Vikings

Early in the 9th Century, some Norsemen settled in the Shetland and Orkney Islands, north of Britain, and gradually encroached on the territory of the Picts and Scots from 835. The Hebrides Islands, off the west coast, became the base for Viking raids upon Ireland. They were called the *Sudreyjar* ("Southern Isles") by the Norsemen. Thorgils (Turgeis) led the first Viking intrusion into the interior of Ireland in 832. Although numerous, the Celtic inhabitants were no match for the well-armed and determined Norsemen. Brushing aside the uncoordinated defenders, Thorgils captured the principal strongholds, gaining hegemony over Ireland.

8

Meanwhile, a far greater threat appeared in the North Sea. Frisians, occupying the coast of the North Sea from the Rhine to the Weser, had long been the leading merchants and pirates of that stormy sea. By the 8th Century, they were conducting a brisk trade with Scandinavia from their port of Ribe on the west coast of Jutland. Charlemagne had subjugated the Frisians, and when he also defeated the Saxons and extended his realm to the Ejder River, the ruler of Denmark and southern Norway, King Godfred, became alarmed. He took a fleet of 200 longships south in 810, raiding the Frisian islands and the environs of the Zuider Zee. At the mouth of the Rhine, the Frisian capital, Dorestad, was sacked five times before it received protection.

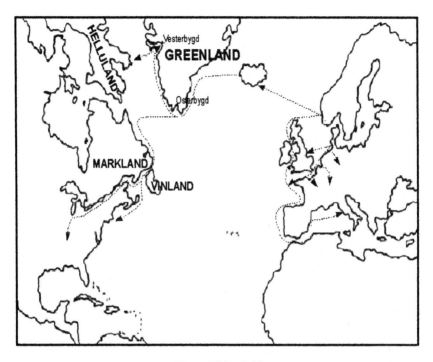

Western Vikings Raids

Charlemagne charged a vassal with the defense of Frisia. The Danish Viking chief Harald was established in a feudal fief on the island of Walcheren. Godfred countered by initiating the construction of the Danevirke, a giant dike across the Jutland peninsula just south of Hedeby. Danish Vikings appeared at Dorestad again in 820, but were beaten off. Apparently, they were the same raiders that attempted to sail up the Seine later that year, only to be repulsed. Yet, in 834, the Danes succeeded in sacking Dorestad, and raids on the Frankish empire began in earnest. Charlemagne had died in 814, and his sons spent more time fighting each other than fighting the Vikings. Rouen was burned in 841, as was Quentowic the following year. When longships pushed up the Seine again, opposition was light and Paris was sacked in 845. Charles the Bald bought them off with 3,000 kilograms of silver, the first of thirteen *Danegeld*s paid by the French over the next 80 years.

Meanwhile, the Norse Vikings had established themselves in Ireland and had also begun raiding France. However, while the Danes were busy plundering northern France, the Norsemen struck south of the Brittany peninsula, reaching Aquitaine in 799. Noirmoutier Island at the mouth of the Loire River was occupied in 835, and became a forward base for Norse depredations. They sailed up the Loire in 843 and attacked Nantes. Bordeaux was ravaged so severely by the Vikings that the once prosperous commercial center became nearly depopulated. The terrified Franks fled into the high country of the Haut-Limosin, Burgundy, the Ardennes and the Auvergne. Yet, the freebooters were not satisfied.

Moorish Spain was the richest kingdom of the time. With a nose for plunder, Vikings ventured to attack Seville in 844, captured it, and held it for a week before vengeful Moors savagely attacked them. They barely escaped, but the next year the chastened Moors sent an emissary to the Viking chieftains in an attempt to end the galling raids. The negotiations were futile, for the expeditions had merely whetted the Viking appetite for plunder.[8]

Viking operations were greatly facilitated by their famous longships, quite superior to contemporary vessels in hull and rudder design, keel strength, and sail size. The unique clinker construction made their hulls light for easy portage, yet strong and flexible to ride over the choppy waves encountered in the North Sea and Atlantic Ocean. They were capable of being rowed at 13 kilometers per hour. Early longships, of the 9th Century, had 15-20 pairs of oars.

**Viking Longship**
800-1100 A.D., 25 tons, 40-80 men

As time passed, they grew larger. Royal vessels of the 11th Century had as many as 25-35 pairs of oars. Crews of three men per oar were apparently carried on expeditions (one rowed, one shielded the rower from missiles, the third fought boarders).

Voyages over the open sea were generally limited to the months from April to early October. The raiders clung to the coasts most of the time, beaching their boats to eat and sleep ashore each night. Upon reaching their destination, they grounded the longships and poured inland in bands of 1-200 men dressed in leather jackets (some later wore mail shirts) with leather or metal helmets and carrying round shields. Long continued feudal squabbling back home had allowed the Vikings to perfect the *strandhogg*, a lightning thrust inland to capture supplies, followed by an equally rapid retreat before armed resistance could develop. These tactics have led some to conclude that the Vikings had little stomach for battle. However, when cornered, Vikings were fierce fighters. Against the inferior militia they encountered in Europe during the 9th Century, they were invincible. With broadaxes, spears, and swords they cut their way through the ill-led masses of levies. Sometimes, charges were preceded by flights of arrows, for the Vikings were among the few Europeans of the time to use the bow. Often, they would establish a base on an island, or other inaccessible place, then mount raids into the nearby mainland, returning to the base when satiated or hotly pursued. When they had devastated an area, they left in search of another.

10

## The Viking Invasion of England - 9th-10th Centuries

From Frisia, Vikings sailed up the Thames and attacked London in 842, one of many contemporary raids on England. The Danes found the Anglo-Saxon kingdoms of Mercia, Kent, Wessex and Northumbria vying for predominance, and exploited the rivalries. From the environs of Paris, following the bribe by Charles the Bald in 845, the huge Viking fleet turned westward. Leaving Frisia in 850, 350 ships arrived to winter at the island of Thanet in the mouth of the Thames, raiding up the river during the following year. A Viking fleet carried around 500 men to Northumbria in 865, where they raided and plundered to such an extent that their numbers were exaggerated to a "great heathen host" by the unfortunate victims. Wintering in East Anglia, they took York in 866 and overran Mercia the following year. The Saxons finally managed to halt their rampage and a boundary was established in 878 along a straight old Roman road running northwest from London to Chester. Eight years later, Alfred of Wessex concluded a treaty which confined them to a "Danelaw" east of the boundary. Danish families poured into the territory and settled into farming, largely abandoning their wandering.

In the north of Britain, the Celtic Picts and Scots united in 844 and formed the Kingdom of Scotland. Although Norse Vikings made heavy inroads into what they called *Sudreland* ("Southern Land"), they were never able to conquer the kingdom. The Viking objective of a Norse Ireland and a Danish England also went unfulfilled. Isolated from the ravages of the Great Migrations, the Celts of Ireland had preserved much of the ancient wisdom throughout the Dark Ages. Tragically, this rich culture was largely destroyed during the savage conflicts with the Vikings.

Thorgils (Turgeis), who had taken a large fleet of longships to Ireland in 839, built forts at Dublin, Limerick, Waterford and other sites. Unlike most Vikings, he destroyed the Catholic institutions he found and introduced the worship of Thor. After his death, the Danes captured Dublin in 851 and defeated a Norse fleet off Carlingford the following year. Olaf the White reestablished Norse supremacy at Dublin in 853 and ruled for twenty years. In western England, the Celts were also driven away from the rich coastal land, although they maintained the three kingdoms of Strathclyde, Wales and Cornwall. Irish forces overran the great Viking base of Dublin in 902, forcing many Norsemen to flee to the safety of Northumbria and Mercia.

The Norse chieftains of Dublin forged close ties with the Saxons of Wessex through the town of Chester, later Bristol. Aethelstan the Saxon took an army into Northumbria in 926 and succeeded in wresting control from the Norsemen. Olaf Kvaaran of Dublin mounted a great expedition in 937 to regain the lost kingdom, but was defeated by Aethelstan at the Battle of Brunanburgh. Olaf seized the throne after the death of Aethelstan, but his successor, Erik Blood-Axe, died at the Battle of Stanmoor in 954. Britain lost her last Norse king.

Many adventurers were unready to settle down to a domestic life in the newly conquered lands and left Britain to raid the Continent. Sixty-two longships, commanded by the Viking chieftains Hastein and Bjorn, left the Loire in 859 and passed around the coasts of Spain. Sailing through the Straits of Gibraltar, they sacked Algeciras, then made a brief excursion to the coast of North Africa before turning northward. After plundering the rich Moorish coasts, the Vikings sailed toward France, sweeping through the Balearic Islands in passing. They went into winter quarters on the Rhone delta. Sailing upriver on the spring flood, they ravaged Arles, Nimes and Valence before being driven back by the Franks. Moving on to Italy, the Vikings sacked Pisa and Luna (apparently mistaken for fabled Rome). Some may have ventured into the eastern Mediterranean before the chieftains decided to retire from the sea with their plunder. However, they were met by a Moorish fleet when they tried to renegotiate the straits into the Atlantic. Spurred by the depredations they had suffered, the Moors attacked. The weary, booty-laden Vikings were easy prey for the vengeful Moors. Only a score of longships regained the Loire in 862.

The disastrous conclusion of this great expedition apparently discouraged further attacks until 966, when 80 vessels tried unsuccessfully to penetrate the Straits of Gibraltar. Moorish civilization was now well developed and the adventurers were turned back. However, 18 cities in the Asturian kingdom of northern Spain were sacked.[9]

## Explorations of the Western Vikings

From *Hjaltland* (Shetland Islands), Norse explorers found the Faroe Islands, a further two days journey from Norway. The Faroes became a stepping stone from Norway to volcanic Iceland, which had been discovered in 800. With rudimentary sextants, Norse sailors could use the sun and stars to sail latitude lines until they arrived at their destination. Around 20,000 Norse settlers had migrated to Iceland by 930, when the first *althing* was convened to organize a republic. A new wave of immigration began in 980, bringing the population to 70-80,000. Even more daring sailors reached *Svalbard* (Spitzbergen) and Novaya Zemlya in the Arctic Ocean. The migrants were fleeing the autocratic King Harald "Fairhair", who tried to stop the loss by levying a tax on emigration. Largely because of the experience, the Icelandic *althing* rejected a king, leaving a decentralized government of cooperating families.

About 900, the Viking Gunnbjörn had been blown off course and sighted Greenland, only 2-3 days sailing west of Iceland. Erik the Red, outlawed in both Norway and Iceland for murder, sailed to Gunnbjörn's land, which he then advertised to famished Icelanders as "Greenland". Twenty-five longships left Iceland in 984 and fourteen of them reached the new land. Eventually, two small settlements were formed by 2,000 Icelanders, the only agricultural communities established by Europeans in the Arctic. They got timber from *Markland* (Labrador) and traded seal skins, walrus rope-skins and walrus ivory to Europe for other supplies. Life on Greenland was precarious, and by the Middle Ages most of the population had died or been merged with the native Eskimos. Yet this brief colonization gave credence to later Scandinavian claims to the region.

Bjarni Herlufsson accidentally discovered *Vinland* (Newfoundland or New England) when he was blown off course while en route to Greenland. He cruised the shores of *Markland* and *Helluland* (Baffin Island) before eventually reaching his destination. About 990, the son of Erik the Red, Leif Eriksson, led an expedition to the mainland. He had made the first deep-sea voyage over the Atlantic by sailing directly from Norway to Greenland without stopping at Iceland. Crossing to *Helluland*, he sailed south along the shore of *Markland*. In 1000, he apparently landed around the Gulf of the St. Lawrence River, perhaps farther south. Later, Leif's brother Thorvald built a settlement somewhere in *Vinland*. The largest expedition took 160 settlers in 3 ships under Thorfinn Karlsefni to the new land. However, the native Americans, called *skraellings* by the Norsemen, attacked the interlopers. Realizing his charges could not long maintain themselves so far from Europe, Thorfinn abandoned the colony.[10]

12

## Swedish Vikings Rule Russia

During the 8th Century, settlements had been established by the Svear on the eastern shore of the East Sea. Agricultural colonies developed in southwestern Finland and along the coast of Estonia and Livonia. The Svear pushed up the rivers of western Russia to gain the headwaters of the two magnificent river systems of Russia - the Dneiper and the Volga. These early Vikings oppressed the natives and were driven out by the Novgorodian and Krivichian Slavs. About the middle of the 9th Century, a band of Svear moved up the Dvina River and settled on the highlands of the great Valdai forest. They apparently intended to establish a base from which to raid down the Dneiper to Byzantium and navigate the Volga to the rich Arab countries.

Viking traders had been plying the Volga and Dneiper for many years, but the former waterway was better known, as the Dneiper was plagued by navigation difficulties. From their secure fastness, the new Vikings began to develop the route along the Dneiper. Raids were made upon the littorals of the Black and Caspian Seas and Viking delegates reached Byzantium as early as 839. The Byzantines officially referred to the Vikings as *Varangians* (peddlers), or *Rus* (referring to their place of origin in *Ruotsi* or *Roslagen* on the point of Sweden adjacent to the Åland Islands, the first step on their long journey.

Traders navigating the Volkhov through Lake Ilmen, and sailing up the Dvina from the Gulf of Riga, found it necessary to portage their craft from the upper reaches of the streams to the headwaters of the Dneiper (which was called the *Austrvegr* by the Svear).

At this critical communications point developed the Viking town of *Gnezdovo* (Smolensk). From that town, only the most daring traders attempted the float down the *Austrvegr* to the Black Sea, for there were dangerous rapids to negotiate at the point where they entered the territory of the hostile Khazars. Those who succeeded in escaping all perils were rewarded with the riches of *Myklegard* (Constantinople), where the *Varangians* found ready markets for the furs, hides, honey and slaves they had taken among the Slavs (from which unfortunate people derives the term "slaves").

About 860, the Svear chieftain Hrörekr (Rurik) settled in *Holmegaard* (Novgorod) on Lake Ilmen and established hegemony over the surrounding region. As punishment for the breaking of a treaty, he sent two of his retainers, Askold and Dir, with 8,000 men in 200 boats on a raid against Byzantium in 862. Emperor Michael III had just left to campaign against the Saracens, and the secrecy and swiftness of the attack surprised the Byzantines. The Varangians blockaded the city from land and sea and devastated the surrounding territory, much as their Norse brethren were doing in western Europe. However, a messenger reached the Emperor in time. Askold and Dir prudently retired to Kiev, a Slavic town on the middle Dneiper which they occupied and fortified. Other Slavic cities along the Dneiper were seized and fortified as armed strongholds. From them the Svear subjugated the local Slavs and collected tribute to support themselves. Hrörekr also sent retainers to take control of Polotsk, Rostov and Beloozero on the Volga. The conquests were accomplished with apparent ease because the Slavs were divided by tribal animosity, preventing confederation to oppose the fierce and energetic invaders. One by one, the Slavic tribes were absorbed. Although beginning to lose its position as the chief Varangian city, *Holmegaard* mounted a campaign against the Volga Bulgars (traders descended from the Huns).

Pechenegs, Asian nomads related to the Cumans, lived between the Volga and the Urals in the 9th Century and preyed on the Khazars. In 860, the Khazars and the nearby Ghuz united to drive the pesky Pechenegs to the west, where they replaced the Magyars along the Don River. In 889, they drove the Magyars over the Dneiper and became a menace to Viking traffic along that waterway. Against them, the Varangians employed equal numbers of infantry and cavalry in summer campaigns when forage was plentiful. The cavalry, and part of the infantry, marched along the river bank, the rest of the infantry riding in boats on the stream with the supplies. Knowing that nomads protected their mobile bases with tenacity, they advanced toward the Pecheneg tent camp upon reaching the southern steppes. The Pechenegs harassed the marchers with flights of arrows, hoping to disorganize their formations. If they succeeded, they would attack with lances and swords. An enemy attack would be parried by refusing battle and retiring to resume their harassment. The Varangians countered their tactics with similar ones, trying to slow down the elusive Pechenegs with showers of arrows from their archers and horsemen. Often these were Pecheneg mercenaries in the pay of the Varangians. If successful in reaching the nomad's base camp before it could pack up and flee, the Varangian infantry would form up in a deep phalanx-like formation and charge the defenders.

Helgi (Oleg), the successor of Hrörekr as the prince of *Holmegaard*, began to build stockaded towns in the countryside along the upper *Austrvegr*, and impose tribute on the inhabitants. To protect their cities from incursions by the Pechenegs, the Varangian princes built earthen walls, interspersed with wooden forts, along the frontier rivers. As the nomads had no siege trains, they could not pass these barriers and were limited to brief raids. These unique fortifications in a land of primitive tribes earned the region the name of *Gardarike* ("realm of forts"). Local Slavic chieftains vied for affiliation with the admired Viking princes, initiating assimilation.

Kiev, a crossroads of international trade routes, began to take precedence over Novgorod at the beginning of the 10th Century. Kiev became known as the "mother of Russian cities" and the capital of the *Varangians*. At this time, the prince of Kiev took the title of Grand Duke, and the name *Rus* (thus Russia) was first applied to the principality, the first geographical-political appellation for the eastern Slavs.

There were no fixed territorial boundaries, cities being abandoned and new ones formed when desired. At the time, *Gardarike* included Kiev, Perezaslavl and Chernigov, together with the surrounding territory. The Varangian princes were largely independent, possessing a personal bodyguard as the core of their military power. The bodyguards varied in size, that of the 11th Century Grand Duke Yaroslav the Wise containing 1,000 men, although lesser princes had

14

only a few hundred. They wore leather clothing, with pointed metal helmets, although wealthy warriors had chain mail and visors on their helmets. All carried wooden shields covered with leather and rimmed with metal, behind which they wielded double-edged swords, battleaxes, and short spears. Light troops employed javelins and bows. The infantry formation had developed into a strong center with two wings. The Varangians were skillful boatmen, navigating rivers and seas in boats carrying 12-40 men (later boats were built to carry up to 100). The members of the bodyguard were supplied all necessities, and their senior officers administered the principality. Varangians filled all ranks until the early 11th Century when Slavs were admitted for the first time. The princes were members of a loose alliance. They could unite their bodyguards for a military campaign, and levy troops from the subject Slavs. In addition, they could readily hire mercenaries from back in Sverige.

During the off season, the prince and his retainers toured his principality, collecting furs, honey and wax in tribute from his Slavic subjects. To the north of Kiev, Varangian supervisors kept Slavic laborers busy hollowing out tree trunks to make boats for the coming trading season. When the river ice broke in the spring, they were floated to Kiev and prepared for the journey.

As soon as the ice disappeared from the Dneiper in April, the prince returned to Kiev to await the finished boats, which were hauled up on the bank for rigging with double rudders, oars, and a single square sail in the Viking fashion. They were then loaded with merchandise. In June, the prince set out down the Dneiper to Vitichev, 50 kilometers to the south. When joined by boats from Novgorod, Smolensk, Lubiech, Chernigov and Vishgorod, the fleet

**Varangian Longship**
800-1100 A.D., 5-20 men

descended the lower Dneiper and sailed along the Black Sea coast to Byzantium. The most dangerous part of the trip was the Dneiper rapids, 40 kilometers long, where the cargo had to be portaged on the backs of the slaves. A detachment of troops was deployed eastward into the steppes to ward off the Pechenegs. After passing the Danube delta, the detachment withdrew to the homeland to meet the expedition upon its return. Princely sales of goods and slaves were supplemented by those of private traders who accompanied the expedition. They returned to Kiev with the products of the rich Middle East: gold, silks, fruit and wine.

Prince Helgi of Novgorod lured the aged Askold and Dir out of Kiev in 907, executed them, and seized their principality. He enlarged *Gardarike* by subjugating more Slavic tribes along the Dneiper, then recruited their warriors for the second expedition against *Myklegard*. In a doubtful 2,000 boats carrying 20,000 men, the infantry floated down the river, with the cavalry marching along the banks. It turned out to be merely an enlarged raid of the type the *Varangians* had been conducting in the Black Sea for decades. Whatever its size, the army was large enough to compel the Byzantine emperor to pay tribute and conclude a commercial treaty in 911 that was favorable to the Varangians. A generation later, another Kievan fleet arrived off the bejeweled city of half a million inhabitants.

In 941, Ingvar (Igor) (913-945), Helgi's successor and the first truly historical Varangian prince, led 10,000 men southward in boats.   At the entrance to
the Bosphorus, they were attacked by a fleet of much larger Byzantine vessels,
which used the mysterious Greek fire to inflict severe losses.   Ingvar retired
westward, landed on the coast, and raided into Asia Minor, but returned home
with little to show for it.
   The persistent Ingvar gathered a much larger force in 944, including Pecheneg
mercenaries.   Warned by the Crimean Greeks and Danubian Bulgars that a
huge army was approaching, the Emperor offered a large tribute, and granted
permission for Varangians to trade within the city walls.   With this wise con-
cession, the Byzantine emperor satisfied the greedy Vikings and dispersed their
armed horde, thus preserving the Khazars, who acted as a buffer between the
sophisticated Byzantines and the barbarians.   By mid-century, Varangian trade
with *Myklegard* was flourishing.   Their goal achieved, the robust Vikings ravaged Bulgaria, then turned their attention to their other trade route to the trea-
sures of the East - the Volga River, which flows into the Caspian Sea.
   The Volga provided much more trading for the Vikings than did the Dneiper.
It lacked the series of rapids that obstructed the latter stream, and led directly to
the Eastern Caliphate of the Arab Empire, which possessed silver mines south
of the Aral Sea.   Bulgar, on the Volga near modern Ulyanovsk, was the crossroads of trade in the area.   Caravan routes led from there to the silks of China
and the silver of Chorezm (Khiva).   The *Rus* could also float down the Volga to
Itil, capital of the Khazars, and sail the Caspian to reach fabulous Baghdad.
For most of the period, the Vikings had to pay tribute to both the Bulgars and
the Khazars for the privilege of using the Volga as a trading route.
   Ingvar's son, Sviatoslav, sought to end the practice.   The last half of the
century was marred by his numerous wars.   Although bearing the first Slavic
name of any Varangian prince, he behaved more like a Viking adventurer.   Leaving his mother, Olga, as regent in Kiev, he led an expedition to the Oka  River
to subdue Slavic tribes that had long resisted Varangian control.   Then, in 966,
he campaigned against the Khazars on the lower Volga, capturing their stone
fort, Sarkel, their pre-7th Century capital, Semender, and their current resplendent capital, Itil.   He continued into the northern Caucasus.   The following
year, he attacked the Bulgars on the upper Volga, sacked their capital, then
sailed down the river to the Caspian to make contact with the rich Arab kingdoms on its south shore.   Although he certainly did not enrich his principality,
the spoils he took at least paid for the expeditions and ended the Khazar hegemony on the lower Volga that had persisted for several centuries.
   After returning to Kiev, he was offered a large sum in 968 to aid Byzantine
Emperor Nicephorus Phocas in subduing the Danube Bulgars.   Sviatoslav attacked from the Black Sea, while the Emperor advanced on land.   Despite having to rush back to Kiev to drive off besieging Pechenegs, he returned to capture
Bulgarian King Boris II.   The success led him to consider adding Bulgaria to
his realm, a proposal the Byzantines naturally opposed.   When Sviatoslav
marched toward Byzantium to enforce his decision, new Emperor John Zimisces
decisively defeated him at Arcadiopolis, near Adrianople.   The Byzantine Navy
drove the Varangian fleet away from the mouth of the Danube while the Emperor inflicted another defeat at Dorostalon early in 971.   After a two month
siege, Sviatoslav was captured in the fortress of Dristra (Silistria).   While returning to Kiev with a tiny remnant, he was killed by the Pechenegs at the
Dneiper rapids.

A son of Sviatoslav won the dynastic struggle following his death, and entered Kiev in 980 as Grand Duke Vladimir I, the Great (980-1015). He faced repeated incursions by the Pechenegs, and made systematic expeditions against the northern Slavic tribes. He invaded Poland in 981, probably to obtain the salt deposits near Halich and Przemysl, and occupied the ancient territory of the Croats on the upper Dneister. Together with Czerwien, they remained under Kievan control until 1018. Possibly the most important event of his reign occurred in 988 when Vladimir was baptized into the Byzantine Orthodox church, greatly altering the subsequent history of eastern Europe.

The following year, he invaded the Crimea (Byzantine territory) and captured Korsun on the south coast near modern Sevastopol. He signed a treaty with the Byzantines and became their staunch ally after marrying the sister of Emperor Basil II. Vladimir enlarged and stabilized *Gardarike*, founding many new cities on the tributaries to the Dneiper. However, he did not rule a cohesive state, rather a coalition of armed camps.

The increasing Slavicization of the *Rus* was reflected in the name of the Swedish Vladimir. With several lines of fortresses along the banks of the *Austrvegr*, he made *Gardarike* the most powerful state in Russia, establishing his sons as rulers of the borderlands. Large numbers of Swedish settlers were pouring into the realm, and many at home began referring to it as "Greater Sweden". Utilizing the excess population of *Sverige* to create a professional army, he attempted to break the Bulgar hegemony on the upper Volga, defeating them twice in battle. Nevertheless, late in the 10th Century, trade along the Volga declined as the mines of the Eastern Caliphate became depleted.

From the 9th Century, when first contact was made with Byzantium, Vikings took service in the Imperial Bodyguard. Not until late in the 10th Century was a distinct unit of Varangians organized within the famous guard. So many Scandinavians entered the Emperor's employ that the unit commonly came to be known as the "Varangian Guard" during the ensuing 11th Century, and was used as an elite reserve in battle. However, after the Norman invasion of England in 1066, many Saxons and Danes came to Byzantium, and the Guard lost its Swedish character.

Vladimir's ablest son, Yaroslav, was made the prince of *Holmegaard*, but rewarded his father by revolting in 1014. The aged Vladimir died while preparing to march against him. Yaroslav captured Kiev in the following year to end the dynastic struggle. Taking advantage of the distracted *Rus*, Polish King Boleslaw, the Brave had occupied the salt mines. Yaroslav was beaten by the skilled Pole when he tried to recover them. On 22 July 1018, they faced each other across the Bug near Volyn. Yaroslav had 3-5,000 troops, a thousand of which were Pecheneg mercenaries.

The Poles launched a surprise attack over bridges they had built across the river, causing Yaroslav to flee to Novgorod. Boleslaw marched on Kiev and replaced Yaroslav on the ducal throne with his more-agreeable brother to free his rear for operations in western Europe. However, after Boleslaw left for Poland, Yaroslav returned in 1019 and drove his brother out of Kiev, becoming Grand Duke Yaroslav, the Wise (1019-1054). Decisively defeating the Pechenegs in 1026, he ended their depredations for years. Ineffective raids were made into Lithuania and Poland from 1038-47.

He opened the **Sixth Varangian War** against Byzantium in 1043. With his son Vladimir in command, the fleet crossed the Black Sea while an experienced field commander, Vyshata, led 6,000 men along the shore. The Varangian flotilla encountered the Byzantine fleet at the mouth of the Bosphorus.

17

After patiently watching the Varangians form a ragged line facing his own, the Emperor signaled his triremes to advance. The smaller Varangian vessels surrounded the triremes, trying to break their oars and punch holes in the hulls with large wooden beams. The Byzantines fought back with oars, catapulted stones and Greek fire, throwing the Varangians into great confusion. Although the Emperor sent his reserves into the battle, the Rus resisted fiercely until a sudden gale sank many of the damaged Varangian boats, and the survivors fled. Vyshata tried to retire, but was intercepted and captured by the Byzantines.

Nevertheless, Yaroslav accumulated great wealth during his reign and made Kiev a beautiful city admired throughout the world. He divided *Gardarike* into provinces overlapping tribal boundaries to discourage tribal conflicts. He compiled the oldest legal code of the eastern Slavs - the *Pravda*. However, his was the last reign that could be termed truly Varangian. From the middle of the century, Slavs began to replace Varangians in the prince's bodyguard and administration.

There was still no Russian nation, and no national army. When Yaroslav died in 1054, the Kievan state began to disintegrate in civil war, accelerated by the incursions of the Polovtsians (Cumans), Turkish nomads from Asia who subdued the Pechenegs and raided Kievan territory.

The Mongol invasion of 1221 ended Varangian influence in Russia. The remaining Vikings were absorbed in the Slavic population, forming the basis for the modern Ukrainians and White Russians. Russia passed from the Viking to the Byzantine Age, for Vladimir had accepted the Greek Orthodox doctrine in 988. The Church gathered many of the reins of power, and the state adopted the Slavic tongue. When the Turks sacked Constantinople in 1453, Orthodox Kiev became the repository of much of the rich Byzantine culture. Subtle changes were also taking place in Western Europe that were to result in the termination of Viking activities and the advent of the modern Scandinavian nations.

# WESTERN

# SCANDINAVIA

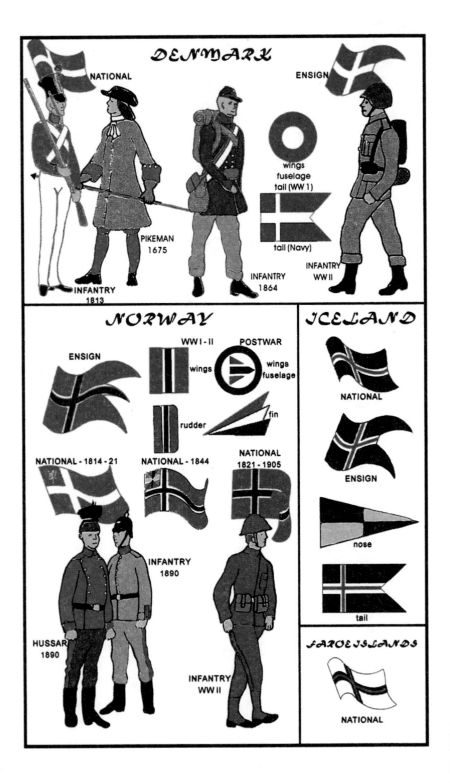

# DENMARK

NATIONAL

ENSIGN

wings
fuselage
tail (WW 1)

tail (Navy)

PIKEMAN
1675

INFANTRY
1864

INFANTRY
WW II

INFANTRY
1813

# NORWAY

ENSIGN

WW I - II          POSTWAR

wings                    wings
fuselage

rudder                    fin

NATIONAL - 1814 - 21      NATIONAL - 1844      NATIONAL
                                              1821 - 1905

INFANTRY
1890

HUSSAR
1890

INFANTRY
WW II

# ICELAND

NATIONAL

ENSIGN

nose

tail

# FAROE ISLANDS

NATIONAL

# Denmark

Even before the Viking Age, Denmark established a royal dynasty. It became a united kingdom under Godfred at the beginning of the 9th Century, with *Things* meeting in Jutland, Sjaelland and Skåne. Kings Hemming and Horik maintained the Danish cohesion, but atrophy began upon the latter's death at mid-century. Gorm the Old restored royal power about 936 and fathered a line of powerful Danish kings. His son, Harald "Bluetooth" (940-985), consolidated the kingdom, introduced Catholicism, and established a Viking stronghold at the mouth of the Oder River that became the most powerful military force in northern Europe. With these men, Harald resumed raiding England in 980. Plundering, rather than conquering, his men struck Southampton, Cheshire, Devon and Cornwall. London was burned in 982. By the last decade of the century, Olaf Tryggvason of Norway was leading joint expeditions. Harald had earlier invaded Norway, but left the conquest for his son to complete.

Sweyn "Forkbeard" (985-1014) extended Danish control in England, but his expeditions differed from earlier Viking forays. He gathered professional soldiers and mercenaries at four great military camps in northern Jutland and Sjaelland. Carried across the North Sea in scores of longships, they sacked Exeter, Wilton, Salisbury, Norwich and Thetford. The raids served the political/financial purpose of prodding King Aethelred to buy off the invaders each year. Ironically, the bribes were used by Sweyn to maintain his army for future forays. As a new millennium began, he confronted Norway with a fleet including longships of his temporary ally, Olaf Skottkonung of Sweden. Off the west coast of the island of Rügen in **1000**, they destroyed Olaf Tryggvason and his fleet during the Battle of Svalde, then divided Norway between them.

At his death, Sweyn left his English possessions to his son Canute and his Danish realm to Harald, another son. When Aethelred died in 1016, and Harald perished two years later, Canute became king of both England and Denmark. As Canute the Great (1018-1035), he brought Danes back into Norway, where Olaf Haraldsson had seized power. Although Olaf forged a hostile alliance with Swedish King Anund Jacob, Canute shrewdly promised independence to the Norwegian Viking chieftains if they would join him. He beat a Swedish fleet at the Battle of Stangbjerg in 1026, then destroyed a combined Swedish-Norwegian fleet at the Battle of Helgeaa in **1028**. Landing in Norway, Canute found Olaf supported by few Norwegians and forced him to flee to *Gardarike*, under the protection of Yaroslav. Canute then wrested territorial concessions

21

from Anund, building Lund into the market and manufacturing center of Skåne. Denmark retained a firm grip on the southern peninsula.[11]

Canute died in 1035 and his empire was divided between his sons. England was allotted to Harald "Harefoot", Norway to Sweyn, and Denmark to Harthacanute. Dynastic strife robbed Harald of his throne, and the Danes were driven back to the Orkney Islands after the Normans successfully invaded England in 1066. Sweyn was quickly expelled from Norway in favor of Magnus the Good, a son of Olaf Haraldsson. When Harthacanute died in 1042, Magnus also became King of Denmark. The Wends had been pressing into the base of the Jutland peninsula, but Magnus defeated them at the great Battle of Lysborg in **1045**. However, Magnus died later in the campaign and a former Varangian Guard, Harald Hardraade, attempted to reconquer Denmark for the Norwegian dynasty, burning Hedeby in 1050. Sweyn Estrithson, a nephew of Canute the Great, finally succeeded in ridding the country of Norwegians. Nearly a century of peace settled over Denmark.

# DENMARK MASTERS THE BALTIC

German towns had been quietly cooperating to bring the Baltic trade under their control while the last of the Viking monarchs struggled for the thrones of Scandinavia. They began building cogs of 100 tons that were superior to the Viking knorrs as cargo vessels. With the much larger capacities of the cogs enabling them to levy a smaller carrying charge, the Hansa traders soon captured most of the Baltic commerce. Visby, on the island of Gotland, was the first Hansa base. During the chaos in Denmark following the death of Canute, nearby Lübeck became the Baltic commercial center of the Hanseatic League.

Not until the middle of the 12th Century did Danish King Valdemar I, the Great (1157-1182) regain sufficient control to extend Danish authority into northern Germany, southern Sweden, and Livonia in the eastern Baltic. The Slavic Wends continued their raids into southern Jutland as late as 1150. The Danes built fortresses at threatened locations along the coast and constructed a great brick wall at the Danevirke to keep the Wends out of the peninsula. Absalon, a remarkable soldier-statesman assisting Valdemar I, took an army over the Ejder River into Wendish territory, capturing their island stronghold of Rügen in **1169** and Pomerania in 1184.

Canute VI (1182-1202) ruled the strongest nation in northern Europe. A population of 700,000 occupied 50,000 square kilometers, guarded by some 160,000 armed men and 1,400 longships. From a nation of only 10 inland towns, sheltered from the Wendish pirates, Denmark had developed to 80 coastal towns as a result of the defeat of the pirates. Her location astride the northern trade routes soon brought wealth. Ribe was the largest town and had a heavy commerce with the Rhineland, Flanders and England.

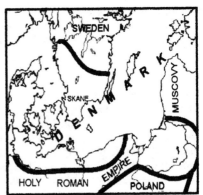

22

Danish ships carried horses, cattle, grain, meat, dairy products and timber southward, returning with building stone, salt, wine and cloth. Already, the center of commerce was moving eastward as the herring fishing grounds of Skåne developed. The most important fishing village was Havn on Sjaelland. There, Absalon built castles, and foreign merchants began settling. Little Havn was transformed into Köbenhavn (Copenhagen). Continuing his role, Absalon defeated a Pomeranian attempt to wrest control of the Baltic from Denmark with a great victory at the naval Battle of Strela (Stralsund) in **1184**. Denmark had become a great power in Europe, positioned astride the land and sea trade routes to the north.

The Holy Roman Emperor was still the legal feudal lord of the Danish kings. Denmark became embroiled in imperial politics because Valdemar's son was the Duke of Schleswig. The Count of Holstein had founded Lübeck in 1143 to displace Schleswig/Hedeby as the chief Baltic port. The customs duties from the lucrative portage trade to the North Sea then went to Holstein, rather than Denmark. Furthermore, the Lübeckers were usurping Danish trade by purchasing herring in Skåne. Every August, they brought it to Lübeck, along with salt and other merchandise, for sale in Germany. The Danes aggressively restored their monopoly. At Skånor, the principal port at the southwest tip of Skåne, they confiscated ships of Lübeck in 1201 and imprisoned the merchants.

At the same time, the Duke of Schleswig crossed the Ejder River and over-ran Holstein, forcing Lübeck to accept Danish suzerainty. The Duke became King Valdemar Sejr (the Conqueror) in 1202. He supported the current German Emperor in his struggle to retain power and was rewarded with the acquisition of all land north of the Elbe and Elde Rivers in 1214. When he led a crusade to Estonia in 1219, he narrowly evaded annihilation to win the Battle of Lyndanis on **15 June 1219**. It was there that he saw a vision of the banner that soon became the Danish flag, the oldest still in use in the world. Yet, the Germans persisted in trying to diminish Danish power. In the summer of 1223, the Count of Schwerin captured the king while hunting and imprisoned him until he agreed to cede all of the southern Baltic coast. After his release, he tried to regain the lost territory, but in 1227 was defeated at the Battle of Bornhöved in Holstein.

Valdemar's empire largely disintegrated after his death in 1241. The break-down of feudalism had begun. A vigorous middle class was developing around the herring fisheries and cattle industry. Craft guilds formed in the cities. The social strains of these developments brought about a civil war when Valdemar died. Rifts developed between Pope and king, king and nobles. The noble landlords, led by the Count of Holstein, wielded actual power. Denmark entered the 14th Century with the kingdom divided, and Sweden in possession of Skåne just across The Sound.[12]

## The Hanseatic Wars - 14th-16th Centuries

To restore order at the strategic crossroads of its sphere of interest, the son of the last weak Danish monarch was crowned King Valdemar IV Atterdag (1340-1375) by the Lübeck Council. Craftily, he restored most of the old Danish empire, although he sold Estonia to the German Knights of the Sword. Progress was delayed by a catastrophe. The Plague originated in the interior of Asia, reached Europe in 1346, and arrived in Denmark two years later. Denmark escaped relatively lightly, losing a fourth of her population to the terrifying disease.

In the summer of 1361, Valdemar unexpectedly attacked Gotland and exacted tribute from the wealthy burghers after winning several battles with his well-equipped troops. This high-handed action stirred the Wendish towns to form a league with Sweden and Norway against Denmark. Under command of the mayor of Lübeck, Johan Wittenberg, a large Wendish fleet sailed for Denmark in the spring of **1362** and besieged the castle of Helsingborg. Approaching from the rear, King Valdemar attacked the Hansa fleet, took many ships, and forced Lübeck to sign an armistice. In the autumn of 1367, Hansa envoys of Wendish, Prussian and Dutch towns met at Cologne to form an alliance against the Danes. As allies, they gained King Albrecht of Sweden, disaffected nobles of Jutland, and the Princes of Schleswig and Holstein. Denmark's hegemony in the Baltic commercial network was in dire jeopardy.

**Danish Warship**
14th Cent.

A united fleet of 41 war cogs sailed to Copenhagen, forcing Valdemar to flee. Most Hansa vessels were merchant cogs, but Lübeck and Hamburg maintained fleets of war cogs. Danish war vessels were not as advanced, most being longships with fore and stern castles attached. Troops landed at Copenhagen leveled its castle and plundered the city. Over the next year, the fleet continued on to capture all of the castles on the west coast of Skåne.[13]

The Peace of Stralsund in **May 1370** gave the Hanseatic League practical immunity from local laws, allowing them a stranglehold on Danish affairs. After the death of Valdemar Atterdag, his daughter became regent as Queen Margaret. Perceived weakness was dispelled when she sent Danish troops against Swedish King Albrecht in response to the Swedish noble's objections to Albrecht's attempts to Germanize his realm. In Västergotland, they defeated him in **February 1389** and took him prisoner. The victory made Margaret regent of Sweden also, although Albrecht's supporters still held Stockholm, Gotland and Finland. Denmark, Norway and Sweden were now joined in a union of her person. German influence was gradually eradicated. Schleswig was presented to the Count of Holstein, creating peace and security on Denmark's southern border. With the deposition of Albrecht, Mecklenburg rule in Sweden ended. A lengthy conflict with the Hansa representatives in the Baltic ended with their expulsion from Stockholm in 1398. Yet, Denmark and Sweden were elective monarchies and could separate at the first royal election. Margaret tried to secure the union by promoting her nephew, Duke Erik of Pomerania, as heir to all three thrones.

### The Kalmar Union - 1397

Margaret convened a Council of Kalmar in June, 1397 and proposed a joint constitution ruled by a common king. The three nations were to be self-governing but bound to a common foreign policy. She neutralized opposition from her own nobles by ignoring the Danehov and settling authority over domestic issues on the provincial *Thing*s. She kept a close watch on the administration of her bailiffs, traveling from castle to castle.

When the Duke of Holstein died in 1404, Margaret purchased tracts in Schleswig, gradually gaining control of the province. Her death in 1412 left her son, Erik VII, with the Schleswig problem that would plague Danish foreign policy for two centuries. He became imbued with the Renaissance idea of the

24

idea of a king independent of his nobles, and centralized power in the Council of Kalmar. He set about using his assumed powers to renovate his kingdom.

Trouble developed when Erik persuaded the Danish courts to abrogate Holstein's claim to South Jutland (Schleswig). He envisioned a Danish North European empire along the Baltic coast to Pomerania, gained with the assistance of the Holy Roman Emperor (his cousin) and England (his mother's homeland). A desultory war began in **1422**, with Erik repeatedly defeated. The Count of Holstein recaptured most of Schleswig by 1431. His inability to marshal the military resources of the Union forced Erik to agree to an armistice in 1432. The disruption of the vital Hansa trade caused a revolt against Erik by the miners of Sweden, where he had replaced Swedish bailiffs with unpopular Danes. During the autumn of 1434, the Swedes won battle after battle, capturing most of the royal castles. Yet, Erik retained most of his privileges after skillfully managing a conference of Swedish leaders in January 1435. Erik was finally deposed in 1439 and the nobles regained power.

The nobles wished to retain the Union and appointed Christopher of Bavaria as king. However, his death in 1448 initiated twenty years of instability. The Danes elected Christian of Oldenburg as Christian I (1448-1481). He immediately moved to regain Danish suzerainty over Norway and Sweden. The Norwegians elected him as king, but the nobles revolted in 1451. Christian I emerged the victor after six years of conflict. He occupied Gotland, and included Schleswig and Holstein in his domain, thus becoming the most powerful northern king since Canute the Great. In 1468, he gave the Hebrides, Shetlands, Orkneys and the Isle of Man as a dowry for the marriage of his daughter to the King of Scotland. Thus were lost the territories first gained by the Norwegian Vikings centuries earlier.

However, Christian I was unable to reestablish the centralized power enjoyed by Margaret. He convened the first Danish Rigsdag in October 1468 to counter the Swedish aristocracy. When the Swedes refused to accept him, he sailed with a strong army up the coast of Sweden and landed near Stockholm. Sten Sture met him with a peasant militia that routed the Danes in **1471** at the Battle of Brunkeberg Bridge, just outside the city. Sture occupied Finland, Gotland and Skåne, building a strong Swedish state that spelled the end of the Kalmar Union.

When Christian died in 1481, his son Hans (1481-1513) was elected king. Although made King of Norway in 1483, Hans lost much of his power to the nobles. Yet, he proved an able ruler. To counter the power of the aristocracy, Hans appointed many burghers to positions on the Council. At the same time, he sought to reduce the power of the Hanseatic League by attacking its capital of Lübeck. For this campaign, Hans built the first Danish Navy, manned by the sons of Danish burghers. On the other hand, the Army continued to be composed of German mercenaries, paid by the king. While Sweden was occupied in conflicts with Muscovy, Hans landed near Stockholm with his German mercenaries and inflicted a severe defeat upon Swedish forces. He was then made King of Sweden, also. However, the Union was not restored and, when Hans was defeated at the Battle of Ditmarschen in **1500**, he lost the Swedish throne.

Christian II (1513-1523) was supported by the Catholic Church against the Swedes, who were attempting to rid the country of clerical control. Years of skirmishing climaxed in **1520** with the Battle of Åsund in Västergotland, where the well-armed German mercenaries of Christian II fought onto the ice of Lake Mälaren. Sture was killed in the battle and the Danes marched on to Stockholm, where Christian was crowned King of Sweden. When he ordered the mass execution of the leading men of Sweden in the infamous "Stockholm bloodbath", however, Gustav Vasa led a successful rebellion against him. Christian II and his administrators were driven out of the country and the Union of Kalmar ended.

The Hanseatic League was also declining. The lower Rhine towns had withdrawn early in the century. Nevertheless, when Christian II returned to Sweden in 1523, forcing Gustav Vasa to flee to Lübeck, the Hanseatic fleet was still strong enough to relieve Stockholm and restore Vasa. The following year, the Hansa fleet captured Copenhagen and overran Zealand. Christian II fled to Holland, and the Duke of Holstein was placed on the Danish throne as Frederik I. Nobles, burghers and the monarchy vied for control, and the Reformation added the clergy to the conflict. The peasants and burghers, led by the Hanseatic Count of Oldenburg, were initially successful in the ensuing civil war. However, after the great general, Johann Rantzau, swept through Jutland with his Holstein and German troops, the Protestant Duke of Holstein was elected by the Rigsdag as Christian III (1536-1559) to succeed his father. Monasteries and churches were confiscated and the bishops imprisoned.

Commanding a fleet including Swedish and Prussian vessels, Peder Skram defeated the Hanseatic fleet in a battle within the Little Belt in 1535. Most trade privileges were stripped from the League two years later. The Danish Council of the Realm declared Norway a province of Denmark, ending its status as a separate nation under the crown. The Hanseatic League still had strong "counters" (counting houses) at Bergen and Oslo, but the new restrictions rapidly eroded shipping from Norway. Schleswig and Holstein also came into the Danish sphere of influence as Lübeck declined.[14,15]

The northern power structure was changing. As the Hanseatic League declined, the burghers of Holland gained an increasing share of the Baltic trade. Danish agricultural prospects improved when the Dutch began buying Danish corn for shipment to southern Europe. The Danish merchant navy also increased greatly, bringing prosperity to its owners. The nobles became rich, at the expense of the peasants. Nearly half of the land was owned by the aristocracy, the rest by the Church and the Crown. The peasants were landless. Yet, the power of the nobles decreased as their numbers dwindled by half during the Sixteenth Century.

## Northern Seven Years War - 1563-1570

Denmark was now the dominant power in northern Europe. She possessed Norway, the Swedish provinces of Jämtland and Härjedalen, as well as almost the entire southern and western coasts of Sweden, along with the islands of Gotland and Bornholm. The ambitious Vasas would not long permit the Danes to isolate them from trade with the West. The sons of the two old Scandinavian kings came to blows on the eastern shores of the Baltic, where Denmark possessed Ösel Island and Sweden held Estonia and Finland. However, Erik XIV of Sweden made his main attacks against the Danish territories adjoining Sweden. He captured a section of the coastland in northern Halland Province in 1563, which he immediately began to use for trade with the West. Both sides brutally ravished the inhabitants of the border regions. After capturing Ronneby in 1564, Erik put all of its citizens to death because they had been intercepting the trade of Småland Province, which should have gone to his crown city of Kalmar. Frederik II (1559-1588) moved to protect his threatened empire.

26

The Danish fleet included many Lübeckers, but the other Hansa towns remained neutral and the Hanseatic League disintegrated. After many years of determined building, the Swedes had finally achieved parity at sea. The two fleets first met between the islands of Öland and Gotland in 1564. In a two day battle, Herluf Trolle led the Danish fleet to victory over the Swedes, under Jakob Bagge. The severe northern climate prevented operations during the winter, but the Danes returned the following summer. Off Bukow, east of Lübeck, on 4 June 1565, Herluf Trolle took 28 Danish and Lübeck ships against the Swedish fleet. Neither side gained an advantage, but Trolle was mortally wounded. Without its famous admiral, an Allied fleet of 36 ships was beaten on 7 July 1565 in an action on the open sea between Rügen and Bornholm. Klas Horn, with 46 Swedish ships, was the victor. However, both sides suffered heavy losses. The following year, Lübeck's seapower was largely destroyed when, after an action with the persistent Swedish fleet off Visby, 9 of their ships, and 11 Danish vessels, ran aground. The Hanseatic League was finished (the last counter, in London, was closed in 1598). With the discovery of the Americas had come new, more important, trade routes across the North Atlantic to richer sources of the same goods that northern Europe had hitherto provided. Trading power shifted to the states on the Atlantic seaboard.

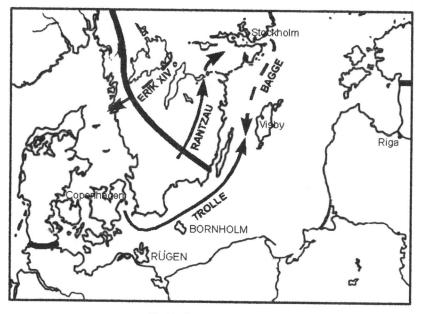

The Northern Seven Years War

With his maritime communications now secure, Daniel Rantzau, the very capable commander of the German mercenaries that made up the Danish Army, crossed the frontier into central Sweden. He ravaged the rich province of Östergotland, then advanced on Stockholm. However, supplies failed to reach him from Skåne, and he was forced to begin a retirement on 24 Jan 1568. Although he skillfully extracted his forces with few losses, both sides were financially exhausted. Erik XIV now committed excesses in his realm that resulted in his deposition in January 1569. The Peace of Stettin ended the

27

war in 1570. Denmark remained the dominant Baltic power, gaining Estonia and having Jämtland and Härjedalen restored to Norway. [16] Denmark had no minerals or timber, and the soil was poor. Corn, cattle and horses were the only exports. Her position at the mouth of the Baltic was her main asset, the "Sound Dues" collected from every ship passing between the Baltic and North Seas forming a major source of revenue to the Danish crown from 1430.

Christian IV (1588-1648) became King of Denmark and Norway in 1588. After reaching his majority and taking control of the government, he began a series of projects that vastly increased the influence of Denmark. He established factories in the homeland, then formed trading companies to place Danish merchants in favorable positions along the world's trade routes. Oslo was renamed Christiania to become the center of burgeoning Norwegian commerce. Norwegian copper mining was encouraged, and the naval stores (spars, rope, tar) industry developed. The northern routes became a bone of contention when the Dutch discovered Spitzbergen (now Svalbard) in 1596, stimulating their whaling and trading in the north. Dutch, English and German merchants began trading with Murmansk by way of the Arctic shore of Finnmark. The Danes moved to block them.

Christian IV strengthened the Danish Navy until it rivaled that of Sweden. In April 1599, he took a fleet of 8 ships to Vardöy, his base in Finnmark, to restore Denmark's monopoly of the trade to northern Russia. The action exacerbated friction with Sweden, which was also trying to acquire Finnmark for the same purpose. The Kalmar War of 1611-3 was the result. Campaigning from Skåne, Christian captured the two strongest Swedish frontier posts, Kalmar and Ålvsborg. Gustavus Adolphus, with his last troops, succeeded in stopping the Danish advance and the Peace of Knäred was signed. This proved to be the high water mark of Danish ambitions in Scandinavia, for Sweden gained dominance by mid-century.

## Thirty Years War - 1618-1648

Protestants and Catholics had come to blows in Germany. Christian IV decided to intervene on 9 July 1624. Great efforts were made to build up the Danish Army. Hitherto, the Danish kings had principally employed mercenaries in their military forces. Now, Christian established a national cadre.

Hertig Johann Ernst, Hertig Frederik, Pfalzgraf, Quernheim, Hagen, Wersabe, Sterling, Baudissin, Nell, Fredag, Hertig Friedrich, Rheingraf, Norprath, Buchwald, Courville, Solms, Ohr, Bremer, Brandenburg etter Administrator, Ercken, Daniel, and Kochtitzky Horse Regiments.
Livregiment, May, Linstow, Lippe, Limbach, Frenking, Rantzau, Neuhof, Speth, Görtzen, Beck, Brandenburg, Liebenstein, Beaton, Kruse, Sehested, Mecklenburg, Solms, Hünecken, Hatzfeld, Mackay, Kolbe, Rohr, Puteitz, Morian, Gent, Frijs, Falk Lykke, Rosenkrantz and Vognsen Infantry Regiments.
1 French mercenary dragoon regiment
1 French, 4 English and 3 Scottish mercenary infantry regiments [17]

Christian IV led an army up the Weser River into Germany in 1625, but failed to gain much support from England and Holland. Count Albrecht von Wallenstein, with 20,000 men, prevented Count Ernst von Mansfeld from crossing the Elbe to support the Danes. Although Wallenstein pursued Mansfeld to Silesia, Gen. Johan Tserclaes (Count Tilly) still had sufficient troops at the Battle of Lutter on 24-7 Aug 1626 to defeat Christian IV. The Danes withdrew northward to lick their wounds, but remained in the field.

28

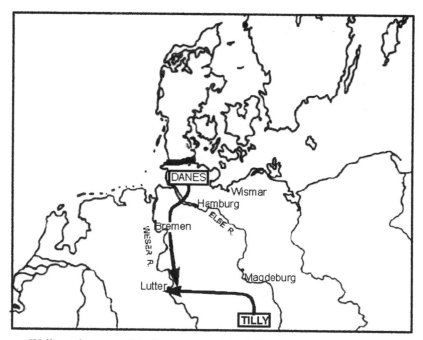

Wallenstein returned during autumn of the following year and marched down the Elbe with Tilly, driving the Danes into Holstein. He occupied Mecklenburg and Pomerania, then captured Wismar, forty kilometers east of Lübeck, to build a naval base from which to attack the Danes and Swedes. When it proved unsuitable, he moved to build the base at Stralsund. Christian IV joined Gustavus Adolphus in an expedition of 1628 that saved the city. However, the Danish Council of nobles, not wishing to promote their ancient rival, repudiated the king's cooperation with Sweden. Beaten again at the Battle of Wolgast on 2 Sept 1628, Christian IV signed the Peace of Lübeck on 7 June 1629. Under pressure from the nobles, he gave up Holstein and other territories in northern Germany and withdrew from the war without gain.

Christian IV was not done meddling. With Swedish troops deeply involved in Germany, he attempted to eliminate part of Sweden's treaty exemption from the Sound Dues by excluding her new conquests from the exemption. Sweden reacted quickly. Torstensson was ordered north into Holstein while another Swedish army invaded Skåne. Christian was not prepared for this predictable result of his actions. Swedish troops quickly overran Jutland and Skåne. From Zealand, the Danes fought back. Christian IV accompanied his admiral, Jorgen Wind, in bringing the Danish fleet against the approximately equal Swedish fleet of 40 ships under Klas Fleming. Off the island of Femern, 50 kilometers north of Wismar, the two fleets fought to a draw on 11 July 1644. However, a Danish squadron of 17 ships under Pros Mund was annihilated by Wrangel's fleet of 42 ships off Laaland on 23 October of that year. At the Peace of Brömsebro in 1645, Denmark lost Jämtland, Härjedalen, Halland, Gotland and Ösel Island to Sweden. The loss of Halland was especially painful as the vital resources of eastern Norway passed through that province. The advantages gained by the fine domestic reforms of the popular king were nullified by his disastrous foreign policy. Christian IV died in 1648, and the disgruntled nobles seized power.

# THE WARS WITH SWEDEN

Fearing domination by its ancient foe, Denmark bided its time. While Sweden's Charles X was busy expanding his empire in 1657 with a campaign in Poland, Frederik III (1648-1670), a puppet of the Danish nobles, moved to regain the lost possessions. The new national Danish Army was devoid of mercenaries.

> Gyldenlöve, Urup, Huass, Jens, Buchwald, Sehested, Rantzau, Henrik Ahlefeld, Detlef Ahlefeld, Trampe, Rigsmarskalk Bille, Dronning og Konungs Livregiment, Eberstein, Schack, Kruse, Dronning, Gyldenlöve, Brockenhus, Tott and Urne Horse Regiments
>
> Gyldenlöve and Rigsmarskalk Bille Dragoon Regiments
>
> Bredow, Both, Rosenkrantz, Lange, Frijs, Lindenow, Ulfeldt, Gyldenlöve, Eckerich, Brockdorff, Powisk, Linderoth, Ziegler, Rigsmarskalk Bille, Lobbrecht, Körber, Eberstein, Bremer, Befälhavare Schack, Livregiment, Bentfeld, Pivisk and Dronning Infantry Regiments [18]

The Dutch allies of Sweden feared the growing power of their ally and had switched sides in 1649. A reconciliation in 1656 left them reluctant to help Denmark. Yet, when Russia and Austria pledged support, Frederik III persuaded the Danish Council to declare war on the Baltic's greatest military power.

Charles X immediately marched through Pomerania to Stettin, received the support of Hamburg, and routed the Danes at Bremen. With 6,000 troops he overran Holstein and Jutland. The Danish Army fled to the fort of Fredericia, newly constructed to command the Little Belt. Expecting the Danish fleet to hold off the roughly equal Swedish Navy, the Danish troops planned to hold the fort until Polish, Brandenburg and Austrian forces arrived to cut the Swedes off in the peninsula. However, Marshal Bille was unable to defeat the assault of Count Wrangel's 4,000 men, and 3,000 Danes were surrendered with the fortress. Then the two Belts froze over during the extremely cold winter. At the end of **January 1658**, the Swedes made a remarkable march over the ice and across Fyen and Laaland to Zealand. Unable to counter the move, the Danes sued for peace and the Treaty of Roskilde on 26 Feb 1658 gave Skåne, Blekinge, Halland and Bornholm to Sweden. Sweden also gained a second outlet to the West with the acquisition of Bohuslän and Trondheim across central Norway. The Western maritime powers were pleased to see the shores of the Öresund under the control of two rival nations that would prevent each other from getting a stranglehold.

Treaty negotiations were protracted, and an exasperated Charles X renewed the conflict in July 1658. Count Wrangel was ordered to attack Copenhagen, Kronberg (Elsinore) and Christiania. Copenhagen was surrounded on land and sea. Frederik III rallied the Danes on Zealand to patriotic fervor and the capital was saved. However, Kronberg fell in September. Alarmed at the possibility of Sweden obtaining the same control of the Öresund previously exploited by Denmark, the maritime nations of Holland, England and Brandenburg came to Denmark's aid. A Dutch fleet joined the Danes off Copenhagen on 29 October and drove away the Swedish blockaders. The Brandenburg Army overran Jutland, but the Swedish forces still held Zealand. On **8 Nov 1658**, the Dutch fleet of 35 ships under Wassenaer defeated Wrangel's fleet of 35 ships in a bitter battle in the Öresund. Both sides lost heavily, but the Dutch gained control of Danish waters. The Swedish vessels soon returned, but the Dutch again relieved Copenhagen on 11 February 1659. They landed 2,000 Dutch troops on Zealand, then escorted 9,000 Danish troops from Jutland to Fyen, where they defeated 6,000 Swedes under Philip of Sulzbach in the Battle of Nyborg. Charles X died early the following year and the Swedish nobles sought peace. The Treaty of Copenhagen of June 1660 confirmed Skåne as a Swedish province and returned the Norwegian provinces. The two nations guaranteed passage of the Öresund to foreign ships. Thus, the Baltic maritime situation changed little.

## The Scanian War - 1674-1679

Paradoxically, the disastrous war resulted in the strengthening of Denmark while Sweden floundered under a regency for the boy-King Charles XI. The ruin of Denmark forced the erring nobles to yield much of their power. The Mayor of Copenhagen, Hans Nansen, and the Bishop of Zealand led the lower estates in establishing an absolute hereditary monarchy in October 1660 for Frederik III. His less able son, Christian V (1670-99), was assisted by one of Denmark's greatest statesmen, Peder Schumacher (Count Griffenfeld). He formed a French-style Privy Council to advise the king and greatly increased the Danish Navy and merchant marine. However, Denmark became increasingly dependent upon Norwegian timber and fish for revenue. When it was discovered that Griffenfeld was maneuvering himself into a position of power, he was accused of treason in 1676 and imprisoned.[19]

Adventurous Danes launched expeditions to the rich New World. Danish planters made permanent settlements on the West Indies island of St. Thomas in 1672. Slaves were imported the following year to work very profitable sugar plantations. Because sufficient military bases had not yet been constructed along the newly established trade routes, most of the European merchant ships were well armed to repel pirates and the flotillas of petty tyrants. The Danes chartered merchantmen from their burghers to bolster their fleet in wartime:

ARMED MERCHANT VESSELS

East India Company
*Spes, Oldenburg* - 34
*Phönix, Neptunus, Fortuna* - 24

West India Company
*Regina Dania, Havmanden* - 34
1 galiot, 2 jagts

Copenhagen
*Dronningen af Danmark, Prins Friderich,*
*Nye Kjöbenhavns Waaben, Tygeren* - 34
*Charitas, Kjöbenhavns Slot* - 24
*Emanuel, Pelicanen, Mercurius* - 12
*Forgyldte Ören, St. Jörgen* - 6

Nyborg
1 ship

Aalborg
*St. Johannes* - 12

Bragenes
*Statholder Gyldenlöve* - 34

Bergen
*Charlotta Amalia, Prins Friderich,*
*Prosperitet af Bergen,*
*St. Franciscus,* 2 others - 34
*St. Maria, Gyldenlöve,*
*Nordstjernen, Havridderen* - 12
*St. Andreas, Oranienbom* - 6

Trondheim
*Patientia,* 2 others - 34
*Salvator Mundi* - 12
*Unge Tobias* - 6

Christiansand
*Christiansand* - 34

Langesund
*St. Maria* - 34

Skien
1 ship

31

During the Seventeenth Century, the Dutch took over the Baltic trade lost by the Hansa merchants. Utilizing the naval stores thus obtained, they were able to build ships at a third the cost of their chief competitors, the English and French, and gained a monopoly on European maritime commerce. Of an estimated 20,000 merchant ships in world service, 15-16,000 were Dutch. England possessed only half as many, the French little more than a tenth. The Dutch had large colonies in Moscow and Riga to control trade with Russia, and had created an Arctic trading post at Archangel. Göteborg was established to siphon off trade with Sweden. The Danes favored the munificent Dutch dues-payers during wartime, closing the Sound to English shipping. The Danish Navy possessed 21 ships of the line, mostly small fourth rates.

**Danish Fleet** (Admiral Niels Juel)

SHIPS OF THE LINE

First Rate
*Christianus Quintus, Sophia Amalia* - 96

Second Rate
*Prins Georg, Norske Löve* - 90
*Tre Kroner* - 86

Third Rate
*Churprinsen* - 80
*Enighed* - 70

Fourth Rate
*Charlotta Amalia* - 62
*Anna Sophia, Fridericus Tertius,*
  *Christianus Quartus, Tre Löver* - 60
*Nellebladet, Gyldenlöve, Färöe,*
  *Svanen, Lindormen, Christiania* - 50
*Delmenhorst, Hummeren, Kjöbenhavn* - 46

**FIRST RATE** 96 gun ship of the line
1650, 1500 tons, 750 men,
28-32 pdrs, 28-24 pdrs,
28-12 pdrs, 12-6 pdrs

FRIGATES

Fifth Rate
*Falken, Anthonette, Lossen,*
  *Havfruen, Havmanden* - 32
*Jageren, Fisken* - 30

Sixth Rate
*Hjorten* - 22
*Vildmanden, Trefoldighed,* 2 more - 18

**FOURTH RATE** 60 gun ship of the line
1650, 1000 tons, 400 men
26-24 pdrs, 24-12 pdrs,
10-6 pdrs

**FIFTH RATE** 32 gun frigate
1650, 300 tons, 120 men,
8-9 pdrs, 20-6 pdrs,
4-4 pdrs

**SIXTH RATE** 18 gun frigate
1650, 200 tons, 70 men,
14-6 pdrs, 4-4 pdrs

20

To counter Hapsburg ambitions, France allied itself with Sweden in 1674. Fearful of a power monopoly in the north, a coalition of Brandenburg, Austria, Holland and Denmark formed to oppose Sweden. In 1675, the Brandenburg Army destroyed the Swedish Army's reputation for invincibility. Christian V decided to join the victors in relieving Sweden of its Pomeranian and Scånian possessions, and led an army through Mecklenburg. The outcome depended upon whether Sweden could retain command of the Baltic Sea. Sweden's navy was in poor shape and its commanders, Baron Creutz and Klas Horn, were inexperienced in naval warfare. Danish Admiral Niels Juel was more competent, but also inexperienced. His fleet was made up of relatively small vessels.

A Dutch fleet, under Cornelius Tromp, joined the Danes to cruise against the larger Swedish fleet. Off the east coast of Rügen on 3-4 June 1676, the three fleets met as dusk approached. The Battle of Jasmund dragged on throughout the night until midday on the 4th. There were few casualties, and no decision, as both sides maneuvered for favorable positions. Two days later, Tromp assumed command of the combined fleet to better coordinate its operations. With 25 ships of the line (including 10 Dutch) and 10 frigates, the Allied fleet was now a little stronger than that of Sweden. On 11 June, the Allies came up with the Swedes off the coast of Öland Island. Swedish Admiral Creutz tried to double back with his van and take the Allies between two fires, but his flagship capsized in the strong wind and the Swedish line was thrown into confusion. Tromp moved in and the Swedes lost 4 ships, the Allies none.

Niels Juel had already captured Gotland. Now Bremen, Verden and Pomerania were overrun by the Danish Army. While Gyldenlöve advanced from Norway into Västergotland with 10 regiments of volunteers, the main Danish Army of 20,000 men, under Christian V, crossed to Skåne.

> Arenstorff, Liebreich, Rantzau, Sandberg, Sehested, Kruse, Gyldenlöve, Livgarde, Baudissin, Gottfried, Geveke, Steensen, Hörnumb and Grandvilliers Horse Regiments
>
> Oertzen, Rantzau, Walter, Ramsted, Fleischer, Brahe and Schönemaker Dragoon Regiments
>
> Lütken, Baudissin, Martin, Bibow, Bülow, Lützow, Ellebracht, Harloff, Witmake, Schönfeld, Martens, Brinck, Nimpffen, Stuart, Lehndorf, Flönnies, Netzow, Ufm Keller, Grandvilliers, Tecklenburg and Braun Infantry Regiments [21]

Christian IV had intended to introduce uniforms for his royal regiments even before the Thirty Years War, but not until 1691 was that accomplished. The two Fyen (Fünen) regiments were combined into one regiment in 1676, with the uniform of the 2nd Regiment.

> **Kings and Queens Life Guards** wore a red coat and breeches with green, blue or yellow cuffs and stockings. Black tricorn and shoes.
> **Grenadiers** had a red coat with white braid and blue facings, red breeches, blue stockings, a red conical hat with blue plate. Black shoes.
> **The Prince's Regiments** wore a dark blue coat and breeches with various facings. The tricorn and boots were black.
> **Line Infantry** wore light grey coats with cuffs, breeches and stockings of various regimental colors. The tricorn and shoes were black.
> **The 1st Fyen Regiment** had grey coats with green cuffs, breeches and stockings. The tricorn and shoes were black.
> **The 2nd Fyen Regiment** wore medium green coats and breeches with dark yellow cuffs and stockings. The tricorn and shoes were black.
> **Dragoons** had light grey coats and hats, with cuffs of red, blue or green. Boots were black, and some black hats were coming into use.

A Grenadier Corps formed in 1701 with men drawn from the line regiments. The red uniform was introduced in 1711 for the line infantry, but was still not universally worn by 1720.

The young Charles XI proved a courageous and energetic Swedish king. Holding Halland, he marched against the Danes in Skåne during the autumn of 1677. At the Battle of Lund, the two armies fought the bloody climax of their centuries-old rivalry. The 15 Danish infantry regiments were armed with a mixture of pikes, still useful in repelling cavalry, and flintlock muskets (which had just replaced matchlocks). The invention of the paper cartridge made it possible to arm the cavalry as dragoons, with short muskets called carbines. More than 10,000 Scandinavian brothers died on the battlefield. The Danes were forced out of Skåne. With the expulsion of the Swedes from Germany, the modern boundaries of the Scandinavian states were established.

The conflict resumed at sea. The inhabitants of little Moen Island, south of Zealand, had watched a Danish squadron of 9 ships of the line and 2 frigates, under Niels Juel, capture 5 of Admiral Sjöblad's 7 Swedish ships of the line on 11 June. A month later, the two rivals engaged in a major battle. The Swedes expected the arrival of another Dutch squadron, and were very anxious to achieve a decisive victory before it could reinforce the Dano-Dutch fleet already in the Baltic. East of Zealand, on 11 July 1677 the fleets met. With the wind coming over the port bulwarks, they both sailed 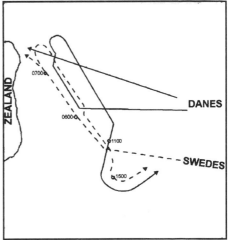 westward toward Zealand, the Danes to the north of the Swedes. Shortly before 0600, they turned northwest to parallel the coast.

The wind was now from the west. While rounding into Kjöge Bay, close to the shore, the Swedish *Draken* went aground about 0700. From *Victoria*, the Swedish flagship, Field Marshal Henrik Horn detailed 6 other ships of the line to protect it and turned in succession to a southeasterly course toward the open sea. Admiral Niels Juel left 6 Danish ships of the line to attack the Swedish detachment while he led the pursuit of the main Swedish fleet with his flagship *Christianus Quintus*. After a sharp fight between the two detachments, the *Draken* and two other ships were forced to surrender.

The six Danish ships then crowded on sail to catch up with their main fleet. After a running fight with the fleeing Swedish fleet, Niels Juel broke through their line between the center and rear squadrons about 1100. At this moment, the detached Danish ships arrived to place the Swedish rear between two fires. The battle broke up into numerous ship-to-ship encounters that persisted until nightfall. The Swedes lost 6 ships of the line and 3 fireships. The toll mounted the following day when the 4 ships that escaped from the fight over the Draken were taken. The Danes had only 4 ships seriously damaged and lost 350 men, while the Swedes suffered casualties of 1,500 dead and wounded, with 3,000 more captured. Niels Juel's tactical skill had gained control of the western Baltic for Denmark. The war ended with the Peace of Nijmegen of 1679. [22]

34

## The Great Northern War - 1700-1721

Sweden hungered for peace. Her neighbors hungered for revenge. Russia wanted a "window to the west" in the eastern Baltic. The new state of Prussia coveted Pomerania. The Poles and Saxons wished a share of the spoils. In April 1697, Danish diplomats met with Peter the Great in Moscow to discuss the defeat of their common enemy. They were buoyed by the news that the Swedish king had died while they met, to be succeeded by a mere boy - 15 year old Charles XII. The "Great Northern League" moved to attack Sweden without declaring war.

Frederik IV had been growling at the Duke of Holstein-Gottorp for some time. When Sweden reinforced Rügen to 7,000 men in support of the Duke, Frederik moved 20,000 men into Schleswig late in 1699, but then puzzled Charles XII by halting. The reason for the pause was soon revealed.

While Russia prepared to move on Narva, King Augustus of Poland-Saxony attacked Riga on 11 Feb 1700. However, the Swedish forces in Livonia repulsed the attack and Charles XII turned on his nearest foe.

Still clothed in the grey uniforms of the Scanian War, the Danish Army mustered 15 regiments, totaling 25,000 men armed with new flintlock muskets. On 20 March 1700, Frederik sent his 20,000 waiting men into Holstein, in position to annihilate the scattered Swedish garrisons. Opting to let the forces of Holland and Hanover defeat the Danes on land, Charles XII gathered 16,000 men in southern Sweden, awaiting the arrival of an Anglo-Dutch fleet that would free the Swedish fleet to operate in the eastern Baltic Sea. Another 10,000 Swedes defended the Norwegian border against Danish incursions. Frederik attempted to use his fleet to block Swedish movements to the south. The Danish Navy was little larger than that of Sweden, but had a longer maritime tradition, particularly on the high seas. Frederik IV tried to bring the Swedish fleet to battle before the Allies arrived, but the Swedes stayed safely in their base at Karlskrona. Then he attempted to capture Göteborg and cut Swedish communications with the west, but was repulsed.

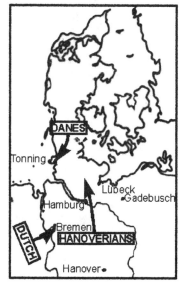

Dutch troops were now closing on Bremen, and a Hanoverian army picked up Swedish reinforcements before moving into Holstein to bolster the 5,000 troops of the Duke of Holstein-Gottorp. On 19 May 1700, Frederik started toward the vital Tönning fortress, on the northwestern coast of Holstein, to capture it before the Dutch arrived. The reinforced Hanoverian Army of 20,000 men crossed the Elbe into Holstein, forcing Frederik to lift the siege of Tönning and hurry to block them.

At this critical moment, ominous news reached him of the sailing of the Anglo-Dutch fleet. The Allies, 13 Dutch and 12 English ships of the line, arrived off Göteborg on 9 June, then moved south to the vicinity of the Öresund, awaiting the Swedish fleet. The Danes, with 29 ships of the line, watched their enemies close in.

35

**Danish Fleet** (Admiral Gyldenlöve)

SHIPS OF THE LINE

First Rate
*Fridericus Quartus, Christianus Quintus* - 110

Second Rate
*Dannebrog* - 94
*Elephanten* - 90
*Tre Kroner, Prins Friderich* - 84

Third Rate
*Norske Löve* - 82
*Mars* - 80
*Dronning Lovisa, Tre Löver* - 78
*Sophia Hedevig, Prins Christian* - 76
*Churprinsen, Mercurius* - 74
*Prins Georg* - 70

Fourth Rate
*Charlotta Amalia* - 60
*Christianus Quartus, Gyldenlöve,*
*Fridericus Tertius* - 56
*Prins Carl, Prins Wilhelm* - 54
*Nellebladet, Oldenborg,*
*Svärdfisken, Tumleren* - 52
*Slesvig, Engelen* - 50
*Delmenhorst* - 48

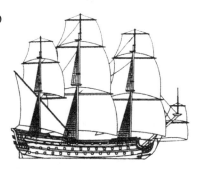

**FIRST RATE** 110 gun ship of the line
1700, 2000 tons, 850 men,
30-32 pdrs, 30-24 pdrs,
30-18 pdrs, 20-9 pdrs

Fifth Rate
*Neptunus* - 44

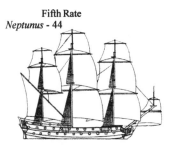

**FOURTH RATE** 52 gun ship of the line
1700, 900 tons, 300 men,
22-18 pdrs, 22-9 pdrs,
8-6 pdrs

**THIRD RATE** 78 gun ship of the line
1700, 1300 tons, 600 men,
22-32 pdrs, 24-18 pdrs,
24-9 pdrs, 8-6 pdrs

FRIGATES

Fifth Rate
*Söhunden* - 40
*Hummeren* - 32

Sixth Rate
*Dragonen* - 28
*Hvide Falk, Lossen* - 26
*Den blå Heyren, Kongens jagt Kronen* - 24
*Örnen, Mågen* - 20

**SIXTH RATE** 26 gun frigate
1700, 500 tons, 150 men,
22-9 pdrs, 4-6 pdrs

36

SLOOPS

Brigs

*Sværmeren, Packan, Fröken Elsken,*
  *Jagt Elephanten* - 16
*Makrelen, Snarensvend, Phönix,*
  *Flyende Abe, Vindhunden* - 12
*Flyende Fisk* - **8**

Bomb Vessels

*Arche Noa* - 34
*Hekla* - 25
*Postillionen* - 18
*Pram* - **8**

**SLOOP** 12 gun brig
1700, 200 tons, 80 men,
12-6 pdrs          [23]

Danish shipwrights had improved their product a good deal over the quarter century since the last war. Although the number of vessels in the Navy remained about the same, the line of battle ships were more powerful. More significantly, reliance on armed merchant ships commandeered from the shipping companies had nearly ceased. Although the merchant seamen were sailors as good as anyone, their enthusiasm for warfare was suspect.
The Swedes left Karlskrona on 16 June with 38 ships of the line. However, the Allied admirals would not subordinate themselves to Swedish Admiral Wachtmeister and agreed only to cooperate. Skillfully, Danish Admiral Niels Juel had positioned the Danish battle fleet between the enemy fleets in such a way that they could attack him only in unfavorable conditions. The Allies succeeded in concentrating on 4 July. However, their combined fleets did nothing, for the Dutch and British wished to maintain the Baltic naval balance while the Swedes wanted to destroy the Danish fleet and gain Baltic control.
Frederik IV still had his army largely intact, but most of the troops were deployed away from the capital.

Ahlefeld and Ditmarschen Cuirassier Regiments
Rothstein, Glücksburg and Wurttemberg Dragoon Regiments

Grenadiergarde Regiment
1., 2., 3., 4. Danish Imperial Infantry Regiments

Brockdorff, Boisset, Mohrstein, Plessen, La Pottrie, Ende, Malzahn, Scholten,
  Württemberg, Harboe and Delwig Infantry Regiments

Jutland and Zealand Landstorm Dragoon Regimets
Östsjöland, Västsjöland, Fünen, Aalborg, Aarhus, Ribe, Vyborg, and Oldenburg
  Landstorm Infantry Regiments [24]

Despite the naval inaction, the Allies had control of the sea, for Niels Juel was forced to retire to the protection of Copenhagen. Utilizing this indirect support, the Swedes passed 4,000 men to Zealand, near Ringsted, on **24 July**. By early August, 10,000 infantry and cavalry had landed. As Frederik IV had only 5,000 men cooped up in Copenhagen, he sued for peace on 11 August. The Treaty of Travendal, signed a week later, returned Schleswig to the Duke of Holstein-Gottorp and forbade Danish hostilities against Sweden. However, the Danish fleet remained intact.[25]

37

At Poltava in 1709, Charles XII lost his entire army, and Frederik IV saw an opportunity to regain some territory. He sent troops into Schleswig, and captured Bremen and Verden. The latter two were given to Hanover as inducement to enter the war. Frederik then sent an army into Skåne, while another force joined the Polish-Saxon Army in invading Swedish Pomerania. However, the last project came to nought, as did the invasion of Skåne. Swedish General Magnus Stenbock fought the Danes at the Battle of Helsingborg in **February 1710**. Although the Danish Grenadiers and Foot Guards stood firm, the rest of the army was routed and the Danes were forced to withdraw over the Öresund. A second Battle of Kjöge Bay sealed the issue. On **4 Oct 1710**, the Danish fleet of 26 ships of the line under Admiral Gyldenlöve was surprised by the Swedish fleet. Although the *Dannebrog* blew up, two Swedish ships also were lost.

After defeating the Danish invasion, Sweden concentrated upon strengthening her position in northern Germany. A Danish army was defeated at the Battle of Gadebusch in 1712. On **28 Sept 1712**, a fleet of 95 Swedish transports landed troops on Rügen, with the protection of a fleet of 29 ships of the line under Admiral Wachtmeister. Danish Admiral Gyldenlöve managed to evade Wachtmeister and get into the defenseless Swedish transports off Cape Arkona, burning 40 of them and capturing 15 others, unhindered by the Swedish battleships which sailed off without giving battle.

Things came to a head when Charles XII declared war on Prussia, whose troops were encroaching on Pomerania. On **24 April 1715**, Danish Rear Admiral Gabel took 9 ships of the line and frigates against a Swedish squadron of 6 ships of the line and frigates cruising west of Femern. The Swedes fled before the superior Danish force, but were forced aground in Kiel Bay the following day and surrendered.

Denmark and Hanover came to the support of Prussia. At the siege of Stralsund, 28,000 Danes participated with a like number of Prussians and Saxons. A new red uniform had been adopted in 1711 for the Danish troops. Little was done to implement the change until after 1720, for the Danes were busy assisting the Germans in driving the Swedes from their shores.

A Swedish squadron was cruising in the Greifswalder Deep, south of Rügen, and there were strong Swedish batteries on Rügen, Wollin and Usedom Islands. On 18 July, the Danish fleet attempted to enter the Deep, but were preempted by the untimely arrival of a Swedish battle fleet from Karlskrona. Frederik IV made a second attempt on **8 August 1715**.[26]

**Danish Fleet** (Admiral Raben)

| SHIPS OF THE LINE | FRIGATES |
|---|---|
| *Elephanten* (new) - 90 | *Hummeren* - 32 |
| *Justitia* - 86 | *Höjenhald, Hvide Örn* - 30 |
| *Dronning Lovisa* - 78 | *Lossen* - 26 |
| *Sophia Hedevig, Prins Christian* - 76 | |
| *Nordstjernen* - 72 | |
| *Jylland, Havfruen, Wenden* - 70 | |
| *Ebenetzer, Beskærmeren* - 64 | |
| *Anna Sophia, Svanen* - 60 | BRIGS |
| *Prins Wilhelm, Prins Carl* - 54 | *Packan* - 16 |
| *Oldenborg, Fyen, Nellebladet* - 52 | *Hummeren* - 8 |
| *Laaland, Delmenhorst* (new), *Island* - 50 | |

FIRESHIPS
*Sorte Hane*
*Concordia* [27]

38

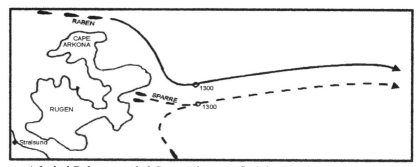

Admiral Raben rounded Cape Arkona to find the Swedes anchored in three squadrons along the coastal shoals. Swedish Admiral Sparre managed to form line on an easterly heading with the wind abeam. The two fleets, each of 21 battleships, began a running battle at 1300. In disciplined line ahead, with no maneuvering, they slugged it out until 2000. Neither sank any ships, but both sides reported around 600 casualties. The Danes anchored off Rügen the following day, severing Sweden's communications with Stralsund. When the Swedish fleet retired to Karlskrona, Raben sailed to Copenhagen for repairs.

Joined by 8 heavy British ships of the line, the Danish fleet returned during the autumn and cruised between Bornholm and Rügen, preventing Swedish ships from resupplying Stralsund. On **15 November**, the Danes and Prussians mounted a perfect amphibious operation from 330 coastal vessels. Within a few hours, 12,500 infantry and 5,000 cavalry landed on Rügen, completely encircling Stralsund, which capitulated on December 23.

Charles XII moved into Norway in **February 1716** to capture Christiania. Two columns, totaling 7,000 men, converged on Christiania. The Danish corps of General Lutzow fell back to join the reserve corps of General Sehested in shielding the capital. Although he drove the Dano-Norwegians out of the capital, Charles XII could not take the Åkerhus fortress or destroy the combined Danish army of 7,000 men northeast of the city. The Swedes paused to await reinforcements from Karlskrona.

The Swedish fleet was slow in fitting out. Danish Vice Admiral Gabel took a squadron of 7 ships of the line and 4 frigates into the Skagerrak in March, blocking Swedish movements. Unable to supply his forces over the ice-bound mountains, Charles was forced to withdraw from Christiania on 18 April. The Swedes encamped near Frederikshald (Halder) fortress in southeastern Norway to prevent the junction of the Danish armies in Norway and Denmark for an invasion of Skåne during the summer of 1716. A Swedish attempt to storm the fortress on 22 June was repulsed with heavy loss. The Swedish transport fleet was sheltered at Dynekilen, just to the south of Frederikshald, but could not dare the open sea until the Göteborg squadron came out to escort it. The Swedes were barely maintaining themselves with coastal vessels that sailed along the shore, safe from the heavy Danish ships. Rear Admiral Tordenskjold brought a flotilla of small Danish craft northward to ferret them out. In the Battle of Dynekilen on **8 July**, he destroyed the transport fleet, forcing Charles XII to withdraw into Sweden.

Frederik IV believed the time ripe to invade Skåne. He had 30,000 men ready, and had commandeered nearly the whole merchant fleet to transport them. The Russians had gathered 40,000 men at Danzig to make a simultaneous landing.

| SHIPS OF THE LINE | FRIGATES |
|---|---|
| *Elephanten* - 90 | *Höjenhald* - 30 |
| *Justitia* - 86 | *Fortuna* - 26 |
| *Dronning Lovisa, Tre Löver* - 78 | *Löwendahls Galley, Svenske Sophia* - 20 |
| *Prins Christian, Sophia Hedevig* - 76 | |
| *Nordstjernen* - 72 | SNOWS |
| *Wenden, Havfruen, Jylland* - 70 | *Galley von Bergen* - 14 |
| *Beskærmeren, Ebenetzer* - 64 | *Snarensvend* - 12 |
| *Prins Carl, Prins Wilhelm* - 54 | |
| *Oldenborg, Fyen* - 52 | SCHOONERS and JAGTS |
| *Island, Delmenhorst, Laaland* - 50 | *Vindhunden, La Diligente* - 4 |
| | *West Wlieland* - 2 |

FIRESHIPS
*Sorte Hane, Maria Margretha*     28

When his ships returned from Norway on **8 Aug 1716**, Frederik IV joined his fleet to that of the Coalition. Assembling in Kjöge Bay, the fleet sailed for Bornholm, intending to destroy the Swedish fleet. With Czar Peter the Great in overall command of the combined fleet, 19 British ships of the line (Admiral Norris) were in the van, the 24 Russian ships of the line in the center, while Admiral Gyldenlöve brought up the rear with the Danish fleet. However, the Swedes had prudently retired to the protection of Karlskrona, and the Coalition fleet was restricted to blockading the Swedish base for a month. Czar Peter decided on 19 September that the season was too far advanced for a successful assault on the strong Swedish defenses and departed eastward. When the British fleet also left for home, a dismayed Frederik IV had no choice but to end the promising expedition. With the Swedish Army growing ominously larger in Skåne during 1717, Frederik IV sent Rear Admiral Tordenskjold to attack the base of the reinforced Swedish Göteborg squadron. When he was repulsed in May and July, the king replaced him with Admiral Rosenpalm.

Charles XII advanced into Norway on **15 August 1718** with an army of 21,000 infantry and 13,000 cavalry. To oppose him, the Danes deployed:

**Army of Norway** (Gen. Lutzow) - 29,000 men
Sponeck's Corps (Lt.Gen. Sponeck) - Svinesund-Testedal
Gaffron's Corps (Maj.Gen. Gaffron) - Christiania

The Danes retired before the oncoming Swedes and, in the north, Trondheim was soon besieged. However, while supervising the siege of the main Danish fortress guarding Christiania, Charles XII was shot through the head on 30 November and died. After a council of war, the Swedish commanders decided to abandon the Norwegian campaign.[29]

Danish forces followed as the Swedes retired down the coast of the Kattegat. The Swedish Kattegat squadron of 5 ships of the line, 1 frigate and 10 smaller vessels lay in Marstrand harbor, north of Göteborg. Rear Admiral Tordenskjold was ordered to make a third attempt to destroy it and, on **21 July 1719**, he approached with 7 ships of the line, 2 frigates and a dozen galleys and gunboats. Landing marines and artillery on the north shore of the main island, the Danes shelled the harbor defenses until they were able to storm the base on 26 July, capturing all vessels not scuttled by their crews. Sweden was now sealed off from communication to the west. The Treaty of Nystad was signed on 30 August 1721, ending the war. Denmark profited little from her efforts, being required to return all of her conquests except Schleswig.

40

Conflicts and commercial changes caused Denmark's agricultural trade to decline during the early years of the Eighteenth Century. The inconclusive wars with Charles XII had laid a burden of taxes on Denmark that left the peasants in poverty. The nobles regained much of their old power while the peasantry practically reverted to serfdom. Floods and droughts struck the land, and a disease killed 100,000 cattle in 1745. Denmark's merchant fleet declined to only 400 ships, half strength.

In the middle of the century, exotic products from the East Indies and the Caribbean came into demand in Europe. During the 17th Century, Denmark had emulated other European countries in forming East and West Indies Trading Companies. As a base for the Caribbean trade, Denmark had acquired St. Thomas in the Virgin Islands. The Danes crossed to neighboring St. John in 1717 and the Danish West Indies became known as the world's largest slave market. The slaves rebelled in 1733 and drove the planters off of St. John. To compensate, the Danes purchased nearby St. Croix from the French the same year. Although of little economic value, Charlotte Amalia on St. Thomas and Christiansted on St. Croix were two of the finest harbors in the West Indies. Danish warships and merchantmen plied the Atlantic.

The frequent colonial wars between the Dutch, English and French greatly benefited the neutral Danish merchants. Resulting prosperity promoted the permanent release of Danish peasants from serfdom in 1788. Although the Russians blockaded the Danish straits against Sweden in 1757, Denmark was little affected by the Seven Years War, and other conflicts of the century. The Dutch resumed carrying Danish corn and the newly-freed peasants prospered.

Although Denmark diligently avoided engaging in the wars raging over the Continent, she kept an appraising eye on Sweden. When full-scale conflict broke out between Sweden and Russia in 1788, Denmark saw an opportunity to seize the maritime provinces of Sweden. With the main fleets of the two antagonists at each other's throats in the eastern Baltic, Russian Admiral von Dessen took the White Sea squadron (4 ships of the line and 2 frigates) out of Archangelsk, and rounded the North Cape of Norway to join a Danish squadron of 3 ships of the line and 9 frigates under Admiral Povalichen. The combined fleet was intended to intercept the Swedish fleet as it returned to Karlskrona for the winter. At the time, Denmark had a fleet of 14 small ships of the line (1-74, 5-70s, 3-64s, 3-60s, 2-50s), 11 frigates (1-46, 1-40, 6-36-8s, 1-32, 1-28, 1-24) and 60 xebecs. Morale and training were high within the Danish fleet, and their ships were of good design. The Allies should have been able to snap up many of the exhausted Swedish ships, but after only a month of station keeping, Von Dessen retired to Copenhagen and the Swedes gained Karlskrona, unmolested. With meagre prospects, Denmark exited the war again late in 1788.

*The Second Armed Neutrality* - 1801

England passed Navigation Acts to promote her merchant fleet. They prohibited foreign vessels from carrying goods to England that had not been produced in the owner's own country. Thus, foreign companies, particularly those of Holland, could not economically participate in a trade carrying goods from one country to another as England was the chief consumer. To enforce the Act, the British Navy began stopping foreign merchant ships at gunpoint and searching them for transient stores. Such harassment led Russia, Prussia, Sweden and Denmark to form a coalition called the Second Armed Neutrality. They began convoying their merchant vessels with men of war.

# BRITANNIA BREAKS DANISH POWER

On 25 July 1800, the Danish frigate *Freja*-40 was convoying 6 merchant-men (2 ships, 2 brigs, 2 galliots) when it encountered a British squadron with the frigates *Prevoyante* - 40, *Terpsichore* - 32 and *Nemesis* - 28 with the corvette *Arrow* - 18 and the lugger *Nile* - 10. The British lowered a boat to search, but the *Freja* fired into *Nemesis*, which returned fire. The Danes resisted stoutly for 20 minutes before striking to the much superior British force. The irritated British determined to break the coalition, one piece at a time. Early in 1801, they embargoed 150 Baltic merchantmen, occupied the Danish East and West Indies, and sent a fleet of 18 ships of the line and 21 smaller craft to coerce the recalcitrant Danes. When they refused to withdraw from the coalition, British Admiral Parker decided to attack their capital. Russia was unable to come to their aid, for the Gulf of Finland iced over each winter, trapping the Baltic Fleet. Copenhagen was guarded by shore batteries and the Danish fleet. Olfert Fischer arranged his motley collection of floating batteries, razees, East Indiamen and hulks in a line along the outer edge of the shoal offshore. The Sound Squadron was also at anchor, in the mouth of the harbor. From north to south, the fleet comprised:

**Battle Line** (Adm. Olfert Fischer)
*Mars* - 74
*Elephanten* - 70
*Hjaelperen* - 20
*Infödstretten* - 64
*Holsteen* - 60
*Söhesten* - 18
*Charlotta Amalia* - 26
*Sjaelland* - 74
*Aggershuus* - 20
*Gerner* - 24
*Elven* - 6
*Dannebrog* (flag) - 62
*Haien* - 20
*Kronborg* - 22
*Svärdfisken* - 20
*Jylland* - 48
*Nyborg* - 20
*Rendsborg* - 20
*Valkyrien* - 48
*Prövesteen* - 56
12 xebecs (gunsloops) - 4

**Sound Squadron** (Commodore Bille)
*Danmark* - 74
*Trekroner* - 74
*Iris* - 40
*Sarpen* (snow) - 18
*Nid Elven* (snow) - 18

Fortresses
Trekronor (two)
30-24 pdrs
38-36 pdrs
Six smaller batteries

The Danish fleet had been allowed to decline through the last years of the Eighteenth Century. Although ten ships of the line were on the stocks in various stages of completion, just ten others could be activated to face the British, and most of those were unseaworthy. Only the Sound Squadron, ship of the line *Holsteen*, frigate *Hjaelperen* and tiny sloop *Elven* were ready for sea.

Admiral Nelson was to take his van division, reinforced to a total of 12 ships of the line, and make an attempt on the Danish position. After two nights of work by his sounding boats, he brought his ships through the passage east of the Middle Ground on the First of April. With a southeast breeze, he weighed and approached the south end of the anchored Danish line at 0930 on **2 April 1801**. The poorly-trained and inexperienced Danish crews could only watch in admiration as the expert British seamen navigated the difficult approaches to their line, although three enemy battleships did go aground.

The Danish Sound Squadron remained in the harbor mouth, out of the action. The battle would be fought by the anchored vessels.

When the firing began at 1000, the Danes fought fiercely. As the British battle line slowly progressed along the line of Danish ships, the cannonading increased, reaching a peak about 1130. The British then put out stern anchors, and for three hours the brave Danes exchanged broadsides with their heavier antagonists. The gun vessels of both fleets busied themselves with attacks on exposed and crippled ships. British Adm. Parker had been unable to beat up against the wind to gain a position from which to bombard the strong *Trekronor* fortresses at the north end with his 8 ships of the line, having to content himself with sending 4 frigates to annoy them. He feared that Nelson would have to run the gauntlet of the shore batteries if he continued. Parker then exhibited his timid leadership.

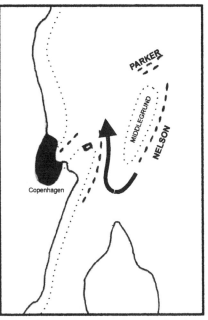

Perceiving no slackening of Danish fire, and seeing three badly damaged ships of the line drift away to go aground, he hoisted the "recall" signal, allowing Nelson one of his famous moments. The insubordinate admiral put his glass to his blind eye and announced that he could not make out the signal!

The Danes were expecting assistance from the Swedish fleet, but it could not make headway against the contrary winds. Nelson persisted in his attack, and the battered Danes began drifting away about 1400, some striking their colors. While a truce, arranged with Crown Prince Frederik, was being forwarded to Parker for approval, Nelson prudently sailed past the dangerous forts to the safe waters of the Öresund.

The Crown Prince had learned of the death of Czar Paul I a week earlier, thus was amenable to the peace overtures. An agreement was reached on 9 April, and the British fleet sailed into the Baltic three days later to force a similar pact on the Swedes. The Danes had suffered losses of 480 dead, 570 wounded and 2,000 captured, while inflicting casualties upon the enemy of 256 killed and 688 wounded. By the peace treaty of 23 October, Denmark had to evacuate the Hanseatic cities of Hamburg and Lübeck. However, Britain returned her captured troops and colonies. [30]

Required to adhere to the conditions of the British Navigation Laws, the Scandinavian countries looked to their own interests, sometimes working against each other. Denmark reorganized its army. When Napoleon sent troops to northern Germany in preparation for an attack on Prussia, Denmark moved strong forces into Holstein and debated whether to join the coalition against him. The Danes were in a difficult strategic position. On their southern doorstep was the most powerful army in the world, yet their vital islands were more vulnerable to the British Navy. In the event, the decision was taken from them.

The new Danish Army mustered:

15 infantry regiments (1 Guard, 2 Life Guard)
4 heavy cavalry regiments (1 Life Guard)
2 hussar regiments
3 light dragoon regiments (1 Life Guard)
1 lancer regiment (from 1808, Bosniaks earlier)

**12 pdr Field Gun**
121 mm, 1000 kg, 5 kg ball,
1656 m max, 828 m eff

**Infantry** wore a red tunic with facings of light blue, light yellow, green, white or black, white waistcoat, dark blue breeches and leggings (white in summer) with various facings, and a black shako or bearskin grenadier hat. By 1813, dark gray breeches, black gaiters and black shakos were worn.

**Jagers** wore dark green overall with black facings (yellow for mounted jagers).

**Artillery** wore the infantry uniform with dark blue facings, dark blue breeches and black gaiters.

**Life Guard of Horse** wore yellow tunics with red facings, yellow breeches, black light dragoon helmets with black crest, black boots.

**Heavy Cavalry** wore a red coat with yellow, dark blue, light blue or light green facings, buff breeches, black bicorn and black boots.

**Hussars** had a light blue dolman with crimson collar and cuff, a crimson pelisse with black piping, buff leather breeches, black fur hat and hussar boots.

**Light Dragoons** wore a red tunic with a plastron, cuffs and collar of black, green or light blue, dark blue breeches, a black light dragoon helmet and black boots.

**Lancers** wore a light blue kurtka with red facings, light blue breeches, red-topped black czapka, black boots.

**Bosniaks** wore a long, light blue coat and baggy breeches, both trimmed in red, red fez with white turban, lances.

The diversification and romanticization that permeated other European armies of the Napoleonic period had found their way into the Danish Army with the reorganization that followed the disasters of 1801. The trend was especially evident in the cavalry units, although the "Bosniaks" were replaced by conventional "Lancers" in 1808.

## *The Third Coalition* - 1805-1807

In July of 1807, Napoleon signed the Treaty of Tilsit with Russia and Prussia. Secret clauses of the treaty required the signatories to persuade other nations to close their ports to British goods. Although Napoleon would easily overrun Holstein and Jutland if they resisted, the Danes believed they could hold out on Sjaelland (Zealand), and maintain communications with Norway, if they were assisted by the British Navy. Learning of the secret plans of the coalition, Britain decided to neutralize Denmark before it fell into the hands of Napoleon.

The Danish Navy had made up the losses of 1801 by the time it faced the new threat. Twenty ships of the line were in commission, with 3 more almost completed on the stocks. There were also 12 snows, 24 smaller sloops and 26 gun vessels.

# Danish Fleet (Commodore Bille)

### SHIPS OF THE LINE

**Second Rate**
*Christian VII, Neptunus, Waldemaar - 84*

**Third Rate**
*Prindsesse Caroline, Prindsesse Sophia Frederik,
     Kronprinds Frederik, Kronprindsesse Marie,
     Arveprinds Frederik, Fyen, Odin, Norge,
     Trekroner, Skjold, Danmark, Justitia - 74
Ditmarschen, Seierherre, Mars,
     Prinds Christian Frederik, Nassau - 64*

### FRIGATES

**Fifth Rate**
*Perlen, Rota - 38
Harfrue, Havfruen, Nymphen,
     Freija, Venus, Iris, Nayaden - 36
Frederikscoarn - 32
Frederiksteen, Triton - 28*

### CORVETTES

**Sixth Rate**
*Lille Belte, St. Thomas, Fylla - 24
Elven, Gluckstad - 20*

### SLOOPS

**Snows**
*Glommen, Mercurius, Sarpen,
     Nid Elven, Delphinen - 18
Allart, Coureer, Euderen, Phipps - 16
Brevdrageren, Flyvendefiske - 14*

**Schooner**
*Örnen - 12*

11 gunsloops
15 gunyawls

**SECOND RATE** 84 gun ship of the line
1780, 1600 tons, 650 men,
26-32 pdrs, 26-18 pdrs
26-12 pdrs, 6-9 pdrs,
8 carronades

**THIRD RATE** 74 gun ship of the line
1780, 1400 tons, 600 men,
28-32 pdrs, 30-18 pdrs,
16-9 pdrs, 8 carronades

**FIFTH RATE** 36 gun frigate
1780, 700 tons, 200 men
26-18 pdrs, 10-9 pdrs,
8 carronades

**SLOOP** 24 gun corvette
1780, 500 tons, 150 men,
22-9 pdrs, 2-6 pdrs,
8 carronades

45

**SLOOP** 18 gun snow
1780, 300 tons, 100 men,
18-6 pdrs, 8 carronades

**SLOOP** 8 gun sloop
1780, 120 tons, 50 men,
8-6 pdrs
(Baltic Sloop)

**SLOOP** 6 gun jagt
1780, 80 tons, 40 men,
6-4 pdrs

**GUNYAWL** 1 gun
1780, 60 tons
1-24 pdr              31

A Marine Corps had formed in 1798, initially with 6 companies. By 1803, this had grown to a Marine Regiment of 4 battalions.

**Marines** wore a red double-breasted coat with a dark blue collar, lapels and cuffs, red cuff flaps, white turnbacks, white waistcoat and breeches, a black bicorn hat with a white plume, and black boots.

A British fleet left Yarmouth on 26 July and, by 1 August, was off Göteborg. To prevent reinforcements from reaching Sjaelland from Jutland, a squadron of 4 ships of the line, 3 frigates and 10 brigs entered the Great Belt. The main fleet of 25 ships of the line, 40 frigates and smaller vessels anchored off Helsingör on 3 August. The fleet was joined by more than 380 transports carrying 29,000 troops. The Danes were caught by surprise. Crown Prince Frederik, in charge of his incapacitated father, was campaigning in Holstein with the Danish Army. No Danish ships were ready for sea.

Maj.Gen. von Peymann readied the Copenhagen fortresses and sent couriers to the Crown Prince to draw the army back from Holstein. Frederik ordered concentration on 9 August, the same day Von Peymann received an ultimatum from the British. The Crown Prince called up the reserves when he reached the capital two days later. After unsuccessful negotiations with the enemy, he sailed with his ailing father to Koldring, severely damaging the morale of the troops left behind. Nevertheless, 14,000 men had gathered to defend Copenhagen by the time the British ordered an invasion.

On **16 August 1807**, the British landed at a point six kilometers north of the capital. With their fleet cutting off seaborne sustenance, the British troops proceeded to surround the Danes on the landward side. Some 9,000 British troops had disembarked on Rügen early in July to assist the Prussians. They were transported to Kjöge Bay on 21 August, where they defeated 10,000 Landwehr troops of Gen.Lt. von Castenskjold during an unproductive armistice lasting from 28-30 August. Weak sorties by the Copenhagen garrison were easily repulsed. After the Danes rejected a demand to surrender their fleet, British gunboats began bombarding Copenhagen at 0730 on **2 September**, continuing throughout the next day. Heated shot and Congreve rockets from special boats caused many fires, killing more than 1,600 civilians and injuring 1,000 more. Following this display of British ruthlessness, the Danes surrendered on the 6th. Entering the Danish fortresses, British soldiers burned what they could not use. The high quality Danish ships were carried off by British crews, but most were lost in a storm at sea and only four ships of the line were taken into the Royal Navy. Denmark had suffered the worst defeat in her history.[32]

### *Denmark's Struggle to Regain Power* - 1807-1814

Crown Prince Frederik refused to ratify Peymann's agreement and remained determined to defeat Britain. Defenseless, with his fleet gone, he concluded an alliance with France and Russia on 31 October 1807. Four days later, Great Britain declared war. As Frederik VI, he ascended the Danish throne early in 1808, and declared war on Sweden in February, although he had little martial strength.

Years would be required to rebuild the Danish battle fleet. From the few ships that went aground in the Öresund while being carried off by the British, 2 ships of the line and 29 other vessels were salvaged. Although the Danes launched another ship of the line, 4 frigates and 8 brigs over the next six years, their main effort involved the building of numerous small boats, similar to those of Sweden and probably designed by Chapman. However, the 160 Danish gunsloops and 70 gunyawls differed in having two lugsails, a fore-sail and a small jigger instead of the lateen sails favored by the Swedes. The gunsloops carried two 24 pdrs and six 4 pdr howitzers in their tiny hulls.

**REVENUE CUTTER** 10 gun
1780, 120 tons, 40 men,
10-4 pdrs

Napoleon was determined to force Sweden to break with Britain and join the Continental system. With the blessing of his new ally, he sent Marshal Bernadotte into Jutland at the head of a corps of French troops. Concentrating on Fyen, Bernadotte was preparing to cross to Sjaelland and invade Sweden when British seapower intervened. One of the Danish ships of the line, *Prinds Christian Frederik*-64, sailed southward from Norway to drive away a British frigate that was preventing the French crossing of the Öresund. Off Seirö, she was intercepted by a British squadron of 2 ships of the line, a frigate and 2 corvettes. The Danes put up a hard fight, but eventually were forced to beach their ship, which was then burned. Bernadotte could not cross to Skåne without secure communications, and eventually withdrew from Denmark. The Danes kept up the fight with their gunboat fleet, attacking British warships and merchantmen that ventured into the Öresund, and chartered numerous privateers that preyed on English shipping, taking 335 prizes.

Frederik saw the danger of losing Norway when his commander in the province, Prince Christian August von Augustenborg, was elected as heir apparent to the Swedish throne in July 1809. He hastily made peace with Sweden, improved administration in Norway, then breached his agreement with Napoleon by allowing the Norwegians to resume trade with Britain.

The crisis reappeared in 1810 when Christian August died. The new Swedish crown prince, former French Marshal Bernadotte, had energetic plans for developing the strength of his new realm.

47

When Bernadotte broke with Napoleon to join a coalition of Great Britain and Russia, Denmark was left exposed beyond Napoleon's immediate sphere of interest. Her isolation was emphasized on **6 May 1812** with the loss of a small squadron on the Norwegian coast of the Skagerrak. The new frigate *Najaden* and three 18 gun brigs were at anchor in a bay near Arendal when the light British ship of the line *Dictator*-64 boldly sailed into the shoal waters, beached herself alongside the Danish frigate, and shot her to pieces.

**MERCHANT** galeas
1780, 200 tons, 60 men

The danger increased in 1813 when Bernadotte, now known as Crown Prince Karl Johan, was given command of a Northern Army of Prussians and Swedes to operate on the right wing of the Coalition forces converging on Napoleon at Leipzig. Sweden demanded that Denmark cede Norway to her, but Frederik VI stubbornly clung to Napoleon. Declaring war on Sweden in September 1813, he moved troops into Holstein to face the oncoming Army of the North. Frederik lost his dangerous gambit when Napoleon was defeated at the Battle of Leipzig in October. Karl Johan, divested of all but his Swedish troops, turned northward and advanced on the now unsupported Danes. Frederik VI asked for an armistice on 15 December. By the terms of the Peace of Kiel of **14 Jan 1814**, Denmark gave up Norway to Sweden, but retained the islands of the North Atlantic that had been occupied by Scandinavians since Viking times. Helgoland was lost to Great Britain, but Denmark did receive monetary compensation and the remaining Swedish possessions in northern Germany.[33]

## TEUTONIC COUP DE GRACE

Denmark had fallen from her former glory. She had lost the main source of her wealth, the forest products, fish and furs of Norway, for which the rather poor North German provinces did not fully compensate. Now she was a small, poor nation with few resources. Furthermore, the Pomeranian possessions involved Denmark in every German dispute, a dangerous situation for a nation as weak as Denmark in a Europe whose social structure had been disrupted by the recent wars. When the pan-European revolt against authoritative government erupted at Paris in July 1830, the two German duchies cried for local autonomy. Reactionary King Frederik VI realized that granting such freedom would create similar demands in Denmark proper. He managed to derive a conservative Estates Constitution in 1834 that established separate assemblies for Holstein, Schleswig, Jutland and the islands. However, strong opposition developed when he tried to muffle the critical Danish press.

His successor, Christian VIII (1839-48), ruled a relatively peaceful realm. However, when he died in January 1848, the Schleswig-Holstein problem reappeared. The two duchies were important to Denmark because of their bountiful agricultural production.

## The First Schleswig War - 1848-1850

Schleswig had been bound to Denmark since the Danes had taken control of the ancient commercial city for which the duchy was named. Although the rural citizens of Schleswig were Danes, the ruling classes were German, creating a natural affinity with Holstein, which had been an early adherent to the Holy Roman Empire.

King Frederik VII had barely ascended his new throne when the vocal Holsteiners demanded that Schleswig be united with them under a common constitution allowing membership in the new German Confederation. As the Danish majority in Schleswig wished to remain with Denmark, the king refused the request on 4 March 1848.

The infection had already spread. On 21 March, a massive demonstration in the streets of Copenhagen so shook the king that he proclaimed himself a constitutional monarch and promised reform. Seeing an opportunity, the German aristocrats of Schleswig and Holstein instigated a revolt, establishing a provisional government at Kiel. Conspiratorial Prussia quickly granted the new government recognition on 12 April. The Prussian Diet authorized sending troops to Kiel under General Friedrich Wrangel to support the rebels. Alarmed by the Prussian alacrity, Danes flocked to arms.

Denmark possessed a small navy of well-founded vessels:

SHIPS OF THE LINE
*Valdemar, Frederik VI* - 84
*Dannebrog* - 72
*Skjold* - 64

FRIGATES
*Thetis* - 48
*Rota, Havfruen, Bellona* - 46
*Tordenskjold* - 44

CORVETTES
*Galathea* - 26
*Valkyrien* - 20

BRIGS
*Najaden* - 14
*Saga* - 12

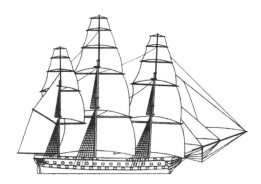

SECOND RATE 84 gun ship of the line
1830, 2000 tons, 700 men,
26-32 pdrs, 26-18 pdrs,
32-12 pdrs, 10 carronades

FOURTH RATE 46 gun frigate
1830, 1600 tons, 500 men,
24-32 pdrs, 4-20 cm shell guns,
22 carronades

SLOOP 20 gun corvette
1840, 800 tons, 200 men,
18-32 pdrs, 4-20 cm shell guns [34]

49

The Army received new uniforms, for the red coats had been replaced:

**Infantry** wore dark blue tunics with scarlet collar patches and piping, light blue cuffed trousers, a soft light blue kepi (planned spiked helmet did not come into use), black boots

**Jagers** and **Light Infantry** wore a dark brownish green overall (dark gray trousers from 1849) with scarlet collar and piping, soft green kepi, black boots

**Artillery** and **Dragoons** wore the same as the infantry, but with crimson facings

**Engineers** wore the same as the infantry, but dark blue overall

The Danish Army had been completely reorganized in 1842. Not only were the uniforms changed from the scarlet Napoleonic style to the completely new dark blue "field" style sweeping Europe, the old line regiments were abolished and replaced by numbered battalions.

Supported by Prussia, Schleswig-Holstein volunteers marched northward in March, but were defeated by Danish regulars on **9 April 1848** at the Battle of Bov (near Flensburg) and driven back to Schleswig. Off Helgoland, the Danish North Sea Squadron blockaded the Prussian coast of the North Sea to prevent communications with Britain. However, when the corvette *Valkyrien* pressed the operation too closely, three Prussian paddle steamers drove her away. Anxious to curb Prussia's growing power, the other European powers applied sufficient pressure to force her to sign the Convention of Malmö on 26 August.

However, the Convention proved to be merely a truce, and fighting broke out again on **3 April 1849**. The main Danish Army left Fredericia and reinforced the forces at the Danevirke. Desultory fighting continued until Czar Nicholas I induced Prussia to sign the Treaty of Berlin on **2 July 1850**, restoring the situation after the Napoleonic Wars. After Prussia's withdrawal from the conflict, Denmark marched into Schleswig and Holstein to coerce them into acknowledging Danish suzereignty. Although the insurgents made a stand at Isted, north of Schleswig, on **25 July**, the Danes prevailed. The duchys were restored to the Kingdom of Denmark, for the time being.

Danish citizens gained more democracy when a new constitution was approved by King Frederik VII on 5 June 1849. Lawmaking was now vested in a bicameral legislature. Once again, Danish burghers could busy themselves with profitable trade. However, now it was more localized than in the past for their possessions in the West Indies had become unprofitable. The slave trade had been prohibited by Denmark in 1803, and emancipation was extended to the slaves in 1848, after repeated rebellions. With free labor ended, and competition from nearby planters more richly endowed with sugar-producing land, the economy stagnated. During the latter half of the 19th Century, the population of the Virgin Islands decreased by half.[35]

## The Second Schleswig War - 1864

At home, the Schleswig-Holstein question continued to plague Denmark. The line of succession in the duchies was settled by a Protocol of London on 8 May 1852. Denmark gained general control, but Holstein was allowed to take part in the German Confederation. Instead of solving the conflicts, these arrangements created new ones. When Prussia protested the passage of laws in 1861 by the Danish Rigsdag, without consulting the duchies, the Danes ignored her. The situation was exacerbated on 30 March 1863 when the king announced that Schleswig was now considered part of Denmark, and that Holstein would be administered by her. Frederik VII died before he could sign a new constitution of 15 November, uniting Denmark and Schleswig. When his successor, Christian IX (1863-1906) approved the document, Otto von Bismarck of Prussia seized the opportunity to promote German solidarity against a common foe.

The Diet of the German Confederation sent 12,000 Saxon and Hanoverian troops into Holstein on 24 December to establish a government under Duke Frederik VIII. Bismarck persuaded Austria to sign an annexation agreement on 16 January 1864. Denmark was in a precarious position, for Russia had been crippled by her Crimean War while France had lost interest in Baltic events. The wily Bismarck not only maneuvered the Danes into war, he made them appear the aggressors. Publicly conjecturing that Great Britain would come to Denmark's aid if he attacked, he elicited the desired bombastic defiance from the Danish government. Claiming ample proof of Denmark's intractability, he set his forces in motion.

The Danes have always presumed the large Baltic islands of Sjaelland, Fyen, and Laaland to be their seat of power. Jylland (Jutland) was considered an outback useful as a buffer against invasion. Now they decided to defend the Danevirke (the ancient line of defense across the base of the peninsula) with part of their army. The vital position was established at Dybböl, along the east coast, where the movements of troops over Alsen Island to the arsenals of Fyen could be escorted by the much superior Danish Navy.

The Danes had plenty of men, but many years of neglect had left the Army an ill-trained militia. Although nominally possessing 80,000 men, the Danish Army mobilized slowly around Flensburg, in rear of the Danevirke, and on the Schlei River to the east of Schleswig. Rudimentary fortifications were constructed around Schleswig to form the main point of resistance.

With mobilization, the Danish battalions were organized into regiments again. The uniform remained similar to that of the first war, although the greatcoats were made heavier and the boots lengthened. Most of the infantry wore the 1858 model field cap, although the 18. Regiment used the 1858 model shako officially prescribed. By the end of January, an army of 30,000 men had deployed along the Danevirke:

**Danish Army** (Gen. de Meza)
1 cavalry division
3 infantry divisions
1 reserve infantry brigade

**Grindreng Breechloading Rifle**
1840

The uniforms had changed little since the first war, except that the expedients adopted in the field were standardized. The result was one of the first true field uniforms in Europe.

> **Infantry** wore a dark blue tunic with scarlet facings, light blue trousers, dark blue cap, black boots
> **Artillery** wore dark blue overall, with crimson facings
> **Dragoons** wore light blue overall, with crimson facings, black crested helmet, black boots
> **Engineers** wore dark blue overall, crimson facings, black hat

Rank was indicated by devices on the epaulettes: generals- 1-3 large 6-ptd stars on gold cords, field officers- 1-3 stars and rosettes, company officers- 1-3 rosettes. Non-commissioned officers had 1-3 chevrons on both lower arms. All devices were the color of the uniform buttons.

51

The allies assembled their forces on the frontier of Schleswig:

**Austro-Prussian Army** (Field Marshal Wrangel)
Austrian Army Corps (Marshal Gablenz) - 10,000 men
  1 cavalry brigade
  4 infantry brigades
Prussian Army Corps (Prince Frederik Charles)
  24,000 men
Prussian Guard Division - 11,000 men
  2 infantry divisions

**12 pdr Field Gun**
120 mm, 1000 kg, 5.5 kg ball
1800 m max, 900 m eff

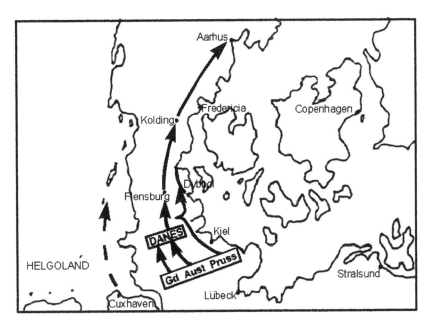

Confederation forces intended to confront the main Danish line at the Dane-virke, the Austrians mounting a holding attack while the Prussians wheeled around the Danish left flank, through Eckernforde. As the Austrians crossed the Ejder River on **1 February 1864**, the forward Danish units fell back toward the Danevirke. At Jagel, on 3 February, they made a stubborn stand that blocked the main road to Schleswig. The more numerous Austrians eventually drove them back into the Danevirke, establishing two brigades at Königsberg, near Schleswig.

While the Austrian troops maintained their snow-covered positions through intense cold, the Prussians marched eastward through the peninsula south of the Schlei River, crossing the river at Arnis on the 5th. The Danes did not wait to be enveloped. They evacuated the Danevirke during the night and were well on their way to Flensburg when the Prussians circled west. Realizing that the badly outnumbered Danes had retired, Marshal Gablenz sent an Austrian bri-gade in pursuit at 0400. Meeting the groping Prussian envelopment, they drove the Danish rear guards into Flensburg. There, General de Meza divided his forces. With 6½ brigades, he fell back to Dybböl, while the remainder of the Danish forces continued northward

52

Extending for 6 kilometers along the coast, the troops of the Dybböl position were in communication with the Danish headquarters on Fyen. General Hekermann was sent with 1 cavalry division and 2 infantry brigades toward Kolding, to shield the important fortress of Fredericia. Count Wrangel ordered the Austrians to pursue northward while the Prussians masked Dybböl. Austrian advance guards reached Kolding on 18 February.

Over British objections, the Austrians marched into Jutland on **8 March**, the Prussian Guard Division reaching Fredericia the same day. General Hekermann had placed most of his forces around Veile. Gablenz moved his Austrians forward to attack, pinning the Danes frontally and enveloping their right flank. Routed, the Danes streamed northward. There was no pursuit as Gablenz had been ordered to stay near the Fredericia fortress, which was defended by part of General Hekermann's force. Hekermann fell back to Viborg with most of his troops. The Austrians followed, hoping to invest that place and capture Aarhus without opposition. Fredericia was evacuated by the Danes on **29 April**. Practically all of the Jutland peninsula was now occupied by Confederation troops.

Towards the end of March, when the Austrians arrived, the Prussian Guard Division had been sent south from Fredericia to join the forces of Prince Frederick Charles in attacking the Dybböl entrenchments. While they waited for a siege train to arrive, 150 small vessels were gathered to transport the anticipated victors to Alsen Island nearby. Trench parallels were begun on 28 March, after 56 siege guns were emplaced in support. Only two Danish brigades were defending the position, with their backs to the sea. As the Prussians had only a few small warships. the Danish Navy enjoyed complete control of that sea:

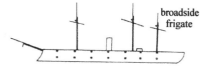

**Danmark** 1864, 4,572 tons, 18 km/h,
**Peder Skram** 12-20 cm, 13 cm armor

broadside frigate
**Dannebrog** 1863, 3,106 tons, 14 km/h,
16-60 pdr, 12 cm armor
converted from ship of the line

screw frigate
**Niels Juel** 1855, 2,388 tons, 42 guns
**Sjaelland**

screw frigate
**Tordenskjold** 1861, 1,745 tons, 34 guns
converted from frigate

screw corvette
**Thor** 1851, 1,016 tons, 12 guns

gunboat
**Fylla** 1862, 551 tons, 16 km/h,
**Diana** 3-15 cm

**Rolf Krake** 1863, 1,346 tons, 12.6 km/h,
2-20 cm, 11 cm armor

screw ship of the line
**Skjold** 1858, 2,590 tons, 64 guns
converted from ship of the line

screw frigate
**Jylland** 1860, 2,459 tons, 44 guns

screw corvette
**Hejmdal** 1856, 1,194 tons, 16 guns
**Dagmar**

armored gunboat
**Absalon** 1862, 517 tons, 18 km/h,
**Esbern Snare** 3-15 cm, 5 cm armor

36

The monitor *Rolf Krake* moved into the inlet south of Dybböl and bombarded the attacking allies. However, its fire was insufficient to prevent the storming of the Danish position on the morning of 18 April. After suffering 1,800 casualties, the Danes were driven off of the peninsula, leaving 3,400 prisoners behind. Nevertheless, they still controlled the sea around their large Baltic islands, for Austria was the only member of the German Confederation that possessed a seagoing fleet.

Word was received that an Austrian squadron had passed northward through the English Channel and put in at the Prussian base of Cuxhaven. Although the Austrians had intended to send a squadron of armored ships to match those of Denmark, they were not ready for sea. It was the Levant Squadron (screw frigates *Schwarzenberg*-51 (flag) and *Radetzky*-37, gunboat *Seehund*-4) that was sent instead. In any event, the Danish armored ships were kept in the Öresund to protect the vital islands. Admiral Edouard Suenson had been dispatched to the North Sea with a small squadron of wooden screw frigates and corvettes to blockade the Confederation traffic emanating from the Elbe and Weser Rivers. He cruised near Helgoland with his North Sea Squadron of the screw frigates *Niels Juel*-42 (flag) and *Jylland*-44, and the screw corvette *Hejmdal*-16.

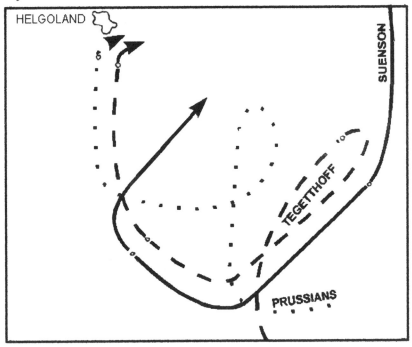

The Austrian commander, Admiral Wilhelm von Tegetthoff, was aggressive. Joined by a Prussian paddle-wheel steamer, the *Preussischer Adler*-4, and the two small gunboats *Blitz* and *Basilisk*, he boldly weighed from Cuxhaven and sailed toward Helgoland on **8 May 1864**.

Suenson turned south toward the oncoming Confederation squadron, the *Niels Juel* leading the *Jylland* and *Heimdal*. The two Austrian frigates circled northward with the Prussian gunboats on their port beam. Fire was opened from 4,000 meters. Both groups of Confederation vessels turned in succession

54

to parallel the Danes. With the range gradually closing, the Austrian and Danish frigates slowly exchanged broadsides. Swenson was cheered by the flames his shells created on the flagship *Schwarzenberg*, which was astern of the *Radetzky*. Tegetthoff was compelled to break off the action and shelter near Helgoland. Swenson's ships also had been roughly handled. He retired to Norway to effect repairs, leaving the Confederation in command of the North Sea. Thus ended the Battle of Helgoland, the last battle in history between squadrons of wooden ships.[37]

Great Britain brokered an armistice on 25 April in an effort to negotiate a peace that would leave Denmark as a strong buffer to Prussian expansion. Bismarck parried every British initiative and the Confederation moved again on 26 June. Danish forces had concentrated on Fyen. While the Austrians at Fredericia mounted a demonstration of crossing to Fyen, the Prussians made passage to Alsen Island. The *Rolf Krake* attempted to interfere with the crossing, but was driven off by the Prussian siege batteries. At 0200 on **29 June**, the Prussians began to cross and established two brigades on the island within an hour. The Danes on Alsen retired to Fyen. Tegetthoff cruised with his squadron to the Frisian Islands, off the west coast of Jutland, and landed troops. With Jutland completely in Confederation hands, the Danes sued for peace on 1 August. Restricted to their Baltic islands, they were amenable to the terms of the Peace of Vienna, by which they renounced their claims to Schleswig-Holstein on **30 October**.[38,39,40]

## *The Turn to Neutrality* - late 19th Century

Having lost 40% of her territory as a result of the war, Denmark was no longer capable of influencing events around her. With the heavy grain production of Schleswig impossible on the poor soils of Jutland, Denmark changed from an exporter to an importer of corn.

The Rigsdag was split on the question of defense. Some wished to reduce the army to a militia, capable only of frontier management. Although some advancements were made, such as the first use of observation balloons in 1887, the land defenses were generally allowed to deteriorate. In 1867, Remington rifles and carbines were adopted for the infantry and dragoons.

It was decided that a balanced navy would be maintained as a coastal defense force. The old broadside frigates continued to serve, their armament and armor inefficiently spread throughout the ships. But rapidly developing naval technology was beginning to change the old broadside warship into the modern configuration. Commemorating the victory over the Austrians of the previous decade, the flagship of the new navy was the *Helgoland*, a large specimen of the new type of heavily-armed and armored cruising warships designated casemate frigates. To permit protection of the vital machinery and guns with heavy armor, their armament was concentrated in a central position, the first step in the evolution of what would become the modern battleship.

The addition of steam-powered propellers to the old sailing ships had resulted in screw frigates and corvettes. These were now developing into the modern cruiser with increased speed, shell-firing guns, and armor in the larger vessels. The advent of the self-propelled torpedo was also revolutionizing naval warfare. With it, small torpedo boats were capable of destroying heavy warships from a safe distance. All navies immediately set about constructing large numbers of the inexpensive wasps, particularly for use in coastal waters. Others, such as the torpedo ram, *Tordenskjold*, would develop into the destroyer.

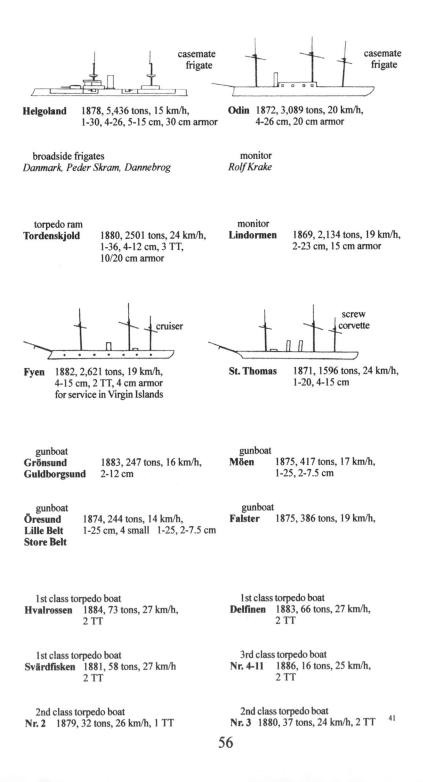

casemate
frigate

**Helgoland**  1878, 5,436 tons, 15 km/h,
1-30, 4-26, 5-15 cm, 30 cm armor

casemate
frigate

**Odin**  1872, 3,089 tons, 20 km/h,
4-26 cm, 20 cm armor

broadside frigates
*Danmark, Peder Skram, Dannebrog*

monitor
*Rolf Krake*

torpedo ram
**Tordenskjold**  1880, 2501 tons, 24 km/h,
1-36, 4-12 cm, 3 TT,
10/20 cm armor

monitor
**Lindormen**  1869, 2,134 tons, 19 km/h,
2-23 cm, 15 cm armor

cruiser

screw
corvette

**Fyen**  1882, 2,621 tons, 19 km/h,
4-15 cm, 2 TT, 4 cm armor
for service in Virgin Islands

**St. Thomas**  1871, 1596 tons, 24 km/h,
1-20, 4-15 cm

gunboat
**Grönsund**  1883, 247 tons, 16 km/h,
**Guldborgsund**  2-12 cm

gunboat
**Möen**  1875, 417 tons, 17 km/h,
1-25, 2-7.5 cm

gunboat
**Öresund**  1874, 244 tons, 14 km/h,
**Lille Belt**  1-25 cm, 4 small  1-25, 2-7.5 cm
**Store Belt**

gunboat
**Falster**  1875, 386 tons, 19 km/h,

1st class torpedo boat
**Hvalrossen**  1884, 73 tons, 27 km/h,
2 TT

1st class torpedo boat
**Delfinen**  1883, 66 tons, 27 km/h,
2 TT

1st class torpedo boat
**Svärdfisken**  1881, 58 tons, 27 km/h
2 TT

3rd class torpedo boat
**Nr. 4-11**  1886, 16 tons, 25 km/h,
2 TT

2nd class torpedo boat
**Nr. 2**  1879, 32 tons, 26 km/h, 1 TT

2nd class torpedo boat
**Nr. 3**  1880, 37 tons, 24 km/h, 2 TT  41

# DENMARK AND THE GREAT WAR

Germany was obviously preparing to gain hegemony in central Europe, her rapid increase in shipbuilding making the moats surrounding Denmark's principal islands ineffective. Thus, the anxious socialist government was shaken by the outbreak of war on 1 August 1914. The army of 50,000 men was called up.

**Danish Army**
5 infantry brigades - 7000 men
4 dragoon regiments
2 field artillery regiments
Army Troops
Danish Guard
1 Foot Guard battalion
1 Hussars of the Guard regiment
6 garrison artillery companies
1 engineer regiment

**Infantry** wore a dark blue kepi and tunic with scarlet facings, light blue trousers.

**Artillery** and **Engineers** had a dark blue tunic and trousers with crimson facings. Dark blue kepi for artillery, black for engineers

**Foot Guards** wore medium gray tunic with white facings, light blue trousers, and a black helmet with a black fur crest.

**Hussars of the Guard** had a black kepi, light blue tunic and trousers with white braid and facings.

**Dragoons** wore a light blue tunic and trousers with crimson facings, black helmet and boots.

From 1915, the uniform was changed to medium gray overall for all branches of service. The insignia of rank for officers was worn on the collar:

Generals - large 6-ptd silver stars
    General - 3
    Lieutenant General - 2
    Major General - 1
Field Officers - small 6-ptd gold stars
    Colonel - 3
    Lieutenant Colonel - 2
    Major (nonexistent in Danish Army)
Line Officers - small 5-ptd gold stars
    Captain - 3
    1st Lieutenant - 2
    2nd Lieutenant - 1

Major
General

First
Lieutenant

The insignia of rank for senior non-commissioned officers were gold buttons worn on a narrow shoulder piece with red edging, and small red chevrons, point up, above the cuff for junior officers.

Senior Non-commissioned Officers
    Staff Sergeant - 3 buttons
    Senior Sergeant - 2 buttons
    Sergeant - 1 button
Junior Non-commissioned Officers
    Senior Corporal - 3 chevrons
    Corporal - 2 chevrons
    Lance Corporal - 1 chevron

Senior
Sergeant

Corporal

Germany tested the Rigsdag's resolution on 5 August by enquiring if Denmark intended to mine her coastal waters, implying that she would if the Danes did not. After some hesitation, Denmark laid the mines, satisfying both German demands and British desires. As Europe went up in flames, Denmark walked a tightrope, carefully informing both sides of every move she made. Convinced of her neutrality, both Germany and Great Britain eventually signed agreements respecting Denmark's foreign trade. Having control of the oceans, the Allies could readily obtain their raw materials. Germany, on the other hand, was severely limited as to sources. Denmark became her chief supplier of meat, and animal fats for nitroglycerine. The Allies sought to limit this trade, but were only partially successful.

Even so, Denmark nearly became involved in the war, for Britain's imaginative First Lord of the Admiralty, Winston Churchill, conceived of a plan to descend upon the Baltic coast of Germany in January 1915, then drive southward and split the Central Powers. The Danish Army that would have faced these movements had been reorganized, but still consisted of 50,000 men in 15 infantry regiments, 4 cavalry regiments, 2 field artillery regiments, 4 garrison artillery battalions and 3 engineer battalions. The troops were now organized into a division on Sjaelland (Zealand) and another on Jylland (Jutland), a composition that remained nearly unchanged throughout the war:

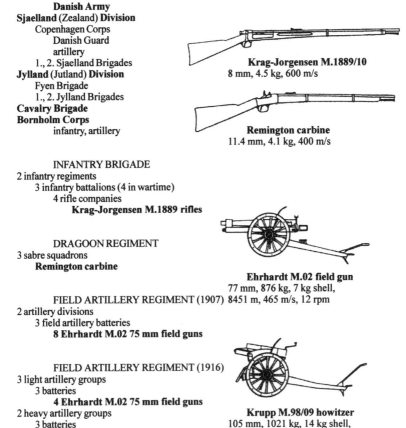

**Danish Army**
**Sjaelland (Zealand) Division**
Copenhagen Corps
Danish Guard
artillery
1., 2. Sjaelland Brigades
**Jylland (Jutland) Division**
Fyen Brigade
1., 2. Jylland Brigades
**Cavalry Brigade**
**Bornholm Corps**
infantry, artillery

**Krag-Jorgensen M.1889/10**
8 mm, 4.5 kg, 600 m/s

**Remington carbine**
11.4 mm, 4.1 kg, 400 m/s

INFANTRY BRIGADE
2 infantry regiments
3 infantry battalions (4 in wartime)
4 rifle companies
**Krag-Jorgensen M.1889 rifles**

DRAGOON REGIMENT
3 sabre squadrons
**Remington carbine**

**Ehrhardt M.02 field gun**
77 mm, 876 kg, 7 kg shell,
FIELD ARTILLERY REGIMENT (1907) 8451 m, 465 m/s, 12 rpm
2 artillery divisions
3 field artillery batteries
**8 Ehrhardt M.02 75 mm field guns**

FIELD ARTILLERY REGIMENT (1916)
3 light artillery groups
3 batteries
**4 Ehrhardt M.02 75 mm field guns**
2 heavy artillery groups
3 batteries
**4 Krupp M.98/09 105 mm howitzers**

**Krupp M.98/09 howitzer**
105 mm, 1021 kg, 14 kg shell,
7042 m, 302 m/s, 8 rpm

The military application of the new flying machines was revealed by a flight over the Öresund in 1910. Accordingly, the first army aviator was trained in 1912 and an indigenous B & S monoplane was purchased in July. The following year, a Maurice Farman M.F.7 and a Henri Farman HF.20 were acquired from France. The new airmen were part of the Army's engineer branch, although observation balloons remained with the Artillery. The unsuccessful B & S monoplane crashed in 1914, but when the Great War began, a Caudron G.III and a Bleriot XI brought to four the number of French aircraft equipping the air service.[42]

A Donnet-Leveque, Progenitor of the Danish Flying Boats

The Danish Navy entered the air age before the Army, two officers beginning pilot training in December 1911. A Henri Farman was acquired in March 1912, followed by a Maurice Farman. Operations began from Klövermarken in central Copenhagen.

Both Farmans had become nonairworthy by the end of 1913, but the future course of naval airmen of the Submarine and Flying Boat Division was established the same year with the purchase of two Donnet Leveque flying boats from France. A flying boat base was inaugurated at the Slipshavn naval station in Copenhagen in April 1915.

**Danish Navy**

Coast Defense Division
   5 coast defense battleships
Cruising Division
   4 3rd class cruisers
West Indies Station
   1 3rd class cruiser
Torpedo Boat Flotilla
   29 torpedo boats
Submarine and Flying Boat Division
   14 submarines
   17 flying boats
   4 floatplanes

3rd class battleship

**Herluf Trolle**   1899-1920, 3,526 tons, 27 km/h,
**Olfert Fischer**   2-24, 4-15 cm, 3 TT,
**Peder Skram**   7/28 cm armor
**Niels Juel**   first two stricken 1932-6

59

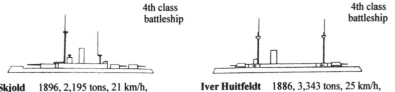

4th class
battleship

4th class
battleship

**Skjold** 1896, 2,195 tons, 21 km/h,
1-24, 3-12 cm, 4 TT, 5/30 cm armor

**Iver Huitfeldt** 1886, 3,343 tons, 25 km/h,
2-26, 10-5 cm, 4 TT,
5/28 cm armor

The building of modern armored warships began with the Fourth Class Battleship *Iver Huitfeldt* of 1886. She was rebuilt in 1904 with a modernized secondary armament of quick-firers. A decade later, the *Skjold* initiated the pattern to which all succeeding Danish armored ships were built. She possessed the low freeboard and sparse heavy armament typical of monitors. The ultimate *Herluf Trolle* class differed chiefly in being larger and faster. They were rated as Third Class Battleships until all of the Danish armored ships were designated as Coast Defense Battleships in 1914. Wartime shortages postponed the completion of *Niels Juel* until 1920, allowing her design to be considerably altered. The Danish coast defense battleships were capable of fending off enemy cruisers, but had neither the firepower nor protection to face sea-going battleships.

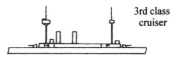

3rd class
cruiser

3rd class
cruiser

**Gejser** 1892, 1,311 tons, 26 km/h,
**Hejmdal** 2-12 cm, 4 TT, 3 cm armor

**Hekla** 1890, 1,311 tons, 28 km/h,
2-15 cm, 5 TT, 4 cm armor

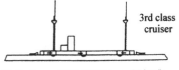

3rd class
cruiser

**Valkyrien** 1888, 2,946 tons, 25 km/h,
2-20 cm, 5 TT, 6 cm armor

3rd class cruiser
**Fyen** 1882, 2,621 tons, 19 km/h,
4-15 cm, 2 TT, 4 cm armor

As would be expected in a coastal navy, the Danish cruisers were old and slow. The most modern vessels, *Gejser* and *Heimdal*, could make only 26 kilometers per hour, and possessed but two guns of any size. The ancient *Fyen* was used as a tropical sloop to show the flag in the Virgin Islands.

The situation was better in the torpedo fleet, for Denmark had noted the tactical and financial advantages of purchasing numerous small vessels capable of deadly use among the Danish archipelago. Thirty small craft of modern design entered service by the end of the war. Denmark also invested in more than a dozen submarines of the latest coastal design. The Danes hoped to discourage violation of their waters by belligerent vessels of importance.[43]

torpedo boat

| | | |
|---|---|---|
| **Springeren** | **Stören** | 1916-9, 110 tons, |
| **Havkatten** | **Saelen** | 39 km/h, 1 TT |
| **Nordkaperen** | **Makrelen** | |
| **Söhunden** | **Sölöven** | |
| **Havhesten** | **Narhvalen** | |

torpedo boat

**Hvalrossen** 1914, 170 tons, 42 km/h,
**Svärdfisken** 1-7.5 cm, 4 TT
**Delfinen**

torpedo boat

**Söridderen** 1911, 240 tons, 44 km/h,
**Flyvefisken** 2-7.5 cm, 5 TT
**Söulven** 2250 km

torpedo boat

**Tumleren** 1911, 250 tons, 44 km/h,
**Spaekhuggeren** 2-7.5 cm, 5 TT
**Vindhunden** 2250 km

torpedo boat

torpedo boat
**Ormen** 1907, 97 tons, 50 km/h, 4 TT

**Hajen Söbjörnen** 1896, 144 tons,
**Havörnen** 43 km/h, 1 small, 4 TT

torpedo boat

**Nordkaperen** 1893, 114 tons, 35 km/h, 4 TT
**Makrelen**

t orpedo boat

**Havhesten** 1888, 95 tons, 35 km/h, 4 TT
**Narhvalen**

torpedo boat

**Stören** 1887, 90 tons, 37 km/h, 4 TT
**Sölöven**

sub
**Rota** 1918, 374 tons, 26/15 km/h, 4 TT
**Bellona**
**Flora**

sub
**Aegir** 1916, 237 tons, 24/13 km/h,
**Nepton** 3 TT
**Ran**
**Galathea**
**Triton**

sub
**Havmanden** 1911, 206 tons, 19/24 km/h,
**Havfruen** 3 TT
**Nymphen**
**2 den April**
**Najaden**
**Thetis**

61

Denmark's First Falcon - a Nielsen og Winther Aa

Neutrality restricted Denmark's access to aircraft of the belligerents, although the worn out prewar aircraft had been replaced in 1915 by 2 Thulin B monoplanes from Sweden and 2 Henri Farman H.F.23s. To enlarge its tiny air arm, the Danish Army decided to take the same course as the Navy and construct its own aircraft. In 1916, the *Töhjusvaerkstoederne* (Arsenal Workshops) built prototypes of two designs based on the Maurice Farman M.F.11. Although these were not proceeded with, the Arsenal did manage to produce a small air force before the war ended:

**Danish Flying Battalion** - Klövermarken (Copenhagen)
    fighters:
   6 Nielsen og Winther Aa
    reconnaissance:
   12 Vickers F.B.5
   9 Töhjusvaerkstoederne Type H

**Nielsen og Winther Aa**
1917, 8 m span, 150 km/h,
16/3000 m, 1 mg

**Vickers F.B.5**
1914, 11 m span, 113 km/h, 580 km,
16/1500 m, 2750 m SC, 1 mg

**Töhjusvaerkstoederne Type H**
1918

In addition to the main base, the aircraft operated from forward airstrips at Viborg, Ringsted and Odense. Due to the belated appearance of the new aircraft, their performance was not up to contemporary standards. Furthermore, the engines installed were unreliable, resulting in many fatal accidents during the last years of the war.[44]

The Navy continued to be the most important defense service as the bulk of the population was concentrated on the large islands and the Baltic shore of the Jutland Peninsula. Denmark persisted in its policy of maintaining a squadron of armored ships to protect the island heartland, with a few cruisers to probe the surrounding seas. The flotilla of coastal torpedo boats was greatly increased, with a number of submarines added. However, interest in her Caribbean colonies had dwindled and only the old *Fyen* continued to show the flag there.

Belligerent actions by the British and German navies early in the war provided impetus for the development of Danish naval aviation. The *Örlogsvaerftet* (Naval Dockyard) used the two French flying boats as a pattern to produce a series of similar aircraft over the next several years, beginning with the F.B.I in December 1914. As time went on, some of the earlier models were rebuilt, and new ones produced. The 2 F.B.Is were followed by 4 F.B.IIs in 1914, 8 F.B.IIIs in 1915, 3 F.B.IVs in 1917 and 3 F.B.Vs in 1919. A German Sablatnig floatplane that washed ashore inspired the *Örlogsvaerftet* to design one of their own, and produce 4 examples as the H.B.I in 1918.[45]

The F.B. series was comparable to similar designs popular in the Austrian and Italian Navies. From their shore base, Danish naval airmen flew their little flying boats over the waters of the straits, providing long-range reconnaissance for the vigilant surface units.

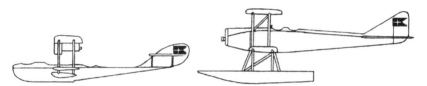

**Örlogsvaerftet F.B.III**
1917-9, 17 m span, 130 km/h, 4 hrs,
3500 m SC, 650 kg B

**Örlogsvaerftet H.B.I**
1918, 19 m span, 130 km/h, 4 hrs,
3800 m SC, 1 mg

With her decline following the Schleswig wars, Denmark found that the Virgin Islands had lost their value. Sparsely populated by former slaves, the islands were protected only by a small civic guard clothed in khaki overall, with brown shoes and khaki leggings. On the white tropical helmet was a large brass badge bearing the Danish arms. The collar and piping were red. Officers were distinguished by a broad red stripe on the trousers and gold cords on the cuffs. The men were armed with Remington carbines.

From the 1860s, the United States had been proposing purchase of the islands. The building of the Panama Canal placed the islands halfway along a strategic route to the American east coast, increasing their value to that nation. In December 1916 the Rigsdag agreed to sell the islands to the United States. In return, the United States acknowledged Denmark's interests in Greenland.

Of much more immediate import to the Danes was the initiation of unrestricted submarine warfare by Germany in February 1917, resulting in the loss of 667 seamen by the end of the war. Together with the Allied blockade of German trade routes through the North Sea, the result was the disruption of the Danish economy. Denmark had to stretch her neutrality, for only by bending to some Allied demands could she obtain imports vital to her welfare. Germany could only protest. As the war drew to an end, the Rigsdag passed the Act of Union on 1 December 1918 that gave Iceland independence from Denmark, but confirmed her control of Greenland.[46]

# DANISH PACIFISM

Following the Armistice on 11 Nov 1918, the Danish armed forces were quickly demobilized and the wartime defenses of Copenhagen were dismantled. The military aviators also felt the knife. Noting the rash of late war crashes, in April 1919 the War Office banned all flights with unreliable engines. Although large quantities of modern planes became available as war surplus, the Danish government purchased none. The Army was left with only 6 airworthy aircraft. Even pilot training was curtailed, requiring that Danish airmen be trained abroad. Eventually, in 1920, 3 L.V.G. B.IIIs were purchased, followed by 4 Breguet 14A.2s the following year. However, these aircraft were used mainly for carrying mail. Military flying practically ceased. The Navy also got into the mail-carrying business, using 5 Friedrichshafen F.F.49s (H.B.II) to fly between Copenhagen and Stege. Three of the five additional floatplanes purchased in 1922 were cannibalized for parts.

The Fokker IO Served in the dual Trainer/Reconnaissance Role

The government initiated social reconstruction programs in 1919. Large estates were discouraged by a measure abolishing total inheritance by the eldest son (a practice dating from Viking days, and the right of nobility from 1671). The government purchased part of each estate and distributed the land to small landholders. Shortly after Denmark joined the League of Nations on 8 March 1920, an "Easter Crisis" developed when the king dismissed officials bent on reuniting Schleswig with Denmark. Negotiations averted a civil war. Economic difficulty reappeared in 1922 with the rapid deflation of the *krone*. The government left it up to the banking system to remedy the situation. As the economy worsened, an election of 11 April 1924 placed the Social Democrats in power, with Stauning as prime minister. Socialist legislators attempted to abolish the Army altogether, substituting an 800 man "watch" that was little more than a police force. Although the Defense Act of 1 Feb 1923 reduced the wartime strength, the Army was retained.

Analysis of the aerial operations during the last yer of the war in France indicated the need for reorganization of the Danish Army air service. The aircraft were withdrawn from the Engineers and organized as the separate *Haerens Flyverkorps* (Army Flying Corps) under Army control. Lack of financing imposed severe restrictions on operations. A new designation system was introduced which utilized a letter indicating the type of aircraft (J-*jager*: fighter, R-*rekognosceringsplan*: reconnaissance, M-*molleplan*: autogyro, S-*skoleplan*: trainer, O-*overgangsplan*: advanced trainer), preceded by Roman numerals indicating the chronological order of the model, from the first of the type purchased.

Under the financial restrictions imposed by the socialist government, the Flying Corps was reduced to a single operational squadron and a flying school. Eight new Potez 15s were purchased from France in 1923 for the active squadron. War-surplus German aircraft equipped the flying school.

**Haerens Flyverkorps**
1 escadrille
 **8 Potez 15.A2**
 **18 Fokker IR** (1926)
Flyverskole
 **5 L.V.G. B.III, 2 Fokker C.I**
 **15 Fokker IO** (1925)

**Potez 15A.2**
1923, 14 m span, 190 km/h, 467 km,
5185 m SC, 2-3 mgs

**Fokker IO, IIO**
1918, 9 m span, 185 km/h, 1.5 hrs,
6000 m SC, 3 mgs
(modified Fokker C.I)

**Fokker IR**
1924, 13 m span, 222 km/h,
5400 m SC, 2 mgs, 50 kg B
(Fokker C.VB)

The worn war-surplus trainers of the Flyverskole were replaced from 1925 by modified Fokker C.Is built by the *Töhjusvaerkstoederne*. Three pattern aircraft were followed by 22 developments (15 two-seat, 7 single-seat) known as *O-Maskinen*. Intended as advanced trainers, the new craft were often used as observation planes by the equipment-starved Flying Corps. The Potez 15 had proven unsatisfactory and Denmark cast about for a replacement. Early in 1926, 5 Fokker C.VBs were purchased from the Netherlands and 13 copies were built by *Töhjusvaerkstoederne*. Operations moved to Kastrup in 1928.

The Navy also felt the stingy hand of the Rigsdag. During the decade following the Great War, no new warships were launched. However, the short-lived naval aircraft were replaced. A Hansa-Brandenburg seaplane, acquired as the war was ending, proved so successful that 16 more were built by the *Örlogsvaerftet* from 1921-7. Naval aviators ceased consorting with submariners on 15 Sept 1923 when the *Marinen Flyvevaesenets* (Naval Air Service) was established as a separate branch. The wartime system of designation was expanded, with the initial character indicating the environment (L-*land*: landplane, H-*hydro*: seaplane, F-*flyvebaad*: flying boat), a second character indicating the configuration (B-*biplan*: biplane, M-*monoplan*: monoplane) while Roman numerals indicated the chronology of the model.

65

Two Luftflotille (air flotillas) were organized in 1926. Landplanes were based at Ringsted while the seaplanes were provided a harbor at Copenhagen:

**Marinen Flyvevaesenets**
　1. Luftflotille - Copenhagen
　　**16 Hansa-Brandenburg H.M.I**
　2. Luftflotille - Ringsted
　　**3 Hawker L.B.II**

**Hansa-Brandenburg H.M.I**
1918, 13 m span, 179 km/h, 4 hrs,
6/1000 m, 2-3 mgs
(Hansa-Brandenburg W.29)　　47

The strains of the worldwide economic depression caused unemployment to rise to 89,000 men, a third of Danish workers. General dissatisfaction allowed Leftists to gain control of the government on 14 December 1926. Some success was achieved in restoring the economy and, by 1931, a recovery had been made.

Norway had become a much more active seafaring nation than Denmark. She had built a large merchant marine and, during the decade after the Great War, made a number of scientific and colonizing expeditions into the Arctic and Antarctic. Those ice-bound lands were of doubtful ownership, and Norway laid claim to several of them. Norwegian Vikings had discovered and settled Greenland during the Dark Ages. Based on medieval allocations, Norway announced her intention to establish fishing settlements on the east coast of that island. The Danes began transferring settlers from the island's west coast to forestall Norwegian encroachment. Conflict was imminent.

Outnumbered two to one by Norwegian ground forces, the Danish Army had a mobilized strength of 105,000 men with 53,000 rifles and 120 field guns. It was organized into three divisions, two on Zealand and one on Jutland. However, its equipment was of Great War vintage and the men were poorly trained.

**Danish Army**

**1. Division** - Zealand
　Life Guards Regiment
　　2 battalions
　4 infantry regiments
　Hussar of the Guards Regiment
　1 artillery regiment

**2. Division** - Zealand
　4 infantry regiments
　1 dragoon regiment

**3. Division** - Jutland
　3 infantry regiments
　1 dragoon regiment
　1 artillery regiment

**Bornholm Garrison**
　infantry, artillery

Army Troops
　1 heavy field artillery regiment
　　**Krupp 15.5 cm howitzers**
　1 engineer regiment　　48

The Army's air unit still had only one operational eskadrille, but the Lorraine-Dietrich inline engines of its Fokker C.VBs had been replaced by 440 horse-power Bristol Jupiter VIA radials in 1929.

**Haerens Flyverkorps**
  1 escadrille
    **18 Fokker IR**
  Flyverskole
    **5 Fokker C.I, 15 Fokker IO**

**Fokker IR**
1924, 13 m span, 225 km/h,
5400 m SC, 2 mgs, 50 kg B
(re-engined Fokker C.VB)

The Excellent Heinkel H.M.II Became the Navy's Jack-Of-All-Trades.

The Navy had languished since the end of the Great War. Except for the launching of a couple of small submarines and two fishery protection vessels, nothing had been done to strengthen it. On the other hand, the Naval Air Service had been much improved with the arrival of all Hawker Dankok fighters and the replacement of the aging Hansa-Brandenburg with its descendant, the Heinkel He.8, which gave excellent service as the H.M.II.

**Marinen Flyvevaesenets**
  1. Luftflotille - Copenhagen
    **16 Heinkel H.M.II**
  2. Luftflotille - Ringsted
    **15 Hawker L.B.II**

**Heinkel H.M.II**
1927, 17 m span, 209 km/h,
5800 m SC, 2 mgs, 200 kg B
(Heinkel He.8)

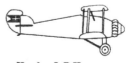

**Hawker L.B.II**
1925, 10 m span, 233 km/h, 2½ hrs,
6954 m SC, 2 mgs
(Hawker Dankok)      49

67

Unprepared, Denmark looked to come out the loser in the dispute with Norway. However, the recognition of Danish sovereignty over Greenland, provided by the United States in 1917, gave Denmark's claim legal standing. With both sides rattling sabers, and Norwegians already fishing the Greenland Sea, the question was put to The Hague Tribunal of the League of Nations. When that court found for Denmark in April 1933, Norway withdrew its fishermen and tension ended between the two former allies. Denmark's resolve was to be tested again within a decade.

## DENMARK REARMS

Its helplessness in the face of such a minor provocation diverted the Danish Rigsdag from reliance upon the good will principle in foreign relations. Furthermore, National Socialism was ominously gaining control of Denmark's southern neighbor. The result was the Defense Act of 1 Nov 1932, which reorganized the armed forces and set in motion a rearmament program.

The Modern Sloop Ingolf was Used for Fishery Protection.

Unlike the other Scandinavian nations, Denmark eschewed new armored coast defense ships for its Navy. The *Olfert Fischer* and *Herluf Trolle* were stricken from the active rolls. Propulsion machinery of the *Niels Juel* was modernized in 1935-6 and the *Peder Skram* was rebuilt to carry a floatplane on deck. Three classes of sloops were constructed to look after things in the Faroes and Greenland, with *Hvidbjörnen* and *Ingolf* each carrying a floatplane. However, most naval attention was given to the torpedo fleet. A class of four modern coastal submarines was completed, as were two of coastal torpedo boats.

In the Army, infantry and artillery weapons were not replaced, although the Madsen M.1939 joined the collection of earlier models already in service. The Army tested two tanks, the Italian Fiat 3000B and the French NC.2, but Denmark was not prepared to fund such expensive weapons. Mechanization was to be limited to the purchase of reconnaissance vehicles. Tests were conducted with a tiny Vickers Carden-Loyd Patrol tank and a Landsverk L.185 armored car purchased in 1932. For cavalry, two Landsverk L.181s were added in 1935.

**Vickers Carden-Loyd Patrol**
1932, 2 tons, 1 mg,
48 km/h, 180 km, 11 mm, 2 men

**Landsverk L.185**
1933, 4.6 tons, 1-20 mm, 2 mgs,
60 km/h, 240 km, 6/4 mm, 5 men,
20 mm/500 m P

The 1932 Defense Act reorganized Army aviation as the *Haerens Flyvertropper*, which was to expand to five eskadrilles. Initially, there were sufficient aircraft on hand to equip only three eskadrilles, which began moving to Vaerlose in 1934. Four Bristol Bulldogs were acquired for working up the 1. Eskadrille as a fighter unit. A Gloster Gauntlet was purchased from Britain, and the *Haerens Flyvertropper Vaerksteder* began licence construction of 17 copies, which entered service between 1936-8. The 2. Eskadrille received the 18 Fokker C.VBs. The old Fokker IO advanced trainers equipped the 3. Eskadrille, and 8 more were licence-built in 1932 as the IIO. To upgrade the reconnaissance squadrons, a pattern aircraft preceded 23 taper-winged Fokker C.VEs licence-built by the *Vaerksteder* from 1933-5, the first 12 of which replaced the old Fokkers of the 3. Eskadrille. By 1 Aug 1935, receipt of the second dozen allowed formation of the 5. Eskadrille. The 4. Eskadrille was to be a second fighter squadron, but it was never established.

With obvious signs of crisis appearing all around it, the Danish Rigsdag reduced the expansion plans with the Defense Act of 1937. The Army did not receive tanks, and acquired only a handful of armored cars. However, when Landsverk offered the much improved Lynx, eighteen were ordered. Three of these were received in 1939, but the other 15 were retained in Sweden when Denmark fell. If the program had been completed, by 1941 the Danes could have fielded:

**Danish Army**
2 infantry divisions
**1 mechanized cavalry regiment**
9 Landsverk Lynx armored cars
4 infantry regiments
1-2 field artillery regiments

**MECHANIZED CAVALRY REGIMENT**
3 mechanized squadrons
1 armored car troop
**3 Landsverk Lynx**
1 motorcycle troop
1 machinegun troop
**4 Madsen M.1939 lmgs**

Preparations were made to produce under licence 12 Fokker D.21s to replace the Gauntlets in the 2. Eskadrille. Twelve potent Fokker G.Ibs (with an option for 24 more) were ordered to equip 3 eskadrilles, but none arrived. Thus, by 1941 the Army would have possessed:

**Haerens Flyvertropper**
1.,3.,5. Eskadrilles (army cooperation)
  **12 Fokker IVR**
2. Eskadrille (fighter)
  **12 Fokker IIIJ**
Artillery Observation Battalion
  **2 Avro IM**
  observation balloons

**Fokker IVR**
1937, 17 m span, 430 km/h, 1380 km,
8706 m SC, 2-20 mm, 3 mgs, 400 kg B
(Fokker G.Ib)

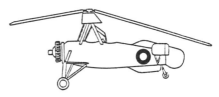

**Avro IM**
1934, 11 m rotor, 161 km/h, 400 km,
5/1000 m   (Cierva C.30A)

The Avro IM Gyroplane Was Intended for Observation of Artillery Fire.

Observation balloons were transferred from the artillery to the Air Force. Tests found two Cierva gyroplanes capable of artillery observation duties, but cost prohibited replacement of the vulnerable balloons.

70

The Naval Air Service was to be completely modernized and enlarged. For the first time, an offensive capability was to be provided by a state-of-the-art light bomber. The main naval base would have had the protection of an effective, modern fighter by 1941.

1. Luftflotille
   **Heinkel He.114B**
2. Luftflotille
   **Macchi C.200**
3. Luftflotille
   **Fairey P.4-34**

**Macchi C.200**
1937, 11 m span, 504 km/h,
6/5000 m, 8900 m SC, 2 mgs, 320 kg B

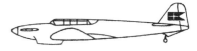

**Heinkel He.114B**
1936, 14 m span, 335 km/h, 1050 km,
4800 m SC, 1 mg, 100 kg B

**Fairey L.M.I**
1937, 14 m span, 456 km/h, 1610 km,
8113 m SC, 2 mgs, 227 kg B
(Fairey P.4/34)

By 1936, 10 licence-built Hawker Nimrod Mk.IIs joined 2 purchased from Britain to replace the Hawker Dankoks defending the Copenhagen naval base in the 2. Luftflotille. Soon, the rapid pace of world progress made the Nimrods obsolete and it was necessary to seek better equipment, the Italian Macchi C.200 being selected. Highly maneuverable, the lightly-armed Macchi would probably have been designated the L.M.II. Another Heinkel product, the He.114 (probably H.M.III), was slated to replace the well-liked He.8 floatplanes. Two Hawker Dantorp (Horsley) torpedo bombers were acquired in 1933, but funds were lacking to equip a squadron before the type was obsolete. The sleek Fairey P.4-34 (later developed into the Fulmar) was ordered as a light dive and level bomber for a new *luftflotille*. The naval aircraft factory began tooling up for licence production in 1939, but none were completed. A single Dornier Wal (F.M.I) flying boat, purchased from Lufthansa in 1938, was limited to survey work over Greenland, in company with He.8s.

Since 1864, Danish defense policy had been one of doing nothing to antagonize Germany, the nearest great power. The northern half of Schleswig, lost to the German Confederation at the end of the war, was populated mostly by Danes. At the end of World War I, the Versailles Treaty awarded northern Schleswig to Denmark. This was a mixed blessing, restoring a rich, heavily populated territory to Denmark, but providing a possible point of conflict with Germany. However, the fact that Denmark did not press for more concessions at a time of German weakness was to stand her in good stead in the future.

The rapid spread of fascism, and the rearmament of Germany, increased Danish anxiety. Denmark relied upon the League of Nations against aggrandizement by great powers, but was becoming concerned that it was too weak to defend Denmark while involving her in non-neutral operations. Recognizing the new domination of the Baltic by Germany, Great Britain entered into a naval agreement with Hitler in 1935, effectively abandoning the area to the Germans. During the summer of 1936, Denmark declared that League of Nations military decisions would no longer be binding.

# WORLD WAR II

Denmark refused to accept the possibility of becoming involved in the coming European conflict. The Allies anticipated that Germany would show little interest in Scandinavia, but they reckoned without proper appreciation for modern air power. Hitler planned to occupy Norway to gain a flanking position for his bombers, bases for his commerce-raiding warships, and a guaranteed supply of high-grade Swedish iron ore. Denmark lay in his path, and would serve as a convenient staging point for *Operation Weserubung*. From the airfields of Aalborg, near the northern tip of Jutland, he could control North Sea communications. The units of the German Special Command that gathered in Schleswig went unnoticed in the torrent of westward troop movements that followed the Polish Campaign. Determined on neutrality, the Rigsdag did not even mobilize its forces:

**ROYAL LIFE GUARD REGIMENT**
2 infantry battalions
    4 rifle companies
    1 machinegun company

**Madsen M1924**
7.92 mm, 11 kg, 680 m/s, 450 rpm

**CAVALRY REGIMENT**
1 armored car troop
    **3 armored cars**
2-3 cyclist squadrons (Hussars of the Guard)
4 horse squadrons (3 in Hussars of the Guard)
1 anti-tank troop
    **4 Solothurn 20 mm AT guns**

**Madsen M35**
37 mm, 341 kg, 0.80 kg shell,
900 m/s, 55 mm/500 m P

**INFANTRY REGIMENT**
3 infantry battalions
    3 rifle companies
        **Krag-Jorgensen M.1889/10 8 mm rifle**
    1 machinegun company
        **9 Madsen M.1919, M.1924,**
            **M.1939 8 mm lmg**
    1 weapons company
        **4 Solothurn 20 mm AT guns**
        **6 Rheinmetall 81 mm mortars**
    1 anti-tank company
        **8 Madsen M35 37 mm AT guns or**
        **Bohler M35 47 mm AT guns**

**Bohler M35**
47 mm, 336 kg, 1.45 kg shell,
670 m/s, 35 mm/1000 m P

**FIELD ARTILLERY REGIMENT**
2 light artillery groups
    3 light artillery batteries
        **8 Ehrhardt M.02 75 mm field guns**
1 heavy artillery group
    3 heavy artillery batteries
        **8 Krupp M.98/09 105 mm howitzers**, or
        **Krupp M.13 150 mm howitzers**

**ANTI-AIRCRAFT BATTALION**
4 batteries
    **4 Madsen 23 mm AA guns**

**Sjaelland Division** - Copenhagen
  Royal Life Guard Regiment
  Hussar of the Guard Regiment
    2 Landsverk L.181, 1 L.185
  1.,4.,5. Infantry Regiments
  1.,2. Field Artillery Regiments
  13. Anti-aircraft Artillery Battalion
  1 engineer battalion
**Jylland Division** - Viborg
  Jutland Dragoon Regiment
    3 Landsverk Lynx
  2.,3.,6.,7. Infantry Regiments
  3. Field Artillery Regiment
  14. Anti-aircraft Artillery Battalion
  2 engineer battalions
Army Reserve
  2 heavy artillery groups

**Landsverk L.181**
1933, 7.8 tons, 1-20 mm, 3 mgs,
80 km/h, 290 km, 9/5 mm, 5 men,
20 mm/500 m P

**Landsverk Lynx**
1938, 7.8 tons, 1-20 mm, 3 mgs,
70 km/h, 250 km, 18 mm, 6 men,
20 mm/500 m P

In 1923, the uniform was officially changed to a khaki color. However, the Rigsdag allocated no funds for new uniforms. As officers and non-commissioned officers purchased their own uniforms, they wore the new style, but the men continued to wear the gray of 1915. All grades wore the M.1923 khaki helmet in the field.

Insignia of rank for officers was worn on shoulder straps bordered with broad braid of branch color (infantry-scarlet, artillery-carmine, hussars-white, dragoons-carmine, engineers-light red):

Generals - large 6-ptd gold stars
  General - 3
  Lieutenant General - 2
  Major General - 1
Field Officers - medium 6-ptd gold stars
  Colonel - 3
  Lieutenant Colonel - 2
  Major (nonexistent in Danish Army)
Line Officers - small 6-ptd gold stars
  Captain - 3
  Captain-Lieutenant - 2, with boss in center
  1st Lieutenant - 2
  Lieutenant - 1, with boss at top
  2nd Lieutenant - 1

General

Captain-Lieutenant

Insignia of rank for non-commissioned officers was worn on shoulder straps bordered with braid of branch color, or as chevrons above the cuff:

Senior Non-commissioned Officers - gold buttons and bars
  Sergeant Major, 1st class - 2 buttons, 1 bar in center
  Sergeant Major, 2nd class - 2 buttons
  Sergeant Major, 3rd class - 1 button, 1 bar above
  Sergeant Major, 4th class - 1 button
  Staff Sergeant - 2 bars
  Sergeant - 1 bar
  Cadet - 1 boss
Junior Non-comm. Officers - yellow chevrons
  Corporal - 2
  Soldier, 1st class - 1

Corporal

Sergeant Major,
3rd class

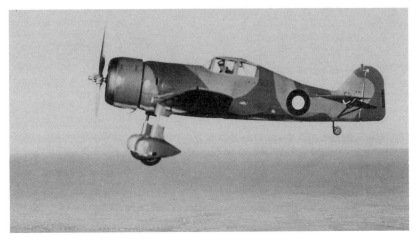
The 2. Eskadrille Was Still Working Up Its Fokker IIIJs When the War Began.

The Army Air Service continued upgrading its equipment. The first Danish Army fighter squadron formed after the World War had not filled out until 18 licence-built Gloster Gauntlets were delivered by the *Haerens Flyvertropper Vaerksteder* in 1938. They were followed by a handful of Dutch Fokker D.21s early in 1940.

**Haerens Flyvertropper** (Col. Foerslev)

Sjaellandving - Vaerlose
  1. Eskadrille
    **13 Gloster IIJ**
  3. Eskadrille
    **9 Fokker IIR, 2 Fokker IR**

Jyllandving - Vaerlose
  2. Eskadrille
    **7 Fokker IIIJ, 3 Fokker IR**
  5. Eskadrille
    **12 Fokker IIIR, 2 Fokker IR,**
    **1 Avro IM**

**Fokker IIIJ**
1936, 11 m span, 460 km/h, 850 km,
8/6000 m, 11000 m SC, 2-20 mm, 2mgs,
100 kg B  (Fokker D.21)

**Fokker IIR, IIIR**
1925, 15 m span, 254 km/h, 1200 km,
7500 m SC, 2 mgs, 50 kg B
(Fokker C.VE)

**Gloster IIJ**
1928, 10 m span, 370 km/h, 733 km,
9/6100 m, 10218 m SC, 2mgs
(Gloster Gauntlet II)

Although a good machine, the Gauntlet was obsolete by the time it entered service.  Events were moving so swiftly that the War Ministry's next acquisition was also behind world progress.  A delight to fly, the licence-produced IIIJ was too slow and too lightly armed for 1940.[50]

74

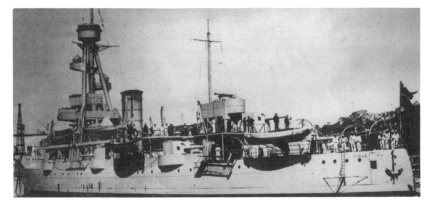

Niels Juel, Flagship of the Danish Navy

By 1940, the Danish Fleet had become purely defensive in concept. Gone were most of the armored ships, and all of the cruisers. The torpedo boats were painted dark brown, the submarines dark green. All others were a light gray.

**Danish Navy**

Coast Defense Division
  *Niels Juel*
  *Peder Skram* {1 **H.M.II**}

coast defense
battleship ¨

Torpedo Division
  *Glenten, Högen, Örnen*
  *Dragen, Hvalen, Laxen*
  *Makrelen, Nordkaperen,*
    *Havkatten, Saelen*
  *Springeren, Stören, Sölöven,*
    *Söhunden, Havhesten, Narhvalen*
  *Hvalrossen*

**Niels Juel** 1920, 3,861 tons, 26 km/h, 6440 km,
10-15 cm, 2 TT, 5/20 cm armor,
modernized 1935-6, stricken 1952

Submarine Division
  *Havmanden, Havfruen,*
  *Havkalen, Havhesten*
  *Daphne, Dryaden*
  *Rota, Bellona, Flora*
  *Ran, Triton, Galathea*
  *Henrik Gerner* (tender)

Mine Division
  *Lindormen*
  *Lossen*
  *Kvintus, Sixtus*
  *Söbjörnen, Sölöven, Söulven,*
  *Söridderen, Söhesten, Söhunden*

Fishery Protection Division
  *Freja*
  *Hejmdal*
  *Ingolf* {1 **H.M.II**}
  *Hvidbjörnen* {1 **H.M.II**}

seaplane
tender

Seaplane Tender
  *Beskytteren* {2 **H.M.II**}

**Beskytteren** 1900, 447 tons, 18 km/h,
2-7.5 cm, 2 seaplanes

75

*Niels Juel* had been completed after the Great War, sporting a tall conning tower, and was overhauled with modern machinery just before World War II. The *Peder Skram*, also had updated machinery, but retained her original appearance. *Beskytteren*, an old fishery vessel, was often used as a tender for the Navy's seaplanes.

Half a dozen torpedo boats and submarines, completed between the wars, were very small coastal vessels. The sloops *Ingolf* and *Hvidbjörnen*, were intended for fishery protection and overseas operations.

torpedo
boat

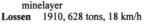

torpedo
boat

| | | |
|---|---|---|
| **Glenten** | 1934, 290 tons, 44 km/h, | |
| **Örnen** | 2-8 cm, 6 TT | |
| **Högen** | stricken 1945 | |

| | | |
|---|---|---|
| **Dragen** | 1930, 290 tons, 44 km/h, |
| **Laxen** | 2-7.5 cm, 8 TT |
| **Hvalen** | stricken 1945 |

sub

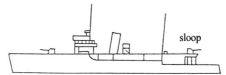

sub

| | |
|---|---|
| **Havmanden** | 1938, 315 tons, 13/28 km/h, |
| **Havfruen** | 5 TT |
| **Havkalen** | |
| **Havhesten** | |

| | |
|---|---|
| **Daphne** | 1926, 302 tons, 13/26 km/h, |
| **Dryaden** | 1-7.5 cm, 6 TT |

minelayer

**Lindormen** 1940, 622 tons, 23 km/h,
2-7.5 cm, 150 mines
stricken 1969

minelayer
**Lossen** 1910, 628 tons, 18 km/h

sloop

**Hejmdal** 1935, 705 tons, 21 km/h,
2-7.5 cm, 6440 km

sloop

**Ingolf** 1934, 1,200 tons, 31 km/h, 5600 km,
2-12 cm, 4 small AA, 1 floatplane
**Hvidbjörnen** 1929, 1,067 tons, 27 km/h,
2-9 cm, 5500 km, 1 floatplane

torpedo
boat

**Nymphen** 1943, 720 tons, 56 km/h,
**Najaden** 2-12 cm, 6 TT, 60 mines
completed in 1947

minesweeper
**Söbjörnen** 1939, 270 tons, 33 km/h,
**Söridderen** 2-7.5 cm, 2 small AA
**Söhesten**
**Sölöven**
**Söulven**
**Söhunden**

The Navy ordered two new ocean-going torpedo boats, the *Najaden* and *Nymphen*, but they had not been laid down by the time Denmark fell. [51]

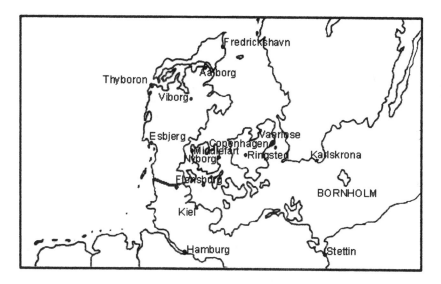

**Marinen Flyvevaesenets** (Commander Grandjean)

1. Luftflotille - Copenhagen
   **13 Heinkel H.M.II**
   **1 Dornier F.M.I**

2. Luftflotille - Ringsted
   **9 Hawker L.B.V**
   **2 Hawker H.B.III**

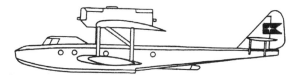

**Hawker L.B.V**
1933, 9 m span, 333 km/h, 491 km,
8540 m SC, 2 mgs, 45 kg B
(Hawker Nimrod)

**Dornier F.M.I**
1922, 23 m span, 185 km/h, 2190 km,
4500 m SC, 2 mgs, 1000 kg B
(Dornier Wal)

Intended for the defense of the principal naval base at Copenhagen, the Hawker L.B.Vs were also capable of dive bombing. After a 60° dive from high altitude, they could release 50 kilograms of bombs from 1200 meters, or they could approach from low altitude, dive briefly at 30°, and drop the bombs from 300 meters above the ground.

The Naval Air Service was incapable of carrying out its mission in the environment of 1940. Its principal interceptor was 300 km/h slower than the Messerschmitts possessed by Germany. The remainder of its aircraft were of 1920s vintage. The Danish government had pursued a policy of non-provocation toward its powerful neighbors, leaving only enough military strength to dissuade petty adventurers. Hitler was no petty adventurer.

With her new, though obsolescent, weapons, Denmark could fend off free-booters and hold her own in minor disputes, but had not the resources to confront a major invasion. Such an invasion erupted in the Spring of 1940. Germany had mopped up pockets of Polish resistance following the tidal wave that had swept over that unfortunate people early in the previous fall. During the ensuing winter, German troop trains hurried their victorious forces to the Rhineland to confront French forces feebly demonstrating in Lorraine. No one noticed that not all of the troops passed by to the west.

The Eyes of the Danish Army - a Fokker IIIR.

Early on **9 April 1940**, Danish anti-aircraft batteries near Flensburg opened fire on unidentified aircraft passing overhead, bringing down at least one large plane. A Fokker IIIR of the 5. Eskadrille was dispatched from Vaerlose to investigate the disquiet in South Jutland. It returned with a report of large numbers of German aircraft intruding Danish air space on a northerly course. The Danish commanders already knew. At 0415, formations of Heinkel He.111 medium bombers of the German KG 4 had roared over Copenhagen. Fortunately, the missiles descending from them were of paper, not explosives.

Vaerlose was not so fortunate. The government had delayed dispersing its air force to safer airstrips, fearing provocation of Hitler. Finally receiving dispersal orders, the aircraft were warming their engines for the move early on the 9th when a report of the German incursions was received. The leading Fokker IIIR took off, but was only 50 meters off the ground when a hail of shells blew it out of the air. The killer was a sleek Messerschmitt Bf.110 of I/ZG 1, which had been escorting the German bombers over the capital. Peeling off from their undisturbed charges, the Bf.110s had swooped down on the vulnerable Danish aircraft lined up on the aerodrome. With their crews scrambling for shelter, no further Danish aircraft attempted to rise. When the *zerstorergruppe* had completed its strafing attack, it had destroyed 11 aircraft and heavily damaged 14 others. Unready to join combat, the 2. Eskadrille lost one of its Fokker IIIJs, with 4 others rendered unserviceable pending major repairs. Within minutes, Denmark was left with no air protection for her Army or population.

Hitler's demand for free passage through the country was opposed only by Danish border guards when German troops crossed the frontier at dawn on 9 April. While Pz.Kw.Is and IIs of Panzer Abteilung 40 helped German infantry mop up the border guards, the 11. Motorized Rifle Brigade raced up the west coast of Jutland. Some Danish infantrymen left their barracks in time to form up, but they were quickly routed. The Germans secured free passage by *coup de main.*

At Esbjerg, the Danish garrison was assailed in three dimensions. Messerschmitt Bf.109Es of II/JG 77 hovered over them while the minesweepers of the German Marine Group X disgorged troops to occupy their strategic base at the head of the North Frisian Islands. Coming by road, the motorized brigade arrived shortly afterward. The Messerschmitts landed on the airfield to defend the west coast from possible Allied raids.

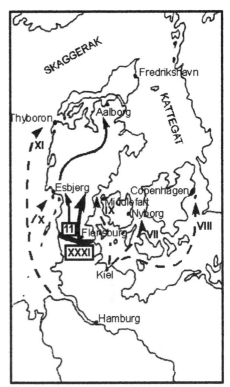

Another hundred kilometers up the coast, a second flotilla of minesweepers (Group XI) took possession of Thyboron, at the mouth of the Limfjord, which formed a sea passage to the strategic interior of northern Jutland.

At 0700, German paratroops began dropping on the two major aerodromes at Aalborg, followed immediately by swarms of Ju.52/3ms bearing troops of the 69. Infantry Division staging toward Norway. The Germans planned to use the airfields to protect the groups of warships plowing through the North Sea. *Peder Skram* was anchored in the roads off Fredrikshavn, near the northern entrance to the Kattegat. Just as the German attack began, its H.M.II floatplane left the water, yet safely reached Fredrikshavn harbor. Messerschmitt Bf.110s of I/ZG 1, and Junkers Ju.87Bs of I/StG 1, landed on the airfields at Aalborg, followed by Dornier Do.18 flying boats and landplanes of Ku.Fl.Gr. 706.

Similar movements were taking place in Baltic waters. The severe winter had blocked the Danish straits with ice, causing the Germans some anxiety as the time for action approached. However, the same severity had forced the Danish Navy to place in storage most of its Heinkel H.M.IIs, and the single Dornier F.M.I flying boat, after they returned from their 1939 survey of Greenland. The Navy deployed two *luftflotille*, one for seaplanes at Copenhagen and one for landplanes at Ringsted, in central Zealand southwest of the capital. In the face of a sky full of fleet Messerschmitts, the Hawker L.B.Vs were helpless and never left the ground, nor did the two lumbering H.B.III torpedo bombers. Two Heinkel H.M.IIs at shore bases escaped attention from the Luftwaffe, but the Danes saw little of the enemy naval forces approaching their islands.

The old German battleship *Schleswig-Holstein* led Marine Group VII through the Great Belt to Nyborg, where troops were landed on the east coast of the large island of Fyen without opposition. Minesweepers of Marine Group IX negotiated the Little Belt to secure Middlefart on the island's west coast. The battleship's guns were not needed, for a minelayer of Marine Group VIII had sealed the *Niels Juel* into its base at Copenhagen. The group's motor torpedo boats waited in vain to pick off Danish warships that ventured out. The most powerful Danish forces were on Sjaelland, defending the capital. With reports pouring in of enemy forces roaring up the Jutland Peninsula, ground troops prepared to face an inevitable landing.

Hussars Patrol in a Landsverk L.181

A Trojan Horse was already present in Copenhagen. Before the invasion began, an infantry battalion of the German 198. Infantry Division had been smuggled into the harbor aboard a disguised troopship. Early on 9 April, it was put ashore north of the city and quickly advanced to the Citadel, an ancient Danish fortress that guarded the route to the capital and the headquarters of the Danish Army. Its garrison of 70 men was quickly captured and the enemy battalion hurried on to Amalienborg Palace, where it clashed with the Danish Royal Guard. Realizing that resistance was useless, King Christian X ordered a ceasefire at 0834. Danish casualties in the war, mainly from the Royal Guard, were 13 killed and 24 wounded.[52,53]

### *The Occupation* - 1940-1942

Technically, Denmark had not been at war with Germany, for she had never ordered her Army to initiate operations. As a result, Hitler allowed a great deal of local control within the country. The Rigsdag continued to meet, although with German "supervision". Denmark had a Nazi party, the *Dansk Samling*, but it played little part in the government. Foreign Minister Munch skillfully deflected many of Hitler's demands. Most naval vessels remained in the possession of the Danes, only the six newest torpedo boats being taken into the German Navy on 5 February 1941 for use as training vessels. Although the Air Force also was permitted to operate, all flying was banned and the remaining airworthy planes were stored (10 IIIJs, 15 IIRs and IIIRs, 8 L.B.Vs, 13 H.M.IIs, 1 F.M.I). Few German troops were quartered in Denmark, which was exhibited to an anxious Europe as a good example of a cooperative Nazi protectorate.

80

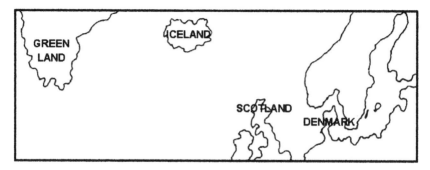

After the German occupation of their homeland, Danes found refuge in many different places. Some had already tasted battle on foreign soil. A battalion of volunteers fought with the Finns during their Winter War of 1939-40, nationality distinguished by a red and white stripe on the collar tabs of their Finnish uniforms. Some Danish seamen, at sea during the German invasion of their country, made their way to England and operated motor minesweepers for the Royal Navy from the autumn of 1943.

Greenland was the spawning grounds for weather systems headed for Europe, making it an important site for meteorlogical parties engaged in forecasting weather on the Continent. As the air war escalated, German units clandestinely operated on the island, hunted by the Allies and Greenlanders alike. The other Danish possessions in the North Atlantic also became involved in the conflict. Iceland became a staging point for Allied units supporting the convoys to Russia. The severance encouraged ideas of independence.

### Danes in the German SS - 1940-1945

Yet, for the most part, Denmark remained a peaceful subject of the Third Reich. In April 1940, the SS Nordland Regiment was formed, under the command of Count Schalburg of the former Danish Royal Guards. Eventually, the regiment mustered 800 Danes and 800 Norwegians. Along with the West European SS Westland Regiment, and the Finnish SS Battalion, it formed the 5. SS Wiking Division of the German Army Group South during the invasion of Russia. As part of Kleist's 1. Panzergruppe, it fought in Galicia and the Ukraine, participating in the capture of Rostov. During 1942, it advanced into the Caucasus Mountains in company with the Slovak Fast Division. It escaped over the Don River with heavy losses after Stalingrad.

Meanwhile, *Freikorps Danemark* had formed on 28 June 1941. By December, it mustered 1,500 Danes. At the beginning of 1942, it was sent to the front with the 1,500 Norwegians of the *Norske Legion*, operating around Leningrad as part of the 3. SS Totenkopf Panzer Division for the rest of the year. The remaining Nordic troops were used to form the 11. SS Nordland Panzergrenadier Division in the spring of 1943. It operated against partisans in Croatia from May-November, then moved to Narva, Estonia at the end of the year. Nearby were 15 former Danish Air Force Fokker C.VEs that had been overhauled and issued to an Estonian squadron for night harassment attacks on the Soviets. In October 1944, the Nordland Division moved to a position south of Riga, Latvia. Evacuated to Germany at the end of 1944, it fought in the defense of Berlin until the war ended. A total of 6-7,000 Danes served in the Waffen-SS.

81

## Resistance Begins - 1943-1945

The situation at home had changed with the German invasion of the Soviet Union during the summer of 1941. Although it announced a state of non-belligerency, the Danish government broke off diplomatic relations with the Soviets and Prime Minister Scavenius expressed support for Finland and Germany in the fight against Bolshevism. The Danish Communist Party, already strong, developed into a formidable resistance group and started a campaign of sabotage in April 1942. Most other Danes initially opposed terrorism, but indiscriminate reprisals by the Germans against the Communist activities fell upon all. Sabotage increased during 1943, and the Communists gained control of the Danish shipyard unions. German brutality in putting down shipyard strikes caused an uprising on 9 August 1943 that quickly spread. After a strike in Odense from 18-23 August ended in bloody rioting, similar strikes broke out across Zealand and Jutland. On 24 August, Hitler demanded that the Danish government execute strikers and saboteurs. In a reply four days later, the government refused to comply. German troops seized Danish Army posts and interned their garrisons. Under martial law, saboteurs were executed.

A great uprising occurred all over Denmark on **29 August 1943**. Acts of sabotage against German facilities were accompanied by destruction of stored aircraft and equipment by Danish military personnel. Defiant units of the Danish Navy put to sea and sailed for Sweden. *Niels Juel* reached the open waters of the Isefjord in northern Zealand, but was bombed by German aircraft and had to be beached. The torpedo boat *Havhesten* was wrecked trying to escape. Four other torpedo boats (*Stören, Narhvalen, Havkatten, Söhunden*) successfully reached Swedish anchorages. The rest of the vessels were scuttled by their crews. Some were later salvaged and put into service by the Germans. The Gestapo began to operate against the Resistance the following month. Many Danish leaders were arrested and sent to the concentration camp at Horseröd, although citizens helped 7,000 Danish Jews to escape to Sweden. A Freedom Council was formed on 16 September to oversee all resistance activities.

## The Free Danes - 1940-1945

When the Army was demobilized in August 1943, most of its officers remained in Copenhagen to prepare for liberation. Danish leaders approached the Swedish government with a plan to smuggle the corps of officers to Sweden and rebuild the Danish Army there. They requested arms for 50,000 men, including tanks and aircraft. In the event, a small group of officers escaped to recruit volunteers for a Danish Corps. With fewer than 500 men in Sweden at the end of 1943, it grew into the Danish Brigade of 5,000 men by May 1945.

At the end of 1944, it was organized into infantry battalions, clothed in Swedish uniforms with Danish insignia, and trained with Swedish weapons. Although no tanks were ever provided by the Swedes, a small squadron of 8 Saab B17Cs was trained to support the ground troops in action.[54]

**Saab B17C**
1940, 14 m span, 435 km/h,
3 mgs, 680 kg B

82

Increasing numbers of fighting men escaped abroad, many gravitating to Great Britain. Several battalions formed up in northern England, wearing British battle dress with an arc on the peak of their shoulders bearing the title "Danmark" in white letters on a red field, and utilizing Danish rank insignia. An additional 774 men joined the British Army. A number of Danish airmen also flew with the Royal Air Force, chiefly in the Norwegian squadrons. Two-thirds of the Danish merchant marine sailed with the Allies. The Allies never organized the Danes into an active combat unit and the Danish government-in-exile never declared war on Germany. Nevertheless, from August 1944, quantities of arms began arriving for the underground, which possessed 43,000 fairly well-equipped men by the time the Danish government-in-exile signed an agreement with the Freedom Council on 1 May 1945.

The Communists were gaining support in Denmark through their untiring fight against the Nazis. A general strike by the population of Copenhagen in July 1944 led to open rebellion throughout the country. German communications were interdicted and supplies destroyed. Danish officials began to fear a Communist takeover of Denmark when the war ended, as the British appeared indifferent to the situation in Scandinavia. The Freedom Council was dominated by Communists, and the Soviet Union was known to desire control of the outlet to the Baltic.

As large numbers of German troops were still in northern Norway, controlling the vital Swedish iron ore and the nickel mines of Petsamo, it was thought that Germany would seek to maintain control of Denmark as an escape route for its northern troops. The Wehrmacht had 200,000 men in Denmark. Three German infantry divisions were deployed along the west coast of Jutland, with a fourth just over the German border and a fifth in Copenhagen. The 233. Reserve Panzer Division was stationed at Horsens, on the southeast coast of Jutland, with a handful of obsolete French tanks.

Increasing pressure was put on Sweden to aid in driving out the Nazis when the war ended. Although the Swedish high command developed such operational plans, when the Allied armies reached the mouth of the Elbe River in the spring of 1945, the German troops in Denmark laid down their arms. King Christian X and the new prime minister, Vilhem Buhl, took charge. The Danish troops from Sweden and England restored order without a fight.[55]

Peace - Cattle Graze Among Abandoned Ju.88s on an Airfield in Denmark

# DENMARK IN THE COLD WAR

From 1947-9, a brigade group of 4,000 men took part in the occupation of Germany, but was reduced to 1,000 men in 1949. Denmark's active army was composed of 2 divisions by 1950, one based on Jutland, the other on Zealand. It retained the British organization, uniforms, weapons and techniques acquired by the independent battalions of exiles that trained in northern Britain during the war.

**Humber Mk.II**
1941, 7 tons, 2 mgs,
72 km/h, 400 km, 15/5 mm, 3 men

In 1946, war surplus Humber Mk.II scout cars, Humber Mk.IV armored cars, and Staghound Mk.III armored cars were obtained from Britain, along with Canadian C 15TA armored personnel carriers. With them, mechanization of the Danish Army began.

A small navy of escorts and submarines, principally of British origin, was assembled after the war.

frigate

frigate

**Holger Danske**   1943, 1,420 tons, 22 km/h,
**Niels Ebbesen**   2-13 cm
(ex-British River class),
stricken 1959

**Esbern Snare**   1941, 1,067 tons, 27 km/h,
**Rolf Krake**   6-10 cm
**Valdemar Sejr**   (ex-British Hunt class),
stricken 1963

coastal
destroyer

**Huitfeldt**   1947, 790 tons, 56 km/h, 2-10 cm
**Willemoes**   rerated Patrol Vessels in 1958,
(ex-Nymfen and Najaden), stricken 1965

corvette

sub

**Thetis**   1940, 1,016 tons, 18 km/h,
1-10 cm, stricken 1963
(ex-British Flower class)

**Saelen**   1942, 550 tons, 18/24 km/h,
**Springeren**   4 TT, (ex-British U class),
**Stören**   stricken 1956

84

## SCANDINAVIAN
## SOLIDARITY

A flare from the Danish Royal Yacht signals the coastal destroyers *Huitfeldt* and *Willemoes* to take station ahead of a division of three Norwegian *Oslo*-class frigates steaming through Oslofjord. Jubilation at the war's end was soon dampened by the growing enmity between the Western democracies and the Soviet Union, succinctly labeled "The Cold War".

Danish seamen were scattered around Western Europe following the uprising of 1943. The new Navy was formed around those deemed loyal to the government-in-exile, who had been trained on British vessels. Only the *Nymphen* and *Najaden*, renamed *Huitfeldt* and *Willemoes* were discharged from German service to join the new escort flotilla.

Danish airmen, returning from wartime service in British and Norwegian air units, were organized into three squadrons:

**Flyvevåben**

721. Eskadrille
    **8 Consolidated PBY-5A**
722. Eskadrille
    **19 Supermarine Spitfire LF/HF.IXe**
    **3 Supermarine Spitfire HF.XI**
    **3 Supermarine Spitfire PR.XI**
725. Eskadrille
    **19 Supermarine Spitfire LF/HF.IXe**

**Supermarine Spitfire IX**
1942, 11 m span, 670 km/h, 700 km,
6.4/6100 m, 13725 m SC, 454 kg B,
2-20 mm, 2 mgs

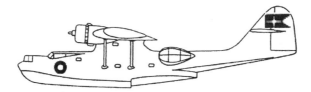

**Consolidated PBY-5A**
1939, 32 m span, 272 km/h, 2670 km,
4480 m SC, 5 mgs, 1820 kg B

## NATO Integration - 1950

Denmark joined the North Atlantic Treaty Organization in 1949, under the sponsorship of the United States. This departure from a century of neutrality was impressed upon the Danes by the vulnerability of their position. For ten months at the end of World War II, the Soviets had occupied the strategic island of Bornholm, from which they controlled access to the Baltic. Astride the sea route giving the Soviet Union access to the Atlantic Ocean, Danish fears were heightened when the Soviets successfully engineered Communist takeovers in eastern Europe. The coast of Marxist East Germany lurked menacingly but 50 kilometers to the south. Would Denmark, with its strong Communist party, be the next satellite?

The Defense Act of 1951 directed reorganization of the Army. American officers began advising the Danish commanders in techniques successful in American experience, and an olive drab British-style uniform with NATO helmet was adopted. A medical team was sent to participate in the United Nations police action in Korea. Mechanization was increased with the arrival of American M3 and M5 halftracks for use as armored personnel and weapons carriers. A battalion of M41 light tanks was purchased from the United States, and initially used in the infantry support role.

The Air Force had been made an independent branch of the Armed Forces on 1 October 1950. Great Britain supplied its initial jet equipment. Two squadrons of Meteors became operational after several years of operational training on the Spitfire IXs that formed Denmark's initial postwar aerial defenses.

By 1952, Denmark possessed:

**Flyvevåben**

721. Eskadrille
**8 Consolidated PBY-5A**
**8 Douglas C-47A, 2 Bell 47D**

722. Eskadrille
**20 Supermarine Spitfire IX**
**6 Supermarine Spitfire XI**

723. Eskadrille
**20 Gloster Meteor F.4**
**20 Gloster Meteor N.F.11** (1952)

**Republic F-84G**
1950, 11 m span, 1001 km/h (0.82), 2367 km,
8/10675 m, 12353 m SC, 6 mgs, 1816 kg B

724. Eskadrille
**20 Gloster Meteor F.8**
**20 Hawker Hunter F.51** (1956)

725. Eskadrille
**6 Republic F-84E** (1951)
**20 Republic F-84G**
726. Eskadrille
**20 Republic F-84G**
727. Eskadrille
**20 Republic F-84G**
728. Eskadrille
**20 Republic F-84G**
729. Eskadrille
**20 Republic F-84G**
730. Eskadrille
**20 Republic F-84G**

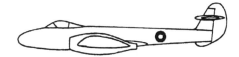

**Gloster Meteor F.4, 8**
1948, 11 m span, 953 km/h (0.78), 1932 km,
12/12200 m, 4-20 mm
**Gloster Meteor N.F.11**
1950, 13 m span, 871 km/h (0.80), 1530 km,
13115 m SC, 4-20 mm

**Hawker Hunter F.51**
1954, 10 m span, 1151 km/h (0.92), 1127 km,
13725 m SC, 4-30 mm, 4 Fireflash SAM

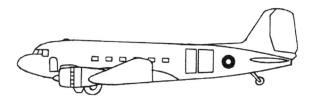

**Douglas C-47A**
1935, 29 m span, 369 km/h, 2415 km,
7300 m SC, 28 troops or 3400 kg C    [56]

The Unswept F-84G Thunderjet Became Denmark's First Standard Jet Fighter

**Danish Army**

2 mechanized divisions - Jutland, Zealand
  2-3 mechanized brigades
    1 reconnaissance squadron
      **12 M41**
    1 tank battalion
      **22 Centurion 3**
    2 mechanized infantry battalions
      **M3, M5 halftrack APCs**
    1 artillery battalion
      **M-101 105 mm field howitzer**
      **M-114 155 mm field howitzer**
    1 engineer company

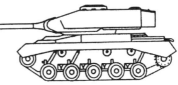

**M41A2**
1949, 23.5 tons, 1-76.2 mm, 2 mgs,
65 km/h, 160 km, 38/30/25 mm,
140 mm/1000 m P, 4 men

Army Aviation
  8 liaison platoons
    **2 Piper L-18C Super Cub** (from 1957)

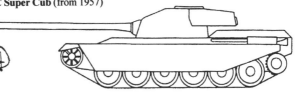

**Piper L-18C Super Cub**
1949, 11 m span, 177 km/h,
4120 m SC, no mg

**Centurion Mk.3**
1948, 49.5 tons, 1-83.4 mm, 1 mg,
34 km/h, 105 km, 152/76/51 mm,
165 mm/1000 m P, 4 men

**M-3**
1935, 10.3 tons, 2 mgs,
72 km/h, 322 km, 13 mm, 13 men

A shift in the supply of armaments had already begun. Having been nurtured, trained and armed in the United Kingdom after the occupation of their homeland, it was logical that the reborn Danish Army should employ British arms, uniforms and methods. However, these were growing old, and replacements were expensive. Although some British aircraft continued to find their way to the Danish squadrons, the purchase of 338 Republic F-84G fighters at relatively low cost under a mutual defense treaty with the United States was only the first of a long line of transactions with American arms suppliers. American advisors accompanied the new armaments, supplying Americanized uniforms and training. However, a British design was selected for the new main battle tank.

It was obvious that heavier armor was needed by the Army and, late in the decade, 217 Centurion Mk.3s were acquired from Great Britain, displacing the M41s to reconnaissance duties. With the new weapons, the Danish Army was reconfigured to produce a more viable defense.

**RIFLE COMPANY**
HQ - **2-.50 cal hmgs**
3 rifle platoons
    HQ - **1-3.5" RL, 1 SMG**
    3 rifle squads
        **1 Madsen or MG 42/59 AR**
        **5 M1 Garand rifles**
        **2 SMGs**
1 heavy weapons platoon
    **5 Madsen or MG 42/59 AR** (with tripod)
    **3-60 mm mortars**
    **2-3.5" RL**

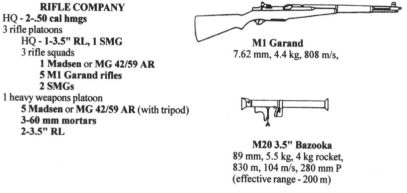

**M1 Garand**
7.62 mm, 4.4 kg, 808 m/s,

**M20 3.5" Bazooka**
89 mm, 5.5 kg, 4 kg rocket,
830 m, 104 m/s, 280 mm P
(effective range - 200 m)

**M2**
12.7 mm, 59 kg, 900 m/s, 650 rpm

**M2**
60 mm, 19 kg, 1.4 kg shell,
1750 m, 158 m/s, 18 rpm      57

Danish troops participated in United Nations peacekeeping operations in Palestine, the Congo, and Cyprus. Denmark also supplied Truce Observers following conflicts in Israel, Lebanon, Yemen and the Kashmir.

With Communist takeovers occurring on her doorstep, Denmark had quickly constructed an aerial umbrella with the financial aid of the American MDAP program, using some of the most advanced warplanes of the time. Although a utilitarian design with few innovations, this very simplicity made the F-84G an ideal high-performance aircraft on which to develop operational techniques for a small air force.

However, this costly project was soon rendered obsolete by the appearance of swept-wing, then supersonic, jet aircraft. The prohibitive cost of keeping up with the rapidly improving technical achievements in military hardware began to plague Denmark.

The war surplus British vessels of the Navy were replaced by Danish-built warships during the 1960s. In 1962, 8 Alouette III helicopters were acquired for use aboard the four frigates employed in fishery protection.

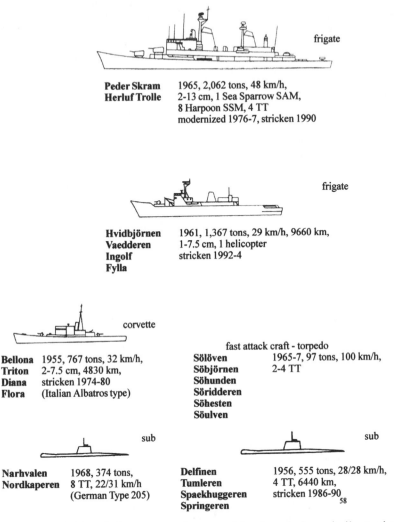

frigate

**Peder Skram**
**Herluf Trolle**

1965, 2,062 tons, 48 km/h,
2-13 cm, 1 Sea Sparrow SAM,
8 Harpoon SSM, 4 TT
modernized 1976-7, stricken 1990

frigate

**Hvidbjörnen**
**Vaedderen**
**Ingolf**
**Fylla**

1961, 1,367 tons, 29 km/h, 9660 km,
1-7.5 cm, 1 helicopter
stricken 1992-4

corvette

**Bellona**  1955, 767 tons, 32 km/h,
**Triton**   2-7.5 cm, 4830 km,
**Diana**    stricken 1974-80
**Flora**    (Italian Albatros type)

fast attack craft - torpedo
**Sölöven**      1965-7, 97 tons, 100 km/h,
**Söbjörnen**    2-4 TT
**Söhunden**
**Söridderen**
**Söhesten**
**Söulven**

sub

**Narhvalen**    1968, 374 tons,
**Nordkaperen**  8 TT, 22/31 km/h
                 (German Type 205)

sub

**Delfinen**       1956, 555 tons, 28/28 km/h,
**Tumleren**       4 TT, 6440 km,
**Spaekhuggeren**  stricken 1986-90
**Springeren**                          58

Danish dockyards began to produce warships for missions similar to those assigned to the Navy before the war. The *Peder Skram* and *Herluf Trolle* embodied the pride of the new Navy, possessing the size and armament to keep an eye on Denmark's three detached possessions, Bornholm, Greenland and the Faroe Islands.

To aid the two flagships in maintaining this far-flung empire, the Danes chose to protect their own coasts with small coastal submarines and the mainstay of small, modern navies - the fast attack boat, of which the first Danish examples arrived in 1965, armed with guns. Communications between Danish possessions were guarded by the *Hvidbjörnen* class of frigates and the *Bellona* corvettes, assisted by on-board hellicopters.

**Flyvevåben**

721. Eskadrille
3 Douglas C-54D
3 Bell 47J

722. Eskadrille
8 Consolidated PBY-6A
7 Sikorsky S-55C

723. Eskadrille
20 North American F-86D
724. Eskadrille
30 Hawker Hunter F.51
725. Eskadrille
20 North American F-100D,F
726. Eskadrille
20 North American F-86D
727. Eskadrille
20 North American F-100D,F
728. Eskadrille
20 North American F-86D
729. Eskadrille
20 Republic RF-84F
730. Eskadrille
20 North American F-100D,F

**Republic RF-84F Thunderflash**
1952, 10 m span, 1093 km/h (0.94), 3540 km,
14020 m SC, 4 mgs, cameras

**Sikorsky S-55C**
1951, 16 m rotor, 180 km/h, 580 km,
1770 m SC, 12 men

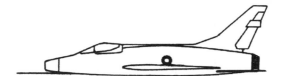

**North American F-86D Sabre**
1951, 12 m span, 1115 km/h (0.91), 885 km,
16650 m SC, 24 F.F.A.R. missiles

**Bell 47J**
1955, 11 m rotor, 169 km/h, 414 km,
3719 m SC, 4 troops

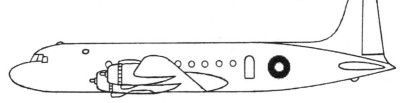

**North American F-100F Super Sabre**
1957, 12 m span, 1230 km/h (1.19), 2415 km,
15250 m SC, 2-20 mm, 4 Sidewinders, 2725 kg

**Douglas C-54D**
1942, 36 m span, 451 km/h, 6280 km,
50 troops or 14515 kg C     59

91

Supersonic Dane - An F-100 Super Sabre

As the decade of the 1960s began, the Danish Air Force was greatly strengthened by the acquisition of all-weather fighters and supersonic ground attack planes. Denmark's first supersonic aircraft, the North American F-100 Super Sabre, arrived to provide Danish airmen with one of the most lethal ground attack weapons in the world. Capable of carrying a heavy load of ordnance, it was also tasked with the mission of day fighter, employing infrared-guided air-to-air missiles. Night interception now was allotted to one of its progenitors, the D model of the F-86 Sabre. Possessing most of the characterics that had mastered the MiG-15 in Korea, the Sabre provided a measure of protection against the night-flying intruders of the Warsaw Pact.

Nevertheless, Denmark remained in a highly vulnerable position, at the focus of one of the strategic routes certain to be contested by the forces of NATO and the Warsaw Pact, yet with insufficient resources to provide an efficient defense. As Denmark's dependence upon NATO grew, so did her conviction that large monetary outlays for modernizing her defenses were futile. There was fear in NATO circles that Denmark would not only fail to fulfill her commitments to the defense of Western Europe, but would retreat into neutrality.

### Facing the Warsaw Pact - 1970-1990

The army was restructured by the austere Defense Act of 1960. All of the Centurions were upgraded to Mk.5 standards during the decade, and 106 of them were rearmed with 105 mm guns and designated as Centurion 5/2s. The rest retained the 83.5 mm gun as Centurion 5s. Some 530 M113 armored personel carriers were purchased (later increased to 600 with the acquisition of M113A1s) to mechanize the active army.

A new Act came into force on 1 January 1970 which integrated the three services into the Defense Command (*Forsvar*). The active army then contained 28,000 men. The Defense Act of 1970 was amended in April 1973 and extended in March 1977. During this period, most of the limited funding was utilized to strengthen the Air Force, with needed modernization of the Army deferred until the aerial buildup was completed. The Army deployed 21,400 men in 5 mechanized infantry brigades. Before the delay ended, a freeze on defense spending was imposed in the mid-1980s. The Army was forced to continue with obsolete weaponry, which it attempted to modernize by modification.

### Danish Army

4 mechanized infantry brigades
  1 tank battalion
    **22 Centurion 5, 5/2**
  3 mechanized infantry battalions
    **28 M113 APC**
  1 artillery battalion

Bornholm battalion group

1 heavy artillery battalion
  **12 M-115 203 mm howitzers**
2 missile battalions
  **Honest John SSM**
1 Army Aviation squadron
  17 helicopters, 28 light aircraft

Reserves - 40,000 men
  2 mechanized infantry brigades
    **22 Centurion 5, 5/2**

Territorial Defense
  15 infantry battalions
  15 artillery batteries

Home Guard - 52,000 men

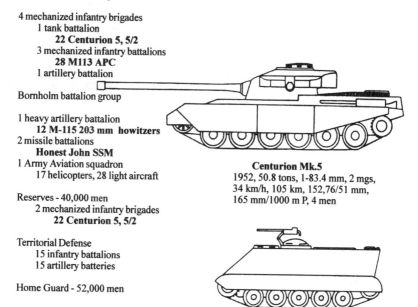

**Centurion Mk.5**
1952, 50.8 tons, 1-83.4 mm, 2 mgs,
34 km/h, 105 km, 152,76/51 mm,
165 mm/1000 m P, 4 men

**M113**
1960, 10.4 tons, 1 mg,
68 km/h, 321 km, 2 crew, 11 men

Danish ground forces did receive some modern weapons to replace the earlier British and American designs of World War II vintage. The infantry of the mechanized brigades was now carried in M113 armored personnel carriers, while the tank battalions were equipped with the still viable Centurion 5 main battle tank. Helicopters and battlefield missiles had also made their way into the ranks.

The satellite states of the Soviet Union posed little threat to Denmark during the early years of the organization's existence, for Poland and East Germany were not trusted by the Soviets and received little military assistance. Denmark was firmly rooted in NATO, relying upon reinforcements to assist her Army in defending the mouth of the Baltic.

The situation changed drastically after the spring of 1968, when Polish troops demonstrated loyalty to the Warsaw Pact in quelling riots in Prague. The USSR lavished more attention on the forces of the North European states. Denmark was forced to acknowledge a much greater capability for rapid deployment and operations by her neighbors. There was now a distinct possibility of isolation before NATO reinforcements could arrive in the Baltic.

93

Although possessing effective aircraft, the Danish Air Force was tiny when compared to the armada it faced. In 1964, 25 Lockheed F-104Gs were delivered, followed by 15 Canadair CF-104s and 7 CF-104Ds in 1971. The early Starfighter had suffered a number of shortcomings and was rejected for widespread service in the United States Air Force. However, development produced a reliable supersonic fighter that was available immediately in large quantities due to the American rejection. It thus offered the West Europeans an economical leap into the first rank of air defense.

### Flyvevåben

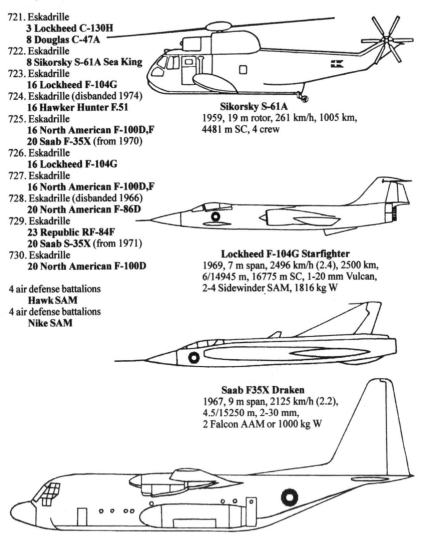

721. Eskadrille
   **3 Lockheed C-130H**
   **8 Douglas C-47A**
722. Eskadrille
   **8 Sikorsky S-61A Sea King**
723. Eskadrille
   **16 Lockheed F-104G**
724. Eskadrille (disbanded 1974)
   **16 Hawker Hunter F.51**
725. Eskadrille
   **16 North American F-100D,F**
   **20 Saab F-35X** (from 1970)
726. Eskadrille
   **16 Lockheed F-104G**
727. Eskadrille
   **16 North American F-100D,F**
728. Eskadrille (disbanded 1966)
   **20 North American F-86D**
729. Eskadrille
   **23 Republic RF-84F**
   **20 Saab S-35X** (from 1971)
730. Eskadrille
   **20 North American F-100D**

4 air defense battalions
   **Hawk SAM**
4 air defense battalions
   **Nike SAM**

**Sikorsky S-61A**
1959, 19 m rotor, 261 km/h, 1005 km,
4481 m SC, 4 crew

**Lockheed F-104G Starfighter**
1969, 7 m span, 2496 km/h (2.4), 2500 km,
6/14945 m, 16775 m SC, 1-20 mm Vulcan,
2-4 Sidewinder SAM, 1816 kg W

**Saab F35X Draken**
1967, 9 m span, 2125 km/h (2.2),
4.5/15250 m, 2-30 mm,
2 Falcon AAM or 1000 kg W

**Lockheed C-130H Hercules**
1955, 41 m span, 607 km/h, 6020 km,
7925 m SC, 92 troops, 23600 kg C

60

Scandinavian Dragon - Acrobatic Saab F-35Xs Over the Baltic

However, Denmark purchased a smaller number of F-104s than did other NATO air forces. The principal reason for the deficit was acquisition of the excellent Swedish Saab J35 Draken, twenty being received in 1970 as the F-35XD fighter, followed by 20 RF-35XD reconnaissance fighters the following year. Although the unique Starfighters were faster, the Saabs were more versatile. In 1971, 15 Hughes 500M (OH-6A) Cayuse were delivered to the Air Force as transport helicopters.

Observing the world-wide increase in Communist activism during the 1970s, Denmark sought to fulfill its responsibilities to NATO without antagonizing its Warsaw Pact neighbors. The Standing Force was equipped with 200 main battle tanks, 650 armored personnel carriers, 72 self-propelled howitzers , and other artillery. Territorial Defense units of 21 infantry battalions and 7 artillery battalions totalled 24,000 men, while the Home Guard comprised 56,500 men. Denmark's Jutland Division was part of the only multinational corps in Western Europe.

With the Warsaw Pact receiving numbers of the latest Soviet tanks, it was imperative that Denmark strengthen its armored forces, as the Centurion was now out of date. Much improvement resulted from the delivery of 120 Leopard 1A3s in 1976-8, displacing the Centurion 5/2s to Augmentation companies and the Centurion 5s to Reserve companies. Laser rangefinders were added to 88 of the Centurion 5/2s in 1984.

In order to create viable reconnaissance vehicles capable of operating on the modern battlefield, 53 M41 light tanks were upgraded by 1988. A diesel engine was installed to greatly increase the range, an NBC system was added, and APFSDS ammunition improved the armor penetration of the 76 mm gun. The resulting vehicle was designated the M41 DK-1.

95

The Army is deployed in two operational commands, one on Jutland and the other on Zealand. Each comprises active "Field Army" and reserve "Territorial Defense" forces. The short distances between Danish localities allow all units to mobilize within 24 hours. Thus, the Scandinavian system of inactive reserves is viable.

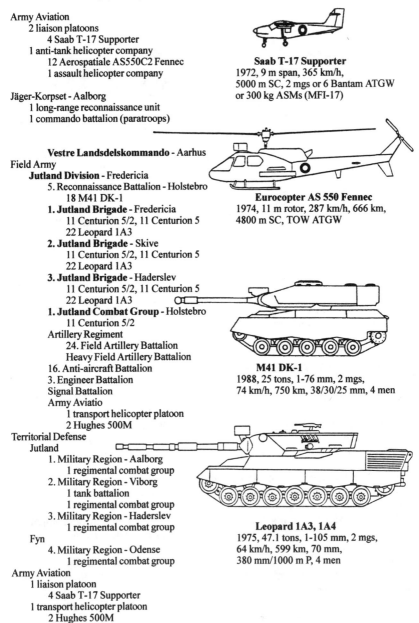

**Danish Army** (Haeren)

Army Aviation
 2 liaison platoons
  4 Saab T-17 Supporter
 1 anti-tank helicopter company
  12 Aerospatiale AS550C2 Fennec
 1 assault helicopter company

Jäger-Korpset - Aalborg
 1 long-range reconnaissance unit
 1 commando battalion (paratroops)

**Saab T-17 Supporter**
1972, 9 m span, 365 km/h,
5000 m SC, 2 mgs or 6 Bantam ATGW
or 300 kg ASMs (MFI-17)

**Vestre Landsdelskommando** - Aarhus
Field Army
 **Jutland Division** - Fredericia
  5. Reconnaissance Battalion - Holstebro
   18 M41 DK-1
  **1. Jutland Brigade** - Fredericia
   11 Centurion 5/2, 11 Centurion 5
   22 Leopard 1A3
  **2. Jutland Brigade** - Skive
   11 Centurion 5/2, 11 Centurion 5
   22 Leopard 1A3
  **3. Jutland Brigade** - Haderslev
   11 Centurion 5/2, 11 Centurion 5
   22 Leopard 1A3
  **1. Jutland Combat Group** - Holstebro
   11 Centurion 5/2
  Artillery Regiment
   24. Field Artillery Battalion
   Heavy Field Artillery Battalion
  16. Anti-aircraft Battalion
  3. Engineer Battalion
  Signal Battalion
  Army Aviatio
   1 transport helicopter platoon
   2 Hughes 500M
Territorial Defense
 Jutland
  1. Military Region - Aalborg
   1 regimental combat group
  2. Military Region - Viborg
   1 tank battalion
   1 regimental combat group
  3. Military Region - Haderslev
   1 regimental combat group
 Fyn
  4. Military Region - Odense
   1 regimental combat group
Army Aviation
 1 liaison platoon
  4 Saab T-17 Supporter
 1 transport helicopter platoon
  2 Hughes 500M

**Eurocopter AS 550 Fennec**
1974, 11 m rotor, 287 km/h, 666 km,
4800 m SC, TOW ATGW

**M41 DK-1**
1988, 25 tons, 1-76 mm, 2 mgs,
74 km/h, 750 km, 38/30/25 mm, 4 men

**Leopard 1A3, 1A4**
1975, 47.1 tons, 1-105 mm, 2 mgs,
64 km/h, 599 km, 70 mm,
380 mm/1000 m P, 4 men

Field Army
  3. Reconnaissance Battalion - Naestved
     18 M41 DK-1
  **1. Zealand Brigade** - Ringsted

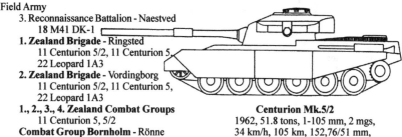

     11 Centurion 5/2, 11 Centurion 5,
     22 Leopard 1A3
  **2. Zealand Brigade** - Vordingborg
     11 Centurion 5/2, 11 Centurion 5,
     22 Leopard 1A3

| **1., 2., 3., 4. Zealand Combat Groups** | **Centurion Mk.5/2** |
|---|---|
| 11 Centurion 5, 5/2 | 1962, 51.8 tons, 1-105 mm, 2 mgs, |
| **Combat Group Bornholm** - Rönne | 34 km/h, 105 km, 152,76/51 mm, |
| 12 M41 DK-1 | 380 mm/1000 m P, 4 men |

Copenhagen Garrison
  Guard Hussar Battalion
     11 Leopard 1A3
  Royal Life Guard Battalion
  Danish Life Guard, Zealand Life Guard Battalions

Territorial Defense
  Zealand
     5. Military Region - Slagelse
     6. Military Region - Copenhagen
  Bornholm
     Bornholm Island Command - Rönne

Army Aviation
  1 liaison platoon
     4 Saab T-17 Supporter
  1 transport helicopter platoon              **Hughes 500M**
     2 Hughes 500M                            1963, 8 m rotor, 241 km/h, 610 km,
                                              4815 m SC, 1 mg, 4 men or 430 kg C

**Reserves**
10 infantry battalions
4 artillery battalions
some anti-tank companies

**Home Guard** (Haerhjemmevaernet)
7 military regions (36 districts)
  540 infantry companies (3 platoons)


As the operational command of Zealand would operate over several large
islands, no division was formed, the two brigades and 4 combat groups being
available for independent deployment when necessary. Reserve and Home Guard
units retained obsolete organization and weapons:

**REGIMENTAL COMBAT GROUP** (Territorial)
3 infantry battalions
  **GM 66 (G-3) 7.62 mm AR**
  **MG 62 (MG 42) 7.62 mm lmg**
  **MW 51 60 mm mortars**
1 artillery battalion
  **M-101 105 mm field howitzers**
  **M-108 155 mm field howitzers**          **M-65 "Carl Gustav"**
1 anti-tank company                          84 mm, 13.2 kg, 2.5 kg shell,
  **M-65 Carl Gustav 84 mm RR**              400 m, 310 m/s, 6 rpm,
1 engineer company                           320 mm/400 m P

97

**BRIGADE**
HQ - 1 anti-tank platoon **(8 TOW on jeeps)**
1 reconnaissance company (disbanded in 1987)
  3 reconnaissance troops (1 Augmentation)
    **2 M41 DK-1, 1 M-113, 4 jeeps**
    **1 M125 SP 120 mm mortar**
1 armored battalion
  HQ - **2 M113**
    1 reconnaissance platoon
    **3 M113**
    1 anti-tank platoon
    **2 jeeps w/TOW**
  2 tank companies
    HQ - **2 Leopard 1A3, 2 M113**
    3 troops
    **3 Leopard 1A3**
  1 mechanized infantry company
    HQ - **2 M113**
    3 rifle platoons
    **GM 66, GM 75 7.62 mm AR,**
    **Hovea m/49 9 mm SMG**
    **MG 62 7.62 mm lmg,**
    **MW 51 60 mm mortar**
    **4 M113 APC**
    1 rifle platoon (Augmentation)
    1 mortar platoon (Augmentation)
    **2 M125 SP 120 mm mortars**
    1 anti-tank platoon
    **2 jeeps w/106 mm RR or TOW**
  1 motorized infantry company (Augmentation)
    3 rifle platoons
    **GM 66, GM 75 7.62 mm AR,**
    **Hovea m/49 9 mm SMG**
    **MG 62 7.62 mm lmg,**
    **MW 51 60 mm mortar**
    1 rifle platoon (Augmentation)
    1 mortar platoon (Augmentation)
    **2 MW 50 towed 120 mm mortars**
    1 anti-tank platoon
    **2 jeeps w/106 mm RR or TOW**
2 mechanized infantry battalions (1 Aug., 1 Res.)
  HQ - **2 TOW, 4 M125 SP 120 mm mortars**
  1 tank company
    HQ - **2 Centurion 5/2, 5, 2 M113**
    3 troops
    **3 Centurion 5/2, 5**
  2 mechanized infantry companies
  1 motorized infanty company (Augment.)
  1 motorized infantry battalion (Reserve)
  HQ - **2 TOW, 4 M125 SP 120 mm mortars**
  4 motorized infantry companies
1 artillery battalion
  HQ - **4 M113**
    2 self-propelled artillery batteries
    HQ - **3 M113 observation vehicles**
    **6 M109 155 mm SP howitzers**
    1 field artillery battery (Augmentation)
    **8 M114A1 155 mm field howitzers**
    1 anti-aircraft battery
    **4 Bofors 40 mm L/60 AA guns**
1 engineer company
  **6 M113 APC**
Army Aviation
  1 helicopter platoon
  **2 Hughes 500M**

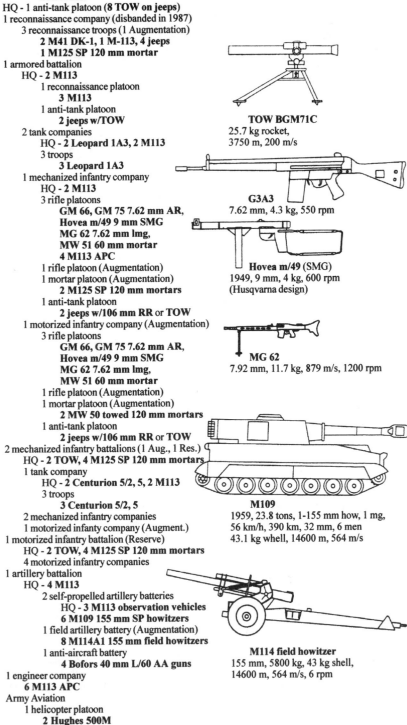

**TOW BGM71C**
25.7 kg rocket,
3750 m, 200 m/s

**G3A3**
7.62 mm, 4.3 kg, 550 rpm

**Hovea m/49** (SMG)
1949, 9 mm, 4 kg, 600 rpm
(Husqvarna design)

**MG 62**
7.92 mm, 11.7 kg, 879 m/s, 1200 rpm

**M109**
1959, 23.8 tons, 1-155 mm how, 1 mg,
56 km/h, 390 km, 32 mm, 6 men
43.1 kg whell, 14600 m, 564 m/s

**M114 field howitzer**
155 mm, 5800 kg, 43 kg shell,
14600 m, 564 m/s, 6 rpm

98

The active artillery batteries were equipped with self-propelled vehicles, but the Augmentation units retained towed howitzers. Army aviation support came from the Swedish Malmö Flygindustri company, which had developed its MFI 15 Safari light plane into an armed reconnaissance model, the MFI 17, of which 32 were supplied to Denmark as the T-17 Supporter for use as a liaison and light anti-tank aircraft, one platoon in each Operational Command. Much more powerful anti-tank capability was possessed by the dozen AS550C2 Fennecs acquired in 1990. In addition, an assault helicopter company was formed to provide mobility to strike units.

**BORNHOLM COMBAT GROUP**
1 light tank company
  **12 M41 DK-1**
2 motorized infantry battalions
  **HQ - 4 TOW, 8 MW 50 120 mm mortars**
  4 motorized infantry companies
1 artillery battalion
  3 field artillery batteries
    **6 M101 105 mm howitzers**
1 anti-aircraft artillery battalion
  3 batteries
    **4 Bofors 40 mm L/60 AA guns**
1 engineer company
1 signal company

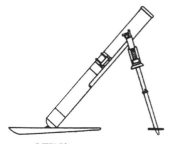

**Bofors M36**
40 mm, 1922 kg, 0.9 kg shell,
4941 m VR, 900 m/s, 120 rpm

**COMBAT GROUP**
1 tank company
  **HQ - 2 Centurion 5/2, 2 M113**
  3 troops
    **3 Centurion 5/2**
2 motorized infantry battalions
  **HQ - 8 M56 106 mm RR,**
    **4 MW 50 120 mm mortars**
  4 motorized infantry companies
1 artillery battalion
  3 field artillery batteries
    **8 M101 105 mm howitzers**

**M101 field howitzer**
105 mm, 2256 kg, 21 kg shell,
11300 m, 472 m/s, 12 rpm

**MW 50**
120 mm, 275 kg, 12 kg shell,
5700 m, 15 rpm

The reconnaissance companies were removed from the brigades in 1987 and grouped into two reconnaissance battalions deployed on Jutland and Zealand under the Operational Commands.

**ARMORED RECONNAISSANCE BATTALION**
2-3 armored reconnaissance companies
  **HQ - 1 M125 SP 120 mm mortar, 1 jeep**
  3 reconnaissance troops
    **2 M41 DK-1, 1 M113 w/81 mm mortars,**
    **1 jeep**

## HEAVY FIELD ARTILLERY BATTALION
2 field artillery batteries
**4 M115 203 mm heavy field howitzers**

## ANTI-AIRCRAFT BATTALION
1 anti-aircraft battery
**12 Bofors 40 mm L/60 AA guns**
3 anti-aircraft batteries
**Hamlet SAM (Redeye) (replaced by Stinger)**          61,62,63

In 1961, a new field uniform of dark and light lime green camouflage was adopted, although the helmet remained the M1948 American style common to NATO. Insignia of rank was changed at the same time. The rank of brigade general was added in 1983, with the rank of general changing from three stars to the three devices described below and the other generals receiving the stars of the former next higher rank.

Generals - gold devices or large 6-ptd gold stars on shoulder straps
    General - crown, crossed batons and wreath
    Generallöjtnant - 3 stars
    Generalmajor - 2 stars
    Generalbrigaden - 1 star

Field Officers - medium 6-ptd gold stars on shoulder straps
    Oberst - 3 stars
    Oberstlöjtnant - 2 stars
    Major - 1 star

Oberstlöjtnant

Company Officers - small 5-ptd gold stars on shoulder straps
    Kaptajn - 3 stars
    Premierlöjtnant - 2 stars
    Löjtnant - 1 star below a triangular gold pip
    Sekondlöjtnant - 1 star

Non-commissioned Officers - buff chevrons, point up, or bars
                  on upper sleeve
    Seniorsergent af 1.grad - 4 chevrons over 3 arcs
    Seniorsergent af 2.grad - 4 chevrons over 2 arcs
    Oversergent - 4 chevrons over 1 arc

    Sergent - 3 chevrons over 1 arc (conscript - no arc)
    Korporal - 2 chevrons over 1 arc (conscript - no arc)

    Overkonstabel af 1.grad - 3 bars
    Overkonstabel af 2.grad - 2 bars
    Konstabel - 1 bar
    Menig (conscript) - no device          Korporal

The Danish Army has needed new equipment for some time  Most revenue during the past two decades had been used for modernizing the Air Force. Then, in the mid-1980s, defense spending was reduced, forcing the Army to retain obsolete equipment. As a result, the Danish Jutland Division was the weakest assigned to the NATO defense of Europe, being the only one still using the venerable Centurion in first-line service.

The Jutland Division would normally be assigned to the Allied Forces Northern Europe (AFNORTH), although it could also be detached to operate with Allied Forces Central Europe (AFCENT). However, its readiness was low, only a fifth of its troops on active duty. Although it could be rapidly mobilized and reinforced with reserves, they were poorly armed. It was considered capable only of reinforcing the German troops defending Holstein.

A Sea King Disgorges Frogmen Into an Icy Northern Lake

The Danish Navy added some new vessels around 1980 and avoided most of the reductions suffered by the other armed forces.

**Danish Navy** (Sövaernet)

Fleet Command (Sövaernets Operative Kommando) - Aarhus

Frigate Squadron
    Peder Skram, Herluf Trolle
    Niels Juel, Olfert Fischer,
    Peder Tordenskjold
Fast Attack Boat Squadron
    Sölöven, Söridderen, Söbjörnen,
    Söhesten, Söhunden, Söulven
    Willemoes, Bille, Bredal, Hammer,
    Huitfeldt, Krieger, Norby,
    Rodsteen, Sehested, Suenson
Mine Combat Squadron
    7 minelayers, 6 minesweepers
Submarine Squadron
    Narhvalen, Nordkaperen
    Delfinen, Spaekhuggeren,
    Tumleren, Springeren
Fishery Protection Squadron
    Beskytteren
    Hvidbjörnen, Vaedderen,
    Ingolf, Fylla

Navy Home Guard (Marinehjemmevaernet)
    3 naval districts
    MHV 53, 64, 70-2, 81-6, 90-5
    6 Askö class

Naval Air Service
    **7 Westland Lynx Mk.80** (from 1979)
    **2 Westland Lynx Mk.91**

frigate

**Niels Juel**     1978, 1,341 tons, 45 km/h, 4025 km,
**Olfert Fischer**   1 Sea Sparrow SAM, 8 Harpoon SSM
**Peter Tordenskjold**   1 helicopter

fast attack craft - missile

**Willemoes Bille**     1976-8, 264 tons, 70 km/h,
**Huitfeldt Bredal**   2-4 Harpoon SSM,
**Hammer Krieger**   1-7.5 cm, 2-4 TT
**Norby Rodsteen**
**Sehested Suenson**

The *Peder Skram* and *Herluf Trolle* were modernized in 1976-7, but were placed in reserve with skeleton crews in 1987. *Beskyttern* and the *Hvidbjornen* class were used for fishery protection in the North Sea and around the Faroe Islands and Greenland. The five frigates each carried a helicopter.

**Westland Lynx Mk.80**
1980, 13 m rotor, 232 km/h, 212 km,
3230 m SC

Eight Westland Lynx Mk.80s were delivered from 1979. Used chiefly for anti-submarine warfare and maritime patrol, they were standard HAS Mk.2s with a more powerful engine. A couple of Mk.91s were later added.

### Battle Scenario - 1990

Would tragedy be triggered? To all outward appearances stronger than ever, the Soviet Union was disintegrating internally. Economic problems were rapidly mounting. The Warsaw Pact satellites were growing restless as evidence of the wealth generated for the common people by capitalism in neighboring nations became increasingly obvious. Would Soviet leaders resort to the same measures employed by their Western political counterparts when in trouble at home - foreign military adventures? If their calculations revealed that a window of opportunity to hegemony over all of Europe was closing, desperation could result in conflict. The nations enclosing the Baltic Sea would be among the first affected.

Much of the shipbuilding for the Warsaw Pact took place in the Baltic, which was considered a base from which Soviet air and naval forces could dominate northern Europe. Two dozen cruisers and destroyers, two dozen frigates, 56 submarines, and nearly 300 fast attack boats were deployed around the shores of the sea.

The Warsaw Pact had such an overwhelming preponderance of force in the Baltic that it probably could have overwhelmed Denmark before it could even mobilize, if Sweden remained neutral. Preemptive air strikes would be made against air bases in Germany, and the north, to gain air superiority. Seaborne and airborne landings would seize Zealand, from where paratroops would drop on bases in southern Norway, permitting the Soviet Baltic Fleet to join the Northern Fleet in operations into the North Atlantic.

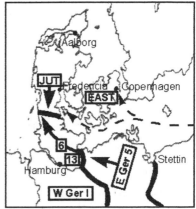

With Zealand, and the shores of the Skaggerak occupied by strong enemy air forces, reinforcements would be hindered from reaching the NATO forces in northern Germany. Under attack from two directions, the ground units of LANDJUT would be diverted from advancing into East Germany. Rather, the East German Fifth Army could advance northward into the Jutland peninsula, supported by coastal landings by the Soviet Baltic Fleet Marine, East German 29. Panzer Regiment, and the Polish 7th Naval Assault Division. Air drops could be made by a Soviet parachute division, the East German 40th Parachute Battalion, and the Polish 6th Air Assault Division. The Warsaw Pact movements would isolate the main Danish forces on Zealand, where they could be dealt with easily. The Jutland Division would be trapped on the move and cut to pieces before it could be reinforced. Denmark was in a hopeless position.

To coordinate the defense of Schleswig-Holstein, Denmark and Norway against Warsaw Pact forces, in April 1951 NATO had established Allied Forces Northern Europe (AFNORTH), with headquarters at Kolsås, Norway (near Oslo). The importance of Denmark in the defensive scheme led to the formation of Allied Forces Baltic Approaches (BALTAP) in 1962, with headquarters at Karup, Denmark. Ground operations were delegated to the Allied Land Forces, Jutland and Schleswig-Holstein (LANDJUT) at Rendsburg, West Germany.

It was expected that, within a week, BALTAP could be reinforced by the 12,500 men of the 6th Field Force, UK Mobile Force, (including 1 reconnaissance battalion of Scorpion/Scimitars and 1 armored battalion of Chieftains). Flying in to support the northern forces would be a squadron of American F-15 interceptors, three squadrons of American F-16 fighters, two squadrons of British Jaguar fighter bombers, and two squadrons of American A-10 anti-tank assault planes. However, a month would be required for the UK-Netherlands Amphibious Force and the American 4th Marine Amphibious Brigade (M-60 MBTs) to arrive. Thus, the initial thrust of the invasion would have to be stopped principally by the forces already in place:

**Allied Land Forces, Jutland and Schleswig-Holstein** (LANDJUT)

Danish Jutland Division - Fredericia
18 M41 DK-1, 66 Leopard 1A3, 44 Centurion 5/2, 33 Centurion 5

West German 6. Panzergrenadier Division - Neumunster
66 Leopard 2

West German Home Defense Group 13 - Eutin
64 M-48

In the event of hostilities, the West German 6. Panzergrenadier Division (1 brigade of Leopard 2s) and Defense Group 13 (64 M-48s) would deploy in place to hold the northern flank of the NATO defenses. While the brigades and battle groups of the Danish Eastern Operational Command sought to prevent landings on the islands of Zealand, the Jutland Division would attempt to advance 1-200 kilometers down the peninsula and join the West Germans.

Although it would be accompanied by the Jäger-Korpset and reserve units, the Jutland Division would have great difficulty in achieving the junction. Danish air cover would break down if the promised reinforcements did not arrive promptly. Reinforcements would eventually reach the multi-national corps, but Denmark would probably be in enemy hands by then. The position of the remaining troops of the NATO corps could then be turned. Denmark would become a base for Soviet operations against Great Britain.[64,65]

103

Following the signing of the Conventional Forces Europe Treaty (CFE) in 1991, Denmark decided not to completely rebuild its fleet of 106 Centurion 5/2s. Instead, she will purchase from Germany 110 used Leopard 1A3/1A4s and upgrade them, and her own 120 1A3s, to 1A5s. The 111 stored Centurion 5s would then be disposed of. Orders have also been placed for 50 M113A2s equipped with Italian OTO-Melara T-25 turrets to produce a Mechanized Infantry Combat Vehicle (MICV). In 1991 there were 353 main battle tanks and 316 armored personnel carriers.[66]

New frigates and coastal submarines had been added to the fleet:

Olfert Fischer at Work

**Danish Navy**

Frigate Squadron
    Thetis, Hvidbjörnen,
        Triton, Vaedderen
    Niels Juel, Olfert Fischer,
        Peder Tordenskjold

frigate

Fast Attack Boat Squadron
    Willemoes, Bille, Huitfeldt,
        Bredal, Hammer, Krieger
    Norby, Rodsteen, Sehested,
        Suenson

**Hvidbjörnen** 1991, 2,642 tons, 34 km/h,
**Vaedderen** 1-7.5 cm, 13685 km,
**Thetis** 1 helicopter
**Triton**

Submarine Squadron
    Tumleren, Saelen, Springeren
    Narhvalen, Nordkaperen

sub

**Tumleren** 1965, 468 tons, 22/33 km/h,
**Springeren** 8 TT, 8050 km,
**Havmanden** purchased in 1987, modernized
**Saelen** (ex-Norwegian Kobben class)

Fighter of the Nineties - the F-16

**Flyvevåbnet**

Tactical Air Force Command (Flyvertaktisk Kommando) - Karup

721. Eskadrille - Vaerlose
**3 Lockheed C-130H, 10 Saab T-17,
3 Grumman Gulfstream III**

722. Eskadrille - Vaerlose
**8 Sikorsky S-61A**

723. Eskadrille - Aalborg
**16 General Dynamics F-16A.**
724. Eskadrille - disbanded 1974
725. Eskadrille - Karup
**16 Saab A-35XD**
726. Eskadrille - Aalborg
**16 General Dynamics F-16A,_**
727. Eskadrille - Skrydstrup
**16 General Dynamics F-16A,B**
728. Eskadrille - disbanded 1966
729. Eskadrille - Karup
**18 Saab S-35XD**
730. Eskadrille - Skrydstrup
**16 General Dynamics F-16A,B**

**General Dynamics F-16A**
1974, 10 m span, 2075 km/h (1.95),
6100 m SC, 1-20 mm, 926 km,
2 Sidewinder or Sparrow SAM,
6810 kg W

Anti-aircraft Missile Group

Zealand - 4 Improved Hawk SAM squadrons
Fyn - 2 Improved Hawk SAM squadrons
Jutland - 2 Improved Hawk SAM squadrons

The Danish Air Force opted to standardize on the American F-16. From 1980-2, F-16s replaced the F-100s, which were sold to Turkey. The 725. Eskadrille was scheduled to replace its aging Drakens with F-16s in 1988, but the new austere program forced them to soldier on. A total of 57 F-16As and 16 F-16Bs were delivered from 1980-1987.

# GREENLAND

Sailing for 2-3 days west from Iceland about 900 A.D., Gunnbjörn, a Norwegian Viking, sighted a lengthy coast near the Arctic Circle. In 982, another Norwegian, Erik the Red, sailed to find Gunnbjörn's discovery, then returned to Iceland 3 years later, regaling the famished Icelanders with tales of a land of plenty he called "Greenland". Within a few years, about 2000 settlers had established two colonies on the west coast: Österbygd to the southwest had 190 farms. Farther north, the Vesterbygd had 90 farms. Trade consisted primarily of walrus skins and tusks. The Viking population grew to 3000 by the time the king of Norway took control in 1261.

However, the Hanseatic League monopolized the trade of Norway and, having no interest in Greenland, left the colonists stranded, the last trading vessel leaving Greenland in 1410. When an English explorer visited the island in 1585, he found no colonists alive, they apparently having died of disease and the genetic complications of inbreeding.

The two colonies were restablished in 1721. Near ancient Vesterbygd, Godthaab became the largest settlement, while Godhavn in the north was the whaling center. Between them, near the remains of Österbygd, grew Julianehaab. Eventually, Denmark gained control of Norway and retained possession of Greenland when Norway was ceded to Sweden in 1814. Seal hunting became important during the Nineteenth Century. Until the 1917 agreement with the United States, Denmark's sovereignty extended only over the west coast. The agreement gave Denmark control of the entire island, creating friction with Norwegian hunters and whalers operating on the east coast. The advent of air power was to greatly increase its importance.

Following the conquest of Denmark in 1940, the Germans had been landing teams on eastern Greenland to set up weather reporting stations, vital for planning military operations on the European continent. The Danes of Greenland signed an agreement with the United States in May 1941 to protect them against such foreign interference. Greenland established its own army of 26 men in the summer of 1941 to patrol its eastern coast. The islanders never had a distinct flag, flying that of Denmark. It is probable that the tiny Greenland Army initially wore Danish uniforms, possibly acquiring American equipment from 1942. Patrols of 3-5 men attempted to cover large expanses of Arctic terrain.

In August 1942, the Germans smuggled two parties, totaling 27 men, onto eastern Greenland in "Operation Holzauge". They evaded capture until they captured a patrol of 3 men from the Greenland Army, and one escaped to report the location. A raid by American B-24s forced the party to be evacuated by a German seaplane in mid-June. To aid in finding such clandestine stations, the Allies set up radio direction finding (RDF) stations. Nevertheless, the Germans maintained another weather station in northern Greenland from September 1943 to June 1944. Quiet returned at war's end.

Discovery of the mineral cryolite at Ivigtut, south of Godthaab, provided the principal export until lead and zinc deposits were discovered on the east coast and mined from 1956. On 1 May 1979, home rule was accorded Greenland and a parliament, the *Landsting*, elected.

# NORWAY

Descendants of the original Finno-Ugrian "hunter-gatherers" of Norway still roam the tundra of northern Scandinavia. With ancestral remains dating from around 6000 B.C., the Lapps form one of the oldest continuous races of man on the earth. However, the encroachments of the Teutons around 1700 B.C. pushed the original inhabitants northward into the obscurity of a little-known region called Finnmark.

Organized civilization began to appear in Norway early in the 9th Century when groups of *fylkir* (local communities) united themselves in three *lagthing*, regional territories corresponding to the natural divisions of the peninsula. The uplands of eastern Norway became the *Eidsivathing*, the area around Nidaros (Trondheim) was the *Eyrathing*, while the *Gulathing* encompassed the fjords of western Norway. Because of their situation near the trade routes between the East (Baltic) and North Seas, the chieftains of the *Eidsivathing* became wealthy. Halfdan Whitebone, of the ancient Viking Yngling family from Uppsala in Svear, during the 7th Century had acquired the *Vestfold* uplands and the *Vik* (the shores of the Foldenfjord, later known as the Oslofjord). His son was murdered by Asa, who ruled the area in the name of their infant son, Halfdan the Black. A basic belief developed in a bevy of mythical beings controlling everyday activities. *Odin* was the chief, as god of wisdom and combat, although *Thor* ran a close second as the god of agriculture and protector against disease and sorcery. The sailors had *Njord*, god of seafaring, while *Freya* watched after women and home life. With community foundations laid, the reign of Asa produced a strong kingdom of *Vik-ings*. Yet, the Norwegian Vikings were impeded by the Danish Vikings, who controlled the *Skager-Rak* and the straits leading to the East Sea. Halfdan the Black's son, Harald Fairhair, set about freeing the Norwegians from Danish influence. He first marched through the uplands, then to Trondelag, securing allegiance of the great chieftains of central Norway. He had much more difficulty with the fiesty Vikings of the southwest, but forced their submission by winning the Battle of Harfsfjord in **872**. From this date, the birth of Norway is reckoned, for he was now master of the settled part of the peninsula. He moved his capital from the Vestfold to Avaldsnes on the southwest coast. Before he died, he designated Erik Blood-axe as heir to the throne, but Erik was unable to gain control and the powerful *jarl* of Trondelag called Haakon from England to rule. The reign of the young king was so peaceful and prosperous that he became known as Haakon the Good. His goodness was in contrast to the ruthlessnes of his successor, Harald Graypelt, who alarmed the Danes by trying to drive them out of the Vik.

The Danish king, Harald Bluetooth, carried Haakon of Trondelag with him as he swept through Norway without opposition. When Harald died, Haakon asserted independence and defeated an expedition under Danish King Sweyn Forkbeard at Hjörungavaag, stirring the first sentiments of Norwegian nationhood. However, Haakon became autocratic as time went on and the famous Viking, Olaf Tryggvason, was able to sail into Trondheimfjord and take control of the country. Having absorbed Roman Catholic doctrine during his Viking days, Olaf alienated the Norwegians by compelling them to accept his beliefs. When Sweyn asserted his claims in Norway, Olaf built a large fleet of longships and activated the *leidang*, squadrons of longships to be supplied by the various coastal districts. However, all abandoned the overbearing king and, when he met Sweyn at the Battle of Svold in **1000**, he had only a few longships. Olaf was killed and Sweyn took control of the Vik.

***Foundation of the Nation of Norway*** - 11th Century, A.D.

It was left to another Viking, Olaf Haraldsson, to end his wanderings and return to unify his homeland. Rebuffed by the proud chieftains of Trondelag, he became the first king to give attention to the inhabitants of the interior of Norway, who enthusiastically joined him. The alarmed Trondelag leaders brought a fleet into the Foldenfjord in the spring of 1016, but were defeated by Olaf at Nesjar. Olaf established the first truly national Norwegian government, with Catholicism as the official religion, but took a fatal misstep by concluding a treaty with the King of Sweden against Denmark. Canute, King of Denmark, shrewdly informed the Norwegian chieftains that he would restore their independence from the crown if they joined him. When Canute sailed north with a large fleet in 1028, Olaf was left unsupported and was forced to flee through Sweden to *Gardarike* in Russia. Two years later, Olaf returned to throw out the Danes. However, on **29 July 1030** at the Battle of Stiklestad, he faced a Danish army twice the size of his own, which took the lives of Olaf and most of his followers. Nevertheless, when the Danes proved more oppressive than he, the Norwegians canonized him as St. Olaf.

The quarrels left over from the Viking Age were ended when King Magnus Olafsson of Norway joined Kings Inge of Sweden and Erik of Denmark in signing the first pan-Scandinavian peace treaty at Konungahella in 1101. The first Norwegian cities were founded and began growing rapidly, particularly from the middle of the 12th Century. From his capital of Bergen, King Sverri (1177-98) ruled over a stable kingdom with a landed aristocracy. The Hebrides Islands and the Isle of Man, old Viking bases, were sold to Scotland in 1266. During the latter part of the century, the capital was moved to Oslo, in the rapidly growing eastern country. Nevertheless, Bergen became the largest and wealthiest city in Norway because of the huge fleets of ships trading there for abundant fish, hides and furs. Much timber was also shipped to the Netherlands. Increasingly wealthy Norwegians were purchasing grain and luxury items from the traders. However, trouble was already appearing. Foreign shipowners were competing with Norwegian merchants for the carrying trade. When King Haakon the Old tried to suppress the growing power of the Norwegian burghers by prohibiting their engagement in overseas trading and by abolishing their craft guilds, the foreign traders gained the advantage. English merchants, particularly, carried most Norwegian goods after 1290. Haakon the Old made another mistake in 1230 when he gave Lübeck, of the Hanseatic League, trading privileges in Norway.

He compounded his mistake by signing a trade treaty with the League in 1250. The aggressive Hansa trade policies were soon enveloping Norway in their tentacles. When Norway struggled to free itself, the League cut off the vital grain trade and the Norwegians relented. Another treaty in 1294 gave them further privileges. As a result, development in Norway was strangled for the next two centuries. Norwegian protests were stifled by Hansa blockades, penetrated by only a few English ships. One of these brought the Bubonic Plague to Bergen in 1349. By the end of the year the disease had killed a third of Norway's population. Of 300 noble families, only 60 survived the century.

From 1381, Queen Margaret of Denmark skillfully maneuvered to gain control of Sweden, Norway and Denmark. She was elected Queen of Norway in 1388. Stockholm was under the sway of the Hanseatic League, which employed privateers from Rostock and Wismar to supply it. Many of them descended to piracy. Margaret finally got control of Stockholm when her candidate, Erik of Pomerania, was elected king of the three Scandinavian nations at a meeting in Kalmar in **1397**. Norway had never become completely feudalized, but the local districts were now going increasingly to Danes and Germans. Erik reinstated Sound Dues on the Hanseatic merchants, who abandoned Bergen in 1429. The piratical privateers sacked and burned the city soon afterward. In its last action, the *leidang* fleet of 100 small obsolete vessels pursued, but could not face the 7 large pirate ships.

Revolts soon cropped up against the weak Erik. However, the nobility in Norway had never fully recovered from the Plagues of the 14th Century and retained Erik as their king. Norwegian dissidents, led by Amund Sigurdsson Bolt, did manage to wrest some concessions from the Danes. When Erik refused to act on their complaints at a meeting in 1439, and allowed a Dutch fleet in his employ to blockade and ravage the Norwegian coast, the Norwegian nobles switched their support to Christopher of Bavaria. His successor, Christian I (1450-81), gave much more attention to Norway than had previous Danish kings. Yet, as time went on, Norway was again neglected. She lost the last of her Viking possessions when the Orkney and Shetland Islands became part of the dowry given to Scotland when Christian took a Scottish queen. Norway nearly broke up into scattered settlements.

## *Union with Denmark* - 1536

Norwegian nationhood was saved when Danish King Hans sent Prince Christian to rule Norway as a viceroy, although Norway continued as a mere province of Denmark. Norway was officially incorporated into Denmark in **1536**. Both nations flew the Dannebrog and Danish noblemen administered the country with all decisions made in Copenhagen. The Hansa merchants had returned to Bergen and Oslo, causing Norwegian shipping to decline. Christian IV (1588-1648) built a large Dano-Norwegian fleet to further his imperial ambitions. Oslo was renamed Christiania in his honor. He sent expeditions to Greenland and Hudson's Bay, hoping to find a Northwest Passage. After the Dutch began interrupting Denmark's monopoly in the carrying trade to Murmansk, he became involved in a war with Sweden, the ally of the Dutch. When Norwegians refused to attack Swedish territories in 1611, nationalism was reborn in their successful defiance. A Norwegian Army was planned, but never organized.

## Swedish Invasions of Norway - 17th-18th Centuries

The outbreak of the Thirty Years War had little effect on isolated Norway until the Dutch joined the Swedes in attacking arrogant Denmark in 1643-5.
The expert Norwegian peasant marksmen were organized into a trained militia by the outstanding Norwegian statesman, Hannibal Sehested. Although not a military man, he directed affairs so well that the militia kept the Swedes out of Norwegian territory. Thus, they were incensed when Christian IV ceded the Norwegian provinces of Jämtland and Härjedalen to Sweden at the end of the war. As stadtholder of Norway for the king, Sehested was determined to strengthen Norway. He managed to gain permission for a separate defense ministry and enlarged the militia and fleet. But the gains were lost when Christian died in 1648. Norway lost Trondelag and Baahus (Bohuslän) provinces, when Danish Frederik III sacrificed most of Denmark's empire by losing a rashly declared war with Sweden in 1657-8.

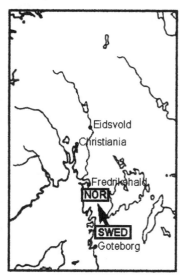

However, Norway was finally beginning to shake off the yoke of Denmark. Wearing the light grey coats of the Danish infantry, with red cuffs, black breeches, a black tricorn and black boots, the Norwegians successfully defended Fredrikshald (Halden) against a Swedish invasion with a small contingent of militia mustered from each district:

Trondheim, Bergenhus, Tönsberg, Åkershus and Bohus Infantry Regiments

Fortunately for the fledgling Norwegian Army, Sweden was preoccupied with defending itself against the Alliance. When Karl X died, the Peace of Copenhagen in **May 1660** restored Trondelag to Norway, whose border then took the configuration maintained to the present.

In 1664, Frederik III sent his son, Ulrik Frederik Gyldenlöve, to be the new stadtholder of Norway. He became the most popular of the many Danish governors. When the Scånian War broke out, the Danish Fleet was under the command of a Norwegian, Curt Adeler, replaced after his death by the Dane, Niels Juel. Containing many Norwegian-manned ships, the fleet fought well against the Swedish Fleet. A coastal defense fleet had also been built up to defend the many ports along Norway's fjord-pierced coast. Unlike the *leidang* fleet of the 15th Century, it was actively trained and under the direct control of the central government. It was capable, however, of little more than the suppression of piracy and smuggling.

When 5,000 Norwegian soldiers participated in the Danish invasion of Sweden after its warrior-king, Charles XII, had been defeated in Russia, Norway became the focal point of much of the military action when he returned to Sweden in **1716**. Charles advanced over the Norwegian border toward Christiania and occupied the capital. However, he was unsuccessful in reducing nearby Åkershus fortress, or destroying the Norwegian Army gathered of the city.

Forced to withdraw, Charles marched on the fortress of Fredriksten, guarding the southeastern border of Norway. Nearby Fredrikshald had a fine harbor, toward which a Swedish transport fleet was slowly making progress with heavy cannon and supplies for a siege. The Norwegian, Peder Tordenskjold, took a Danish fleet of small vessels into the shallows and destroyed the Swedish transport fleet at the Battle of Dynekilen. Left without supplies, Charles retired into Sweden.

Charles XII returned in 1718. One Swedish column advanced on Trondheim while the king, himself, led another against Fredriksten and had it under siege by December. But, on 11 December, a musket ball struck Charles in the head as he watched the action. Demoralized, both Swedish Armies retired from Norway. Employing skillful tactics, Admiral Tordenskjold captured Marstrand, enabling the combined armies of Norway and Denmark to overrun Bohus. The Danes eschewed a full invasion this time and the Peace of Frederiksborg on 3 July 1720 ended the last war between Scandinavian nations.

Along with the Danish Army, Norwegian troops adopted red cutaway coats in 1785. Waistcoasts and breeches were red for the infantry, black for the artillery, and buff for the cavalry, with various facings. Boots, or shoes, gaiters and tricorns were black.

Infantry Regiments
1.,2.,3. Trondheim
1.,2. Bergenhus
1.,2. Åkershus
1.,2. Smaalen
1.,2. Opland
1.,2. Vesterlen

**Musket**

Norske Jagerkorps
Mountain Jagerkorps
Nordenfeld, Söndenfeld Ski Battalions

Dragoon Regiments
Åkershus, Opland, Smaalen, Trondheim

Artillery Brigade [67]

**6pdr Field Gun**
93 mm, 390 kg, 2.7 kg ball,
1300 m max, 750 m eff

Hostilities between the Baltic maritime powers at an end, the Norwegian Fleet declined, but the Army was maintained at full strength. The merchant marine profited from Norway's neutrality in the world war that developed in the aftermath of the American Revolution. From around 550 ocean-going vessels, it rapidly increased to 850, carrying goods to the various belligerents. Although Christiania became the cultural center of the nation as the capital, Bergen continued to grow as a cosmopolitan commercial center, harboring the vessels and merchants of many nations.

Although Denmark became enmeshed in European politics through the Armed Neutrality agreements, Norway steered clear by secret agreements with England, against whose naval might the agreements were directed. During the first seven years of the 19th Century, the Norwegian merchant marine increased to 1,500 vessels. Norway was again growing wealthy from her seamen. Nevertheless, many Norwegians lost their lives in the two attacks made by the British on the Danish Fleet in 1801 and 1807. When Denmark entered an alliance with France and Russia on 31 October 1807, Great Britain declared war four days later. Norway's large trade with England ended and poverty again stalked the unfortunate Norwegians.

The extremely autocratic Frederik VI ascended the throne of Denmark and immediately declared war on Sweden in February 1808. Norway was exposed to Swedish attack, with little hope of succor by Denmark as the Swedes now possessed the intervening provinces of the southern peninsula and had the more powerful fleet. Norwegian infantry of the period wore a short red coat with plastron of regimental color, light blue trousers, and black boots with a black conical hat (changed to a black shako in 1810). Grenadiers had a tall fur hat. Ski troops wore light blue overall with a black fur hat bearing a gold frontal plate. However, the threat never grew into war.

The agitation caused by his inconsiderate policies led Frederik VI to send more able administrators to Norway before the Norwegian-Danish union was jeopardized. Events in Sweden soon nullified his efforts. The new king, Bernadotte, coveted Norway rather than Finland. When he invaded Denmark from the south in 1813, Frederik VI was forced to sign the Treaty of Kiel on **14 January 1814** which ceded Norway to Sweden. Christian Frederik, cousin of the Danish king, tried to rally Norwegians against the Swedes, fortifying the border and skillfully evading demands for the surrender of Norwegian fortresses to their new masters. On 25 February, he declared the independence of Norway, to the delight of the people. Sweden threatened to use military action to enforce its rights under the Treaty of Kiel, but the Norwegians warned that they would not go down without a lengthy fight and countered with a proposal for a union similar to the one they had with Denmark. When Sweden persisted, Christian Frederik issued a call to arms on 9 June. Fighting broke out on **29 July 1814**. As the raw Norwegian militia had no chance against the well-equipped Swedish veterans, the conflict lasted only a couple of weeks. In the uplands, they held their own in three skirmishes, but along the southeastern coast the main Swedish forces advanced, with the support of their fleet. An armistice was arranged at the Convention of Moss on 14 August. Bernadotte had meanwhile become sympathetic to the Norwegian cause and negotiated a treaty that left the Norwegian constitution intact, although Swedish troops were to occupy the eastern territories as far as Christiania. The Norwegian citizenry was incensed by the concessions of Christian and he abdicated on 10 October. The Norwegian parliament, the *Störting*, agreed to unite with Sweden and elected Bernadotte as king of Norway.

Norway was largely left to govern and embellish herself, gaining a measure of equality within the Norway-Sweden alliance through economic and cultural development. The armies of the two nations developed independently. The Golden Lion of St. Olaf, which first appeared in the 13th Century, was added to the canton of the Dannebrog in 1814 to distinguish Norwegian vessels and possessions from those of Denmark. Because of confusion with the flag of Denmark, particularly at sea, in 1821 the Lion was removed and a dark blue cross was superimposed over the white cross of the Dannebrog to produce the modern Norwegian flag.

By 1830, the Army was wearing Swedish uniforms:

> **Infantry** wore dark blue overall (white trousers in summer), with red facings and a dark blue shako.
> **Jagers** wore light grey overall, with a dark blue plastron and shako (or campaign hat).
> **Cavalry** was green overall, with red piping and a black shako.
> **Artillery** wore the same uniform as the infantry, but with carmine piping.

The year 1844 marked the beginning of the modern state of Norway. The new Swedish King Oscar I granted Norway equality in domestic affairs, allowing her to develop completely independent armed forces, pledged only to support Sweden in foreign affairs under the direction of a viceroy. She was allowed to adopt her own flag, which was the old one of 1821 with the addition of the Swedish-Norwegian Union colors in the canton. The naval ensign was similarly marked.

In military dress, Norway joined the world-wide admiration of things Prussian and adopted a dark blue tunic and dark grey trousers for its infantry, surmounted by a black spiked helmet. The artillery differed in having a fur crest on its helmet. Both displayed red facings, although the trouser stripes of the artillery were double-wide. Thus, the cut of the Norwegian uniform remained similar to that of Sweden, although the details began to diverge (red facings rather than the Swedish yellow).

Karl XV (1859-72) did not agree with his father's policy of leniency toward Norway. Prodded by the Swedish aristrocracy, which felt that Sweden had never been accorded the full fruits of the Treaty of Kiel, King Karl initiated a quarrel when he proposed increased Swedish control over Norwegian affairs through a revision of the Act of Union. However, the quarrelling remained limited to diplomatic exchanges. Norway continued to maintain her own military services, including a small navy of sailing warships. During the 1850s, she possessed a handful of cruising warships with two large frigates, a 44 and a 40, providing the principal fighting force supported by two small corvettes, a 16 and a 10.[68]

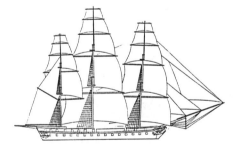

**FOURTH RATE** 44 gun frigate
1850, 1600 tons, 500 men,
24-32 pdrs, 4-8" shell guns,
22 carronades

**SLOOP** 16 gun corvette
1850, 350 tons, 120 men,
16-32 pdrs, 2-8" shell guns

The new autonomy flowered in the 1860s, when many national characteristics appeared in the Norwegian Army. As Otto von Bismarck began to manipulate the factions of Europe to benefit Prussia and unite the Germans, Denmark unfortunately possessed one of the territories desired by the Iron Chancellor. Schleswig and Holstein had long been the frontier between German and Dane. Their rich agriculture and dense mixed populations were important to both nations. For their possession, Denmark fought two wars with the German Confederation. Inevitably, Norway became involved in the conflicts, as a naval refuge for the combatants.

Although Swedish troops had gone to Fyn Island in 1848 to block any advance on Copenhagen, neither Sweden nor Norway moved to support Denmark when she was overwhelmed in 1864. The residual bitterness ended the movement toward pan-Scandinavianism during the rest of the century. At the time of the two wars, Norway possessed considerable armed forces. The lessons of the wars were incorporated in a reorganization following legislation passed by the *Störting* in May 1866:

1. (Åkershus) Infantry Brigade - Christiania
   4 rifle battalions, 2 field batteries, 1 horse battery
2. (Åkershus) Infantry Brigade - Frederikshald
   4 rifle battalions, 2 field batteries, 1 horse battery
   Trondheim Infantry Brigade - Trondheim
   4 rifle battalions, 3 field batteries
   Bergen Infantry Brigade - Bergen
   4 rifle battalions, 1 field battery, 1 mountain battery
   Christiansand Infantry Brigade - Christiansand
   4 rifle battalions, 1 field battery, 1 mountain battery
   Jagerkorps - Christiania
   6 companies (one formed the Royal Guard)
   Cavalry Brigade
   Åkershus Dragoons - Christiania
   5 squadrons
   Opland Dragoons - Hamar
   4 squadrons
   Trondheim Dragoons - Trondheim
   2 squadrons

RIFLE BATTALION
4 rifle companies
**Larsen or Remington rifles**

Larsen rifle

DRAGOON REGIMENT
2-5 squadrons
**sabers, Remington carbines**

ARTILLERY BATTALION
2-3 batteries
**3 *tom* M/1868 75 mm field gun**
**3½ *tom* M/1869 9 mm heavy field gun**
**2½ *tom* M/1869 75 mm mountain gun**
**2½ *tom* M/1869 75 mm horse gun**
**4 *tom* M/1870 121 mm siege gun**

3 *tom* field gun
75 mm, 920 kg, 3.4 kg shell

Measured in *toms*, equal to the caliber in inches, the artillery material was mostly iron rifled muzzleloaders. During the period of the two Schleswig wars, Norwegian artillery used batteries of 6-6 pdr and 12 pdr smoothbore bronze muzzleloaders. Eight company-size Landwehr Divisions, composed of reservists, were attached to each brigade.[64]

The experiences of the First Schleswig War had led to the adoption of a new uniform in 1860:

**Infantry** had a dark blue tunic and kepi with red piping, and dark gray trousers with black boots.
**Artillery** was similar with carmine facings.
**Jagers** had green jackets with no facings, dark gray trousers, and a black Alpini hat with black feathers.
**Cavalry** wore green overall, with red facings and a red kepi.

114

The age of the steamship had dawned and Norway had a small fleet of armored coast defense ships and cruising ships. With headquarters at Horten, the Navy was administered in six naval districts:

1. District - Christiania
2. District - Drammen
3. District - Christiansand
4. District - Bergen
5. District - Trondheim
6. District - Tromsö

monitor

monitor

| | | |
|---|---|---|
| **Skorpionen** | 1866, 1,514 tons, 11 km/h, | |
| **Thrudvang** | 2-28 cm, 30 cm armor | |
| **Mjölner** | | |

**Thor** 1872, 2,002 tons, 14 km/h,
**Odin** 2-28 cm, 36 cm armor

screw frigate
**Kong Sverre** 1860, 3,528 tons, 18 km/h,
44-32 pdrs

screw frigate
**St. Olaf** 1856, 2,217 tons, 16 km/h,
34-32 pdrs

screw corvette
**Nordstjerna** 1862, 1,635 tons, 14 km/h,
16-32 pdrs

screw corvette
**Nornen** 1855, 973 tons, 14 km/h,
**Ellida** 14-32 pdrs

screw gunboat
**Brage** 1878, 264 tons, 14 km/h,
**Nor** 1-27 cm

screw gunboat
**Sleipner** 1877, 571 tons, 16 km/h,
1-26, 1-15 cm

screw gunboat
**Wale** 1874, 229 tons, 11 km/h,
**Uller** 1-26, 1-15 cm

screw gunboat
**Glommen** 1863, 237 tons, 13 km/h,
**Lougen** 1-17, 1-15 cm            [70]

Agitation for complete independence from Sweden increased as the Nineteenth Century drew to a close. In 1872, the thousandth anniversary of the founding of the Norwegian state, the Swedish viceroy was withdrawn. When King Oscar II refused to allow a separate Norwegian consulate, and vetoed a proposal to remove the Union symbol from flags, the Norwegian prime minister resigned in protest in June 1892. The people declared for independence in 1894, but nothing was immediately done, for Norway was in a weak position with no foreign support for its aspirations. Indeed, Germany urged Sweden to act firmly against the Norwegians, raising the spectre of Russia or Great Britain seizing Norwegian territory. The Swedish Riksdag rejected Norwegian demands for a consulate in 1895, and in June of that year the Norwegian Störting withdrew the demands. However, resentment remained high and, to defy Sweden, many Norwegians began displaying the Danish Dannebrog, although the flag used by military forces did not change.

Agitation reappeared in Norway in 1905. After the *Störting* refused to continue under the direction of the Swedish king, a plebiscite was held in August that severed ties to Sweden. During August and September, the Swedish and Norwegian ministers met for three weeks in Karlstad, Sweden to seek an agreement. When an impasse developed over the fate of the fortresses at Halden and Kongsvinger, which were considered vital to screen the mobilization of the Norwegian army, conflict loomed between the two Scandinavian neighbors.

115

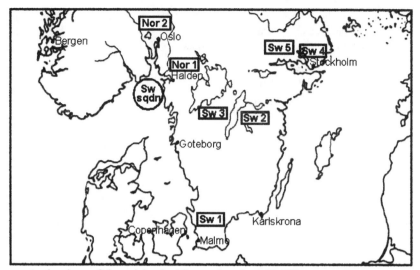

At the time of the crisis, the Norwegians had 22,500 men under arms:

**Norwegian Army**

5 infantry brigades
  2 infantry regiments
    2 infantry battalions
      4 rifle companies
        **Krag-Jorgensen rifles**
Jagerkorps
  5 jager companies
1 cavalry brigade
  4 light dragoon regiments
    2-3 sabre squadrons
5 field artillery battalions
  2 light batteries
    **6 Krupp M/1887 84 mm field guns** or
    **M/1869-93 65 mm mountain guns**
1 siege artillery battalion
  4 light field artillery batteries
    **4 Schneider-Canet M/1898 75 mm field guns**
  2 heavy field gun batteries
    **4 Schneider-Canet M/1901 105 mm heavy field guns**

**Krag-Jorgensen M/1894 rifle**
1894, 6.5 mm, 4.3 kg, 750 m/s

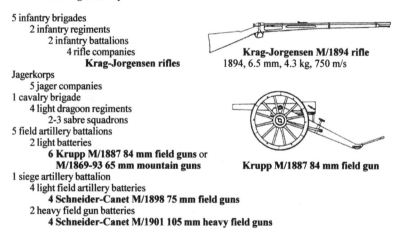

**Krupp M/1887 84 mm field gun**

The siege artillery battalion had been established in 1902. In 1888, the Norwegian Army had returned to the spiked helmet and the uniform was completely changed:

    **Infantry** wore light blue overall, with red piping. The spiked helmet was black and the boots were brown.
    **Jagers** had a medium blue tunic and dark gray trousers, with red facings, and a black Alpini hat with black feathers.
    **Light dragoons** wore a medium green tunic with dark gray trousers and red facings. The kepi was dark gray with a black plume. Boots were black.
    **Artillery** wore a dark gray tunic and black trousers, with red facings and a dark gray kepi.
    **Engineers** wore light blue overall with black facings and a black spiked helmet.

116

Lacking mineral resources and good agricultural land, the Norwegians had turned to the sea for sustenance. By 1905, they possessed the world's fourth largest merchant marine. Nearly 200 steamships were of over 1,000 tons burthen, while 1,200 others displaced from 100-1,000 tons. There were also 700 merchant sailing ships of over 100 tons, half of which were larger than 1,000 tons. The country could provide only weak coastal protection for these assets.

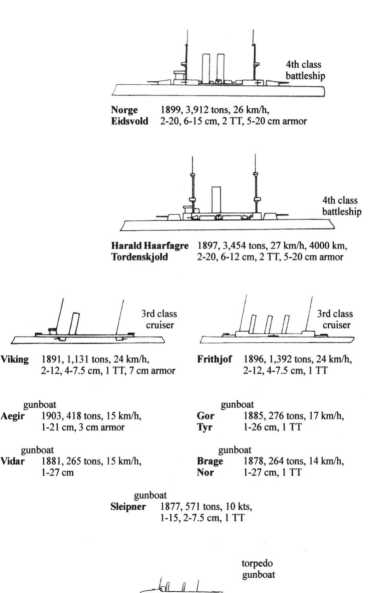

4th class
battleship

**Norge**      1899, 3,912 tons, 26 km/h,
**Eidsvold**   2-20, 6-15 cm, 2 TT, 5-20 cm armor

4th class
battleship

**Harald Haarfagre**   1897, 3,454 tons, 27 km/h, 4000 km,
**Tordenskjold**       2-20, 6-12 cm, 2 TT, 5-20 cm armor

3rd class
cruiser

3rd class
cruiser

**Viking**   1891, 1,131 tons, 24 km/h,
2-12, 4-7.5 cm, 1 TT, 7 cm armor

**Frithjof**   1896, 1,392 tons, 24 km/h,
2-12, 4-7.5 cm, 1 TT

gunboat
**Aegir**   1903, 418 tons, 15 km/h,
1-21 cm, 3 cm armor

gunboat
**Gor**   1885, 276 tons, 17 km/h,
**Tyr**   1-26 cm, 1 TT

gunboat
**Vidar**   1881, 265 tons, 15 km/h,
1-27 cm

gunboat
**Brage**   1878, 264 tons, 14 km/h,
**Nor**     1-27 cm, 1 TT

gunboat
**Sleipner**   1877, 571 tons, 10 kts,
1-15, 2-7.5 cm, 1 TT

torpedo
gunboat

**Valkyrien**   1896, 419 tons, 37 km/h,
4-7.5 cm, 2 TT

|  | 1st class torpedo boat |  | 1st class torpedo boat |
|---|---|---|---|

**Hval** 1897, 103 tons, 37 km/h, 2 TT
**Hai**
**Delphin**

**Storm** 1898, 103 tons, 37 km/h, 2 TT
**Trods**
**Brand**

|  | 2nd class torpedo boat |  | 2nd class torpedo boat |
|---|---|---|---|

**Ravn** 1903-5, 74 tons, 25 km/h, 2 TT
**Örn**
**Jo**
**Lom**
**Grib**

**Hauk** 1902, 75 tons, 32 km/h, 2 TT
**Falk**

|  | 2nd class torpedo boat |  | 2nd class torpedo boat |
|---|---|---|---|

**Hvas** 1901, 65 tons, 31 km/h, 2 TT
**Kjaek**

**Djerv** 1898, 65 tons, 31 km/h, 2 TT
**Dristig**
**Kvik**

|  | 2nd class torpedo boat |  | 2nd class torpedo boat |
|---|---|---|---|

**Lyn** 1896 65 tons, 31 km/h, 2 TT
**Glimt**
**Blink**

**Varg** 1894, 65 tons, 32 km/h, 2 TT
**Raket**

|  | 2nd class torpedo boat |  | 2nd class torpedo boat |
|---|---|---|---|

**Orm** 1887, 40 tons, 32 km/h, 2 TT
**Oter**

**Pil** 1887, 40 tons, 32 km/h, 2 TT
**Rask**

The Navy was alert and ready for action. The 4th Class Battleships were typical examples of coast defense ships of the time. Although rather weakly armed, they were good sea boats. The torpedo gunboat *Valkyrien* was a new type of vessel that would soon develop into the torpedo boat destroyer. The numerous torpedo boats would have been deadly within the restricted waters of the many Norwegian fjords.

Yet, the Norwegians realized they had little chance of winning a conflict with Sweden, which had twice as many soldiers and a superior naval squadron already lurking just outside the Oslofjord.

6 infantry divisions, totaling:
24 infantry regiments
9 cavalry regiments
8 artillery regiments

Seagoing Squadron
7 4th class battleships
4 torpedo cruisers
8 torpedo boats

The ministers reached a compromise, leaving the fortresses in place, but disarmed to mere monuments. On **26 Oct 1905**, Oscar II renounced the throne of Norway and Prince Charles was elected Haakon VII, king of an independent Norway. A neutral zone, 20 kilometers wide, was established along the border with Sweden. The Union colors were removed from the canton of the flag. The newly independent Norwegian Army was a national militia, somewhat like the Swiss, with a rather archaic organization. The various arms were formed during peacetime into "corps", each of one Line, one *landvärn* and one *landstorm* battalion. Each annual class of recruits spent six years in the Line units, followed by six more in the *landvärn* reserves, finally four in the *landstorm*.

> Five Military Command Areas
>   1 brigade
>     4 infantry "corps"
>       3 battalions
>         4 companies
>
> Northern Military Command Area
>   Finnmark Battalion
>     2 companies
>   Nordland, Tromsö Battalion
>     5 companies
>
> Army Troops
>   Jager Corps
>     3 battalions
>   2 cavalry "corps"
>     3 battalions
>       3 squadrons
>   1 cavalry "corps"
>     3 battalions
>       2 squadrons
>   3 field artillery "corps"
>     3 battalions
>       1 division
>         3 batteries
>           6 guns
>   3 heavy artillery batteries
>   2 mountain artillery batteries
>   6 fortress artillery battalions
>   3 engineer battalions

The Active Field Army consisted of 40,000 men of the Line and 35,000 of the *Landvärn*. However, no more than 18,000 of these could be mobilized without the *Störting*'s consent. In reserve were 95,000 men of the *Landstorm*.

> **Norwegian Field Army**
> 2 divisions (1 Line, 1 Landvärn)
>   3 infantry brigades
>     4 battalions
>   3 field artillery batteries
>   1 heavy field artillery battery
>   3 cavalry squadrons
>   4 machinegun detachments
>   engineers
>   1 cavalry brigade
>     6 squadrons

The Army barely had time to savor its new independence before danger stalked the North Sea.

# WORLD WAR I

World War I found the Norwegian Army with much the same composition as that at the end of the previous century. The Army had been reorganized in 1909 into five brigade areas, reestablishing the regiments according to Norwegian lineages that were disrupted in 1818. The Krag-Jorgensen rifle was still the infantry arm, but the field artillery had received new material, Ehrhardt 7.7 cm field guns and 12 cm howitzers. The siege artillery battalion was enlarged to a regiment before the war began.

**Norwegian Army**

1 cavalry brigade
    4 light dragoon regiments
        2-3 sabre squadrons

5 infantry brigades
    1 jäger (cyclist) company
    2 infantry regiments
        2 infantry battalions
            3 rifle companies
              **Krag-Jorgensen M/1894 6.5 mm rifle**
            1 machinegun company
              **Hotchkiss M.11 6.5 mm lmg** or
              **Madsen M.14 6.5 mm lmg**

**Madsen M.14 lmg**
6.5 mm, 11 kg, 680 m/s, 450 rpm

5 field artillery regiments
    2 field artillery battalions
        3 light field artillery batteries
            **4 Ehrhardt M/1901 77 mm field guns** or
            **4 Rheinmetall M/1911 75 mm mtn guns**

**Ehrhardt M/1901**
77 mm, 876 kg, 7 kg shell,
8450 m, 465 m/s, 12 rpm

1 siege artillery regiment
    1 light field artillery battalion
        4 light field artillery batteries
            **4 Schneider-Canet M/1898 75 mm field guns**
    1 heavy field artillery battalion
        2 heavy field gun batteries
            **4 Schneider-Canet M/1901**
            **105 mm heavy field guns**
        4 heavy field gun batteries
            **4 Cockerill-Nordenfeldt M/1904**
            **105 mm heavy field guns**
    1 heavy field howitzer battalion
        2 heavy field howitzer batteries
            **4 Ehrhardt M/1908 120 mm field howitzers**
        2 heavy field howitzer batteries
            **4 Bofors M/1915 120 mm field howitzers**

A new uniform was adopted in 1914, based on the jäger uniform of 1905. The uniform was a pale gray-green overall, with red piping. The kepi was of the same color while all leather was brown. Late in the war, the gray British 1916 helmet was adopted.

With the outbreak of the war, each district trained a regiment for the active army and also formed a *Landvärn* battalion of 6 companies. The *Landvärn* added 30,000 men to the army. By 1916, the army consisted of 80,000 men in 6 brigades totalling 65 infantry battalions, 5 cyclist (skier) companies, 3 cavalry regiments, 27 field artillery batteries, 3 mountain artillery batteries, 9 heavy artillery batteries and 1 engineer regiment.

**Norwegian Army**
6 mixed brigades
2-3 infantry regiments
4 infantry battalions
3-4 cavalry squadrons
1 field artillery battalion
3 batteries
1 heavy artillery battalion
1 engineer company

The Army purchased 3 Maurice Farman M.F.11s and built Kjeller airfield (near Lillestrom, northeast of Oslo). However, the *Störting* did not approve formation of an air unit until the *Haerens Flyvevaesen* (Army Air Unit) was established in 1915. Construction of aircraft for the Army began at a Kjeller factory. Nine copies of the Maurice Farman M.F.7 were built as the FF.1, followed by 15 FF.2s (Maurice Farman M.F.11). The 4 FF.3 *Hydro* of 1917 were enlarged maritime reconnaissance versions of the M.F.11.

**Haerens Flyvevaesen**
Sonnenfjellske Air District
Nordenfjellske Air District
Nord-Norges Air District
11 groups
5 planes
8 independent groups
3 planes

**FF.1**
1913, 16 m span, 95 km/h, 3½ hrs,
4000 m SC, no mgs
(Maurice Farman M.F.7)

**FF.5**
1916, 13 m span, 132 km/h, 4 hrs,
3355 m SC, 1 mg, 105 kg B
(B.E.2E)

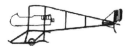

**FF.2**
1914, 16 m span, 106 km/h, 3½ hrs,
15/900 m, 3810 m SC, 1 mg, 130 kg B
(Maurice Farman M.F.11)

By 1917, the Army Air Unit planned to increase to 120 aircraft. As the factory was too small to produce this number in a reasonable time, Norway purchased 12 Farman F.40s from France in 1916 and 18 BE.2Es from Britain in 1917. Nearly identical to the BE.2E, 17 FF.5s were built in 1918, but were relegated to training as the T.1.

When the Great War broke out in 1914, the Norwegian fleet contained:

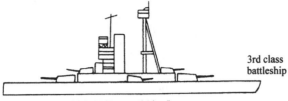

3rd class
battleship

| Bjoergvin | 1914, 5,791 tons, 24 km/h, |
| Nidaros | 2-24, 4-15, 6-10 cm, 2 TT, 5/18 cm armor |

4th class battleship
**Norge**      1899, 3,912 tons, 26 km/h,
**Eidsvold**   2-20, 6-15 cm, 2 TT,
               5-20 cm armor

1st class gunboat
**Viking**     1891, 1,131 tons, 24 km/h,
               2-12, 4-7.5 cm, 1 TT, 7 cm armor

4th class battleship
**Harald Haarfagre**  1897, 3,454 tons, 27 km/h,
**Tordenskjold**      2-20, 6-12 cm, 2 TT,
                      5-20 cm armor

1st class gunboat
**Frithjof**   1896, 1,392 tons, 24 km/h,
               2-12, 4-7.5 cm, 1 TT

destroyer

**Draug**      1908-14, 589 tons, 43 km/h,
**Garm**       6-7.5 cm, 3 TT
**Troll**

destroyer
**Valkyrien**  1896, 419 tons, 37 km/h,
               4-7.5 cm, 2 TT

1st class
torpedo boat

**Teist**      1906-12, 104 tons, 27 km/h,
**Kjell**      3 TT
**Scarv**

2nd class torpedo boats
**Ravn, Grib, Jo, Lom, Örn,
Hauk, Falk, Hvas, Kjoek
Djerv, Dristig, Kwik, Lyn,
Blink, Glimt, Varg, Raket,
Orm, Oter, Pil, Rask**

1st class torpedo boats
**Laks, Sild, Sael, Skrei,
Hval, Hai, Delphin, Storm,
Brand, Trods**

sub
**A1-5**   1909-14, 200 tons, 26/16 km/h, 3 TT

72

The new *Bjoergvin* class were powerful, modern ships, but were not complete when the war began.  They were seized by the British government, rebuilt, and put into service as the monitors *Glatton* and *Gorgon*.  The two cruisers were so small that they were officially rated as 1st Class Gunboats during the war.  Only a single division of destroyers was available.  The numerous torpedo boats were stationed in the myriad Norwegian fjords, with the fleet's larger, more modern ships assigned to protect important ports.  The Norwegian Navy was tied to its coasts.  With the chief naval base at Horten, neutrality patrols were mounted during the war, which went unchallenged.

The Navy became the first service to adopt the new flying machine. A Rumpler Taube was acquired in 1912. With the outbreak of the war, a Maurice Farman M.F.7 on floats arrived. Eventually, the Marinens Flyvefabrikk at Horten built 6 M.F.1 seaplanes, similar to the Army's FF.3 *Hydro*. They were followed by 3 M.F.2s in 1916, 4 M.F.3s in 1917, and 7 M.F.4s in 1918, all based on the FF.3. In 1916, the Storting approved an enlarged Naval Air Unit:

**Marinens Flyvevaesen**
Horten, Kristiansand, Bergen seaplane stations
   13 groups
      4 planes

 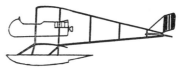

**M.F.5**                           **M.F.1**
1916, 8 m span, 158 km/h, 2 hrs,     1914, 16 m span, 106 km/h, 3½ hrs,
2318 m SC, 1 mg, 25 kg B           15/900 m, 3810 m SC, 1 mg, 130 kg B
(Sopwith Baby)

73

To supplement the Farman types being produced at Horten, the Navy purchased 18 Sopwith Baby seaplanes from Britain in 1917. These were the most modern aircraft in Scandinavia at the time. Nine more were licence-produced in 1918 as the M.F.5.

With Europe obviously on the verge of war, garrisons had been mobilized on 30 July 1914 for the coastal forts protecting Oslo, Kristiansand, Bergen and Trondheim. Norway adopted a neutral stance with the outbreak of the Great War in August. Under the overall command of General Major Holtfedt, the defense minister, the five army districts were placed on alert and 197,000 men mobilized. Unable to face the battle fleets of the Great Powers, Norway was limited to using her numerous torpedo boats for neutrality patrols.

Norwegian products were important to both sides in the conflict, with the result that Norway experienced two of the most prosperous years in her history. However, in August 1916 the belligerents began to attempt to deny each other the fruits of Norway. Great Britain tried to pressure Norway into ending trade with Germany by withholding coal exports to her. Germany began seizing and sinking Norwegian merchant ships. During 1915, 61 Norwegian vessels were sunk, 49 by German submarines. In the fall of 1916, another German U-boat campaign began and, up to January 1917, 170 more Norwegian merchant ships slid beneath the waves.

The announcement by Germany on 1 February 1917 that she would begin unrestricted submarine warfare was a particular threat to the large, unprotected, Norwegian merchant marine. By the end of the war, she had lost 820 vessels, half of her prewar fleet and more than any other nation.

The Allies also tried to involve Norway in the war. Propositions to seize a naval base in southern Norway, from which to flank German naval movements, were entertained by the British from 1916. In September 1917, the British First Lord of the Admiralty, Winston Churchill, advocated stationing an advanced squadron of the Grand Fleet at Kristiansand to block German egress from the North Sea. The strong objections of the Norwegian government to British encroachment were alleviated with the arrival of a division of American battleships late in 1917, the Norwegian naval commander expressing favorable opinions early the next year. However, the Norwegians lost their enthusiasm when the Americans laid a massive barrage of 56,000 mines between the Orkney Islands and Haugesund in March 1918 (the British added 15,000 more), threatening Norwegian neutrality and commerce. A proposal to establish a base at Stavanger for Allied vessels patrolling the east end of the barrage was refused by the Norwegians. [74]

# EXPANSION AND CONFLICT

The dissolution of Russia at the end of the Great War stimulated renewed ambitions to extend Norwegian territory along the Arctic coastline into the White Sea at Murmansk. Facing opposition from the Allies, who were fearful of creating future quarrels, the Norwegians settled for recognition of Norwegian sovereignty on the coal-rich Arctic island of Spitzbergen in 1920. It was officially incorporated into Norway as Svalbard in 1925. Five hundred kilometers north of Iceland lies the desolate island of Jan Mayen, and it, too, came under Norwegian sovereignty in 1929. At the time of little value, except for Svalbard's coal, the islands assumed strategic importance during and after World War II with the involvement of Soviet White Sea naval forces in world affairs. In 1926, drastic cuts were made in the armed forces. The Army was reduced to a cadre around which citizen soldiers were to rally in a national emergency. The Navy would receive two-thirds of the appropriations as the first-line of defense against aggression.

The sea-faring Norwegians continued a modern Viking Age of exploration with expeditions to the south polar region. Roald Amundsen was first to reach the South Pole in 1912. From Svalbard in 1926, he flew over the North Pole in the airship *Norge*. Landings were made by Norwegian parties on the Antarctic islands of Bouvet and Peter I in 1927-9. They then laid claim to a large section of the Antarctic continent in 1939, calling it Dronning Maud Land (Queen Maud Land). Resurrecting medieval claims, Norway next tried to establish fishing settlements on Greenland. However, the treaty that ceded the Virgin Islands to the United States in 1917 contained a clause that recognized Denmark's sovereignty over Greenland. The Danish settlements were on the west coast, but when the Norwegians laid claim to the east coast, the Danes began moving settlers there to forestall them.

At the time of the dispute, the Norwegian Army had:

**Norwegian Army**

1. **Divisjon** - Halden
2. **Divisjon** - Oslo
3. **Divisjon** - Kristiansand
4. **Divisjon** - Bergen
5. **Divisjon** - Trondheim
6. **Divisjon** - Harstad

The composition varied somewhat. The 3. and 4. Divisjons had only 1 mountain artillery battery with no cavalry or engineers. The 4. and 6. Divisjons had 2 independent infantry battalions attached. The 6. Divisjon had no cavalry and only 1 battery of mountain artillery. The Army was equipped with 71,836 Krag-Jorgensen M.94 6.5 mm rifles, 228 Ehrhardt M.01 77 mm field guns and 36 Ehrhardt M.08 120 mm heavy field howitzers.

1 cavalry regiment
  6 sabre squadrons
  1 machinegun troop
3 infantry regiments
  1 cyclist company
  3 infantry battalions
    3 rifle companies
      **Krag-Jorgensen M.1894 6.5 mm rifles**
      **Hotchkiss M.11 6.5 mm lmgs** or
      **Madsen M.14,18 6.5 mm lmgs**
    1 machinegun company
      **Colt M.29 7.92 mm hmgs**
1 field artillery regiment
  3 light battalions
    3 light field artillery batteries
      **4 Ehrhardt M.01 77 mm field guns** or
      **4 Rheinmetall M.11 75 mm mtn guns**
  1 heavy battalion
    3 field howitzer batteries
      **4 Ehrhardt M.08 120 mm** or
      **4 Bofors M.15 120 mm field howitzers**
1 engineer regiment

75

    The Flying Corps was organized into 3 divisions.  To replace the worn out Great War aircraft, war surplus Bristol Fighters were purchased in Britain, and Hauk reconnaissance planes were designed and built in Norway.  In 1927, the *Störting* decided to develop separate roles for the air units of the Army and Navy.  The Navy was to organize the defense of northern Norway, and all Army floatplanes transferred for Navy use there.  Aircraft of the Army were used primarily for training:

*Haerens Flyvevapen*

5 Bristol F.2B
14 Hawag CLV FF.7 Hauk
13 Hansa-Brandenburg W.29, W.33

**Bristol F.2b**
1917, 12 m span, 201 km/h, 3 hrs,
12/3050 m, 6100 m SC, 2 mg, 27 kg B

**Hansa-Brandenburg W.29**
1918, 13 m span, 179 km/h, 4 hrs,
6/1000 m, 2-3 mgs

    The Norwegian Army Air Corps would not have been a good match for its Danish counterpart.  The Danes had equipped their army cooperation squadrons with modern Fokker biplanes.  The indigenous *Hauk* biplanes used in a similar role by Norway were not particularly successful aircraft.  The old Bristol Fighters were of Great War vintage and had lost most of their potency.  The *Störting* had been influenced by economy and Norway's difficult terrain in its policies toward the Army's air arm, not expecting the ground forces to be deployed on foreign soil.

125

The only additions to the Navy of the Great War were the three little *Snögg* class torpedo boats and six small coastal submarines of the *B* class. The M.F.9 floatplane fighter proved too unstable and was withdrawn after five years of use. However, the licence-built Brandenburg W.33s were successful in the reconnaissance role. A small batch of licence-built Douglas DT-2 torpedo planes was still in service when World War II began.

*Marinen Flyvevaben*
15 M.F.9
9 M.F.5
30 Hansa-Brandenburg W.33
8 Douglas DT-2B,C

**MF.9**
1925, 10 m span, 2 mgs

**Hansa-Brandenburg W.33**
1918, 16 m span, 174 km/h, 4 hrs,
13/1980 m, 3 mgs

**Douglas DT-2**
1921, 15 m span, 161 km/h, 440 km,
2260 m SC, 830 kg T

76

However, the military forces of the two nations were never tested, for the League of Nations Hague Tribunal found in favor of Denmark in April 1933 and Norway withdrew its fishermen. This unfavorable outcome led to revisions of Norwegian military policy.

The Army Programme of 1933 proposed a mobilized army of 6 mixed field brigades (feltbrigader) totaling 66 infantry battalions, 12 cavalry squadrons, 15 cyclist companies, 36 artillery batteries, and 12 engineer companies. The *feltbrigader* were to have 5,000 men in the following organization:

**FIELD BRIGADE**
1 cyclist company
4 infantry battalions
3 rifle companies
1 machinegun company
1 artillery battalion
2 field artillery batteries

The Army Air Corps was to be reduced to 36 fighters and 39 reconnaissance planes. It tested the Curtiss Hawk, ASJA J6, Hawker Fury and Gloster Gauntlet before selecting the Armstrong-Whitworth Scimitar as the Army's next fighter, to be named the *Falk*. However, none were ever built and 12 Gloster Gladiators were purchased instead. The reconnaissance units were modernized with Dutch Fokker C.Vs.

Under the new programme, the Navy was scheduled to receive some badly needed small craft. Minelayers, sloops, torpedo boats and destroyers were all laid down. The Naval Air Corps was to have 20 fighters, 24 reconnaissance planes and 20 torpedo bombers. Even this modest modernization was soon to be threatened.

126

Threatening to disarm Norway, a Labour government came to power in 1935, but did not carry out its threat. However, it did cancel a militia that the Defense Law of 1933 had established as a reserve for the tiny "neutrality guard", the only military force capable of rapid mobilization. Training time was drastically reduced, the Labour prime minister, Nygaardsvold, successfully resisting attempts to increase expeditures in 1937. However, a new six year plan was approved in 1938. The Army would have an establishment of 36 fighters and 76 reconnaissance planes and bombers. The Navy would have 24 torpedo bombers and 30 reconnaissance planes. The *Störting* reluctantly agreed to fund the program, but little of the new equipment was received before a new European crisis erupted.

### *Too Little - Too Late* - 1937-9

It was obvious by April 1939 that Norway's defenses were dangerously inadequate, but it was already too late to remedy the deficiency. Not only were defensive preparations weaker than in 1914, the responsibilities of the armed forces were not even defined.

Norway's mountainous terrain was not conducive to large-scale armored operations. However, the Six-year Plan of 1938 proposed partial mechanization of the cavalry regiments. In 1937, the 5. Divisjon at Trondheim had tested samples of the Swedish Landsverk L.120 light tank and two improvised armored cars created by mounting armored boxes on truck chassis (the Landsverk L.185 was considered the eventual armored car equipment). In the aftermath of the severe financial depression, no funds were available to purchase expensive armored equipment and the project was canceled.

The proposed cavalry regiment would probably have had a mixed composition of infantry, cavalry and mechanized units:

**MECHANIZED CAVALRY REGIMENT**
1 reconnaissance company
    **Landsverk L.185, motorcycles**
2 horse squadrons
1 motorized machinegun squadron
1 mortar section
1 tank squadron
    **Landsverk L.120**

It would be discovered by combatants that the mixture of horse and motorized elements would hinder each operationally because of their disparate mobility. In any case, the sparse road net would have limited the use of armor, compounded by Norway's limited liquid fuel resources. The cost of motorized vehicles to a poor nation just recovering from fiscal problems caused the parliament to reject the purchase of armor.

However, the *Störting* did agree to fund the purchase of new aircraft from foreign manufacturers. Orders were placed in Italy for 20 Caproni Ca.312bis, and in the United States for 24 Curtiss Hawk 75A-6s (and a licence to build 24 more). These orders were followed by more to America for 36 Curtiss Hawk 75A-8s and 36 Douglas 8A-5s, all with 1200 hp Wright Cyclone engines for easy maintenance. If the programme had been completed, by 1941 the Norwegians would have possessed:

**Norwegian Army**
1., 2., 5. Divisjons
  **1 mechanized cavalry regiment**
    L.120, L.185, motorcycles
3 infantry, 1 artillery regiments

3., 4. Divisjons
  1 motorcycle company
  2 infantry regiments
  1 mountain artillery battalion

6. Divisjon
  3 infantry regiments
  2 infantry battalions
  1 mountain artillery battalion

**Landsverk L.185**
1933, 4.6 tons, 1-20 mm, 2 mgs,
60 km/h, 240 km, 6/4 mm, 5 men,
20 mm/500 m P

**Landsverk L.120**
1937, 4.5 tons, 2 mgs,
52 km/h, 300 km, 13/10/8 mm, 2 men

1 jagebataljon
  3 jagevingen - Kjeller (Oslo)
    **12 Curtiss Hawk 75A-8**

1 jagebataljon
  2 jagevingen - Fornebu (Oslo)
    **12 Curtiss Hawk 75A-6**
  1 jagevingen - forward airfield
    **12 Gloster Gladiator I,II**

1 bombebataljon
  3 bombevingen - Sola (Stavanger), Kjeller
    **12 Douglas 8A-5**

1 speidebataljon
  1 speidevingen - Gardermoen (Oslo)
    **9 Caproni Ca.312bis**
  1 speidevingen - Sola, Kjevik (Arendal)
    **9 Caproni Ca.312bis**

Trondelagavdelning
  Vaernes (Trondheim)
    **12 Fokker C.VD**

Hålogalandavdelning
  Bardufoss (Narvik)
    **12 Fokker C.VD**

**Curtiss Hawk 75A-8**
1939, 11 m span, 520 km/h, 971 km,
4.9/4575 m, 9974 m SC, 6 mgs

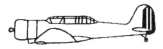

**Douglas 8A-5**
1939, 15 m span, 400 km/h, 1500 km,
9100 m SC, 5 mgs, 300 kg B

**Caproni Ca.312bis**
1938, 16 m span, 430 km/h, 650 km,
8000 m SC, 3 mgs, 400 kg B [77]

Modernization of the Navy, as the first line of defense, was already underway. For the *Marinens Flygevapen*, the Norwegian *Storting* approved purchase of 12 Heinkel He.115A-2s from Germany, four for each *flyavdelning*. All M.F.11s were to be replaced by 24 Northrop N-3PBs ordered from the United States. The dispersal of the vessels among the many coastal stations proved unworkable and ineffective during the invasion of 1940. An earlier appreciation of the advantages of concentration, would have produced a viable fleet upon completion of the programme:

**Norwegian Navy**

Panserskipsdivisjonen
  *Eidsvold, Norge*

1. Jagerdivisjon
  *Draug, Garm, Troll*
2. Jagerdivisjon
  *Sleipner, Aeger*
3. Jagerdivisjon
  *Gyller, Odin*
4. Jagerdivisjon
  *Balder, Tor*
5. Jagerdivisjon
  *ZN4, ZN5*

destroyer

**ZN4-5**  1943, 1,240 tons, 55 km/h,
4-12 cm, 4 TT

1. Torpedobåtdivisjon
  *Snögg, Stegg, Trygg*
2. Torpedobåtdivisjon
  *Kjell, Skarv, Teist*
3. Torpedobåtdivisjon
  *Grib, Jo, Lom, Ravn, Örn*

1. Ubåtdivisjon
  *A2, 3, 4*
2. Ubåtdivisjon
  *B2, 4, 5*
3. Ubåtdivisjon
  *B1, 3, 6*

Mineleggers
  *Olav Tryggvason, Fröya*

Oppsynsskip (fishery protection vessels)
  *Fridtjof Nansen, Senja, Nordkapp*

**1. Flyavdelning**
  Sola (Stavanger) - **4 Heinkel He.115A-2**
  Horten - **4 Northrop N-3PB**
  Kristiansand - **4 Northrop N-3PB**
**2. Flyavdelning**
  Flatöy (Bergen) - **4 Heinkel He.115A-2,**
            **4 Northrop N-3PB**
  Sola (Stavanger) - **4 Northrop N-3PB**
  Aunöya (Trondheim) - **4 Northrop N-3PB**
**3. Flvavdelning**
  Skattöra (Tromsö) - **4 Heinkel He.115A-2**
  Vadsö - **4 Northrop N-3PB**

# WORLD WAR II

The invasion of Finland by the Soviet Union on 30 November 1939 placed Norwegian sovereignty in jeopardy, both from possible Soviet encroachments and from Allied attempts to aid the Finns. Britain and France pressured Norway to allow passage of troops through the Tromsö region into Finland. However, as that would give control of Narvik and the rich Swedish iron ore to them, the Allies realized that the action would precipitate German and Soviet reaction. Nevertheless, the French saw an opportunity to divert German troops from their eastern borders during the "Phony War" and coerced agreement from the British. By the end of February 1940, a first echelon of 15,500 Allied troops was ready to move to Narvik and advance up the railway to the Swedish mines. A second echelon would land at Trondheim and move across the waist of Norway to thwart any German intervention. Alarmed, both Norway and Sweden refused passage. The question became moot when the Finnish War ended on 12 March with a Soviet victory.

The Germans were also planning a preemptive move. Admiral Raeder convinced Hitler that the failure of the High Seas Fleet of World War I was due to its being bottled up in the North Sea because the coast of Norway had not been seized. Hitler was waiting only for the breakup of ice in the Danish straits before moving north.

Aware of the events swirling around it, the Norwegian *Störting* authorized mobilization of the Navy and 7,000 troops. In January 1940, additional troops had been sent north to form a second brigade under General Fleischer's 6. Divisjon at Harstad, in case the Russo-Finnish War spilled over into Norway. Reacting to ominous reports from attaches in Berlin, the General Staff urged on 5 April that the *Störting* allow further mobilization. The request was ignored.

## *Barbarian Invasion* - 9 April 1940

Shrouded by fog, tiny *Pol III* puttered around its assigned patrol station, bobbing over the swells that hinted at the storms whipping up the North Sea. The crew had paid little heed to the scuttlebutt claiming Hitler was coming west this spring, but when a column of shadowy warships intruded into her surreal gray world just after midnight of **9 April 1940**, the watchful patrol boat crackled a warning - "unknown ships entering Oslofjord!"

The intruders were, in fact, Group V of the German Kriegsmarine, instructed to sail serenely northward to Oslo and welcome their Nordic brothers into the bosom of Aryan civilization. A steel fist greeted all who resisted the Nazi embrace. Little *Pol III* died under a hail of bullets from the torpedo boat *Albatros*. Unfortunately, Norway had only a small, rusty shield with which to defend herself.

At the outbreak of the Second World War, the Norwegian Navy was a collection of antiques, recently infused with some modern torpedo craft. Two similar classes of small coastal destroyers had just been completed, and a pair of ocean-going destroyers was on the stocks. A large modern minelayer and a sloop had recently been commissioned. However, most Norwegian vessels were still in their original Nineteenth Century configuration, unsuited to modern naval warfare. They were dispersed around the long coast, defending the numerous fjords and archipelagoes.

**Norwegian Navy** (Adm. Diesen)
**1. Sjöforsvarsdistrikt** (Rear Adm. Smith-Johannsen) - Horten
  3. Jagerdivisjon - Kristiansand
    *Gyller, Odin*
  2. Torpedobåtsdivisjon - Kristiansand, Horten
    *Kjell, Skarv, Teist*
  3. Torpedobåtsdivisjon
    *Grib, Jo, Lom, Ravn, Örn*
  1. Ubåtdivisjon
    *A2, 3, 4*
  2. Ubåtdivisjon - Kristiansand
    *B2, 5*
  1., 3. Minesveiperdivisjon - 6 vessels
  1. Mineliggerdivisjon - 4 vessels
  Minelegger
    *Olav Tryggvason*

destroyer

| | |
|---|---|
| **Odin** | 1940, 640 tons, 48 km/h, |
| **Balder** | 2-10 cm, 2 TT |
| **Tor** | |

sub

| | |
|---|---|
| **B1-6** | 1924-30, 425 tons, 28/20 km /h, |
| | 1-7.5 cm, 4 TT |

minelayer

| | |
|---|---|
| **Olav Tryggvason** | 1934, 1,622 tons, 32 km/h, 4800 km, |
| | 4-12, 1-7.5 cm AA, 4 small, 280 mines |

**1. Flyavdelning**
  Harfsfjord (Stavanger) - **1 Heinkel He.115A-2**
  Horten - **5 M.F.11, 2 Douglas DT-2B,C**
  Kristiansand - **3 M.F.11**
  Gressholmen (Oslo) - **1 Junkers Ju.52/3m**

**2. Sjöforsvarsdistrikt** (Rear Adm. Tank-Nielsen) - Bergen
  1. Jagerdivisjon - Stavanger, Trondheim
    *Draug, Garm, Troll*
  2. Jagerdivisjon - Trondheim, Stavanger
    *Sleipner, Aeger*
  1. Torpedobåtsdivisjon - Trondheim, Bergen
    *Snögg, Stegg, Trygg*
  4. Torpedobåtsdivisjon
    *Brand, Storm, Sael*
  5. Torpedobåtsdivisjon - Trondheim
    *Laks, Sild, Skrei*
  Ubåt - *B6*
  2. Minesveiperdivisjon - 2 vessels
  2. Mineleggerdivisjon - 4 vessels
  Minelegger
    *Fröya*

**MF.11**
1931, 11 m span, 235 km/h, 800 km,
5000 m SC, 3 mgs, 300 kg B

destroyer

| | |
|---|---|
| **Sleipner** | 1937-40, 603 tons, 52 km/h, |
| **Gyller** | 3-10 cm, 2 TT |
| **Aeger** | |

minelayer

| | |
|---|---|
| **Fröya** | 1916, 760 tons, 35 km/h, |
| | 4-10 cm, 3 small, 2 TT |

torpedo boat

| | |
|---|---|
| **Snögg** | 1920, 222 tons, 40 km/h, |
| **Stegg** | 2-7.5 cm, 4 TT |
| **Trygg** | |

**2. Flyavdelning**
  Flatöy (Bergen) - **2 Heinkel He.115A-2,**
              **4 M.F.11, 3 Douglas DT-2C**
  Harfsfjord (Stavanger) - **2 M.F.11**
  Aunöya (Trondheim) - **1 M.F.11**

131

**3. Sjöforsvarsdistrikt** (Commander Hagerup) - Tromsö
Panserskipsdivisjon (Commodore Askim)
    *Eidsvold, Norge*
3. Ubåtdivisjon
    *B1, 3*
Oppsynsskip (fishery protection vessels)
    *Fridtjof Nansen, Senja, Michael Sars,*
    *Nordkapp, Heimdal*

patrol
vessel

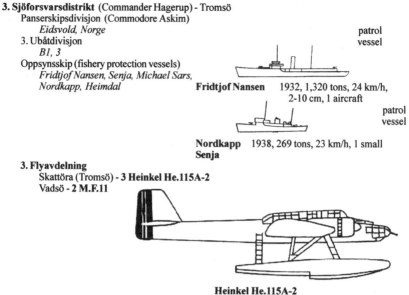

**Fridtjof Nansen**   1932, 1,320 tons, 24 km/h,
                      2-10 cm, 1 aircraft

patrol
vessel

**Nordkapp**   1938, 269 tons, 23 km/h, 1 small
**Senja**

**3. Flyavdelning**
Skattöra (Tromsö) - **3 Heinkel He.115A-2**
Vadsö - **2 M.F.11**

**Heinkel He.115A-2**
1937, 22 m span, 314 km/h, 2800 km,
5200 m SC, 2 mgs, 1250 kg B or T

The outer batteries of Norwegian coastal artillery could not fire because the heavy fog hid the warships. Approaching Drobak, the German column was obliged to enter one of the narrow branches of the main fjord. Only a few meters offshore, the excited defenders of old Oskarsborg fortress descried the enemy intruders. Seizing the opportunity, they fired point blank into the leading vessels, and loosed two torpedoes from underwater tubes. Contre Admiral Kummetz, leading in his flagship *Blucher*, was overwhelmed by the furious barrage. Within minutes, the proud new heavy cruiser was racked by internal explosions and sank. Following the flagship, the "pocket battleship" *Lutzow* was also hit heavily, but managed to reverse course and lead the light cruiser *Emden* and the torpedo boats *Albatros, Kondor* and *Mowe* in an ignominious retirement from the unexpectedly hostile narrows. As they passed Horten, the minelayer *Olav Tryggvason* sank the *Albatros*. Hitler drew back a bloody fist.

Oslo's sailors were not the only Norwegians to see action that fateful night. Unknown to the shore personnel of the *1. Sjöforsvarsdistrikt*, as the first skirmish developed in the Oslofjord, the German light cruiser *Karlsruhe* was approaching the north shore of the Skagerrak in company with the sisters of the torpedo boats thrusting toward Oslo. Group IV sent the *Greif* to land troops at Arendal, then ordered her, *Luchs* and *Seeadler* to surprise the defenses at Kristiansand. However, the same fog that hid them from the shore prevented them from finding the channel into the Trysfjord that led to Kristiansand. The group was still waiting for better visibility when one of three M.F.11s of the *1. Flyafdelning* discovered them at 0600. Alerted by the seaplane's report, the shore batteries drove back the German vessels when they tried to enter at 0620. Five Heinkel He.111s of KG 26 belatedly rained bombs on the determined artillerymen, who resumed an accurate fire on the column of German warships when it tried again to enter at 0655. *Karlsruhe* opened fire on the plucky Norwegian gunners at 0750, but when the three torpedo boats tried to enter

132

the fjord under cover of the bombardment, fog intervened and they lost direction. At 0930, *Karlsruhe* forged ahead despite the fog, and narrowly avoided going aground. As if to atone for its earlier weak action, KG 26 put an entire group of Heinkels over the Norwegian base as the cruiser had its brush with disaster. For an hour and a half they dropped explosives on the forts. The devastated batteries could no longer fire. Group IV entered the anchorage unmolested. The new Norwegian destroyers *Odin* and *Gyller*, surprised by the appearance of the German squadron, were unable to gain the sea through the fog. They were captured without contributing to the defense of their base. The old torpedo boat *Kjell*, and the two little submarines *B2* and *B5* also failed to fulfill their missions.

**Norwegian Army Air Corps** (Col. Thomas Gulliksen)

**Flygebataljonen** - Kjeller (Oslo)
  **Bombevingen**
    Kjeller (Oslo) - **4 Fokker C.VE**
    Sola (Stavanger) - **4 Fokker C.VE,**
        **4 Caproni Ca.310**
  **Speidevingen**
    Kjeller (Oslo) - **8 Fokker C.VD**
    Sola (Stavanger) - **2 Fokker C.VD**
  **Jagevingen**
    Kjeller (Oslo) - **1 Gloster Gladiator II**
    Fornebu (Oslo) - **5 Gloster Gladiator I,**
        **5 Gloster Gladiator II**

**Trondelag flygeavdelning**
  Vaernes (Trondheim) - **1 Fokker C.VD,**
      **8 Fokker C.VE**

**Hålogaland flygeavdelning**
  Bardufoss (Narvik) - **3 Fokker C.VD**
  Banak (Hammerfest) - **3 Fokker C.VD**

Fokker C.VE
1925, 13 m span, 245 km/h, 1200 km,
7300 m SC, 2-3 mgs, 50 kg B

Caproni Ca.310
1937, 16 m span, 347 km/h, 1025 km,
7300 m SC, 3 mgs, 400 kg B

Fokker C.VD
1925, 13 m span, 225 km/h, 1200 km,
7000 m SC, 2-3 mgs, 50 kg B

Gloster Gladiator I,II
1934, 10 m span, 407 km/h, 692 km,
6/4575 m, 10000 m SC, 4 mgs

The *Haerens Flygevapen* was alerted to German movements, but was surprised by the weight of the attack. The first swarm of Heinkel He.111s of KG 26 dropped no bombs as they roared over Oslo on 9 April. They were intended to cow the Norwegian government with a show of force, and coerce the Norwegian citizens with a shower of leaflets. Yet, when reports arrived from Malmö, Sweden of 15 large airplanes (Ju.52/3ms) flying northward, the Norwegians were ready to fight. From Fornebu airfield, southwest of Oslo, Captain Munthe-Dahl ordered his *Jagevingen* into the air. Five Gladiators took off at 0700, followed by two more a few minutes later. Flying at 900 meters in a "V" formation, the first five searched to the southwest of Oslo, noting the smoke from the stricken *Blucher*. Pursuing reports of large formations of enemy planes approaching Oslo from the southwest, the 5 Gladiators were flying westward at 1,700 meters over Steilene when they spotted three dozen planes approaching 600 meters below them. Maintaining their tight formation, the Gladiators dove

133

on the intruders. Time and again they slashed through the enemy bombers, until 3 Heinkels had gone down trailing smoke. Over Sandvika, the tardy pair of Gladiators tore into another bomber stream, detaching an He.111 from its fellows. A Dornier Do.17P pathfinder also got caught in Norwegian gunsights and crashed. Fast Messerschmitt Bf.110 escort fighters bore in on the slow Norwegian biplanes and shot one down in retribution. Low on fuel, the Norwegians headed for home, only to be warned to land elsewhere. Eight Bf.110s of I/ZG 76 were now strafing Fornebu airdrome, destroying two of the Gladiators that had already landed. The remaining Norwegian fighters landed temporarily on frozen lakes all around Oslo. [78]

At Fornebu, the Bf.110s failed to silence the Norwegian anti-aircraft gunners, who took a heavy toll of the German aircraft now circling over the airfield. The loiterers were waiting for a company of 300 paratroops who were to drop on the field and secure the landing area. However, the Junkers Ju.52/3ms of II/ KGzbV 1 that were carrying them had turned aside from bad weather and landed at Aalborg, Denmark to reorganize. Nearly out of fuel, the Messerschmitts took a drastic course. They landed and used their machineguns to subdue the perimeter defenders sufficiently for the Ju.52s of KGrzbV 103 to land with their cargo of airborne infantry. Nevertheless, the Norwegian gunners downed at least 3 of the planes. The tardy paratroops arrived shortly afterward, along with another formation that had been diverted from Stavanger. Combined, the 8 companies of airborne troops marched boldly into Oslo, as if on parade, and captured the capital without opposition.

Although the old coastal fortresses had turned back the seaborne invasion, the Germans had used new-fangled air power to leap over the surface defenses and gain their objective. With the capital in their possession, they pried open the southern door. Two Norwegian M.F.11s from the *1. Flyavdelning* at Horten flew into a hornet's nest of German aircraft and were shot down while attempting to discover the whereabouts of the wounded enemy naval squadron. It appeared again after the Junkers Ju.87Bs of I/StG 1 spent the morning of 10 April bombing the Oskarsborg fortress into shambles. Group V warily probed the upper Oslofjord, but no viable defenses remained. The *Harald Haarfagre* and *Tordenskjold* didn't even raise steam. They and the *Olav Tryggvason, Orn, Lom* and *A2* were captured at Horten, along with the 3 remaining M.F.11s. Others hid among the branches of the fjord for a time. *Teist* was scuttled by her crew after being hunted down at Drange on 14 April. *Skarv* was captured by two German minesweepers. The submarines *A3* and *A4* were scuttled on 16 April, as were *Ravn, Jo* and *Grib* when south of Lyngör the next day.

### *The Battle for Southern Norway* - 9 April-1 May 1940

The interior of southern Norway is a mountain fastness with meagre communications routes. Most of the population resides in cities sited close to the sea along the coasts. The result was a mandatory perimeter defense thrust upon the Norwegian high command. Realizing that any invader would also be hindered by the formidable terrain of the interior, and the lack of maneuvering room along the coasts, the Norwegians had chosen to mobilize local divisions at arsenals near the main cities. Each division would be forced to fend for itself, with the help of the local naval and air forces, and such additional air forces as could be spared from the crucial defense of Östlandet around Oslo. The maritime mobility possessed by the invaders largely frustrated Norwegian plans.

134

Stavanger was to experience the German aerial mobility. Four minesweepers (Group VI) entered the harbor of Egersund to the south, but no naval invasion group approached Stavanger. The city was included in the operational zones of both the *1.* and *2. Sjöforsvarsdistrikt*, an arrangement that caused much confusion and inaction. The modern coastal destroyer *Aeger*, of the *2. Jagerdivisjon*, was paired with the old *Draug* of the *1. Jagerdivisjon*. Of the seaplanes on the Harfsfjord, the Heinkel He.115 was under the command of one district while the two M.F.11s followed the orders of the other. The most formidable weapons at Stavanger were the 6 Fokker C.Vs and 4 Caproni Ca.310s of the *Bombevingen* and *Speidevingen* which were based at Sola airfield on the coastal plain south of the city. The Germans also coveted that location.

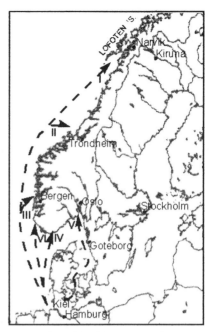

At 0755 on 9 April, reports were received of the fighting around Oslo, and all aircraft were ordered to leave Sola and fly east to Östlandet. When the three serviceable Ca.310s dutifully took off, one crash landed after its engines failed and the other two made emergency landings farther north, along with the accompanying Fokkers. They had hardly left when 11 Junkers Ju.52/3ms emerged from the fog at 0845 and approached Sola from the southeast, dropping a company of paratroops on the field.

Two Messerschmitt Bf.110s left a formation of six from I/ZG 76 that were circling overhead and strafed the Norwegian airfield defenses, destroying the two Fokker C.Vs left behind. The capable paratroops secured the base and sent a platoon to capture the seaplane and naval base at the Harfsfjord.

The Norwegian Navy got in a few licks before it succumbed. When two German cargo vessels tried to enter the harbor prematurely in the early hours of 9 April, the *Aeger* and *Draug* sank them. *Aeger* paid the price at dawn when she was bombed and sunk by Heinkel He.111s of III/KG 4. However, the *Draug* managed to move north to Haugesund and remain concealed during the day. The next day she left for Great Britain. All of the naval seaplanes at the Harfsfjord were captured.

The ancient Hanseatic port of Bergen received more attention. Coast artillerymen manning the shore batteries at the mouth of the Korsfjord awoke to find troops landing from unknown vessels offshore, obviously intending to capture their guns. Nevertheless, they landed a few shells on the intruding warships as they passed. Surviving Norwegian gunners watched as Heinkel He.111s of KG 26 and Junkers Ju.88s of KG 30 were drawn to something offshore at noon. Their target was the British Home Fleet, which was moving in to block what it thought was a German attempt to break out into the Atlantic. For three hours the bombs fell. One hit the battleship *Rodney*, but failed to penetrate her armor. A destroyer was sunk and three cruisers damaged.

The British had discovered that the Luftwaffe, rather than Britannia, ruled the waves of the North Sea. Meanwhile, Group III pushed on up the Korsfjord. The 4 M.F.11s at the Flatöy seaplane base were loaded with 50 kilogram bombs and sent out to look for the approaching enemy squadron. Without bombsights, and flying through thick mists, they were unable to place any bombs on the warships. Group III reached Bergen at 0620. The two Heinkel He.115s at the base left before the Germans arrived, one flying to Scotland, the other to Narvik to join the *3. Flyavdelning*. The light cruisers *Koln* and *Konigsberg* supported the torpedo boats *Leopard* and *Wolf* and 5 motor torpedoboats (S boats) as they winkled out the few units of the Norwegian Navy stationed at the port. The crew of the old minelayer *Fröya* beached her on 13 April. The 20 year old torpedo boat *Stegg* was found at Heröysund in Hardangerfjord and sunk by the gunnery training ship *Bremse* on 20 April. The only other Norwegian vessels were three early-century 100 ton torpedo boats. The *Brand, Storm* and *Sael* were hunted down and either sunk by the S boats or captured. The little submarine *B6* was captured and taken into the German Navy as the UC 2 (sister *B5* became UC 1). The surviving M.F.11s gathered with some from Kristiansand on the Hardangersfjord and Sognefjord, where they continued reconnaissance operations until the south was evacuated. Two then flew north to join the *3. Flyavdelning* at Vadsö.

Unable to equip their Army to modern standards because of the poor economic situation, Norwegians were defended by an infantry force against an enemy well trained and equipped to carry out advanced tactics. The Norwegians were still largely in a World War I condition, as were the armies of many West European nations of the time. An ancient elite unit guarded the king and government in Oslo:

**ROYAL GUARD REGIMENT**
4 rifle companies

The three cavalry regiments had some automatic weapons units dubbed onto their horsed squadrons of dragoons:

**CAVALRY REGIMENT**
2 horse squadrons
1 machinegun squadron
1 cyclist company
1 motor machinegun squadron
1 mortar section

**Colt M.29 hmg**
7.92 mm, 14 kg, 839 m/s, 450 rpm

Sixteen infantry regiments formed the core of the Norwegian ground forces. They were armed with a Nineteenth Century rifle and were woefully short of machineguns and mortars.

**INFANTRY REGIMENT**
4 infantry battalions
   3 rifle companies
     **Krag-Jorgensen M.94 6.5 mm rifles**
     **6 Hotchkiss M.11 6.5 mm lmgs** or
     **Madsen M.14, M.18 6.5 mm lmgs**
   1 machinegun company
     **2-4 Colt M.29 7.92 mm hmg**
     **2 M.35 81 mm mortars**

**M.35 81 mm mortar**
81 mm, 44.5 kg, 4.2 kg shell,
4600 m, 245 m/s, 25 rpm

Three low-country divisions had field artillery regiments. The principal artillery piece was the Ehrhardt 77 mm field gun of the World War I German army, although some heavy field howitzers had been integrated into the regiment when the old siege artillery regiment was disbanded after the war.

**ARTILLERY REGIMENT**
2 light field artillery battalions
   3 batteries
      **4 Ehrhardt M.01 77 mm field guns**
1 heavy field artillery battalion
   3 batteries
      **4 Ehrhardt M.08 120 mm field howitzers** or
      **4 Bofors M.15 120 mm field howitzers** or
      **4 Kongsberg M.32 120 mm field howitzers**

Three divisions located in severe terrain had only a single battalion of mountain artillery.

**MOUNTAIN ARTILLERY BATTALION**
2 batteries
      **4 Rheinmetall M.11 75 mm mtn guns** or
      **4 Kongsberg M.22, M.27 75 mm mtn howitzers**

Most troops wore the uniform of 1914: gray-green overall with a soft kepi and gray gaiters over black boots, with red piping around the collar, top of cuff, and trouser stripe. The little-worn 1934 model had a stiff kepi, no gaiters, and dark green piping. A ribbed, British-style helmet was issued. Rank insignia was worn on collar patches, shoulder straps and cuffs. The collar patches of field and line officers were dark green, those of field officers having a broad border of silver braid.

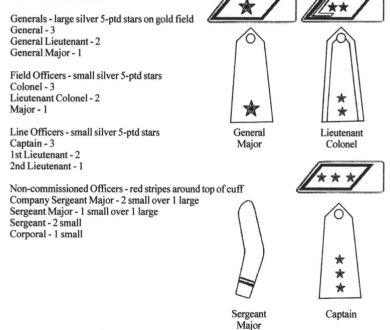

Generals - large silver 5-ptd stars on gold field
General - 3
General Lieutenant - 2
General Major - 1

Field Officers - small silver 5-ptd stars
Colonel - 3
Lieutenant Colonel - 2
Major - 1

Line Officers - small silver 5-ptd stars
Captain - 3
1st Lieutenant - 2
2nd Lieutenant - 1

Non-commissioned Officers - red stripes around top of cuff
Company Sergeant Major - 2 small over 1 large
Sergeant Major - 1 small over 1 large
Sergeant - 2 small
Corporal - 1 small

General
Major

Lieutenant
Colonel

Sergeant
Major

Captain

137

Ephemeral Armor - A Landsverk L.120 Denied By Norwegian Troops

With swift strokes by his aerial and naval forces, Hitler had gained control of all important ports of southern Norway. Debating in the eleventh hour, the Norwegian parliament, the *Störting*, had authorized only partial mobilization, even with unmistakable signs of invasion all around them.

Norwegian Army (Gen.Maj. Laake, Ruge from April 11)

1. **Divisjon** (Gen.Maj. Ericksen) - Halden
   1. Dragoon Regiment
   1., 9., 10. Infantry Regiments
   1. Artillery Regiment
2. **Divisjon** (Gen.Maj. Hvinden Haug) - Oslo
   Royal Guard Regiment
   2. Dragoon Regiment
   4., 5., 6. Infantry Regiments
   2. Artillery Regiment
3. **Divisjon** (Gen.Maj. Liljedahl) - Kristiansand
   3., 7. Infantry Regiments
   1 mountain artillery battalion
   1 cyclist company
4. **Divisjon** (Gen.Maj. Steffens) - Bergen
   2., 8. Infantry Regiments
   1 mountain artillery battalion
   1 cyclist company
5. **Divisjon** (Gen.Maj. Laurantzon) - Trondheim
   3. Dragoon Regiment
   11., 12., 13. Infantry Regiments
   3. Artillery Regiment
   1 engineer battalion
6. **Divisjon** (Gen.Maj. Fleischer) - Narvik
   14., 15., 16. Infantry Regiments
   2 independent infantry battalions
   1 mountain artillery battalion
   1 engineer battalion
General Reserve
   1 anti-aircraft artillery regiment
   1 engineer regiment

With enemy troops landing in their harbors, the Norwegian field units had to hastily draw as many stored weapons as possible from their arsenals and head for the hills to mobilize.

138

While the *Störting* debated, the Heinkel He.111s of KG 26 were already landing at Sola airfield near Stavanger, from where they could easily reach any target in southern Norway. By the end of the first day, there were 180 German planes of all types on the airfield. To secure Stavanger, the German 69. Infantry Division had dropped off some of its troops while the rest of the division went on to Bergen. The exposed detachment was relieved by the 214. Infantry Division on 17 April.

Three days later, the new division advanced southward along the coast road, driving advance elements of the Norwegian 3. Divisjon back into Kristiansand. General Liljedahl had managed to mobilize all of the units of his small 3. Divisjon, and established a blocking position forty kilometers inland on the high ground north of the city. When the 214. Infantry Division began moving northward on **23 April**, the 3. Divisjon held up its advance until dive bombers of I/StG 1 shattered the Norwegian positions. Two days later, the demoralized defenders surrendered, a situation that British and French troops were to experience later in the spring.

Intended for emergency use by the Norwegian Army Air Force, the forward landing strip at Kristiansand was occupied instead by the short-ranged Messerschmitt Bf.109Es of II/JG 77. The Germans now had single-seat fighter cover for their units in southern Norway. The Norwegians were about to learn first hand about the terror of air power.

The 4. Divisjon of General Steffens had a much longer fight than the Kristiansand troops. He had mobilized his two infantry regiments and single mountain artillery battalion at Voss, 70 kilometers northeast of their arsenal at Bergen. After concentrating at Bergen, the German 69. Infantry Division advanced eastward on **17 April**. The small Norwegian division, with only 4,500 men, managed to halt the German advance in the rugged mountain valley. Despite the success, an order was received from the high command for the 4. Divisjon to abandon its strong position and retire eastward. Something had gone wrong at Oslo.

### *Death in the Heartland* - 9 April-4 May 1940

With German bombers overhead on **9 April**, the members of the Norwegian *Störting* had left their exposed chambers in Oslo and retired to Elverum, near the Swedish border 120 kilometers north of the capital. Colonel Otto Ruge had used his detachment to halt a German armored column that was threatening to capture the Norwegian government. When the grateful legislators succeeded in convening briefly at Elverum, they authorized the king and his ministers to make any decisions necessary to prosecute the war. The president of the *Störting*, Carl Hambro, fled to Stockholm, where most of Norway's foreign policy was determined throughout the war. Having proven his fighting spirit, Colonel Ruge was promoted to general and given command of the widely dispersed Norwegian Army on 11 April. His forces were already in desperate straits, fighting to survive.

Östlandet was defended by two army divisions. At Halden, astride the traditional invasion route from Sweden, the 1. Divisjon was unable to mobilize even half of its 9,000 men. When the German 196. Infantry Division left its landing point in Oslo and advanced southward, General Ericksen had only his dragoon regiment, 1. Infantry Regiment, and the second battalion of his artillery regiment in hand. Ericksen's skeleton division was unable to stop the enemy advance and, on 15 April, was driven across the border to internment in Sweden.

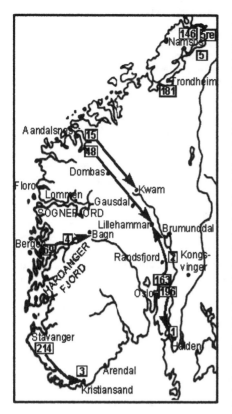

With more maneuvering room, the 2. Divisjon at Oslo fared better. However, the division's commander, General Major Hvinden Haug, also achieved mobilization of only half of his units. The Royal Guard formed the rallying point for the dragoon regiment and the intact 6. Infantry Regiment. However, only two batteries of artillery could be removed from the capital's arsenal before it was overrun. The division was ordered to establish a defensive line between Lillehammer and Rena, blocking the Gudbrandsdal and the Österdal, the two best routes to Trondheim. On **15 April**, the enemy 163. Infantry Division pushed northward toward the western valley. After driving the Norwegian 1. Divisjon into Sweden, the 196. Infantry Division turned about and advanced toward the more easterly Österdal. The Norwegian infantry had no anti-tank guns to confront the company of Pz.Kw.I and Pz.Kw.II tanks of Panzer Abteilung 40 that were leading the attack.

Nevertheless, when the enemy armor reached the forward Norwegian positions between Randsfjord and Kongsvinger, the tanks became restricted to the roads of the rugged, snowbound terrain, and were easily halted by mined obstructions. The resolute Norwegians contested every kilometer, fighting from one roadblock to the next, hoping to delay the Germans until promised Allied reinforcements reached them.

The reinforcements resulted from an Allied decision to try to hold central Norway. Trondheim could be reached by naval forces without unduly exposing them to the demonstrated danger of the Luftwaffe. However, Trondheim was already in German hands. On **10 April**, the Kriegsmarine's Group II had arrived off Trondelag. Supported by a Covering Force, consisting of the battleships *Scharnhorst* and *Gneisenau*, the heavy cruiser *Admiral Hipper* had led the destroyers *Jacobi*, *Riedel*, *Heinemann* and *Eckoldt* into Trondheimfjord at 0400, three of the destroyers landing troops on the shore to subdue the coastal batteries. They met no opposition as they continued up the fjord, dropping anchor at Trondheim at 0530. The landing party quickly captured the arsenal of the Norwegian 5. Divisjon before it could mobilize. The many branches of the fjord offered refuge for the small Norwegian vessels based at Trondheim. The ancient torpedo boats *Lak*, *Sild* and *Skrei* were eventually captured or scuttled by their crews. The old destroyers *Troll* and *Garm* escaped to the Sognefjord for the time being. One of the last torpedo boats commissioned, *Trygg* slipped out of Trondheimfjord with the modern coastal destroyer *Sleipner* and headed south down the coast.

*Trygg* put in at Aandalsnes, but the *Sleipner* fought off repeated aerial attacks as it sailed on down the coast, claiming 5 German planes, and escaped to Britain to become the center for the renaissance of the Norwegian Navy. The lonely M.F.11 at Aunöya attempted to follow it to Scotland, but was shot down by wary British fighters as it approached the coast. Only three battalions of the Norwegian 5. Divisjon managed to mobilize. By 19 April, they had gathered at Vist, at the head of the fjord. The 5. Divisjon was to have been supported by the *Trondelag flygeavdelning* at Vaernes airfield, 40 kilometers northeast of Trondheim. When the alarm was given, its nine Fokkers flew to a frozen lake near Trondheim. With only a fifth of the local ground troops armed, the Norwegian flyers could do little but watch the Germans take over their base. The survivors flew to Narvik.

Over Difficult Mountain Roads Pz.Kw.Is Supported German Columns

The Allies landed on both sides of Trondheim, intending to close the pincers around the occupying German forces and let them dry on the vine. "Mauriceforce" (British 146th Brigade, French 5ʳᵉ Demi-brigade de Chasseurs Alpins) began landing at Namsos, 130 kilometers north of Trondheim, on **14 April**. "Sickleforce" (British 148th and 15th Brigades) came ashore at Aandalsnes, 150 kilometers on the other side of Trondheim. The operations of "Mauriceforce" were stillborn, for on 20 April German bombers from Sola/Stavanger demolished the port facilities of Namsos. Unable to sustain themselves for an offensive, the two brigades stayed near the sea. However, the British 148th Brigade immediately advanced eastward from Aandalsnes, reaching Lillehammer in the Gudbrandsdal on **21 April**. It arrived just as the Germans launched a heavy attack on the main position of the Norwegian 2. Divisjon. Reeling from the assault, the broken Norwegians fell back on the arriving British troops, forcing them to retreat. The weather cleared at this inauspicious moment, and the German Luftwaffe took full advantage.

141

The *Haerens Flygevapen* was no longer capable of defending the troops. From Kjeller airfield, northeast of Oslo, 4 Fokker C.VEs of the Bombevingen and 8 C.VDs of the Speidevingen had made reconnaissance flights at 0540 and 0630 the morning of 9 April, without result. They were then sent north to escape attacking German aircraft. Ski-equipped planes flew to Lake Naerenvann, north of Moelv, while wheeled planes went to Brumunddal. The commander of the *Speidevingen*, Captain Reistad, took command of the heterogeneous collection of aircraft (designated Group "R") on **16 April**. After German bombers found the base, all serviceable aircraft (1 Gladiator fighter, 1 Ca.310 bomber, 5 C.VE light bombers, and 4 C.VD reconnaissance planes) flew to Lake Vangsmjösa, near the eastern head of Sognefjord. Even there, the complete aerial dominance of the Luftwaffe, and the severe shortage of aviation fuel, limited operations to a few liaison and reconnaissance flights over the battle area. The Gladiator and Ca.310 were soon disabled, leaving the confused Allied troops in the Gudbrandsdal with no fighter cover. When the Germans invaded Norway, the British aircraft carriers *Glorious* and *Ark Royal* had been recalled from the Mediterranean. To remedy the aerial deficiency, they approached the Norwegian coast on 23 April with the second-line No.263 Fighter Squadron on board. It had been selected for the operation because its 18 biplane Gloster Gladiators could operate from the primitive landing strips in Norway. They landed on a frozen lake between Aandalsnes and Dombas on the night of **24 April**. However, most of their motors were frozen when they tried to get airborne the following morning as German bombers came over. Ten of the precious fighters lay shattered on the lake at the end of the day. Five survivors flew to Aandalsnes, but they were also gone within two more days. In the meantime, British Fleet Air Arm fighters had been unsuccessful in preventing the far more numerous German aircraft from raiding the port facilities of the Allied Expeditionary Force. It was during these raids that the Norwegian *Trygg* was sunk at Aandalsnes on 25 April and the *Garm* set on fire at Bjordal in the Sognefjord the next day.

For the pursuit, the Germans reorganized their forces on 23 April. The 163. Infantry Division, reinforced with a tank company, was redirected westward to form a flank guard against the Norwegian 4. Divisjon approaching from Bergen. To advance rapidly up the Österdal to Trondheim, a regiment of the 181. Infantry Division was reinforced with two tank platoons and motorized troops from the Hermann Goering regiment. The 196. Infantry Divison, with a platoon of tanks, was to drive the disorganized mass of Allied troops up the Gudbrandsdal to Aandalsnes. Coming up behind the routed 148th Brigade, the British 15th Brigade had established a position at Kvam, 50 kilometers northwest of Lillehammer. There the victorious 196. Division was brought up short on **25 April**. Harassed continually by air attacks, the British brigade held for three days while the broken forward units streamed back through their lines. Instead of an envelopment of the large naval and air bases at Trondheim, the entire operation had deteriorated into a defensive struggle with the advancing German forces, all the while sustaining heavy losses from unopposed air attacks. Bowing to the inevitable, the Allies began reembarking their troops at Aandalsnes on 28 April. Half of the Norwegian 2. Divisjon was trapped at Gausdal the next day and was captured. The other half retired with the British to Aandalsnes. The last of the Allied troops sailed on **2 May**, and the remnants of the Norwegian 2. Divisjon surrendered the following day. Their base in enemy hands, and their vessels out of fuel, crews abandoned the destroyer *Troll* and the torpedo boat *Snögg* at Florö on 4 May.

The Norwegian 4. Divisjon was now in a precarious position. The German 69. Infantry Division had been following close on its heels as it retired from Bergen. Now the Norwegian advance guards were encountering forward troops of the German 163. Infantry Division advancing up the Hallingdal, whose branches led to both the Hardangerfjord and the Sognefjord. In an attempt to block the approaches to both fjords, the Norwegians carried out extensive demolitions along the southern tributary, then moved the bulk of their division to the northern branch. At Göl, where the Hallingdal divides, the 163. Infantry Division split its forces, the main body going on toward the Sognefjord. Three infantry battalions took the south branch, and were stopped by the Norwegian roadblocks. The north column (4 infantry and 1 artillery battalions, 1 tank company) soon encountered the main position of the Norwegian 4. Divisjon at Bagn.

General Steffen's determined troops fought hard, but the Germans broke through the Norwegian positions on **27 April** and the routed defenders streamed back toward the Sognefjord. At Lommen, north of that waterway, the division surrendered on 1 May. The whole of southern Norway was now in enemy hands. Attention turned to securing the routes to Narvik, which the Allies had considered their goal all along.

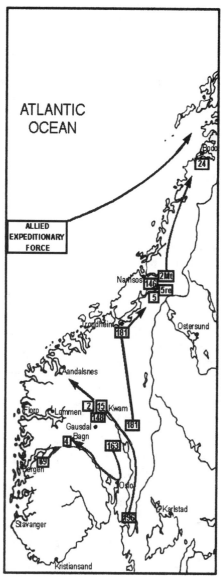

Meanwhile, Group Fischer, the mobile German column racing up the Österdal, had made contact with the rest of the 181. Infantry Division moving inland from Trondheim on 30 April. United, they advanced to Vist at the head of the fjord, where they encountered the fragments of the Norwegian 5. Divisjon and the forward troops of the British and French brigades advancing from Namsos. Adding the Norwegian artillery captured at the Trondheim arsenal to their own, the Germans began driving the Allies northward. The Allied troops had already received the order to leave Norway and fought a delaying action until their troops sailed from Namsos on 2 May. Two days later, the remnants of the Norwegian 5. Divisjon surrendered. The bulk of the Norwegian Army was now *hors de combat*.

143

King Haakon VII had been evacuated from Molde by the British cruiser *Glasgow* on 29 April. General Ruge followed from Aandalsnes on 2 May in the British destroyer *Diana.* They were put ashore at Tromsö to oversee the battle for northern Norway. Several Allied leaders had considered the effort to hold central Norway a vain one in view of the overwhelming German aerial strength. They believed that Narvik, strategically placed to influence activities in Sweden and Finland, should have been the objective all along. The only railroad ran east to the vital Swedish iron mines. An interrupted road of poor quality wound southward. Even aircraft had to wear floats to find a landing place in most of the wild, mountainous area, although there was an airfield at Bardufoss, 80 kilometers north of Narvik.

The British had been the first to initiate operations to control the destination of iron ore from the port. On 5 April, a British minelaying force had left port with its escort. Part of the force was to mine the Vestfjord leading to Narvik, the rest of the ships sowing their deadly cargoes farther south. Troops were embarked on several cruisers, ready to land on the Norwegian coast. The southern mine force was recalled when the German Group II and its Covering Force were discovered and bombed on 7 April. Thinking the enemy intended mischief in the Atlantic, the British Home Fleet (battleships *Nelson, Valiant,* 8 cruisers, 14 destroyers) sailed that evening to intercept them. A fuzzy report by a Sunderland flying boat confirmed British suspicions of a break-out attempt, and the Home Fleet drew off to a blocking position. The waters of the North Sea were then free of surface ships dangerous to the Germans. However, as *Scharnhorst* and *Gneisnau* led the 10 destroyers of Group I toward Narvik, their radar plotted a large vessel at dawn on **9 April**. It was the British battle cruiser *Renown*, covering the Vestfjord mining force. She had steamed south on 8 April, accompanied by the destroyers of the Narvik group, leaving the mouth of the Vestfjord unprotected. Although they opened fire at 0500, the Germans believed they were faced by a fleet and tried to break off action, pursued by the *Renown* through heavy seas. Meanwhile, in the lee of the Lofoten Islands, the German destroyers entered the Ofotfjord at 0400. One destroyer was detached as a picket at the mouth of the fjord, five others landed troops at various points, while three pushed on for Narvik. The Norwegian armored ship *Eidsvold* was patrolling just outside Narvik harbor. As she attempted to close, *Heidkamp* fired a spread of torpedoes that sank the old ship before she could fire a shot. Alerted in the inner harbor, her sister ship *Norge* opened fire as two German destroyers rounded the headlands. Unhurt, *Schmitt* hit the little battleship with several torpedoes and she sank quickly at 0500. Three Norwegian fishery protection vessels in the harbor, the *Michael Sars, Heimdal* and *Senja,* were captured. Five British destroyers entered the fjord early the following morning and attacked the German flotilla. Each side lost two destroyers in a sharp skirmish. The crews of the sunken German destroyers joined the 3. Mountain Division which had gone ashore at Narvik.

A British expeditionary force was already on the way, necessitating destruction of the threatening German naval forces. On **13 April**, the battleship *Warspite* and 9 destroyers arrived in the Ofotfjord, which extended from the head of the Vestfjord. Most of the German destroyers were sunk, the remainder being scuttled by their crews when they ran out of fuel and ammunition. Two days later, the British 24th Guards Brigade made contact with the Norwegians when it landed at Harstad with a troop of Carden-Loyd light tanks. General Major Fleischer's 6. Divisjon had been on an active basis since the Finnish "Winter War" threatened to spread over the border. The Germans had driven the division away from the shores of the Ofotfjord, but it had established a stable position at Gratangen, about 30 kilometers north of Narvik. It was deployed in two brigades, the 6. to the east and the 7. adjacent to the head of Gratangenfjord.

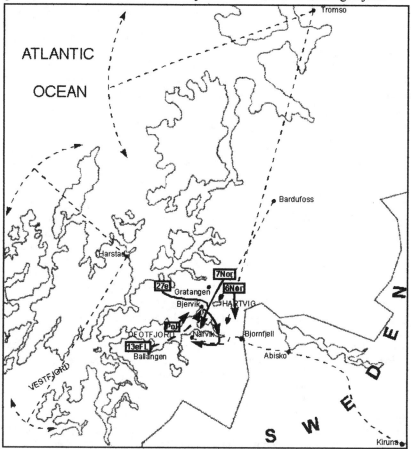

The airfield at Bardufoss housed the *Hålogaland flygeavdelning*, where its six Fokker C.VDs now concentrated, along with others from the *Trondelag flygeavdelning*. On **14 April** they were armed with 3-50 kg bombs and attacked 11 Junkers Ju.52s trapped in soft ice on Lake Hartvig, 15 kilometers north of Narvik. Strafing and bombing, they destroyed all but one of the enemy transports. The Germans were learning a lesson they later taught in many campaigns: offensive operations must be conducted within range of supporting air units. For all practical purposes, the 3. Mountain Division was completely isolated from other German forces.

Two German Navy pilots thought they could get fuel from local Norwegians when they set their Heinkel He.115B-1 floatplanes on the water near Bodö. Their mistake brought to six the number of Heinkels possessed by 3. *Flyavdeling* at the Skattöra seaplane base near Tromsö. The twin-engined floatplanes became the only medium bombers available to the Allies in the north. Collected at that base were also six M.F.11s, two from Vadsö, two escapees from southern fjords, and two returnees from Scotland. The biplanes were employed in watching German naval movements and anti-submarine patrol. However, German U boats had discovered the advantage conferred on them by the restricted passages to the various fjords leading to the Allied bases. Sinkings of cargo vessels were increasing. To aid the Norwegians in hunting down submarines, the Supermarine Walrus flying boats of British Fleet Air Arm Squadron No. 701 arrived at Harstad on 18 May.

On **24 April**, the Norwegian 6. Divisjon attacked from its position 30 kilometers north of Narvik, but was repulsed. Three days later, the French 27ᵉ Demi-brigade de Chasseurs Alpins landed at Harstad. When the two units began to advance southward in concert against the German perimeter, they made little progress. In fact, another month passed before sufficient forces were deployed to uproot the tough German mountain troops. The French 13ᵉ Demi-brigade de Legion Etrangere (Foreign Legion) and the Polish Brigade de chasseurs du Podhale reached Harstad on 5 May. Loaded on the British cruisers *Effingham* and *Aurora*, the two battalions of the Foreign Legion were carried to the head of Herjangsfjord and landed at Bjervik on **12 May**. Two MLC landing boats were launched from the battleship *Resolution*, carrying 4 Hotchkiss H.35 light tanks of the 342ᵉ Independent Tank Company. Fire from the cruiser *Enterprise* and five destroyers covered the landing as Blackburn Skuas from the carrier *Ark Royal* dive bombed German positions on shore. The landing was the signal for a general Allied offensive. The Polish Brigade had been placed across the Ofotfjord from Narvik. Now it began advancing up the west coast of the fjord, aided by naval gunfire. With no German fighters around to harass them, the Norwegian Army's Fokker C.VDs began attacking the positions of the German 3. Mountain Division. Heavier bombs rained from the Navy's Heinkel He.115s during repeated sorties from Skattöra. The French 27ᵉ Brigade struck the left flank of the defenders as the Norwegian 6. Divisjon moved forward. The Allied forces soon linked up at the head of Herjangsfjord, then advanced down the eastern bank of the fjord in conjunction with the Norwegian 6. Brigade. The Germans were steadily driven back over the Kuberg Plateau until they were trapped against the Swedish border at Björnfjell on the railway to Kiruna.

By this time, the Germans were mounting several air raids each day from Vaernes. On 4 May, they sank the Polish destroyer *Grom*. Later, the same fate awaited the British destroyer *Curlew*. With even heavier raids in prospect as the German *kampfgruppen* moved nearly 200 bombers to Vaernes, three weeks were spent clearing snow and lengthening the runways at Bardufoss in preparation for the arrival of British Royal Air Force fighters to oppose them. On 21 May, No.263 Squadron's veterans of Trondheim returned to Norway with a fresh supply of 18 Gladiators flown off the deck of *Furious*. They were followed five days later by Hurricanes of No.46 Squadron ferried by the *Glorious*. These fighters had to fly 80 kilometers from their airfield over difficult country to reach the battle area around Narvik. So long as the Germans had to sortie from Vaernes near Trondheim, 600 kilometers to the south, the Allied flyers held their own. However, the German 2. Mountain Division was pushing north toward Bodö, where they would have a landing ground within 30 minutes flying time of Narvik. Most of the British 24th Guards Brigade was transported to Bodö on **14 May**, where a stand was made in conjunction with two Norwegian battalions. For a week, the troops halted the German advance.

The Allies were on the verge of success. However, events in Western Europe were already beginning to affect the campaign in Norway. German soldiers stood on the banks of the English Channel by 21 May. Three days later, the Allied high command decided that while the security of France and Britain was important, that of Norway was not. King Haakon was informed of the Allied decision to withdraw and preparations began immediately.

It was deemed desirable to prevent German use of the port facilities of Narvik for iron ore loading, but the Germans still occupied the city. Landed on the peninsula south of the city, the Polish Brigade advanced eastward, with the aid of fire from the British cruiser *Southampton*. Thus it threatened to cut off the German troops on the Narvik peninsula. Supported by fire from the British anti-aircraft cruisers *Cairo* and *Coventry*, 5 destroyers, and a sloop, the French Foreign Legion was ferried across Rombaksfjord during the night of 27-8 May. Then, with five Hotchkiss light tanks leading, it advanced westward along the Kiruna railway towards Narvik. Large numbers of German bombers attacked the Allied warships, Junkers Ju.87Bs operating from Mosjöen, only 300 kilometers away. The two British squadrons at Bardufoss kept 3 fighters over the battle area most of the time, and prevented further damage. The Germans evacuated the city before the French arrived. The Allies spent several days demolishing the port facilities so well that the Germans were unable to resume ore shipments for nearly a year.

On 2 June, the German Lufwaffe made a maximum effort. Throughout the day, waves of a dozen bombers or dive bombers, escorted by Messerschmitt Bf.110s, went after the naval base at Harstad. They paid particular attention to the large number of merchant ships gathering to begin the evacuation. Mounting 75 sorties during the day, the two squadrons of Gladiators and Hurricanes so harassed the raiders that many bombs missed. Without loss to themselves, the fighters claimed 9 enemy aircraft.

As the evacuation began the next day, they continued to fly cover, with the assistance of naval fighters from the aircraft carriers *Glorious* and *Ark Royal* off shore. Few casualties resulted, 25,000 men being embarked by 8 June. The two fighter squadrons then flew onto the *Glorious* and the armada sailed for Britain. Unfortunately, the *Glorious* was caught and sunk by the German battleships *Scharnhorst* and *Gneisenau*, but the troop convoy escaped. The unseaworthy Norwegian submarine *B3* was scuttled at her berth, but the warships *Fridtjof Nansen, Nordkapp* and *B1* left with the Allied fleet. King Haakon VII went with them on the British cruiser *Devonshire*. General Ruge remained at Narvik to sign an armistice for midnight of 9-10 June, then spent the rest of the war in a Nazi concentration camp. The Norwegian 6. Divisjon was demobilized. The four Heinkel He.115s remaining at Skattöra flew to the Shetland Islands. Three immobile M.F.11s were captured, but the other three flew to Rovaniemi, Finland. There they were interned, then later confiscated for Finnish use. A handful of Fokker C.Vs also reached Finland from Bardufoss.

The Germans also received a Norwegian largesse. *Gyller* and *Odin* were captured. When *Tor* and *Balder* were completed on their stocks by the Germans, all four destroyers were commissioned in the German Navy as the torpedo boats *Löwe, Panthir, Tiger* and *Leopard*. The old armored ships *Harald Haarfagre* and *Tordenskjold*, which had been decommissioned as depot ships, were taken over by the Germans and rearmed as the floating anti-aircraft batteries *Thetis* and *Nymphe*. However, destroyers ZN4 and ZN5, which were to have been completed in 1943, were sabotaged by the Norwegian underground and largely destroyed on their stocks. [79,80]

147

Vidkun Quisling, leader of the Norwegian Nazi party, the *Nasjonal Samling* (*N.S.*), proclaimed himself leader of Norway on 9 April 1940. Joseph Terboven was designated as *Reichskommissar* by Hitler and set up an Administrative Council on 25 September to depose King Haakon VII and form a national government including many of the 7,000 members of the *Nasjonal Samling*. When the *Störting* refused to approve the scheme, it was dissolved and a bureaucracy was established with *N.S.* members as the titular heads of most of the ministries. Ill-feeling toward the government-in-exile, for its lack of preparedness in meeting the April invasion, was quickly transferred to the inept Quisling, who was quietly ignored by the German military regime,

King Haakon VII had refused to recognize Quisling as the head of the Norwegian government. He took his ministers to Tromsö for the remainder of the campaign, then left for London on 8 June 1940 to organize the *Nygaardsvold*, an exile government. When the Norwegian Army was demobilized in June 1940, officers organized the *X.U.* intelligence groups that reported German military movements to London. By May 1941, some 20,000 former military men were in *Milorg*, an underground army which was recognized as another branch of the Norwegian armed services in November. They were dispersed over the country in sections of 8-10 men, using arms that had been hidden before the demobilization. Although crippled by widespread Gestapo arrests at the end of 1942, their numbers grew to 32,000 at the time of the Normandy invasion, and to 47,000 by the end of the war. However, they were not organized and trained for guerrilla warfare. Rather, they were prepared for a return landing in coordination with the exile units. With the British supporting such a return in 1942, J.C. Hauge became the leader of *Milorg*, and full cooperation was achieved between the high command in London and the units in the field.

A coordination committee (*K.K.*) was formed among the civilian population in 1942 and began publishing illegal newspapers. At a higher level, Chief Justice Paal Berg secretly accepted direction of the resistance movement, in consultation with the *Nygaardsvold* in London.

Quisling assumed the position of "Fuhrer" of Norway on 1 February 1942. The Nazi bureaucracy began to permeate all facets of national life, as it had in other German satellite states. A major campaign was launched to gain the support of the population against Bolshevism and "Western plutocracies". The *N.S. Youth Service*, modelled on the *Hitler Jugend*, was resisted by church and school, resulting in the arrest of many teachers and clergymen. Similarly, when Quisling tried to form a Chamber of Cooperations, as Mussolini had done in Italy, mass resignations of the business leaders scuttled the project. The Norwegian Nazi party grew to only 43,000 members (5% of the population). From the beginning, Norwegians supported the Allies.

Of greatest value to the Allied cause were the 1,200 modern vessels of the Norwegian merchant navy, fourth largest in the world. Its vessels immediately became part of the supply system to British forces in the Mediterranean. Many Atlantic convoys included Norwegian merchant ships. During the critical year of 1941, the Norwegians provided 40% of the foreign tonnage entering British ports. They had a major role in the vital convoys to Murmansk that helped to prop up the teetering Soviet state in 1942. Some 25,000 Norwegian seamen took part in the war after the fall of Norway. Great Britain had few warships to spare for the escaped Norwegians, but 8 motor torpedo boats (followed by

148

12 more later in the war), and the first of 38 whaling boats were acquired for use as minesweepers, patrol boats and escort vessels. The submarine *B1* was attached to the British 7th Submarine Flotilla until April 1944. [81]

In September 1940, the United States Navy transferred 50 old destroyers to Great Britain. Four of these were placed under Norwegian control. Although they were of World War I design, they were twice as large as any previous Norwegian destroyers. *Mansfield* was taken over in December 1940, *Bath* and *St. Albans* in April 1941, and *Newport* in September 1941. They were used mainly for escorting convoys on the northern Atlantic route, patrolling from mid-Atlantic, past Iceland to the coast of Scotland. Under British sponsorship, the Free Norwegians deployed:

destroyer

| | | destroyer |
|---|---|---|
| **Mansfield** | 1918, 1060 tons, 22 km/h, | *Sleipner, Draug* |
| **St. Albans** | 4-10 cm, 12 TT | |
| **Bath** | (ex-U.S. Wickes and Little class) | sloop |
| **Newport** | transferred 1940 | *Nordkapp* |
| **Lincoln** | | |

motor torpedo boats
*5, 6, 50-2, 54, 56, 71*

sub
*B1*

330 Squadron - Reykjavik, Iceland
**18 Northrop N-3PB**

**Northrop N-3PB**
1938, 15 m span, 414 km/h, 1610 km,
7320 m SC, 6 mgs, 908 kg B

In 1941, the first naval air unit moved to Iceland. Designated 330 Squadron within the British Royal Air Force structure, it operated 18 Northrop N-3PBs on convoy escort and submarine patrol missions from April of that year. The Northrops were the fastest floatplanes in the world when they first appeared, and were ordered as replacements for the Höver M.F.11 in patrolling the coasts of Norway. They lacked sufficient range for the long overwater patrols they were called upon to undertake, but were well armed for strafing attacks. The N-3PBs were replaced by 6 Catalina Is in the summer of 1942.

The fish oil factories of Norway were now providing Germany with glycerin for explosives. On **11 April 1941**, *Mansfield* entered Oksfjord, between Tromsö and Hammerfest, and landed parties in the darkness that destroyed the factory there. While escorting a convoy, *Bath* was sunk on 19 August 1941. The worn out *Mansfield* was returned to Britain in February 1942, followed by the *Newport* in June. They were immediately replaced by another old American destroyer, the *Lincoln*.

Norwegian soldiers had greater difficulty in achieving combat readiness. They gradually collected in Scotland from scattered locales. When the Norwegian Brigade was formed in March 1941, there were only sufficient troops for a single infantry battalion and a battery of ex-French Puteaux M.1897 75 mm field guns. In May 1941, the government-in-exile placed Norwegian units under British control for the duration of the war. Although the number of troops grew thereafter, Winston Churchill intended to use them only for a return to Norway. Preparations in 1942, at the urging of Josef Stalin, were halted when his scheme for landing in northern Norway was postponed for lack of troops. The Norwegian government-in-exile feared Nazi reprisals to such landings and believed they would push Sweden into the German camp. The invasion was proposed again in 1943, but again hung fire. Thus, Norwegian soldiers endured the agitation of idleness while their brothers fought the enemy in the air and on the sea.

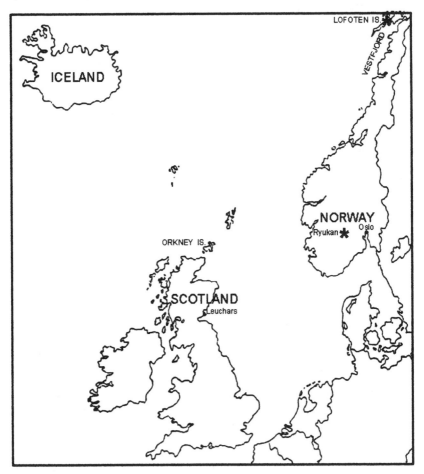

Combat was experienced only by an Independent Company of commandos that was formed in July 1941. It took part in the first British commando raid on the Lofoten Islands in March 1942. Another raid on the Lofotens in December was followed by an attack on the Målöy fortress. Commandos parachuted into the Norsk Hydro plant at Rjukan, 120 kilometers west of Oslo, in February 1943 and destroyed the sole source of heavy water for the Nazi atomic bomb project. When the Germans reacted with severe reprisals against Norwegian civilians, the *Nygaardsvold* forbade further raids.

As there was no room in Great Britain, escaped Norwegian airmen gathered near Toronto, Canada to train for a return to the fray. The American aircraft ordered to reequip the Air Force, 36 Curtiss Hawk 75As, 36 Douglas 8A-5s and 24 Northrop N-3PBs, were delivered to the camp in Canada, which became known as "Little Norway".

Norwegian fighter pilots renewed their quarrel with the enemy when 331 Squadron was formed on 21 July 1941 to fly 20 old Hawker Hurricane Is from bases in Scotland and the Orkney Islands. They soon received a score of the more potent Hurricane IIA,Cs.

From 1941-5, a transport unit at Leuchars, on the east coast of Scotland, flew 12 Lockheed Lodestars on dangerous communications flights between the government-in-exile in Great Britain and the Norwegian exile ministers in Stockholm, Sweden.

**Free Norwegian Army Air Force**

331 Squadron - Scotland
  **20 Hawker Hurricane I,IIB**
1 transport unit - Leuchars
  **12 Lockheed 18 Lodestar**

**Hawker Hurricane Mk.IIB**
1940, 12 m span, 551 km/h, 773 km,
8.2/6100 m, 11133 m SC, 12 mgs, 454 kg B

**Lockheed 18 Lodestar**
1940, 20 m span, 370 km/h, 2720 km,
7750 m SC, 22 troops

Large numbers of Norwegian merchant seamen had been undergoing training in naval procedures and by August 1941 were ready for sea duty. Five British "Flower" class corvettes were transferred for their use. *Eglantine* came in August, *Acanthus* and *Montbretia* in September, followed by *Rose* in October and *Potentilla* in January 1942. They were soon involved in derring-do. British Rear Admiral Hamilton cruised the Vestfjord with a squadron on **26-8 December 1941**. From his flagship, the cruiser *Arethusa*, he led the *Acanthus, Eglantine* and some British and Polish destroyers in to destroy a radio station and other German facilities. During the spring and summer of 1942, the four corvettes were involved in escorting convoys across the Atlantic as Escort Group B6, with the British destroyer *Viscount* as flagship.

Two British "Hunt" class light destroyers were acquired in July 1942. The *Eskdale* and *Glaisdale* joined the English Channel escort force. When an important German convoy was reported to be making its way south along the coast in **December 1942**, they were included in a force of five "Hunt"s sent to stop it. After sweeping along the coast for four days, the Allied force spotted the convoy approaching with torpedo boat and R-boat escorts. The escorts forced two of the Allied destroyers out of action, but the *Eskdale* broke through the line of escorts, sank a *T.1* class torpedo boat and 2 R-boats. Other destroyers passed through the breach and sank two merchant ships, dispersing the convoy.

151

The Free Norwegians also received a submarine. Of the British "U" class, the *Uredd* prowled the shipping lanes along the Norwegian coast, where it sank a large German cargo ship on 15 October 1942. However, it was sunk on 24 February 1943 during another patrol off Norway. It was replaced by a sister, the *Vaerne*, which was renamed *Ula*. The *Ula* also enjoyed success, sinking two German cargo ships off western Norway on 24 November 1943.

As the war reached its critical phase in the fall of 1942, the Norwegians operated a navy of convoy escorts:

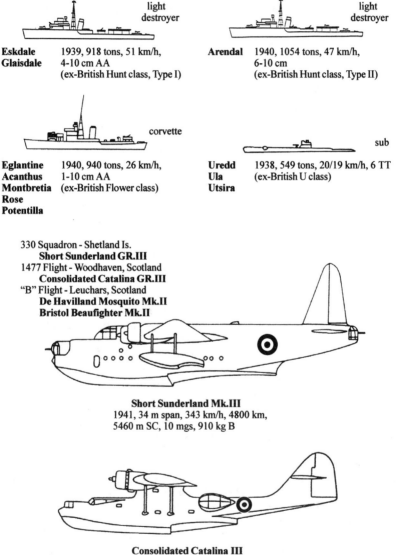

| | |
|---|---|
| light destroyer | light destroyer |

**Eskdale**   1939, 918 tons, 51 km/h,
**Glaisdale**   4-10 cm AA
        (ex-British Hunt class, Type I)

**Arendal**   1940, 1054 tons, 47 km/h,
        6-10 cm
        (ex-British Hunt class, Type II)

corvette

sub

**Eglantine**   1940, 940 tons, 26 km/h,
**Acanthus**   1-10 cm AA
**Montbretia**   (ex-British Flower class)
**Rose**
**Potentilla**

**Uredd**   1938, 549 tons, 20/19 km/h, 6 TT
**Ula**   (ex-British U class)
**Utsira**

330 Squadron - Shetland Is.
   **Short Sunderland GR.III**
1477 Flight - Woodhaven, Scotland
   **Consolidated Catalina GR.III**
"B" Flight - Leuchars, Scotland
   **De Havilland Mosquito Mk.II**
   **Bristol Beaufighter Mk.II**

**Short Sunderland Mk.III**
1941, 34 m span, 343 km/h, 4800 km,
5460 m SC, 10 mgs, 910 kg B

**Consolidated Catalina III**
1939, 32 m span, 272 km/h, 2670 km,
4480 m SC, 5 mgs, 1820 kg B

152

Early in 1943, No.330 Squadron moved with its Catalinas to the Shetland Islands, although a detachment of 2 N-3PBs continued operating from Iceland for a time. Reequipped with 10 Short Sunderland III flying boats, 330 Squadron conducted convoy escort and submarine patrol operations from the Shetlands as far as Iceland and the Faroe Islands, under the direction of No.18 Group of the British Coastal Command, which patrolled the waters off Norway.

Another naval unit was formed at Woodhaven, Scotland in February 1942. Designated No.1477 Flight, it flew 3 Catalinas. A "B" Flight was established at Leuchars at the same time, flying Mosquito VIs and a couple of Beaufighters. In 1943, they were united as No.333 Squadron to fly 7 Catalina IIIs in reconnaissance, submarine patrol and shipping strikes off the coast of Norway.

Norwegian aspirations continued to rise in Great Britain. A second fighter squadron, No.332, was formed in January 1942. Equipped with Spitfire Vs, the two Norwegian squadrons were grouped with two British fighter squadrons in RAF No.132 Wing based at North Weald airfield just north of London, intercepting German raiders and assailing German positions on the French coast. A dress rehearsal for the invasion of Europe was mounted at Dieppe, France on **19 August 1942**. One of the objectives of the operation was to lure 500 German fighters and bombers to their destruction over the beachhead. Thus, the 56 fighter squadrons of No.11 Group, including No.132 Wing, participated. Although the operation was a failure, the Norwegian squadrons inflicted heavy losses on the enemy.

**Norwegian Army Air Force**

No.132 Wing (RAF) - North Weald
331, 332 Squadrons
    **Supermarine Spitfire VB**
1 transport unit
    **Lockheed 18 Lodestar**

**Supermarine Spitfire VB**
1941, 11 m span, 602 km/h, 472 km,
7.5/6100 m, 11285 m SC, 227 kg B,
2-20 mm, 4 mgs

The fine fighting spirit displayed by the Norwegians gained them some of the first Spitfire IXs delivered to the RAF. With them, the Norwegians went on a tear, No.331 Squadron ranking first and No.332 third in the number of enemy aircraft shot down by RAF squadrons during 1943.

Air power required accurate weather forecasts of conditions over targets and airfields. For the North Atlantic and Europe, it was necessary to know of weather fronts approaching from Greenland, the Norwegian Sea and Arctic Norway. The Arctic islands that Norway had acquired between the wars thus assumed a new importance.

The Germans had control of Scandinavia after the spring of 1940, but employed ships, U boats and aircraft to monitor weather in the North Atlantic. The British established a weather station on Jan Mayen Island, but had to withdraw when storms destroyed supply efforts. A second attempt in March 1941 provoked German bombing.

A German Heinkel He.111 landed on Spitzbergen (Svalbard) on 29 April 1941 to make preparations for a permanent station. Spitzbergen was completely evacuated and its coal mines and facilities destroyed in "Operation Gauntlet", when Force K (cruiser *Nigeria* - Rear Adm. Vian, flag - and the destroyers

*Aurora, Icarus, Anthony* and *Antelope*) escorted a passenger liner to the island to remove its population of 3,200 on 25 August 1941. The German weather station was in full operation by 11 November. To destroy it, a company of Free Norwegian ski troops, under Capt. Sverdrup, was landed on Spitzbergen in **May 1942**. Focke-Wulf Fw.200s bombed and sank both supply ships while they were still unloading, also killing Capt. Sverdrup and several troops. Harassed by German planes, the remnants of the company hunted for the German weathermen, who kept on the move. A full British battalion landed on 15 July to aid in the search. The German party was evacuated in the face of certain capture. However, another party, landed on the northeast corner on 25 October, remained through the spring of 1943.

Early in 1943, Norwegian ships were involved in one of the greatest actions in the Battle of the Atlantic. The Allies were succoring the foundering Soviet state with convoys around the North Cape of Norway to the White Sea. During the first week of **January 1943**, a convoy was shadowed by a pack of U-boats. The *Eglantine* hit one of them with gunfire, then dropped depth charges on it. Later the same night, she repeated her performance after a merchant ship caught a torpedo. At the same time, the *Rose*, in company with the British destroyer *Fame*, similarly attacked two more U-boats. The next day, Coastal Command Liberators made successive sweeps over the convoy, sinking a submarine with depth charges in one of ten attacks during the day. The *Potentilla* also probably destroyed one during that day. Bad weather intervened, and it was not until the fourth day that the wolves got back in among the flock. They were prevented from reaching firing positions by the *Rose* and *Potentilla*, in cooperation with the British *Vervain*. Six air attacks were made by British and American planes. Finding the defenses too efficient for them, the U-boats left the scene and the convoy proceeded unscathed.

Hitler requested his inactive surface navy to mount "Operation Zitronella" in mid-1943. An amphibious raid on Spitzbergen, the *Tirpitz, Scharnhorst* and 9 destroyers approached the main village on **7 September 1943**, quickly smothering the Norwegian battery of 75 mm guns, and within 4 hours completing the landing at the quay. However, *Tirpitz* (on its only surface "shoot" of the war) landed shells among its own infantry as it was deploying and the Norwegian garrison largely escaped inland. Unable to hold the island in the face of Allied naval superiority, the Germans withdrew the next day. The Allies set up a new weather station in October.

However, the Norwegians also sustained losses. The corvette *Montbretia* was sunk in action on 18 November 1942. During the night of 13-4 April 1943, while *Eskdale* and *Glaisdale* were escorting a convoy of 6 vessels off Plymouth, England, the German 5. Motor Torpedo Boat Flotilla attacked. *S90* hit the *Eskdale* with two torpedoes. *S112* and *S65* then finished her off. She was replaced by a more formidable warship, the British fleet destroyer *Success*, renamed *Stord* by the Norwegians. The new ship was soon thrown into the fray. On **26 December 1943**, the German battleship *Scharnhorst* attempted to attack a Murmansk convoy moving along the south edge of the ice pack near the North Cape of Norway. With the British battleship *Duke of York* closing in support, four British cruisers skillfully fought off the dangerous predator. The *Scharnhorst* retired but was pursued by a British task group that included the Norwegian destroyer *Stord*:

> *Duke of York*
> *Jamaica*
> *Savage, Saumarez, Scorpion, Stord*

The four destroyers closed on the German battleship and its escort of five destroyers. Launching torpedoes from 1400 meters, they succeeded in crippling the Nazi giant, slowing it sufficiently for the *Duke of York* to catch up. Following a rain of heavy shells, the *Scharnhorst* sank at 1945, 100 kilometers northwest of the North Cape. [82]

American Dive Bombers Strike German Convoys in the Lofoten Islands

German convoys carried Swedish iron ore from Narvik by slipping through the extensive archipelagoes along the Norwegian Atlantic coast, hiding in the numerous fjords when they drew too much attention from the Allies. As the winter of 1943 approached, the Allies mounted Operation Leader to impede the traffic. Supported by two modern battleships, four cruisers, and a screen of 10 destroyers, on **4 October 1943** the American carrier *Ranger* launched a strike while off Bodö.

> *Duke of York, Anson*
> 4 cruisers
> 10 destroyers
> *Ranger*
>    30 SBD, TBF
>    12 F6F

Roaring up the Vestfjord, the formations of dive and torpedo bombers discovered two German convoys, and left 4 merchant ships sinking with 6 others so damaged they had to be beached. Five planes failed to return to the carrier. Although attacks on the German shipping through Norwegian waters continued, the Allies were never able to completely stop the traffic.

Another German party landed on northeastern Spitzbergen in September 1944, while a weather ship from Tromsö hovered to the west of the island. They provided the best weather information that Hitler had received since 1940, at a critical time in the war. However, the ship waited too long, became ice bound, and was never heard from again.

Unable to coerce the Norwegian population into submission to the Nazi takeover, the Germans began cracking down on the resistance. Some 1,300 officers, and 1,000 other citizens, had been deported to concentration camps by the summer of 1943. Yet there were those who embraced the Nazi ideology. Some Norwegians joined the Danes of the *SS Nordland Regiment*, under the command of Count C.F. Schalburg (of the former Danish Royal Guards), when it was formed in April 1940 within the German Waffen-SS. Older volunteers were placed in the *SS Nordwest Regiment*. When the Germans invaded Russia, the *N.S.* established the *Norske Legion* on 29 June 1941 and employed anti-communist propaganda to recruit 1,500 volunteers for service on the Eastern Front. The Legion was sent to the front at the beginning of 1942, attached to the German 3. SS Totenkopf Division near Leningrad. The Norwegians were withdrawn for rest in the spring of 1943, then amalgamated with the *Freikorps Danemark* to join the new 11. SS (Nordland) Panzergrenadier Division formed during the summer. The Legion became its *SS Panzergrenadier Norge Regiment* with 800 men. About the same time, in August 1942, a battalion of SS ski troops was formed and fought with the Finns in Lapland until the Finnish surrender. The Nordland Division was sent to Croatia, where it took part in bitter guerrilla fighting from May-November 1943. At the end of the year, it moved to the east coast of the Baltic Sea. By September 1944, it was at Narva. At the end of 1944, it was evacuated to Germany and fought around Berlin until the war ended. Over 5,000 Norwegians had served in the Waffen-SS during the war.

Hoping to gain more "cannon fodder" through delusion, the *N.S.* in 1944 touted the *Arbeids Tjenesten* (Labour Corps), ostensibly for work projects in Norway. Around 70,000 Nowegian men were conscripted. However, when the Nazis then tried to muster them into the German Army for service on the Eastern Front, the resistance sabotaged the Labour Corp's offices and most of the conscripts disappeared into the forests. Many escaped over the border to join the "police troops" in Sweden.

## *Free Norwegians Prepare to Liberate Norway* - 1940-1945

Norwegian exiles in Sweden did not fare as well as those in Britain. Norwegians were not reticent about expressing their anger at Sweden for allowing the Germans to transport supplies to their beleagured forces in northern Norway while the campaign was still going on. When the Norwegian minister died in Stockholm in October 1940, the Swedish government questioned the legality of the Norwegian legation. Friction developed with the Swedish troops managing the internment camps and Swedish police began harassing the Norwegians. Then, when Norwegian vessels tried to leave Göteborg harbor in March 1942, sixty-two Norwegian sailors were killed by Swedish bullets. The ill-will engendered by these actions lasted into the postwar years. However, during the summer of 1943, the Swedish government allowed the Norwegian representatives in Sweden to assemble 8,700 men for training as "police troops".

Gradually, more Norwegian troops also arrived on the crowded British Isles, until 4,000 men were in training with British equipment. The troops wore British uniforms with Norwegian rank badges. On the upper left sleeve was a patch bearing the title "NORGE". The Norwegian flag appeared on the upper right sleeve and the left side of the helmet.

**Norwegian Brigade**
2 infantry regiments
1 field artillery battalion
**British 25 pdr field gun/howitzers**

**25 pdr. Mk.II Field Gun**
87.6 mm, 3330 kg, 11.4 kg shell,
12328 m, 453 m/s, 10 rpm,
64 mm/1000 m P

When their British support troops were withdrawn for service in the invasion of Normandy, the Norwegians were left without logistical support and were forced to remain in Scotland. However, one of the Scottish divisions involved in the invasion did include 40 Norwegian officers.

With the invasion of Normandy approaching, the Free Norwegian Navy was strengthened by the acquisition of a second fleet destroyer to replace the tired *St. Albans* and *Lincoln*, which had been returned to Britain in February 1944. The Type 2 "Hunt" class light destroyer *Badsworth* was transferred to Norway in November 1944 as the *Arendal* to replace the sunken *Eskdale*. The *Potentilla* was exchanged with the Royal Navy for the *Tunsberg*, a "Castle" class corvette, on 17 April 1944. A "U" class submarine, the *Utsira* (formerly *Variance*) was also transferred at this time. Thus, at the time of the Western Allies reentry into the Continent, the Free Norwegians had increased the capabilities of their Navy to include fleet action:

destroyer

| | | destroyers |
|---|---|---|
| **Stord** | 1943, 1758 tons, 68 km/h, | *Sleipner, Glaisdale, Arendal* |
| **Svenner** | 4-11 cm, 8 TT | |
| | (ex-British S class) | |

corvette

| | | corvette |
|---|---|---|
| **Tunsberg** | 1943-5, 1060 tons, 26 km/h, | *Eglantine, Acanthus, Rose* |
| | 1-10 cm AA | |
| | (ex-British Castle class) | |

motor torpedo boats
*#345, 618-20, 623, 625-7, 631
653, 688, 712*

sub
*Ula, Utsira*

83

Preparation for the huge invasion included crippling the remaining submarine warfare potential of the German Navy to prevent its use against the lucrative armada about to sail from England. The Norwegian submarine *Ula* contributed by sinking *U974* off Norway, as well as two cargo vessels. However, the principal anti-submarine offensive in Norwegian waters was conducted by No.18 Group of the British Coastal Command.Short Sunderland IIIs of the

Norwegian No.330 Squadron joined Catalinas and Liberators of the group in sinking five U-boats off Norway during May and June of 1944. The cudgel was then taken up by the mixed No.333 Squadron, whose Beaufighters and Catalina IIIs helped other Catalinas, Liberators and Fortresses to sink 10 U-boats during June and July. Eleven Sunderland Vs replaced the Mk.IIIs of No.330 Squadron in April 1945.

In the huge Allied fleet at the invasion of Normandy were a number of Norwegian naval vessels, in addition to 60 of their merchant ships.

**Eastern Naval Task Force** (Rear Adm. Vian)
**Force D** (Rear Adm. Patterson) - supporting "Sword" Landing Force
    British battleships *Warspite, Ramillies*
    British cruisers *Mauritius, Arethusa, Frobisher, Danae*
    Polish cruiser *Dragon*
    *Stord, Svenner*, 8 British destroyers
    3 British "Hunt" class light destroyers
**Force E** (Rear Adm. Dalrymple-Hamilton) - supporting "Juno" Landing Force
    British cruisers *Belfast, Diadem*
    7 British destroyers
    *Glaisdale*, 3 British "Hunt" class light destroyers

The *Svenner*, formerly the British S class *Shark*, was sunk by a German S-boat on **6 June 1944** while engaged in the invasion. The general escort forces included the Norwegian corvettes *Eglantine, Acanthus, Rose* and *Tunsberg*. *Rose* was sunk in action on 26 October 1944. The *Tunsberg* saw only brief service at it was mined and sunk on 12 December. It was replaced eight days later by the "Flower" class corvette *Buttercup*. [84]

No.132 Wing helped provide air cover for the invasion, then supported Canadian ground forces as they advanced along the coast of northern France, Belgium and the Netherlands. They flew to forward bases on the Continent before retiring to Britain in April 1945 to prepare a return to Norway.

On 10 November 1944, the Norwegian Army and Navy Air Forces were united with the anti-aircraft units in the *Luftforsvaret*:

**Free Norwegian Air Force**

330 Squadron - Shetland Is.
    **11 Short Sunderland GR.V**
331, 332 Squadrons - Belgium
    **48 Supermarine Spitfire Mk.IX**
333 Squadron - Scotland
    **10 Consolidated Catalina GR.IVB**
334 Squadron - forming
    **10 De Havilland Mosquito F.B.VI**
1 transport unit - Scotland
    **12 Lockheed 18 Lodestar**

**Supermarine Spitfire IX**
1942, 11 m span, 670 km/h, 700 km,
6.4/6100 m, 13725 m SC, 454 kg B,
2-20 mm, 2 mgs

**De Havilland Mosquito F.B.VI**
1943, 16 m span, 612 km/h, 2254 km,
9.5/4575 m, 10065 m SC, 4-20 mm, 4 mgs, 908 kg B

With only 2,600 airmen, the Norwegian air units had been very efficient, destroying 252 German aircraft, sinking 5 U-boats and damaging 19 more.

Following the breakout from the Normandy peninsula, Allied armies quickly swept northward up the coast of the English Channel during the fall of 1944. A Norwegian commando company assisted in the clearance of Walcheren Island within the Scheldt Estuary of Holland. The Allies suffered a severe setback during the winter, however, when the Germans launched a powerful offensive through the Ardennes to capture the major Belgian port of Antwerp before it could be fully repaired to supply the Allied armies. The idle German units in northern Norway began moving southward to reinforce the effort, until *Milorg* sabotaged communications facilities in Norway. By mid-March 1945, few routes remained intact and the German movements ceased.

Norwegian naval operations continued as the war in Europe drew to a close. The submarine *Utsira* found lucrative targets off Norway, sinking a patrol boat on 16 Jan 1945 and a cargo ship on 5 April. *Arendal*, in company with the Polish "Hunt" class destroyer *Krakowiak* and the British destroyer escort *Riou*, drove away the German 4th and 6th Motor Torpedo Boat Flotillas which were laying mines along the Thames River-Scheldt Estuary shipping route on the night of 25-6 March 1945. However, the 9th Flotilla succeeded in laying mines that sank six vessels.

Back in Norway, events took a threatening turn when Soviet forces crossed from Finland into Finnmark late in October 1944. The retreating German forces torched everything of use to the advancing Russians, leaving a mountainous Arctic wasteland to cross in order to pursue them. With the Arctic winter already upon them, the Soviets halted at Kirkenes. As a token of their sovereignty and support, the Norwegians were allowed to send 300 men from Britain, and two companies of "police troops" from Sweden to Kirkenes. American planes ferried more troops from Sweden in April 1945, and General Major Dahl had 3,200 men with which he cleared Finnmark of German outposts before the war ended.

With the war obviously drawing to a close, the Norwegian government-in-exile concentrated on preparing its widespread forces for the return to their homeland. *Milorg* now had 40,000 active members, and there were 13,000 more in the "police" battalions in Sweden. Sabotage of German installations increased, but so did the brutal Nazi reprisals. As Reichskommisar Terboven was a fanatical Nazi, there was a very real possibility of the 400,000 German troops in northern Norway continuing to fight independently of the crumbling home forces. The threat was removed when Admiral Dönitz, heading the German government after the death of Hitler, removed Terboven from command and transferred power to General Bohme on 7 May. Terboven, and other Nazis, committed suicide.

The surrender of Germany on **8 May 1945** created great excitement among the homesick Norwegian exiles. Having lost more than 2,000 men during the war, *Milorg* mobilized openly on the day of the surrender to effect Norwegian control of the country. On 13 May, *Arendal* joined six British warships in escorting Crown Prince Olaf to Oslo. The following day, *Acanthus* and two British destroyers entered Bergen harbor. Fears of resistance by the large numbers of German troops in northern Norway proved unfounded. *Stord* and a British destroyer left Rosyth and arrived at Tromsö on 16 May to look over the situation. Ten days later, the Norwegian Brigade arrived at that port from Scotland. However, the German troops surrendered peaceably and left Norway without the destruction that followed their withdrawal from other countries. No clashes occurred. King Haakon VII returned to his throne on 7 June. [85]

# THE COLD WAR

The first parliamentary election in occupied Europe was held on 8 October 1945. Einar Gerhardsen became the new prime minister, and held office for the better part of two decades. Among the first acts of the new government was the trial and execution of Vidkun Quisling, and other Norwegian Nazis. Eighty thousand prisoners were repatriated to Russia from concentration camps in Norway. Trygve Lie, the foreign minister of the government-in-exile, continued in the new government until he won election to a higher post on 2 February 1946 as the first Secretary General of the United Nations.

Following the war, two light infantry divisions were organized from the cadre of the Norwegian Brigade returning from Scotland

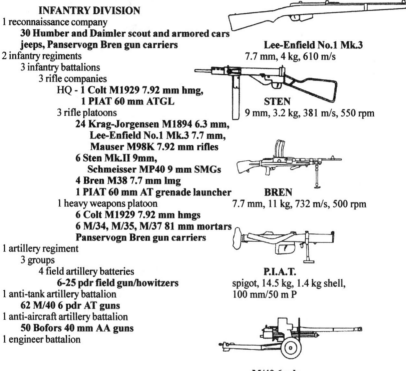

**INFANTRY DIVISION**
1 reconnaissance company
  **30 Humber and Daimler scout and armored cars**
  **jeeps, Panservogn Bren gun carriers**
2 infantry regiments
  3 infantry battalions
    3 rifle companies
      HQ - **1 Colt M1929 7.92 mm hmg,**
        **1 PIAT 60 mm ATGL**
      3 rifle platoons
        **24 Krag-Jorgensen M1894 6.3 mm,**
        **Lee-Enfield No.1 Mk.3 7.7 mm,**
        **Mauser M98K 7.92 mm rifles**
        **6 Sten Mk.II 9mm,**
        **Schmeisser MP40 9 mm SMGs**
        **4 Bren M38 7.7 mm lmg**
        **1 PIAT 60 mm AT grenade launcher**
      1 heavy weapons platoon
        **6 Colt M1929 7.92 mm hmgs**
        **6 M/34, M/35, M/37 81 mm mortars**
        **Panservogn Bren gun carriers**
1 artillery regiment
  3 groups
    4 field artillery batteries
      **6-25 pdr field gun/howitzers**
1 anti-tank artillery battalion
  **62 M/40 6 pdr AT guns**
1 anti-aircraft artillery battalion
  **50 Bofors 40 mm AA guns**
1 engineer battalion

**Lee-Enfield No.1 Mk.3**
7.7 mm, 4 kg, 610 m/s

**STEN**
9 mm, 3.2 kg, 381 m/s, 550 rpm

**BREN**
7.7 mm, 11 kg, 732 m/s, 500 rpm

**P.I.A.T.**
spigot, 14.5 kg, 1.4 kg shell,
100 mm/50 m P

**M/40 6 pdr**
57 mm, 1224 kg, 2.7 kg shell,
8990 m, 885 m/s, 15 rpm,
118 mm/500 m P

**Bofors M36**
40 mm, 1922 kg, 0.9 kg shell,
4941 m VR, 900 m/s, 120 rpm

The Army retained the British uniforms, and Norwegian insignia, of the wartime Norwegian Brigade. Equipment for the 28,000 men in the two divisions included British and American models: 1,300 jeeps and 1,200 other vehicles, 500 motorcycles, 28 reconnaissance vehicles (12 Humber and 7 Daimler scout cars, 9 Daimler armored cars - not including those with the brigade in Germany), 7,000 Sten guns, 1,200 Bren guns, 280-2" mortars, 440 PIAT, 62-6pdr AT guns and 72-25 pdr field guns. From World War II Norwegian stocks came 22,000 Krag-Jorgensen rifles, 100 Colt lmgs, 100-81 mm mortars and 96-75 mm mountain howitzers. For use in the far north, 300 M29C Weasels were acquired in 1945 and used until 1970.

The *Heimevernet* (Home Guard) was formed in 1946 from the *Milorg* Resistance organization, which had been disbanded in July 1945. It had 72,000 men able to mobilize in 4 hours within 18 districts. Equipped for guerrilla warfare, it expected to operate in 8 man teams, sometimes grouped into platoons or companies. From 3-6 teams were supported by each of the 525 parishes within the districts.

When the war ended, only 36 Spitfire IXs were taken to Norway. The Norwegian air units were transferred from Britain and the Continent to airfields at Gardermoen, Sola, Örlandet, Vaernes and Bardufoss, which had been left in excellent condition by the Germans.

## Reorganization of 1947

In June 1946, the *Störting* debated the future structure of Norway's defenses. Legislation approved on 15 June 1947 provided for the purchase of a British *Arethusa* class light cruiser for the Navy (never carried out) and an air force of 186 planes in 3 fighter squadrons of Spitfires, 2 light bomber squadrons of Mosquitos, 1 maritime reconnaissance squadron of Catalinas and a transport squadron.

The Norwegian Army was reorganized into 6 brigades:

Ostlandet
   **1. Brigade** - Skedsmo
   **2. Brigade** - Eidsvold
   **Tank Battalion**
      9 M24, 25 KW III
Sörlandet
   **3. Brigade** - Jaeren
Vestlandet
   **4. Brigade** - Voss
Trondelag
   **5. Brigade** - Vaernes
Nord-Norge
   **6. Brigade** - Tromsö

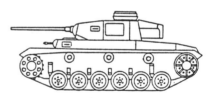

**KW III**
1942, 22.7 tons, 1-50 mm L60, 2 mgs,
45 km/h, 145 km, 77,50/30 mm,
59 mm/1000 m P, 5 men
(Pz.Kw.IIIJ,K,N)

**Bren Carrier No.2**
1938, 3.9 tons, 1 mg,
48 km/h, 9/6 mm

Although the ground units were equipped with reasonably modern British small arms, it was imperative to address the lack of a mobile strike force.

Numerous vehicles of the German Panzer Brigade Norway were left behind in Oslo when the Germans evacuated the country at the end of the war, including 30 Pz.Kw.IIIJ,K, 31 Pz.Kw.IIIN, 10 Sturmgeschutz IIIG, 12 Bergpanzer 38(t), 4 Sd.Kfz.232(8 rad), 4 Sd.Kfz.232(6 rad), and 4 Sd.Kfz.222. These were confiscated by the Norwegian Army. However, many of them were in poor shape and fewer than half were refurbished for use by the Norwegian Army. Twenty-five Pz.Kw.IIIs of mixed models joined the first 9 American M24 light tanks in 1948, forming a tank battalion for training in modern armored operations. Thirty-seven M8 Greyhound armored cars were added to the British vehicles of the reconnaissance companies.

The brigade organization remained constant from 1947-1951:

### FIELD BRIGADE (1947)
1 reconnaissance squadron
3 infantry battalions
1 field artillery battalion
1 anti-tank battery
1 anti-aircraft battery
1 engineer company

Most of the vessels manned by Norwegian seamen at the end of the war were officially transferred to the new Norwegian Navy in 1946. Together with former Norwegian vessels recaptured from the Germans, a considerable naval force was organized.

destroyer

| | |
|---|---|
| **Oslo** | 1944, 1737 tons, 68 km/h, |
| **Bergen** | 3-11 cm, 4 TT |
| **Stavanger** | (ex-British C class) |
| **Trondheim** | stricken 1961-8 |

destroyer
*Stord*
   stricken 1957

coastal destroyer
*Sleipner, Balder, Gyller,*
*Odin, Tor*
   stricken 1956-9

light destroyer
*Narvik, Arendal,*
*Haugesund, Tromso*
   stricken 1961-5

corvette
*Andenes, Nordkyn, Soroy*
   stricken 1956-7

frigate

| | |
|---|---|
| **Draug** | 1942, 1392 tons, 29 km/h, |
| **Horten** | 2-10 cm |
| **Valkyrien** | (ex-British River class) |
| | stricken 1963 |

motor torpedo boat
*Falk, Hauk, Jo, Kjeld, Lom,*
*Ravn, Skarv, Stegg, Teist, Örn*
(ex-British Vosper type)
   stricken 1959

sub

| | |
|---|---|
| **Kaura** | 1940, 781 tons, 31/15 km/h, |
| **Kya** | 1-8 cm, 5 TT |
| **Kinn** | (ex-German Type VIIC) |
| | stricken 1961-4 |

sub
*Uthaug, Utsira, Utstein,*
*Utvaer, Ula*
   stricken 1965-6

Thirty-five captured German Fieseler Fi.156 liaison planes were accorded the Norwegian Air Force in 1945. They were used until 1954, when they were replaced by Pipers. In 1947, from Britain came eighty war surplus aircraft. The first jet aircraft arrived in April 1948. With the new equipment, the *Luftforsvaret* formed:

**Norwegian Air Force**

331, 332 Squadrons
   **47 Supermarine Spitfire IX**
   **3 Supermarine Spitfire P.R.XI**
333 Squadron
   **10 Consolidated Catalina GR.IVA**
334 Squadron
   **18 De Havilland Mosquito F.B.VI**
335 Squadron
   **12 Lockheed Lodestar**
336, 337 Squadrons
   **20 De Havilland Vampire F.3**
   **36 De Havilland Vampire F.B.52**
liaison
   **24 Noorduyn UC-64 Norseman**
   **35 Fieseler Fi.156 Storch**

**De Havilland Vampire F.B. 52**
1949, 12 m span, 883 km/h (0.78), 1960 km,
8700 m SC, 4-20 mm, 900 kg W

**Fieseler Fi.156**
1936, 14 m span, 175 km/h, 240 km,
5100 m SC, 1 mg

With tensions between East and West appearing in the wake of the war, Norway pursued a policy of accomodating both sides. The failure of Czechoslovakia's similar policy, with the Communist takeover of that country in February 1948, created consternation in Norway. Finland was already being pressed to sign a treaty of mutual assistance with the Soviets. Sweden proposed a Scandinavian union, but her vacillating defense policy during the war had created a great deal of resentment among her neighbors. When she stuck to her strict neutrality by refusing to agree to come to the aid of the other parties if they were attacked, she was rebuffed. Under the terms of the treaty, Denmark and Norway would also have been required to greatly increase their defense spending to bring their armed forces up to the level of Sweden. The treaty was stillborn.

On **4 April 1948**, Norway joined the North Atlantic Treaty Organization. The *Störting* passed five "Defense of the Realm Acts" in 1950, expanding the armed forces and organizing them along NATO lines. From Horten, the Navy's headquarters was transferred to the large new base at Bergen. Of greatest immediate assistance to the defense of Western Europe were the eight fighter squadrons Norway deployed, mainly in the north. The outbreak of the Korean War in June 1950 again altered the situation and caused another reorganization of the Norwegian armed forces, and the influx of much American weaponry.

In 1951, Norway received the first American military assistance. Two new reserve brigades were organized, with another forming in 1954. They were followed by three "mobilization brigades" (10., 11., 12.) which would be called up in a national emergency. The Army now mustered:

**Norwegian Army**

Ostlandet
  **1. Divisjonskommando** - Nittedal kirke
    **1., 4., 7., 8. Brigades**
Sörlandet
    **3., 10., 11. Brigades**
Vestlandet
    none
Trondelag
    **9. Brigade**
Nord-Norge
    **6. Divisjonskommando** - Skjold
        **2., 5., 6., 12. Brigades**

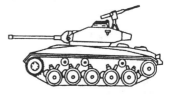

**M24**
1943, 18.4 tons, 1-75 mm, 3 mgs,
55 km/h, 161 km, 37/25/25 mm armor,
85 mm/1000 m P, 4 men

**Jeep**
1939, 1.5 tons, 1 mg,
105 km/h, 480 km, 2 men

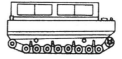

**M29 Weasel**
1942, 2 tons, no mg,
89 km/h, 400 km, 4 men

Delivered in 1953, 124 M24 Chaffee light tanks were in service. With the new American equipment, the brigades were reorganized in 1952:

**FIELD BRIGADE**
1 reconnaissance squadron
  **9 M24, jeeps**
3 infantry battalions
  3 rifle companies
    HQ - **1 Browning M2 12.7 mm hmg**
        **1 M9A1 60 mm RL**
    3 rifle platoons
        **24 M1 Garand 7.62 mm rifles**
        **3 Browning M1918A2 7.62 mm lmg**
        **1 M9A1 60 mm RL**
    1 heavy weapons platoon
        **3 M2 60 mm mortars**
        **3 M18 57 mm RR**
        **1 M9A1 60 mm RL**
  1 heavy weapons company
    **24 M1919A4 7.62 mm hmgs**
    **6 M/34-37 81 mm mortars**
1 field artillery battalion
  3 light batteries
    **6 M2A1, M/16 105 mm howitzers**
  1 medium battery
    **6 M1 155 mm field howitzers**
1 anti-tank battery
    **12 M/40 75 mm AT guns**
1 anti-aircraft battery
    **18 Bofors 40 mm AA guns**
1 engineer company

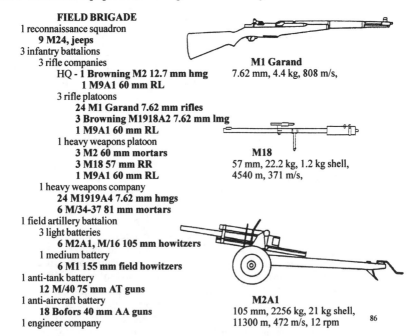

**M1 Garand**
7.62 mm, 4.4 kg, 808 m/s,

**M18**
57 mm, 22.2 kg, 1.2 kg shell,
4540 m, 371 m/s,

**M2A1**
105 mm, 2256 kg, 21 kg shell,
11300 m, 472 m/s, 12 rpm

86

164

Large quantities of American Military Assistance Program aircraft arrived, beginning in 1951. The first of NATO's defenders against Soviet air power, the Republic F-84G Thunderjet was not an outstanding fighter, but was rugged and reliable, serving to introduce small air forces to jet operation. It was intended as an interim model while waiting for the sweptwing F model. In the event, the increasingly important photo reconnaissance mission was the only one fulfilled by sweptwing versions in Norway. The North American F-86K all-weather fighters proved popular mounts, adept in night and bad weather interception. More versatile amphibious Catalinas replaced the older model. In 1956, Norway deployed:

**Norwegian Air Force**

330, 331, 332, 334, 336, 338 Squadrons
  **6 Republic F-84E Thunderjet**
  **200 Republic F-84G Thunderjet**
333 Squadron
  **19 Convair PBY-5A Catalina**
335 Squadron
  **20 Douglas C-47A Dakota**
337, 339 Squadrons
  **64 North American F-86K Sabre**
340 Squadron
  **35 Republic RF-84F Thunderflash**
liaison
  **24 Noorduyn UC-64 Norseman**
  **16 Piper L-18**
light transport
  **10 De Havilland-Canada DHC-3 Ott**
  **14 Bell 47D,G,J**

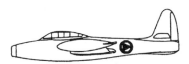

**Republic F-84G Thunderjet**
1950, 11 m span, 1001 km/h(0.82), 2367 km,
8/10675 m, 12353 m SC, 6 mgs, 1816 kg B

**Republic RF-84F Thunderflash**
1952, 10 m span, 1093 km/h(0.94), 3540 km,
14020 m SC, 4 mgs, cameras

**Piper L-18B-C Super Cub**
1949, 11 m span, 177 km/h,
4120 m SC, no mg

**De Havilland DHC-3 Otter**
1954, 18 m span, 258 km/h, 1545 km,
5730 m SC, 9 troops or 1360 kg C

**Bell 47G**
1949, 11 m rotor, 169 km/h, 507 km,
6000 m SC, 1-2 troops

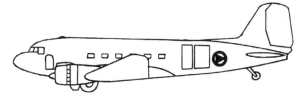

**Douglas C-47A**
1935, 29 m span, 369 km/h, 2415 km,
7300 m SC, 28 troops or 3400 kg C

87

165

*Climax of the Cold War* - 1960-1970

As elsewhere in the Western world, peace and anti-nuclear movements began in Norway during the 1960s, lead by the Socialist People's Party (S.F.). During the 1960s, the Norwegian Army was completely reorganized and re-equipped to conform to NATO standards. American-style olive green uniforms with NATO (American) helmets were worn.

Northern Command - Bodo
**Brigade North** - Bardufoss
Southern Command - Oslo

**M48A2**
1955, 47.2 tons, 1-90 mm, 2 mgs,
50 km/h, 257 km, 110/120/76 mm,
147 mm/1000 m P, 4 men

**M113A2**
1978, 11.7 tons, 1 mg,
68 km/h, 483 km, 2 crew, 11 men

The Army totaled 6 active (regular) brigades and 11 mobilization brigades. In 1964-5, 39 M48A.2s were delivered to equip the first of two tank regiments. They were followed in 1969-71 by 78 Leopard 1s. The field brigades of 1963 had 5,213 men:

**FIELD BRIGADE**
1 reconnaissance squadron
    **9 M24, jeeps**
3 infantry battalions
    3 rifle companies
        **M1 Garand rifles,**
        **9 M1918A2 lmgs,**
        **3 M18 57 mm RRs,**
        **12 M20 89 mm RLs**
    1 support company
        **24 M1919A4 hmgs,**
        **6 M/37 81 mm mortars**
        **6 M40 106 mm RR**
1 heavy mortar company
    **12 M30 107 mm mortars**
1 field artillery battalion
    4 batteries
        **6 M2A1 105 mm field howitzers**
1 anti-tank rocket troop
    **7 SS10/11 ATGW**
1 anti-aircraft battery
    **18 Bofors 40 mm AA guns**
1 engineer company

**M20 rocket launcher**
89 mm, 5.5 kg, 4 kg rocket,
830 m, 104 m/s,
280 mm P (eff. range - 200 meters)

**SS-11 ATGW**
164 mm, 30 kg,
3000 m, 125 m/s, 600 mm P

**M30**
107 mm, 317 kg, 10 kg shell,
6800 m, 18 rpm

88

166

Brigade vehicles included 501 jeeps, 391 trucks and 78 M29 Weasels. Thirty-nine M113A2 cavalry combat vehicles were purchased in 1964 for use by the 1. Infantry Battalion of Brigade North and the Cavalry Regiment. The total of M113 vehicles reached 136.

On the upper left sleeve of the khaki green uniform were short horizontal stripes in the branch color (cavalry - green and yellow, infantry - red, artillery - red and blue, engineers - blue and red, signals - blue and white). Rank insignia of the officers, 5 pointed silver stars, were worn on the collar of the service uniform, and in white on the shoulder straps of the field uniform. Non-commissioned officers wore white chevrons, point down on the upper sleeve. The two senior sergeants also had a white bar across the top of the chevrons, with a white crown above the array of the sergeant major.

Generals - gold lace field, large silver stars
    General - 3
    General Lieutenant - 2
    General Major - 1
Field Officers - silver lace edging, silver stars
    Colonel - 3
    Colonel Lieutenant - 2
    Major - 1
Company Officers - silver stars
    Captain - 3
    Lieutenant - 2
    Ensign - 1
Non-commissioned Officers - white chevrons
    Sergeant Major - 3, bar and crown
    Staff Sergeant - 3, bar
    Sergeant - 3
    Corporal - 2
    Vice Corporal - 1

Colonel
Lieutenant

Sergeant
Major

The importance of Norway to NATO lay in the remarkable ocean Gulf Stream which, as ancient men had discovered, swathed the entire Atlantic coast of Norway in a warm embrace which permitted year-round human travel in the Arctic - westward as well as eastward travel. Free access to the world's oceans from European Russia was possible only from the White Sea along the North Cape of Norway. The bulk of the Soviet fleet of nuclear submarines, and a mass of aerial resources, were based near Murmansk. Norway was in the path of any hostile Soviet advance. Its bases were crucial to the defense of Western Europe and the blocking of a Soviet submarine threat against the American eastern seaboard. Thus, strengthening of the Norwegian defenses received a good deal of attention from NATO.

The American Sabre, which had proven the equal of the Soviet MiG-15 in Korea, replaced the workhorse Thunderjets in the Norwegian fighter squadrons. New Grumman HU-16B Albatross amphibious flying boats were acquired for anti-submarine work. With excellent flying characteristics, and modern mechanical and electronic gear, they were capable of operating from heavy seas, ground runways, and frozen lakes. "Flying Boxcars" greatly improved the airlift capabilities of the transport squadron. New interest in troop airlift was expressed in the Norwegian Air Force with the authorization for formation of a common helicopter unit for the three services. Those duties were now being carried out by 14 Bell 47G,J, 4 Sikorsky H-19-D-4 helicopters and 10 DHC-3 Otter utility transports. The new unit would have 37 Bell 204s (UH-1B). The mission of light aircraft was expanded to tactical observation for the Army with the advent of 27 Cessna L-19As.

167

Since the end of the war, the Air Force had been administered in Eastern, Western, Trondelag and Northern Air Commands. Plans were now afoot to consolidate the first three to form two commands: Nord-Norge and Sör-Norge. By 1962, the *Flyvapnet* had matured into a small, but efficient air force:

**Norwegian Air Force**

330, 333 Squadrons - Andöya
  **18 Grumman HU-16B Albatross**
331, 334 Squadrons - Bodö
332, 336 Squadrons - Rygge
338 Squadron - Örlandet
  **116 North American F-86F Sabre**
335 Squadron - Gardermoen (Oslo)
  **8 Fairchild C-119F,G**
  **4 Douglas C-47A**
337, 339 Squadrons - Rygge
  **64 North American F-86K Sabre**
717 Squadron - Rygge
  **35 Republic RF-84F Thunderflash**
light transport
  **10 De Havilland-Canada DHC-3 Otter**
  **14 Bell 47D,G,J**
  **4 Sikorsky H-19-D-4**
observation
  **27 Cessna L-19A BirdDog**

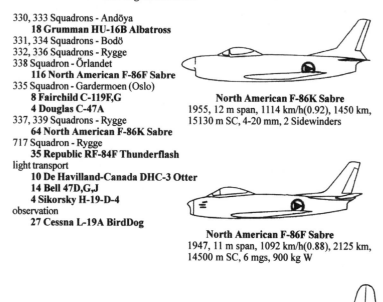

**North American F-86K Sabre**
1955, 12 m span, 1114 km/h(0.92), 1450 km,
15130 m SC, 4-20 mm, 2 Sidewinders

**North American F-86F Sabre**
1947, 11 m span, 1092 km/h(0.88), 2125 km,
14500 m SC, 6 mgs, 900 kg W

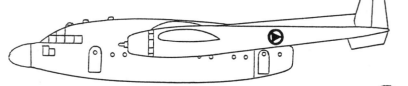

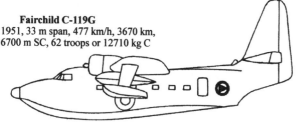

**Fairchild C-119G**
1951, 33 m span, 477 km/h, 3670 km,
6700 m SC, 62 troops or 12710 kg C

**Grumman HU-16B Albatross**
1947, 24 m span, 425 km/h, 4350 km,
6710 m SC, no mgs

**Cessna L-19A Bird Dog**
1950, 11 m span, 185 km/h, 700 km,
5640 m SC, no mgs [89]

The extensive coastline of Norway, and her dependence on maritime trade, together with the recent discovery of large reserves of petroleum in the North Sea, would indicate the need for a large navy. However, Norway's economic limitations, and her total dependence on the naval power of NATO, restricted her naval forces to convoy escorts and coastal defense vessels.

Norwegian naval shipbuilding revived in the mid-1960s. A class of large modern missile frigates replaced the weary vessels acquired from Britain after the war. Surface-to-surface missiles gave them a punch superior to the retired class of fleet destroyers of the same name. A pair of sleek new corvettes took over escort duties. To defend her lengthy coasts, Norway produced a unique class of ten small coastal submarines of the *Kobben* class. While the new submarines prowled the deep waters of the many fjords, eighteen fast attack craft carried surface-to-surface missiles capable of challenging any surface vessel intruding those narrow waterways. Together with a later class of fourteen torpedo craft, they would make things hot for any enemy.

frigate

| | |
|---|---|
| Oslo | 1964, 1,473 tons, 40 km/h, |
| Bergen | 4-7.5 cm, 6 Penguin SSM |
| Trondheim | |
| Stavanger | |
| Narvik | |

corvette

| | |
|---|---|
| Sleipner | 1963, 609 tons, 32 km/h, |
| Aegir | 1-7.5 cm |

fast attack craft
- missile

| | | |
|---|---|---|
| Blink | Glimt | 1965-8, 100 tons, |
| Skjold | Trygg | 59 km/h |
| Kjekk | Djerv | 1-7.5 cm, |
| Skudd | Arg | 6 Penguin SSM |
| Steil | Brann | |
| Tross | Hvas | |
| Traust | Brott | |
| Odd | Brask | |
| Rokk | Gnist | |

| | | |
|---|---|---|
| Hauk | Örn | 1977-80, 120 tons, |
| Terne | Tjeld | 59 km/h, 708 km, |
| Skarv | Teist | 6 Penguin SSM |
| Jo | Lom | 2 TT |
| Stegg | Falk | |
| Ravn | Grib | |
| Geir | Erle | |

sub

| | | | | |
|---|---|---|---|---|
| Kobben | Kunna | Kaura | Kya | 1963-7, 375 tons, 31/19 km/h, 8 TT, |
| Kholpen | Kinn | Sklinna | Stadt | 3 to Denmark in 1987 |
| Stord | Svenner | Ula | Utsira | 6 to be scrapped, 6 modernized |
| Utstein | Utvaer | Uthaug | | |

A Coast Guard was established in 1977 within the Defense Command. It was originally supplied with 6 vessels, plus 7 chartered from private companies. In 1980, it was planned to acquire 2 more ships, plus P-3B patrol planes and 6 Lynx helicopters for the ships. [90]

169

Although purchases of the original Lockheed F-104 interceptor were curtailed by the United States Air Force for lacking all-weather capability, the unique plane was strengthened for NATO use. Fast and formidable, it greatly improved the air defense of Europe at the height of the Cold War. Norway formed one elite all-weather interceptor squadron in 1963 with 23 F-104Gs, later reinforced by a squadron built in Canada. However, the bulk of the new orders went to a sturdy workhorse capable of carrying a heavier load of weapons than any other supersonic aircraft of the time - the Northrop F-5A. There were also 4 batteries of Nike SAMs. By 1978, the Norwegian *Flyvapnet* was organized into two commands:

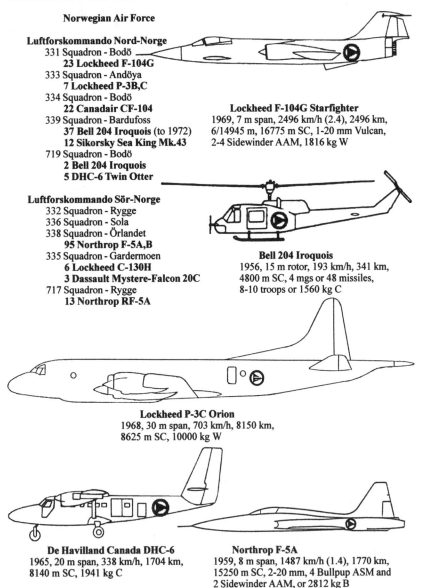

**Norwegian Air Force**

**Luftforskommando Nord-Norge**
  331 Squadron - Bodö
    **23 Lockheed F-104G**
  333 Squadron - Andöya
    **7 Lockheed P-3B,C**
  334 Squadron - Bodö
    **22 Canadair CF-104**
  339 Squadron - Bardufoss
    **37 Bell 204 Iroquois** (to 1972)
    **12 Sikorsky Sea King Mk.43**
  719 Squadron - Bodö
    **2 Bell 204 Iroquois**
    **5 DHC-6 Twin Otter**

**Luftforskommando Sör-Norge**
  332 Squadron - Rygge
  336 Squadron - Sola
  338 Squadron - Örlandet
    **95 Northrop F-5A,B**
  335 Squadron - Gardermoen
    **6 Lockheed C-130H**
    **3 Dassault Mystere-Falcon 20C**
  717 Squadron - Rygge
    **13 Northrop RF-5A**

**Lockheed F-104G Starfighter**
1969, 7 m span, 2496 km/h (2.4), 2496 km,
6/14945 m, 16775 m SC, 1-20 mm Vulcan,
2-4 Sidewinder AAM, 1816 kg W

**Bell 204 Iroquois**
1956, 15 m rotor, 193 km/h, 341 km,
4800 m SC, 4 mgs or 48 missiles,
8-10 troops or 1560 kg C

**Lockheed P-3C Orion**
1968, 30 m span, 703 km/h, 8150 km,
8625 m SC, 10000 kg W

**De Havilland Canada DHC-6**
1965, 20 m span, 338 km/h, 1704 km,
8140 m SC, 1941 kg C

**Northrop F-5A**
1959, 8 m span, 1487 km/h (1.4), 1770 km,
15250 m SC, 2-20 mm, 4 Bullpup ASM and
2 Sidewinder AAM, or 2812 kg B

A number of changes took place during the latter half of the decade of the 1970s. By 1980, there were 21,000 men in the active army, with 85,000 more in the Home Guard. A great deal was done to increase the anti-tank defences of the brigades. The Brigade 78 comprised:

**FIELD BRIGADE**
1 reconnaissance squadron
**Volvo/LandRover**
3 infantry battalions
   3 rifle companies
      **AG 3 7.62 mm rifles**
      **9 MG 3 7.62 mm lmgs**
      **9 M2 Carl Gustav 84 mm RR**
   1 support company
      **4 M/37 81 mm mortars**
      **4 M30 107 mm mortars**
1 field artillery battalion
   3 batteries
      **6 M109G SP 155 mm howitzers**
1 panserjager squadron (in 9 brigades)
      **8 NM 116**
1 anti-tank rocket troop
      **12-24 TOW 152 mm RL**
      **7 Entac RL** (in some)
1 anti-aircraft battery
      **24 NM 45 20 mm AA mgs**
1 engineer company

**LandRover**
1985, 1.4 tons, 105 km/h, 560 km, 690 kg C

**AG 3**
7.62 mm, 4.3 kg, 550 rpm

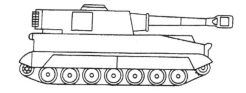

**MG 3**
7.62 mm, 11.6 kg, 1200 rpm

**M2 "Carl Gustav"**
84 mm, 13.2 kg, 2.5 kg shell,
400 m, 310 m/s, 6 rpm,
320 mm/400 m P

**M109G**
1970, 24.1 tons, 1-155 mm how, 1 mg,
56 km/h, 350 km, 32 mm, 6 men
43.1 kg shell, 18100 m, 635 m/s,

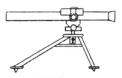

**Bolinder Munktell BV 202N**
1958, 2.9 tons, no gun,
39 km/h, 400 km, 1000 kg C,
2 crew, 10 troops

**TOW**
152 mm, 25.7 kg rocket,
3750 m, 280 m/s, 600 mm P

The 5,155 man brigade organization of 1978 had 320 Volvo/Land Rovers, replacing the former jeeps, along with 349 trucks and 48 tractors. For operations in the far north, 140 BV 202N over-snow vehicles began replacing the Weasels in 1968.

The *Forsvars* (Armed Forces) controlled the *Haeren* (Army), *Marinen* (Navy) and *Flyvapnet* (Air Force). Norway's defensive position was difficult. Its 200 kilometer frontier with the Soviet Union was isolated within the Arctic Circle. Its only link to the south was a single road 2,000 kilometers long skirting a coastline exposed to Soviet amphibious landings or an armored thrust from Murmansk across Swedish Lapland. Though small, the Norwegian Army was skilled in Arctic and guerrilla operations. Norwegian military units participated in United Nations operations in Korea, Kashmir, Congo, Lebanon, Yemen and Egypt.

Since 1972, the Army has been administered in five military regions called "divisions" to commemorate pre-1940 formations.

**Brigade North** (Brigade 90)
3 mobilization brigades (Brigade 90)
10 mobilization brigades (Brigade 78)
5 mobilization brigades (Brigade 90)
1 standing battalion group (Brigade 90)
1 infantry battalion (Brigade 90)

From 1989, the Brigade 78 organization was supplemented by a new one for brigades mobilized during wartime. Called Brigade 90, the new brigade type has increased anti-tank and anti-aircraft strength and greater mobility. Three brigades were to have the organization by 1988, with a total of ten by the late 1990s. Brigades in strategically important areas suitable for tank operations are designated Brigade 90 P-F and have a tank battalion attached.

**FIELD BRIGADE**
1 reconnaissance squadron
    **Mercedes-Benz 230G**
1 tank battalion (in P-F brigades)
    **39 M48A.5, Leopard 1**
3 infantry battalions
    3 rifle companies
        **AG 3 rifles, MG 3 lmgs**
        **M113A1 APCs, NM 135 MICVs**
    1 heavy company
        **M72 hmgs (U.S.), 81 mm mortars**
    1 heavy mortar company
        **107 mm mortars**
1 field artillery battalion
    **towed 105 mm and 155 mm howitzers**
1 panserjager squadron (in 9 brigades)
    **8 NM 116**
1 anti-tank company
    **6 NM 142 w/TOW ATGW**
    **24 LAW 94 mm, 106 mm RR** or
        **Carl Gustav 84 mm ATGW**
1 air defence battery
    **20 mm, 40 mm AA guns**
1 engineer company

**Mercedes-Benz 230G**
1970, 1.7 tons,
134 km/h, 750 kg C

**LAW**
94 mm, 8.8 kg, 4 kg shell,
500 m, 600 mm P

Seventy-two of the obsolete M24 light tanks were upgraded to NM 116 panserjagers in 1975-7 by mounting the light-recoil 90 mm gun used on the French AML armored car. A squadron of eight was assigned to each first-line field brigade where their mobility proved useful in the rugged Norwegian terrain. The remaining unconverted M24s were relegated to airfield defence with the Home Guard. [91]

Sixteen M48A5s were delivered in 1988 and all of the earlier models were upgraded to this standard. Some 136 M113A2s were originally purchased from the United States and 41 still remain in service as armored personnel carriers. Of the rest, 53 were converted to NM 135 *stormpanservogns* (mechanized infantry fighting vehicles) in 1982. Five years later, 36 M113A1s were converted to NM 142 *rakettpanserjagers* (rocket anti-tank vehicles), carrying TOWs. Since then, 44 more have been built on new chassis. About 42 M113s remain in storage and they are gradually being refurbished and returned to service. The peacetime army contains:

**Forsvarskommando Nord-Norge** - Bodo
  6. Divisjon - Harstad
    **Brigade North**
    14., 16. 17. Infantry Regiments
    1 tank battalion
**Forsvarskommando Sör-Norge** - Stavanger
  Distriktskommando Trondelag - Trondheim
    12., 13. Infantry Regiments
  Distriktskommando Vestlandet - Bergen
    9. Infantry Regiment
  Distriktskommando Sörlandet - Kristiansand
    7., 8. Infantry Regiments
  Distriktskommando Östlandet - Hamar
    Cavalry Regiment
    3., 4., 5. Infantry Regiments
    1 tank battalion

**NM 135 stormpanservogn**
1982, 11.7 tons, 1-20 mm, 1 mg,
68 km/h, 483 km, 2 crew, 10 men

**NM 142 rakettpanserjager**
1987, 12 tons, 2 TOW,
68 km/h, 483 km, 4 crew

In 1987, the Army converted from the khaki green combat uniform to a camouflaged one. Although the trousers remain khaki green, the tunic and NATO helmet are camouflaged, and there is a small Norwegian flag displayed on the upper left arm.

Generals - gold lace field, large silver stars
  General - 4
  General Lieutenant - 3
  General Major - 2
Field Officers - silver lace edging, silver stars
  First Colonel - 4
  Second Colonel - 3
  Colonel Lieutenant - 2
  Major - 1
Company Officers - silver stars
  Captain - 3
  Lieutenant - 2
  Ensign - 1
Non-commissioned Officers - white chevrons
  Sergeant - 3
  Corporal - 2
  Vice Corporal - 1

General
Major

Corporal

Rank devices remained largely unchanged, 5-pointed silver stars for the officers (those of generals being larger than the others) and white chevrons, point down, on the upper sleeve for non-commissioned officers. The ranks of sergeant major and staff sergeant were abolished in 1975. Rank insignia on the combat uniform is limited to the shoulder straps where it appears in white on a rectangular slide which is gold for generals, edged in white for field officers and plain for company and non-commissioned officers.

Naval policy remained one of using small vessels in coastal defence. A new class of larger missile attack boats was developed in conjunction with West Germany. They replaced the members of the *Kobben* class decommissioned from 1989.

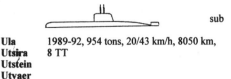

sub

| | |
|---|---|
| **Ula** | 1989-92, 954 tons, 20/43 km/h, 8050 km, |
| **Utsira** | 8 TT |
| **Utstein** | |
| **Utvaer** | |
| **Uthaug** | |
| **Uredd** | |

Three air force squadrons cooperated with the Navy. Long range reconnaissance over the Atlantic was the mission of the Lockheed Orions of 333 Squadron. Sea King helicopters of 330 Squadron conducted sea/air/rescue operations. Operating from Coast Guard vessels, particularly the new *Nordkapp* class, the Westland Lynx patrolled the coasts.

*Facing the Soviet Challenge* - 1980-1990

For defence against an attack by the Soviet Union, the developed armed forces of Norway remained largely in cadre configuration, expected to mobilize in place at short notice with certain readiness units designated to reinforce the active units. Upon mobilization, they would deploy:

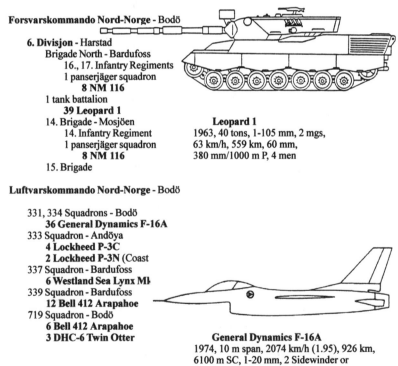

**Forsvarskommando Nord-Norge** - Bodö

  **6. Divisjon** - Harstad
    Brigade North - Bardufoss
      16., 17. Infantry Regiments
      1 panserjäger squadron
        **8 NM 116**
    1 tank battalion
      **39 Leopard 1**
    14. Brigade - Mosjöen
      14. Infantry Regiment
      1 panserjäger squadron
        **8 NM 116**
    15. Brigade

**Leopard 1**
1963, 40 tons, 1-105 mm, 2 mgs,
63 km/h, 559 km, 60 mm,
380 mm/1000 m P, 4 men

**Luftvarskommando Nord-Norge** - Bodö

  331, 334 Squadrons - Bodö
    **36 General Dynamics F-16A**
  333 Squadron - Andöya
    **4 Lockheed P-3C**
    **2 Lockheed P-3N** (Coast
  337 Squadron - Bardufoss
    **6 Westland Sea Lynx Mk**
  339 Squadron - Bardufoss
    **12 Bell 412 Arapahoe**
  719 Squadron - Bodö
    **6 Bell 412 Arapahoe**
    **3 DHC-6 Twin Otter**

**General Dynamics F-16A**
1974, 10 m span, 2074 km/h (1.95), 926 km,
6100 m SC, 1-20 mm, 2 Sidewinder or
Sparrow AAM, 6810 kg W

174

**5. Divisjon** - Trondheim
  12. Brigade - Trondheim
    12. Infantry Regiment
      1 panserjäger squadron
        **8 NM 116**
  13. Brigade - Steinkjer
    13. Infantry Regiment
      1 panserjäger squadron
        **8 NM 116**
  11. Brigade

**NM 116**
1973, 18.4 tons, 1-90 mm SB, 2 mgs,
57 km/h, 400 km, 37/25/25 mm,
320 mm/1000 m P, 4 men

**4. Divisjon** - Bergen
  9. Brigade - Bergen
    9. Infantry Regiment
      1 pansarjäger squadron
        **8 NM 116**
  10. Brigade

**3. Divisjon** - Kristiansand
  7. Brigade - Kristiansand
    7. Infantry Regiment
      1 panserjäger squadron
        **8 NM 116**
  8. Brigade - Stavanger
    8. Infantry Regiment
      1 panserjäger squadron
        **8 NM 116**
  1 tank battalion
    **39 M48A4**

**M48A5**
1973, 49 tons, 1-105 mm, 2 mgs,
50 km/h, 494 km, 110,120/76 mm,
320 mm/1000 m P, 4 men

**2. Divisjon** - Hamar
  Cavalry Regiment - Hamar
  3. Brigade - Kongsberg
    3. Infantry Regiment
      1 panserjäger squadron
        **8 NM 116**
  4. Brigade - Hamar
    4. Infantry Regiment
  5. Brigade - Flisen
    5. Infantry Regiment
      1 panserjäger squadron
        **8 NM 116**
  1 tank battalion
    **39 Leopard 1**

**Bolinder Munktell BV 206N**
1976, 3.5 tons, no gun,
55 km/h, 370 km, 2000 kg C,
2 crew, 15 troops

**Luftvarskommando Sör-Norge**

  332 Squadron - Rygge
  338 Squadron - Örlandet
    **36 General Dynamics F-16A**
  335 Squadron - Gardermoen
    **6 Lockheed C-130H**
    **2 Dassault Mystere-Falcon 20C**
  336 Squadron - Rygge
    **23 Northrop F-5A, RF-5A**
  720 Squadron - Rygge
    **9 Bell 412 Arapahoe**

330 Squadron - Bodö, Banak, Örlandet, Sola
  **9 Westland Sea King Mk.43**

In preparation for a possible conflict with the Soviet Union, the bulk of the active Norwegian forces were deployed around Bodö and Tromsö, opposite the "Finnish wedge" which nearly severs northern Norway from the rest of the country. The Garrison in Sör-Varanger (GSV), along the Russian border, consisted of a reduced infantry battalion group of elite troops. It served as an alert force, possessing only a few Carl Gustav and TOW anti-tank weapons and some 81 mm mortars mounted in BV 206BK over-snow tracked vehicles. Support for the forward battalion was provided by the Garrison in Porsanger (GP), a reinforced battalion group of the 17. Infantry Regiment at Alta.

The headquarters of Brigade North at Bardufoss was accompanied by a battalion of Leopard 1 main battle tanks and a battery of M109 155 mm SP howitzers. The northern troops were supplied with BV 202 over-snow vehicles, supplemented by BV 206Ns from 1983. Two tank companies of Leopard 1s and two batteries of M109s were also deployed at Bodö and Andöya. The nearby airfields were defended by RB-70 SAMs, which replaced old Bofors 40 mm AA guns. Lockheed P-3Bs at Andöya patrolled the North Atlantic as far as Bear Island (halfway to Svalbard), in cooperation with British Nimrods. At Bodö, were a squadron of F-104G interceptors and a squadron of CF-104 ground attack fighters, which could also strike ships with Bullpup ASMs. Tactical reconnaissance was the mission of the RF-5As at Bardufoss. A squadron of Sea King helicopters at the same base provided search and rescue services.

If an attack materialized, the northern forces were to be deployed to the Soviet border to face two Soviet Category I divisions advancing from Murmansk. They were to be reinforced by units from the south. The first to arrive would have been the F-5A (later F-16) ground attack planes of 336 and 338 Squadrons. Within one day, the 13. Infantry Regiment at Steinkjer, north of Trondheim, would be airlifted northward, while the 14. Infantry Regiment from Mosjöen, south of Bodö, would reach the area by surface transport within 2-5 days. The 5. Infantry Regiment at Flisen, northeast of Oslo, would follow within a week. The weapons for these reinforcements were already stored in northern Norway. Three squadrons of fast missile attack boats could reach northern Norway within 3 days, along with 8 Kobben-class attack submarines.

The only standing forces in the south were a weak infantry battalion (the Royal Guard at Oslo), a squadron of Leopard 1s, some M24 light tanks guarding airfields, and two artillery batteries. However, seven more regiments were to mobilize within 3 days while the movements to northern Norway were going on. As the rugged Norwegian terrain would prevent ready concentration, the southern regiments would have operated in largely independent zones.

Acquisition of the new F-16s from 1980-2 provided the Air Force with a high performance fighter combining the capabilities of the F-5 and F-104.

176

The airlift capability of the Air Force was greatly increased with the purchase of Bell Arapahoe transport helicopters. Twelve Westland Sea King helicopters displaced the Bell 204s. The Westland Sea Kings are used for search and rescue missions while the Sea Lynx is a Coast Guard helicopter. In addition, during wartime the helicopters of the private petroleum companies would be at the disposal of the government, providing six squadrons of Chinooks, Pumas and Sea Kings for transport missions. Many light helicopters would also be available.

In view of northern Norway's strategic position, particularly with regard to Soviet naval movements from the White Sea, it was planned to deploy an Allied Mobile Force to reinforce the Norwegian ground units. The first units could have arrived within a few days, but a month would have been required for full deployment:

**Allied Mobile Force**
3rd British Royal Marines Commando Brigade
W Company, Royal Netherlands Marines
4th Amphibious Brigade, U.S. Marine Corps
5th Canadian Air/Sea Transportable Brigade Group

Aiding NATO in the defense of its northern flank was the forbidding nature of the terrain. The mountainous Arctic wastes of the North Cape restrict an approaching invader to a few easily blocked routes. The defensive scheme was never tested, for in 1992 the Soviet Union disintegrated, eliminating the immediate threat. Financially strapped Norway immediately set about reducing its military expenditures. A reorganization of the armed forces began in 1993, a process still going on. [92]

After the signing of the Conventional Forces Europe (CFE) treaty, it was decided to purchase surplus Leopard 1s from the German Army to achieve uniform equipment. All Leopards are being upgraded to Leopard 1A5 configuration. Spain, Turkey and Italy are interested in purchasing Norway's M48A5s.

# FAROE iSLANDS

Norsemen navigating westward along a latitude line during the 9th Century A.D. encountered a group of rugged islands 600 kilometers off the coast of Norway. Bathed by the Gulf Stream, the islands proved to have a mild climate, although strong westward winds hinder forestation of the rather bleak surface. Because of the difficult agricultural conditions, the inhabitants turned to that hardy animal providing food and fiber - the sheep. By the time Denmark took over the islands in 1386, there were so many of the wooly creatures that they had become known as the "sheep islands" - Faroe Islands
in Danish. However, in time fishing became a more important industry.

During the 16th Century, English buccaneers made life miserable for the inhabitants until a local seaman, Magnus Heineson, led Danish warships in suppressing the pirates. However, navigation of the numerous fjords between the islands is dangerous because of strong tidal currents and maritime activity came to be concentrated at the capital of Thorshavn. Most trade is conducted with Norway and Denmark.

In 1852, the Danes allowed the Faroese to form their own *lagthing* for settling local questions. Some instigation for independence has been going on since 1910. The Faroese gained control of domestic government under their own parliament in 1948. The ultimate authority in foreign affairs, and responsibility for the defense of the islands, remains with Denmark. Although still under the Danish crown, the Faroese have been flying their own national and merchant flag since 1931. Of the same pattern as that of Norway, it consists of a white field with a red cross bordered in blue (azure from 1959).

# iceland

Norse adventurers, sailing westward from the Faroe Islands in 874 A.D., descried land rising from the sea at the edge of the Arctic Circle, eight hundred kilometers northwest of Scotland. They found only a few Irish hermits living on a large, fjord-pierced island. Smoke, and bubbling hot water, issued from the ground in many places, for the newcomers were standing on volcanoes rooted in the sea bed. Later, fleeing tyrannical conditions in western Norway, Viking families sailed westward along the 65th parallel, seeking the new land reported by the explorers. The swarm of Norse settlers established 4,000 homesteads on the island they named *Island* (Iceland). Joined by Irish families displaced by Viking incursions into their homeland, the Icelanders reached a population of 50,000 by 1100. At the same latitude as southern Greenland, Iceland became a natural way point for adventurers measuring the positions of the sun and stars with crude sextants to find their way westward through the Great Sea to the new lands. Life in Iceland was turbulent, but free of meddling Viking tyrants.

179

However, the kings of Norway desired to control the new lands to the west and, in 1263, a treaty placed the Icelanders under the Norwegian crown. The Union of Kalmar transferred Iceland to Danish control in 1280. From that time, Iceland declined in population and became isolated from the world.

As the Seventeenth Century dawned, English, Gascon and Algerine pirates ravaged the helpless island. During the following century, plagues of smallpox, anthrax and famine, together with two violent volcanic eruptions, wiped out two-thirds of the population. The miserable island, shaken by frequent earthquakes, had been transformed from the promising enterprise it once was into a hopeless derelict.

Not until the Nineteenth Century did the lot of the Icelanders improve. When Norway separated from Denmark in 1814, Iceland remained with Denmark. A parliament was established in 1854, and the islanders gained free trade privileges. Under the leadership of Jon Sigurdsson, Iceland received its own constitution in 1874.

Agitation for independence began during the Great War, a flag appearing that later became the national flag. The Act of Union of 30 November 1918 placed Iceland on an equal basis with Denmark, under the Danish king. Development of the country began. Only a fourth of the surface was inhabited. Reykjavik, the capital, was the only large town with 28,000 residents. A network of roads had been built since the turn of the century, but there were no railroads. An eighth of the interior was covered by a glacier. There were 107 volcanoes, a fourth of them active.

Half of the population was engaged in raising sheep and cattle on the low grasslands of the southwest coast. The principal industry was fishing, the shallow shelf around Iceland teeming with fish flourishing in the warm waters of the Gulf Stream that provided a moderate climate for such a high latitude. Iceland's rich fishing grounds were to prove an irritating attraction for foreign fishermen. Products of the fisheries constituted 90% of Iceland's exports, most of which went to Great Britain, Spain and Denmark. Such basic necessities as food, textiles and fuel had to be imported.

Iceland, as a possession of Denmark, had no army or navy. However, its popular fishing grounds required supervision and the *Lanhelgisgaezlan* (Coast Guard) was established to rescue fishermen in trouble and keep foreign vessels beyond its four-mile fishing limit. Aided by a few old aircraft, several small boats accompanied two larger dark gray vessels in the tasks:

cutter                    cutter

**Aegir**  1929, 500 tons, 23 km/h, 1-6 cm        **Thor**  1922, 300 tons, 16 km/h, 1-6 cm
      stricken 1968                                     purchased 1931, stricken 1964

These two vessels, together with the small *Gautur* and *Saebjorg*, led rather peaceful lives as the four-mile limit caused little conflict with the fishing boats of foreign nations. The foreign fleets were relatively small, and composed of small craft not capable of heavy fishing pressure. There were plenty of fish for all, a situation that was to change drastically after the terrible conflict that was shaping in Europe. At the time, Iceland was the extreme northwestern outpost of Europe, but soon to become involved in the continental affairs.

# WORLD WAR II

Icelanders had the misfortune of occupying the most important strategic point in the North Atlantic. Following the invasion of Scandinavia by the Germans, an innocuous vessel circled Iceland for two and a half months in 1940. It was actually a German meteorology ship, reporting the incoming weather that exerted a vital effect upon the air operations Hitler was conducting against Great Britain. The ship's relief vessel was captured, suffering the fate of the secret operation for which they were performing reconnaissance.

Iceland was favorably placed for air and naval attacks on Great Britain's supply lines across the Atlantic to America. After the fall of Norway, the German unit that accomplished it, Group XXI, was ordered to provide staff and troops for another daring enterprise dubbed Operation Icarus. From Tromsö, Norway, the 163. Infantry Division, reinforced with a tank battalion (2 tank companies - 17 Pz.Kw.38(t), 1 armored reconnaissance company - 13 Pz.Kw.II), engineers, and mobile heavy weapons, was to sail to Iceland in 3-4 days and disembark in the harbors of Reykjavik and Akureyri.

Realizing the strategic importance of Iceland, British Marines had landed on the island on 11 May 1940, and were replaced five days later by the 147th Infantry Brigade. Soon, two Short Sunderlands began searching for approaching invaders. The Germans could have overcome this weak force, but supplying and defending the isolated occupation forces would pose a problem. The German Navy was reluctant to risk scarce warships on such a rash venture until Luftwaffe units could be established on Iceland. The opportunity vanished when the British 49th Division arrived on 27 June as the "Alabaster Force". By autumn, artillery had been established at eight likely coastal landing sites.

His resources inadequate to carry off Icarus, Hitler canceled the operation at the end of June. The United States agreed to take responsibility for the defense of Iceland a year later. The American First Marine Brigade landed at Reykjavik on 7 July 1941, followed a month later by 30 Curtiss P-40Es of the 33rd Pursuit Squadron. American Army troops began arriving during the autumn, allowing the last British troops to withdraw in 1942. The Germans gave no further serious thought to invading Iceland.

At first, Iceland was used as a base for British and Norwegian maritime reconnaissance planes. Later, as relief operations to Russia increased, it became a teeming staging point for the Arctic convoys.

## *Independence* - 1944

With Denmark occupied by the Nazis, elements in Iceland urged severance of political ties. On 17 June 1944, the leaders declared her an independent republic and adopted the red on blue flag as the national emblem. In swallowtail form, it had been flown by the Coast Guard vessels since 1918. Iceland joined NATO in 1949, but this resulted in an agreement that has been regretted ever since. The agreement established the Iceland Defense Forces, consisting of American air units which occupied the Keflavik airbase from 5 May 1951. Supported by 3,000 NATO troops, they operated fighter, reconnaissance and sea-air-rescue aircraft.

Further irritation came from the vastly increased foreign fishing that followed the availability of war surplus patrol boats, converted to trawlers.

181

To aid the Icelandic cutters in patrolling the territorial fishing waters, a Catalina flying boat left behind by the American Navy was salvaged and put into service:

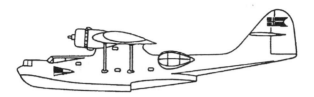

**TF-RAN**
1944, 32 m span, 287 km/h, 2260 km,
16200, SC, 5 mgs, 1820 kg B
(Consolidated PBY-6A Catalina)

From 1956-62, the flying boat did patrol and rescue work, stopping 14 foreign trawlers violating the new fishing limits. Aircraft of the Division of Air Operations were registered with the names of Norse gods.

Foreign firms rapidly increased their makeshift initial efforts to modern commercial fleets including large refrigerated trawlers. As catches by the native Icelanders began to decrease, pressure increased in the *Althing* to force the foreigners away. It responded by declaring in 1958 that Iceland's territorial limits were being extended from 6 to 20 kilometers off the shore.

cutter

**Aegir** 1968, 1,168 tons, 31 km/h,
**Tyr** 1-6 cm , 1 helicopter

cutter

**Arvakur** 1962, 725 tons, 19 km/h,
1 small, 1 helicopter,
purchased 1969, refitted 1976

cutter

**Odinn** 1960, 1,016 tons, 29 km/h, 1-6 cm,
1 helicopter, refitted 1975

cutter

**Albert** 1957, 200 tons, 21 km/h, 1-5 cm,
1 helicopter, refitted 1972

cutter

**Thor** 1951, 930 tons, 27 km/h, 1-6 cm
1 helicopter, refitted 1972

**TF-HUG, MUN**
1949, 11 m rotor, 169 km/h, 507 km,
6000 m SC, 1-2 troops
(Bell 47G)

93

The old Coast Guard vessels had been retired and new ones built. They were sent into action, cutting the nets of any trawlers found within the new limits. The resulting uproar was settled by an agreement in 1961 with Ireland, Great Britain and West Germany. GNA, Iceland's only large helicopter, served from 1972-5 while the little Hughes flew from 1976 until it crashed in 1981. The Catalina was replaced in 1962:

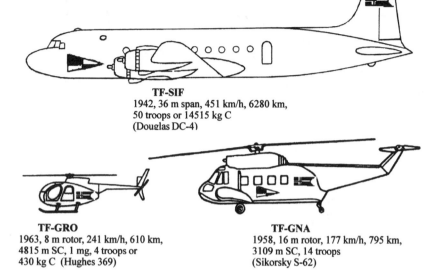

**TF-SIF**
1942, 36 m span, 451 km/h, 6280 km,
50 troops or 14515 kg C
(Douglas DC-4)

**TF-GRO**
1963, 8 m rotor, 241 km/h, 610 km,
4815 m SC, 1 mg, 4 troops or
430 kg C  (Hughes 369)

**TF-GNA**
1958, 16 m rotor, 177 km/h, 795 km,
3109 m SC, 14 troops
(Sikorsky S-62)

*The Cod War* - 1975-1976

As foreigners continued to take fish that the Icelanders considered to be theirs, the pot boiled over again in 1973 when the harassed parliament increased territorial limits to 80 kilometers. Powerful Great Britain came to a temporary agreement with the determined fishermen later in the year. The International Court of Justice ruled in favor of the British, but the feisty Icelanders reacted in July 1975 by declaring a territorial limit of 320 kilometers and initiating actions to drive foreigners beyond it. Tiny Iceland was able to confront the much larger foreign nations by exploiting the strategic importance of the NATO airbase at Keflavik where an American fighter squadron and a maritime patrol squadron were usually stationed.

Although West Germany and Belgium agreed to observe the new limit, the British persisted in negotiating a major presence by their fishing fleet, dreading heavy unemployment. Iceland proposed decreasing the British catch to half its current level, but the British refused. An enraged Prime Minister Hallgrimsson broke off negotiations and demanded the British end all fishing. Captain Sigurdsson deployed his force of modern cutters, ready for action. The impasse benefitted the Icelandic Communists as Soviet trawlers had carefully observed the new limits. Iceland threatened to expel NATO forces. The result was a campaign of intimidation, which became known as the "Cod War".

When British trawlers ignored Hallgrimsson's declaration, four cutters of the Icelandic Coast Guard sortied and cut their nets. Reluctantly, lest they appear a bully, the British dispatched seven frigates and three ocean tugs to protect their fishermen. A series of incidents occurred, in which vessels of both sides threatened to ram those of their opponent. In December 1975, the British tug *Euroman* damaged the Icelandic cutter *Thor*, futilely claiming accident. In retaliation, the *Thor* fired on another tug, the *Lloydsman*, which was closing the shore of Iceland to escape a storm.

When the dogged *Thor* again bored in on British trawlers in March 1976, the frigate *Yarmouth* set a parallel course. The two antagonists veered toward each other, the frigate sheering off part of *Thor*'s bridge, but causing no casualties. The Icelanders got in their share of licks. *Tyr* struck the frigate *Scylla*, then rammed her sistership, *Juno*, amidships. [94]

The Icelandic cutters were assisted by a search plane acquired in 1972. *SYR* was a Fokker F.27 airliner equipped with long-range tanks under the wings, which British journalists reported as bombs. Very successful, she was joined by *SYN* four years later, which is still flying.

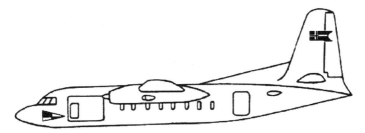

**TF-SYR, SYN**
1957, 29 m span, 613 km/h, 1060 km,
8970 m SC, 6810 kg C
(Fokker F.27 Friendship)

Following further clashes, the United States and Norway brokered negotiations, during which the Icelandic Foreign Minister Agustsson signed an agreement with the British Foreign Secretary, reducing Britain's fishing within the 320 kilometer limit to a fourth its former size.

Despite her threats during the "Cod Wars", Iceland has allowed the Keflavik NATO base to remain. Stationed there are 3,000 troops of the Iceland Defense Forces, a squadron of 18 F-15 fighters, one of 9 P-3C maritime patrol planes, plus rescue, early warning and service units. Iceland has never had formal armed forces, but several of the current organizations approach that status:

**National Police** - 457 men
    "Viking" counter-terrorist squad
**Lanhelgisgaezlan** (Coast Guard)
    7 patrol vessels
    2 maritime patrol planes
    1 helicopter

The police wear blue-black uniforms and are armed with American small arms. The Coast Guardsmen wear naval uniforms of a similar color. The vessels fly a swallow-tail version of the national flag, while the aircraft display a similar emblem on the tail with a blue/yellow checkered pennant on the nose. All vessels have provisions for carrying a helicopter when needed.

184

# EASTERN

# SCANDINAVIA

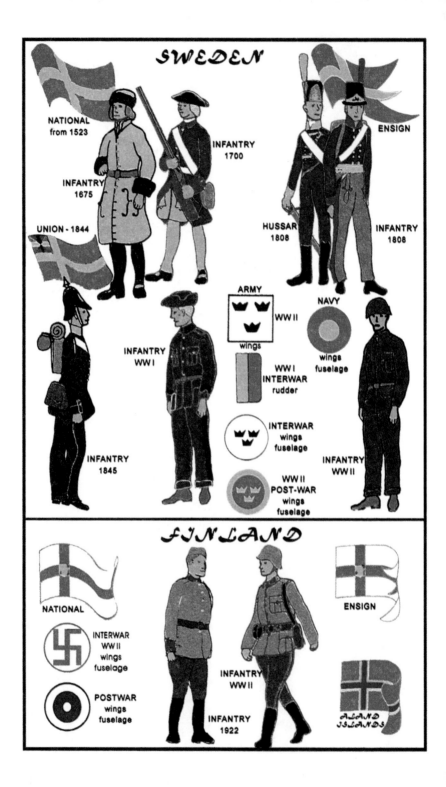

# SWEDEN

NATIONAL
from 1523

INFANTRY
1675

UNION - 1844

INFANTRY
1700

ENSIGN

HUSSAR
1808

INFANTRY
1808

INFANTRY
1845

INFANTRY
WW I

ARMY

WW II

wings

WW I
INTERWAR
rudder

NAVY

wings
fuselage

INTERWAR
wings
fuselage

WW II
POST-WAR
wings
fuselage

INFANTRY
WW II

# FINLAND

NATIONAL

INTERWAR
WW II
wings
fuselage

POSTWAR
wings
fuselage

INFANTRY
1922

INFANTRY
WW II

ENSIGN

ALAND
ISLANDS

# SWEDEN

Despite their commercial intercourse with much of Asia, the Svear had little contact with the advanced civilizations of Western Europe. As a result, at the end of the Viking Age they were more primitive than their brethren in Denmark and Norway. In the middle of the 10th Century, Olaf Skottkonung established a kingdom that became the strongest state of Northern Europe. To rid his realm of dissolute paganism, he introduced Catholicism. In coalition with Sweyn Forkbeard of Denmark, he overthrew Olaf Trygvasson in 1000, occupied southeastern Norway, and annexed the Trondheim area. However, Olaf Haraldsson succeeded in driving the Swedes and Danes out of Norway fifteen years later.

The Danes soon returned. Swedish King Anund Jacob (1021-1050) cooperated with Norwegian King Olaf Haraldsson in opposing this incursion by Canute the Great, but lost a naval battle at Stangbjerg in 1026. Two years later, the Danes defeated the combined fleet of Swedish and Norwegian longships at Helgeaa, forcing Sweden to cede the coastal province of Blekinge to them.

Norway's Harald Hardrada took advantage of Anund's weak successor, King Steinkel (1050-1066), and invaded the Swedish lake country, gaining territory from the settlement forced upon Sweden. When Steinkel died, civil war broke out between the Svear and Goths for domination of the country. The kingdom shattered in anarchy. Fortunately, the Danes were also involved in civil strife at this time, and the Swedes were left to squabble without interference.

After his accession in **1134**, King Sverker restored order by permanently amalgamating the two rival factions. Later, Eric IX organized a Catholic hierarchy in Sweden and undertook a crusade against the still pagan Finns. The Catholic ecclesiastical center of Uppsala became the nation's philosophical foundation. However, traders from German towns had banded together to wrest Baltic trade from the Scandinavians. Their capacious cogs were more economical than the narrow-beamed knorrs used since Viking times, and soon dominated Baltic commerce. Visby, on the island of Gotland, became the banking and accounting center of the Hanseatic ("Confederation") League. It was the only first-rank city in northern Europe.

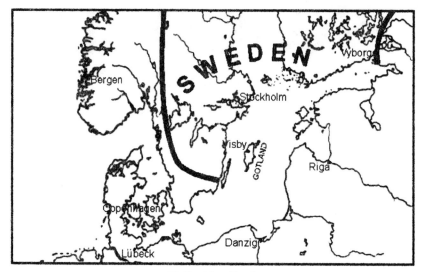

Medieval Scandinavia

Around the middle of the 13th Century, Birger Jarl (Earl) Magnusson emerged as a leading statesman in medieval Europe. He successfully fended off the *stormän* (magnates-nobles) and practically ruled as the sovereign from 1248-1266, although his son was actually on the throne as the first king of the "Folkung" dynasty. Concluding a trade agreement with the Hanseatic League, in **1251** he founded Stockholm with the construction of a large castle. He also prepared the way for the abolition of serfdom in Sweden.

King Magnus Ladulas (1275-1290) furthered Birger Jarl's work. Lübeck had superseded Visby as the Hansa administrative center, and the king meddled in a dispute between the Swedish and German citizens of Gotland, eventually acquiring both the island and its capital. Magnus established a hereditary nobility in 1280. In exchange for exemption from taxes, the nobles were required to provide heavily armed men that became the core of a strong medieval Swedish Army of foot and horsemen. The nobles were periodically summoned to a Council of the Realm, which thereafter replaced the *Thing* as the arbiter of Swedish history. The leading magnates were designated *Drots* (civil officials) or *Marsk* (military marshals). Marsk Torgils Knutsson drove the Slavs out of western Karelia in Finland and founded Vyborg as a stronghold against them. However the Duke of Södermanland had the popular marshal killed and carved out his own realm in western Sweden, supported by Norway and Denmark. King Birger, son of Magnus, invited his brothers to a banquet, where they were murdered. Birger thus gained sole control of the "Folkung" heritage, only to be banished by the outraged nobility, ending the dynasty.

Although the "Folkung" dynasty had dissipated its strength in dynastic squabbles, it had done much to develop the economy of Sweden. Mines in central Sweden now exported silver, copper and iron. Most of the exports were carried in Hansa cogs, which traded salt, spices, cloth, glass and ornaments for the metals. The old commercial towns of Kalmar, Söderköping and Tälje were joined by new trading centers, the most important of which was Stockholm. Hansa merchants settled in the bustling towns, establishing the first craft guilds. They built substantial stone houses and began dominating Swedish life.

188

# UNION OF KALMAR

Magnus II, the hereditary ruler of Norway, was also elected King of Sweden in 1319, uniting the two nations. His Dutch queen introduced the highest culture of Europe to backward Sweden. Establishing universal Common Statutes, Magnus initiated Swedish unification. However, conditions worsened at mid-century. The Plague entered Sweden in 1349, eventually claiming a fourth of the population. Denmark reconquered Skåne, and also took Öland. Utilizing the general dissatisfaction, the Swedish nobility succeeded in eroding Magnus' power, openly revolting in 1356. To counter their demands, he summoned the first Riksdag (parliament) in 1359. Nevertheless, he was forced to abdicate, and the nobles took control of the government. After Denmark captured Gotland in 1361, the magnates aligned Sweden with the Hanseatic League to expel the invaders, but their combined fleets were defeated by the Danes in the naval Battle of Helsingborg in **1362**. Two years later, Duke Albrecht of Mecklenburg was enthroned as the puppet king of the Swedish nobility. He pursued a policy of Germanization of all Swedish institutions. The command of castles was gradually transferred to German nobles loyal to him. Albrecht's coat-of-arms consisted of three golden crowns on a blue field, Sweden's symbol ever since.

By 1370, Denmark had fallen into civil war and the Hanseatic League gained the upper hand throughout the Baltic. Scandinavians suffocated under the ensuing Hansa monopoly. The Germanization process ended in February 1389 with the defeat of Albrecht in Västergotland by the Danish/Norwegian troops of Margaret, regent for Eric of Pomerania. At a convention at Kalmar in 1397, Eric was elected King of Denmark, Norway and Sweden within a Union of Kalmar. Stockholm was finally wrested from German control in 1398. Yet, the Union failed in its primary purpose of breaking the monopoly of the hated Hanseatic League.

Eric ruthlessly worked to make Sweden a vassal state of Denmark. His attacks upon Lübeck interrupted the Hansa trade with Sweden. Salt and cloth became scarce and Swedish metals could not reach their markets. Under the leadership of Engelbrecht Engelbrechtsson, the Swedish miners and peasants revolted in **1434**. Engelbrechtsson displayed military skill in leading his ragtag army to capture castle after castle. The following year, he formed a Riksdag consisting of nobles, priests, burghers and peasants, establishing a parliament that has endured to the present. However, the nobles maneuvered him out of power, making Karl Knutsson Bonde the leading statesman and soldier with the title of Marsk. Engelbrechtsson was ambushed the following year, and the rest of the peasant leadership was scattered. The nobles regained firm control.

Following the death of Engelbrechtsson, times were troubled. An alternation of Swedish regents and Danish kings attempted to rule. From mid-century, twenty years of turmoil resulted. Karl Knutson Bonde left Finland and arrived in Stockholm with a large peasant army. With skill, he maneuvered himself to the thrones of both Sweden and Norway. Danish opposition soon deprived him of the Norwegian part of his realm, resulting in six years of open warfare from 1451-7. Danish King Christian emerged the victor and Bonde was forced to flee to Danzig. Bonde was later restored to the throne of Sweden, but as nothing but a figurehead for the ruling magnates. When he died in 1470, the country was impoverished, with hatred for the Danish oppressors increasing rapidly.

Danes and Norwegians populated Skåne. The Hanseatic League controlled Swedish trade. Sweden was a stifled land of provincially divided peasants.

The Axelsson family led the ruling aristocrats, becoming the bailiffs of many Swedish and Danish castles with more actual power than any Scandinavian king. When one of their relatives, Sten Sture, was elected Regent to the young Swedish monarch, Danish King Christian I decided to assert his claim under the Union of Kalmar. He sailed up the Swedish coast in **1471** and landed at Stockholm with a large army. At the head of numerous peasants and miners, Sten Sture met him just outside the city, at Brunkeberg Bridge, and inflicted a severe defeat. Sture then proceeded to ruthlessly organize a strong central government and a small professional army. His burgeoning power inevitably brought conflict with the Axelssons during the 1480s. They worked with the nobility to regain their influence. He managed to prevent them from giving King Hans of Denmark the three Scandinavian crowns, but was distracted by events east of the Baltic Sea..

Duke Ivan III was creating an empire for the state of Muscovy. After conquering Novgorod, he sent troops into Finland. Sten Sture defeated him twice, establishing a boundary between the two powers in 1497. King Hans took advantage of his preoccupation to seize the Swedish throne for a time, but Sture returned in 1500. When both claimants died three years later, power brokering began again, from which Sten Sture the Younger emerged as the front runner. However, he alienated the Catholic Church and many nobles. The Danes marched northward from Skåne under their new king, Christian II, and defeated the younger Sture on the ice of Åsund in Västergotland when he tried to stop their triumphant march to Lake Mälar and Stockholm. Sture was killed during the battle, and Christian II was crowned King of Sweden in the fall of 1520. Suits brought by the Catholic archbishop resulted in the execution by Christian of the leading men of Sweden. This "Stockholm Blood Bath" alienated Swedes, ending the Kalmar Union and provoking rebellion among the subject people. [95]

# WARS OF THE VASA KINGS

Christian laid waste to the Swedish provinces of Östergötland and Småland as he retired southward. A young Swedish nobleman, Gustav Eriksson, released from prison in Denmark, made his way to the mining country of Dalecarlia after learning of his father's execution at Stockholm. Peasants and miners flocked to the charismatic leader, and the rebellion quickly spread throughout the country. He was elected Regent of the Realm in August 1521 and, by the end of the year, succeeded in driving the Danes from all but the large castles of Stockholm, Kalmar and Älvsborg. He gained arms and soldiers from Lübeck to aid in reducing these strongholds and to secure Finland. The Hanseatic Fleet forced the surrender of the Danes in Stockholm and, on **6 June 1523**, Gustav was elected king. The ensuing dynasty came to be known as Vasa, from the vase displayed in the family arms. As the symbol of the new Swedish state, a yellow and blue flag was adopted, remaining unchanged to the present day.

Shrewdly, Gustav gained the support of the Swedish nobles with plans to confiscate much of the property of the Catholic Church and place it under Royal and aristocratic control, at the same time entertaining leaders of the Reformation movement. The new revenues allowed him to create a large central government, an army of mercenaries, and a strong fleet that left him an absolute monarch, dominant over both clergy and nobility. He was so strong that, when protests greeted his imposition of several taxes to reimburse Lübeck, he executed the leaders of the protests without even consulting the nobility.

He negotiated a rapprochement with Denmark, then aided it in defeating Lübeck. Although the Germans occupied Copenhagen and Malmö for a time, with the aid of the Hansa fleet, the commercial monopoly of the League was broken. However, Gustav's ambitious schemes to increase Swedish commerce caused a serious revolt in Småland when he prohibited trade across the border to Danish Skåne, the principal destination of Smålaning trade. An agreement in 1542 with the rebel leader, Nils Dacke, ended this most serious challenge to his reign.

Sweden was still largely isolated from Western Europe. Only a small strip of Swedish territory, between Norwegian Båhus and Danish Halland, reached the Kattegat at Älvsborg fortress. North of the Swedish mining district, Norway held sway, while Skåne, Bornholm and Gotland were Danish possessions. Gustav's next project was to eject Denmark from peninsular affairs. His opportunity came when the Teutonic Order disintegrated in 1526. Muscovy eagerly moved into the power vacuum on the eastern shore of the Baltic, occupying Narva. To forestall a brutal Russian invasion, Reval requested Swedish administration of Estonia. The Swedes obligingly crossed from Finland late in the 1550s, precipitating a conflict that was to rage intermittently for two centuries. In 1561, the Danes occupied Ösel Island, and a nearby section of the coast of Courland. Polish troops moved up the Lithuanian coast into Livonia. The struggle was basically one for control of trade between Russia and Western Europe.

## *Northern Seven Years War* - 1563-1570

Gustav Vasa died in 1560, but his son, Erik XIV, was determined to make Sweden the strongest northern power. He greatly increased Sweden's military forces. Founding an indigenous arms industry, he created an army unique for the time. Rather than employing mercenaries, as did most European monarchs, he created a standing army of well-armed and trained Swedish peasants. As a reserve in time of war, provincial levies were given considerable training.

The Swedish fleet encountered the Danes off Bornholm in May 1563, without conclusion. Danish troops were thrown across the Kattegat, soon capturing the fortress of Älvsborg. Sweden was now completely cut off from the West. To reopen vital supply routes, Erik attacked the weakest point of the Danish empire - Norway. Under a French mercenary officer, Claude Collart, Swedish troops moved into Jämtland against negligible opposition and captured Trondheim in 1564. Collart intended to continue south along the coast to Bergen, the most important Scandinavian outlet to the Atlantic, but was forestalled by a Danish counteroffensive under Erik Rosenkrantz. Rosenkrantz moved northward from Bergen and recaptured Trondheim. Sweden was denied an Atlantic port, but did manage to hold on to Jämtland, thus creating a buffer between Danish territory and Stockholm.

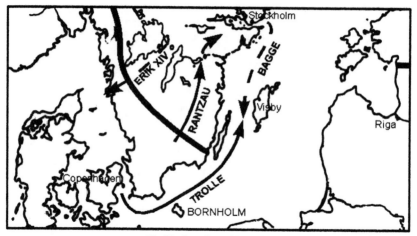

The Northern Seven Years War

Another offensive was mounted into southeastern Norway in 1567. From Jämtland, a Swedish army crossed the frontier and gradually overran the eastern provinces of Norway, until they were halted at Åkershus fortress. The citizens of Oslo burned their town to deny housing to the invaders. Erik called on the Norwegians to throw off the "yoke of the Jutes", but few complied.

Farther south, more frequent clashes had occurred. The Norwegian fortress of Båhus was besieged several times, but never reduced. Then Erik made the mistake of besieging Halmstad in Halland just before the winter of 1563 began. Frigid weather took its toll on the exposed Swedish troops and they were repulsed. As they retired, they were attacked by the Danes and routed. Älvsborg similarly resisted recapture. However, a well-executed siege of the Varberg fortress in northern Halland was successful, opening the needed communications route to the North Sea.

Along the frontier between the two bitter enemies, the loyalty of the populace was divided. Each side took malicious pleasure in devastating the adherents of the other. In the style of ancient conquerors, Erik slaughtered all the inhabitants of Ronneby in August 1564 because they had drawn away his profitable trade through Kalmar.

With his other military improvements, Erik XIV started a shipbuilding program that produced a fleet equal to that of Denmark. However, the Danes had long navigated the high seas, while Swedish experience had been largely limited to the archipelagoes of the Baltic and the rivers of Russia. Thus, Danish seamen possessed a strong moral edge. Admiral Jakob Bagge lost a two-day battle with the Danes between Öland and Gotland in 1564. However, the victor, Herluf Trolle, was mortally wounded during another encounter on 4 June 1565, a loss that would later be decisive in the sea war. Admiral Klas Kristersson Horn took the Swedish Fleet against 28 Danish and Lübeck ships off Bukow, on the coast of Mecklenburg. Although the battle was inconclusive, the Swedes gained confidence from the competence displayed by their men and vessels.

The Swedes won their first great sea victory the following month. Between Rügen and Bornholm, Klas Horn led 46 ships in an attack on 36 Danish and Lübeck ships. Both sides suffered heavy losses, but the Swedes were the clear victors. The Danes largely became fugitives after the battle.

192

The following year, an inconclusive action off Gotland ended in disaster for the Danes when 11 of their ships, and 6 of Lübeck, ran aground at Visby. Lübeck never again gained maritime prominence and the Danes were crippled for some time. The blockade was broken, with supplies reaching Sweden from northern Germany. On land, the Swedes fared worse. The Danes had a very capable commander, Daniel Rantzau, who took an army into Östergötland, one of the richest provinces of Sweden, in the autumn of 1567. Plundering as he went, Rantzau advanced on Stockholm. He was halted at the end of long supply lines when reinforcements from Skåne failed to reach him. He began a retirement on 24 January 1568, harassed by Swedish soldiers. Skillfully, he regained the frontier in mid-February with few losses.

Erik began suffering recurring bouts of insanity, which led to his imprisonment in September 1568, and eventual dethronement the following January. In the absence of success, both sides lost interest in the conflict and peace was concluded at Stettin in 1570. Sweden had to give up most of her gains and Denmark remained the dominant power in the Baltic.

## SWEDEN'S BID FOR EMPIRE

The next Swedish king, Johan III, sought to ensconce himself at the mouths of the Russian rivers, in control of the trade routes plied by his Viking ancestors. Slowly, Sweden overran Estonia and Livonia. At the Battle of Wenden in **1578**, the Swedes beat the troops of Ivan the Terrible. The following year, they occupied Polotsk, astride the Dvina River upstream from Riga. At the Peace of Teusina in 1595, Russia gave up Narva, and all of Estonia. Sweden enjoyed little of her success, for Johan III had died in 1592 and the rivalries of his successors plunged Sweden into one of her most violent periods. Sigismund, the son of Johan III and King of Poland, was a fervent Catholic. He took a Polish army into Sweden to oust his Protestant uncle, Duke Karl of Södermanland. The Duke skillfully manipulated the religious revolution going on, calling an ecclesiastical council at Uppsala in 1593 that made the Protestant Church of Sweden the official state church. Devout Sigismund was levered out of Sweden, and Karl ruled in conjunction with the Council of the Realm. Sigismund returned to Sweden in 1598 with a Polish army, but was defeated on **25 September 1598** at the Battle of Stägebro and was driven back. The Riksdag removed his crown and he retired to Poland. Many of the nobles had supported the absentee king, as his absence gave them much leeway in Swedish affairs. Now they paid with their lives as Karl took control of the government.

### First Polish-Swedish War - 1600-1611

Sweden made Reval its capital in Estonia. Narva had not become the Russian trade center the Swedes had expected, for the Dutch had developed a new route around the North Cape of Norway to the White Sea. In an effort to gain Riga, the most important Baltic port of the Russian river trade, Duke Karl of Södermanland set out southward from Estonia in 1600, overrunning Livonia. However, the Poles, under Hetman Jan Chodkiewicz, drove him back, capturing Dorpat and Reval the following year.

193

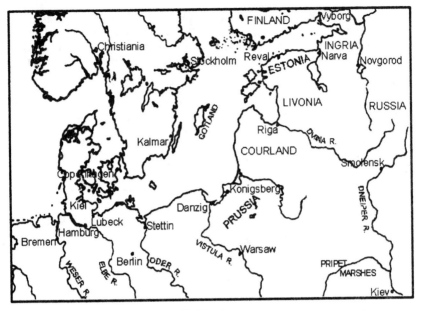

The Vasa Arena

Södermanland, now King Karl IX (1604-1611), returned in **1604**, landing with an army of 14,000 men and marching toward Riga. However, Chodkiewicz, with only 3,500 men, used his famous Polish cavalry in a headlong charge that routed the Swedes with 9,000 dead. The king narrowly escaped, and lost interest in the conflict thereafter.

Meanwhile, the Poles were thrusting deeply into Russia during its "Time of Troubles". To match the Polish expansion, Karl IX advanced eastward, occupying Novgorod. When Poland insisted upon placing its candidate on the Russian throne, and twice defeated Russian armies sent against it, Czar Basil offered Finnish Karelia to Karl IX in exchange for his help. A combined army of 30,000 Russians and 8,000 Swedes, under Russian General Shuisky, marched to relieve the Polish siege of Smolensk, but was surprised in **September 1610** by only 3,000 Poles under Hetman Zolkiewski. In the Battle of Klushino, the allied army was annihilated, losing 15,000 men. The Poles occupied Moscow, but a rebellion of 1611 threw them out of the country. Karl IX managed to hang on to Livonia, which became the breadbasket of Sweden. [96]

### The War of Kalmar - 1611-1613

Over the previous century, the Vasas had changed Sweden from a primitive nation of brigands to one of law-abiding culture. Its citizens enjoyed freedoms accorded few others in the world of the time. The nation was poised to assume leadership in the Baltic. Frustrated in his quest for a Baltic entrance to Russia, Karl IX sought to control the new route around the North Cape by acquiring Finnmark, the Arctic region of Norway. He was challenged by Christian IV of Denmark, who planned to resurrect the Kalmar Union. During the ensuing war, the Danes captured Älvsborg castle on the Kattegat, then went on to besiege Kalmar castle on the Swedish east coast. Karl died shortly thereafter.

194

Sixteen year old Crown Prince Gustav distinguished himself during the campaign, and now took charge of the operations. After two further years of fighting, the Peace of Knarod ended the war in January 1613, with Finnmark still in Danish hands.

Crowned Gustav II Adolph in 1611, the young monarch was to become the most remarkable leader in Swedish history. His abilities were soon tested. Shortly after the War of Kalmar ended, Russia sent a force to reclaim Novgorod. The Swedes occupying that ancient stronghold of the Vikings beat them back. Gustavus Adolphus, as his name is rendered in Latinized form, invaded Muscovy the following year, but was repulsed at the frontier fortress of Pskov. The Treaty of Stolbovo ended the war in 1617. Under its terms, Gustavus evacuated Novgorod, but Russia ceded to Sweden the provinces of Karelia and Ingria, its last Baltic possessions.

This favorable outcome was largely achieved by the remarkably able Chancellor of State, Axel Oxenstjerna. The experienced statesman steadied the young monarch, and left him free to utilize his many talents. Gustavus Adolphus was a great organizer. He developed the mining industry of Sweden, endowed the University of Uppsala, and enlarged the army and navy. With the aid of Dutch merchants, he established the port of Göteborg in 1621 to open Swedish markets to West European trade. [97]

## *Second Polish-Swedish War* - 1617-1629

Shrewdly, the young king moved in on the crownlands of Poland while the Catholic Vasas were distracted by major conflicts with both Russia and Turkey. After recapturing several Estonian ports in 1617, he arranged an armistice with the Poles until he could gather his strength. Three years later, he landed in Estonia with 12,000 men and marched south in company with 4,000 Estonians. Overrunning Livonia, he captured Riga on **15 September 1621**. Following another armistice with the desperate Poles, he disembarked at Riga in 1625 and proceeded to occupy all of Livonia and Courland against negligible opposition.

The Vasa armies were changing from a composition heavy with mercenaries (13 Swedish, 10 mercenary regiments during the war with Russia) to a national army employing mercenaries only when manpower ran low. During the second war with Poland, Sweden fielded:

Upland, Södermanland, Ostgota, Västgota, Småland and Streiff Horse Regiments
Tott, Ekholt and Wrangel Finnish Horse Regiments
La Barre Dragoon Regiment

3 German mercenary horse regiments

Livgarde Infantry Regiment
Taube, Andersson Cruus, La Gardie, Baner, Södermanland, Ostgota, Västgota, Mansfeld,
    Seaton, Clodt, Thurn, Armin, Plato, Kagg, Ribbing, Saltzburg, Muschamp,
    Scheiding, Teuffel, Bagge, Hand, Klitzing, Soop, Hemmingsson, Stackelberg,
    Torstensson, Rosladin, Upland, Gray, Antonissen and Sperreuter Infantry Regiments
Rosencrantz, Flemming, Cobron, Wrangel, Essen, Grass, Horn and Bürtz
    Finnish Infantry Regiments

7 German mercenary infantry regiments
4 Scottish mercenary infantry regiments
3 English mercenary infantry regiments [98]

Utilizing his already considerable experience, Gustavus began improving contemporary weapons and tactics, introducing more flexible formations than the clumsy pike-walled "Spanish squares" then in vogue. He trained his musketeers to deploy into six ranks behind and on the flanks of the pikemen. The leading two ranks would fire their pieces, then break to allow the next ranks to advance through them while they formed up in the rear to reload. In this way, each squadron gradually moved forward in a slow, rolling charge. Upon reaching the enemy lines, the pikemen delivered the decisive final charge. To increase the supporting firepower, Gustavus adopted a light "leather gun", issuing one to each brigade to be used at the colonel's discretion.

Determined to end the Vasa squabbles, Gustavus landed at Pillau in 1626 with 15,000 men and quickly overran all of northern Prussia. Danzig remained the Pole's only access to the Baltic. The king left forces to blockade the port and returned to Sweden. Hetman Koniecpolski attempted to reopen the Vistula and relieve Danzig with 9,000 men, but could not cut Swedish communications with Pillau. When Gustavus returned with reinforcements in May 1627, he took 14,000 men against the Poles and defeated them at the Battle of Dirschau. The improvements wrought by Gustavus bore fruit, as the Swedish cavalry fought that of the Poles on even terms for the first time. Sigismund III attempted to interrupt Swedish Baltic communications by chartering privateers to prey on Swedish commerce. They managed to harass Swedish ships, but Admiral Stjernskjold took a squadron of 6 galleons, including the *Tigern* (flag), *Pelikan* and *Solen*, to blockade their principal base of Danzig. On **28 November 1627**, they were standing off the Hel peninsula when a Polish squadron of 10 privateers, including 2 galleons, weighed anchor and sailed out to attack them. The Poles succeeded in capturing the *Tigern* and blowing up the *Solen*, after which the rest of the Swedish fleet fled. Yet, Sweden retained control of the sea. [99]

Reinforced to 32,000 men, Gustavus moved south in 1628, driving Koniecpolski back. He then turned to give support to the Protestant princes of Germany. The Poles renewed their offensive, defeating the Swedish cavalry at the Battle of Sztum in 1629 and nearly capturing Gustavus. From the ensuing Truce of Altmark, Gustavus gained the use of all Prussian ports (except Danzig, Puck and Königsberg) for a period of six years. The Truce had been arranged by Cardinal Richelieu of France who, alarmed by Imperial successes in Germany, wished to release the brilliant young Swedish soldier-king for operations against the Hapsburgs.

### The Reforms of Gustavus Adolphus

When the Seventeenth Century opened, armies were still fighting in massed formations little changed from the phalanx employed by Alexander twenty centuries earlier. The principal infantry weapon was a clumsy pike of 5-6 meters in length, as firearms weighed around 10 kilograms and required a forked rest to get off just one shot every two minutes.

Gustavus Adolphus had been trained by veterans of the wars of Maurice of Nassau. Youthful admiration for that great Dutch commander resulted in the adoption of many of his reforms by the Swedish Army, particularly regarding organization, logistics, discipline and engineering. In 1626, Swedish articifers lightened the matchlock musket to 5 kilograms, allowing it to be fired without a rest. The rests were replaced by much lighter "Swedish feathers" - thin, double-pointed spikes that were planted in a palisade to ward off enemy cavalry.

Even more importantly, Gustavus adopted a prepared paper cartridge containing powder and a 14 gram ball, doubling the rate of fire of his musketeers to a shot a minute. Each musketeer carried 15 cartridges in a bandolier. Ranks were reduced to six, which deployed into three for battle. The front rank kneeled so that all three ranks could fire a volley. This contrasted with other European armies, which formed their infantry into huge squares 10-45 ranks deep. Armed with a clumsy musket requiring 94 motions to load, they were outflanked and beaten by the firepower of Gustavus' smaller army. He organized his new mobile infantrymen into brigades (regiments) numbering from 1,000-2,000 men:

**INFANTRY BRIGADE**
2-4 squadrons
4 companies
1 troop (center)
54 pikemen
2 troops (wings)
36 musketeers

Gustavus reduced the length of the pike to 3 meters. His pikemen, wearing a steel helmet and cuirass, were commanded by the captain of each company. The lieutenant and first sergeant were responsible for the musketeers, who wore a steel helmet above a sleeveless peasant smock, loose breeches and woolen stockings, all of drab homespun. Except for the uniformed Royal Life Guard, the Swedish troops presented a crude appearance compared to the splendid mercenaries of other European armies, who were clothed by their patrons. Nevertheless, the dress was practical, and the natural fighting spirit of the men was heightened by the king's practice of promoting officers on the basis of ability rather than birth or seniority.

In artillery, too, the young Swedish king overturned prevailing practice. Though powerful, contemporary European artillery was nearly immobile, once deployed on the battlefield. Requiring 20 horses to move them, cannon were supplied at the rate of one per thousand infantrymen. They were useful in initial harassing fire and in punching holes in the enemy infantry line, but were silenced by the advance of their own troops as they could not maneuver to open positions. Similarly, Gustavus employed "position" artillery on the wings and center of his infantry line, the principal weapon being the 9 pdr, an excellent fieldpiece. He also used batteries of 6, 12, 16 and 30 pdrs. In addition, he assigned two light "battalion guns" to the colonel of each brigade. He went a little too far in his quest for mobility when he invented the unique "leather guns", composed of copper tubes bound by iron bands and swathed in leather. They were replaced by more substantial equipment after the Second Polish War. Their successors, two little 4 pdrs, weighed but 230 kilograms, and could be maneuvered in the field by 2 horses and served by just 3 men, as could the 9 pdrs. The light 4 pdr "battalion guns" made up half of his artillery. Using solid shot and canister in wooden cartridges, Swedish artillery could fire three times as fast as the enemy, and now numbered six cannon per thousand infantrymen. Other European armies soon imitated Gustavus, with Germany, France and Austria successively leading.

Gustavus also gave much attention to his cavalry. The European gentry clung to their obsolete heavy armor and caracoling tactics in massed formations. Gustavus' heavy cavalry continued to wear the cuirass and helmet, but he reduced its ranks to three. Organized into eight troops of 70 men, the regiments were trained to charge at a trot, directly at the enemy, in the manner of the French Huguenots. As the men in the first rank fired their pistols, then

197

drew their swords to close with the enemy, the second and third ranks accompanied them, but reserved fire until the hostile line broke. Most of the firepower for the charge came from musketeers stationed between the regiments, which fired as the charge began, then reloaded in preparation to support a second charge or a retirement. Regimental guns (but not true horse artillery) added their fire to the attack. Again imitating the Huguenots, Gustavus organized regiments of dragoons for use as light cavalry. Without armor, they fought from horseback with carbine and saber during an offensive, but dismounted as infantry on the defensive. By tying his cavalry to the infantry, Gustavus sacrificed much of its mobility. Nevertheless, the Swedish cavalry contributed greatly to his early victories.

The progressive field engineering practices of Maurice of Nassau were adopted almost intact. A large number of sappers accompanied the army, and all ranks, including the cavalry, were trained in building pontoon bridges and erecting field fortifications.

In battle, Gustavus generally deployed his infantry brigades in three lines, with intervals between those in each line. The second line supported the first, the third acting as a reserve. Cavalry and artillery were deployed in the intervals, with more cavalry on the flanks of the line and the "battalion guns" in front of each brigade. The formation of each brigade (which could vary from 2-4 squadrons) was flexible, being adapted to the tactical situation. Commonly, one squadron was deployed in advance, the pikemen to the front, with the troops of the other squadron(s) echeloned to the right and left rear. In any case, the intent was to form a wedge of pikemen to protect the musketeers as they sortied and retired. The result was a checkerboard of pikemen and musketeers:

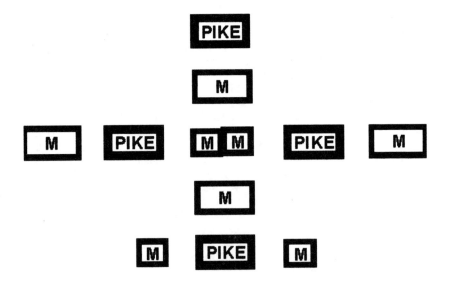

Tactical cooperation of the three arms was Gustavus' greatest contribution to the science of warfare. The mixed battle groups permitted a degree of coordination that best utilized the capabilities of all units in mutual support. His "linear" tactics persisted to the early years of the Twentieth Century, with some features still in use today. [100,101]

# THIRTY YEARS WAR

Nearly 100,000 troops of the Holy Roman Empire gathered on the south shore of the Baltic Sea in 1628. They had just defeated the Danes, who retired to their island strongholds. No Protestant army of any size remained to oppose the victorious Catholics. The Imperialists had been unable to pursue the Danes, or even capture coastal German Protestant cities, for they had no warships.

In November 1629, Gustavus Adolphus warned the Council of the Realm of the danger in the south. Although the Swedish Navy of 54 ships ruled the Baltic, he knew it was only a matter of time until Emperor Ferdinand II decided to stamp out the last heretics. The king urged the Riksdag to impose greater exactions on the populace to strengthen the armed forces. By 1630, three quarters of their taxes went to the army. However, Gustavus' policy of making war nourish war brought the ratio down to one quarter within a couple of years. In **June 1630**, he landed with 13,000 men at Usedom, in Pomerania. The Emperor sneered at his little force of rough peasants. Yet, Gustavus had gained respect for the fighting qualities of his men during two decades of campaigning. He said of them, "My troops are rude, and ill-dressed, but they smite hard and they shall soon have better clothes."

The core of Gustavus' early military campaigns was the Home Army:

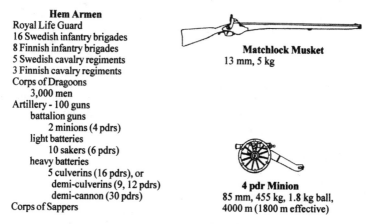

**Hem Armen**
Royal Life Guard
16 Swedish infantry brigades
8 Finnish infantry brigades
5 Swedish cavalry regiments
3 Finnish cavalry regiments
Corps of Dragoons
   3,000 men
Artillery - 100 guns
   battalion guns
     2 minions (4 pdrs)
   light batteries
     10 sakers (6 pdrs)
   heavy batteries
     5 culverins (16 pdrs), or
     demi-culverins (9, 12 pdrs)
     demi-cannon (30 pdrs)
Corps of Sappers

**Matchlock Musket**
13 mm, 5 kg

**4 pdr Minion**
85 mm, 455 kg, 1.8 kg ball,
4000 m (1800 m effective)

When the Swedish Home Army was reorganized in 1636, the ratio of brigades was changed to 14 Swedish and 9 Finnish. The brigades were distinguished by sashes and silk flags of white, yellow, red, green, blue and black, on which were embroidered emblems and mottoes. Brilliant young Lennart Torstensson was in command of the artillery, while doughty old Johan Baner led the cavalry.

## Consolidation of Northern Germany - 1630-1631

Bringing his army to full strength by gathering a like number of garrison troops from Pomerania, Gustavus set out to rekindle the Protestant cause. However, while he was meticulously recapturing more than eighty places in Pomerania and Mecklenburg, the Protestant German princes displayed total apathy toward him. Richelieu arranged the Treaty of Bärwalde on 23 January 1631, persuading the French king to finance the Swedish campaign against his

Hapsburg rival, in exchange for Gustavus' promise not to molest territories in which Catholicism was already well established.

The Swedish invasion caused a change in the Imperialist camp, also. Under pressure from the Protestant princes who were outraged by the excesses of Wallenstein, Emperor Ferdinand II dismissed the old marshal on 24 August 1630. Enough of his disgruntled troops enlisted in the Swedish Army to form several brigades of mercenaries. In time, these would swell to 30,000 men, including half a dozen cavalry regiments. However, 40,000 of his troops joined Count Tilly, who then had 70,000 men to begin the infamous Siege of Magdeburg in **November 1630**. The Imperial troops suffered more than the determined defenders, for they were repeatedly repulsed and found little sustenance in the denuded countryside.

Gustavus' successes encouraged the Protestant German princes. Under the leadership of John George of Saxony, they issued a Manifesto from Leipzig on 28 March 1631 demanding that Ferdinand end his excesses. When the Emperor ignored their protests, the princes established an army on 14 May, under the command of Hans Georg von Arnim.

Hoping to force Tilly to lift the siege of Magdeburg, Gustavus made a brilliant surprise march to the Oder River on 13 April and captured Frankfurt. Tilly kept his teeth embedded in Magdeburg. On 20 May, he and Count Pappenheim stormed the fortifications. Their starved troops got out of hand and sacked the city. Only 5,000 of its 30,000 inhabitants survived the horror. The Elbe was choked with mutilated corpses. Thus, the Thirty Years War began to earn its reputation as the most horrible in modern history. Weakened by supply deficiencies and disease, the Swedish Army entrenched itself at Werden on the banks of the Elbe. Tilly approached during July and twice assaulted the maze of field fortifications with 22,000 men. Case shot from the battalion guns cut swaths in the Imperial ranks as they approached in close order and the defenders threw them back with losses of 6,000. Tilly had no choice but to leave barren Mecklenburg and enter Saxony for sustenance.

### Campaign in Saxony - 1631

As Tilly feared, the ravages of the starved Imperial troops drove John George to place his Saxon Army at the disposal of Gustavus Adolphus on 11 September. Four days later, Tilly's troops entered the Saxon capital, Leipzig, and set about looting the rich city. Tilly would have preferred to retire southward, but he could not get his men to abandon their booty. He heeded Count Pappenheim's advice and formed up his army of 36,000 men on the plain of **Breitenfeld**, six kilometers north of Leipzig. The Swedish Army throughout Germany included:

Livgarde, Wetberg, Gehlen, Breitenbach, Zülow and Bremen Horse Regiments
Wunsch, Wrangel and Ekholt Finnish Horse Regiments
Aderkas (Livonian) and Dönhoff (Kurlander) Horse Regiments
Taupadel Dragoon Regiment
39 German mercenary horse regiments
5 German mercenary dragoon regiments

Livgarde, Pithan, Merretich, Livgarde Hertig Adolf Friedrich, Lohausen, Görtzke,
    Livgarde Hertig Hans Albrecht, Müffel, Leubelfing, Livgarde Hertig Wilhelm,
    Schenk, Skaraborg, Teuffel, Bagge, Seaton, Hand, Klitzing, Soop, Hemmingsson,
    Stackelberg, Torstensson, Rosladin, Bremen and Upland Infantry Regiments
Vyborg, Wrangel, Essen, Grass, Horn and Bürtz Finnish Infantry Regiments
36 German, 5 Scottish and 4 English mercenary infantry regiments [102]

The Swedish *Hem Armen* of 26,000 men, and John George's 16,000 Saxons, joined forces at Düben, forty kilometers north of the Saxon capital. As they approached Breitenfeld on **17 September**, they found the Imperial forces already in battle array. Long experienced in classic Spanish practice, the seventy-two year old Tilly deployed his forces in the familiar pattern. Eleven huge "squares" of infantry, averaging 1,500 men, were disposed in two lines, with the cumbersome artillery pieces distributed across their front. Pappenheim's 7 regiments of cavalry were on the left wing, with the 5 cavalry regiments of Tilly on the right. In full view of the waiting enemy, Gustavus' ragged Swedish troops marched into position on the right wing, while the more conventional Saxon troops took their place on the left. Two thousand Imperial light horsemen advanced to harry the Allied deployment, but the Swedish dragoons demonstrated their capabilities by driving them back. Gustavus' deployment evoked bewilderment among the watching Imperial officers, for not a single "square" appeared. Instead, 8 brigades of infantry formed two lines in "brigade order". Most of the Swedish heavy cavalry was on the right wing, supported by interspersed infantry and light artillery, with some on the left wing and in reserve behind the center. The Saxons were drawn up in more conventional fashion on the left wing, their cavalry on both flanks of an infantry phalanx.

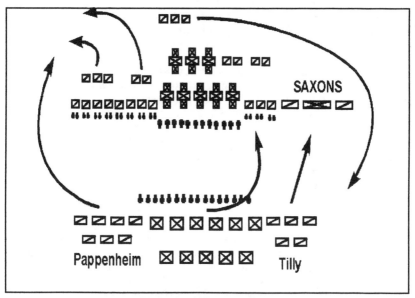

Battle of Breitenfeld - 17 September 1631

After the customary artillery bombardment, in which the Swedish guns fired three times to the Imperialists one, Tilly began the tilt in conventional fashion by sending his cavalry forward from both wings. Pappenheim swept around the Allied right wing with his 5,000 Black Cuirassiers and attacked the Swedish reserves. However, the mobile Swedish heavy cavalry of the second line wheeled at right angles to the first, forming a salient against which the vaunted cuirassiers vainly charged seven times. With regimental guns firing, the doughty Swedish cavalrymen and musketeers alternately sortied and shielded each other,

201

eventually putting the battered Imperialists to flight. On the other wing, the Croat light cavalry of Tilly struck the inexperienced Saxon Army. The raw Saxon troops broke before an avalanche of red-cloaked Croat horsemen, the best in Europe, and fled the field. With their allies gone, the rustic Swedish troops were badly outnumbered by the gaily-dressed Imperialists. Skillfully, Tilly advanced against the exposed left flank. Gustavus' veterans calmly changed front, then met the Imperial advance with a devastating storm of musketry. The gunners of Lennart Torstensson rapidly tore holes in the enemy ranks. Gustavus led his reserves in a sweep around Tilly's right flank and captured both the Saxon and Imperial artillery. Riddled by frontal and enfilade fire, the faltering Imperial line broke and fled as the Swedish pikemen pressed home their steady charge. The Swedes rode into the confused mass of fleeing Imperialists to avenge the Magdeburg massacre. Of his 36,000 man army, Tilly escaped with only 2,000 survivors. Twelve thousand had been killed or badly wounded and another 7,000 were captured. Swedish casualties amounted to 2,100. Further, Tilly lost all of his artillery and baggage trains.

Few battles in history have been more decisive than Breitenfeld. The best tenets of the well-tried "Spanish system" had been skillfully applied by an experienced master, but the old system was beaten by equally skilled application of the new "linear system". The combined-arms concept of Gustavus would now sweep across Europe, relegating the old method to the dustbin of history.

Vienna appeared to be his for the taking, but Gustavus was unsure of either his Protestant allies or his lines of communication should he march on the Imperial capital. Instead, he chose to plunder the Hapsburg provinces of western Germany. Despite the objections of Cardinal Richelieu, who considered them to be in the French sphere of interest, Gustavus invaded the Rhineland, capturing Erfurt. Turning south, he entered Franconia. After taking Mainz on 22 December, he settled in to winter there. Meanwhile, Saxon troops occupied Prague. Gustavus and his allies had 108,000 troops roaming the crumbling Holy Roman Empire by Christmas 1631. Of these, 18,000 were on the Rhine, 20,000 on the Main, 8,000 in Hesse, 13,000 on the Elbe, 17,000 in Mecklenburg, 20,000 in Bohemia and 12,000 in various garrisons. Only a quarter of them were Swedes.

### *Invasion of Bavaria* - 1632

In desperation, Emperor Ferdinand II recalled the disgraced Wallenstein in April 1632, granting him almost dictatorial powers. As Duke of Friedland, Wallenstein had organized the first totalitarian military state in Europe, putting the entire population of his duchy to work producing munitions. Before the duke could raise a new army, Gustavus invaded Bavaria. There Tilly had gathered a new Imperial army and waited with Maximilian of Bavaria on the steep heights overlooking the Lech River.

Overnight, Gustavus' engineers built a bridge of boats and sent across 300 Finns who threw up earthworks to shelter the troops that crossed later. On **16 April**, the Swedish artillery fired for six hours into the Imperial camp, killing Tilly and causing 3,000 casualties. Abandoning both baggage and guns, Maximilian retreated. He was saved only by a windstorm that blocked the roads to the pursuing Swedish cavalry. Gustavus advanced to occupy Augsburg, Munich and all of southern Bavaria. The incensed Swedish king began to hear of depredations perpetrated by his German mercenaries.

202

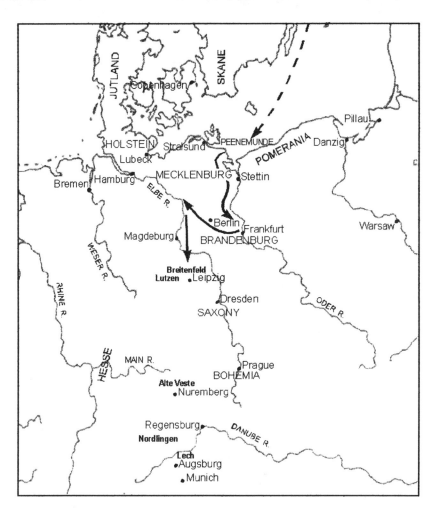

Theatre of the Thirty Years War

Wallenstein now had 40,000 mercenaries under his command. He treated them to plunder in Saxony before marching south. Gustavus had only 20,000 men at hand, and entrenched them at Nuremberg to await him. Joined by the 20,000 men Maximilian had saved from the Lech, in August Wallenstein encamped on the height of **Alte Veste** above Nuremberg and settled in to let attrition take its course. Daily, both sides buried scores of corpses taken by disease and injury. Wallenstein drew supplies from Friedland, but had wasted the country around Nuremberg, ensuring the more rapid decline of the Swedish Army. Gustavus sent for reinforcements. When they arrived to provide him an army of 45,000 men, he decided to attack. On **4 September**, Gustavus ordered successive charges for 10 hours, but Wallenstein had chosen his position well. In the rough ground, covered by heavy brush, the superior Swedish cavalry could not operate and the artillery was greatly hampered. The fight was a bloody frontal encounter with entrenched infantry. Gustavus finally admitted defeat and withdrew with losses of 4,000 dead.

Wallenstein did not pursue, for his army was also nearly starved. The Swedes retired to the northwest, while Wallenstein renewed his rape of Saxony. Reinforcements crossed from Sweden and many Germans were now enlisting in Gustavus' command, for his spectacular accomplishments had made him the hero of the Reformation. New units included:

Mützschaphal, Uslar and Eisleben Horse Regiments

24 German and 2 French mercenary horse regiments
11 German mercenary dragoon regiments

Uslar, Mützschephal, Schonberg, Ehlen, Heiden, Schlammersdorf, Tetzel, Steinbach
    and Riese Infantry Regiments
Åbo Finnish Infantry Regiment

34 German and 2 Scottish mercenary infantry regiments [103]

Concerned with the preservation of his lengthy line of communications to the homeland, Gustavus made the swiftest march of the war to Erfurt, 400 kilometers in 18 days. Accustomed to the leisurely pace of contemporary warfare, Wallenstein believed the Swedes would pause for replenishment, and detached Pappenheim's 8,000 cavalrymen for a plundering foray to Halle. Gustavus' scouts told him of the movement and he decided to attack, catching Wallenstein with but 20,000 men at **Lützen**, 24 kilometers west of Leipzig. Only two hours of daylight remained when the Swedes arrived, so the two armies spent the night facing each other across a road. Fog shrouded the dawn of **16 November**, delaying the Swedish advance until 1100. Gustavus' battle formation was essentially unchanged from that used at Breitenfeld. As the 18,000 troops in the army included many German mercenaries, Bernard of Saxe-Weimar was given command of the left wing while Gustavus personally took charge of the right. The Imperial infantry was formed up in five squares, four of which were deployed in a "lozenge" arrangement in the center with the fifth supporting the cavalry of the right wing. Cavalry was also on the left wing, the artillery in front, and skirmishers in a ditch along the road.

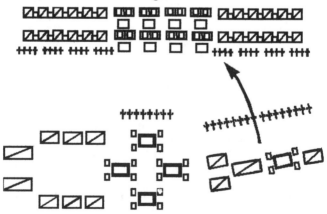

Battle of Lützen - 16 November 1632

Gustavus' cavalry charged that of Count Heinrich Holk on the Imperial right flank and drove it back on the artillery. Wallenstein set fire to Lützen. Smoke from the burning town billowed into the fog, enshrouding the battlefield. Groups of men groped for each other in the murk, illuminated fitfully by artillery discharges. The central Swedish infantry began its slow charge, overrunning the Imperial skirmishers and capturing the artillery. Seeing the accompanying Swedish cavalry slowed by the ditch, Wallenstein sent his cavalry against the exposed infantry. The stout Swedes held their position and Gustavus galloped forward to urge them on, with his artillery firing into the Imperial squares at point blank range. Just as the enemy began to waver, word spread wildly through the ranks that Gustavus was dead.

Their morale shaken, the Swedish troops pulled back. Bernard took command and ordered another advance, but at this moment Pappenheim returned with his horsemen and drove the Swedes back with a counterattack. The conflict now became a series of dogged hand to hand encounters with the nearest enemy in the smoky hell. Pappenheim was fatally wounded and, just before darkness fell, Bernard urged his exhausted men forward in a final charge that cleared the ditch, captured the artillery, and drove Pappenheim's cavalry from the field. Wallenstein withdrew toward Halle, leaving behind his artillery, baggage and 12,000 casualties. The Swedes lost 10,000 men. Both sides paraded regiments of only a few men at the next muster.

The death of Gustavus left the Protestant cause in chaos. His leadership had rallied the German princes, and raised morale with victory after victory over the powerful Imperialists. Now, there was no acknowledged leader. For a dozen years, Count Axel Oxenstierna became the de facto ruler of Sweden. Gustavus' gifted daughter, Christina, promoted royal extravagance as the queen, while her people lapsed into poverty. The war lost direction, but dragged on in fifteen more years of meaningless carnage. Only seven more Swedish regiments joined the fray during the remaining fifteen years of the conflict. The Swedish generals commanded mercenary troops recruited to replace the gruesome piles of corpses left on every battlefield. New units included 172 regiments of German horsemen and 123 of German footmen. Few men of other nationalities were now involved in the war.

An attempt was made at unity. Oxenstierna was elected to lead the League of Heilbronn, established in **March 1633** as a coalition of German principalities. He renewed the Franco-Swedish alliance, but despite his competent management, there was no clear objective for the campaigns that followed.

### *Operations in Bavaria* - 1634

Wallenstein was assassinated after conspiring with the Swedes to displace the Emperor. King Ferdinand of Hungary took nominal command of the Imperial Army, although Matthias Gallas was the actual field commander. The situation had crystallized sufficiently by the summer of 1634 for new campaigns to begin. Bernard of Saxe-Weimar took credit for the bloody victory at Lützen and demanded overall command of the Protestant armies. Rejected, he attempted to dominate the direction of the field operations. He and Swedish General Gustavus Horn marched from Augsburg with 20,000 men. Hoping to distract the Imperial Army from its advance on Regensburg, they moved toward Bohemia. Undaunted, Gallas took Regensburg and Donauwörth, then besieged **Nordlingen**, where he was joined by a Spanish army under Ferdinand.

205

Formed up for battle, the combined armies watched the Swedes approach on **6 September 1634**. The 15,000 Imperial troops of Gallas were entrenched on a hill, with the Spanish contingent of 20,000 men on a plain to their left. The Swedish Army of 16,000 infantry and 9,000 cavalry was ordered to pin the Hapsburg army and envelop its right flank.

Bernard advanced frontally against the Spaniards, holding them in position while Horn took his Swedes against the Imperialists on the hill. Their first charge was successful, but was thrown into confusion when the powder magazine of the captured artillery exploded. Ferdinand sent his unoccupied Spanish troops to counterattack and drove the Swedes from the hill. The Imperialists then joined the Spaniards in an attack on the isolated troops of Bernard, which turned and fled. The Swedish Army was in turn attacked. Nearly surrounded, the remnants of the finely-tuned army that had landed in Pomerania four years previously perished. Made prisoner were 4,000 men, while 17,000 more dead and wounded lay on the battlefield.

The rivalry between the houses of Bourbon and Hapsburg, which had been the underlying cause of many of the war's events, now came into the open. Cardinal Richelieu entered the war on 30 April 1635 with the Treaty of Compiegne, while the Imperialists and Protestant princes partially reconciled their differences with the Peace of Prague a month later. The war became a purely political one, fought by mercenary armies. France adopted the Swedish linear system, calling its squadrons "battalions", a term that persisted subsequently in European armies.

### *Swedish Mercenary Armies Ravage Germany and Bohemia* - 1635-1642

Several Swedish generals continued to lead mercenary armies, primarily in northern and eastern Germany. From August 1635, Johan Baner operated along the Elbe, defeating the Saxons at the Battle of Goldberg in November. He inflicted a crushing defeat upon them on **4 October 1636** at Wittstock. With the assistance of Lennart Torstensson, he lured the Saxons off of a hilltop, then struck them from three directions, putting them to flight. The two Swedish generals marched on Leipzig the following spring, but were halted by Gallas' Imperial army in Saxony.

Imperial forces, under Bavarian General von Geleen drove the Swedish Army away from the Elbe in 1638. Baner retired to the Oder. He barely escaped being trapped by Gallas and joined reinforcements under Count Karl Gustav Wrangel in Pomerania. During a miserable winter there, the Swedish Army suffered heavy losses to disease.

The following spring, Baner advanced into Saxony and beat John George at the Battle of Chemnitz on **14 April 1639**. He then invaded Bohemia, but was repulsed before Prague. The old campaigner was suffering from hard usage, along with the men he had led across Europe. Disease and famine took their toll. He died on 20 May 1641.

Lennart Torstensson took sole command after Baner's death. In the spring of 1642, he crossed the Elbe and besieged Leipzig, then retired to Breitenfeld when an Imperial army under Archduke Leopold William approached. As the Imperialists were forming a battle line on **2 November 1642**, Torstensson led a cavalry charge against their left flank, smashing it before it could deploy. He turned and struck the exposed flank of the Imperial center as the Swedish infantry charged frontally. The flight of their infantry left the Imperial cavalry on the right wing to receive the next attack. Many were captured before flight. [104]

## The Invasion of Denmark - 1643-1645

Following this Second Battle of Breitenfeld, Torstensson ravaged Bohemia and Moravia, but was recalled by the outbreak of war with Denmark. King Christian IV had issued an edict excluding recent Swedish acquisitions from the Sound Dues exemptions accorded Sweden by the Treaty of Knäred since 1613. Chancellor Oxenstierna ordered Torstensson to march north into Holstein. At the same time, another Swedish army was sent into Skäne. Both Jutland and Skåne were quickly overrun, for Denmark was unready for war.

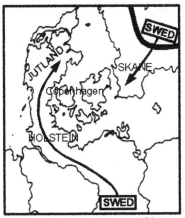

At sea, there was more parity. The Swedish Navy had 30 ships and frigates (plus a dozen smaller vessels), including three large flagships for the admirals commanding the divisions of the fleet:

**Flottan** (Amiral Klas Fleming)

FLAGSHIPS (GALLEONS)
*Scepter* - 56 (Amiral Fleming)
*Kronan* - 68 (Amiral Åke Ulfsparre)
*Arken* - 72 (Amiral Löjtnant Klas Bjelkenstjerna)

GALLEONS AND FRIGATES
*Draken* - 40
*Göteborg* - 36
*Svärdet, Stockholm, Samson* - 34
*Mars, Nyckeln* - 32
*Leoparden* - 30
*Raphael, Westervik, Mercurius* - 26
*Andromeda, Apollo* - 24
*Recompens, Katten* - 22
*Månen, Svanen, Tigern* - 18
*Jupiter, Regina, Enhörningen,*
    *Jägaren, Achilles*
*Gamla Fortuna, Westerviks Fortuna*
    *Smäländska Lejonet, Westgötha Lejonet*

**GALLEON** 34 guns
1600, 400 tons, 150 men,
12-12 pdrs, 20-6 pdrs,
2-3 pdrs

**FRIGATE** 18 guns
1600, 190 tons, 70 men,
2-12 pdrs, 14-6 pdrs,
2-3 pdrs    105

Because of Holland's desire to break the Danish bottleneck to the Baltic, she had encouraged Sweden to enlarge her fleet. Swedish shipbuilders were strongly influenced by the Dutch, for the Baltic abounded in the shoal waters common to the coast of Holland. Swedish ships acquired characteristics peculiar to the Baltic: broad-beamed, shallow draft construction, and mounting a unique spritsail instead of a triangular topsail when gaffsails replaced lateen sails on the mizzenmast.

A Swedish squadron was fitted out in Holland, but was intercepted off Blåvands Huk in May 1644 and scattered by the Danish Fleet. From Sweden, the main fleet sortied during the summer. On **11 July 1644** it met the Danish Fleet of equal size off the island of Femern, 50 kilometers north of Wismar. The rival admirals, Klas Fleming and Jorgen Wind, maneuvered and cannonaded for ten hours without losing a ship. The fleets finally separated without reaching a decision.

They met again in the autumn. Count Wrangel had 42 ships in company off the south cape of Laaland on 23 October when he encountered Pros Mund with 17 Danish ships. The unequal fight lasted for six hours. Mund was killed, and his squadron annihilated, only 3 ships escaping.

Coupled with the disasters on land, the Danish sea losses forced them to the Peace of Brömsebro in 1645, which awarded Sweden the western provinces of Jämtland, Härjedalen and Halland. Gotland and Ösel Island (off Livonia) also came into Sweden's possession, greatly improving her strategic maritime position. Sweden retained exemption from the Sound Dues. To Sweden's victorious fleet, by 1648 were added a number of mostly small vessels that were handy in the Baltic:

### GALLEONS AND FRIGATES

| | |
|---|---|
| *Äpplet* - 66 | *Salvator, Hjorten* - 22 |
| *Caesar* - 46 | *Falken* - 18 |
| *Wismar* - 34 | *Fama* - 16 |
| *Tre Kronor* - 32 | *Oxen* - 14 |
| *Hafsfrun* - 24 | *Höken* - 12 |

Torstensson resumed his operations in Bohemia. At the Battle of Jankau on **6 March 1645**, he defeated a force of Bavarians and Imperialists under Von Werth. Count Wrangel then relieved Torstensson, but was held up by a long siege at Brünn and forced to withdraw to Hesse to obtain provisions.

The Swedes returned in June 1648, this time under the command of Count Hans Cristoph Königsmarck. He laid siege to Prague and was preparing to assault the city when word arrived of the Peace of Westphalia. This agreement of **24 October 1648** left Sweden with Stettin, Wismar and Bremen. Swedish arms had gained a reputation as the most feared in Europe.

The cost had been terrible. The Swedes were charged with the destruction of 1,500 towns and 18,000 villages, probably an exaggeration. Germany did suffer 7,500,000 deaths, and the chaos of the war continued for many years. The malaise of German aggression in Europe's future may have had its roots in this inhuman war.

In Sweden, returning soldiers were forced to beg on the streets, with their families. Queen Christina apparently felt unable to cope with the distress and abdicated in 1654, ending the Vasa dynasty. The Count of the Palatinate was chosen to succeed her as Karl X Gustav, initiating the Palatine dynasty.

# THE STRUGGLE FOR THE BALTIC

*The First Northern War* - 1655-1660

Northern Europe was in turmoil. Germany was a wasteland, the Holy Roman Empire in tatters. The Poles had been given a respite by Sweden's distraction, and had gained strength. Karl X proposed to enlarge Sweden's holdings on the Baltic by invading Poland from Pomerania and simultaneously driving south from Livonia through Lithuania. During the war, the king would call upon 107 horse and dragoon units and 59 infantry regiments.

Sinclair, Ridderhielm, Oxenstierna, Drottning, Schönleben, Skåne, Trondheim,
    Lindtworm and Bohus Horse Regiments
Adelsfahne, Taube and Horn Finnish Horse Regiments
Riksskattmästere La Gardie, Fältmarskalk, Welling, Uhlefeld, Skytte, Toll, Vietinghoff,
    Wilhelm Yxkull, Renn, Taube, Budberg and Burmeister Baltic Horse Regiments

57 German mercenary horse regiments
7 Danish mercenary horse regiments

Småland and Skåne Dragoon Regiments
Behrens Finnish Dragoon Regiment
Radziwill, Korff, Riksskattmästere La Gardie, Uhlenbrock, Schwengel, Lagercrantz,
    and Mecken Baltic Dragoon Regiments

16 German mercenary dragoon regiments
1 Danish mercenary dragoon regiment

Livgarde Infantry Regiment
Rosenkrans, Fleming, Kühn, Halland, Skåne, Blekinge, Bohuslan and Trondheim
    Infantry Regiments
Radziwill, Greve Jacob, Uhrquardt, Fältmarskalk, Helmfeld, Bock, Schwengel, Gunther,
    La Coutiere, Sprengtport and Schultz Baltic Infantry Regiments

38 Germany mercenary infantry regiments
5 Danish mercenary infantry regiments
3 Scottish mercenary infantry regiments
3 English mercenary infantry regiments
3 Dutch mercenary infantry regiments
1 Polish mercenary infantry regiment [106]

In western Poland were 17,000 Swedish troops under Count Arvid von Wittenberg. Karl joined him during the summer of 1655 with 32,000 more, then advanced into central Poland. He captured Warsaw on 8 September, and Cracow soon afterward. At the same time, Russians and Swedes overran Lithuania. The Elector of Brandenburg thought he saw a chance to gain some of the spoils and occupied West Prussia. Karl immediately drove him back and besieged Berlin during the winter of 1655-6. The Treaty of Königsberg made Brandenburg a vassal of Karl X.

Atrocities and plundering by the Swedish troops in Poland caused a general uprising of the populace against them. Karl marched into Poland in the spring of 1656 with 10,000 Swedish troops. However, he was trapped by John Casimir against the Vistula and San Rivers, then surrounded by superior Polish forces near Sandomierz. With extraordinary skill and bravery, Karl X fought his way out of the encirclement, but lost most of his troops to avenging Polish partisans. He reached Brandenburg with only 4,000 men.

209

Accompanied by the 18,000 men of the Brandenburg Army, Karl returned to Poland in June 1656. The following month, he confronted 50,000 Poles at Warsaw and defeated them in a three day battle. However, the Elector of Brandenburg refused to venture farther into Poland, and Karl was forced by lack of numbers to end his advance. Other problems now appeared. Alarmed at the success of Sweden, which had become the most powerful nation in northern Europe, Holland had concluded a defensive alliance with Denmark in 1649. Although Karl X made a similar agreement with the Dutch in 1656, Austria, and particularly Russia, urged Denmark to take advantage of Sweden's involvement in Poland to reduce its empire. On the basis of their support, for Denmark's defenses were in poor shape, Frederik III declared war on **1 June 1657**. Brandenburg switched sides shortly afterward. Threatened by enemies on every side, Karl X had no choice but to cut short his Polish adventure and withdraw to Pomerania.

With only 6,000 troops, he marched westward from Stettin during July, having the tacit approval of the Duke of Holstein-Gottorp. Aided by Hamburg, he routed the Danish troops in Bremen and Holstein, then overran Jutland. Three thousand Danish remnants holed up in the fortress of Frederiksodde, where Swedish Count Wrangel assaulted them with 4,000 men on 24 October. Danish Marshal Bilde was killed and his men surrendered, leaving Karl in possession of the peninsula. A triple alliance of Brandenburg, Austria and Poland was concluded in **January 1658**. Troops of the Alliance threatened to trap Karl on Jutland, with a hostile Dutch fleet joining that of Denmark to deprive him of supplies and reinforcements from Sweden. Karl's next move was one of the most brilliant in the annals of war. He took the Swedish Army over the frozen Little Belt to Fyn, then crossed over the Great Belt by way of the islands of Taasinge, Langeland, Laaland and Falster. With Copenhagen now exposed to capture, the Danes agreed to the Treaty of Roskilde on 27 February, whereby Sweden gained possession of Skåne, Blekinge, Halland and the island of Bornholm, also the Norwegian provinces of Trondheim and Bohuslän.

However, the implementation negotiations were protracted and Karl threatened to invade Denmark again and annex it as three provinces of Sweden. The Dutch began to give support to the Danes, for they did not wish Sweden to have a monopoly in the Baltic. With the intent of gaining control of the Sound, Karl sent Count Wrangel to attack Copenhagen, Kronberg (Helsingör) and Christiania (Oslo). The Swedes besieged the capital from land and sea, but Frederik III rallied the citizens and presented Karl with the prospect of a long and bloody siege. The Elector of Brandenburg led troops of the Triple Alliance into Holstein, then Jutland. Kronberg fell in September before they could intervene, giving Sweden control of the Sound. [107]

Alarmed by events, Holland sent a fleet of 35 ships of the line to escort 30 transports bearing 2,000 Dutch troops to aid in lifting the siege of Copenhagen. In the early morning of 8 November 1658, Dutch Admiral Wassenaer took advantage of a northerly wind to sail into the Sound. At Helsingör, Count Wrangel awaited him with a Swedish fleet of 35 ships of the line and 8 frigates. A sharp battle developed at 0800, with heavy casualties on both sides. The Dutch lost several ships and 1,700 men while the Swedes lost 3 ships and a like number of men. Nevertheless, the Swedish Fleet drew off and Copenhagen was relieved. Numerous combats continued between the shallows flotillas of the antagonists throughout the Danish archipelago. Trondheim and Bornholm were recovered by Denmark, and the Danish population of Skåne rebelled. The three great maritime powers entered into the Hague Concert to impose a settlement based

210

on the Treaty of Roskilde. However, France refused to join Holland and England in an actual attack as it wished to enlist Sweden in reducing Hapsburg power on the Continent.

In **November 1659**, Dutch Admiral De Ruyter escorted 9,000 Danish troops to Fyn, where they defeated the Swedish garrison of 6,000 men under Philip of Sulzbach in the Battle of Nyborg. Karl X died in February 1660 and the nobles immediately sought peace. In May, the Treaty of Oliva settled things with Poland, Sweden retaining Livonia. Arranged with Denmark in June, the Treaty of Copenhagen formally confirmed Skåne as a province of Sweden. Sweden emerged as one of the largest nations of Europe, possessing the most powerful army on the continent. However, she was surrounded by states intent on reducing her empire.

### *The Scånian War* - 1675-1679

Karl XI succeeded his father as a four year old boy. His Regency was headed by Magnus Gabriel de la Gardie, an incompetent nobleman. The Regent did make an important alliance with France in 1672, as Louis XIV was planning expansion at his neighbors' expense and desired support from Europe's foremost power. However, Sweden's power had become illusory. Partly due to the poor financial condition of the nation following the long wars, De la Gardie allowed the Navy to decline and drastically reduced the supply of munitions to the Army.

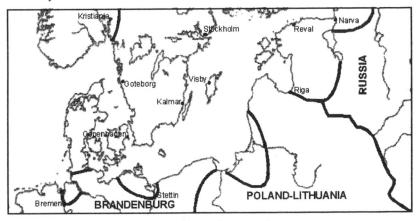

Theatre of the Northern Struggle

Denmark chafed at her losses. When the Franco-Swedish agreement was announced, she joined a coalition with Brandenburg, Holland and Austria to oppose them. Sweden played into their hands. From Pomerania, a force of 12,000 Swedish troops invaded Brandenburg. The Elector had greatly enlarged his army during recent years and defeated the invaders at the Battle of Fehrbellin on **28 June 1675**. He followed up by invading Pomerania, capturing Stettin, Stralsund and Griefswald. The reputation for invincibility of Swedish arms had been destroyed. Denmark was emboldened to march through Mecklenburg with an army to support Brandenburg. In September 1675, Danish King Christian V signed an agreement with Elector Frederick William to fight until they had prevailed at the expense of Sweden. [108]

211

The Swedish Navy was still based at Stockholm, far to the north of the disputed seas. Given little opportunity to exercise at sea, because of financial and climatic restrictions, the under-trained Swedish seamen were commanded by two men with no naval experience, Baron Creutz and Field Marshal Henrik Horn. The fleet included the largest warship in the world at the time - the *Kronan*, with 126 guns on four decks.

**Flottan** (Amiral Creutz)

SHIPS OF THE LINE

First Rate
*Kronan* - 126

Second Rate
*Nyckeln* - 88
*Svärdet* - 86
*Äpplet* - 84

Third Rate
*Victoria* - 76
*Hieronymus, Solen, Mars* - 72
*Jupiter* - 68
*Mercurius* - 66
*Saturnus, Draken* - 64
*Venus* - 62

Fourth Rate
*Wrangel* - 60
*Wismar* - 58
*Carolus, Caesar* - 56
*Hercules* - 54
*Svenska Lejonet* - 52
*Amarant* - 50
*Göteborg, Andromeda* - 48

**FIRST RATE** 126 gun ship of the line
1668, 1500 tons, 750 men,
12-36 pdrs, 16-30 pdrs, 40-24 pdrs,
2-18 pdrs, 36-12 pdrs, 20-6 pdrs

**SECOND RATE** 86 gun ship of the line
1650, 1300 tons, 650 men,
26-32 pdrs, 26-18 pdrs,
22-9 pdrs, 12-6 pdrs

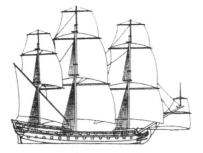

**THIRD RATE** 72 gun ship of the line
1650, 1100 tons, 500 men,
16-24 pdrs, 10-18 pdrs, 22-12 pdrs,
2-8 pdrs, 8-6 pdrs, 14-4 pdrs

**FOURTH RATE** 48 gun ship not of the line
1650, 600 tons, 200 men
22-18 pdrs, 20-9 pdrs, 6-6 pdrs

FRIGATES

Fifth Rate
*Spes* - 46
*Neptunas* - 44
*Månen, Falken* - 42
*Västervik* - 40
*Abraham* - 36
*Phoenix, Örnen* - 34
*Sundsvall, Fredrika Amalia, Hjorten* - 32

Sixth Rate
*Uttern* - 24

SLOOPS

Jakt
*Jägaren* - 26
*Postiljon* - 22

**FIFTH RATE** 32 gun frigate
1650, 300 tons, 120 men,
8-6 pdrs, 14-4 pdrs,
10-2 pdrs          109

The Swedish Navy had nominal command of the sea, for Brandenburg had a tiny fleet and the Danes had but 19 small ships of the line. However, the Dutch were quick to send reinforcements under some of their best admirals. The Danish admiral, Niels Juel, was a far more competent and enterprising sea captain than the Swedish landlubbers. In **May 1676**, he descended upon Gotland and captured it, unopposed by the larger Swedish Fleet. On 3-4 June, Baron Creutz finally came up with the Danes off Jasmund, on the island of Rügen. By this time, the Danes had been reinforced by Dutch warships. The battle developed towards evening and continued fitfully throughout the night. Both fleets attempted to outmaneuver the other and there was little gunfire, thus few casualties. About midday on 4 June, they separated without conclusion.

Dutch Admiral Cornelius Tromp took command of the allied fleet. He pursued the Swedes as they sailed northward along the Swedish coast on **6 June 1676**. With 19 small Danish ships of the line, 10 Dutch ships of the line, and 10 frigates, Tromp was slightly superior to the Swedes. He overtook them as they passed close to the island of Öland. Tromp achieved the weather gage by daring to sail through shoal water inshore of the Swedes. Creutz tried to break through the allied line just ahead of the Dutch flagship, *Christianus V*, in order to take the enemy line between two fires.

However, in the strong westerly crosswind, the monstrous *Kronan* capsized with the admiral aboard, throwing the Swedish van into confusion. Tromp swooped down on the melee, sinking 4 Swedish ships of the line. The Swedes suffered 2,000 casualties and 600 prisoners, the allies few. 110

Without the support of the Swedish Fleet, the troops in Germany could not be supplied. Pomerania, Bremen and Verden were overrun and Wismar was captured. While General Gyldenlöve took an army of Norwegian troops into Västergotland, King Christian V crossed the Öresund to invade Skåne, where the Danish peasants rose up to greet him. Harassed by Danish partisans, the Swedish Army was in danger of being overwhelmed.

213

Passive to this time, young King Karl XI suddenly took charge of the government in the crisis and moved energetically to save the nation. In Halland, he threw back Gyldenlöve, then turned to face the Danes in Skåne. At Lund, across the Öresund from Copenhagen, he confronted Christian V in the autumn of 1676. His army was armed principally with obsolete weapons left over from the Thirty Years War. However, the troops had been issued their first true uniforms:

> **Infantry** wore a long coat of gray (9 regts.), red (7 regts.), yellow (3 regts.), blue (3 regts.) or green (2 regts.) derived from the coats of arms of the home district of each regiment. A few regiments wore brown or green coats not symbolic of a particular district. Men wore a low fur busby with a bag of the coat color, while officers wore a black, wide-brimmed hat.
>
> **Cavalry** wore a silver breastplate and cutaway coats of regimental color. The head was covered with a broad hat.

In a long, bloody battle, both sides lost about 10,000 men, but the Swedes retained the battleground and the Danes had to retreat. Determined operations during the following year drove the Danes from Skåne. With new leaders, the Swedish Fleet moved to threaten the Danish home islands. Admiral Sjöblad stood off the south coast of Moen Island on **11 June 1677** with 7 ships of the line, but was intercepted by a Danish squadron of 9 ships of the line and 2 frigates under Niels Juel. The Danes boarded 5 of Sjöblad's ships during a decisive action. The following month, the Swedes returned, this time with 25 ships of the line and 11 frigates under Field Marshal Henrik Horn. With his flag in *Victoria*, Horn approached Kjöge Bight on a northwesterly course. He intended to defeat the Danish Fleet before the expected arrival of another Dutch squadron. Niels Juel, on a parallel course in *Christianus Quintus*, lead 19 ships of the line and 6 frigates. An independent fight developed around the Swedish *Draken*, which went aground at 0700. The bulk of the two fleets turned in succession and engaged in a running battle to the southeast. Three Swedish ships of the line sank and 7 others were captured. Losses of 3,000 prisoners and 1,500 dead and wounded contrasted with Danish casualties of only 350 men and 4 damaged ships.

This disastrous naval battle gave Denmark control of the western Baltic, precluding any Swedish attack on Zealand. The lost territories in northern Germany could not be reclaimed. Nevertheless, Sweden had preserved control of her peninsula. France sponsored the Treaty of Saint-Germain in 1679, by which Brandenburg returned Pomerania to Sweden. Together with the Treaty of Fontainebleau involving Denmark, France preserved a strong Swedish state in the Baltic.

The exactions of the war caused hardships in Sweden. Karl XI took firm control, permanently reducing the power of the nobles and making himself an absolute monarch. A skilled administrator and financier, he began to strengthen the Army. The nation was divided into military districts responsible to raise and train territorial regiments at the disposal of the king in time of war. This system of "military tenure" remained in force into the Twentieth Century. To position the Navy closer to the usual scene of conflict, he initiated construction of a major naval base at Karlskrona in 1680. Strife was still in prospect, for both Brandenburg and Denmark had emerged strong from the Scånian War. Karl XI was inept at foreign affairs, which he left to his advisors. In April 1697, Denmark sent emissaries to Moscow to begin negotiations against Sweden. When Karl died later in the year, Sweden was again being threatened. [111]

214

# GREAT NORTHERN WAR

When fifteen year old Karl XII succeeded his dead father in 1697, Sweden's enemies perceived that his inexperience and imperiousness should provide them opportunity to end his nation's dominance of the Baltic. During the spring, Denmark, Russia and Poland-Saxony joined in a "Great Northern League" to wrest territory from Sweden. Sweden faced formidable foes. The Danes mustered an army of 25,000 men, Brandenburg had 30,000, Poland-Saxony could field 30,000, while enigmatic Russia possessed unknown resources. The young king wisely sought the advice of experienced military officers. General Karl Rehnskjold emerged as the best Swedish commander. He was placed in charge of the most important operations, at first with King Karl by his side.

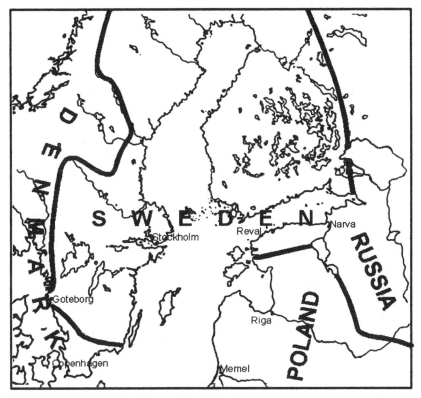

Swedish Empire

Word of the first moves by the Great Northern League reached Karl XII on 6 March. He left Stockholm, never to return. The Swedish forces in the Baltic provinces were sufficient to hold out for some time, but he could not campaign in the east with a potent enemy in his rear. Realizing that it was the old nemesis, Denmark, at the center of the conspiracy against Sweden, he went to Skåne to prepare for a crossing of the Sound.

The *Indelta* system of "military tenure", initiated by his father, provided Karl XII with a home army of 36,000 men. There were also 23,500 paid professional soldiers garrisoning the 90 forts and castles of the Swedish Empire.

Livgarde Dragoon Regiment
Kruse, Ulfsparre, Gyllenstierna, Ramsay, Wrangel, Apoloff, Hierta and Kirchbach
    Cavalry Regiments
Rehbinder Finnish Cavalry Regiment

Stenbock, Barnekow and Von der Nath Dragoon Regiments
Knorring Finnish Dragoon Regiment
Albedyll, Velling, Schlippenbach Baltic Dragoon Regiments

12 German and 1 French mercenary dragoon regiments

Bärenhjelm, Löwenhaupt, Putbus, Köhler, Skytte, Sinclair, Krusenstierna, Stjeinastrale,
    Maijdell, Rohr, Wessmanny, Morath, Bjornberg, Noth, Patkull, Hamilton, Halland,
    Ostskåne, Västskåne, Ribbing, Horn and Beckern Infantry Regiments
Tiesenhausen, Lode and Gyllenström Finnish Infantry Regiments
La Gardie, Vellingk, Nieroth, Liewen, Stackelberg, Zöge, Mellin, Schwengel, Pahlen,
    Rehbinder, Mengden, Buddenbrock and Baner Baltic Infantry Regiments

4 German, 4 Saxon, 1 French and 1 Swiss mercenary infantry regiments [112]

The men of the home army trained once a month with their local company, then gathered once a year with their district regiment. The system produced a force of adequately trained, loyal and patriotic troops, but one which was slow to mobilize because of the scattered locations of the units. Infantry and cavalry regiments were composed of two battalions armed with standard weapons:

**INFANTRY REGIMENT** - 1200 men
2 battalions
    4 companies
    17.3 mm, 4 kg

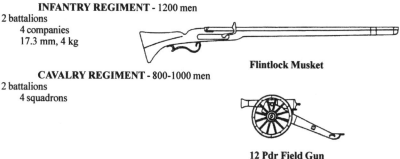

**Flintlock Musket**

**CAVALRY REGIMENT** - 800-1000 men
2 battalions
    4 squadrons

**12 Pdr Field Gun**
121 mm, 3000 lbs, 12 lb ball,
1500 yds max, 700 yds eff

Infantrymen were well equipped with new flintlock muskets mounting bayonets. Although the bayonet was introduced by France to eliminate the pike late in the Seventeenth Century, the Swedish Army retained a few pikemen. Mobility was improved by subdividing the mass of troops into subordinate divisions, brigades, regiments and battalions. Infantry tactics had changed little since the Thirty Years War. Ranks had been reduced to four, with the rear ranks loading the muskets for the first two. After approaching to within 40 meters of the enemy line, the rear two ranks would fire a volley over the kneeling men in front. The front two ranks would hold their fire until the last moment, then follow their volley with a bayonet charge - the feared Swedish "cold steel".

216

Heavy cavalry continued to wield a long, straight sword, although Karl XII initially prohibited the use of firearms on horseback and abolished all armor. He trained his troopers to charge at full speed. Flintlock pistols were re-issued just before the invasion of Russia in 1708. Dragoons carried flintlock carbines. Freed from its infantry-support role, the Swedish cavalry gained much mobility and retained its reputation as among the best in Europe. It played an important part in each Swedish military operation.

Howitzers and mortars had been introduced into European armies, but England and Holland were the primary exponents of these shell guns. Most armies relied upon ball and canister fired from 4, 6, 8, 12, 18, 24 and 36 pounder field guns, of which there were an average of 4 per 1,000 infantrymen in the Swedish Army. Since the time of Gustavus Adolphus, the artillery of Sweden had steadily grown in importance to battle tactics. [113]

A standard uniform had replaced the myriad of regimental uniforms in 1687. The Life Guards received their own resplendent uniform in 1699.

**Life Guards** wore a dark blue cutaway coat with yellow facings, waistcoat and stockings. Officers had gold braid trim on the coat, but no facings. All wore a black tricorn.

**Infantry** had a dark blue cutaway coat with facings of regimental color, yellow waistcoat, yellow stockings, and a black tricorn.

**Artillery** wore the infantry uniform, but without facings.

**Cavalry** had a buff (later dark blue) cutaway coat, facings of regimental colors, buff trousers, black boots and tricorn.

Karl XII inherited the fine fleet his father had built. Sweden also possessed an ocean-going merchant fleet of 300 vessels. Swedish seamen were less experienced than those of Denmark, and lacked a morale-building maritime tradition. Most of the naval officers had served in foreign navies and were unfamiliar with Baltic conditions.

**Swedish Fleet** (Amiral Wachtmeister)

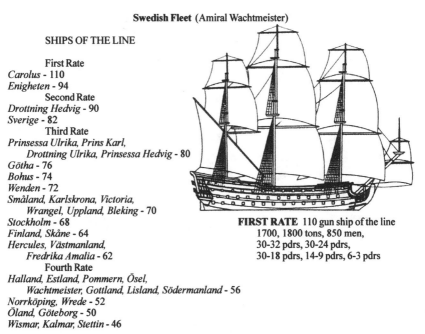

SHIPS OF THE LINE

First Rate
*Carolus* - 110
*Enigheten* - 94
Second Rate
*Drottning Hedvig* - 90
*Sverige* - 82
Third Rate
*Prinsessa Ulrika, Prins Karl,*
    *Drottning Ulrika, Prinsessa Hedvig* - 80
*Götha* - 76
*Bohus* - 74
*Wenden* - 72
*Småland, Karlskrona, Victoria,*
    *Wrangel, Uppland, Bleking* - 70
*Stockholm* - 68
*Finland, Skåne* - 64
*Hercules, Västmanland,*
    *Fredrika Amalia* - 62
Fourth Rate
*Halland, Estland, Pommern, Ösel,*
    *Wachtmeister, Gottland, Lisland, Södermanland* - 56
*Norrköping, Wrede* - 52
*Öland, Göteborg* - 50
*Wismar, Kalmar, Stettin* - 46

**FIRST RATE** 110 gun ship of the line
1700, 1800 tons, 850 men,
30-32 pdrs, 30-24 pdrs,
30-18 pdrs, 14-9 pdrs, 6-3 pdrs

# FRIGATES

**Fifth Rate**
*Wachtmeister* - 48
*Phoenix* - 44
*Reval, Vyborg* - 40
*Ebenezer* - 36
*Svarte Örn* - 32

**Sixth Rate**
*Jarramas, Örnens Pris* - 30
*Falken* - 26
*Välkomsten, Rushenfeldt* - 24
*Postiljon* - 22
*Anclam, Kisken*

**SECOND RATE** 80 gun ship of the line
1700, 1400 tons, 650 men,
26-32 pdrs, 24-18 pdrs,
24-9 pdrs, 6-6 pdrs

**FOURTH RATE** 56 gun ship not of the line
1700, 1000 tons, 400 men,
24-24 pdrs, 24-12 pdrs,
8-6 pdrs

**THIRD RATE** 62 gun ship of the line
1700, 1200 tons, 500 men,
26-24 pdrs, 26-12 pdrs,
10-6 pdrs

**FIFTH RATE** 40 gun frigate
1700, 500 tons, 200 men,
20-12 pdrs, 20-6 pdrs

**SIXTH RATE** 22 gun frigate
1700, 350 tons, 150 men,
22-6 pdrs                    114

## SLOOPS

Snows - five
Jakts - three
Bombs - four

218

## Invasion of Denmark - 1699-1700

Denmark's Frederik IV invaded Schleswig in April 1699 with 20,000 troops, which the Duke of Holstein-Gottorp could oppose with only 5,000. Karl XII mobilized 2 infantry and 2 cavalry regiments to send to his aid. On **21 October 1699**, under escort of 12 ships of the line and 4 frigates, they landed at Peenemunde and joined garrison troops already in Pomerania to form a mobile army of 7,000 men under General Nils Gyllenstierna.

Hoping to free his fleet for operations in the eastern Baltic, Karl XII awaited the arrival of an Anglo-Dutch fleet in the spring of 1700. On the Norwegian border, 10,000 men were mobilized, with another 16,000 men formed up in southern Sweden prepared to operate against Denmark or Poland-Saxony. The Danish Fleet attempted to entice the Swedish Fleet into battle before it was reinforced, but the Swedes stayed in port. A landing was made at Göteborg to interpose between Sweden and its approaching allies, but the Danes were repulsed. Dutch and Hanoverian troops came to the aid of the Duke of Holstein-Gottorp, allowing Karl XII to concentrate on affairs with the Baltic powers.

The fleet of 13 Dutch and 12 English warships arrived off Göteborg on **9 June 1700**. Karl XII sailed from Karlskrona on 16 June and the allies moved south to the Sound to meet him. The allied commanders refused to subordinate their fleet to the inexperienced Wachtmeister, so the two fleets operated by consultation. With the Swedish Fleet at sea, Niels Juel skillfully placed his fleet of 40 Danish ships of the line in the Sound between the cooperating allied fleets, in a position where it would be difficult to attack. Aboard the *Carolus*, Karl's problem became one of effecting a junction with the allies.

**Swedish Fleet** (Amiral Wachtmeister)

Second Squadron (Van) (Amiral C. Ankarstjerna)
*Småland, Sverige, Hercules, Halland, Estland, Västmanland, Enigheten* (flag), *Karlskrona, Wismar, Pommern, Prinsessa Ulrika, Bohus, Kalmar*

First Squadron (Center) (General Amiral H. Wachtmeister)
*Finland, Prins Karl, Götha, Ösel, Fredrika Amalia, Carolus* (flag), *Drottning Hedvig, Wachtmeister, Norrköping, Gottland, Victoria, Wrangel, Wrede*

Third Squadron (Rear) (Amiral F. Taube)
*Öland, Uppland, Wenden, Stettin, Skåne, Drottning Ulrika* (flag), *Stockholm, Lisland, Göteborg, Södermanland, Prinsessa Hedvig, Bleking*

To evade the waiting Danish Fleet until the allied fleets could rendezvous in overwhelming strength, Karl XII ignored his admirals and sent all but the heaviest ships through the *Flintrännan*, the treacherous flats close to the Swedish shore. Passing through on 3-4 July, they joined the Dutch-English fleet, but nothing came of the venture because of the lack of cooperation among the allies. Niels Juel retired to Copenhagen, where Swedish bomb vessels harassed his ships with a desultory fire. Four thousand Swedish troops, under General Karl Rehnskjold, sailed at 0700 on 24 July and rendezvoused with the combined fleets. Feinting at Ringsted, the convoy hove to offshore nearby and landed the troops, with the fleet bombarding the few Danish defenders. The rest of the Swedish army was then ferried across in waves and, by 2 August, some 10,000 men were ashore. The 5,000 Danish troops on Zealand withdrew to Copenhagen, while the allies closed in on land and sea to capture the capital and the fleet. Frederick IV quickly asked for peace, saving his fleet. Karl XII was now free to campaign in the east, but with the nagging worry of that intact Danish fleet in a potentially dangerous position to his rear.

### Campaign in the Baltic Provinces - 1700-1704

Poland-Saxony had invaded Livonia on 11 February 1700, but General Dahlberg was prepared to defend Riga and Augustus II had to halt to await siege artillery. In May, the main Saxon Army was defeated by troops under Major General Maidel and was forced back over the Dvina River. However, in mid-July, the Saxons got 17,000 men over the river, forcing General Vellingk away from Riga, which was placed under siege. The Danish capitulation freed Swedish troops for operations in Livonia. Augustus II pulled back over the river and appealed for Russian help.

Six Swedish ships of the line escorted transports carrying 5,000 men across the Baltic. Karl XII, in the flagship *Västmanland*, directed their landing at Pernau on **6 October 1700**. Another 5,000 followed shortly. Gathering garrison troops to form an army of 11,000, Karl began moving eastward on 13 November. Czar Peter the Great had invaded Ingria with 40,000 men in August, and initiated a siege of Narva on 4 October. General Horn was tenaciously holding the city with a garrison of only 2,000 men. Under the direction of General Rehnskjold, the Swedish Army stormed the Russian camp on the morning of 20 November, inflicting 8-10,000 casualties, and sending the rest streaming into Russia. The Swedes captured 140 new cannon, but the 2,000 casualties they sustained were nothing compared to the losses they suffered from disease after occupying the polluted Russian camp. Karl XII played his subordinate role well and soon took full direction of the war. He set up a string of outposts to the east to keep the Russians at bay while he tended to the Saxons.

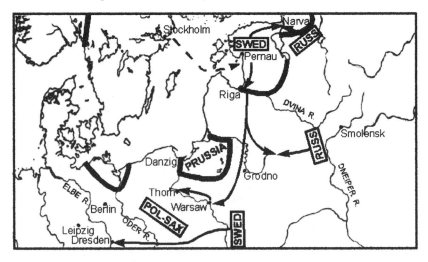

Campaigns in the East

220

Augustus II had been besieging Riga for almost a year, and now began raiding into Livonia. On **17 June 1701**, Karl moved swiftly southward from Dorpat with his main army and relieved Riga. Although 10,000 Russians were marching to their support, General Steinau's 9,000 Polish-Saxon troops were still dispersed along the Dvina River when boats, carrying hay bales to stop bullets, emerged out of a smoke screen on 9 July. The pioneers were followed by 6,000 Swedish troops, who established a bridgehead. When the Livonian troops of General Paijkull failed to throw them back, General Steinau ordered a retreat. The Swedish cavalry could not get across the river for pursuit. Not until the end of the month did Karl XII learn that Steinau had withdrawn to Kovno in Poland. The Swedes made Courland their base of operations, for from Riga they could prevent a junction of Russian and Polish-Saxon forces, invade Poland, yet keep an eye on the Baltic provinces.

*Invasion of Poland* - 1702-1706

Unwisely, in the light of future events, Karl XII decided that Poland-Saxony was more dangerous to Sweden than was Russia. In April 1702, he followed Augustus II into Poland. Polish-Saxon forces concentrated at Cracow. The Saxon Army of 22,300 men faced 16,230 Swedes at the Battle of Kliszow on **9 July 1702**. It was another classic Polish-Swedish conflict, with the cavalry playing a prominent role. The 21 Swedish cavalry squadrons (2,100 men) outfought the 34 Polish-Saxon squadrons. Swedish casualties of 1,500 were more than offset by the 2,000 lost by the enemy.

After wintering in Warsaw, Karl XII marched westward on 18 April 1703 and surrounded a force of 6,000 Saxon infantry at Thorn, whose cavalry had been detached to Pultusk. Seeing an opportunity to free Poland of Saxon control, the Polish nobles formed a Confederation. Its army assisted the 8,000 Swedish troops of General Rehnskjold in driving the Saxons out of Poland. Thorn capitulated on 4 October.

Russia now took a hand, helping Augustus II to recapture Warsaw in August 1704. Other Russian forces pressed through Courland to aid the Saxons. Swedish General Lewenhaupt defeated them at the Battle of Jakobstadt in Lithuania on 18 July. He was then charged with keeping the Russians out of Poland while Karl XII and General Rehnskjold moved westward from Lemberg toward Warsaw. Augustus II did not wait for them, but fled with 3,000 Saxons. Failing to cross the Vistula in time to trap him, Karl XII turned to pursue another force of 4,000 Saxons under General Schulenburg. He caught it at Punitz, near the border, on 28 October 1704, but the Saxons escaped.

Leaving General Rehnskjold to supervise 10,000 men spread along the western Polish frontier, Karl XII turned to attack the Russians while their streams and bogs were frozen by the cold. He left Warsaw on 29 December 1705 with 20,000 men and surprised a League force of 30,000 men at Grodno on **15 January 1706**. The enemy force broke up, the Russian troops escaping into the Ukraine. Augustus lead the Polish-Saxon contingent westward to attack Rehnskjold. A thaw prevented a Swedish campaign into Courland.

Before Augustus could take him in rear, General Rehnskjold marched against a Saxon army twice his size. At Fraustadt on 3 February 1706, the Swedish infantry pinned a larger force of Saxon infantry while the strong Swedish cavalry struck both Saxon wings in a classic double envelopment. Two hours of fighting routed the Saxons with heavy losses. Karl XII rewarded Rehnskjold with a promotion to Field Marshal.

221

*Invasion of Saxony* - 1706

The king decided to drive the pesky Saxons out of the war. On 7 July 1706, he broke camp at Jaroslav in Volhynia and marched surreptitiously westward, passing through Silesia during the last week of August. The remnants of the Saxon Army fled before him into Thuringia, and he reached Leipzig on 4 September. With Swedish troops approaching the capital of Dresden, the Saxon Council sent emissaries, which began negotiations to end hostilities. Augustus II relinquished his throne. The Treaty of Altranstadt on **24 September 1706** broke up the Great Northern League and ended Catholic persecution of Protestants in the Holy Roman Empire. [115]

*War with Russia* - 1701-1709

As the war with Poland-Saxony drug on, many in Sweden began to doubt the wisdom of campaigning in Poland while leaving Russia to build up its strength. Peter the Great was initially limited to maritime commerce through Archangelsk. Sweden had sent 7 sloops of war into the White Sea during the summer of 1701. They cruised the sea, burning coastal villages and capturing Russian fishing vessels before returning home on 21 July. Czar Peter ordered construction of small warships in the primitive shipyards of Archangelsk. Some of the vessels were moved to Lake Onega, then portaged to Lake Ladoga.

The Swedish flotillas on the lake, under Admiral Nummers, were defeated in several actions by squadrons of sloops of war and gunboats. In conjunction with the lake offensive, Peter invaded Ingria. General Schlippenbach opposed him with 8,000 men, but was defeated on **7 January 1702** at the Battle of Errestfer. On 27 June, 18 boats carrying 700 Russian soldiers surprised the Swedish squadron of 3 brigantines, 3 galleys and 2 boats on Lake Ladoga and sent them fleeing. Defending Ingria, General Krongiort's 7,000 men were beaten at Hummselsdorf on 18 July, laying the Neva Valley open to the Russians. The lake squadron was defeated again on 7 September, when 20 Russian boats attacked them near Kexholm. Sweden was unable to prevent Russian acquisition of Ingria and the great lakes.

Slowly, Peter the Great was fulfilling his dream of acquiring a "window to the west", taking advantage of the respite accorded him by Karl XII's campaign against Augustus II. Swedish access to northern Russia and Lake Ladoga was blocked when the fortress of Noteburg, at the source of the Neva, was captured by the Russians on 2 October 1702. The mouth of the Neva was secured the following spring. In May 1703, boarding parties captured the Swedish brigantines *Astrel*-14 and *Hayden*-10 in the Neva. The island of Kotlin, at the head of the Gulf of Finland, was occupied. By the end of 1703, Russia had achieved its outlet to the Baltic.

To broaden the corridor, Peter tried to capture Lake Peipus. A Swedish squadron of 4 sloops of war had seized control of the lake in 1702. Reinforcements increased the Swedish flotilla to 14 jakts and sloops by the spring of 1703. Commanded by Commodore Löschen af Herzfeldt, the flotilla encountered 90-100 Russian boats, carrying 5,000 men, on **7 August 1703**. Displaying disdain for Russian fighting qualities, he waded into the swarm, destroying 20 boats. The jakt *Vivat*-4 was sent to scout out the Russian anchorage, but was surrounded by enemy boats and blown up. Then, on 17 May 1704, Russian shore batteries destroyed most of the flotilla when it was trapped by a boom constructed across the mouth of its river base.

222

Russia now controlled a strip of the Baltic shoreline, which Peter immediately put to good use. Fortifying Kotlin Island, he established a naval base at Kronstadt, with shipyards at his new capital of St. Petersburg on the nearby mainland. By 1705, Peter possessed a squadron of 9 ships of the line, 4 brigs and 32 smaller warships. For the first time, the Swedish Navy had to face a second major fleet in the Baltic. Sweden had made a serious mistake in not constructing a naval base on the Gulf of Finland.

A squadron of 7 Swedish ships of the line and 5 frigates appeared off Kronstadt in **June 1705**, challenging the young Russian Navy to a fight. However, Peter had ordered his fleet commander, General-Admiral Fedor Apraksin, not to accept battle until the navy was fully ready. Eight Russian frigates were anchored between Kronstadt and Kotlin, but were protected by a boom, shore batteries, and a line of gunboats. Two Swedish attacks on 26 June were repulsed. The following day, the Swedes bombarded the anchorage, but with little effect. The anxious Swedes returned for a second bombardment on 3 July, with similar ineffectiveness, and an attempted landing on 2 August was thrown back. Sweden was reduced to blockading the mouth of the Neva, unable to make use of her naval superiority. [116]

Karl XII gathered his land forces to deal with Russia. His troops were employed in garrisoning the widespread empire:

Sweden
Field Army
9,000 men
Reserve and Garrison Troops
17,000 men

West Pomerania
Field Army (Karl XII)
32,000 men
Reserve and Garrison Troops
11,000 men

Baltic Provinces
Field Army (Gen. Lewenhaupt)
11,400 men
Reserve and Garrison Troops
11,000 men

Finland
Field Army (Gen. Lybeker)
14,000 men

Karl XII took his army across the Oder River on **7 September 1707** and made camp at Slupca, east of the Warta River. There, 9,000 fresh troops from Pomerania joined him. His army now contained:

7100 heavy cavalry
9600 dragoons
14200 infantry
1500 Tovarich (Valloches)
10000 other troops

The Tovarich, Polish light cavalry, were excellent reconnaissance troops. They kept Karl apprised of the Russian positions and movements. Thus, when Prince Menshikov was found at Warsaw, his retirement to a planned defensive position at Pultusk, on the Narew, was duly reported. On 28-30 December,

223

Karl crossed the frozen Vistula between Plock and Thorn, well to the north of the Russians. He advanced in three columns, the Polish-Lithuanian forces to the north of his main army, with the Valloches and dragoons providing a flank guard to the south. A forced march through the Masurian marshes to Grodno surprised the enemy, turning his position without fighting. The Polish Crown Army was still cooperating with Russia. To support the Polish-Lithuanian Commonwealth troops of Stanislaus Leszczynski, Karl attached to them 8,000 German mercenaries at Danzig, Posen, Elbing as well as Pomerania, under the command of General Krassow.

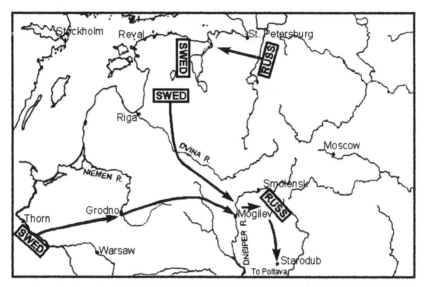

Campaign in Russia

At the end of **June 1708**, General Lewenhaupt started south with 7,500 infantry and 5,000 cavalry to join his king. General Stromberg was placed in charge of the 10,000 men left in Livonia. He was to cooperate with General Lybeker's 14,000 man army of Finland in driving General Apraksin's Russian troops from St. Petersburg. A fleet of 22 Swedish warships appeared off the coast of Ingria in support. However, using his interior lines of operation, Apraksin attacked the divided Swedish forces in turn. He beat Stromberg at Wesenberg in Estonia before Lybeker could cross the Neva on 29 August. Lybeker accepted exaggerated reports of Russian strength, lifted his siege of St. Petersburg, and sailed for Sweden with the Fleet.

The Tovarich found the Russian main army entrenched at Gorki. Karl XII paused at Mogilev on 9 July, delaying his crossing of the Dneiper River until 5 August. He marched southeast for a few kilometers to draw the Russians from their position, but could not leave the Dneiper far behind until Lewenhaupt reached him with supplies. At Cherikov, he first encountered large numbers of Russian troops on 21 August. Two days later, he turned northeast toward Smolensk. Peter the Great formed up 4,000 dragoons and 9,000 infantry behind a marsh shielding the town, then attacked through a thick mist on 1 September. They inflicted 800 casualties on the Swedes during two days of fighting, the first time Russian troops had stood firm before Swedish steel.

Peter initiated a series of rear guard actions, forcing the Swedes to deploy, then retiring before battle was joined, burning everything of use to them. The sharp counterattacks displayed to the Swedes that the new Russian Army, created by Peter while Karl XII was campaigning against Augustus II, was far more formidable than that he had possessed when the war began.

The Russian border was crossed on 11 September. Lewenhaupt did not reach the Dneiper until 21 September, by which time provisions were in short supply in the main army, for Peter's "scorched earth" policy was depriving the Swedes of the plunder they expected. Karl XII decided to diverge from the Smolensk-Moscow route to forage for provisions. An elite force of 1,000 cavalry and 2,000 infantry, under General Lagercrona, was sent south on 14 September to capture Starodub, capital of Severia. Peter followed with his main army, but Lagercrona diverged from the direct route and did not reach Starodub until after the Russians had occupied it.

Further bad news reached the king. On 29 September, the Russians won their first battle with a Swedish army, defeating Lewenhaupt at the Doza River, and forcing him to retire away from Karl. The ragged Swedish troops marched on, hoping to be afforded winter quarters and supplies by Mazeppa's Cossacks in the Ukraine. Lewenhaupt finally got round to the main army with only 7,000 of his men left. The combined forces broke over the Desna River at Mezin on 2 November, against increasing Russian opposition. The determined Swedes beat the Russians to Romny and went into winter quarters under Mazeppa's protection.

Karl XII belatedly broke camp at the end of April and moved southward. Hopes for cooperation with the Poles, Tartars or Turks faded, and Swedish morale began to suffer as Russian harassment increased.

**Poltava** - 28 June 1709

Karl XII advanced on Voronezh, stopping on 2 May to invest the Russian fortress of Poltava. Czar Peter marched to its relief with an army of 80,000 men (61 infantry battalions, 23 cavalry regiments, 72 cannon). The Swedish Army was seriously short of ammunition. Karl's problems were compounded by a ball through his foot on 17 June, followed by a debilitating infection. Recovering, he issued orders for an attack on the Russian camp, knowing he could fight only a short battle.

**Swedish Army** (Field Marshal Rehnskjold)

Infantry (Gen. Lewenhaupt)
24 battalions - 9,000 men
Cavalry (Gen. Creutz)
41 squadrons - 13,000 men

Most of the 30 cannon were left with the baggage trains as there was sufficient ammunition to supply only 4 of them in action.

The Swedes advanced at 0400 on 28 June. They encountered two lines of redoubts barring their way to the Russian camp. The six main fortifications blocked a passage, while the approaches were segmented by four more redoubts projecting forward from the main line. The Swedes soon took the first two redoubts, but the third resisted stoutly, devouring six infantry battalions. At 0900, reports were received that the main Russian Army was advancing. A heavy double line of 18,000 infantrymen appeared, supported by 72 cannon.

Rehnskjold tried to boost the morale of his weary troops by attacking first, but a gap developed between his wings and the Russians poured into it. The single line of Swedish infantry began to waver, and the cavalry on the right wing was forced back. The battle was over in half an hour, with the Swedish infantry annihilated. Exemplifying courage and leadership, Karl XII steadied his remaining cavalry into an orderly retreat. The Russians pursued slowly, for their infantry was badly shaken by their encounter with the best troops in the world. Some 6,901 Swedish lads lay dead on the battlefield, and 2,760 were made prisoner. Russian casualties amounted to 4,635 dead and wounded. A watershed in the European power struggle had been passed.

Karl intended to retire to Poland with his remaining 16,000 men, mostly cavalry. However, his officers convinced him that the plan was impossible and persuaded him to escape to Turkey with the Cossack leaders while they led as much of the army to the Crimea as they could. Unfortunately, with Karl XII dead, General Lewenhaupt surrendered the army when a much smaller force of 6,000 Russian cavalry and 2,000 Cossacks appeared on a nearby height. Sweden's fine army was gone and the empire was in peril. [117]

### Loss of the Swedish Empire - 1709-1714

Peter marched westward into Poland, restoring Augustus II to his throne by the end of 1709. Other Russian forces occupied Karelia, Estonia and Livonia, seizing Vyborg, Reval, Elbing and Riga. They immediately began construction of a second naval base at Reval. Russia now had complete control of the Gulf of Finland. A fleet was sent to sea in May 1713 under command of General-Admiral Feodor Apraksin. He cruised the coast of Finland, but finding no Swedish ships, retired to Reval. Commodore Raab took a squadron of 3 Swedish Fourth Rates (2-56s, 1-46) to reconnoiter Reval. He anchored at Hogland during the night of 10 July, but at 0300 discovered the Russian Fleet approaching under full sail, and was forced to take shelter under the guns of Helsingfors. A coastal flotilla of 200 gunboats later assisted the Russian Fleet in the capture of Helsingfors, Åbo, and other places on the Finnish coast.

Determined to have its share of the spoils, Denmark took Schleswig and Bremen-Verden. A Danish army crossed the Sound and invaded Skåne. However, when the Danes joined a Polish-Saxon force in invading Swedish Pomerania, the Swedish garrison repulsed them. The excursion into Skåne also came to grief. At the Battle of Helsingborg in **February 1710**, General Magnus Stenbock defeated the invading Danish army and forced it back across the Sound. Stenbock then sailed to Pomerania to organize its defense.

Admiral Wachtmeister staged a surprise descent upon the Danish Fleet anchored in Kjöge Bay. On the morning of 4 October 1710, he took 21 ships of the line against the 26 anchored Danish ships of the line. During a brief exchange of fire, the Danish *Dannebrog*-82 blew up. Two Swedish ships of the line had to be burned after running aground. The principal gain to Sweden was the moral one of "bearding the lion" in his den.

Sweden succeeded in holding Pomerania against all antagonists, largely because she maintained command of the sea. On one occasion, that control was severely damaged. Off Cape Arkona, the northern tip of the island of Rügen, Danish Admiral Gyldenlove destroyed 55 transports bringing supplies and reinforcements. A Swedish fleet of 95 transports was landing cargoes on **28 September 1712** when Gyldenlove slipped between the transports and their escort with his fleet, wreaking great destruction. Admiral Wachtmeister could not intervene before the deed was done and simply sailed away with his 29 ships of the line. Wachtmeister retired in 1714, and development of the Swedish Fleet was assumed by Admirals von Liewen and Klas Sparre. [118]

### *The Empire at Bay* - 1714-1721

Sweden was given respite by the entrance of Turkey into the conflict against Russia. When the Sultan's army pinned Peter the Great against the Pruth River, he negotiated instead of destroying the Russians. Karl XII remained in Turkey, haranguing the Sultan to renew hostilities. The irritated pasha finally ordered him to leave. From the Aegean port of Demotika, Karl made a remarkable ride all across Europe. Arriving at Stralsund in Pomerania on 11 November 1714, he set about revitalizing the Swedish war effort. He should have negotiated at least a temporary peace, but unwisely decided to continue the conflict.

The Loss of the Swedish Empire

227

Sweden had already lost much of her empire during his absence. An army had been transported to Pomerania for an invasion of Poland, but was forced back into Holstein, where it surrendered. As a result, Brandenburg occupied Stettin, Bremen was lost to Hanover, and Russia placed a heavy hand on the Baltic provinces.

Russian troops began advancing through southern Finland, plundering and killing as they went. After capturing Helsingfors, they pushed westward along the Finnish coast. A few skirmishes occurred between the rival navies as they approached. The Russian Baltic fleet now had 10 ships of the line and 7 frigates. In the spring of 1714, Admiral Wattrang put to sea with 15 Swedish ships of the line and harassed the Russian shallows flotillas. Blockaded in the archipelago near Åbo, the Russians tried to escape eastward on **6 August 1714** by portaging their galleys on rollers. Rear Admiral Ehrensköld boldly anchored 9 little gunboats athwart their course. For hours, he held off nearly 100 Russian boats, severely damaging or sinking 40 of them before retiring. Although of doubtful credit to the Russian Navy, this Battle of Hangö Head (or Gangut) is celebrated as its first historical victory.

In the spring of 1715, 16 Swedish ships of the line cruised to Reval. Entering the harbor, they bombarded the Russian squadron stationed there, but with little damage inflicted by either side. This proved to be the last offensive effort by the Swedish Fleet, as the West European maritime powers now began to take a hand in the Baltic.

Swedish privateers were making inroads on Dutch and British shipping to Russia by 1714. The allies sent a combined fleet of 20 British and 12 Dutch ships of the line to the Baltic the following year to convoy their vessels. There were no encounters as the Swedish Fleet remained in port. The Danes were more successful. Off Femern on 24 April 1715, a squadron of 9 ships of the line put 6 Swedish ships of the line to flight, during which they grounded and were captured in Kiel Bay the following day.

In June 1715, General-Admiral Apraksin cruised the western Baltic with 18 ships of the line, 4 frigates and 2 snows. He was joined by 7 British ships of the line during the summer. Over the winter of 1715-6, the Danes and Russians had worked out a plan for landing on the coast of Skåne. For that purpose, the combined squadrons of Russia, Denmark and Britain gathered at Copenhagen in overwhelming force. Learning of their intentions, Karl XII deployed 20,000 men to Skåne. The allied fleet sailed from Kjöge Bay with British Admiral Norris in the van, Admiral Gyldenlöve's Danish ships in the rear, and Czar Peter in overall command from his squadron in the center. They learned, upon reaching Bornholm, that the Swedes had retired into Karlskrona. Dissension developed among the allies and no attack was ever made. The Russians went to Mecklenburg and the British sailed for home.

Sweden's enemies were closing on her. By July 1715, 28,000 Danes and 27,000 Prussians and Saxons had gathered around Stralsund. They were held at bay by strong Swedish batteries on the islands of Usedom, Ruden and Rugen. The Swedish squadron cruising the Greifswalder Deip was joined by most of the battle fleet on 18 July. They arrived just in time to prevent a descent by the Danish Fleet with the intention of gaining control of those waters. Some 3,500 Prussian, 2,300 Hanoverian and 5,000 Danish troops initiated a close siege of Stralsund on 2 November. The Swedish garrison consisted of 4,000 men.

Frederik IV then made a second attempt to control the Pomeranian seas. Twenty-one Danish ships of the line approached the anchored Swedish Fleet on 8 August.

228

Second Squadron (Van) (Amiral Johan Lillje)
*Skåne, Brähmen, Öland, Pommern,
Prins Karl* (flag), *Småland, Ösel*

First Squadron (Center) (Amiral Klas Sparre)
*Riga, Stockholm, Götha Lejon* (flag),
*Prins Karl Fredrik, Västmanland, Estland*

Third Squadron (Rear) (Amiral M. Henck)
*Gottland, Verden, Enigheten* (flag)
*Fredrika Amalia, Lisland, Wenden, Karlskrona*

2 frigates, 1 snow, 1 jakt

At 1300, both fleets stood out to sea on parallel courses to the east of Rügen. A cannonade continued until 2000, with no maneuvering. Each side inflicted 600 casualties on the other, but sank no ships. Admiral Sparre withdrew to Karlskrona. The Danes went to Copenhagen for repairs. Joined by 8 British ships of the line, seaworthy Danish ships cruised between Bornholm and Rügen, preventing Swedish reinforcements from reaching Pomerania. The Danes and Prussians conducted a perfect amphibious operation on 15 November, landing an army of 12,500 infantry and 5,000 cavalry on Rügen, which fell the following day. Karl XII escaped to Sweden just before Stralsund, now isolated, capitulated on 23 December. Wismar fell to the allies on **19 April 1716**. Sweden had been forced off of the Continent. [119]

## *The Campaign in Norway* - 1716-1719

Karl XII conceived of a way to distract his enemies. Announcing support for the Jacobite opponents of King George I, he invaded Danish Norway, simultaneously approaching the Jacobites and diverting Denmark from Skåne.

From Värmland, he crossed the border on **26 February 1716**, advancing on Kristiania with 3,000 men. General Mörner joined him in converging on the capital with a march to Moss by his 4,000 men. A feint was made at Svinesund in the south by 800 cavalry under General von Ascheberg. The Jämtland Regiment crossed to Röros to prevent the Norwegian border forces from retiring on the capital. The Norwegians had 7,000 men shielding Kristiania, with a corps of 1,000 men in an advanced position. A heavy snowstorm delayed the Swedes long enough for the Norwegians to build up their defenses. Karl XII skillfully used valleys and frozen lakes to avoid the Norwegian fortresses and occupied Kristiania on 10-11 March, without opposition.

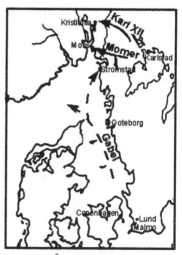

However, the Norwegian Army remained intact. Åkershus fortress could not be taken until siege artillery arrived by sea from Göteborg. The Swedish Fleet was slow in fitting out for the 1716 season and Denmark took advantage to gain control of the sea. Unable to supply his troops, Karl was forced to withdraw from Kristiania on 18-9 April. He intended to remain in Norway to block an invasion of Skåne from the west. Making Torpum his headquarters, he distributed his troops around Frederikshald and supplied them with coastal vessels until the Göteborg squadron arrived. Rear Admiral Tordenskjold attacked the Swedish base at Göteborg, but was repulsed. Danish Vice Admiral Gabel had taken a squadron of 7 ships of the line and 4 frigates to the Skagerrak at the end of March. On 8 July, he sent 5 attached British ships of the line to support Tordenskjold's shallows vessels in an attack on Strömstad at the entrance to Dynekilen Fjord, destroying a galley flotilla commanded by Rear Admiral Sjöblad. The Swedish coastal traffic was disrupted, isolating Karl's troops. The Danish moves threatened an invasion of Skåne.

While scout vessels watched for the appearance of an invasion fleet in Denmark, Karl XII collected forces at Malmö, intending to march to their support with his forces if an invasion occurred. He left Major General de la Gardie in command in Norway and traveled to make his new headquarters at Lund between his two concentrations. The Danes had commandeered nearly their whole merchant fleet to carry 30,000 men across to Skåne.

Another threat was forming to the east. As a Russian shallows flotilla ravaged the settlements along the Swedish coast from Stockholm to Norrköping during July 1717, some 40,000 Russian troops gathered at Danzig, preparing to board transports. Apraksin mounted a raid on Gotland, landing troops at Östergarn to pillage. The dreaded Rus were closer to the homeland than they had ever been. However, the Coalition was in trouble. Britain's George I had his hands full with the Jacobites, and did not support his allies as vigorously as in the past. A combined fleet finally formed in August 1717 with 18 Danish, 19 British and 24 Russian ships of the line. A Dutch squadron of 6 Fourth Rates convoyed Dutch and British commerce to the eastern Baltic while the combined fleet cruised off Bornholm, watching Karlskrona, where the Swedish Fleet had shut itself up. Believing it was too late in the season to prosecute a successful campaign, the Czar abandoned the operation on 19 September. The Coalition split into Russo-Prussian and Dano-Hanoverian factions.

Admiral Klas Sparre took the Swedish Fleet to sea with the intention of falling upon the abandoned Danes, but Admiral Norris had left 7 ships of the line behind when he sailed home to England and they reached the Danes in time to discourage Sparre. He then sailed eastward to do battle with a Russian squadron of 12 of the line, but they retired into Reval when he approached. Sweden had proven stronger than the Coalition had thought.[120]

The breakup of the Coalition gave Karl XII time to organize his forces for a renewed campaign in Norway. By October 1718, he had 65,000 men mustered into 37 infantry and 23 cavalry regiments. A Holsteiner, Georg Heinrich von Görtz, remarkably scraped together a new army from Sweden's remaining meagre human resources, although it was not the rag-tag force of derelicts once reported by historians. The principal difference from the levies of earlier years was the presence of numbers of skilled workers previously exempted from military service. The infantry was thoroughly trained and the artillery improved. Heavy artillery benefited particularly, eighteen 48 pdrs being the largest cannon ever cast in Sweden. Each infantry regiment had thirty-two 3 pdrs drawn by 4 horses, and sixteen 6 pdrs drawn by 8. Employing cartridges, they could fire 12-14 shots per minute, ten times the rate achieved by artillery using separate charges of powder and shot.

The Swedish Army, still regarded as possessing the best fighting spirit and discipline in Europe, was composed of regulars, reserves, and mercenaries. The regiment was the only permanent unit. Established for the purpose of recruiting and training within its home district, it was the repository of morale within the army. Regiments were sometimes organized into "columns" to undertake specific missions. Brigades contained troops of one branch and class (regulars, reserves, mercenaries). Some divisions lacked artillery. This organization was later adopted by other European armies.

**DIVISION**
2-3 infantry, cavalry and artillery brigades
2-3 regiments
2 battalions

Uniforms remained little changed, although some regiments were reduced to wearing homespun gray due to the shortage of cloth.

The Navy increased to 22 ships of the line and included a force of Marines for the first time. The main fleet was still based at Karlskrona, with the Army bivouaced nearby. To protect the maritime lines of operation, the Göteborg Squadron of frigates and galleys was strengthened. The Stockholm Squadron consisted of the shallows flotillas and a fleet of 145 merchant ships available to transport 17,500 men by sea.

Karl XII ordered his forces forward on 15 August 1718:

**Swedish Army**
Jämtland Corps (Gen.Lt. Armfelt)
7,500 men
Main Army (Karl XII) - 21,000 infantry, 13,000 cavalry
Northern Column (Gen.Lt. von Albedyhl) - Värmland
10 cavalry squadrons
5 infantry battalions
Central Column (Karl XII) - Västra Ed
33 cavalry squadrons
22 infantry battalions
Southern Column (Fredrik von Hesse) - Strömstad
59 cavalry squadrons
12 infantry battalions

The Jämtland Corps was intended to pin Norwegian forces in the north. It was broken up into outposts along the border after its mission was fulfilled. Danish General Lutzow divided his army of 29,000 men into two corps, one to guard the eastern approaches to the capital and one to block the advance from Värmland. By dispersing his columns, Karl XII anticipated Napoleon's technique of advancing in separate corps that could be concentrated in any direction to surprise the enemy. The Northern Column had easy going as the Norwegians withdrew to rear defensive positions. As the Main Army drove the enemy back from Fredericksten fortress, the Jämtland Corps cleared eastern Norway as far as the Glommen River. It then marched on Trondheim, but was too weak to capture the city and settled down to a siege. The king was dissatisfied with the performance of the Northern Column and replaced Albedyhl with General Major Leutrum. General von Schwerin was placed in charge of the siege of Fredericksten, a well-built fortress. As he was observing the progress of the attack from the Swedish trenches at 2100 on **30 November,** the king took a ball through the head. Fredrik von Hesse replaced the dead king and decided to abandon the campaign after a council of war with his officers. War weary Sweden did not long mourn the warrior king's demise. [121]

231

Under the leadership of Hesse, the government made overtures to England/ Hanover and Denmark, with the goal of isolating Russia. This policy was aided in 1719 by a breach in relations between England and Russia. The Czar's vessels were now cruising at will in the Baltic. On **24 May 1719**, three Russian 50 gun ships came up with a Swedish squadron north of Gotland. In what came to be known as the Battle of Ösel Island, the Swedish frigate *Rushenfeldt*-24, a 16 gun snow and a schooner were quickly overtaken as the squadron steered for Sandhamn. The frigate *Wachtmeister*-48 resisted stoutly and was about to escape when two more Russian 50s appeared ahead, forcing her to strike after a strong fight.

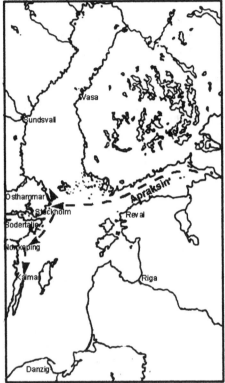

The feared Russian invasion force appeared off the Swedish coast on 9 July. Thirty ships of the line, under General-Admiral Apraksin, escorted 150 galleys and transports carrying 30,000 men to the coast of Uppland, north of Stockholm, where they pillaged many villages. The fleet then split up. While one squadron remained on station in the Stockholm archipelago, a second sailed on 14 July, destroying Nyköping, Södertalje, Norrköping and many intermediate villages as far south as Kalmar, before returning 3 August. A third squadron made a similar foray northward, ravaging the coastal towns of the Roslagen peninsula. It destroyed Östhammar and Norrtälje, along with many iron and timber industries, before returning on 19 August. Some 6,000 Russian soldiers were put ashore near Stockholm on 13 August, but were driven back to the sea by the Södermanland Regiment and reembarked on their ships.

Britain did not wish to see Sweden subjugated by Russia and sent a fleet of 16 ships of the line to join the Swedish Fleet in September. Apraksin sailed for Reval on 20 August, before the allies could attack him.

Conflict with Denmark was winding down. Before settling with Sweden, the Danes were determined to regain their trade in naval stores from the Scandinavian peninsula. The Swedish Göteborg Squadron of 5 ships of the line, 1 frigate, and 10 smaller vessels was anchored at Marstrand, just to the north of its home base, when a Danish squadron of 7 ships of the line, 2 frigates, and a dozen shallows craft approached on 21 July 1719. The Danes landed Marines and artillery, which bombarded the Swedish ships in the harbor, most of which were scuttled by their crews. After negotiations, Sweden submitted again to the Danish Sound Dues. Karl XII's adventures had spilled much Swedish blood with little benefit to the nation.

The naval war with Russia continued. British Admiral Norris again entered the Baltic in the spring of 1720 to prod the demoralized Swedish Fleet to attack the Russians.

**Swedish Fleet** (Flottan Amiral Klas Sparre)
Flagships
*Prins Fredrik Karl* - 70 (Adm. Sparre)
*Karlskrona* - 70 (Adm. Wachtmeister)
*Stockholm* - 64 (Vice Adm. Wachtmeister)
*Pommern* - 64 (Vice Adm. Sjöblad)
Ships of the Line
*Bremen* - 64
*Wenden, Götha, Skåne* - 60
*Werden* - 56
*Öland* - 50
Frigates
*Reval, Svarte Örn, Jarramas, Ebenezer, Kisken,
Anclam, Örnens Pris, Phoenix*
Snows - five
Bombs - four
Armed Merchantmen - seven
Fireships - two
Galleys - eleven

The allied fleet sailed north, but off Reval fell to quarreling about command arrangements and failed to bring the Russian Fleet to battle. Apraksin evaded them and sailed into the Gulf of Bothnia in May. He plundered the Swedish coast without interference, destroying Umeå and nearby villages. The Russian shallows flotillas also made several destructive raids along the Swedish coast. On 7 August, a Swedish squadron of 4 ships of the line, 6 frigates, and some smaller vessels went after them off the Åland Islands in the mouth of the Gulf of Bothnia. The shoal water restricted the movements of the Swedish deepwater ships and the Russians captured 4 of the frigates, although they lost 45 of their galleys in the action. A disgruntled Norris returned to England in November.

The naval campaign resumed in May 1721 when Norris arrived with 21 ships of the line to join the Swedish Fleet off Reval:

**Swedish Fleet** (Adm. Sparre)

Ships of the Line
*Götha Lejon, Enigheten* - 92
*Ulrika Eleonora* - 84 (flag)
*Prins Fredrik Karl* - 70
*Stockholm, Bremen* - 64
*Fredrika Amalia, Västmanland, Skåne* - 60
*Werden* - 56
*Öland* - 50
Frigates
*Svarte Örn, Jarramas, Ebenezer, Örnens Pris*
Bombs - two
Scout Boats - two

Again, Apraksin slipped by them into the Gulf of Bothnia, where he devastated Söderhamn, Sundsvall and Härnösand. Obviously, the British Navy was of little help to the weakened Swedes. Ninety small shallows vessels had been lost to the Russians, with 64 more destroyed by Denmark. The Russian Fleet dominated the Baltic with 29 ships of the line Sweden was now in third place

233

as Denmark had 25 ships of the line to the Swedes 24. The Treaty of Nystad, signed on **10 September 1721**, confirmed Prussian possession of Stettin and most of Pomerania and ceded the Baltic provinces to Russia. [122]

# THE AGE OF FREEDOM

War weary Sweden was disenchanted with an absolute monarchy that could involve them in distant conflicts of doubtful value to the country. In January 1719, the Diet of the Estates met in Stockholm to draft a new constitution that would severely limit the power of Queen Ulrika Eleonora, the sister of Karl XII. They established a Regent to supervise her activities. She abdicated in 1720, in favor of her husband, Fredrik af Hesse. Crowned Fredrik I, he was relegated to a mere national figurehead by the restrictions placed on the monarchy. A century of centralized authority had dissipated.

**MERCHANT** krayer
1750, 300 tons, 80 men

The President of the Chancellery, Arvid Horn, succeeded in accruing much of the former royal power. He led a hybrid government, with governing power resting in the Council of the Realm which, however, was required to have the consent of the Diet of the Estates. Horn, a skilled politician, gathered able men around him and governed Sweden in a careful manner that restored stability. By the end of his tenure, Sweden's iron exports had expanded to 50,000 tons annually. A number of outstanding leaders appeared during this period: the philosopher Emanuel Swedenborg, the chemist Anders Celsius, and the botanist Karl von Linne (Linnaeus).

*Russo-Swedish War* - 1741-1743

In 1738, Horn's "Caps" party was ousted by the "Hats" party, which took Sweden on a more radical course. Desiring to regain the territories lost to Russia, they negotiated support from France, then declared war on Russia on **24 July 1741**. Crossing the new Russian frontier in eastern Finland, 6,000 Swedish troops were confronted by 10,000 Russians at Villmanstrand and routed. While the Russians had 2,400 casualties, Sweden lost 1,300 prisoners in addition to 3,300 casualties. The survivors fell back along the coast to Helsingfors where the main Swedish army of 17,000 men was deployed. Admiral Karl Leuwenhaupt bombarded Vyborg with his 12 ships of the line and 11 frigates, but without result. The Russians used the summer campaign of 1742 to cut the coastal road west of Helsingfors, bringing about the surrender of the army. Swedish forces were driven out of Finland by the end of the year.

The Rus were once again threatening the homeland as the winter of 1743 ended. Russian Admiral Golovin went looking for the Swedish Fleet with 17 ships of the line, 5 frigates and 48 galleys (for work in the archipelago). Off Hangö Head, he encountered Admiral Johan von Utfall with 16 ships of the line, 5 frigates, 2 snows, 2 bomb ketches and some smaller craft. In command of the only armed force now capable of keeping the Russians from the Swedish shore, Utfall retreated after exchanging a few long-range shots. Golovin eschewed pursuit and retired to Reval. Cornered, the "Hats" government signed a peace treaty on **7 August 1743**, ceding still more Finnish territory to the Russians.

## Seven Years War - 1751-1762

The "Hats" survived by blaming the Army and executing its highest officers. They energetically reorganized Sweden's defenses to better operate in Finland. They built a large fortress at Sveaborg, near Helsingfors, which became the long-needed naval base on the Gulf of Finland. A special *Schärensflotten* (shallows fleet), of specialized craft suited to operations within the Finnish archipelago, was constructed.

When Frederick the Great lashed out at his neighbors in an attempt to secure Prussian space in central Europe, Sweden moved to protect the small territory remaining to her at the mouth of the Oder River. Judging Frederick to be incapable of defeating his numerous foes, the "Hats" threw in with the probable winners and declared war on Prussia. This placed Sweden in the ironic position of supporting her former enemies, Russia and Denmark. [123]

Poorly equipped and badly led, the Swedish Army achieved nothing with its 32 infantry regiments. It had not progressed far beyond that of the Great Northern War. The uniforms were rather old-fashioned, with all infantry facings restricted to yellow from 1756:

> **Infantry** wore dark blue coats with yellow facings, waistcoats and breeches, white gaiters, black tricorn and shoes.
> **Cavalry** wore dark blue coats with facings of white, yellow, red, blue or buff, buff waistcoats and breeches, black tricorn and boots.

The Navy had 26 ships of the line (Denmark had 27, Russia only 20 in the Baltic):

### Swedish Fleet

SHIPS OF THE LINE
First Rate
*Konung Fredrik* - 92

Third Rate
*Konung Karl* - 74
*Göta Lejon, Enigheten,*
   *Prins Gustav, Drottning Lovisa Ulrika* - 72
*Prins Karl Fredrik, Friheten,*
   *Hessen-Cassel, Konung Adolf Fredrik* - 64
*Prins Karl, Prinsessan Sofia Albertina* - 62

Fourth Rate
*Göta, Bremen, Stockholm, Finland, Fredrik Rex,*
   *Pommern, Prins Vilhelm, Fredrika Amalia,*
   *Prinsessan Sofia Charlotta,* - 60

**FIRST RATE** 92 gun ship of the line
1720, 1600 tons, 750 men,
28-32 pdrs, 28-24 pdrs,
26-18 pdrs, 10-9 pdrs

235

Fifth Rate
*Sparre* - 56
*Uppland, Södermanland* - 48
*Svarte Örn* - 42
*Illerim, Prins Gustav, Phoenix* - 36
*Jarramas* - 34

Sixth Rate
*Mercurius, Jägaren, Postiljon* - 26

**FIFTH RATE** 36 gun frigate
1720, 450 tons, 200 men,
18-12 pdrs, 18-6 pdrs

**SIXTH RATE** 26 gun frigate
1720, 400 tons, 150 men,
26-6 pdrs

In August 1760, Russian Admiral Mishukov was supported by Danish and Swedish squadrons when he attacked Kolberg, unsuccessfully.

**Swedish Squadron** (Vice Adm. Lagerbjelke)
Ships of the Line
*Prins Gustav, Enigheten, Adolf Fredrik, Friheten,*
*Södermanland, Sophia Charlotta*

Frigates
*Illerin, Ekolmsund*

Mishukov tried again the next year, this time with 40 vessels, including 15 Russian ships of the line and the Danish and Swedish squadrons.

**Swedish Squadron** (Commodore Psilandersköld)
Ships of the Line
*Prins Gustav, Prins Karl, Sophia Charlotta,*
*Bremen, Sparre, Uppland*

Frigates
*Illerin, Jarramas* 124

Appearing off Kolberg on **16 December 1761**, the fleet bombarded the shore positions in support of a landing by troops that captured the fortress. However, Sweden's military aims were not achieved, despite her exertions. The "Hats" were loudly denounced in the Diet of 1765. They were replaced by a group of young idealists who ruined their program by moving too rapidly, causing an economic crisis. The "Hats" regained power, but were challenged by the lower Estates. In the midst of the struggles, Adolf Fredrik died.

Gustav III became king in 1771. Taking advantage of the general public dissatisfaction, he initiated a bloodless coup d'etat on **19 August 1772**, regaining absolute power after jailing the government leaders. The Age of Freedom was over.

# THE WARS WITH RUSSIA

*Russo-Swedish War* - 1788-1790

Although promoting cultural advances, Gustav III tried several unwise economic policies that alienated him from the common people. He attempted to increase his popularity through foreign initiatives. St. Barthelemy was first occupied by the French in 1648. It was ceded to Sweden in 1784. The treeless island had fertile soil and exported small quantities of tropical fruits, but its principal value was as a Caribbean base for enterprising Swedish merchants. Gustav III wished to subdue Denmark, but it was plain that Russia would not idly allow him to gain control of the exits to the Baltic. To avoid a war on two fronts, he decided to attack Russia first. He was aided in his objective by the current involvement of Catherine II (the Great) in a war with Turkey. Developing his war plans during 1787, he gathered his councilors to his castle for secret discussions the following spring. His fleet was to destroy the Russian Baltic Fleet in the Bay (Gulf) of Finland, opening the way for his army to land and capture Catherine's capital, St. Petersburg. To avoid triggering the mutual defense provisions of the Dano-Russian treaties, the king intended to contrive border incidents, then go to Finland to halt the "aggressor". His schemes failed.

Gustav III took personal command of the army and appointed his brother, Karl, Duke von Södermanland, to head the navy. Both were completely unqualified for their commands. The border incident occurred at Nyslott, as planned. Södermanland left Karlskrona with the Swedish fleet on 9 June and sailed to Hangö where he rendezvoused with a flotilla of 28 galleys and 30 gunsloops escorting 8,000 troops on transports. The united force continued on, arriving in Helsingfors on **2 July 1788** as the king declared war. In preparation for the coming conflict, he had built his fleet into a considerable force.

**Örlogsflotten** (Adm. Karl von Södermanland) - Karlskrona

SHIPS OF THE LINE

Third Rate
*Adolf Fredrik, Fadernesland,*
    *Gustav III, Morgenstjernan, Victoria* - 74
*Göta Lejon, Louise Ulrika,*
    *Enigheten, Prins Gustav* - 70
*Drake, Dristigheten, Tapperheten*
    *Leopard, Hedvig Elisabeth Charlotta,*
    *Prins Karl, Försiktigheten,*
    *Sophia Magdalena, Gustavus Adolphus* - 64
*Hertig Ferdinand, Omheten,*
    *Prins Gustav Adolph, Rattvisa* - 62

Fourth Rate
*Riksens Ständer* - 60
*Finland, Torborg* - 56

**THIRD RATE** 70 gun ship of the line
1780, 1400 tons, 600 men,
28-32 pdrs, 28-18 pdrs,
14-9 pdrs, 8 carronades

# FRIGATES

Fifth Rate
*Camilla, Uppland,
Wismar* - 44
*Zemire* - 42
*Venus* - 40
*Illerin, Jarramas, Jarislavits* - 32

Sixth Rate
*Jägaren, Postiljon* - 26
*Trolle* - 24

SLOOPS
*Mercury, Minerva, Phoenix, Pollux,
Sceptre, Swan* (snows)

**THIRD RATE** 64 gun ship of the line
1780, 1300 tons, 500 men,
26-24 pdrs, 26-18 pdrs,
12-9 pdrs, 8 carronades

**FIFTH RATE** 32 gun frigate
1780, 650 tons, 200 men,
26-18 pdrs, 6-6 pdrs,
8 carronades

**FIFTH RATE** 44 gun frigate
1780, 800 tons, 250 men,
20-18 pdrs, 22-12 pdrs,
2-6 pdrs

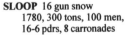

**SLOOP** 16 gun snow
1780, 300 tons, 100 men,
16-6 pdrs, 8 carronades

**SLOOP** 12 gun jakt
1780, 150 tons, 50 men,
12-4 pdrs
(Roslagen jakt)

**BOMB** 8 gun ketch
1780, 180 tons, 40 men,
8-6 pdrs, 2-25 cm mortars

In time of war, Sweden followed the common practice of purchasing merchant ships into the navy as auxiliary cruisers, liaison craft and transport vessels. Scandinavian merchant ships displayed distinctive characteristics, such as spritsails, lug gaff-topsails, and unusual combinations of various types of sails. Swedish ship design was strongly influenced by the Dutch, who also had to deal with shoal waters like those in the Baltic. Swedish seamen were experienced sailors, but were accustomed to the calmer waters of the Baltic and were not as prepared as other Scandinavian navigators to sail the open ocean. From the mid-Eighteenth Century, Sweden was fortunate to be served by one of the world's foremost naval architects, Frederik H. Chapman. Not only did he bring Swedish deep-water designs up to world standard, he also designed most of the sophisticated craft employed so successfully among the skerries of the Baltic.

### Schärnsflotten

**HEMMEMAS**
*Styrbjörn, Hjalmar* - 28
*Oden* - 26

**TURUMAS**
*Sallan Varre, Ragvald, Björn Jerssida* - 24
5 others

**UDEMAS**
three

**GALLEYS**
*Seraphims Orden, Svärdsorden, Stockholm,*
*Taube, von Höpken, von Seth, von Rosen,*
*Posse, Västöta-Dal, Hälsingland, Älvsborg,*
*Nyköping, Småland, Kalmar, Närke, Wrede,*
*Västervik, Västmanland, Halland, Jämtland* - 12

**GUNSLOOPS**
*No.1-70*

**ESPINGARS**
*No.1-28*

The Swedish "Shallows Fleet" was only beginning to mature when the war broke out. By 1790, it had increased to around 350 craft. For the initial battles it was organized into two squadrons, one intended to defend the Stockholm Archipelago, the other to operate along the Finnish coast.

### Schärnsflotten

Swedish Squadron - Stockholm
28 galleys, 30 gunsloops, 28 espingars, 3 jakts

Finnish Squadron (Adm. Ehrensvärd) - Helsingfors
3 hemmema, 8 turuma, 3 udema, 40 gunsloops

From Helsingfors in June 1788, the Swedish army of 36,000 men advanced eastward in two columns. Gustav III led the main column along the coast and besieged Frederikshamn to open the way to St. Petersburg. A smaller northern column left St. Michel (Mikkeli) and marched on Villmanstrand.

239

Russia was not prepared for war with Sweden as she was fully involved with Turkey. In Finland were 19,000 men under General Pushkin, but they were scattered in various garrisons. Catherine II (the Great) hastily sent her Guard infantry and cavalry from St. Petersburg to the Finnish frontier to shield her capital. The Swedish Army was repulsed at the fortress of Svatiapol (Svartholm) through the bumbling of Gustav and his officers. Thereafter, desultory action resulted in a dreary campaign of attrition, with little gain to either side.

Admiral Grieg was preparing a fleet to go to the Mediterranean and attack the Turks. Instead he was ordered to destroy the Swedish fleet. He weighed from Kronstadt on 3 July with the Russian Baltic Fleet of 17 ships of the line and 8 frigates. The next day, elements of the Swedish fleet captured the Russian frigates *Jaroslavits*-36 and *Giktor*-26 off Reval. Learning of the Russian sortie, Södermanland sailed eastward, sighting the Baltic Fleet northwest of Hogland Island on **17 July**. The more numerous Swedish ships were smaller than those of the enemy, leaving Grieg with a slight advantage in weight of broadside. During the preliminary maneuvers to form battle lines and gain tactical advantage, the Russian fleet became disordered. Although Södermanland maintained good order, when the fleets closed he found his flagship, *Gustav III*-74, and the adjacent *Fadernesland*-74 attacked by Grieg's flagship, the *Rostislav*-100. Ten Swedish ships of the line fought seven in the Russian van. In the center, six concentrated their fire on three Russians. The Russian rear division had to content itself with long-range fire. The cannonading began at 1500 and lasted until nightfall. Although the Russians had heavier metal, they were able to cripple and board only the *Prins Gustav*-70, while the Swedes captured the *Vladislav*-74 and severely battered the *Mstislav, Rostislav* and *Iziaslav*. Södermanland had lost 1,200 men while inflicting 1,800 casualties on the Russians. Yet, Grieg had kept the Swedish fleet from attacking the capital. The Swedes withdrew to Sveaborg where they were blockaded until winter set in. In November, they weighed anchor and left for Karlskrona.

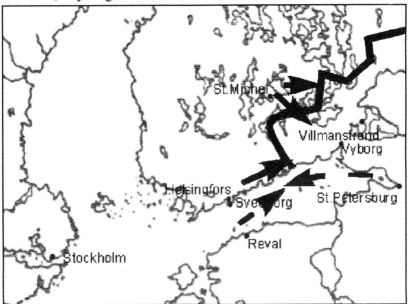

Swedish Operations, 1788

240

Russian Admiral von Dessen had been cruising the western Baltic with a small squadron when the war began. He put into Copenhagen on 8 July and was reinforced with two ships of the line and a frigate. He sailed for Archangelsk with two storeships, but the three large Swedish frigates at Göteborg managed to sink the storeships without being brought to action by the powerful escort. Gustav III could not reinforce his army in Finland for he had not duped Denmark. In August, the Danes launched an invasion from Norway, threatening Göteborg and requiring the king to withdraw troops from Finland. Russian Admiral V.P. Fondezin, with 9 ships of the line and 2 frigates, was joined by a Danish squadron of 3 ships of the line and 9 frigates under Admiral Povalichen. He sailed to Karlskrona and loitered for a month, hoping to catch fragments of Södermanland's fleet of 18 battleships returning to winter at their base, and greatly hindering the progress of the Swedish troop transports. He left well before any Swedes arrived, and wintered at Copenhagen.

Emboldened by his successes, Russian Admiral Grieg went on the offensive. Attacking a squadron of 3 Swedish battleships and 4 frigates anchored at Sveaborg on 5 August, he succeeded in working in close through a heavy fog before firing into the surprised Swedes. In the frenzy to escape, the *Prins Gustav Adolf*-62 went aground and was lost. Fortunately for Sweden, the energetic Grieg died on 16 October, and his successor, Admiral Koslianinov, did little before laying up for the winter at Reval early in November. With a more southerly base, Duke Karl delayed a month before doing the same.

Both antagonists prepared industriously for the campaigns of the next summer. Denmark left the war, leaving Gustav III to concentrate on the Russians. Although the 21 ships of the line of the Swedish fleet were badly outnumbered by the 35 Russia had collected by spring, Catherine's battleships were divided into three widely separated fleets. At Kronstadt, Admiral Spiridov could sail with 14 ships of the line. Admiral Chichagov commanded a fleet of 10 at Reval. Far to the southwest, Admiral Koslianinov was at Copenhagen with 11 ships of the line, 4 frigates, and 3 smaller vessels in position to dispute the Danish straits or take a sortie by Södermanland from the rear. As the Russians at Reval and Kronstadt were locked in by ice for a much longer period that the fleets in the southern Baltic, Södermanland had an opportunity to defeat Koslianinov before he could be sufficiently reinforced.

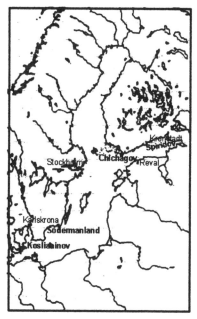

However, Duke Karl did not quit Karlskrona until 6 July, with a fleet of 21 ships of the line, 13 frigates and 8 smaller warships. Chichagov absorbed the Kronstadt fleet and left Reval with 20 ships of the line, 6 frigates and 19 smaller ships. As Koslianinov weighed from Copenhagen with 11 battleships, 4 frigates and 3 smaller vessels, he was escorted by a Danish fleet of 11 ships of the line and 3 frigates. Södermanland was faced with overwhelming opposition, but was in a central position from which he could strike each in turn. However, he was unable to contrive a suitable course of action and cruised aimlessly. The Russian fleets used the delay to converge upon him off Öland Island on **26 July 1789**. Koslianinov had not closed up when Chichagov's 21 ships of the line engaged a similar number of Swedish battleships on a northerly course. With their frigates keeping company on the off side, the two battle fleets exchanged a desultory fire at long range, with little damage to either fleet. After a day of fruitless maneuvering, Duke Karl retired to Karlskrona. The Russian fleets united on 1 August, and the now vastly superior enemy initiated a blockade of the Swedish base the next day. It appears that Chichagov was also an indecisive commander, for after a few days of cruising off Karlskrona, he left for home.

With the major fleets retired from the sea, and operations stalled on land, the focus of the conflict shifted to the shallows fleets of the combatants. The *skärgård* of the Finnish coast allowed small craft to operate without fear of attack from sea-going warships. Hangö was accessible to deep-water vessels, and was fortified. The lack of fortifications at the similarly deep harbor of Porkkala, west of Helsingförs, allowed the Russians to send Admiral Sheshukov with a ship of the line and 3 frigates to support a landing there. Athwart communications, he was able to disrupt Swedish coastal traffic. On the night of 14-5 June, the Swedes moved to drive him away with 17 gunsloops, but failed. A smaller attempt on 2 July was also unsuccessful.

Sweden began attacking Russian shipping. The Finnish Squadron of Admiral Ehrensvärd included 62 craft at Sveaborg and 65 at Svensksund. During June 1788, they began taking Russian merchantmen in the Gulf of Finland. To oppose them, the Russians employed the small sea-going Vyborg Squadron of 2 ships of the line, 2 frigates, 2 bombs and 15 shallows craft under Rear Admiral Kruse, and a flotilla of 86 shallows craft under Rear Admiral Nassau-Siegen at Fredrickshamn (Hamina). When the Russian Vyborg Squadron appeared off the eastern approaches to Kotka, Admiral Ehrensvärd sank vessels to block the channels between the chain of islands guarding the Svensksund, leaving 2 galleys and 11 gunsloops to prevent their removal. Then he arrayed the remainder of his flotilla between two islands at the south entrance to the sound. His two echelons totaled 3 hemmemas, 8 turumas, 3 udemas, and 35 gun vessels.

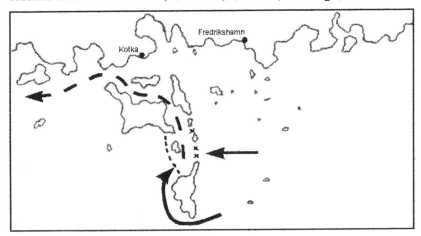

First Battle of Svensksund, 24 August 1789

The First Battle of Svensksund began at 0630 on **24 August 1789** with an attack on the main Swedish flotilla by 20 of the Russian Fredrickshamn flotilla under Major General Balle. Nassau-Siegen, in overall command, was with the remainder of the flotilla and the Vyborg Squadron when they attacked the eastern defenses three hours later. The southern echelon was halted after advancing for only half an hour. Rigorous combat resulted in its repulse at 1400, with heavy losses. However, at 1900 the Russians broke through between the eastern islands, and a running fight ensued with the large Swedish vessels. The Vyborg Squadron sank the hemmema *Oden*, the turumas *Sallan Varre, Ragvald* and *Björn Jerssida*, and the small frigate *Trolle*. Although he lost 16 gun vessels in the fighting, and had to burn 14 transports, Ehrensvärd escaped to heavily fortified Svartsholm with most of his flotilla, followed by the Russians. Skirmishes with Russian sea-going warships continued to the middle of September, but the coastal flank of the Swedish Army was now exposed and Gustav had to withdraw from Lovisa.

Gustav III made a supreme effort in 1790. He commissioned 25 ships of the line, 16 frigates, 16 sloops and 349 shallows craft for the campaign. Catherine activated only part of her fleet, 29 ships of the line, 13 frigates and 200 shallows craft. Again, the Russian admirals made the mistake of dividing their forces into isolated squadrons, but Denmark had signed a peace treaty with Sweden and Copenhagen was no longer available to them.

This time Duke Karl von Södermanland acted as soon as the ice broke up. He sailed from Karlskrona on 30 April with 22 ships of the line, 12 frigates and 13 smaller vessels. He intended to rectify his indecisiveness of the previous year and destroy the squadron at Reval (Tallinn) before it could be joined by the ships based at Kronstadt.

Admiral Chichigov, commanding at Reval, was ready for him. He had deployed his 10 battleships in an outer line, with his 5 frigates in a second line, and an inner line of 2 bombs and 6 shallows craft. Södermanland approached in three columns on **11 May 1790**, then formed a single line ahead as he approached the anchored Russian fleet.

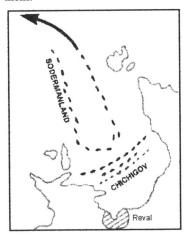

Firing began at 0630, the Swedes attempting to double the Russian battle line. However, just as the maneuver began, a very heavy gale began to blow and the Swedish battle line became disorganized, the *Tapperheten*-64 going aground. A dozen Swedish battleships sailed rapidly by the Russian line, achieving only some long-range cannonading. The closely-anchored Russians did much better, heavily damaging the *Adolf Frederik*-74, *Forsightigheten*-64, *Prins Karl*-64 and *Sophia Magdalena*-64. Duke Karl recalled his disordered fleet, but the fourth-rate *Riksens Ständer*-60 grounded on the way out of the roads and had to be burned. Russian casualties were negligible, but the Swedes lost more than 700.

On 8 May, Sweden attempted the destruction of another tough Russian base. The Sveaborg flotilla of the Finnish Squadron left port under the direct command of Gustav III for an attack on Frederikshamn. Admiral Slysov had 63 shallows craft to defend his base, but the Swedes attacked before he was ready.

Gustav III had twice as many guns on his 110 shallows craft, but Slysov conducted a skillful retirement and lost only 26 vessels when their ammunition ran out. Taking refuge under the guns of Fredrikshamn fortress, the Russians repelled four Swedish attempts to land between 16-8 May. The king recalled his forces, finally convinced he could not take the base.

As soon as the Swedish *Örlogsflotten* had licked its wounds from the action at Reval, and had been reinforced with the *Hertig Ferdinand*-62, *Finland*-56 and *Illerin*-32, it sortied to the island of Hogland in the Gulf of Finland, south of Svensksund. This move prevented the junction of the Reval and Kronstadt fleets and threatened St. Petersburg. Hurriedly commissioning 8 reserve ships of the line to bring his total to 17, Admiral Kruse quit Kronstadt and sailed slowly westward with his 9 frigates scouting ahead.

**MERCHANT** East Indiaman
1750, 600 tons, 200 men,
18-9 pdrs, 4-6 pdrs

They encountered the 6 frigates of the Swedish fleet off the Styrsudd, halfway between Kronstadt and Vyborg. The Battle of Styrsudd (or Kronstadt Bay) began early on **3 June 1790** with brief skirmishes between the two battle lines. Swedish attempts to double the line, or attack with shallows craft, were thwarted by sorties of the Russian "rowing frigates" under Rear Admiral Denisov. Södermanland had missed his chance, for at 2100 Admiral Chichigov's Reval squadron appeared out of the sunset, adding 11 ships of the line and 5 frigates to the Russian fleet.

Completely outnumbered, Duke Karl sought shelter in the Bay of Vyborg, where Gustav III was idling with 175 shallows craft and 120 transports carrying 12,000 troops for the investment of St. Petersburg. Another 40 Swedish shallows craft were approaching from the west. On the other hand, the Russian flotillas were scattered, 10 gun vessels being at Reval, 59 still at Fredrikshamn with Admiral Slysov, and 42 at Vyborg under Admiral Koslianinov. Admiral Nassau-Siegen was in command in the Tragesund, south of Vyborg Bay, with 3 ships of the line, 2 frigates, 6 "rowing frigates", 82 other shallows craft, and 20 transports.

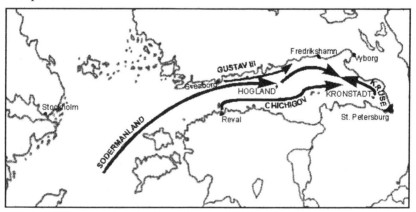

Swedish Advance on St. Petersburg, Summer, 1790

Patiently, the Russians waited until the Swedes ran low on provisions, forcing them to either accept battle or surrender. The Swedes perceived the inevitable on **3 July**. Deploying 6 warships, 20 galleys, and 60 gunsloops under Admiral von Stedingk to prevent Nassau-Siegen from joining Koslianinov at Vyborg, Admiral Törning led 65 gunsloops and 8 bombs, with 120 transports carrying 12,000 troops, northward behind the main Swedish line.

**MERCHANT** packet
1780, 100 tons, 40 men

Södermanland had deployed his 21 ships of the line and 15 frigates across the main entrance to Vyborg Bay, south of a large shoal. Chichigov's much larger combined fleet of 31 ships of the line and 19 frigates stretched far beyond the Swedish line, leaving Rear Admiral Povalichin with 5 battleships and 5 frigates to screen the narrow Kryssebort Channel north of the shoal. Shortly after midnight, Törning's gunsloops attacked the Russians in the northern channel, and were repulsed as expected. At 0600, the entire Swedish fleet got under way and took the course reconnoitered by Törning six hours earlier. Chichagov alerted his captains, but did nothing else. The Swedish fourth-rate *Finland*-56 grounded immediately, but the rest of the fleet, led by *Dristigheten*-64, broke through the division of Russian ships of the line in the northern channel, raking the *Sviatoslav Petr*-74 and *Vseslav*-74 as they passed. By 0830, more than half of the Swedish fleet was through the channel, and still Chichigov had not moved.

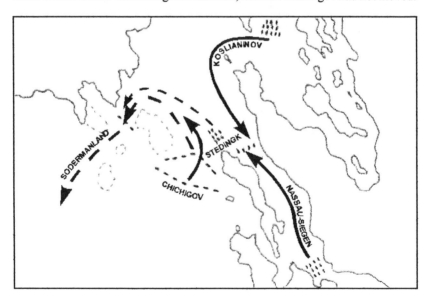

Disaster then struck the Swedes. A fireship was set ablaze to drift down on the stationary Russians, but collided with the *Enighheten*-70 instead. This battleship struck the frigate *Zemire*-42 and the tangled ships blew up. In the resulting confusion, the trailing ships of the line *Hedvig Elisabeth Charlotta*-64, *Omheten*-62, *Louise Ulrika*-70, the frigates *Uppland*-44 and *Jarislavits*-32, a schooner, and 3 galleys went aground on the shoal. However, by 1000 the

245

rest of the Swedish fleet had escaped and was fleeing westward, with Chichagov in tardy pursuit. The Swedish shallows flotilla worked its way westwards through the inshore islands, immune to the attack of Russian sea-going vessels. Nevertheless, by 2000 the slowest Swedish ships were within range of the Russian van. The *Sophia Magdalena*-64 gave as good as she got in a fight with *Mstislav*-74, but was forced to strike at 2230. Most of the rest of the *Örlogsflotten* reached Sveaborg safely during the night. However, daybreak revealed *Rattvisa*-62 and *Göta Lejon*-70 alone on the sea. Attacked by *Izraslav*-66 and *Venus*-44, *Rattvisa* was captured, but the other battleship escaped.

The Battle of Vyborg was one of the greatest disasters ever suffered by the Swedish Navy. Along with 6,000 casualties, it had lost 7 ships of the line and 3 frigates without inflicting much damage on the enemy. Nevertheless, Chichagov had let a golden opportunity slip through his grasp. Losses of 7,000 men, and 11 badly damaged ships of the line, galled him as he watched the Swedes escape certain destruction. He could only blockade their fleet in Sveaborg. [125]

After struggling through bad weather, the Swedish *Schärensflotten* gathered at Svensksund with 12 rowing frigates, 1 jakt, 18 galleys, 153 gunsloops, 10 espingars and 8 mortar vessels. Nassau-Siegen caught up with them on 7 July with a flotilla of 30 sailing ships (including 9 rowing frigates), 23 galleys, 3 floating batteries, 77 gunsloops, 8 bomb vessels and 161 smaller craft. Again, the Swedes had blocked the eastern approaches to the sound, so the Russians formed up for an attack through the southern entrance. There, Gustav III drew up his flotilla in a concave line between two large islands, leaving his center weak to entice attack, with a large reserve of gunsloops behind it. From the shelter of the islands, he could concentrate the fire of his strong wings upon enemy vessels taking the bait.

Without a preliminary reconnaissance, Nassau-Siegen sent his left wing forward first, against the northern limb of the Swedish deployment. When the attack faltered in strong winds and a choppy sea, the king struck its flank with his reserve gunsloops. The flight of the Russian left wing exposed their center to fire from the Swedish right wing, causing fearful casualties as it pushed in to attack the tempting Swedish center. By 1900, the Russians were engaged in a confused retreat, smothered by Swedish fire that caused 3,000 casualties and destroyed 64 vessels.

When Gustav III ordered an advance the following day, the Russians fled to Aspo, leaving 6,000 captives in the hands of the Swedes, who lost only 4 boats. Nassau-Siegen was relieved by Admiral Kozlianinov, who called for reinforcements before he would act.

Vyborg had been avenged, and both Catherine II and Gustav III desired peace. The Treaty of Värälä on **14 August 1790** restored the prewar borders. However, Russia now possessed 46 battleships, while the Swedes retained only 16. Until the rise of the German Navy in the Nineteenth Century, Russia dominated the Baltic.

Gustav III had alienated the Swedish aristocracy with his use of public opinion to crush their opposition to renewal of royal absolutism. Now, the unfavorable outcome of the war eroded his popular support. At a masked ball on 16 March 1792 he was shot, and died two weeks later. However, Duke Karl von Södermanland forestalled an aristocratic resurgence by taking over as regent for his underage nephew, who ascended the throne in 1796 as Gustav IV Adolph. The king's secret police took care of most of the opposition. His reign was marked by an obstinate short-sightedness that would soon contribute to the ruin of Sweden. [126]

Like other maritime nations, Sweden had suffered piratical depredations as her shipping passed through the western Mediterranean. The Barbary States of Morocco, Algiers, Tunis and Tripoli garnered much wealth by running down rich merchant ships with swift xebecs and tartanes, often holding the crews for ransom. Treaties with the Moorish rulers were discarded as soon as the emissaries departed. Depredations increased as the new century arrived, Sweden losing eleven ships during the summer of 1800. Finally, Colonel Lieutenant Tornquist was sent to the Mediterranean on the frigate *Thetis* to negotiate at the muzzle of a gun. He joined the American officers Dale and Bainbridge in escorting both Swedish and American ships through the dangerous waters. In 1802, the frigates *Camilla, Sprengtporten* and

MERCHANT kof
1780, 250 tons, 80 men

*Jupiter* accompanied smaller warships to reinforce Tornquist. They forced favorable terms from the Pasha of Tripoli by blockading his port. As they cooperate with American ships in convoying ships, the piracy gradually decreased.

## *Russo-Swedish War* - 1808-9

The horrors of the French Revolution instilled a hatred in King Gustav IV Adolph for the ruthless leader that emerged - Napoleon Bonaparte. He sided with the Third Coalition against France during the disastrous campaigns of 1805-7, and lost Pomerania and Stralsund as a result.

Livgarde Cavalry Regiment
Livgarde, Konungen, Drottningen, Jägare, Drottningenänkling
    and Engelbrechten Infantry Regiments (elite)
Liv-Grenadiere Infantry Regiment

Skåne and Mörner Hussar Regiments
Västgota, Småland and Adelsfana Cavalry Regiments
Nyland and Bohuslän Dragoon Regiments
Skåne Carabiniers
Karelen Finnish Dragoon Regiment

Dal, Södermanland, Västgota-Dal, Kronoberg, Västerbotten, Älvsborg, Jönköping,
    Kalmar, Jämtland Lätt, Västmanland, Nerike-Värmland, Hälsingland, Uppland,
    and Skaraborg Infantry Regiments

Nyland, Savolaks, Österbotten, Björneborg, Tavastehus and Åbo
    Finnish Infantry Regiments
Tavastehus Finnish Jägarebataljon [127]

The Swedish Army was now a completely national one, with no foreign mercenaries employed by the king. However, a considerable portion of the troops were Finnish, an important addition for the coming conflict. Infantry now included riflemen, with hussars added as light cavalry.

Following European fashion, military coats had been shortened to coatees while headgear ran to tall hats and crested helmets. The basic color remained a dark blue, however.

**Infantry** and **Artillery** wore a dark blue coatee with red facings, long gray trousers with black shoes, and a tall, round black hat.

**Life Guards of Horse** wore a white coatee with light blue facings, blue breeches with black boots, and a black, crested helmet.

**Life Guard Dragoons** wore a dark blue coatee with white facings, blue breeches with black boots, and a black, crested helmet.

**Hussars** wore a dark blue coatee with yellow braid, blue breeches with black boots, and a tall, round black hat.

**Dragoons** wore a dark blue coatee with various facings, buff breeches with black boots, and a round black hat.

Although Russia insisted that Sweden act against British maritime policies, Gustav refused to renew membership in the Armed Neutrality. Therefore, General K.N. von Klercker was not surprised when a courier arrived at his headquarters in Helsingfors, Finland on **1 February 1808** with news of an impending invasion of this important Swedish province. Field Marshal Vilhelm Klingspor, the overall commander in Finland, possessed a force of around 23,000 well-trained Finnish militiamen, but was in Stockholm as Sweden had expected a negotiated end to the conflict and the king was an indecisive monarch. Two brigades, totaling 6,800 men, were on the Kymene River frontier in southern Finland, under the command of Generals von Klercker and Adlercreutz. Colonel Cronstedt's third brigade of 2,900 men was in the interior, north of St. Michel (Mikkeli). Another 2,500 men were scattered in small units throughout Finland. The remainder of the militia was along the northern coast of the Gulf of Bothnia.

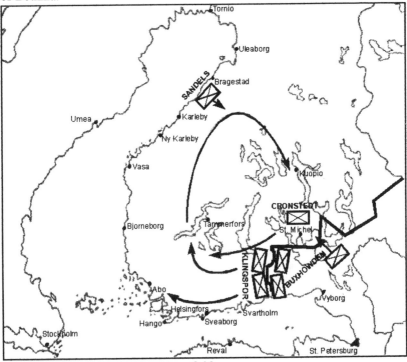

When Russian General Buxhöwden violated the Finnish frontiers early on **21 February 1808**, without a declaration of war, he met little resistance. Two columns, under Generals Kamensky and Bagration, crossed the Kymene River with 16,000 men. Another force of 8,000 men, under General Tuchkov, advanced into central Finland. Swedish dragoons clashed with swarms of Cossacks racing ahead of the enemy columns. Klingspor ordered the Swedish land forces to withdraw northward along the coast, leaving large garrisons to defend the naval bases of Svartholm, Sveaborg (7,000 men, 2,000 guns), Hangö and Åbo. Rather than defend the fortress of Sveaborg, which guarded the capital of Helsingfors (Helsinki), Field Marshal Klingspor withdrew to Tammerfors on 7 March with his main force and ordered the rest of his forces to concentrate there. Buxhöwden had entered Helsingfors five days earlier. On 11 March, General Bagration began the pursuit of Klingspor. Tuchkov was sent along the interior road to cut him off, but he was too late. Klingspor reached Tammerfors safely, where Adlercreutz's brigade was attacked near Tammerfors on 11 March, the Russians crossing the Kumo River a week later. By 16 April, they were approaching the important port city of Uleåborg on the north coast of the Gulf of Bothnia. Klingspor had withdrawn to Bragestad, 50 kilometers to the south of the city.

Capitalizing on their easy progress, Czar Alexander had already proclaimed his annexation of Finland on the first day of the month. However, the Swedes were not through. A brigade under Colonel Johan Sandels advanced upstream from Bragestad in mid-April, and caught two Russian detachments unprepared. The Russian advance was stopped, the troops of Generals Tuchkov and Bulatov falling back upon Kuopio without being pursued. [128]

As in most Scandinavian countries of the time, the army that controlled the coasts of Finland controlled communications, for the interior was poorly served by roads. Russian forces started from their base of Svensksund (Kotka) at the border. The besieged Swedish naval bases on the Gulf of Finland were of modern construction and well supplied. Although the small Svartholm fortress fell on 18 March, the Sveaborg fortress, protecting Helsingfors from its location in the archipelago south of the city, should have been a tough proposition. Its commandant, Admiral Cronstedt, had more defenders than the Russians besieging him.

The Swedes had developed a sophisticated fleet of vessels designed for fighting through the treacherous Baltic archipelagoes. This specialized fleet, known variously as the *Schärensflotten* (Shallows Fleet) or *Armensflotten* (Army Fleet), was first organized in 1756. It was intended for fighting the similar Russian flotillas, transporting the army to landing points, and supporting it with artillery fire and provisions. Initial equipment consisted of galleys, rowed by 40-44 oarsmen, but also carrying lateen sails to permit sailing lengthier courses. Soon, however, the ship list began to bristle with specialized types of craft. Handier gunsloops, with 20-30 oarsmen, and the still smaller 10-20 oared gunyawls, proliferated. Mortar and howitzer boats were developed to bombard defiladed positions. The new carronades inspired the building of a number of small 14-16 oar *espingars* to carry them. Schooners, cutters, luggers and jakts were employed as scouts and liaison craft. Stores, blacksmith, ammunition, cooking, ambulance and other services were provided by special craft.

However, attempts to develop larger specialized vessels were not as successful. The earliest was the *turuma*, a bark-rigged galley type with heavy guns below the outriggers supporting 38 oars. The *udema* had two spritsails, with a jigger and headsails for sailing balance, and 36 oars for close work.

249

However, its most unique feature was a row of heavy guns on the centerline that could fire to either side, although not while being rowed. The largest, and most successful, was the *hemmema*, a frigate-like vessel employing lateen sails on three masts and 40 oars below the gundeck. Sweden also had a shallows flotilla on the Kattegat and, to allow use of the large vessels on either coast, Chapman developed the *pojama*, a smaller version of the hemmema that could pass through the internal waterways from Stockholm to Göteborg. It used a square mainsail and a gaff mizzen with 32 oars, and was armed with two heavy guns both at bow and stern. These vessels proved too small to combat the conventional seagoing warships, yet too unwieldy to efficiently support the little gun vessels. To supplement the cruising elements, Sweden purchased and armed merchantmen in time of war. By 1808, the shallows fleet was more efficient than the *Örlogsflotten*.

**Schärensflotten** or **Armensflotten** (Rear Adm. Hjelmstjerna)

ROYAL SHIPS
*Amphion* (schooner) - 16
*Amadis* (jakt) - **8**
*Esplendian* (jakt) - **8**

HEMMEMA
*Styrbjörn, Hjalmar, Starkotter* -34
*Erik Segersäll* (1809) - 32
*Birger Jarl* (1809) - 32

**HEMMEMA** 34 guns
1790, 400 tons
24-36 pdrs, 2-12 pdrs, 8-2 pdrs

ARMED CRUISERS
*Der Biederman* (ex-Danish corvette) - 24
*Fredrik* (brig) - 18
*Economien* (brig) - 16
*Svalan* (brig) - 16
*Johanna Christina* (brig) - 14
*Blomman* (brig) - 14
*Freden* (brig) - 14
*Celeritas* (schooner) - 18

SCHOONERS
*Fröja* - 16
*Jehu* - 16
*Eglee* (ex-Russian) - 10
*No.2-6* - 4

**TURUMA** 30 guns
1770, 300 tons
22-18 pdrs, 8-2 pdrs

CUTTERS
*Kottka* (ex-Russian) - 8
*Gripen* - 9
*Ystad* - 8

LUGGER
*Nortstjärnan* - 8

JAKTS
*Tokan* - 8
*Tärnan* - 4
*Gustava* - 2
*Orust* - 2

**UDEMA** 13 guns
1780, 300 tons
9-12 pdrs, 2-18 pdrs, 2-8 pdrs

250

GALLEYS
*St. Petersburg, Penny, Tytters,*
*Orell, Seskjär, Woronna, Korotcka* - 22
(captured from Russians in 1790)
*Seraphims Orden, Svärdsorden, Stockholm,*
*Taube, von Höpken, von Seth, von Rosen,*
*Posse, Västgöta-Dal,*
*Hälsingland, Nyköping*
*Wrede, Västmanland,*
*Kalmar, Älvsborg*
*Västervik, Småland, Närke,*
*Jämtland, Halland* - 12

| | |
|---|---|
| HALF-GALLEY | MORTAR VESSELS |
| *Arendal* - 12 | *No.1-6* - 1 |
| | |
| GUNSLOOPS | HOWITZER BOATS |
| *No.1-130* - 6 | *No.1-2* - 2 |
| | |
| DECKED GUNSLOOPS | GUNYAWLS |
| *No.1-13* - 6 | *No.1-56* - 1 |
| | |
| CARRONADE ESPINGARS | DECKED GUNYAWL |
| *No.1-33* - 3 | *No.1* - 7 |

**POJAMA** 14 guns
1810, 200 tons
4-24 pdrs, 10-24 pdr carr.

**GUNSLOOP** 6 guns
1780, 100 tons
2-24 pdrs, 4-3 pdrs

**GUNYAWL** 1 gun
1800, 60 tons
1-24 pdr

**GALLEY** 12 guns
1750, 200 tons
2-24 pdrs, 10-3 pdrs

**MORTAR VESSEL** 1 gun
1800, 90 tons
1-60 pdr mortar

The Army Fleet was subdivided into squadrons, battalions and divisions that included 12 storeships, 18 ammunition boats, 23 cook sloops, and 5 ambulance boats. Under full complement, the battalions were to have:

### GUNSLOOP BATTALION

1 hemmema
12 gunsloops
2 mortar boats
3 avisos (reconnaissance vessels)
Train
    3 cook, 1 water, 1 ammunition, 1 ambulance vessel

### GALLEY BATTALION

3 galley divisions
    2 galleys
6 espingars
1 aviso
1 water vessel [129]

251

The Russians assaulted the first Sveaborg fortifications on 17 March, making good progress. Inept Admiral Cronstedt permitted the enemy to breach his positions, one by one, then prematurely ordered his troops to destroy the fortress on **4 May**. With this act, Cronstedt not only precluded future use of the base by the Swedish fleet, he also failed to order destruction of the large fleet of shallow-water vessels in the harbor. The Russians had been handicapped in the battles among the Finnish archipelago by their shortage of such vessels. At Kronstadt, they had only 60 gunsloops and gunyawls when the war began, with 10 more at Svensksund. The 34 gunsloops on the great Russian lakes were landbound. At Sveaborg, the Russians more than doubled their shallows fleet with the capture of 2 Swedish hemmemas, 8 jakts, 83 gunsloops and 36 gunyawls, a decisive windfall.

With the aid of the ex-Swedish vessels, the Russians moved to occupy the traditional bridge to the Swedish mainland - the Åland Islands. General Buxhöwden advanced with 12,000 men to Åbo where he found 4 jakts, 43 gunsloops and 45 gunyawls, 50 of which were burned by the Swedes. He then started through the *Skärgård*. Alarm sparked Sweden, for of 40,000 men in the country, only 13,000 were formed up for defense of the east coast as there was a very real danger of a Danish invasion in the south and west. They were soon to be needed in parrying several Russian maritime thrusts.

By the end of the Eighteenth Century, Russia possessed the second most powerful seagoing navy in the world. Her Baltic Fleet, based at Kronstadt near St. Petersburg, consisted of 9 ships of the line, 7 frigates, and a dozen smaller warships. Admiral Bodisco appeared off the strategic island of Gotland and landed 1,700 men on 21 April. With the hated *fiend* on their doorstep, the Swedes were stirred to action. Activating most of the ships retained from 1790, they had a large *Örlogsflotten* (War Fleet) ready for sea:

**Örlogsflotten** (Adm. Karl, Duke von Södermanland)

SHIPS OF THE LINE
Third Rate
*Gustav IV Adolf* - 78
*Vladislaff* -76
*Adolf Fredrik, Dristigheten,*
    *Fadernesland, Gustav III, Morgenstjernan* - 74
*Fredrik Adolf, Manligheten,*
    *Åran, Försiktigheten, Tapperheten* - 64

FRIGATES
Fifth Rate
*Euridice* - 46
*Chapman, Uppland, Wismar* - 44
*Camilla, Bellona* - 42
*Jarramas* - 34
*Illerin* - 32

SLOOPS
16 snows, schooners, jakts

Rear Admiral Cederström was placed in command of a squadron of 6 ships of the line, 2 frigates and a few smaller ships. At the end of April, he appeared off the Åland Islands and snared the garrison of 500 Russian troops. On **14 May**, he landed 1,900 men and 6 guns at Sandviken on the east coast of the island of Gotland. They took the road to Visby and captured the Russian force two days later. Swedes breathed easier.

252

Finns in the occupied part of Finland took to the forests and began guerrilla warfare under Swedish officers. Colonel Sandels was particularly successful in eastern Finland, where his men harassed the Russians at Neishlot and Wilmansstrand, forcing them to withdraw into defensive camps.

Yet, events in Finland soon confirmed Sweden's worst fears of "the terrible Rus". When a Russian column reached the coast at Vasa on 24 June, the troops got out of hand and sacked the town. Later, the Swedes succeeded in regaining control of this important port.

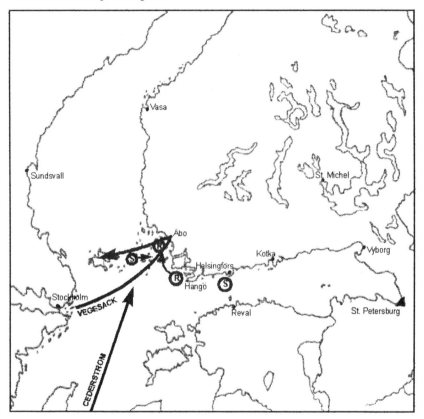

Operations in the Skärgård

Fearful that the Russians would advance across the Åland Islands to the Swedish mainland, Admiral von Södermanland dispatched the Swedish fleet to block them. Rear Admiral Cederström left Karlskrona on 17 June with 11 ships of the line, 2 frigates and 8 smaller vessels and sailed to Åbo. Escorted by a squadron of 20 gunsloops from the Stockholm Squadron under Rear Admiral Hjelmstjerna, General Lieutenant Eberhard von Vegesack passed from Stockholm to Åbo with 3,000 men. Led by the Royal Life Guards, they landed at Lemo on **19 June**, just southeast of Åbo. However, the Russians had 3,500 men formed up, and they drove the Swedes back to their boats with a bayonet charge. The arrival of 90 vessels of the Russian shallows fleet threatened to cut off their retreat. Vegesack retired to the Åland Islands three days later, leaving the gunsloops at Korpo Island, halfway to Åbo.

253

Early in August, the Russians made another attempt to gain control of the *Skärgård*. The main Russian fleet of 90 gunsloops and gunyawls was at Åbo. A second fleet of 70 craft left Hangö to join it. To prevent their consolidation into an overwhelming force, Rear Admiral Hjelmstjerna deployed his 22 gunsloops across the narrow Sandöström through which the Russians were passing from Hangö. Russian General Buxhöwden built fortifications on both sides of the channel, necessitating the landing of 1,000 Swedish troops on Kimito Island to destroy them. However, these were men of the Swedish Landwehr reserves and could make no headway against the Russian regulars. When the Russian shallows fleet approached on **2 August**, the batteries joined them in attacking the Swedish gunsloops. At 0900, Hjelmstjerna was forced to retire, leaving the Russians in control of the vital communication route.

Ironically, the Finnish Squadron of the Swedish *Schärensflotten* lay idling near Hangö while this battle was in progress. Having failed to concentrate their forces, the Swedes now faced the prospect of a superior Russian force operating on interior lines between their Finnish and Stockholm squadrons. At Hangö were the vessels captured earlier from the Swedes at Sveaborg. The officers of the Finnish Squadron decided to utilize the 2,000 troops with them to recapture or destroy the captured fleet. On the moonless night of 17-8 August, the Swedes succeeded in boarding several vessels, but were able to cut out only a few gun vessels, as the rudely awakened Russians cannonaded the hemmemas *Styrbjörn* and *Hjalmar*, driving off the boarders. [130]

It was obvious that Sweden was rapidly being beaten. More than a century of frequent warfare had depleted her human and material resources. Now she was facing enemies on two fronts. Great Britain decided to act before Sweden dropped out of the war and left the Baltic to Napoleon. Vice Admiral Saumarez was dispatched with a fleet of 1-100, 9-74s, 2-64s, 5 frigates and many brigs, sloops, bombs and fireships deemed useful in the skerries of Scandinavia. Accompanying him was a

**MERCHANT** West Coast koster
1780, 80 tons, 30 men

convoy of 200 transports carrying 14,000 troops under General Moore. Rear Admiral Keats, with three 74s and several of the smaller vessels, distracted Denmark by attacking Fyen at Nyborg on 9 August. While he remained in the Öresund to watch the Danes, Saumarez sent his other rear admiral, Hood, ahead with two 74s to reinforce the Swedish fleet and prod it into action. He arrived just in time, for the Russians had finally left the shelter of their base.

To counter the Swedish moves, Admiral Khanykov took the Russian Baltic Fleet (9 ships of the line, 3-50s, 6 frigates, 2 corvettes, 2 brigs, 2 cutters and 9 smaller vessels) out of Kronstadt at the end of July and passed to Hangö, where he could watch the Swedes. Disgusted with Cederström's inactivity, the king had replaced him with Rear Admiral Nauckhoff on 1 July. When Hood joined the *Örlogsflotten* on 20 August, the Russian fleet weighed from Hangö and took station off Åbo. After standing in during the evening of the 22nd, it retired to Hangö Head. A third of the Swedish seamen were ill with scurvy, making their ships inefficient. Nevertheless, they sailed on **25 August**, sighting the Russian fleet southeast of Hangö Head at 0900. The Russians made off to the southeast under full sail. Uncoppered, the Swedish battleships fell behind.

254

By 1600, Hood's two 74s were only 7 kilometers astern of the Russians, but the Swedes lagged 16 kilometers behind. Khanykov ordered his ships to scatter, in an attempt to save his fleet. Hood came up with the *Vsevolod*-74 and battered her into striking. However, Russian ships came to her rescue and she was towed to safety by a frigate. About noon, the Russian fleet anchored in Baltischport (Paldiski) on the northwest coast of Estonia. Saumarez joined the blockaders on 30 August with his flagship *Victory*-100, 2-74s and a 64. Early in October, the Swedish frigate *Camilla*-44 and the British frigate *Salsette*-36 reconnoitered the anchorage preparatory to sending in fireships, but found their plans thwarted by a boom across the harbor mouth. With winter approaching, the allies withdrew, allowing Khanykov to move to the safety of Kronstadt.

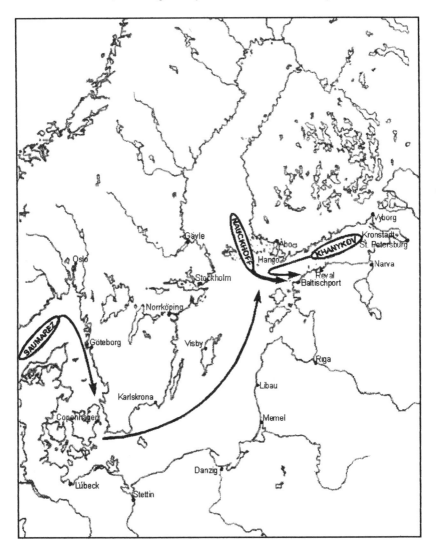

Baltic Naval Operations

255

Once powerful Sweden had put up feeble resistance to the enemy, due largely to the incompetency of the high command. Unprepared for the war that he had initiated, Gustav IV now found his army fragmented into three isolated combat zones, incapable of mutual support.

**Swedish Army** (King Gustav IV Adolph)

Western Army (Gen. Adlersparre) - central and southern Sweden
35,000 men

Southern Finland Army (Gen.Lt. von Vegesack)
5,600 men - Åland Islands
3,000 men - Björneborg

Northern Finland Army (Field Marshal Klingspor) - NW Finland
11,000 men

**12 pdr Field Gun**
121 mm, 3000 lbs, 12 lb ball,
1500 yds max, 700 yds eff

Klingspor had not exploited the successful counteroffensive of April, halting 70 kilometers southeast of Vasa on a line Kristinestad-Kauhajoki-Alavo, while the Russians withdrew to Kuopio to lick their wounds.

By 14 August, the Russian commander in the north, General Kamensky, was ready to resume his advance. From Tammerfors, his columns converged on Vasa, the seaport at the narrowest part of the Gulf of Bothnia. Colonel Georg von Dobeln blocked the route through Kauhajoki with 2,300 men. A second confrontation, near the coast at Lappfjard, also resulted in a Russian reverse. Swinging southwest from Töysä was General Major Gripenberg with 1,500 men on the Swedish left flank. Thirty kilometers behind him, General Major Johan Cronstedt marched with a brigade of 2,800 men from Salmi toward the main Russian forces a hundred kilometers inland. Sent ahead to Alavo, Major Adlercreutz mounted a turning movement with the advance guard and routed the Russian point, gaining time for the Swedes to concentrate for a more formidable defense.

However, on the last day of August, three Russian armies threatened the defenders. General Kamensky broke through the Swedish lines at Alavo with 9,000 Russian troops. Enveloping the Swedish east flank from Saarjarvi, General Vlastov hovered with 4,500 men. General Uschakov was poised to sweep along the coast from Lappfjard with 6,000 men. Field Marshal Klingspor had only about 5,000 Finnish

256

militiamen left to face them. Gripenberg made a brave stand at Ruona with 6-6 pdr and 4-3 pdr artillery pieces sited on a knoll commanding the approaches to the town. The Swedish troops were formed up on the bluffs to the north. Attacking westwards from the valley, the Russians drove the Swedes back to Salmi, where they rallied to stop the enemy advance. A Russian column attempted to cut them off by marching up the west shore of Lake Kuortane, but a brigade had been stationed there to block such a move. By evening of **2 September**, the Swedes were in a bad way, having lost 1,000 men in three days of fighting. Klingspor ordered a retirement on Vasa. Kamensky followed through Lappo to the coast at Ny Karleby, north of Vasa. Vlastov pressed northward to Gamla Karleby. With Ushakov at Lappfjard, Vasa was now surrounded. Following another defeat at Orovats, north of the port, Klingspor negotiated a truce with Buxhöwden on **17 September**. Despite the fatigue of his troops, and the onset of winter in these high latitudes, Czar Alexander repudiated the truce and renewed the offensive, his troops advancing with little resistance. The situation now hopeless, Klingspor left for Sweden after transferring command to General von Klercker. By the terms of an armistice with Kamensky at Olkijoki on 11 November, Gustav IV agreed to withdraw from Finland. Klercker retired toward Tornio, unmolested. Russian troops occupied all of Finland by the end of the month. At Uleåborg, the Russians confiscated 2 jakts and 25 gunsloops. The carefully assembled *Schärensflotten* was largely gone.

With enemy troops poised just across the Gulf of Bothnia, Sweden sent an expeditionary force to seize Åbo and preempt a possible Russian move across the steppingstones of the Ålands archipelago into Sweden. On 30 August, with 19 gunsloops Admiral Hjelmstjerna attacked 20 Russian gunsloops and 4 gunyawls in the Grönvikssund near the edge of the archipelago north of Åbo. He was successful in driving them through the Palvasund leading to Lemo. On Sunday morning, **17 September**, General Major Lantingshausen's 2,600 men disembarked from Swedish transports and landed just south of Nystad. Admiral Rayalin was placed in command of the Finnish Squadron of the *Schärensflotten* and ordered to force the Russian flotillas out of the Palvasund. The following day, he deployed 34 gunsloops across the sound in a line stretching for more than two kilometers to Palva Island. At 0300, Rear Admiral Mäsojedov advanced through the fog to strike the Swedish line in front with his 7 "rowing frigates", 28 gunsloops and 52 gunyawls. He intended to use his superior strength to envelop both ends of the Swedish line, then break through to destroy the Swedish transports. By 0600, the Russian left wing had been repulsed, but the Swedish left wing was also giving way. The Swedes retired in good order to the Grönvikssund after losses of 150 men and 1 gunsloop. The Russians lost 200 men and 3 gunsloops. The Swedes tried again on 26 September. Two detachments of 10 gunsloops were sent ahead while 33 more escorted a transport force traversing the Grönvikssund. Skillfully, the advanced gunsloops kept the Russians at bay for a week until the troops landed. The route to Sweden across the archipelago was blocked, but their efforts were in vain. Finland was already lost.

Sweden was in grave danger. Her moat, the Gulf of Bothnia, was freezing over for the winter. Alexander was outraged that the Swedish Army had been allowed to escape. In December, he replaced Buxhöwden with General Knorring and ordered him to invade Sweden. The new commander gathered three armies to cross on the ice. The plan was for General Schuvalov to advance southward from Tornio along the coast of Sweden to Umeå. There, it would be joined by a second column crossing the ice from Vasa. However, as with many Russian

257

operations, delays postponed the advances until 10 March, by which time the spring thaw was imminent.

To face the Russian invasion, Field Marshal Klingspor commanded a Northern Army from his headquarters at Härnösand with 9,000 men in two divisions. Holding the Tornio River frontier at the head of the Gulf of Bothnia was the first division of General Gripenberg. The second division, under General Cronstedt at Sundsvall, was deployed in the Umeå-Piteå area along the northern coast of Sweden. General von Dobeln was in command of the 9,000 man Southern Army protecting Stockholm. Thus, the Swedes had 18,000 men to face 26,000 Russians bent on their destruction.

**MERCHANT** West Coast galeas
1780, 200 tons, 70 men

Trouble was brewing at home for King Gustav IV. Denmark had lost effective control of Norway after her fleet was carried away by the British in 1807. The Swedish king tried to acquire the valuable province by force. However, when General Adlersparre crossed the frontier with his Western Army, he was thrown back by Norwegian troops under Prince Christian August von Augustenborg. The victorious Norwegian troops could invade Jämtland or Värmland, slicing through the heart of Sweden. Furthermore, Napoleon had decided to force Sweden into his Continenal System and had sent Marshal Bernadotte to Fyen with a considerable force. The French were preparing to join the Danish Army on Sjaelland, from where they could cross the Öresund to Skåne. Sweden had 50,000 troops under arms, but had to keep a large number of them idly watching the Danes. The king's inept management of the war fomented palace conspiracies. General Adlersparre instigated rebellion in Värmland and marched on Stockholm. Before he arrived, General Adlercreutz put the king in custody. On **13 March 1809**, Karl, Duke von Södermanland, was elected King Karl XIII.

At the moment of crisis, Sweden was threatening to break up in civil war. The Swedish troops on the Åland Islands were moved to Stockholm to control the situation. Thus, when General Bagration advanced from Åbo with 20,000 men, he had no opposition. Passing through the islands, he reached the frozen Ålands Haf on **14 March**. Five days later, five hundred Cossacks and 3 hussar squadrons crossed the ice and occupied Grisslehamn. Swedish General von Dobeln hurried northward with 3,500 men and deployed within 15 kilometers of the Russian cavalry. He began negotiating an armistice, fearing that the Russians would advance through Roslagen to Stockholm before he could be reinforced. Help came in the form of a southerly gale that threatened to break up the ice in the Ålands Haf and trap the Russian forces in Roslagen. General Knorring ordered Bagration to withdraw his advance guard to the Åland Islands. Stockholm was safe, for the present.

Five hundred kilometers to the north, other Russian forces had also invaded Sweden. Off Umeå lies the northern *Qvarken*, a chain of islands stretching across the Bothnian narrows to Vasa in Finland. The first of 5,000 men left Vasa on **17 March**, under the command of General Barclay de Tolly, and crossed on the ice to reach the estuary of the Ume River three days later. Three thousand men were soon formed up and quickly forced Umeå's 1,100 man garrison to surrender, although the Swedes did burn the gunsloops in the harbor.

258

With his full army on Swedish soil, Barclay de Tolly started south along the coastal road toward the heart of Sweden.

The third invasion began with the taking of Torneå by Schuvalov's army on **18 March**. At Kalix, 40 kilometers west of the frontier, the Russians trapped much of General Gripenberg's division, and he surrendered the remainder on 25 March. The king signed an armistice two days later. However, Czar Alexander repudiated the agreement and continued operations. As the Swedish and British fleets could operate northward once the Bothnian ice broke up, Russian General Kamensky was cautious in his advance southward along the coastal road.

British Vice Admiral Saumarez returned to Karlskrona early in June 1809, this time with 10 ships of the line and 17 smaller vessels. He conducted raids on the coast of the Gulf of Finland and blockaded Kronstadt, Reval and Riga. Russian coastal vessels scurried for cover, but the forces threatening Sweden did not retire. The presence of the British fleet also suppressed Danish participation. Apparently hoping to bring about union with Norway, in July the Swedish Riksdag elected the Danish commander in Norway, Prince Christian August, as successor to the childless Karl XIII. Denmark concluded a hasty peace to prevent a Swedish takeover of its prized province.

This armistice released many troops for use in the east, and Swedish Admiral von Puke was given command of an expedition to trap the Russians at Umeå. With a fleet of 3 ships of the line, 5 frigates, 6 galleys, 6 decked gunsloops, 36 gunsloops, and 4 mortar vessels, he put to sea from Härnösand on 15 August, in company with 40 transports carrying 11,000 troops of General Wachtmeister. Each ship of the line towed a battalion of gunsloops, with the frigates towing the other small vessels. The following day, he put in at Ratan, 40 kilometers north of Umeå, and was joined by 2 galleys, 18 gunsloops and 3 others. [131]

With his troops disembarked, Wachtmeister started south toward Umeå on **17 August**, but was brought up short at Säfvar by 9,000 Russians under General Kamensky. Ineptly, Wachtmeister tried to use his superior numbers in a frontal attack, lost 1,000 men in 10 hours of fighting, and was driven back to Ratan.

259

The beaten Swedish army took refuge on a peninsula in the harbor. Admiral Puke formed up his *Schärensflotten* beyond the narrow Ratansund, where he could enfilade the Russians as they approached the peninsula. The mortar vessels and the galleys were at the southern end of the line, while 4 gunsloops in a basin adjacent to the peninsula pounded every Russian battle line as they formed up. The army was saved, but the expedition failed in its mission of destroying bridges to cut off Kamensky's retreat. Puke retired to Stockholm. Although the approach of General Cronstedt's division forced Kamensky out of Umeå, the Swedish government had exhausted its resources. With his signature on the Treaty of Fredrikshamn of **17 September 1809**, King Karl XIII reduced Sweden to a minor power, losing Finland, part of northern Sweden, and the Åland Islands, although Pomerania was restored.

## The Coalition Against Napoleon - 1813-1815

With elderly King Karl XIII losing his faculties, the death in May 1810 of Prince Christian August, his chosen successor, precipitated another search. A proposal to invite one of Napoleon's most independent-minded marshals to the throne brought immediate approbation. Jean Bernadotte won election in August as Crown Prince Karl Johan. One of his first steps was to declare war on England, but he did little to assist Napoleon.

When his former emperor declared war on Russia in 1811, Karl Johan realized it would be unwise for Sweden to try to regain Finland at Russia's expense. He initiated a new foreign policy aimed at acquiring Norway instead. Napoleon's occupation of Swedish Pomerania in March 1812, without a declaration of war, facilitated rejection of his old master. To further good relations with Russia, he entered into agreements with Czar Alexander in April 1812. On 7 July, he finally broke relations with Napoleon and concluded peace with England.

The new policy bore fruit when Napoleon was defeated following his invasion of Russia in the fall of 1812. Karl Johan bided his time until the issue was decided, then moved 28,000 Swedish troops and 62 guns into Pomerania early in 1813. As Napoleon was forced back through Prussia, Karl Johan slowly moved his army southward to Berlin. On **16 August 1813** he was given command of the Prusso-Swedish Army of the North.

**Army of the North** (Crown Prince Karl Johan)
Swedish Army
40,000 men, 62 guns
Bülow's, Winzingerode's Corps
70,000 Prussians

Each of the Swedish infantry battalions contained a jäger company. The army had updated its uniforms to include some of the appointments popular in other European armies of the time:

**Lifeguard of Horse** wore a white coatee with light blue facings, blue breeches with black boots, black shako.
**Lifeguard Dragoons** wore a blue coatee with white facings, blue breeches with black boots, black shako.
**Infantry** and **Artillery** wore a dark blue coatee with red facings, gray trousers with black shoes, black shako.
**Dragoons** wore a dark blue coatee with yellow facings, buff breeches with black boots, black shako.
**Hussars** (4 regiments) wore a dark blue coatee with yellow braid, blue breeches with black boots, black busby.

260

Napoleon tried to block the advance of the Crown Prince with Marshal Ney's Corps, but he trapped Ney at Deanewitz on 6 September, inflicting 10,000 casualties. The 7,000 men he lost in victory increased Karl Johan's caution. He has been roundly criticized for the dilatory nature of his subsequent operations, but he had more than the defeat of Napoleon in mind. With 80,000 men, he approached Rosslau, on the Elbe near Wittenberg, and established bridgeheads over the river on 24 September. When he was unable to make further progress, Marshal Blucher was sent north with the 60,000 Prussians of his Army of Silesia. The success of Blucher in breaking out of the bridgehead on 3 October did much to elevate him to a prominent position in the Coalition army. Napoleon left Dresden and moved north to confront the two armies pouring over the Elbe. However, when he advanced toward Blucher on 9 October, the wily Prussian moved west, and the thrust missed its mark. Napoleon had to withdraw to Dresden with Blucher in pursuit.

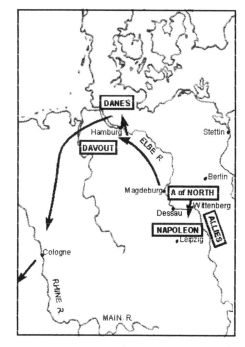

Karl Johan reluctantly followed from Dessau, for he had hoped to advance northward and pressure Denmark into giving up Norway. Stubbornly adhering to Napoleon, Danish King Frederik VI had foolishly declared war on Sweden in September, giving Karl Johan a perfect opportunity to fulfill his ambition. As Blucher attacked the north edge of Leipzig, Karl Johan was avoiding action, although he did advance later on the Prussian left and aid in driving the French back into the city.

To conduct the pursuit, Bülow's Prussian corps was sent west toward Antwerp while the rest of the Army of the North was directed northward to surround Davout's Corps at Hamburg and continue the siege of Magdeburg. Of greater interest to Karl Johan was the Danish Army deployed in Holstein. When the Swedish Army confronted them, with their benefactor retiring into France, the isolated Danes sued for peace on 15 December. The Peace of Kiel of **14 January 1814** awarded Norway to Sweden and Pomerania to Denmark. Karl Johan had attained his objective.

The Allies had become disenchanted with the recalcitrant Swedish crown prince. During a council of war at Bar-sur-Aube, France on 25 February, Bülow's and Winzingerode's Corps were detached from the army of the outraged Swedish prince and transferred to Marshal Blucher's command. Maneuvering 60 kilometers north of Blucher, Bernadotte reached the Meuse at Sedan. However, while the Prussians crossed to pass through Champagne to Paris, the Swedes stayed at Sedan. Thus, the Swedish Army played little part in the final operations before the Treaty of Fontainebleau ended the war on 16 April.

# THE UNION OF SWEDEN-NORWAY

The Peace of Kiel of 14 January 1814 had transferred Norway from Denmark to Sweden. Although some Norwegians were in favor of such a union, most desired independence. The peremptory nature of the transaction, without consulting any leaders, angered many Norwegians. The Danish viceroy refused to leave the country, and conducted an election to form a government. However, pressure was applied by the allies of Sweden to accept her rule. Norwegians took up arms, but the well-trained Swedish Army overwhelmed them. The Convention of Moss on 14 August confirmed Sweden's claims on Norway. Swedish King Karl XIII was formally declared King of Norway on 4 November, but the Act of Union assured home rule for Norway. Karl Johan became Karl XIV when the old king died shortly after the war ended. Although an anti-monarchist revolutionary at the turn of the century, he displayed autocratic tendencies as a king. The Council of the Realm became a mere bureaucracy to carry out his programs. He viewed the Diet of the Estates with a jaundiced eye, evading its deliberations by devious means. Sweden was threatened with return to an absolute monarchy. There was conflict with both his Swedish and Norwegian subjects. However, he did much to reduce Sweden's war debts and saw the Göta Canal opened in 1832. He maintained a battle fleet of 9 ships of the line (*Cesar, Hercules, Johannes, Karolus, Morgenstjernan, North Star, Pelikan, Södermanland, Tre Kronor*), a reasonable Baltic force in an age of fewer, but more expensive, battleships. The Baltic remained placid until mid-century.

## *Friendship with Denmark* - 1848, 1864

Karl XIV's son, Oscar I (1844-59), eased the domestic tensions. He left the Norwegians with more home freedom, although foreign affairs continued to be administered by Sweden. At the time of his coronation, the Swedish-Norwegian Union colors were placed in the canton of the flag. The years of his reign were peaceful ones. Many social reforms were effected and industry promoted. The first railroad was built by British engineers in 1855. However, the general European unrest of 1848 was also felt in Sweden, where there were demonstrations in the streets for greater participation in government. In an unprecedented gesture of friendship toward its ancient rival, Sweden sent an army to the Danish home island of Fyen in 1848 when Denmark was threatened with a Prussian invasion of Jutland during the war with the German Confederation. At the time, the Swedish Army contained 6 jäger and 21 line infantry regiments. A new uniform had been adopted in 1845, ironically embodying many Prussian characteristics:

>    **Infantry** wore a dark blue single-breasted tunic with yellow collar patches and piping, shoulder straps of regimental color, dark blue trousers and spiked helmet, black shoes.
>    **Artillery** wore a similar uniform, but with a dark blue collar patch and shoulder strap.
>    **Cavalry** wore a dark blue tunic with white braid, dark blue trousers, black helmet and boots.

Realizing that Prussian occupation of Denmark would threaten Sweden's sovereignty, the Swedish force blocked a move on the Danish capital.

As friendship with Denmark had increased, the size of the Swedish Navy continued to decrease. By 1848, it had only 8 ships of the line.

**Swedish Fleet**

SHIPS OF THE LINE

Third Rate
*Karl XIII - 74*
*Karl XIV Johan, Försiktigheten - 72*
*Gustav Den Store - 68*
*Prins Oskar, Stockholm - 66*
*Fädernesland, Manligheten - 62*

SHIPS NOT OF THE LINE

Fourth Rate
*Desiree - 50*

FRIGATES

Fifth Rate
*Göteborg - 44*
*Josephine, Eugenie - 36*
*Norrköping - 32*

Sixth Rate
*Von Chapman - 24*

CORVETTES
*Jarramas - 20*
*Lagerbjelke, Najaden, Karlskrona - 18*

**THIRD RATE** 74 gun ship of the line
1830, 1800 tons, 600 men,
28-32 pdrs, 30-18 pdrs,
16-9 pdrs, 8 carronades

**SLOOP** 18 gun corvette
1840, 400 tons, 120 men,
18-9 pdrs, 8 carronades

Some attention was given to development of maritime trade. Slavery was abolished on St. Barthelemy in 1848. Its principal value to Sweden lay in possession of its port of Gustavia, providing access to the West Indies trade.

When Oscar I died in 1859, he was succeeded by his son. Karl XV (1859-72) was a popular king, but a more extravagant statesman than his father. Louis de Geer abetted the king as the President of the Council of the Realm. Together, they nearly involved Sweden in the disastrous Austro-Danish War of 1864 by guaranteeing Sweden's support, without consulting either the Diet or the Council.

However, a bill to enlarge the Army, in light of the continental conflicts in progress, was rejected. The infantry musket was converted into a type of needle gun using the Swedish Karle mechanism. Late in the 1860s, the Hagstrom rifle, a breechloader using paper cartridges, was tested, but 30,000 Remington M.1867s were purchased in 1868, with more licence-built later.

The Navy had begun to build steamships, initially by conversion of sailing ships of the line. Most of the sailing ships of the earlier Danish war were still in commission, with the addition of the ship of the line *Skandinavien*-62.

screw ship of the line
**Karl XIV Johan**    1852, 2608 tons, 72 guns, 12 km/h
(converted from ship of the line)

screw ship of the line
**Stockholm**    1856, 2846 tons, 66 guns, 12 km/h
(converted from shp of the line)

screw corvette
**Orädd**    1853, 810 tons, 10 guns, 19 km/h

screw corvette
**Gefle**    1848, 1260 tons, 8 guns, 17 km/h

side-wheel corvette
**Thor**    6 guns

screw gunboats - 2

The overwhelming victory of the German Confederation forestalled the promised Swedish expedition. Tumult in the Riksdag followed revelation of the guarantee to Denmark, creating a crisis. De Geer led a reorganization of the Riksdag in 1866 that changed it from a body of four Estates to one of two chambers, one elected by city councils, the other by popular suffrage.

# DISSOLUTION OF THE UNION

Oscar II (1872-1907) presided over greater changes than did his father. St. Barts was sold to France in 1877, as Sweden had lost most of her Caribbean trade. The Army of 1882 adopted the kepi and cut of the French uniform.

**Swedish Army**

2 guard infantry regiments
1 guard cavalry regiment

2 grenadier regiments
17 line infantry regiments
4 chasseur battalions

4 hussar regiments
2 dragoon regiments
1 chasseur a cheval corps

3 artillery regiments
22 field, 6 horse, 2 position batteries

Little naval construction took place during the two decades following the Austro-Danish War. Vessels were becoming increasingly expensive, with the new designs for heavily-armed and armored warships. As Sweden did not participate in the growing Franco-German rivalry, there was little impetus for defence development. Thus, by 1880, the Swedish Navy had reached the nadir of its fortunes.

monitor

**John Ericsson**　**Thordon** 1865, 1,500 tons, 10 km/h,
**Tirfing**　　　　　2-24 cm, 25 cm armor

monitor
**Loke**　1871, 1,600 tons, 10 km/h,
　　　　2-24 cm, 46 cm armor

armored gunboat
**Berserk**　**Hildur**　1872-5, 460 tons, 13 km/h,
**Folke**　　**Sölve**　1-24 cm, 36 cm armor
**Gerda**　　**Ulf**
**Björn**

armored gunboat
**Garmer** 1880, 260 tons, 10 km/h,
**Fenris** 1-24 cm, 25 cm armor
(lake vessels)

armored gunboat
**Skjöld**　　1877, 240 tons, 6 km/h,
　　　　　1-24 cm, 20 cm armor
　　　　　(lake vessel)

screw ship of the line
**Stockholm**　　1856, 2,892 tons, 11 km/h,
　　　　　　66-30 pdrs

screw ship of the line
**Karl XIV Johan**　1852, 2,650 tons, 11 km/h,
　　　　　　　　64-24 pdrs

screw frigate
**Vanadis**　1862, 2,164 tons, 19 km/h,
　　　　　16-32 pdrs

screw corvette
**Balder**　　1870, 1,910 tons, 14 km/h,
　　　　　6-14 cm

screw gunboat
**Saga**　1878, 1554 tons, 15 km/h,
　　　7-14 cm

side-wheel corvette
**Skagul**　　1877, 545 tons, 23 km/h,
**Skäggald**　1-28, 1-12 cm
**Skuld**
**Rota**
**Verdande**
**Urd**

265

| screw gunboat | | | |
|---|---|---|---|
| **Svensksund** | **Högland** | **Motala** | 1878, 193 tons, 13 km/h, |
| **Carlsund** | **Allog** | **Astrid** | 1-12 cm |
| **Ingegud** | **Sigrid** | **Alfhild** | |
| **Gunhild** | | | |

| screw gunboat | torpedo gunboat | |
|---|---|---|
| **Blenda** 1874, 508 tons, 21 km/h, | **Ran** 1879, 638 tons, 21 km/h, 1-17 cm | |
| **Disa** 1-28, 1-12 cm | | 132 |

The question of defense preparations was debated for several years, until Russia began to enlarge its navy in 1880. The Riksdag began considering changes in its defence policy and came to preliminary agreement in 1891. From 1901, the Swedish Army began a reorganization, to be completed in 1914. The old *Indelta* system of "military tenure" was abolished. The result was an army resembling the Dutch, with regular volunteers supported by conscripted reserves. The training period for infantry was increased from 90 to 240 days, becoming even longer in the Navy.

Sweden soon had its own internal conflict to resolve. The terms of the Act of Union had never been very clear, and Norway constantly tried to improve its position toward equality with Sweden. Parliamentary government had progressed much further in Norway than in Sweden, putting the monarchy in an awkward position. From 1891, the Norwegian *Storting* demanded that consulates within its borders be held by Norwegians, and in 1898 voted to remove the Union emblem from its flag. Sweden did the same shortly afterward. The negotiations over joint control of consular and foreign affairs stirred opposition in both countries in 1903, precipitating a crisis. Norwegians charged breach of faith in the negotiations. Sweden was astonished when the *Storting* declared the Union dissolved on 7 June 1905. Some advocated settling the question by arms. The Swedish Army was organized into six divisions, recently rearmed:

**ARMY DIVISION**
1-3 cavalry regiments

3-5 infantry regiments
    2 infantry battalions
        4 rifle companies
        **Remington M.1867 12.2 mm rifles**

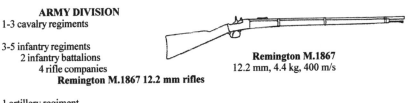

**Remington M.1867**
12.2 mm, 4.4 kg, 400 m/s

1 artillery regiment
    3 divisions
        2 batteries
            **6 Krupp 76.6 mm or 96.2 mm field guns**

**Krupp field gun**
96.2 mm,

        **HUSSAR REGIMENT**
6 sabre squadrons

        **DRAGOON REGIMENT**
8 horse squadrons
**Remington M.1870 12.2 mm carbines**

## Swedish Army

**I. Army Division** - Hälsingborg
2 hussar, 1 dragoon regiments
3 infantry, 1 artillery regiments
3 infantry, 1 transport battalions

**II. Army Division** - Linköping
1 hussar, 4 infantry, 1 artillery regiments

**III. Army Division** - Skövde
1 hussar regiment
1 rifle corps
5 infantry, 2 artillery regiments
1 engineer, 1 transport battalion

**IV. Army Division** - Stockholm
1 life guard cavalry regiment
3 life guard regiments
1 infantry, 2 artillery regiments
1 engineer, 1 transport battalion

**V. Army Division** - Stockholm
1 life guard dragoon regiment
3 infantry, 1 artillery regiments

**VI. Army Division** - Härnosänd
1 light horse corps
1 dragoon regiment
1 rifle, 3 infantry, 1 artillery regiments
1 transport battalion

**Gotland Troops**
1 infantry regiment
1 artillery corps        133,134

Uniforms were now based on French practice, and had become much more practical in the field.

**Life-guard Cavalry** wore light blue tunic, trousers and helmet with a white plume, epaulettes, plastron and trouser stripe.

**Life-guard Infantry** wore a dark blue tunic and trousers, with white epaulettes and scarlet facings, and a kepi with a black plume.

**Hussars** wore a dark blue tunic, attila, trousers and kepi with a black plume and boots. The attila had a white lining. Bars of braid on the chest and the attila were yellow.

**Dragoons** wore a white tunic with a medium blue plastron and trousers. Epaulettes were white. Bars of braid on the chest, and the trouser stripe, were yellow. Helmet and boots were black with yellow trim.

**Jämtlands Light Horse** wore a dark blue tunic and kepi, with light blue trousers. The plume and boots were black. Facings were yellow.

**Infantry** wore a dark blue tunic, trousers and kepi with yellow facings. Life-guards had scarlet facings with white epaulettes and a black plume.

**Rifles** wore a dark green tunic, trousers and hat with green feathers. Facings were black.

**Artillery** wore a dark blue tunic, trousers and kepi with yellow facings. Bars of braid on the chest were black.

**Engineers** wore a light blue tunic, trousers and kepi with yellow facings. The plume was black.

267

Rank insignia was worn on a dark blue pointed cuff piece, which had a top knot added for officers.

Generals - small gold stars below a very broad gold stripe
    General - 3 stars
    General-lieutenant - 2 stars
    General-major - 1 star

Field Officers - narrow gold stripes below a broad gold stripe
    Colonel - 3 stripes
    Colonel-lieutenant - 2 stripes
    Major - 1 stripe

Line Officers - narrow gold stripes
    Captain - 3 stripes
    Lieutenant - 2 stripes
    Ensign - 1 stripe

Non-commissioned Officers - narrow gold or yellow cloth stripes
    Staff Sergeant - 2 gold stripes
    Sergeant - 1 gold stripe
    Staff Corporal - 3 cloth stripes
    Corporal - 2 cloth stripes
    Lance Corporal - 1 cloth stripe

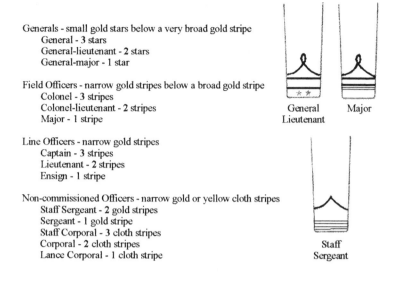

General
Lieutenant

Major

Staff
Sergeant

Menacingly, the Russians had been rapidly increasing their Baltic Fleet as the Nineteenth Century came to a close. In response, Sweden began construction of a fleet of coast defense battleships. Never able to meet the Russians on the open sea, they would, nevertheless, have been dangerous opponents among the skerries of the Swedish coast. The fleet generally operated in two cruising squadrons:

Seagoing Squadron
*Dristigheten*
*Oden, Thor, Njord*
*Svea, Göta, Thule*
4 torpedo cruisers
8 torpedo boats

Coastal Squadron
*Loke*
*John Ericsson*
*Thordon, Tirfing*
1 torpedo cruiser
4 torpedo boats

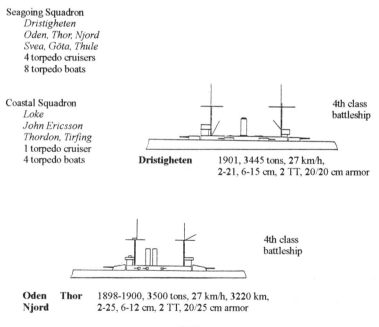

4th class
battleship

**Dristigheten**    1901, 3445 tons, 27 km/h,
    2-21, 6-15 cm, 2 TT, 20/20 cm armor

4th class
battleship

**Oden**  **Thor**    1898-1900, 3500 tons, 27 km/h, 3220 km,
**Njord**    2-25, 6-12 cm, 2 TT, 20/25 cm armor

268

4th class
battleship

| Svea | Göta | 1891-4, 3300 tons, 26 km/h, 3220 km, |
| Thule | | 2-25, 4-15 cm, 2 TT, 20/25 cm armor |
| | | 1-21, 6-15 cm (as rebuilt) |

torpedo
cruiser

| Örnen | Klas Horn | 1896-1900, 863 tons, 31 km/h, |
| Jakob Bagge | Klas Uggla | 2-12 cm, 1 TT |
| Psilander | | |

1st class
torpedo boat

| Komet | Blixt | Stjerna | 1898, 85 tons, 37 km/h, |
| Meteor | Orkan | Bris | 1450 km, 2 TT |
| Vind | Virgo | Mira | |
| Sirius | Orion | Kapella | |

1st class
torpedo boat

2nd class
torpedo boat

| Freka | 1886-93, 60 tons, 29 km/h, | Agda | Blink | 1882-91, 40 tons, 31 km/h, 2 TT |
| Gere | 1047 km, 2 TT | Agne | Blixt | (Blixt lost) |
| Gondul | | Bygve | Bylgia | |
| Gundur | | Galde | Nars | |
| Munin | | Nörve | | |

As passions rose over the issue of Norwegian independence, both brother-nations made preparations for armed conflict. The Swedish Army was twice the size of that of Norway, was more thoroughly trained, and had more specialized units. Norway had nothing to match the Swedish hussars, and the Swedes could also deploy light rifle units and heavy dragoons.

The Swedish Seagoing Squadron prepared to move through the Kattegat to interrupt Norwegian commerce in the face of the tiny hostile fleet. Small coastal battleships formed the core of both hostile squadrons. Each national coast was guarded by more than a score of torpedo boats.

However, the Norwegians would be fighting for their freedom and home-land, with heavy casualties probably awaiting both sides. Increasingly pacifist Swedish citizens were unconvinced of the necessity for armed force in settling the question. In the event, the dispute with Norway was settled peaceably. Negotiations resolved the question of disarming two old fortresses shielding the mobilization of the Norwegian Army. On **26 October 1905**, Oscar II renounced the throne of Norway.

# SWEDISH QUANDARY - THE GREAT WAR

Oscar II died on 8 December 1907 and was succeeded by Gustav V. Rear Admiral Arvid Lindman had become the prime minister earlier in the year and ordered construction of a modern cruiser. When he left office in 1911, the cruiser was canceled by a Liberal ministry. However, alarmed by Russian arming in Finland and espionage in Sweden, the people purchased the cruiser (*Sverige*) by subscription. The Liberal prime minister, Karl Staaff, neglected defense during his tenure from 1911-1914, causing 30,000 peasants to gather in Stockholm in February 1914 to demand a coherent defense policy. The crisis was alleviated when Hjalmar Hammarskjold succeeded Staaff.

In 1908, the Great Powers had agreed to a status quo in the Baltic. Shortly afterward, King Gustav V made several visits to Berlin, sparking rumors that Sweden had placed herself under the protection of Germany. In preparation for military use, the Russians connected Finnish rail lines to their own by 1910. The Baltic Fleet was enlarged and a new naval base was built at Reval. The rising tension was eased when King Gustav V conferred with Czar Nicholas in July 1912.

On 2 August 1914, Sweden learned of the outbreak of World War I. The government ordered partial mobilization and declared neutrality. Russia believed that Sweden had a secret alliance with Germany and would soon declare for the Central Powers, so the Russian Baltic Fleet prepared to attack Gotland and Fårösund. Russia was expected to fortify the Åland Islands, in violation of the treaty of 1856.

The Field Army of 100,000 men consisted of seven divisions of regulars:

**Swedish Army**

1 cavalry division
  4 cavalry regiments
  1 horse artillery division
6 infantry divisions
  1 cavalry regiment
  4 infantry regiments
  1 field artillery regiment
  1 engineer company
  1 pontoon train
  1 telegraph detachment

The conscripts were administered by the *Beväring*, of which the first *uppbåd* (ban) had 100,000 men and the second had 80,000 men. The home defense reserves of the *Landstorm* totalled 175,000 men.

In 1910, a new service dress of grey-brown-green was adopted, with a tricorn headgear called a Caroline (Charles XII) hat. The tunic had a blue collar and cuff, which was chevron-shaped. The trousers had a rolled cuff, covering the boots, and a broad blue stripe. Rank insignia remained on the cuff of the tunic.

Their German cousins had heavily influenced the Swedes. The army was organized and trained on Prussian principles. Many German traditions were practiced by the populace. However, admiration for things German was mostly limited to the upper classes, as the common people aspired to the democratic freedoms enjoyed by the French and British. The result was a nation united in opposition to Russia, but divided on whether to support Germany or the Western Allies.

The twelve-company regiments and artillery units of the Swedish Army generally followed German organization:

**INFANTRY REGIMENT**
3 battalions
    4 rifle companies
        **Mauser M.96 6.5 mm rifles**

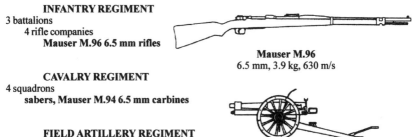

**Mauser M.96**
6.5 mm, 3.9 kg, 630 m/s

**CAVALRY REGIMENT**
4 squadrons
    **sabers, Mauser M.94 6.5 mm carbines**

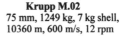

**FIELD ARTILLERY REGIMENT**
11 batteries
    **4 Krupp M.02 75 mm field guns**

**Krupp M.02**
75 mm, 1249 kg, 7 kg shell,
10360 m, 600 m/s, 12 rpm

**HORSE ARTILLERY DIVISION**
3 batteries
    **4 Krupp 75 mm cavalry gun**

There was also a position artillery regiment of seven heavy batteries and a garrison artillery regiment.

Sweden first investigated the new flying machines for military purposes when it purchased a handful of French aircraft in 1911. They were organized into a *Flygkompaniet* (Flying Company) the following year.

**Flygkompaniet**
2 Nieuport 4M, 2 Bleriot XI,
1 Breguet U-1, 1 Henri Farman HF.23

**Nieuport 4M**
1910, 11 m span, 90 km/h, 3 hrs,
no mgs (militarized 4G)

**Bleriot XI**
1910, 10 m span, 106 km/h, 3½ hrs,
14/900 m, no mgs

Three more licence-built Henri Farman HF.23s were later added to the Flying Company, along with a licence-built Bleriot XI.

The cabinet of Prime Minister Hammarskjold was upper class, thus pro-German. However, it was thwarted by the lower house of the Riksdag, thus forcing a compromise policy of neutrality. In January 1915, it declared that war material could not be transported through Swedish territory. Conflict loomed when Norway and Sweden refused to allow Britain to send much needed war materials through northern Scandinavia to Russia. The crisis passed when the Allies decided to send supplies through the Dardanelles instead. The decision was fortunate for Sweden, for her fleet was no match for two of the greatest seapowers on earth.

Oscar II Slices Through a Choppy Sea

Eleven small coastal battleships had been built around the Turn of the Century for use in defending the chief ports from enemy armored ships and as a seagoing cruising squadron in offensive operations. They were classified by the Swedish Navy as First Class Coast Defense Ships (monitors were Second and Third Class). Although possessing the speed and armor of many predreadnoughts of the day, the Swedish coast defense ships had the armament of cruisers. Effective against raiding enemy armored cruisers, they could face hostile battleships only in waters that restricted enemy movements. The three-stack *Oscar II* was the largest and fastest of the type. However, armored cruisers had already appeared as successors and it was the last of the type.

4th class
battleship

**Oscar II**   1905, 4390 tons, 29 km/h, 4800 km,
2-21, 8-15 cm, 2 TT, 10/15 cm armor

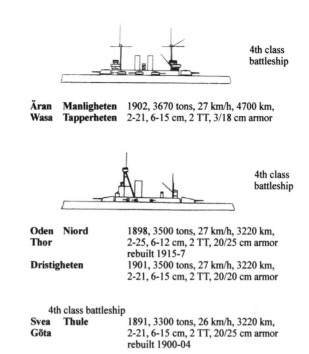

4th class
battleship

| Äran | Manligheten | 1902, 3670 tons, 27 km/h, 4700 km, |
| Wasa | Tapperheten | 2-21, 6-15 cm, 2 TT, 3/18 cm armor |

4th class
battleship

| Oden | Niord | 1898, 3500 tons, 27 km/h, 3220 km, |
| Thor | | 2-25, 6-12 cm, 2 TT, 20/25 cm armor |
| | | rebuilt 1915-7 |
| Dristigheten | | 1901, 3500 tons, 27 km/h, 3220 km, |
| | | 2-21, 6-15 cm, 2 TT, 20/20 cm armor |

4th class battleship
| Svea | Thule | 1891, 3300 tons, 26 km/h, 3220 km, |
| Göta | | 2-21, 6-15 cm, 2 TT, 20/25 cm armor |
| | | rebuilt 1900-04 |

The *Fylgia* was the smallest armored cruiser in the world. As the flagship of the scouting flotilla, it was built to be more powerful than any light cruiser in the Baltic. In the *Sverige* class, Sweden had modern armored ships comparable to those of other navies, although they were rather small. They were intended to form a more effective cruising squadron. However, only the *Sverige* was completed during the war and, unfortunately, nearby navies were already receiving much more powerful battle cruisers.

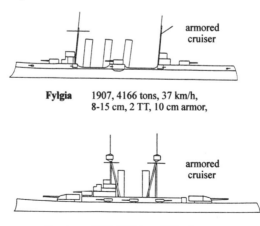

armored
cruiser

| Fylgia | 1907, 4166 tons, 37 km/h, |
| | 8-15 cm, 2 TT, 10 cm armor, |

armored
cruiser

| Sverige | 1915, 7214 tons, 35 km/h, |
| | 4-28, 8-15 cm, 2 TT, 20 cm armor |

273

torpedo cruiser

| | | |
|---|---|---|
| **Örnen** | 1896, 863 tons, 31 km/h, | |
| **Jakob Bagge** | 2-12 cm, 1 TT | |
| **Klas Horn** | | |
| **Klas Uggla** | | |
| **Psilander** | | |

destroyer

| | |
|---|---|
| **Wale** | 1906, 467 tons, 50 km/h, 1300 km, |
| **Ragnar** | 4-7.5 cm, 2 TT |
| **Sigurd** | |
| **Vidar** | |
| **Hugin** | |
| **Munin** | |

destroyer

**Magne** 1905, 466 tons, 50 km/h,
6 small, 2 TT

destroyer

**Mode** 1902, 456 tons, 50 km/h,
6 small, 2 TT

torpedo boat
**Nr. 5-15** 1904-8, 59 tons, 34 km/h,
1130 km, 2 TT

torpedo boat
**Nr. 79, 81, 83, 85** 1902, 49 tons, 32 km/h,
1130 km, 2 TT

torpedo boat

| **Plejad** | **Astrea** | **Pollux** | **Iris** | 1905-10, 120 tons, 43 km/h, |
|---|---|---|---|---|
| **Spica** | **Vega** | **Antares** | **Argo** | 1930 km, 2 small, 2 TT |
| **Altair** | **Polaris** | **Regulus** | **Rigel** | |
| **Castor** | **Thetis** | **Perseus** | **Arcturus** | |
| **Vesta** | | | | |

sub

**Hajen    Sälen** 1917, 397 tons, 28/17 km/h,
**Valrossen** 4 TT

sub
**Hvalen** 1909, 180 tons, 28/18 km/h,
1600 km

sub
**Hajen** 1904, 109 tons, 19/13 km/h,
stricken 1917    [136]

   The Swedish Navy had no cruisers, but four divisions of fast destroyers had recently slid down the building slips.  They followed a class of vessels, the torpedo cruisers, with which the world's navies were experimentally carrying the new automobile torpedo into fleet operations at sea.  Thirty small torpedo boats were confined to coastal work in defense of Swedish ports, along with a handful of little submarines.  The Swedish Fleet was a small, but balanced, navy, not slow in grasping new developments in naval warfare.

274

The Navy had actually got the jump on the Army with respect to aircraft, having organized a shore-based unit in 1911:

**Marinens Flygvasende**
1 Nieuport 4M, 1 Bleriot XI,
1 Henri Farman HF.23, 1 Donnet-Leveque

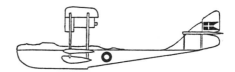

**Donnet-Leveque**
1910, 17 m span, 90 km/h, 3 hrs,
3500 m SC

Had Winston Churchill persuaded his government to send the British Navy through the Oresund in January 1915 and land an expeditionary force on the Baltic coast of Germany, Sweden would have been in a predicament. Not only would contact with friendly Germany have been lost, a supply line to Sweden's mortal enemy, Russia, would have passed along her coasts. The antagonists would seek to deny Swedish bases to the other, as the Kiel Canal allowed the German battle fleet to shift between the North Sea and the Baltic. It is certain that Sweden would have become involved in the conflict - but on which side? The abandonment of Churchill's harebrained scheme precluded an answer.

In 1916, Germany proposed an alliance with Sweden, promising possession of Finland upon the successful conclusion of the war. The Swedish government clung to neutrality, but food shortages strengthened the demands of the pro-German faction. Prime Minister Hammarskjold resigned on 5 March 1917 and a Liberal-Socialist coalition formed a government with Nils Eden as prime minister. Sweden inevitably became involved in the maritime war, losing 29 cargo vessels to German U boats attacking the coal and iron traffic to Britain between September 1916 and January 1917. The Navy conducted mining and anti-submarine operations as the threat increased. Spies from the combatant nations found Sweden a productive base of operations throughout the war. [137]

Due to the government's favorable inclination toward Germany, the Army was able to obtain some modern munitions despite the embargoes, although its establishment remained around 100,000 men.

**Swedish Army**

**I. Division** - Hälsingborg
   Attached
      **Cavalry Division**
**II. Division** - Linköping
**III. Division** - Skövde
**IV. Division** - Stockholm
**V. Division** - Stockholm
**VI. Division** - Härnösand
**Gotland Regiment** - Visby
   2 field artillery batteries

Army Troops
   1 siege artillery regiment
      6 batteries
   1 garrison artillery regiment
      10 companies

The principal changes were the integration of machineguns into the infantry battalion and the welcome addition of heavy field artillery.

**INFANTRY DIVISION**
1 cavalry regiment
    4 horse squadrons
    **sabres**
    **Mauser M.94 6.5 mm carbines**
2 infantry brigades
    2 infantry regiments
        3 infantry battalions
            3 rifle companies
            **Mauser M.96 6.5 mm rifles**
            1 machinegun company
            **Hotchkiss M.1900 6.5 mm mgs**
            **Madsen M.1906 6.5 mm mgs**
1 field artillery regiment
    3 groups
        3 batteries
        **4 Krupp M.02 75 mm field guns**
    2 batteries
    **4 Krupp M.07 105 mm field howitzers**
1 engineer company
1 pontoon train
1 telegraph detachment

**CAVALRY DIVISION**
2 cavalry brigades
    2 cavalry regiments
    2 cavalry regiments
        4 horse squadrons
        **sabres**
        **Mauser M.94 6.5 cm carbines**
1 brigade-division
    3 horse artillery batteries
    **4 Krupp M.02 75 mm field guns**  138

**Krupp M.07 field howitzer**
105 mm, 1020 kg, 14 kg shell,
7040 m, 300 m/s, 8 rpm

Rank insignia was moved from the cuff to the collar in 1916 and, two years later, a helmet was adopted. It was based on the French type, with a plate on the front bearing three crowns.

Generals - gold braid field, large 5-ptd gold stars
    General - 3 stars
    General-lieutenant - 2 stars
    General-major - 1 star
Field Officers - gold border on front and top of collar,
    5-ptd silver stars
    Colonel - 3 stars
    Colonel-lieutenant - 2 stars
    Major - 1 star
Line Officers - plain collar, 5-ptd silver stars
    Captain - 3 stars
    Lieutenant - 2 stars
    Ensign - 1 star

Senior Non-commissioned Officers - small gold chevrons
    Staff Sergeant - 3 chevrons
    Sergeant - 2 chevrons
Junior Non-commissioned Officers - yellow vertical bars
    Staff Corporal - 3 bars
    Corporal - 2 bars
    Lance Corporal - 1 bar

Colonel-lieutenant

Staff Sergeant

Corporal

276

An Albatros B.II arrived as a pattern for 15 more licence-built for training duties with the Army flying unit. Most combat aircraft were foreign designs built under licence by the indigenous Thulin company. The single Thulin A was a Bleriot XI. A Morane-Saulnier M.S.3L inspired 2 Thulin Ds, which were followed by 4 Thulin Es and 7 Thulin FAs. The company developed its own design in 1917, basing it on the Morane N. The 2 Thulin Ks and 5 Thulin Ls were intended as fighters, but were obsolete by the time they appeared and were used by the Army as unarmed scouts.

**Albatros B.II**
1914, 13 m span, 119 km/h, 700 km,
10/800 m, 3000 m SC, no mgs

**Thulin K**
1917, 9 m span, 150 km/h,
5500 m SC, no mgs

The coasts were defended by torpedo boats, with the small armored coast defense ships stationed at the major ports. To watch the approaches, the Navy purchased a Henri Farman HF.23 and had 9 more licence-built. Two Friedrichshafen FF33Ls were procured, along with three FF33Es. Thulin constructed two Bs (copies of the Morane-Saulnier G) and five of their own design, the Thulin G.

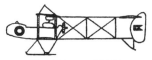

**Henri Farman H.F.23**
1913, 16 m span, 100 km/h, 3½ hrs,
2750 m SC, no mgs

**Friedrichshafen FF33L**
1917, 17 m span, 116 km/h, 2 mgs

Food shortages resulted in riots throughout the country on 17 April 1917. Sweden was close to its first revolution since the end of the Russo-Swedish War in 1809. The Great Reform Acts, initiated in 1918 and completed in 1921, brought democracy to Sweden. When the economic disintegration of Germany interrupted vital imports, Sweden established full trade with the Western Allies on 18 June 1918, practically abandoning neutrality.

Sweden benefitted from the results of the war. The militant German Empire was replaced by the weak Weimar Republic. Equally important, the perennial Russian enemy was now fenced away by a row of new buffer states in the eastern Baltic. The Åland Islands remained a sensitive thorn in Sweden's side. When Red Russians and White Finns converged on the Russian garrison, the islanders appealed to Sweden for annexation to rid themselves of the usurpers. A military expedition left Sweden on 13 February 1918, landing in time to arbitrate an evacuation by the contending factions. However, when Sweden sent a machinegun battalion to demilitarize the islands, the Finns objected. Germany landed a *fliegerabteilung* of warplanes and took possession. However, Sweden refused to join Germany in driving the Reds from Finland. She kept her troops on the islands until 16 May, when the Germans agreed to destroy the Russian fortifications. Sweden retired behind her new security perimeter. [139]

# INTERWAR STRINGENCIES

Scandinavia had largely been ignored by the warring factions during the Great War. Germany's short-ranged fleet did not have the capability of operating beyond the Baltic and North Seas for any length of time. In the Baltic, she had practically no enemies for the Russians had few vessels on that sea. Aircraft were in an initial stage of development that rendered them suitable mainly for short-range operations in support of ground and naval forces. As a result, the war brushed Scandinavia mainly as the side effects of the naval war in the North Sea, as the Allies sowed mines to fence in the German High Seas Fleet.

Following the war, the disintegration of Russia into civil war, and the length of the gestation of the Soviet Union, left Sweden with few enemies. She had been perceived as a German sympathizer during the war, but felt few repercussions from her association in a postwar corner of the world considered unimportant by most of the victorious nations. She was left to develop her resources. Many German arms manufacturers opened "branch companies" in Sweden to circumvent the restrictions of the Versailles Treaty. Thus, Swedish military engineering was given a strong boost.

Nils Eden served as Prime Minister until March 1920, when Hjalmar Branting formed the first purely Social Democratic administration. Little change had occurred in the army of isolated Sweden during the Great War. By 1921, it possessed:

**Swedish Army**
1 cavalry division
4 cavalry regiments
1 horse artillery division
6 infantry divisions
1 cavalry regiment
4 infantry regiments
1 field artillery regiment
1-2 engineer companies
1 pontoon train
1 telegraph detachment

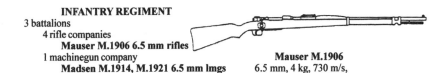

**INFANTRY REGIMENT**
3 battalions
  4 rifle companies
    **Mauser M.1906 6.5 mm rifles**
  1 machinegun company
    **Madsen M.1914, M.1921 6.5 mm lmgs**

**Mauser M.1906**
6.5 mm, 4 kg, 730 m/s,

**CAVALRY REGIMENT**
4 squadrons
1 machinegun section

**FIELD ARTILLERY REGIMENT**
11 batteries
  **4 Krupp M.02 75 mm field guns** or
  **Krupp M.07 105 mm field howitzers**

**Madsen M1921**
7.92 mm, 11 kg, 680 m/s, 450 rpm

**HORSE ARTILLERY DIVISION**
3 batteries
  **4 Krupp cavalry guns**

140

278

Conservatives and socialists alternated governments for the next several years. Sweden initiated a policy of "collective security" within the League of Nations. The Socialists passed the Defense Act of 1925, reducing Sweden's defenses by half. Just one of every two of the annual conscripts was selected for a period of training, which was also reduced from one year to but three months. Four cavalry, nine infantry and two artillery regiments were disbanded, while the remainder were reduced to minimum cadres. The result was a reduction of the army from 12 to 4½ divisions. The uniform had changed in 1923, retaining the previous cut and helmet, but removing the blue facings.

Following the end of the Great War, large numbers of surplus aircraft allowed small nations to establish air forces utilizing the latest equipment developed by the belligerents. Sweden went to Austria for most of its new equipment. The principal fighter was the *Phonixjagaren* (1 Phonix D.III, 30 Phonix D.II), supplemented by 10 Nieuport-Delage 29C.1s. As the Phonix had been the first postwar fighter in service, when the new numbering system was adopted, the Nieuport-Delage was designated the J2. The chief army cooperation aircraft was also a Phonix product. Between 22-30 *Dront*s (Phonix C.I) were joined by 10 more modified in Sweden. Only a handful of bombers were acquired - 3 Fiat B1s (BR) and 2 Fiat B2s (BR.1).

**Phonixjagaren (J1)**
1918, 10 m span, 201 km/h, 2 hrs,
5.4/1980 m, 6800 m, 2 mgs
(Phonix D.II)

**Nieuport-Delage J2**
1918, 10 m span, 238 km/h, 600 km,
11/4000 m, 8000 m SC, 2 mgs
(Nieuport-Delage NiD.29C.1)

**Phonix Dront (A.1, E.1)**
1917, 11 m span, 177 km/h, 3¼ hr,
5400 m SC, 2 mgs, 50 kg B
(Phonix C.I)

Ironically, the Swedish Navy was again dominant in the Baltic, for the Germans had scuttled their battle fleet and the Russian Revolution had crippled the vessels of the Czar. Naval air units equipped themselves primarily with the Heinkel He.1, a direct development of the wartime Hansa-Brandenburg. They also had 5 Friedrichshafen FF.33s and 4 FF.49Cs.

**Heinkel S2, S3, S4**
1920, 16 m span, 185 km/h,
2123 m SC, 2 mgs
(Heinkel He.1)

279

Pride of the Navy - Sverige, as Modernized in 1926

The navy suffered less from fiscal austerity than did the army, although the operational lives of its ships were extended. The *Sverige* class of armored cruisers was completed, and a few small destroyers and submarines were commissioned. In 1929, the old torpedo cruiser *Jakob Bagge* was rebuilt as a seaplane tender with stern gun removed to provide room to hoist a seaplane aboard. At the same time, the old battleship *Dristigheten* was converted to a seaplane carrier capable of carrying more than its usual complement of 3 Heinkel S5s. Later, she carried a Heinkel J4 fighter and a Heinkel T1 torpedo bomber, but was decommissioned in the summer of 1939 as a depot ship for the Heinkel T2s.

**Heinkel J4**
1928, 11 m span, 215 km/h,
6400 m SC, 2 mgs
(Heinkel HD.19W)

**Heinkel T1**
1928, 18 m span, 180 km/h,
3300 m SC, 2 mgs, 1 T
(Heinkel HD.16W)

seaplane carrier

seaplane
tender

**Dristigheten**   1900, 3322 tons, 26 km/h,
4-7.5 cm, 2 small AA, 3 seaplanes
rebuilt 1929-30, stricken 1946

**Jakob Bagge**   1896, 863 tons, 31 km/h,
1-12 cm, 1 TT, 1 seaplane
reblt 1929, stricken 1936

280

On 1 July 1926, the army and navy air forces were united in a single *Flygvapnet*, as part of a general reorganization of the armed forces that also saw the establishment of a tank corps. The aircraft were now grouped into a naval flying corps (2.) and an army flying corps (3.), with specialized tasks indicated by their designations (J - fighter, B - bomber, A - attack, E - artillery, S - reconnaissance, T - torpedo bomber). The naval units received J4 floatplane fighters and S5 coastal reconnaissance floatplanes. It also experimented with a couple of Heinkel HD.16 torpedo bombers (designated T1) with little success. The Phonix fighters were redesignated J1, while the *Dronts* became specialized as E and A types.

**Flygvapnet**
1. **Flygkåren** - Vasterås
   (forming)
2. **Flygkåren** - Hagernås
   6 Heinkel J4
   13 Heinkel S2, S3, S4
   26 Heinkel S5
   2 Heinkel T1
3. **Flygkåren** - Malmslatt
   9 Phonix J1
   10 Nieuport-Delage J2
   14 Fokker J3
   11 Phonix E1
   5 Fiat B1, B2
4. **Flygkåren** - Östersund
   8 Phonix A1

**Heinkel S5**
1926, 17 m span, 132 km/h,
5800 m SC, 2 mgs, 200 kg B
(Heinkel He.5)

**Fiat B2**
1925, 18 m span, 246 km/h, 1000 km,
6250 m SC, 2 mgs, bombs
(Fiat BR.2)                    141

Sweden's faith in the League of Nations was shattered when it proved incapable of dealing with the invasion of Manchuria by Japan and of Ethiopia by Italy. When Hitler dissolved the Weimar Republic in 1933, Sweden altered its foreign policy to one of neutrality. The Army began receiving weapons licence-built in Sweden to foreign designs. A tank battalion, manned by the elite Life Guards, tested tanks and tactics.

**Swedish Army**

**Southern Division** - Hälsingborg
**Western Division** - Skövde
**Eastern Division** - Stockholm
   Göta Life-guard Regiment
   I. Battalion (infantry)
   II. Battalion (Col. Buren)
      12 Strv m/21-29
**Northern Division** - Östersund
**Eastern Brigade** - Linköping
   2 infantry regiments
**Övre Norrland Militärområde** - Boden
   1 cavalry squadron
   2 infantry, 1 artillery regiments
**Gotland Militärområde** - Visby
   1 infantry, 1 artillery regiments
1 army artillery regiment
1 anti-aircraft artillery regiment
1 fortress artillery regiment

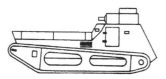

**Stridsvagn m/21-29**
1921, 9.8 tons, 1 mg,
21 km/h, 100 km, 14 mm, 4 men

INFANTRY DIVISION
1 cavalry regiment
  3 horse squadrons
    1 heavy squadron
      m/29 hmgs, mortars
    1 mechanized squadron
      Pb m/31
2 infantry brigades
  2 infantry regiments
    2 infantry battalions
      2 rifle companies
      1 heavy company
        m/29 hmgs, mortars
1 artillery regiment (2 in East and West Div.)
  2 groups
    3 batteries
      4 Krupp M.02 75 mm field guns
    2 batteries
      4 Krupp M.07 105 mm field howitzers
1 engineer company

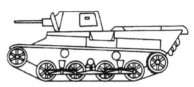

**Stridsvagn m/31**
1931, 11.6 tons, 1-37 mm, 2 mgs,
40 km/h, 240 km, 24 mm, 4 men,
40 mm/500 m P

142

Prohibited by the Versailles Treaty from developing armored vehicles in Germany, Krupp established Landsverk in Sweden, which became a leading arms manufacturer. Krupp's wartime LK.II design was developed into the Strv m/21-29, purchased by the Swedish Army. From a wheel/track hybrid, the company developed a light medium tank, three of which were given trials in 1934 as the Strv m/31. The stringent economic situation prevented its introduction into service. However, Landsverk did succeed in marketing two models of armored cars to foreign armies, the L.180 and L.185.

The Flygvapnet managed to maintain its meagre strength with modern equipment built to foreign designs. However, the J6 Jaktfalk fighter was generally superior to the Bristol Bulldog, and represented an important first step in establishing an indigenous aircraft industry.

**Flygvapnet**

1. **Flygkåren** - Vasterås
   11 ASJA J6, J6A (1931)
   10 Bristol J7
   30 Hawker B4, S7
2. **Flygkåren** - Hagernås
   36 Heinkel S5
   8 Hawker S9 - on *Gotland*
3. **Flygkåren** - Malmslatt
   7 ASJA J6B (1935)
   43 Fokker S6
4. **Flygkåren** - Östersund
   9 Fokker S6
   27 Hawker B4 (1937)
5. **Flygkåren** - Ljungbyhed
   flying school

**ASJA J6**
1929, 9 m span, 310 km/h, 550 km,
11/5000 m, 9300 m SC, 2 mgs

Fokker J3, S6
1925, 15 m span, 245 km/h, 1200 km,
7300 m SC, 2-3 mgs, 50 kg B
(Fokker C.VE)

Bristol J7
1927, 10 m span, 287 km/h, 450 km,
9000 m SC, 2 mgs, 36 kg B
(Bristol Bulldog IIA)

282

A Defense Commission of 1936 proposed a 50% increase in the defense budget. After its overwhelming victory in the election later in the year, a new Social Democratic government, led by Prime Minister Per Albin Hansson, had rejected Conservative demands for more defense spending. The Social Democrats embraced doctrinaire Marxist views as an opposition party, but now Hansson abandoned most of them. He was to prove a brilliant statesman, skilled in parliamentary compromise. Although no longer calling for the nationalization of industry, he did initiate greater central control of the economy and promoted a welfare state.

The iron ore at Kiruna in the far north formed the basis of Sweden's economy, but transportation from the remote site was a major problem. For several months each year, the Gulf of Bothnia is blocked by ice, and a single railroad has difficulty traversing the ice-bound coast. In 1902, while Norway was still a part of Sweden, the ice-free port of Narvik had been developed specifically to export the ore. After the dissolution of the union only three years later, Sweden tried to shift operations to Luleå, but found its efforts stifled by the ice of Bothnia. Arrangements were made with Norway to continue shipping over the railway to Narvik. A thousand freighters were kept busy carrying seven million tons of ore annually, two-thirds of it to Germany in exchange for coal and coke.

In April 1938, the four Scandinavian foreign ministers made a joint declaration of withdrawal from the European power alliances. The Austrian Anschluss, and the signing of the Munich Agreement in September 1938, revealed Germany's intentions, prompting Hansson to take the first steps toward rearmament while reiterating Sweden's adherence to neutrality.

Birger Furugård founded the Swedish National Socialist Party in 1930, but it remained weak. Groups of Nazis infected Sweden soon after Hitler came to power in Germany, but none ever managed to get elected to the Riksdag. However, a group of 2-3,000 German workers were in Sweden, organized as the Landesgruppe Schweden der NSDAP. Its leader, Heinz Bartels, was deported in 1936 when it was revealed that funds it collected were going to the Nazis. It posed a possible wartime danger to the industries in which its members worked, and was carefully watched by Swedish police.

The German-Soviet Pact of 23 August 1939 startled Sweden into a realization of danger, as it gave the Russians free rein in the north. Since Sweden was the world's largest exporter of iron ore, there was little likelihood of Scandinavian neutrality in the coming conflict. Movement of its high-grade ore to any belligerents was bound to be challenged.

King Gustav V had a German queen, and much of Sweden's aristocracy sprang from German families. Large numbers of Swedish officers had been trained there since the late-Nineteenth Century. During World War I, the Swedes had strongly favored Germany, but they had no sympathy for the Nazis that now governed that state. Nevertheless, the Swedish royal family and aristocrats maintained ties with their relatives in Germany. They were not antipathetic towards the French or British, but despised the Russians. Thus, the leaders of Sweden had to follow a narrow and twisting path through the coming conflagration. Most of their subjects favored the Allies, although remaining staunchly neutralist. Yet, the nation's officials, with whom they must work on a daily basis, were leaning in the opposite direction. In an attempt to unify the country, Hansson invited all parties (except the Communists) to participate in governance when the war began. In December 1939, they formed a "National Government", much like the coalescence of Britons around Churchill. [143]

283

# WORLD WAR II

As war clouds gathered over Europe, Sweden found itself in a dangerous situation, occupying a strategic position without the financial resources or manpower to defend itself. Only limited progress had been made by the outbreak of World War II. At that time, 217,000 regular and 185,000 reserve troops could be mobilized in a half-trained state. Regiments were the largest permanent units in the Swedish Army. In dispatches, their designations were abbreviated to I - infantry, K - cavalry, A - artillery, and P - tank. The Army evinced interest in the tiny Landsverk L.100, but it lost out to the less expensive Czech CKD AH IV, of which 48 were licence-built as the Stridsvagn (Strv) m/37. A larger Landsverk design, the L.60, was adopted as the Strv m/38 to support the tiny Czechs. Four independent tank companies had been organized in 1938:

**TANK COMPANY**

HQ - **1 Strv m/37**
3 platoons
   **3 Strv m/37**
1 platoon
   **3 Strv m/38**
reserve
   2 Strv m/37, 1 Strv m/38

A pugnacious little Strv m/37 confronts intruders as a column of its fellows is herded along the high road by a Strv m/38.

There was an acute shortage of officers and non-commissioned officers, although they were highly-regarded by foreign observers. Swedish infantry regiments had but half the heavy machineguns of German and Russian regiments. Only 2 anti-tank guns were available to each regiment, while the Russians had 6 and the Germans had 12. Foreign regiments had the support of a battery of field guns while Swedish artillery was light and obsolete. There was a general shortage of ammunition, and no land mines at all.

284

Germany invaded Poland on **1 September 1939**. Sweden joined the other Nordic nations at Copenhagen on 18 September to establish a mutual policy of cooperation and neutrality. A small number of infantry and artillery battalions were immediately mobilized to deal with surprise attacks. The country was organized into five Milo (Militärområde - Military Areas) to administer the training and supply of the units stationed within them:

**Swedish Army (Gen.Lt. O.G. Thörnell)**

Militärområde Södra (Col. Winberg) - Kristianstad
  I. Division
Militärområde Västra (Gen.Maj. Malmberg) - Skövde
  III. Division
Militärområde Östra (Col. Beskow) - Stockholm
  IV. Division
Militärområde Norra (Gen.Maj. von det Lancken) - Östersund
  II. Division
Militärområde Övre Norrland (Col. Bratt) - Boden
  Övre Norrland Forces
Gotland (Gen.Maj. Törngren) - Visby
  Gotland Forces

The wartime grey-brown-green uniform was adopted in 1939. Originally developed from the French type in 1923, the helmet reached its modern form in 1937. In the field, officers wore breeches tucked into brown boots. The men had short brown boots, into which were wrapped the long trousers. On the tunic's open collar were worn branch devices. From 1939, rank insignia were displayed in gold on the shoulder straps, which were of the same cloth as the uniform.

Generals - gold field, large 5-ptd stars above
  two crossed batons
  General - 3 large stars
  General-lieutenant - 2 large stars
  General-major - 1 large star
Field Officers - plain field, broad gold border,
  stars above regimental number
  Colonel - 3 large stars
  Colonel-lieutenant - 2 large stars
  Major - 1 large star
Line Officers - plain field, narrow gold border,
  stars above regimental number
  Captain - 3 stars
  Lieutenant - 2 stars
  Ensign - 1 star

General-major    Colonel-Lieutenant

Senior Non-commissioned Officers - plain field
  with narrow gold border,
  medallions above regimental numbers
  Staff Sergeant - 3 medallions
  Color Sergeant - 2 medallions
  Sergeant - 1 medallion
Junior Non-commissioned Officers - plain field,
  bars above regimental numbers
  Junior Sergeant - 2 chevrons
  Senior Staff Corporal - 4 bars
  Staff Corporal - 3 bars
  Corporal - 2 bars
  Lance Corporal - 1 bar

Color Sergeant    Staff Corporal

285

Regular and reserve troops were called to 18 months of service and given considerable advanced training. Annual classes of conscripts received a year of instruction by their local depot regiments, then were posted to field battalions for 6 months emergency service as "cover troops". About 400,000 untrained elderly conscripts received 6 months of basic military instruction, then were sent to the front as service personnel. A large number of militia units were converted into frontier and coast defense guards. Anti-aircraft artillery was to be expanded under the 1936 Defense Plan, but still comprised only 4 troops of mobile 70 mm guns, 13 troops of mobile 40 mm guns, 35 batteries of static 70 mm guns and 52 troops of static automatic anti-aircraft guns when World War II began.

The Swedish Navy was better prepared for war. It was ordered to be fully mobilized, nearly all vessels being placed on a war footing.

**Coastal Fleet** (Adm. de Champs)

Armored Ship Division (Adm. de Champs)
*Gustav V, Drottning Victoria, Sverige*
Scouting Group (Capt. Bjorklund)
*Gotland* {**6 S9**}
*Klas Horn, Klas Uggla*
*Nordenskjöld, Ehrenskjöld*
*Göteborg, Stockholm, Malmö*
Submarine Division
*Svea* - tender
*Sjöhunden, Sjöbjörnen, Nordkaparen, Delfinen*
*Draken, Ulven*
*Dristigheten* - aircraft depot ship
7 depot and supply ships

**Hawker S9**
1930, 11 m span, 283 km/h, 395 km,
7625 m SC, 2 mgs
(Hawker Osprey)

light cruiser

Gotland    1934, 4,851 tons, 45 km/h,
           6-15, 4-7.5 cm AA, 6 TT, 5 cm armor,
           11 floatplanes, refitted in 1944

destroyer

| Göteborg | Stockholm | 1936-41, 1,057 tons, 63 km/h, 2600 km, |
|---|---|---|
| Karlskrona | Malmö | 3-12 cm, 6 TT, stricken 1971-4 |
| Norrköping | Gävle | |

destroyer

| Ehrensköld | Nordenskjöld | 1927-31, 1,036 tons, 56 km/h, 2600 km, |
|---|---|---|
| Klas Horn | Klas Uggla | 3-12 cm, 6 TT, stricken 1958-63 |

286

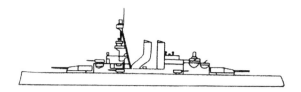

Sverige

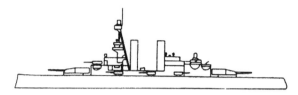

Drottning Victoria

Gustaf V

armored cruiser
**Sverige**           1915-8, 7,234 tons, 37 km/h,
**Drottning Victoria**   4-28, 5-19, 4-7.5 cm AA, 20 cm armor
**Gustaf V**               rebuilt 1929-1940

sub

| | | |
|---|---|---|
| **Sjölejonet** | **Sjöhästen** | 1936-41, 588 tons, 28/19 km/h, 6 TT |
| **Sjöhunden** | **Sjöormen** | |
| **Sjöbjörnen** | **Sjöborren** | |
| **Svardfisken** | **Dykaren** | |
| **Tunlaren** | | |

sub                                    sub

| | | | |
|---|---|---|---|
| **Delfinen** | 1935, 547 tons, 28/19 km/h, | **Draken** | 1927-30, 676 tons, 28/17 km/h, |
| **Nordkaparen** | 1-10 cm, 4 TT | **Gripen** | 9000 km, 4 TT |
| **Springaren** | | **Ulven** | |

The Coastal Fleet operated at sea from April to October of each year, as the severe northern winter froze the Gulf of Bothnia and blocked many Swedish ports. To the division of rebuilt *pansarschiffen* had been added a unique hybrid cruiser/carrier, the *Gotland*. She was capable of launching scout seaplanes from a catapult while underway, then recovering them from the water.

## Stockholm Squadron

Armored Ship
*Äran*
Gunboat
*Svensksund*
30 service and patrol vessels

### Göteborg Squadron

Armored Ship
*Manligheten*
Destroyer Division
*Wrangel, Wachtmeister*
Submarine Division
*Hajen, Sälen, Valrossen*
19 service and patrol vessels

cadet cruiser

**Fylgia** 1905, 4,700 tons, 35 km/h,
8-15 cm, 10 small AA, 10/5 cm armor
refitted 1939-40 as cadet ship

### Karlskrona Division

Armored Ship Division
*Oscar II, Tapperheten*
Destroyer Division
*Ragnar, Sigurd*
Submarine Division
*Illern, Uttern, Bävern, Valen*
16 service and patrol vessels

destroyer

**Wrangel** 1918, 471 tons, 36 km/h,
**Wachtmeister** 4-7.5 cm, 4 TT

### Malmö Division

19 service and patrol vessels

### Visby Division

Destroyer Division
*Munin, Vidar*
7 service and patrol vessels

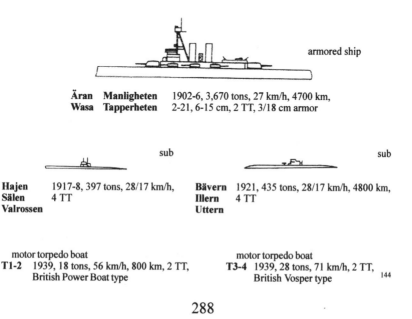

armored ship

**Äran    Manligheten** 1902-6, 3,670 tons, 27 km/h, 4700 km,
**Wasa    Tapperheten** 2-21, 6-15 cm, 2 TT, 3/18 cm armor

sub                                                    sub

**Hajen** 1917-8, 397 tons, 28/17 km/h,    **Bävern** 1921, 435 tons, 28/17 km/h, 4800 km,
**Sälen** 4 TT                              **Illern** 4 TT
**Valrossen**                               **Uttern**

motor torpedo boat                          motor torpedo boat
**T1-2** 1939, 18 tons, 56 km/h, 800 km, 2 TT,    **T3-4** 1939, 28 tons, 71 km/h, 2 TT,
    British Power Boat type                          British Vosper type              144

288

The Swedish Navy was mostly obsolete, only 6 small destroyers and 9 coastal submarines being modern. Ammunition was adequate, but mines and torpedoes were perilously scarce, as was fuel. A number of new ships were authorized, but there was insufficient time to build them before the outbreak of war forced conservation of strategic materials. The *Fylgia* was extensively rebuilt for use as a cadet training ship and a reserve cruiser.

To replace the *Fylgia* and the minelayer *Klas Fleming*, construction of the *Gotland* was authorized as a seaplane carrier with a complement of 11 floatplanes (a maximum of 8 could be carried on deck, with 3 more below). However, the design was altered to a unique hybrid cruiser/carrier with a complement of 6 Hawker S9s. Her commissioning in 1934 was the culmination of repeated attempts to provide the fleet with aerial scouts.

Two new 8,000 ton coast defense battleships, with four 25 centimeter guns, were ordered in 1939 to replace the ancient craft guarding major Swedish naval bases. They were never laid down, as the war left naval materials in short supply, while the terrible efficiency of aircraft against coastal surface ships made them vulnerable in any case. In the restricted waters of the Baltic, only mobile surface ships and small or under-sea vessels had a chance of surviving. Their specification was changed to two 8,000 ton light cruisers, which were completed postwar.

coast defense ship

**proposal**    1939, 8000 tons, 37 km/h,
4-25, 6-12 cm AA, 8 small AA

To redress the shortfall, in March 1940 Sweden purchased from Italy two destroyers, renamed *Psilander* and *Puke*, two torpedo boats, the *Romulus* and *Remus*, and four motor torpedo boats. On their way to Sweden, they were detained in the Orkney Islands by Great Britain, but were eventually released and reached their destination on 1 July. Unfortunately, the Italian vessels suffered mechanical troubles throughout their period of service. Other classes of modern destroyers were available to screen fleet movements while small submarines prowled the coastal waters. Surface ships were painted a light gray (later in the war they had a dazzle camouflage) and submarines were dark green. [145]

During the greater part of the interwar years, the efficiency of the Flygvapnet had been maintained by timely reequipment programmes. Air units were reorganized from *Flygkåren* (corps) into *Flygflottilj* (wings). The *flygflottilj* (F) was the operational unit of the air force. Each was divided into 3 *divisioner* (squadrons) of 15 fighters or 12 other aircraft, which were styled 1.,2.,3./F#. The 1936 Defense Plan had called for expansion of the Flygvapnet to 1 fighter, 1 heavy bomber, 3 light bomber, 1 army cooperation, 1 naval cooperation and 1 flying school wings. However, on the eve of World War II, the aftermath of the worldwide economic depression, pacifism, and uncertainty as to Hitler's intentions led the government to hesitate, one year too long, in procuring modern equipment. Due to shortage of aircraft, only 5 of the 7 combat wings had formed by September 1939.

Striking Power for the Flygvapnet - a New Junkers B3

Two new companies were organized to produce aircraft for the burgeoning Air Force. ASJA (Aktiebolaget Svenska Järnvägsverkstäderna) was established at Linköping in 1930 to build its new fighter and produce the Hawker Hart under licence. The firm then began design of the B8, two prototypes of which were ordered by the Air Force late in 1938 as the B17. However, Saab took over ASJA early in 1939. Saab (Svenska Aeroplan Aktiebolaget) had been formed at Trollhättan in April 1937 to manufacture the Junkers Ju.86 under licence. It became the principal supplier to the Swedish Air Force, and developed some of the most advanced postwar designs.

**Swedish Air Force** (Gen.Lt. Friis)

Flygflottilj 1 - Vasterås
   3 bomber divisioner
     **53 Junkers B3**
Flygflottilj 2 - Hagernås (Stockholm)
   5 reconnaissance divisioner
     **6 Hawker S9**
     **11 Heinkel S12, 20 Heinkel S5**
   1 torpedo bomber division
     **12 Heinkel T2**
Flygflottilj 3 - Malmslatt
   4 reconnaissance divisioner
     **34 Fokker S6**
Flygflottilj 4 - Östersund
   3 light bomber divisioner
     **39 Hawker B4**
Flygflottilj 5 - Ljungbyhed
   flying school
Flygflottilj 6 - Karlsborg
   3 light bomber divisioner
     **24 Hawker B4**

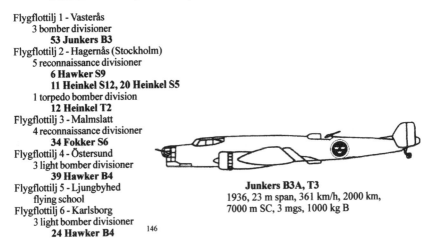

**Junkers B3A, T3**
1936, 23 m span, 361 km/h, 2000 km,
7000 m SC, 3 mgs, 1000 kg B

146

Although modern Junkers B3 medium bombers had entered service in 1938 with a bomber wing based west of Stockholm, the rest of the Flygvapnet flew old army cooperation biplanes. A panic situation developed as no fighters were available to shield Sweden from the fleets of bombers possessed by Europe's great powers.

290

Plans were made to expand the Flygvapnet to 13 flygflottilj by placing orders with foreign manufacturers. A balanced, modern air force would have resulted from fulfillment of the programme in 1941:

**Swedish Air Force** (proposed)

Flygflottilj 1 - Vasterås
**Junkers B3**
Flygflottilj 2 - Hagernås (Stockholm)
**Heinkel S12, Heinkel T2**
Flygflottilj 3 - Malmslatt
**Breguet S10 or Dornier S11**
**Fokker S13**
Flygflottilj 4 - Östersund
**Douglas B5**
Flygflottilj 5 - Ljungbyhed
flying school
Flygflottilj 6 - Karlsborg
**Douglas B5**
Flygflottilj 7 - Satenås
**Fokker B7**
Flygflottilj 8 - Barkarby (Stockholm)
**Seversky J9**
Flygflottilj 9 - Göteborg
**Seversky J9**
Flygflottilj 10 - Ängelholm
**Vultee J10**
Flygflottilj 11 - Nyköping
**Seversky B6**
Flygflottilj 12 - Kalmar
**Fokker B7**
Flygflottilj 13 - Norrköping
**Vultee J10**

**Breguet S10**
1938, 15 m span, 485 km/h, 1350 km,
7/4000 m, 8500 m SC, 1-20 mm,
4 mgs, 400 kg B
(Breguet 694)

**Dornier S11**
1939, 18 m span, 470 km/h, 2000 km,
8800 m SC, 6 mgs, 1000 kg B
(Dornier Do.215A-1)

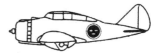

**Vultee J10**
1940, 11 m span, 547 km/h, 1370 km,
9/6000 m, 8600 m SC, 6 mgs
(Vultee 48C)

**Seversky B6**
1938, 12 m span, 459 km/h, 1087 km,
9150 m SC, 3 mgs, 420 kg B
(Seversky 2PA-204A)

**Fokker B7, S13**
1937, 17 m span, 430 km/h, 1380 km,
9.1/5000 m, 8706 m SC, 2-20 mm, 3 mgs, 400 kg B
(Fokker G.Ib)

Gloster J8s began to arrive late in 1939. Of 55 ordered in 1937, 12 were sent to Finland with Swedish volunteers. The remaining 43 were attached to F8. In June 1939, the first of 120 EP-106 fighters were ordered from Seversky, along with 52 two-seat 2PAs for use as anti-ship strike fighters. Vultee was the recipient of orders for 144 of its potent Model 48C fighter in September 1940.

291

To replace the obsolete Hawker B4 in the light bomber role, 103 Douglas 8A-1s would be licence-built by ASJA. Reconnaissance and ground attack were the missions of 18 Fokker G.Ibs ordered in March 1940. An option for 77 more was also negotiated with Fokker. For long-range reconnaissance, 12 Breguet Br.694s were ordered. When they were retained in France with the outbreak of war, a substitute order for 12 Dornier Do.215A-1s was placed in Germany, where 27 Heinkel He.114B-1s had also been ordered to succeed ancient He.5s in the maritime reconnaissance role.

Order after order was placed, only to have embargoes, confiscations and invasions curtail shipment of most of them. Sixty EP-106s were delivered by June 1940, but the United States Army Air Corps confiscated the remaining 60 as P-35A fighters, along with 50 of the 2PAs for use as AT-12 advanced trainers. It also seized all of the Vultee 48Cs, which were designated P-66s and eventually sent to the Chinese Nationalists. The Netherlands was overrun before the Fokker G.Is could be supplied. Germany allowed a dozen Heinkel He.114Bs to be delivered in 1939, but the high-performance Dornier Do.215As were seized and converted to Do.215Bs for the Luftwaffe.

Only Italy, because of her need for foreign currency, agreed to supply aircraft in quantity. Unfortunately, most of them were not up to world standard. The obsolescent Fiat J11 was acquired in place of one of the wings of Severskys. Only one wing of lightly-armed Reggiane J12s (redesignated J20s) could be obtained to replace the J10s. Least effective were the delightful Caproni B16/S16 light twin-engine aircraft that replaced the formidable Fokker G.Is. Just 10 flygflottilj could be equipped. [147]

## *Swedes in the Finnish Winter War* - January-February 1940

Danger stalked Sweden from the moment her inveterate foe crossed the frontier of Finland on **30 November 1939**. Massive Russian blows struck the brave Finns just as winter was beginning. Clumsy Soviet mechanized columns were channeled by the Finnish terrain, allowing the Finns to ambush and destroy them. Their gallant resistance stirred many nations to send aid, most of which arrived too late. Fearing that Swedish involvement in the war would end shipments of high-quality Kiruna iron ore to Germany, Hitler demanded strict neutrality of Sweden. Nevertheless, several battalions of volunteers were allowed to resign from Swedish service and join the Finns.

Emergency preparations in Sweden had been reduced after the end of the war in Poland. Now they were reinstated with even greater urgency. The Swedish 2. Corps was mobilized with two divisions to defend the Swedish-Finnish frontier in the far north. To coordinate the mobilized units, General Lieutenant O.G. Thörnell, the Chief of the Defense Staff, was appointed the Commander-in-Chief. Through the exceptionally cold winter of 1939-40, the raw troops were welded into efficient fighting units.

Despite overflights by German aircraft, and sinkings of her merchant ships, Sweden persisted in neutrality. Nevertheless, it appeared that she would be drawn into the war. Many nations began the century's fifth decade by offering to send aid to the hard pressed Finns. France, Great Britain, the United States, Denmark, Norway, Belgium, Hungary, Italy, Germany, even South Africa pledged nearly 700 artillery pieces, more than 6,000 infantry weapons, and 200 aircraft to their cause. Although her own defenses were woefully inadequate, Sweden authorized shipment of 77,000 rifles and 188 artillery pieces. Few reached Finland in time to be of use.

292

Column of Swedish Sledges on a Finnish Road

Early in 1940, a Volunteer Brigade of 8,000 men in Swedish uniforms landed in Kemi, at the head of the Gulf of Bothnia, accompanied by an air unit:

**Swedish Volunteer Brigade** (Gen. Linder)
8,257 men

**Flygflottilj 19** (Maj. Beckhammar)
12 Gloster J8 (from F8)
5 Hawker B4 (from F4)

**Hawker B4, S7**
1928, 11 m span, 296 km/h, 750 km,
6500 m SC, 2 mgs, 240 kg B
(Hawker Hart)

At a meeting with the Finns on 15 December, it had been decided to send a small air unit to support the Swedish-Norwegian ground forces assembling in the Arctic. From a frozen lake near Kemi, F19 began operations with an attack on Soviet positions at Märkäjärvi (near the Russian border fifty kilometers northeast of Kemijärvi) on **12 January 1940**. Two B4s destroyed several supply dumps before Soviet fighters rose from a nearby airfield. A climbing Polikarpov I-15 was shot down by the escorting J8s, and two more were destroyed on the ground by B4s before they could take off. Yet, three Soviet I-16s managed to take off and slash into the Swedish formation. A B4 went down and two more collided after being damaged.

After the heavy losses at Märkäjärvi, the aircraft of F19 were dispersed to small satellite fields, in the Finnish manner. A flight of 4 J8s was flying a reconnaissance mission near Salla on 17 January when it spotted a like number

293

of Soviet fighters flying below at 500 meters. Diving on the surprised enemy, the Swedes downed two planes. However, F19 pilots found it difficult to dispatch Soviet fighters because their bullets could not penetrate the pilot's armored seats. Dogfights with Soviet fighters on 23 January resulted in the loss of a J8, with no compensating victory.

On **1 February 1940**, heavily reinforced Soviet forces launched attacks on the Finnish positions far to the south in the Karelian Isthmus. On the same day, 40 Soviet SB-2s bombed the port of Oulu in five waves. The Gladiators guarding this important supply base of the Swedish Volunteer Brigade could not get up in time to meet the first bombers, but waded into the succeeding waves and harvested two of the fast SBs. The Swedes envisioned the crushing of Finnish resistance, and a Russian appearance on the narrow Gulf of Bothnia. They feared that such an advance would be followed by a German invasion of Sweden to prevent Russian domination of the Baltic (the Swedes did not know of the secret agreement between Hitler and Stalin).

The British and French governments offered to send an expeditionary force to Finland, if permission could be gained from the Norwegians and Swedes for passage. This offer placed the Swedish government in a difficult position. The populace of Sweden was strongly in favor of helping the Finns, particularly as many of the Finnish upper class were ethnic Swedes. However, Sweden lacked the armaments to defend herself, let alone another nation. She was scrambling to mobilize her half-trained reservists. Yet, the government authorized the formation of more volunteer units from its regular army units. But when Hansson refused transit privileges to the Allies on 17 January, the resulting public outcry threatened to topple the government until King Gustaf V appealed for calm.

Meeting on 19 January, the British Cabinet examined plans to occupy Narvik and the Swedish iron ore fields at Kiruna, then transport supplies and troops across northern Sweden to Finland. Since such an action would precipitate the feared German invasion through southern Sweden, the British calculated that, while 2 brigades were sufficient for the northern landings, another 4 brigades would be required to support the outnumbered Swedish defenders in Skåne. Both Allied and Swedish plans were stillborn, for events in Finland moved too swiftly.

Despite stubborn resistance in the Karelian Isthmus, Russian firepower was overwhelming and the Finns began to waver. When the Finnish 6th Division was sent southward, the Swedish volunteers moved up to relieve it around Lake Kemi. Ten Soviet bombers raided Rovaniemi on 21 February. Four J8s intercepted and downed one of them. The Mannerheim Line was breached on 27 February and Russian aircraft began penetrating deeply into Finnish air space. On 10 March, Rovaniemi was rocked by bombs from a formation of Tupolev TB-3s, although a J8 did manage to send one of the giants to earth. Hawker B4s attacked the Russian columns moving westward on 11 March, but the end was near. An armistice was signed on **13 March 1940**. The Swedish brigade had seen little action, but F19 claimed a total of 8 Soviet planes shot down in the air and 4 more destroyed on the ground. The Swedes lost 3 B4s and 3 J8s.

The Soviet Union obtained a lengthy lease on Hangö, from which it could control movements in both the Gulf of Finland and the Gulf of Bothnia. Stalin required Finland to build a railway along which troops and supplies could move to the menacing base on Sweden's doorstep. Powerful forces of competing totalitarian states were now but a short sea passage from the ancient shores of the Svear. Would Sweden be their next objective? [148,149]

Shortly after daylight on **9 April 1940**, observers at Malmö reported a formation of 15 large aircraft flying northward up the Öresund. They were Junkers Ju.52/3ms of the KGrzbV 103, carrying German airborne infantry for a vertical envelopment of Oslo. German airborne descents to Danish and Norwegian airfields engendered as great a shock in Stockholm as they did in the kindred nations to the west. Disquieting messages from Copenhagen described German warships swarming around Danish coasts. Soon enemy troops were racing up the Jutland peninsula and pouring ashore near the capital. Alarms raced through Sweden, for Malmö was but 25 kilometers across The Sound from Copenhagen. Did German plans involve a crossing into Skåne and an advance on Göteborg?

The government had learned early in April of impending German movements, but failed to act. As a result, few defenses were in place to meet an attack, particularly in the south. The Swedish units deployed on the Finnish border were moving southward, no longer needed with the end of the Russo-Finnish War, when emergency orders reached them. Leave canceled, they were rushed to the southern and western borders. The Swedish armed forces were swiftly mobilized in a series of subtle call ups, intended to convince Germany that they were not mobilizing, only reorganizing. [150]

Heavy Machinegunners on Alert

Initial deployment was dictated by the proximity of German territory to the south coast. Two corps headquarters were formed, one to control the operations in Skåne and the other along the Norwegian border. As the primary danger was a seaborne invasion from the south, the best infantry divisions were deployed to Skåne as they mobilized. A fifth division was added to bolster the southern corps facing Denmark. Both of the Army's mobile units were attached to the I. Division as corps reserve.

**Swedish Army** (Gen.Lt. O.G. Thörnell)

**1. Corps** (Gen.Maj. von Edholm) - Kristianstad
   I. Division (Gen.Maj. von Klercker)
      I. Cavalry Battalion
      7., 10., 16. Infantry Regiments
      3. Artillery Regiment
      Attached
         **1. Cavalry Brigade** (Gen.Maj. Peyron)
            I., II., III. Cavalry Car Battalions
               3 Pb m/31, 9 Pb m/39, trucks
            Artillery Battalion
            **Tank Battalion** (Maj. Holmgren)
               1., 2. Tank Companies (3. Comp. detd.)
               32 Strv m/37, 11 Strv m/38
   IV. Division (Gen.Maj. Testrup)
      IV. Cavalry Battalion
      3., 8., 11. Infantry Regiments
      1. Artillery Regiment
   V. Division (Gen.Maj. Hanngren)
      V. Cavalry Battalion
      4., 6., 12. Infantry Regiments
      5. Artillery Regiment
Militärområde Södra (Col. Winberg)


**2. Corps** (Gen. Nygren) - Skövde
   II. Division (Gen.Maj. Holmquist)
      III. Cavalry Battalion
      2., 13., 14., 21. Infantry Regiments
      4. Artillery Regiment
   III. Division (Gen.Maj. Malmberg)
      II. Cavalry Battalion
      9., 17., 20. Infantry Regiments
      2. Artillery Regiment
   Group Göteborg (Col. Salander)
      15. Infantry Regiment
Militärområde Västra (Gen.Maj. Malmberg)


Militärområde Östra (Col. Beskow)
   1. Infantry Regiment
   **3. Tank Company**
      12 Strv m/37, 6 Strv m/38


**Group Mora** (Col. Anden) - Mora
**Group Jämtland** (Gen.Maj. Ohlsson) - Östersund
   5. Infantry Regiment
Militärområde Norra (Gen.Maj. von det Lancken)


**Övre Norrland Forces** (Gen.Maj. Douglas) - Boden
   19. Infantry Regiment
   I. Ski Battalion
   Boden Fortress
Militärområde Övre Norrland (Col. Bratt)


**Gotland Forces** (Gen.Maj. Törngren) - Visby
   18. Infantry Regiment
   7. Artillery Regiment       151

The success of the large tank forces of Germany in Poland had stimulated Swedish testing of larger armored units. The first essay was a battalion of 46 tanks, organized in September 1939 by combining the tanks from 3 of the 4 existing tank companies, nearly doubling the tanks in each company:

**TANK BATTALION**
2 tank companies
HQ - **3 Strv m/37**
3 platoons
**5 Strv m/37**
1 platoon
**5 Strv m/38**
1 anti-tank company
**18 Bofors 37 mm AT guns**

Although under command of the 1. Corps in Skåne, the two mobile units, the 1. Cavalry Brigade and the Tank Battalion, were deployed near Jönköping at the southern tip of Lake Vattern, in position to intervene to the west or the south. The remaining independent tank company was detached to defend Stockholm in Milo Östra. Swedish troops were ordered to train intensively and construct several lines of field fortifications. A Home Guard of 80,000 under-age and overage men was established for local defense purposes.

Seasoned Warrior - Gustav V at Anchor

The Swedish Navy, preparing to begin its usual summer maneuvers, was placed on a war footing. A large number of secret naval anchorages, protected by anti-aircraft guns, were prepared in the Stockholm archipelago for use by vessels of the Coastal Fleet. While the base squadrons defended their harbors, the Coastal Fleet began patrolling Swedish territorial waters, warning away stray vessels of the combatants and watching for hostile descents. They were assisted by the seaplanes of the naval air wing, Flygflottilj 2 near Stockholm.

Sweden's Principal Fighter Defense - a Flight of J8s

**Swedish Air Force** (Gen.Lt. Friis)

Flygflottilj 1 - Vasterås
  3 bomber divisioner
    **53 Junkers B3**
Flygflottilj 2 - Hagernås (Stockholm)
  4 reconnaissance divisioner
    **6 Hawker S9**
    **11 Heinkel S12, 20 Heinkel S5**
  1 torpedo bomber division
    **12 Heinkel T2**
Flygflottilj 3 - Malmslatt
  4 reconnaissance divisioner
    **34 Fokker S6, 19 Fieseler S14**
Flygflottilj 4 - Östersund
  3 light bomber divisioner
    **39 Hawker B4**
Flygflottilj 5 - Ljungbyhed
  flying school
Flygflottilj 6 - Karlsborg
  3 light bomber divisioner
    **24 Hawker B4**
Flygflottilj 8 - Barkarby (Stockholm)
  3 fighter divisioner
    **38 Gloster J8, 15 Seversky J9**

**Gloster J8**
1934, 10 m span, 407 km/h, 692 km,
6/4575 m, 10000 m SC, 4 mgs
(Gloster Gladiator I)

**Fieseler S14**
1936, 14 m span, 175 km/h, 240 km,
5100 m SC, 1 mg
(Fieseler Fi.156)

152

298

As would be expected, Sweden's aerial defenses were concentrated around the capital. Her air forces were comparable to those of most other European nations of similar size, with one glaring exception - fighters. During the autumn of 1939, fighter interception of the massive bomber forces possessed by the Great Powers was to be accomplished by only forty obsolescent Gloster Gladiator biplanes based at Stockholm. From there, they could cover operations throughout most of populated Sweden, although Malmö and Göteborg were at their extreme range. Forward airfields would bring them closer to the front, to which army cooperation planes could also be detached from their home base of Malmslätt to support ground units. From January 1940, the J8 biplanes of Flygflottilj 8 were supported by a division of Seversky monoplanes. As more of the modern fighters arrived during the summer, the J8s went to F9 and F10 to prepare pilots for their new mounts.

Two wings of Hawker Hart light bombers were positioned strategically opposite the Jämtland Gap and at Karlsborg between the two great lakes. From those bases, they could attack throughout the industrialized territory of Sweden. Much more potent Douglas B5s began replacing the old Hawker biplanes in April 1940. B3 heavy bombers could range over the entire peninsula from their base at the tip of Lake Mälaren. Carrying four times the bomb load of the light bombers, the Junkers would be used to attack concentrations of enemy troops, supply dumps, and communications routes.

General von Edholm soon had three full infantry divisions in position to block a German incursion across the Danish straits. However, the two German divisions that occupied Denmark never made a move to cross. Attention shifted to the German forces rampaging through Norway.

General Nygren's 2. Corps had only two divisions, and one of those had to be deployed far to the north to block egress through the Jämtland Gap. His remaining III. Division was spread along a 300 kilometer front from Lake Siljan in Dalarna to Uddevalla, just north of Göteborg. Worse yet, a German infantry division was advancing toward his southern wing, driving the remnants of a Norwegian division before it. However, after the Norwegians crossed the border and surrendered their arms to Swedish units, the Germans turned about and advanced northward. Heavy fighting developed north of Oslo on 14 April, but the line of the German advance carried them away from Sweden. Bofors 40 mm anti-aircraft guns of 2. Corps shot down a stray Ju.52 over Uddevalla on that day.

The Germans launched their main assault on the British-Norwegian positions on **20 April**. Inevitably, German bombers supporting the assault strayed over the nearby Swedish border as the battle raged over unfamiliar terrain. Three Heinkel He.111s flew southward into Värmland about 1530. An hour later, anti-aircraft guns ringing Göteborg fired upon them, splashing one into the sea. The following day, four Heinkels of KG 54 came to grief. Anti-aircraft guns hit three He.111s that overflew Gotland about 1915, forcing them to crash land on that island and Bornholm. Meanwhile, over Marstrand on the opposite coast, Swedish naval vessels fired on a Heinkel of the same unit about 2000. One of the oldest of Swedish naval aircraft, an S5 of F2 detached for service around Göteborg, gave chase. The German bomber was faster than the ancient floatplane, which opened fire at the last moment and set an engine on fire. The Heinkel crashed in a field, the only victory by a Swedish aircraft during the war. The Swedes also occasionally suffered casualties. On 20 May, a Dornier Do.18 flying boat crossed the coast in the wrong place and strafed Swedish troops around the railroad station at Vassijaure, killing one soldier. [153]

299

By the end of April, Norwegian and British units in the south of Norway had been mopped up. The Germans turned to a fundamental reason for the Norwegian campaign - the vital high-grade iron ores mined at Kiruna in the Swedish Arctic and shipped through the ice-free Norwegian port of Narvik. At Narvik, the British Navy had sunk all of the German destroyers initially deployed there and began landing troops on 14 April. Germany exerted pressure on the Swedish government to allow troops and supplies to pass from Denmark to Narvik on Swedish railways, for the British Navy now controlled the Norwegian Sea. Reichsmarschall Göring harangued his Swedish acquaintances, proposing subterfuge to conceal from the Allies the true nature of the Swedish trains he demanded for shipping sustenance to the beleagured troops in northern Norway.

A high ranking Nazi, Hermann Göring had married a Swedish aristocrat. Although his blustery and bullying manner provoked many, he was a useful contact. Realizing that a refusal of Göring's demands may mean war with Germany, Hansson calmly instructed his emissary to reiterate Sweden's ban on shipment of arms and ammunition, and placed the armed forces on highest alert. When the Swedish delegation on 11 May apprised Göring of the government's position, Hermann displayed his characteristic rage and launched into a tirade during which he darkly threatened to use his vaunted Luftwaffe against the recalcitrant Swedes. After a meeting with Nazi Foreign Minister Ribbentrop, Arvid Richert, the Swedish ambassador, warned Hansson of an imminent invasion and recommended acceptance of Nazi demands. The commander-in-chief of the Swedish armed forces, General-Lieutenant Olof Thörnell, who was considered to be pro-German, also recommended cooperation, calling attention to the unready state of Swedish defenses. King Gustav V expressed his unwillingness to risk war, causing many in the government to waver. However, Hansson remained firm.

Per Albin Hansson was often reviled during the war by Nazis and Allies alike. Yet, taking into account the overwhelming pacifist sentiments of his constituents, he did a remarkable job of handling foreign affairs for the benefit of his countrymen. To gain time to complete mobilization, he now instructed Richert to return to Ribbentrop on 18 May with a proposal to establish a neutral zone around Narvik, under Swedish supervision. [154]

The Allied offensive at Narvik began on 28 May. Soon, the Norwegian 6th Division forced the German 3. Mountain Division back to the Swedish border, where it was faced with surrender or internment in Sweden. Other German forces appeared to be concentrating along the Swedish border east of Oslo. Would the Germans attempt to overwhelm the stubborn Swedes by slicing through central Sweden, then racing up the Bothnian coast to link up with their forces at Narvik? To counter such a possibility, the IV. Division had been detached from the southern 1. Corps and sent to the 2. Corps on 25 April while the V. Division was withdrawn to General Reserve five days later. Work accelerated on the Stockholm defenses.

Just as the Germans reached their limits of resistance, the crisis in France forced the Allies to withdraw from Norway. First destroying the iron ore facilities at Narvik, the Allies gathered an evacuation fleet at Harstad. On **2 June**, the Luftwaffe made a maximum effort to destroy it. Swarms of level and dive bombers attacked the cargo vessels and warships in the harbor. A Swedish armored train was blocking the Narvik-Kiruna railroad at the nearby border and shot down a Ju.52 filled with paratroops intended to reinforce the 3. Mountain Division astride the railroad. The sharpshooting train also hit a Ju.87B of StG 1 and brought it down on the shore of the Torne Träsk.

Prewar Sweden had buffer states on all sides that both insulated her from boundary disputes with great powers and provided some reaction time. With the occupation of Denmark and Norway by Germany, and the presence of Russian forces at Hangö, Sweden was exposed to aggression from all sides.

German armies were rolling to an easy victory in France. Swedes were left to wonder when Hitler would invite them to enjoy the Teutonic embrace. The extended configuration of Sweden posed a problem for the Army High Command. Its rugged terrain was not conducive to rapid movement, decreasing the effectiveness of centrally located mobile forces. As it was necessary to mobilize an extraordinary proportion of Sweden's limited manpower, the Defense Staff worked out a "Shield and Sword" system that allowed the majority of mobilized personnel to return to their civilian occupations between alarms.

The "Shield" consisted of the "cover troops", conscripts undergoing tactical training with their field battalions. They were to delay the advance of an enemy across the frontier, particularly using road blocks to interrupt the progress of mechanized units. Older conscripts guarded the border between the frontier posts where the "cover troops" were concentrated. They were supported by the local Home Guard units.

The main operational units of the Army formed the "Sword". These units had not been demobilized after the alert of early 1940, but had been transferred to field depots and most of their personnel sent home. At the field depots, managed by small staffs, materiel was dispersed and organized for quick distribution. The personnel on leave could be called to arms by a secret radio network. [155]

Intended for use in counterattacks, a large mobile unit had been organized for the first time in April 1940 and held in General Reserve:

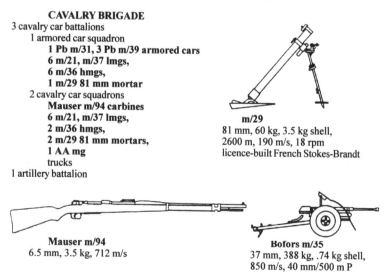

**CAVALRY BRIGADE**
3 cavalry car battalions
  1 armored car squadron
    **1 Pb m/31, 3 Pb m/39 armored cars**
    **6 m/21, m/37 lmgs,**
    **6 m/36 hmgs,**
    **1 m/29 81 mm mortar**
  2 cavalry car squadrons
    **Mauser m/94 carbines**
    **6 m/21, m/37 lmgs,**
    **2 m/36 hmgs,**
    **2 m/29 81 mm mortars,**
    **1 AA mg**
    trucks
1 artillery battalion

**m/29**
81 mm, 60 kg, 3.5 kg shell,
2600 m, 190 m/s, 18 rpm
licence-built French Stokes-Brandt

**Mauser m/94**
6.5 mm, 3.5 kg, 712 m/s

**Bofors m/35**
37 mm, 388 kg, .74 kg shell,
850 m/s, 40 mm/500 m P

Fifteen Pansarbil m/39s, built for Denmark, were confiscated after Denmark was overrun and quickly issued to the cavalry. In the 30 Pb m/40s subsequently built, the Scania-Vabis engine was replaced by a Volvo.

301

Due to the impossibility of obtaining substantial arms from other countries during wartime, the structure and weapons of the Swedish infantry division remained relatively stable throughout the war.

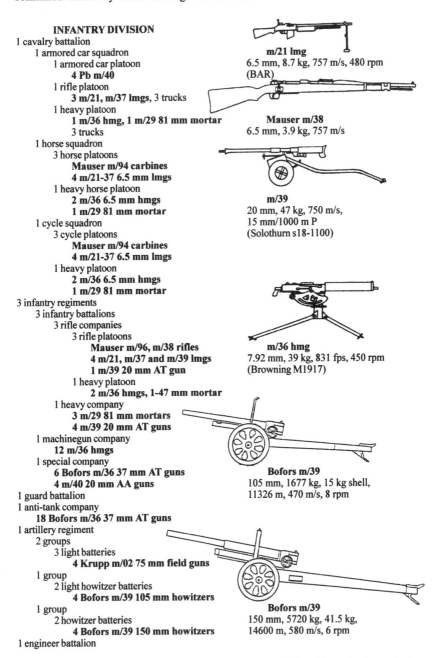

**INFANTRY DIVISION**
1 cavalry battalion
  1 armored car squadron
    1 armored car platoon
      **4 Pb m/40**
    1 rifle platoon
      **3 m/21, m/37 lmgs, 3 trucks**
    1 heavy platoon
      **1 m/36 hmg, 1 m/29 81 mm mortar**
      **3 trucks**
  1 horse squadron
    3 horse platoons
      **Mauser m/94 carbines**
      **4 m/21-37 6.5 mm lmgs**
    1 heavy horse platoon
      **2 m/36 6.5 mm hmgs**
      **1 m/29 81 mm mortar**
  1 cycle squadron
    3 cycle platoons
      **Mauser m/94 carbines**
      **4 m/21-37 6.5 mm lmgs**
    1 heavy platoon
      **2 m/36 6.5 mm hmgs**
      **1 m/29 81 mm mortar**
3 infantry regiments
  3 infantry battalions
    3 rifle companies
      3 rifle platoons
        **Mauser m/96, m/38 rifles**
        **4 m/21, m/37 and m/39 lmgs**
        **1 m/39 20 mm AT gun**
      1 heavy platoon
        **2 m/36 hmgs, 1-47 mm mortar**
    1 heavy company
      **3 m/29 81 mm mortars**
      **4 m/39 20 mm AT guns**
  1 machinegun company
    **12 m/36 hmgs**
  1 special company
    **6 Bofors m/36 37 mm AT guns**
    **4 m/40 20 mm AA guns**
1 guard battalion
1 anti-tank company
  **18 Bofors m/36 37 mm AT guns**
1 artillery regiment
  2 groups
    3 light batteries
      **4 Krupp m/02 75 mm field guns**
  1 group
    2 light howitzer batteries
      **4 Bofors m/39 105 mm howitzers**
  1 group
    2 howitzer batteries
      **4 Bofors m/39 150 mm howitzers**
1 engineer battalion

**m/21 lmg**
6.5 mm, 8.7 kg, 757 m/s, 480 rpm
(BAR)

**Mauser m/38**
6.5 mm, 3.9 kg, 757 m/s

**m/39**
20 mm, 47 kg, 750 m/s,
15 mm/1000 m P
(Solothurn s18-1100)

**m/36 hmg**
7.92 mm, 39 kg, 831 fps, 450 rpm
(Browning M1917)

**Bofors m/39**
105 mm, 1677 kg, 15 kg shell,
11326 m, 470 m/s, 8 rpm

**Bofors m/39**
150 mm, 5720 kg, 41.5 kg,
14600 m, 580 m/s, 6 rpm

The number of regiments in a division was variable, although the majority possessed 3 infantry regiments.

Sweden alleviated her armaments shortage by producing foreign designs under licence. To the prewar licence-built Browning machineguns and Stokes/Brandt mortars were added Finnish Tampella 120 mm mortars, licence-built from 1942. Acquired directly from Germany were ex-Czech Z.B.26 light machineguns and some 105 mm howitzers. From Switzerland came excellent, but obsolete, Solothurn s18-1100 20 mm anti-tank guns. However, the Ljungman AG42 semiautomatic rifle was an indigenous design, from 1943 issued a few to each rifle squad to supplement the bolt-action Mausers. Artillery pieces remained mostly those from the excellent Bofors factory.

Armored Car Squadron on the Road

The tank battalion became the I. Tank Battalion when it was enlarged to three companies:

**TANK BATTALION**
3 tank companies
HQ - **1 Strv m/37**
3 tank platoons
**5 Strv m/37**
1 tank platoon
**5 Strv m/38**

The 1. Corps was reduced to only one division. Although it still retained Major Holmgren's tank battalion, now grown to 63 tanks, its role became secondary as it appeared that there was no German concentration in Denmark. An invasion appeared imminent farther north when the German mountain troops in northern Norway moved eastward along the Arctic coast, and the dispersed infantry regiments in the south began to concentrate around Oslo. The result was the greatest mobilization of Swedish forces that was to occur during the war, reaching a peak of 240,000 regular troops and 115,000 Home Defense troops by **June 1940**. Radios crackled in many Swedish villages.

303

# Swedish Army (Gen.Lt. O.G. Thörnell)

1. **Corps** (Gen.Maj. von Edholm) - Kristianstad
    I. Division (Gen.Maj. von Klercker)
        I. Cavalry Battalion
        6., 7., 11., 16. Infantry Regiments
        3. Artillery Regiment
        **I. Tank Battalion** (Maj. Holmgren)
        48 Strv m/37, 15 Strv m/38
    Militärområde Södra (Col. Winberg)

2. **Corps** (Gen. Nygren) - Skövde
    II. Division (Gen.Maj. Holmquist)
        III. Cavalry Battalion
        2., 20., 21. Infantry Regiments
        4. Artillery Regiment
    III. Division (Gen.Maj. Malmberg)
        9., 17. Infantry Regiments
        2. Artillery Regiment
    IV. Division (Gen.Maj. Testrup) - attd. 11 May
        3., 8., 10. Infantry Regiments
        1. Artillery Regiment
    Group Göteborg (Col. Salander)
        15. Infantry Regiment
    Militärområde Västra (Gen.Maj. Malmberg)

    Militärområde Östra (Col. Beskow)
        1. Infantry Regiment

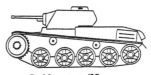

**Stridsvagn m/37**
1937, 4.5 tons, 2 mgs,
48 km/h, 150 km, 15 mm, 2 men
(CKD AH-IV)

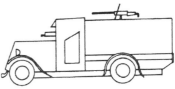

**Stridsvagn m/38**
1938, 8.6 tons, 1-37 mm, 1 mg,
45 km/h, 240 km, 13 mm, 3 men
40 mm/500 m P

**Group Mora** (Col. Anden) - Mora
    13. Infantry Regiment
**Group Jämtland** (Gen.Maj. Ohlsson) - Östersund
    5. Infantry Regiment
Militärområde Norra (Gen.Maj. von det Lancken)

**Övre Norrland Forces** (Gen.Maj. Douglas) - Boden
    VI. Division - formed 22 June
        II. Cavalry Battalion
        14., 45. Infantry Regiments
        11. Artillery Regiment
    Abisko Group
        19. Infantry Regiment
        Skier Battalion
    Militärområde Övre Norrland (Col. Bratt)

General Reserve
    V. Division (Gen.Maj. Hanngren)
        4., 12. Infantry Regiments
    **1. Cavalry Brigade** (Gen.Maj. Peyron)
        I., II., III. Cavalry Car Battalions
        3 Pb m/31, 9 Pb m/39
        1 artillery battalion

**Pansarbil m/31**
1931, 4 tons, 1-37 (20) mm, 1 mg,
60 km/h, 150 km, 6 mm, 6 men
40 mm/500 m P (20 mm/500 m P)
(rearmed with 1-20 mm in 1941)

Gotland Forces
    18. Infantry Regiment
    7. Artillery Regiment     156

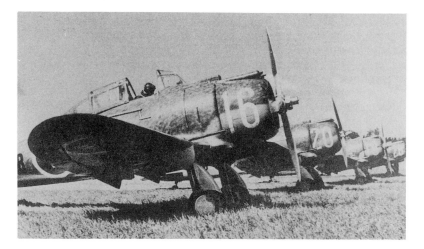

Flygflottilj 8 Prepares to Take its J9s Into the Air

The flurry of activity to purchase foreign aircraft brought a small measure of modernization to the Flygvapnet. First entering service in April 1940, 103 Douglas 8A-1s were built by ASJA as the B5 light bomber. By the end of 1941, all had been delivered to two wings. Although retaining a fixed undercarriage, the B5 was actually the most potent version of the Douglas 8A series and provided the Army with much needed support. However, the Seversky J9s remained the only modern fighters defending Sweden. By the summer of 1940 there were:

**Swedish Air Force** (Gen.Lt. Friis)

Flygflottilj 1 - Vasterås
  **53 Junkers B3**
Flygflottilj 2 - Hagernås (Stockholm)
  **11 Heinkel S12, 12 Heinkel T2**
Flygflottilj 3 - Malmslatt
  **34 Fokker S6**
Flygflottilj 4 - Östersund
  **32 Douglas B5**
Flygflottilj 5 - Ljungbyhed
  flying school
Flygflottilj 6 - Karlsborg
  **32 Douglas B5**
Flygflottilj 8 - Barkarby (Stockholm)
  **55 Seversky J9**
Flygflottilj 9 - Göteborg
  **13 Gloster J8**

**Seversky J9**
1938, 11 m span, 500 km/h, 1000 km,
9580 m SC, 4 mgs, 160 kg B
(Seversky EP-106)

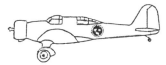

**Douglas B5**
1937, 15 m span, 410 km/h, 1465 km,
9110 m SC, 5 mgs, 300 kg B
(Douglas 8A-1)

While conducting constant reconnaissance missions for the Army, the Flygvapnet trained for its planned expansion. Units were detailed to cooperate with the "cover troops" during their training maneuvers. Techniques of support for the ground units were worked out in preparation for an invasion by the German forces in Norway:

**German Army of Norway**

North Norway
2., 3. Mountain Divisions
South Norway
3. Motorized Division
69., 163., 181., 196., 214. Infantry Divisions
Panzer Abteilung 40
3 light tank companies
22 Pz.Kw.I,II

1.(F)/120 - Ju.88D
I/JG 77 - Bf.109E
I/ZG 1 - Bf.110C
I/ZG 76 - Bf.110C
I,II/KG 26 - He.111
I,III/KG 30 - Ju.88A
Ku.Fl.Gr. 506 - He.115A
Ku.Fl.Gr. 706 - He.60, Do.18

Sweden was now cut off from the west, completely dependent upon the whims of Germany. Ribbentrop insisted that he be allowed to use Swedish railways to transport troops and supplies to German garrisons in Norway, and told Ambassador Richert that a refusal would be considered an unfriendly act. Richert warned his government that, with France now completely subjugated, the German government was prepared to force Sweden to her knees. When the Swedish ambassador to Great Britain communicated that Churchill would be deposed and peace made with Hitler, Richert's appreciation was reinforced.

The Swedish high command believed that a German invasion would come across the rolling country to the south of the mountains. Passing on either side of the great lakes, the invaders would drive on Göteborg or Stockholm. A secondary attack would be made through the Jämtland Gap into the Swedish mining country. General Nygren blocked the flanking movement with his II. Division, defended the route passing north of the lakes to Stockholm with the IV. Division, and shielded Göteborg with the III. Division.

At Jönköping, the 1. Cavalry Brigade and the I. Tank Battalion waited to counterattack in any direction. Three German tank companies, with 66 Pz.Kw.Is and IIs, had been involved in the fighting in Norway. The 63 Strv m/37s and m/38s of the Swedish I. Tank Battalion were of the same quality and should confront them successfully. General Douglas now had the small VI. Division at Boden near the Finnish border, with the Abisko Group deployed forward to block the railroad to Kiruna.

The *Flygvapnet* had improved its efficiency and was training assiduously in cooperation with the ground forces. Forty-five more Seversky J9s arrived in June to protect Stockholm, leaving one *division* available for the defense of Göteborg. This allowed the J8s to deploy to forward positions in Skåne and the west coast. One wing of the new Douglas B5 dive bombers was allotted to the II. Division defending the Jämtland Gap while the other supported the units of the 2. Corps in the lake country. Initial strikes would be made by the Junkers B3s from Vasterås upon enemy troop concentrations and supply dumps, but the two groups of German Bf.110Cs would be quite effective against them. They could also be used for strafing Swedish ground units in conjunction with bombing by He.111s and Ju.88s. Only the Seversky J9s would have enough speed to counter them. However, the Germans had only one group of single-seat Bf.109s, evening the odds somewhat. Furthermore, if the Swedish defenses proved difficult to crack, the Stukas of I/StG 1 could return from France to continue their devilish work.

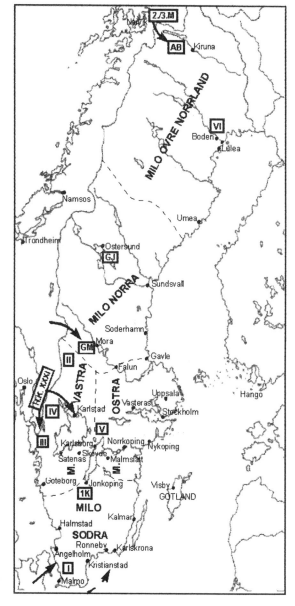

The Expected German Invasion of Summer 1940.

All in all, an invasion would probably succeed, as the Germans had seasoned troops while the Swedes, though inspired by defense of their homeland, were inexperienced and only half-trained. Swedish nerves were further strained when a Dornier Do.17P long-range reconnaissance plane cruised over the positions of the 2. Corps early in the afternoon of 6 July. Downed by anti-aircraft fire, the Germans claimed to have lost their way while flying from Stavanger to Oslo. But had they, or was this a reconnaissance preliminary to an invasion?

With Norway now out of the war, and no friends in position to help, the Swedish cabinet voted on 18 June to allow transit of German military cargoes. Three days later, Hansson informed the Riksdag in secret session. He justified the unpalatable agreement to the Swedish people as the only alternative to being occupied as had seven other European nations. Great Britain recognized the agreement as a realistic response, but in October the United States decided its munitions could be better used in active opposition to fascism and embargoed 110 of the planes still on order by Sweden. As if in penance for giving in to Germany, Sweden leased to the Allies the half of her merchant fleet caught away from home when the war began. A secret agreement allowed Germany to close the Öresund to submarines with nets.

During the following war years, Germany was to ship two million soldiers and 75,000 loads of arms over Swedish railways, violating Sweden's policy of neutrality. Sweden had little choice, for her defenses were too weak to withstand a serious German invasion. Her policy became one of making the fewest possible concessions while building her armed forces to a strength that would make a German invasion too costly for the rewards to be gained. This policy bore fruit when Germany became involved in widespread conflict, leaving insufficient troops available for a campaign in Sweden.

As summer stretched into Autumn 1940, it was realized in Berlin that an invasion of Sweden would probably instigate a Soviet occupation of Finland, a very undesirable event as far as Germany was concerned. Thus, as German forces became occupied in southern Europe, the threat to Sweden abated. She reduced her field forces to only 89,000 men, even her Home Defense units decreasing to 52,000 men. Late in June 1940, the burgeoning regiments in 2. Corps had been divided and the IX. Division formed. At the same time, VI. Division in Övre Norrland was reorganized as the X. Division.

Sweden used the respite to increase the quality of her armaments. Landsverk improved the Stridsvagn m/38 for the infantry-support role by replacing its turret with a much larger one which had twice the armor and unique double machineguns alongside the main armament. A score of the resulting Strv m/39s were built as the year ended.

Strengthening air defense remained the principal concern. The *Flygvapnet* finally received modern aircraft in quantity as Italy began an erratic delivery schedule. The competent Seversky J9s were joined, from mid-1940, by biplane Fiat J11s stationed at Göteborg. Late in 1940, Reggiane J20s began collecting on the aerodrome at Ängelholm, across the Sound from Denmark. They became the most active Swedish aircraft engaged in intercepting belligerent warplanes that strayed into Swedish territory. Less auspicious was the debut of Caproni B16 light bombers that began flying north in November 1940. Possessing good handling qualities, the light twins had been constructed with poor workmanship. Several were lost on the delivery flight from Italy and the type was plagued by mechanical difficulties throughout its career, causing the death of more Swedish airmen than any other type. More warlike qualities were exhibited by the Douglas B5s.

Sweden was encouraged by the continued belligerency of Great Britain, creating hope that she could yet avoid the German yoke. Public opinion hardened against the Nazis. From Norway had come tales of German brutality, resulting in attacks o  Swedish Nazis by outraged Swedes.

Gotland, with Hawker S9s on deck.

It was the Navy that first became involved in great events. *Gotland* was patrolling the Kattegat on **20 May 1941** when a massive form loomed through the sea mists. She radioed her startling discovery to the naval command on shore: The giant Nazi battleship *Bismarck* was at sea! *Bismarck* had left the Polish port of Gdynia two days earlier, picking up an escort of 3 destroyers and some minesweepers before entering The Sound off Denmark. *Gotland*'s report was intercepted by British intelligence and, on 21 May, the *Bismarck* was sighted by patrol aircraft. The British Home Fleet put to sea to begin an odyssey that resulted in the death of the battleship.

### *Teutons Attack the Rus* - June 1941

As spring came to 1941, General Lieutenant Thörnell alarmed the government with reports of threatening German movements. The North German plain was teeming with troop concentrations, supply dumps, and aerial activity. German "tourists" and "technicians" vacationed in Sweden during April-May, returning to Germany with much valuable information. Much of the German Navy had moved to the Baltic and was cruising the waters south of Sweden. Had Hitler decided to occupy Sweden after all? The surprising answer appeared on the first day of summer.

The German ambassador, Karl Schnurre, presented the Swedish government with a list of demands on the morning of **22 June 1941**. Nazi troops were already pouring into Russia, initiating the largest invasion of history - Barbarossa. Reading Ribbentrop's declaration that Sweden's war aims now matched those of Germany, Schnurre demanded waiver of the 24-hour neutrality law against the replenishment of warships, and permission for German planes and troops to pass over Swedish territory without opposition. The Germans had not appreciated the excellent marksmanship displayed in 1940 by Swedish anti-aircraft gunners. He also wanted the Swedish Navy to escort German vessels through Swedish territorial waters and help lay minefields along the east coast to protect German commerce. However, the most immediate demand was permission to transport the German 163. Infantry Division from Norway to Finland for use against the Russians.

309

As he did throughout the war, King Gustav V advocated acceptance of the Nazi demands, the prime minister concurring. However, many in parliament were outraged by the Nazi pressure, resulting in the most divisive political wrangling of the war years, the Midsummer Crisis of 1941. The Riksdag was torn between repugnance at Nazi atrocities in Norway and a desire to assist Finland. However, this time the Swedes considered the Finnish advance into the Soviet Union as aggression. The resulting acrid debate even led to calls for the king's abdication. However, appeals from the Finnish ambassador led to a reluctant acceptance of German terms on 25 June. Fifteen thousand men of the German division began using Swedish rails that very night. [157,158]

The army had been partially mobilized in June when German movements began in preparation for Barbarossa:

**Swedish Army** (Gen.Lt. O.G. Thörnell)

**1. Corps** (Gen.Maj. af Edholm) - Kristiansand
  I. Infantry Division (Gen.Maj. von Klercker)
    11. Infantry Regiment
    4 infantry battalions
    1 artillery battalion
  **I. Tank Battalion** (Maj. Holmgren)
    48 Strv m/37, 16 Strv m/38, 20 Strv m/39
  Militärområde Södra (Col. Winberg)

**2. Corps** (Gen. Nygren) - Skövde
  II. Infantry Division (Gen.Maj. Jung)
    14. Infantry Regiment
  III. Infantry Division (Gen.Maj. Malmberg)
    9. Infantry Regiment
  IV. Infantry Division (Gen.Maj. Testrup)
    8. Infantry Regiment
  IX. Infantry Division
    37. Infantry Regiment
  Militärområde Västra (Gen.Maj. Malmberg)

Militärområde Östra (Col. Beskow)
  **8. Motor Brigade**
    12 Pb m/39
    3 infantry battalions

**Group Jämtland** (Gen.Maj. Ohlsson)
  5. Infantry Regiment
  Militärområde Norra (Gen.Maj. af det Lancken)
    3 infantry battalions

**Övre Norrland Forces** (Gen.Maj. Douglas)
  X. Infantry Division
    X. Cavalry Battalion
    46., 47., Infantry Regiments
    15. Artillery Regiment
  Militärområde Övre Norrland (Col. Ehrenborg)

**Gotland troops** [159]

310

The army had made little progress in mechanization as priority had been given to rebuilding the dangerously obsolete air force. In the autumn of 1940, the cavalry brigade was converted into the 8. Motor Brigade to create a more integrated mobile unit:

**MOTOR BRIGADE**
3 motor battalions
    1 armored car squadron
        1 armored car platoon
            **4 Pb m/39**
        1 rifle platoon
        1 heavy platoon
            **1 m/36 hmg, 1 m/29 81 mm mortar**
    2 cavalry car squadrons
            **2 m/36 hmgs, 1 m/29 81 mm mortar**
1 motor artillery battalion
    **18 Krupp m/02-10 75 mm field guns**
1 anti-aircraft company
    **6 Bofors m/36 40 mm AA guns**
1 engineer company

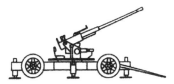

**Bofors m/36**
40 mm, 1922 kg, 0.9 kg shell,
4941 m VR, 900 m/s, 120 rpm

Delivery of the 20 new Stridsvagn m/39s allowed the tank battalion to be increased to 4 companies. The new Strv m/39s provided increased firepower, but the battalion was still basically a light infantry-support unit:

**TANK BATTALION**
4 tank companies
HQ - **1 Strv m/37, m/38** or **m/39**
2 tank platoons
    **5 Strv m/37**
2 tank platoons
    **5 Strv m/38** or **m/39**

In August 1941, the Swedish government rejected further demands for passage of German troops and supplies to Finland. It was berated by the Nazi press for avoiding responsibility in the fight against Bolshevism. Sensitive to the Russian boil festering at the southwestern tip of Finland, the government permitted a battalion of 816 men to assist in the investment of the Soviet base at Hangö until the Russians evacuated it. A company of volunteers also fought with the Finns on the Svir River throughout the war. Swedish Nazis joined the German 5. SS "Viking" Division on the Russian front.

The Swedish Navy suffered a grievous loss on 17 September 1941 when a mysterious explosion severely damaged the destroyers *Klas Uggla, Klas Horn* and *Göteborg* to such an extent that the *Klas Uggla* had to be scrapped. The *Öland* and *Uppland* were ordered built to replace them.

Early in 1941, the Allies began naval raids on the Norwegian coast. Especially troubling was a descent upon Narvik by British, Norwegian and Polish ships on 26-8 December. They steamed into the Vestfjord and destroyed German installations. German Grossadmiral Raeder initiated ominous naval movements early in 1942. At Trondheim, the battleship *Tirpitz* was joined in March by "pocket battleships" *Admiral Scheer* and *Lutzow*, heavy cruisers *Admiral Hipper* and *Prinz Eugen*, 6 destroyers and 3 torpedo boats. Three British air attacks had failed to damage *Tirpitz*, but a torpedo from a British submarine sent *Prinz Eugen* back to the Baltic for repairs. In May, *Lutzow* joined sister ship *Admiral Scheer* and 3 torpedo boats in moving north to protect Narvik.

At a naval conference on 22 January 1942, Hitler strongly urged Sweden to join Germany in resisting any Allied landing in Norway. He promised Narvik and Petsamo as prizes if she acquiesced. Concerned that the Allies would mount an operation to capture the vital mine at Kiruna, Hitler became enraged when the recalcitrant Swedes refused to approve his scheme and began to consider a preemptive occupation. A flood of warnings from Swedish Ambassador Richert arrived at Stockholm during February. Junkers Ju.88D reconnaissance planes flew at high altitude over Swedish military installations. It appeared that Germany was about to mount an invasion. Sweden began to mobilize on **19 February 1942** and, by the end of the month, had 182,000 regular and 78,000 Home Defense troops under arms for the *Marskrisen* (March Crisis).

The Pansarschiffe Division Sails an Evasive Course Through Submarine-infested Baltic Waters.

The Swedish Navy considered the possibility of German landings in Skåne, or along the shore of the Kattegat. Karlskrona and Göteborg were shielded by old armored coast defense ships, old destroyers, and small coastal submarines. The *Kustflottan* (Coastal Fleet), based at Stockholm, prepared to cruise against German naval forces. Composed of the most modern Swedish ships, it was not equipped for extended operations at sea. The three *Sverige* class armored cruisers had been extensively rebuilt just before the war and were good sea boats capable of contending with the two remaining Nazi "pocket battleships". However, the hybrid *Gotland*, intended for launching seaplanes as scouts for the fleet, was the only modern cruiser in the navy. Swedish destroyers, though fast, were small and short-ranged. The fleet efficiently performed its main mission throughout the war - neutrality patrols in Swedish territorial waters. The Navy patrolled the coasts effectively and escorted merchant vessels through Swedish territorial waters. In conjunction with the German Navy, large minefields were laid between the east coast and the Åland Islands, and along the southern and western coasts. A convoy system was organized to guard Swedish shipping against submarines.

Milo Västra was divided between the 1. Corps in Dalarna and Värmland, with the much reduced 2. Corps restricted to the western great lakes.

**Swedish Army** (Gen.Lt. O.G. Thörnell)
**1. Corps** - Karlstad
IV. Infantry Division
   3., 4., 8. Infantry Regiments
XIII. Infantry Division
   45., 47. Infantry Regiments
XVI. Infantry Division
   2., 13., 22. Infantry Regiments
**II. Tank Battalion** (less 6. Tank Comp.)
   63 Strv m/40L
GHQ Reserve
   XIV. Infantry Division
     33., 38. Infantry Regiments

**Stridsvagn m/39**
1939, 9.1 tons, 1-37 mm, 2 mgs,
45 km/h, 240 km, 24 mm, 3 men
40 mm/500 m P

**2. Corps** - Skövde
III. Infantry Division
   15., 16., 17. Infantry Regiments
GHQ Reserve
   9. Infantry Regiment

**3. Corps** - Kristianstad
I. Infantry Division
   6., 11., 12. Infantry Regiments
XI. Infantry Division
   26., 41., 42. Infantry Regiments
Corps Reserve
   7., 46. Infantry Regiments
**I. Tank Battalion**
   48 Strv m/37, 16 Strv m/38, 20 Strv m/39
7., 8. Anti-tank Companies
GHQ Reserve
   **8. Motor Brigade** (Col. Toren) (less I. Motor Bn.)
   8 Pb m/39
   11. Anti-tank Company

Militärområde Östra - Stockholm
1., 10. Infantry Regiments
GHQ Reserve
   **I. Motor Battalion**
   4 Pb m/39
   34. Infantry Regiment

**Pansarbil m/39-40 Lynx**
1938, 7.8 tons, 1-20 mm, 3 mgs,
70 km/h, 250 km, 18 mm, 6 men
20 mm/500 m P

**Group Jämtland**
II. Infantry Division
   5., 14., 21 Infantry Regiments
XII. Infantry Division
   35., 43., 44. Infantry Regiments
**6. Tank Company**
   21 Strv m/40L
4., 9. Anti-tank Companies
**Övre Norrland Forces**
XV. Infantry Division
   19., 20., 51. Infantry Regiments
GHQ Reserve
   50. Infantry Regiment   160

Some units of each command were held in GHQ Reserve. The lonely 50. Infantry Regiment was stationed on the Finnish border east of Boden, the XIV. Infantry Division and the 9. Infantry Regiment were held between Lakes Vänern and Vättern. The 8. Motor Brigade was stationed at Enköping, on the north shore of Lake Malaren, blocking the main route to Stockholm.

J20s Confront Intruders Over Skåne

**Swedish Air Force** (Gen.Lt. Friis)

Flygflottilj 1 - Vasterås
   **53 Junkers B3**
Flygflottilj 2 - Hagernås (Stockholm)
   **11 Heinkel S12**
   **12 Heinkel T2**
Flygflottilj 3 - Malmslatt
   **37 Caproni S16**
Flygflottilj 4 - Östersund
   **53 Douglas B5**
Flygflottilj 5 - Ljungbyhed
   flying school
Flygflottilj 6 - Karlsborg
   **44 Douglas B5**
Flygflottilj 7 - Satenås
   **45 Caproni B16**
Flygflottilj 8 - Barkarby (Stockholm)
   **55 Seversky J9**
Flygflottilj 9 - Göteborg
   **52 Fiat J11**
Flygflottilj 10 - Ängelholm
   **57 Reggiane J20**    161

**Caproni B16, S16**
1940, 16 m span, 436 km/h, 800 km,
7300 m SC, 3 mgs, 400 kg B
(Caproni Ca.313 R.P.B.1)

**Fiat J11**
1939, 10 m span, 430 km/h, 780 km,
4/3000 m, 10200 m SC, 2 mgs
(Fiat CR.42)

**Reggiane J20**
1939, 11 m span, 530 km/h, 840 km,
6/6000 m, 11200 m SC, 2 mgs, 200 kg B
(Reggiane Re.2000)

314

If the Allies managed a considerable landing despite the German arrangements, the trapped Army of Norway planned to fight its way into Sweden, take control of the country, and use it as a base for further operations against the invaders. Far to the north, a division of the Swedish *Övre Norrland Forces* defended the iron mines of Kiruna. From Trondheim, the German XXXIII Corps would send its 181. and 196. Infantry Divisions through the mountains by way of the Jämtland Gap. Supported by a company of Pz.Kw.39-H 735(f) (Hotchkiss H.39) light tanks, and the 702. Reserve Infantry Division, the corps would execute **Operation I** to capture Östersund and establish a position from which to control communications in northern Scandinavia, leaving the *Ovre Norrland Forces* to dry on the vine.

Strv m/40Ls Maneuver Near Strängnäs

Group Jämtland was organized to stop such a move. In the rugged vale of the Storsjön, the II. and XII. Infantry Divisions would go into position behind a screen of two companies of anti-tank guns. Sallying from the mountains, the leading German tanks would be peppered with armor-piercing shot from the waiting Swedish guns as B5 dive bombers of Flygflottilj 4 based at nearby Östersund struck the German columns. A successful counterattack by the 21 Strv m/40Ls of 6. Tank Company against the little Pz.Kw.39-Hs on the point of the enemy advance would help the infantry block the defile.

Farther south, another invasion route between Oslo and Stockholm passes just to the north of the great lakes. Mindful of the danger, the Swedish high command had constructed two fortified lines between the lakes and the east coast, blocking both invasion routes. The principal line ran northeast from Lake Vänern to Falun, then east to Gävle. A fall back position passed from the western tip of Lake Mälaren to Gävle. Railroads and roads running parallel to each position allowed the rapid shifting of troops behind the lines. Deployed forward of the fortifications were the strongest forces of the Swedish Army. From its headquarters in Karlstad, at the north tip of Lake Vänern, the 1. Corps

315

controlled three infantry divisions deployed across Värmland to central Dalarna. A fourth division was held east of Lake Vänern at the disposal of Army General Headquarters, along with the newly-formed II. Tank Battalion, which provided a mobile armored reserve for the corps:

**II. TANK BATTALION**
4 tank companies
HQ - **1 Strv m/40L**
4 tank platoons
**5 Strv m/40L**

The Strv m/40 was the definitive model of the Landsverk L.60 design and was the first to be mass-produced. Little different from the m/39, it embodied several detail improvements but retained the light armor that made the entire series vulnerable even to light anti-tank guns. However, it was a match for the light tanks possessed by the German forces in Norway.

Warming Up the S16s of F3 for a Reconnaissance Mission.

As one passes southward through Värmland, the mountains diminish through rolling hills to a lake-filled basin stretching from the Skagerrak to the Baltic. From ancient times, this lake country has hosted many invasions and migrations. Plucky Swedish airmen flying unreliable Caproni S16s of Flygflottilj 3 would descry approaching infantry columns of the German Army of Norway. The LXX Corps (214. and 280. Infantry Divisions, 710. Reserve Infantry Division) was to make a frontal attack to take Karlstad, penetrate the southern wing of the Swedish fortified zones, and advance to Lake Mälaren.

Across its path lay the Swedish 1. Corps, its IV. Infantry Division astride the route passing north of the great lakes, with the XIII. and XVI. Infantry Divisions holding a line stretching north over rugged terrain to Lake Siljan. Forty-five B16 light bombers of F7 waited on the eastern shore of Lake Vänern. The fast little Italian bombers were a delight to fly, but were crippled by engine, hydraulic and electrical weaknesses. Rising from their airfield at Satenäs, they would assist the more rugged B5s of Flygflottilj 6 in slashing at the German concentrations.

To prevent a flank march around the south end of the great lakes, the III. Division of the Swedish 2. Corps was deployed along the south and west sides of Lake Vänern, where it was in position to block an advance on Göteborg. The battlefield was well within range of fighters based at Stockholm and Göteborg. Nazi bombers would have difficulty getting at the Swedish ground forces under the umbrella of J9s from F8. Fiat J11 fighter bombers of F9 would find their most effective opposition coming from the anti-aircraft guns accompanying the enemy infantry, for the Germans had few fighters available for operations in Scandinavia.

Thus, the Nazi frontal advance would have to force the principal Swedish defensive lines in order to break into the industrial heart of the country. Swedish forces appeared equal to the challenge.

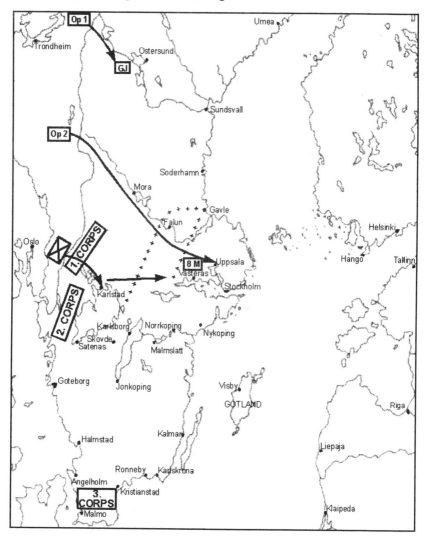

Marskrisen - German Invasion Plan of 1942

317

A Division of B5s from F4 Roars Over the Storsjön

Anticipating the strength of the defenses guarding the industrial region of Sweden, the Germans prepared a decisive blow to the northern wing. The historically belligerent mining province of Dalarna includes a long valley, the Dalälven, that points like a dagger at the Uppland heart of Sweden. Mora, on Lake Siljan, marked the junction between the Swedish 1. Corps and Jämtland Group and was now rather sparsely held, as the Germans were expected to advance through the easier routes to the north and south.

The Germans selected this weakened point for **Operation II**, a blitzkrieg down the Dalälven toward Stockholm. It was to be led by the 25. Panzer Division, organized in May with 20 Pz.Kw.IIs, 40 Pz.Kw.39-H 735(f)s (Hotchkiss H.39) and 15 Pz.Kw.35-S 739(f)s (Somua S.35). Following in its wake was the partially motorized 69. Infantry Division. The first 100 kilometers of the advance would be through a narrow valley between mountains rising to 4,000 meters above sea level. But the defense of the route would be shared by two commands, always a difficult task. In this case, both commands were already distracted by heavy attacks in other sections of their front. It was likely that the Germans would succeed in escaping attention until they reached the more open basin of Lake Siljan. Although the Douglas bombers of Flygflottilj 4 from Östersund would dive on them, the Nazi tanks would face no armor, as the II. Tank Battalion was nearly 200 kilometers away with the 1. Corps.

At Falun, the German columns would strike the main Swedish defense line. Bunkers, artillery, anti-tank guns - all would serve to delay the advance. However, this was the northern flank of the Swedish defenses, where little danger was expected. If the 25. Panzer Division could punch through it, and overrun the second position at Avesta before the Swedes could fall back, it would debouch into rolling lowlands with few natural obstacles. The lethal thrust would be battered by Junkers B3s from Vasterås, now only 50 kilometers away. From Karlsborg and Satenäs, B5s and B16s would strafe and bomb in a desperate attempt to halt the advance.

318

By this time, the II. Tank Battalion and the 8. Motor Brigade would be in position to attack the south flank of the panzer division, while the I. Tank Battalion took responsibility for supporting the Swedish forces west of Lake Vänern. The 63 Strv m/40Ls of the II. Battalion would be effective against most of the Nazi tanks, although the Somuas could destroy them. Fortunately, the Germans possessed little more than a dozen of the ex-French medium tanks. Should the Swedes react in time, the ill-supported thrust of the German armor could be blunted before it ravaged Uppsala and flushed the government from Stockholm. Left without much mobile reserve, the 3. Corps in Skåne anticipated no crossings from Denmark, for the German actions would have been stimulated only by an Allied invasion of Norway. Hopefully, the situation to the north would stabilize before invasion forces appeared off southern shores.

Would Sweden have been able to stave off defeat at this stage in the war? Although the Swedes had good terrain to defend, the mobility of the Germans could have disrupted General Thörnell's plans if he did not act swiftly. The question was not put to the test as no Allied landings appeared in Norway and the German plan was never put in motion. Swedes began to breathe easier. When Gustav V assured Hitler that Sweden would resist any Allied incursion, the Germans backed off, influenced by Sweden's vigorous mobilization and her value as a pliable economic partner rather than a reluctant satellite state.

As the danger of a German invasion diminished, Swedish units were deactivated, but retained in reserve. However, the Riksdag had been sufficiently shaken to approve an enlarged five-year defense plan in January 1942. As Sweden's manpower was being fully utilized, an improvement in strength could be achieved only by increasing firepower. To that end, a number of new weapons were purchased.

The ground forces were reorganized on **1 October 1942**, to coordinate and train the enlarged army. The Militärområde were made more important, with larger headquarters staffs. The western Milo was divided into two parts. The number of divisions was increased to ten, but still had no fixed organization. A total of 36 infantry regiments were organized, but not brigaded. Recruiting regiments established two field regiments that were rotated to the front to gain operational experience.

**Swedish Army** (Gen.Lt. O.G. Thörnell)

I. Militärområdet (Gen.Maj. von Klercker) - Kristianstad
  I., XI. Infantry Divisions
  **I. Tank Battalion**
    48 Strv m/37, 16 Strv m/38, 20 Strv m/39
II. Militärområdet (Gen.Maj. Jung) - Östersund
  II., XII. Infantry Divisions
III. Militärområdet (Gen.Maj. Högberg) - Skövde
  III., XIII. Infantry Divisions
  **II. Tank Battalion**
    84 Strv m/40L
IV. Militärområdet (Gen.Maj. Testrup) - Stockholm
  IV., XIV. Infantry Divisions
  **8. Motor Brigade**
    8 Pb m/39
V. Militärområdet (Gen.Maj. Rappe) - Karlstad
  XVI. Infantry Division
VI. Militärområdet (Gen.Maj. Rosenblad) - Boden
  XV. Infantry Division
VII. Militärområdet (Gen.Maj. Åkerhielm) - Visby
  Gotland Forces          162

319

A subtle, but fundamental, change in the Swedish posture occurred with the first major setbacks suffered by German arms in November 1942. When the myth of German invincibility was shattered at Stalingrad and El Alamein, Swedish resistance to German demands stiffened. For some time, the Western Allies had been urging termination of German privileges. Sweden responded by ending grants of commercial credits in December 1942. However, trade with Germany actually increased, for vital coal, coke and chemicals were shipped to Sweden in exchange for the Kiruna iron ore that met 27% of Germany's requirements. During the ice-free months, Germany could circumvent the hassles of transportation through Sweden by sending merchant convoys through the Gulf of Bothnia to the Finnish port of Kemi. They were watched by Heinkel T2 seaplanes flying neutrality patrols over the broad territorial waters between the mainland and Gotland. Coastal waters in the Gulf of Bothnia were surveyed by Heinkel S12s. On 11 February 1943, an Arado Ar.196A-3 flying a similar mission between Copenhagen and Bornholm turned north too soon and flew into the Bay of Hanö where it was brought down about 1600 by fire from a Swedish naval vessel.

Early in 1943, Hitler's anxiety concerning the Allies' designs on Norway reached a peak. He cut Sweden off from the West by blockading Göteborg from mid-January to May and brought in the LXXI Corps to defend Narvik with the 27., 199. and 230. Infantry Divisions. Dependent upon the food, textiles and petroleum supplied by the Allies, Sweden entered trade negotiations in London during the summer. After a series of convolutions, Hansson bravely terminated German transit privileges over the Swedish railways in **July 1943**. Anticipating a violent German reaction, 300,000 men were mobilized.

**Swedish Army** (Gen.Lt. O.G. Thörnell)

**3. Army Corps** - Kristianstad
  I., XI. Infantry Divisions
  **I. Tank Battalion**
    48 Strv m/37, 16 Strv m/38, 20 Strv m/39

**III. Militärområdet** - Skövde
  III. Infantry Division
**1. Army Corps** - Karlstad
  IV., XII., XIII., XVI. Infantry Divisions
  **II. Tank Battalion**
    84 Strv m/40L

**Stridsvagn m/40L,K**
1940, 9.6 tons, 1-37 mm, 2 mgs,
45 km/h, 240 km, 24 mm, 3 men
40 mm/500 m P

**II. Militärområdet** - Östersund
  II. Infantry Division

**VI. Militärområdet** - Boden
  XV. Infantry Division

**VII. Militärområdet** - Visby
  Gotland Forces

GHQ Reserve - Stockholm
  XIV. Infantry Division
  1., 9., 10., 41. Infantry Regiments
  **8. Motor Brigade**
    12 Pb m/39
  **III. Tank Battalion**
    84 Strv m/41 SI

**Stridsvagn m/41 SI**
1938, 10.6 tons, 1-37 mm, 2 mgs,
45 km/h, 200 km, 25/25/20 mm,
40 mm/500 m P, 3 men    164

Hindered by lack of interest, armor plate, and expertise, Swedish tank development was far behind world progress, an alarming situation in light of the obvious importance of tanks on the modern battlefield. Armor plate was difficult to manufacture, but at last a sufficient quantity was being obtained to produce quantities of tanks in Sweden. At the time of the general reorganizeation of the Army in October 1942, an Armored Corps had been formed from 1 cavalry and 2 infantry regiments to permit development of specialized doctrine and training. Swedish armor improved dramatically from that moment. By the time of the Summer Crisis of 1943, a third tank battalion had formed. The agile Strv m/40L had been supplemented by another licence-built Czech design. Developed in 1938, the CKD TNH was one of the best light-medium tanks in the world, being used by Germany through 1942. It was provided with a new turret of Swedish design, and designated the Strv m/41 SI. The later SII model of 1944 was slightly longer and had spaced center bogies. More reliable than the m/40L, the excellent m/41 was capable of fighting the lightly armored tanks possessed by the German forces in Norway. However, the Tigers and T-34s now clashing on the Russian plains were another matter.

At the moment of greatest danger, Hitler had the rug pulled from under him. Italy surrendered, forcing him to transfer the newly-arrived troops south to keep the Allies from penetrating the Alpine barrier. Some time passed before the Swedish high command realized that the Germans no longer had the forces available to invade Sweden. Once the situation was clarified, the general staff prepared a plan for eliminating the recurring threat to central Sweden, at the same time cutting German communications to northern Norway should the opportunity arise. The 1. Corps was given the task of advancing toward Oslo on a broad front, aided on its left flank by the II. Infantry Division of the III. Milo. Communications with Narvik would be severed with a short thrust by the XV. Division to Mo-i-Rana, south of Bodo on the Atlantic coast of Norway. Held in abeyance, the plan was resurrected at the end of the war as a way of disarming German troops.

The backwardness of Swedish military technology was brought home in November 1943 when the first German V-1 ramjet flying bomb landed in Sweden. Ironically, the seven unarmed V-1s that came down in Sweden by the end of the war were test launched from former Swedish territory - Karlshagen in Pomerania. Great Britain was soon to feel the full potential of the radical weapon.

*Swedish Defenses Mature* - 1943-1944

As the government's foreign policies succeeded in keeping Sweden both independent and non-belligerent, Hansson's stature at home grew to that of a great statesman. Observing the progressive weakening of Germany, he allowed *Landorganisationen*, the largest union in Sweden with a million members, to rail against cooperation with Germany, while Swedish newspapers vilifyed Nazi policies, causing the Nazis to characterize his government as "swine in dinner jackets". Swedish sympathy for the Allies grew rapidly.

As the war wore on, the United States of America increasingly goaded Sweden. Having no history of involvement in European politics, the Americans viewed Sweden mainly as a weak spot in Hitler's *Fortress Europa*. They believed that she was selfishily maneuvering to gain a dominant economic position in postwar Europe. A Swedish mechanical invention, the ball bearing, became the principal bone of contention.

321

Manufactured by the SKF company from fine Swedish steel, ball bearings were used in the engines of aircraft, tanks and other vehicles critical to modern warfare. Realizing that the most direct way of crippling the production of mobile German weapons was to deny them the vital bearings, American heavy bombers had begun raiding German ball bearing plants, only to have Sweden ship more to them. Still dependent upon Germany for vital supplies, Sweden stubbornly refused to lower its exports of the irritating little spheres. More friendly was the treatment accorded the thousand American airmen interned in Sweden during the war. The first crew crashlanded their crippled bomber in a Swedish field on 24 July 1943.

Sweden had used its vast forests to produce scarce materials: automobile fuel, rayon and cellulose wool textiles, even food. The panic defense situation of 1940 had evolved through a stage of perilous jousting by 1943. Foreign weapons, scavenged from every quarter, had armed the early military forces while every effort was made to develop an indigenous munitions industry from meagre resources. The results of the program began to appear in 1943.

Scandinavian Heavy Armor - Stridsvagn m/42s

The Strv m/41 was followed by the first true medium tank produced in Sweden. Designated the Stridsvagn m/42 "heavy" tank, the first models (TM, TV) had mechanical gearboxes, but most of the production run (EH, TH) used hydraulic transmissions. The speed and armor of the Strv m/42 were comparable to other medium tanks of the period, but its 75 mm gun lacked sufficient armor-piercing qualities. At the time, Germany was building Tiger tanks, and the Soviet Union had large numbers of T-34s, KVs and Stalins. Fortunately, such monsters were not available to the Nazis in Scandinavia.

Sweden's first combined arms armored units appeared after the authorization of three *pansarbrigaden* on 1 July 1943. Initially, the 8. Motor Brigade converted to the 8. Pansarbrigade. At the time, only the little tanks of the first two tank battalions were available. With them, training began. Two more tank battalions were forming with new Strv m/41s and Strv m/42s, but most of the required equipment had yet to be ordered and produced. By the summer of 1944, all six wartime tank battalions had been organized.

322

The army possessed the 84 early tanks, with new equipment including 100 Strv m/40Ls, 116 Strv m/41 SIs and 70 Strv m/42s, yet the 8. Pansarbrigad still had only 3 companies of light tanks under its command. The first of 500 *Terrangbil* m/42 armored trucks, manufactured by Scania-Vabis (SKPF) and Volvo (VKPF), arrived in 1944 to serve as armored personnel carriers for the infantry of the armored brigades.

### ARMORED BRIGADE
HQ - 3 light tanks, 2 heavy tanks, 2 APCs
2 tank battalions
   HQ - 1 light tank, 2 heavy tanks, 1 APC
      1 reconnaissance platoon
         5 light tanks
      3 light companies
         HQ - 3 light tanks
         2 light platoons
            **5 Strv m/41, m/40**
         1 heavy platoon
            **5 Strv m/42**
         1 engineer platoon
            **4 Tgbl m/42 KP APCs**

      1 heavy company
         HQ - 3 heavy tanks
         3 heavy platoons
            **5 Strv m/42**

**m/37**

         1 engineer platoon
            **4 Tgbl m/42 KP APCs**

6.5 mm, 9.5 kg, 757 m/s, 480 rpm
(development of BAR)

      1 depot company
         6 light tanks, 2 heavy tanks
1 armored infantry battalion
   HQ - **2 Pb m/31, 8 Tgbl m/42 KP APCs**
   3 rifle companies
      HQ - **1 Tgbl m/42 KP**
      1 armored car and anti-aircraft platoon
         **1 Pb m/31, 1 Tgbl m/42 KP**
      3 rifle platoons
         **3 m/37 lmgs, 1-47 mm mortar**
         **2 Tgbl m/42 KP**
      1 heavy platoon
         **2 m/36 hmgs, 2 m/29 81 mm mortars**
         **2 Tgbl m/42 KP**
   1 heavy company
      HQ - **1 Tgbl m/42 KP**
      1 armored car and anti-aircraft platoon
         **1 Pb m/31, 1 Tgbl m/42 KP**
      1 machinegun platoon
         **4 m/36 hmgs, 2 Tgbl m/42 KP**
      1 mortar platoon
         **3 m/29 81 mm mortars**
         **3 Tgbl m/42 KP**
      1 anti-tank platoon

         **6 m/36 37 mm AT guns** or
         **6 m/43 57 mm AT guns** (from 1944)

**m/43**

         **6 Tgbl m/42 KP**
1 motorcycle company

57 mm, 1224 kg, 2.7 kg shell,
8990 m, 885 m/s, 15 rpm,
118 mm/500 m P

   HQ - **1 Tgbl m/42 KP**
   3 motorcycle platoons
      **3 m/37 lmgs, 30 motorcycles** (10 with sidecars)
1 motorized artillery battalion
   3 batteries
      **4 Bofors m/39 105 mm howitzers**
1 anti-aircraft company
   **5 m/40 20 mm, 10 m/36 40 mm AA guns**
2 engineer companies

164

The Swedish high command saw little reason to alter the triangular infantry organization. The chief improvements came to the heavy weapons units, with heavy mortars and more powerful anti-tank guns added. Sweden had neither the finances nor the fuel to mechanize its infantry. In any event, Russian mechanized forces had achieved little in Finland.

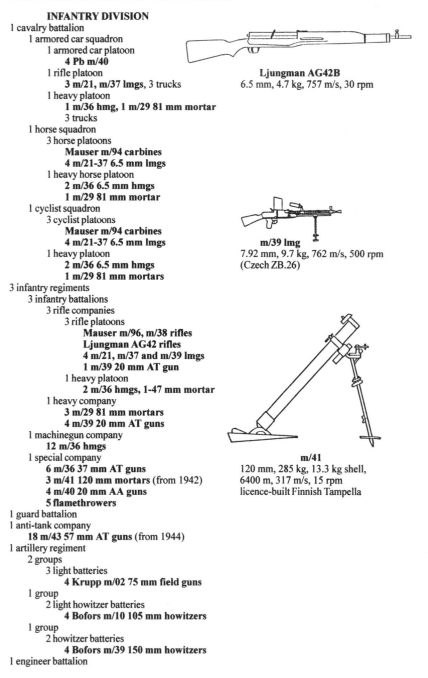

**INFANTRY DIVISION**
1 cavalry battalion
  1 armored car squadron
    1 armored car platoon
      **4 Pb m/40**
    1 rifle platoon
      **3 m/21, m/37 lmgs**, 3 trucks
    1 heavy platoon
      **1 m/36 hmg, 1 m/29 81 mm mortar**
      3 trucks
  1 horse squadron
    3 horse platoons
      **Mauser m/94 carbines**
      **4 m/21-37 6.5 mm lmgs**
    1 heavy horse platoon
      **2 m/36 6.5 mm hmgs**
      **1 m/29 81 mm mortar**
  1 cyclist squadron
    3 cyclist platoons
      **Mauser m/94 carbines**
      **4 m/21-37 6.5 mm lmgs**
    1 heavy platoon
      **2 m/36 6.5 mm hmgs**
      **1 m/29 81 mm mortars**
3 infantry regiments
  3 infantry battalions
    3 rifle companies
      3 rifle platoons
        **Mauser m/96, m/38 rifles**
        **Ljungman AG42 rifles**
        **4 m/21, m/37 and m/39 lmgs**
        **1 m/39 20 mm AT gun**
      1 heavy platoon
        **2 m/36 hmgs, 1-47 mm mortar**
    1 heavy company
      **3 m/29 81 mm mortars**
      **4 m/39 20 mm AT guns**
    1 machinegun company
      **12 m/36 hmgs**
    1 special company
      **6 m/36 37 mm AT guns**
      **3 m/41 120 mm mortars** (from 1942)
      **4 m/40 20 mm AA guns**
      **5 flamethrowers**
1 guard battalion
1 anti-tank company
  **18 m/43 57 mm AT guns** (from 1944)
1 artillery regiment
  2 groups
    3 light batteries
      **4 Krupp m/02 75 mm field guns**
  1 group
    2 light howitzer batteries
      **4 Bofors m/10 105 mm howitzers**
  1 group
    2 howitzer batteries
      **4 Bofors m/39 150 mm howitzers**
1 engineer battalion

**Ljungman AG42B**
6.5 mm, 4.7 kg, 757 m/s, 30 rpm

**m/39 lmg**
7.92 mm, 9.7 kg, 762 m/s, 500 rpm
(Czech ZB.26)

**m/41**
120 mm, 285 kg, 13.3 kg shell,
6400 m, 317 m/s, 15 rpm
licence-built Finnish Tampella

During the war, the Swedish Air Force gained more operational experience than any other branch of service. Some Swedish airmen even engaged in combat. Neutrality patrol by the fighter wings brought increasing incidents as the air war over Europe escalated. Damaged and lost aircraft straying into Swedish air space were intercepted and escorted to internment. The J20s of F10 opposite Denmark were particularly busy and got into numerous scraps with both Allied and German planes that refused their invitation to land, firing warning shots into the air. They were aided increasingly by the new J22s as they progressively equipped new wings. However, no aircraft were shot down by Swedish fighters during the war.

**Swedish Air Force** (Gen.Lt. Nordenskjold)

**1. Flygeskadern** - Stockholm

Flygflottilj 1 - Vasterås
  **60 Saab B18A**
Flygflottilj 4 - Östersund
  **49 Saab B17B**
Flygflottilj 12 - Kalmar
  **55 Saab B17B**

**2. Flygeskadern** - Göteborg

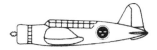

**Saab B18A, S18A**
1942, 17 m span, 465 km/h, 2200 km,
8000 m SC, 3 mgs, 1500 kg B

Flygflottilj 6 - Karlsborg
  **48 Saab B17B**
Flygflottilj 7 - Satenås
  **76 Saab B17B**
Flygflottilj 9 - Göteborg
  **60 FFVS J22**

**3. Flygeskadern** - Stockholm

Flygflottilj 8 - Barkarby (Stockholm)
  **52 Seversky J9**
Flygflottilj 10 - °ngelholm
  **42 Reggiane J20**
Flygflottilj 13 - Norrköping
  **60 FFVS J22**
Flygflottilj 16 - Uppsala
  **54 FFVS J22**

**Saab B17B, S17B**
1940, 14 m span, 396 km/h,
3 mgs, 680 kg B

**4. Flygeskadern** - Stockholm

Flygflottilj 2 - Hagernås (Stockholm)
  **47 Saab S17BS**
Flygflottilj 11 - Nyköping
  **58 Caproni S16** (from F3 and F7 in 1943)
Flygflottilj 17 - Ronneby
  **12 Junkers T3**
  **12 Junkers B3**

Independent Flygflottilj
Flygflottilj 5 - Ljungbyhed
  flying school
Flygflottilj 3 - Malmslatt
  **8 FFVS J22**
  **18 Fieseler S14**
  **44 Saab S17B**   165

**Saab S17BS**
1940, 14 m span, 346 km/h,
3 mgs, 680 kg B

Saab B17s of F4 on Patrol Over the Storsjön

The Flygvapnet was reorganized in 1944. Bombers of the eastern zone were grouped in the 1. Flygeskadern and those of the west in the 2. Flygeskadern. The 3. Flygeskadern controlled all fighters, except for F9 guarding Göteborg. Maritime operation was the mission of 4. Flygeskadern. The army reconnaissance wing near Linköping was established as an independent unit. The Saab B17 became the most common aircraft in the Swedish Air Force after 1942. The first modern aircraft of indigenous design, this not very distinguished, but adaptable and reliable, design became a dive bomber, tactical reconnaissance plane and maritime seaplane. Unavailability of suitable engines retarded its introduction past its peak period of effectiveness. The low-powered B17B first entered service, followed by the more powerful C model and ending with the A model mounting the engine originally intended.

With light metals in short supply, and Saab fully occupied producing bombers, the government directed a design team to develop a fighter using as much steel and wood as possible. The *Flygförvaltningens Verkstad* (FFVS) at Bromma, near Stockholm, was to do final assembly of the new fighter. F9 received its first J22s in September 1943 to replace the old Fiat biplanes defending Göteborg. A maneuverable aircraft with excellent handling qualities, the J22 was too slow and lightly armed for late-war aerial combat. Results of tests against an interned Messerschmitt Bf.109F-1 in 1944 were not published, but it represented a first step in self-sufficiency for Sweden.

The Saab B18 started as a long-range reconnaissance plane to replace the French and German models withheld in 1940. The prototype was reconfigured as a bomber, with its unique canopy offset to improve the pilot's ground view. It began displacing F1's Junkers B3s in June 1944. The weary Junkers were shunted to the naval wing and modified as torpedo bombers (T3) and minelayers (B3). The Flygvapnet finally had mainly indigenous aircraft.

326

**Coastal Fleet**

Armored Ship Division
  *Gustav V, Sverige,*
  *Drottning Victoria*
Destroyer Squadron
  *Öland, Uppland*
  *Visby, Sundsvall*
  *Malmö, Norrköping,*
  *Gävle, Stockholm*
  *Mjölner, Munin,*
  *Mode, Magne*
Submarine Group
  *Sjöhästen, Sjöormen,*
  *Sjöborren,Sjölejonet,*
  *Sjöhunden, Sjöbjörnen,*
  *Svärdfisken, Tumlaren,*
  *Dykaren,Näcken,*
  *Najad, Neptun*
Picket Boats
  *Jägaren, Väktaren*
6 motor torpedoboats
Aircraft Depot Ship
  *Dristigheten*
Flygflottilj 2
  I. Division - **Heinkel T2**
  II. Division - **Heinkel S12**

**Norrlands Group**

Gunboats
  *Waria, Warun*
9 minesweepers and patrol vessels

**Stockholm Squadron**

Armored Ship
  *Tapperheten*
Destroyers
  *Vidar, Hugin*
Gunboats
  *Isbrytaren II, Runeberg*
28 minesweepers and patrol vessels

**Visby Group**

8 minesweepers and patrol vessels

**Karlskrona Group**

Armored Ship
  *Oscar II*
Destroyer Division
  *Ragnar, Sigurd,*
  *Ehrenskjöld, Nordenskjöld*
3 motor torpedoboats
23 minesweepers and
  patrol vessels

**Malmö Group**

Gunboats
  *Poseidon, Triton*
25 minesweepers and patrol vessels

destroyer

**Visby**      1943, 1,163 tons, 63 km/h, 2600 km,
**Sundsvall**    3-12 cm, 6 TT, stricken 1978-81
**Hälsingborg**
**Kalmar**

destroyer

**Öland**     1943, 2,032 tons, 56 km/h, 4000 km,
**Uppland**   4-12 cm, 6 TT, 60 mines, stricken 1978

**Heinkel S12**
1936, 14 m span, 335 km/h, 1050 km,
4800 m SC, 1 mg, 100 kg B
(Heinkel He.114B)

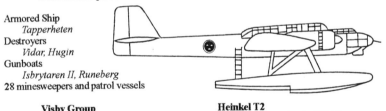

**Heinkel T2**
1937, 22 m span, 314 km/h, 2800 km,
5200 m SC, 2 mgs, 1250 kg B or T
(Heinkel He.115A-2)

destroyer

**Magne**    **Mode**     1942, 644 tons, 48 km/h,
**Mjölner**   **Munin**    3-10 cm AA, 3 TT
                   stricken 1966-8

327

**Göteborg Squadron**

Armored Ship
*Manligheten*
Destroyer Division
*Karlskrona, Göteborg,*
*Puke, Klas Horn*
Submarine Division
*Springaren, Nordkaparen,*
*Delfinen, U4-6*
3 motor torpedoboats
Gunboats
*Skagerrak, Odin*
24 minesweepers and patrol vessels

sub

Näcken  Najad      1943, 558 tons, 30/19 km/h,
Neptun             4 TT, stricken 1957

**Vänern Group**
Picket Boats
*Iris, Thetis*

Sea War School Group

patrol
boat

Cruisers
*Fylgia, Gotland*
9 minesweepers and patrol vessels

Jägaren     Kaparen   1933, 296 tons, 39 km/h,
Snapphanen  Väktaren   2-7.5 cm

destroyer

destroyer

Remus   1934, 647 tons, 55 km/h,
Romulus 3-10 cm, 4 TT,
        purchased 1940, stricken 1958
        (ex-Italian Astore, Spica)

Psilander   1926, 949 tons, 37 km/h,
Puke        4-12 cm, 4 TT,
            purchased 1940, stricken 1947
            (ex-Italian Sella class,
            G. Nicotera, B. Ricasoli)

sub

motor torpedo boat
T11-4   ex-Italian MAS boats,
        purchased 1940

U1-9   1941-4, 367 tons, 26/17 km/h, 4 TT
       U1-3 stricken 1961-4,
       U4-9 rebuilt as Aborren class

anti-aircraft
cruiser

Gotland   1944, 4,851 tons, 45 km/h,
          4-15, 13 small AA, 5 cm armor,
          refitted in 1944, stricken 1961      166

In the fleet, the *Gotland* was converted to an anti-aircraft cruiser during 1943-4 and the rebuilt *Fylgia* entered service training cadets. Two new classes of small destroyers completely modernized the fleet's screening forces.

An *Ehrenskjöld* scans the dangerous waters between two *pansarschiffen* on patrol.

Throughout the war years, the Coastal Fleet hunted hostile submarines. To aid the search efforts, the old battleship *Dristigheten* had been completely refurbished as a seaplane tender, nursing the old T.2s for long-range patrols. Swedish vessels plying the Gulf of Bothnia were being attacked off the Åland Islands by Soviet submarines. Saab S17BS seaplanes now patrolled the coastal waters while the broad seas around Gotland were watched by the S16s of F11 (B16s displaced from F7 by new B17s). On 14 May 1944 an inquisitive S16 was shot down east of Gotland by a Messerschmitt Bf.109G.

329

## The Perilous Last Summer - 1944

Early in 1944, Britain attempted to deprive Germany by purchasing increased quantities of ball bearings, but the SKF company merely built more factories and enjoyed the largesse. The Swedish Air Force was offered 200 Spitfires by the Allies and 200 Messerschmitts by the Germans to alter exports of bearings and iron ore. However, in April Sweden rejected both offers and continued shipments at the 1943 level, to the immense annoyance of the Allies. Sweden did surreptitiously begin to restrict shipments by inducting miners into the armed forces, delaying the opening of ice-bound ports in the spring, and restricting German movements across Sweden. Later in the year, the Soviet Navy solved the problem by making shipping too dangerous.

On 31 March 1944, General H.V. Jung had succeeded General Thörnell as commander in chief of the Swedish Army. The Allied invasion of Normandy set off the final mobilization of the Swedish armed forces:

**Swedish Army** (Gen. H.V. Jung)

**3. Corps** - Kristianstad
  I., XI. Infantry Divisions
  **8. Pansarbrigad** - Helsingborg
    2. Armored Regiment
      I., V. Tank Battalions
        90 Strv m/40K
        57 Strv m/42 EH, 15 TH

**III. Militärområdet** - Skövde
  III. Infantry Division

**1. Corps** - Karlstad
  IV., XII., XIII., XVI. Infantry Divisions
  **9. Pansarbrigad** - Skövde
    4. Armored Regiment
      II., VI. Tank Battalions
        100 Strv m/40L
        72 Strv m/42 TH
**II. Militärområdet** - Östersund
  II. Infantry Division
**VI. Militärområdet** - Boden
  XV. Infantry Division
**VII. Militärområdet** - Visby
  Gotland Forces
    2 tank companies
    48 Strv m/37

GHQ Reserve - Stockholm
  XIV. Infantry Division
  **10. Pansarbrigad** - Strängnäs
    10. Armored Regiment
      III., IV. Tank Battalions
        116 Strv m/41 SI
        73 Strv m/42 TM-TV
  1., 9., 10., 41. Infantry Regiments
  **VII, VIII Tank Battalions** (from 1945)
    104 Strv m/41 SII
    38 Strv m/42 TH, 17 TV

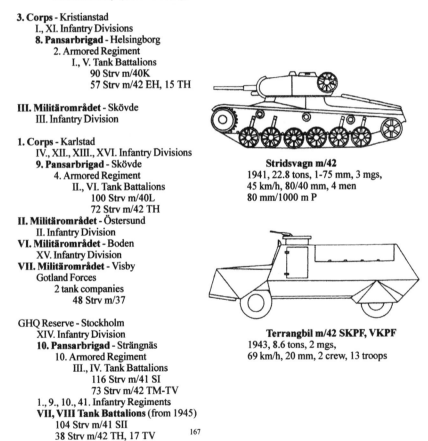

**Stridsvagn m/42**
1941, 22.8 tons, 1-75 mm, 3 mgs,
45 km/h, 80/40 mm, 4 men
80 mm/1000 m P

**Terrangbil m/42 SKPF, VKPF**
1943, 8.6 tons, 2 mgs,
69 km/h, 20 mm, 2 crew, 13 troops

167

New tanks were finally reaching the Army. However, the armored brigades were only partially equipped, as production was slow. Gotland received the little Strv m/37s when they were displaced by new Strv m/41s.

**Swedish Air Force** (Gen.Lt. Nordenskjold)

**1. Flygeskadern** - Stockholm

Flygflottilj 1 - Vasterås
   **60 Saab B18A**
Flygflottilj 4 - Östersund
   **49 Saab B17B-C**
Flygflottilj 12 - Kalmar
   **55 Saab B17A-C**
Flygflottilj 15 - Söderhamn
   organizing as the war ended

**2. Flygeskadern** - Göteborg

Flygflottilj 6 - Karlsborg
   **48 Saab B17B-C**
Flygflottilj 7 - Satenås
   **76 Saab B17A**
Flygflottilj 9 - Göteborg
   **60 FFVS J22** (1943)
Flygflottilj 14 - Halmstad
   organizing as the war ended

**FFVS J22A,B**
1942, 10 m span, 576 km/h, 1270 km,
9300 m SC, 4 mgs

**3. Flygeskadern** - Stockholm

Flygflottilj 8 - Barkarby (Stockholm)
   **52 Seversky J9**
   **FFVS J22** (May, 1945)
Flygflottilj 10 - Ängelholm
   **42 Reggiane J20**
   **60 FFVS J22** (March, 1945)
Flygflottilj 13 - Norrköping
   **60 FFVS J22**
Flygflottilj 16 - Uppsala
   **54 FFVS J22**
   **46 North American J26** (March, 1945)

**4. Flygeskadern** - Stockholm

Flygflottilj 2 - Hagernås (Stockholm)
   **47 Saab S17BS**
Flygflottilj 11 - Nyköping
   **58 Caproni S16**
   **13 Junkers B3** (from F1 in 1945)
   **Seversky J9, Hawker S9C** (1945)
Flygflottilj 17 - Ronneby
   **12 Junkers T3**
   **12 Junkers B3**

**Saab B17C,A**
1940 (1944), 14 m span, 435 km/h,
3 mgs, 680 kg B
(A was a later model than C)

   Independent Flygflottilj
Flygflottilj 5 - Ljungbyhed
   flying school
Flygflottilj 3 - Malmslatt
   **8 FFVS J22**
   **18 Fieseler S14**
   **44 Saab S17B**              168

Allied bombing raids escalated during the spring of 1944 as they sought to cripple the German armaments industry. The result was a number of British and American bombers straying over Swedish air space, of which five were forced down by Swedish fighters. At times, the Swedes had to fire on aircraft whose recalcitrant pilots resisted internment.

A J22 Soars Above the Clouds

More German aircraft also attracted Swedish shells. A lost Messerschmitt Me.410A-1 of ZG 26 approached anti-aircraft positions at Simrishamn on the southeast coast at so low an altitude that the gunners thought it was attacking and shot it down. A month later, 13 May, an anti-aircraft battery at Ystad on the south coast involved itself in the air war. Observing the attack of a Messerschmitt Me.210 on a crippled American B-17 trying to reach the Swedish coast, the gunners fired on the fighter as it passed overhead about 1400, bringing it down into the sea.

The success of the Allied landings in Normandy encouraged the Swedish government to restrict German privileges still further. However, on 13 June, Sweden was reminded that Hitler was not yet done. At low altitude over Kalmar, a violent explosion marked the demise of a German V-2 rocket bomb that had strayed from its test site at Peenemunde, just 100 kilometers south of the coast of Skåne. From the debris of the Uppsala explosion, the Swedes deciphered the horrifying truth about the unguided terror weapon, soon to pose insuperable defensive problems for the British in a final blitz. Fortunately, the Allies were steadily exterminating the Nazis.

The Soviets launched a maximum offensive against Finland on 9 June. The weary Finns soon showed signs of weakening. Fearful that she may become a satellite, or even a republic, of the Soviet Union, in July Prime Minister Hansson urged Marshal Mannerheim to get Finland out of the war while she was still independent. He did so the following month and, on 4 September, the Finns capitulated. As the Germans reluctantly left to trudge westward toward Norway, Sweden gathered forces along the Finnish border and warned the Germans not to encroach on Swedish territory.

During September, British and American forces pushed the Germans back to the Rhine. Ever fearful of Russian intentions, on **9 September 1944** Sweden ended German transit privileges across the country, then closed her ports to foreign ships (mainly German), hoping to keep Soviet submarines from entering Swedish waters to attack the German shipping. Sweden had abandoned neutrality and was now a pro-Allied non-belligerent state.

Sweden was being enveloped by the military forces of two unfriendly powers. The German presence in Norway was greatly strengthened by the troops streaming back from Finland. Twentieth Mountain Army settled into northern Norway, shielding Narvik/Kiruna from a Soviet advance. Its three mountain corps possessed 6 divisions, which remained in the area - *Festung Norwegen* - to the end of the war. Early in 1944, the Germans had:

**Army of Norway** (General von Falkenhorst)

```
LXXI Corps - Narvik
     199., 230., 270. Divisions
XXXIII Corps - Trondheim
     14. Luftwaffe, 196., 295., 702. Divisions
LXX Corps - Oslo
     89., 269., 274., 280., 560., 710. Divisions
     Panzer Brigade Norway
        47 Pz.Kw.III

     Luftflotte 5
Fliegerführer 3
     44 reconnaissance planes
     I/SG 5
        54 Focke-Wulf Fw.190F,G, Junkers Ju.87D
Jagdführer Norwegen - Oslo
     III/JG 5
        23 Messerschmitt Bf.109G
     13./JG 5
        16 Messerschmitt Bf.110G
```

Panzer Brigade Norway had formed after the 25. Panzer Division left for France in August 1943 to prepare for service on the Russian Front. Much of Luftflotte 5 had been expended in the fight for Finland. During the autumn of 1944, the German forces in Norway were reorganized, all units being placed under General Dietl's Twentieth Mountain Army. The Luftwaffe units were reinforced. Two wings (II,III/KG 26) of Ju.88As replaced SG 5. Fighters were increased to 113 Bf.109Gs and Fw.190As in III,IV/JG 5. The old Bf.110s were replaced by fast Me.410s of IV/ZG 26.

Some of the air war again spilled over into Sweden. Two actions occurred on 6 October in Skåne. J20s of F10 intercepted a Junkers Ju.88G-1 south of Malmö in midafternoon and forced it to land at the nearby airfield. A Messerschmitt Me.210 was not so well treated, being shot down into the sea after it inadvertently crossed the coast near Trelleborg. Many FFVS J22s were now entering squadron service, but most of them were stationed in the industrialized areas of central Sweden and saw little action.

To counter the superior German and Soviet fighters, the Flygvapnet ordered the unique fast and well-armed Saab J21A pusher fighter for introduction in early 1945. However, delivery of this excellent aircraft was delayed and 46 North American P-51Ds were purchased as a stopgap. Delivered to F16 at Uppsala in March 1945 as the J26, they quickly became the favorite mounts of Swedish fighter pilots.

Flights of J20s from Ängelholm Scrapped With Many Intruders

Germans were now primarily interested in escaping the oncoming Soviet forces. The pilots of two J20s patrolling off Ystad on **8 April 1945** rubbed their eyes in disbelief at the weird aerial procession leaving a fog bank far below them. Carrying German personnel from East Prussia to Berlin, an old Junkers W.34 light transport led nine Fieseler Fi.156C liaison planes to refuel on Bornholm before turning south to Berlin. Missing the island in the fog, they came out over the Swedish coast. The J20s forced six of them to land near Ystad. Fifty more formidable Ju.88A-6s left Trondheim, Norway on 8 May for a similar mission to Liepaja, Latvia. When one of them decided to cut across Sweden, it was intercepted at mid-morning by a Saab B17. Mistaken for a fighter, the Swedish light bomber succeeded in escorting the bomber to Kalmar. Defections were also beginning. On 30 April, after strafing Russian columns approaching Berlin, a Focke-Wulf Fw.190A-8 flew north. Crossing the south-western tip of the Swedish coast, it was greeted by two FFVS J22s of F10 and escorted to an airfield south of Malmö.

During the war, 126 German, 63 British and 141 American aircraft either crashed, or were forced to land, in Sweden. Most of the German activity occurred in 1940-2, while most Allied intrusions occurred in 1944-5.

In May 1945, there were still 350,000 combat-ready German troops in Norway, with 200,000 less efficient troops in Denmark. If the Germans refused to withdraw, Soviet troops may enter Norway to drive them out and establish a Communist government. Concerned that the Germans would ravish the Scandinavian countryside in leaving, as they had done in other countries, the Swedish government directed the high command to draw up plans to aid Sweden's neighbors in protecting their people. [169]

Operation *Rädda Norge* ("Save Norway") could have involved the central units of the Swedish Army against the German Army of Norway. The Flygvapnet now possessed 300 fighters and a like number of bomber and reconnaissance planes. It would seek to surprise the weakened Luftflotte 5 on its airfields. Fighter sweeps by J9s and J22s of the 3. Flygeskadern would occupy the few remaining fighters of JG 5, allowing Saab B18As to leave Vasterås and plaster German airfields and communications.

Six depleted Nazi infantry divisions awaited the 1. Corps offensive toward Oslo. The only real threat was posed by Panzer Brigade Norway. Properly handled, the 72 Strv m/42s of the 9. Pansarbrigad should have been able to handle it. However, Nazi bombers would have to be kept off the Swedish armored columns. With Oslo in Swedish hands, and the Atlantic sea lanes controlled by the British Navy, the 7 German divisions in central and northern Norway could be left to wither on the vine. If they decided to fight, the two infantry divisions of the VI. and II. Milos could be bolstered by units from the GHQ Reserve, including the 189 tanks of 10. Pansarbrigad. Soviet forces at Petsamo would pin Arctic units.

Operation *Rädda Danmark* was a different problem. Any move toward Denmark, in rear of the Nazi forces on the Rhine, would receive immediate attention. Although the German surface naval vessels were largely inactive, the Swedish Navy would be involved in protecting the invasion fleet from submarines. For this purpose, Sweden now had a fine modern force of small destroyers of the *Visby* and *Göteborg* classes, the *Mode* class torpedo boats, and the *Jägaren* class of submarine hunting gunboats. They would have plenty of air cover from the nearby fighter bases of F9 and F10, while old Junkers B3s were now stationed at Ronneby as T3 torpedo bombers and B3 minelayers to attack ships.

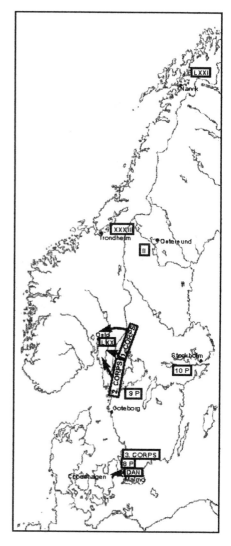

The Proposed Rädda Offensives
1945

In Denmark were only 4 weak German infantry divisions and a nominal panzer division. Raids by the Saab B18As from Vasterås would precede a crossing. The Swedish-trained Danish Brigade of 3,500 men, supported by a squadron of 8 Saab B17Cs, would land on Zealand with the two infantry divisions of the Swedish 3. Corps. Attacks by the B17s of F12 at Kalmar would assist the ground forces in securing Copenhagen and crossing to Jutland. There, the 8. Pansarbrigad could take a leading role in any drive southward, but increasing German resistance at the base of the peninsula would require Allied assistance for further progress.

Sweden did not activate either plan, despite protests from the exiled Danes and Norwegians, pleading fears that German resistance and atrocities would increase if they did so. Despite Allied advice that the Swedes should take no action, the Norwegians considered the inaction merely the last example of a wartime full of Swedish sloth.

A Strv m/42 and a SKPF Traverse a Snowy Forest

### The Terrible Rus - 1940-1945

A major concern for Sweden was the ultimate objective of the Soviet Union. Many of the Danish resistance fighters were Communists, and would welcome a Soviet expedition to the western Baltic. Postwar Soviet possession of Danish islands in position to control communications to the Atlantic was unacceptable to Sweden. Worse, if the Soviet Union occupied Finland, Sweden would be under constant apprehension that postwar disagreements would spill over into her territory. Russia had constructed a base at Hangö under a long term lease provided by the treaty that ended the Russo-Finnish "Winter War" in 1940. When the conflict erupted again in 1941 with the German invasion of Russia, the Swedish government quickly approved a "Hangö Battalion" of 800 volunteers that assisted the Finns in besieging the menacing outpost, which the Russians abandoned in the autumn of 1941.

Drottning Victoria Trains on a Chase Off Her Port Bow

Now, there was fear that the Soviets would occupy the Åland Islands, gaining control of the maritime routes to Sweden's vital northern natural resources. To guard the capital against such an event, around Stockholm were concentrated the GHQ Reserve, the fighters of the 3. Flygeskadern, and the maritime 4. Flygeskadern cooperating with the Coastal Fleet. However, Soviet Baltic surface vessels were largely hors de combat near Leningrad.

Poised along the Finnish border were the Soviet 14 Army (6 divisions), 7 Army (14 division), 21 Army (14 divisions) and 23 Army (12 divisions). In addition, they had more than 1,000 tanks in independent tank brigades and battalions. They were supported by the 1,500 aircraft of the 13 Air Army (including La-5 and Yak-9 fighters, Il-2 and P-39 ground attack planes, and DB-3F and Il-4 medium bombers). A Soviet advance to the Gulf of Bothnia would have posed a dilemma. Resistance to the 50 Soviet divisions would have been hopeless without enlisting the aid of the German forces in Norway. As the Soviets were clearly defeating the Germans on every front, collaborating with the Germans at such a late date would have been foolhardy, inviting the invasion and occupation of Sweden.

Fortunately for Sweden, the Soviets contented themselves with the occupation of Petsamo, leaving most of Finnish territory inviolate. Negotiations with the Western Allies had left Scandinavia in the British sphere of interest. In Norway and Denmark, the German troops left peaceably after the Armistice. No assistance was needed from Sweden, whose government had decided not to break its neutrality, in any case, by initiating the *Rädda* offensives. The Norwegian and Danish troops trained in Sweden gladly left for their homelands, disgruntled with their Swedish sojourn. On **7 May 1945**, the Nazi ambassador in Stockholm announced his government's dissolution. Sweden had survived.

337

# SWEDEN AND THE COLD WAR

Sweden found herself in an ambiguous position following World War II. Although the humanitarian efforts of Count Bernadotte had given freedom to many Nazi political prisoners, and Sweden had cared for thousands of refugees while training their young men to regain their countries, her government had created much ill will by waffling when faced by decisions affecting her neutrality. Norway had been outraged by transit of Nazi troops to Narvik over Swedish railways while fighting was still going on. The Finns were disgusted with Swedish refusal to give them active support against Russia during the entire war, feeling that the Swedes were hiding behind Finnish fighting men.

As a result, when Sweden attempted to negotiate a neutral Scandinavian union after the war, she found resistance among her neighbors. Although the antagonism soon abated, and Scandinavian cooperation resumed, Denmark and Norway elected to join the North Atlantic Treaty Organization (NATO) for defensive protection, while Finland was obligated to abide by defensive treaties with the Soviet Union. Sweden found herself isolated at a time of renewed military menace. The fighting of the world war had metamorphosed into a "Cold War" with numerous points of conflict that could ignite a new conflagration. Sweden was left with no choice but to defend herself, a task for which she prepared admirably over the ensuing decades, producing armed forces more formidable than those possessed by several NATO countries. Nuclear shelters were prepared for her populace, and much of her industry burrowed underground.

Sweden's demobilization euphoria in 1945 was haunted by the memory of her helplessness at the start of the war when frantic orders for foreign weapons had been rebuffed, leaving Swedish field units without modern, mobile capability. However, the persistent engineering efforts were now bearing fruit in numbers of quality weapons rapidly flowing to Swedish units.

**A Strv m/40K Supports a Picket**

338

The Army maintained 3 cavalry, 13 infantry, 6 mechanized infantry, 3 armored, 7 artillery and 3 anti-aircraft regiments.

**ARMORED BRIGADE**
HQ - 3 light, 2 heavy tanks, 2 APCs
1 tank battalion
  HQ - 1 light, 2 heavy tanks, 1 APC
  2 light companies
    HQ - 3 light tanks
    2 light platoons
      **5 Strv m/40, m/41**
    1 heavy platoon
      **5 Strv m/42**
    1 engineer platoon
      **4 Tgbl m/42 KP**
  1 heavy company
    HQ - 3 heavy tanks
    3 heavy platoons
      **5 Strv m/42**
    1 engineer platoon
      **4 Tgbl m/42 KP**
2 armored infantry battalions
  HQ - **10 Tgbl m/42 KP**
  3 rifle companies
    **11 Tgbl m/42 KP**
  1 heavy company
    **4 m/36 hmgs**
    **3 m/29 81 mm mortars**
    **6-57 mm AT guns**
    **14 Tgbl m/42 KP**
  1 special company
    **3 Strv m/40, m/41**
1 motorized artillery battalion
  **12 Bofors m/39 105 mm howitzers**
1 self-propelled anti-tank company
  2 platoons
    **3 Pvkv m/43**
1 self-propelled anti-aircraft company
  **4 Lvkv fm/43**
2 engineer companies

**10 ANTI-TANK COMPANIES**
  2 platoons
    **3 Pvkv m/43**

**6 ASSAULT ARTILLERY COMPANIES**
  2 platoons
    **3 Sav m/43**

**6 INFANTRY CANNON COMPANIES**
  2 platoons
    **3 Ikv 72**      170

**Pansarvärnskanonvagn m/43**
1943, 23 tons, 1-75 mm, 2 mgs,
45 km/h, 40 mm, 4 men
150 mm/1000 m P
(redesignated Pvkv 71 in 1953)

**Luftvärnskanonvagn fm/43**
1943, 17 tons, 2-40 mm,
55 km/h, 20 mm, 4 men,
5000 m VR, 120 rpm,
50 mm/1000 m P

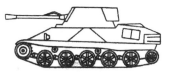

**Stormartillerivagn m/43**
1943, 12.1 tons, 1-105 mm how.,
43 km/h, 25 mm, 4 men

**Infanterikanonvagn 72**
1947, 8.6 tons, 1-75 mm,
57 km/h, 200 km, 20/10/10 mm,
80 mm/1000 m P, 4 men

The Riksdag approved a new Defense Act in **June 1948** which gave procurement of fighters top priority, so the Army had to improvise new armor. In 1944, 18 Sav m/43s had converted from Strv m/41 SIIs as the *Pansarartillerivagn* (Pav) m/43, attached to the artillery, with 18 later built new. After the war, it became the *Stormartillerivagn* and was used as infantry assault artillery. Mounting 75 mm field guns, 38 Ikv 72s arrived in 1947 as mobile infantry cannon. Eighty-seven Pvkv m/43s were introduced the same year, utilizing many components of the Strv m/42 and the heaviest anti-tank gun available in Sweden.

339

Utilizing two excellent Bofors 40 mm anti-aircraft guns on the chassis of the stillborn prewar Strv 33 light tank, 17 Lvkv fm/43 appeared in 1947.

However, further development of Swedish armor was curtailed by the widely-held belief that the day of the tank had ended with the proliferation of effective small anti-tank infantry weapons and the advent of nuclear weapons. Sweden began to regard its tanks as infantry-support assault guns.

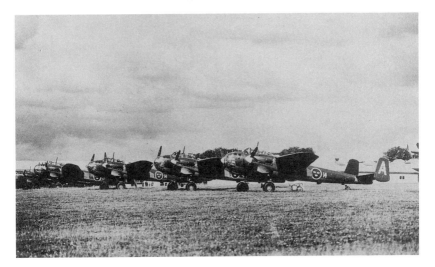

From Halmstad, Flygflottilj 14 flew the potent Saab B18B

The *Flygvapnet* was now almost fully equipped with indigenous aircraft developed during the war. The Saab 18 was a remarkable achievement for the Swedish aircraft industry. Unable to obtain suitably powerful engines, SFAB copied a Pratt and Whitney Twin Wasp from a DC-3 airliner and placed it in production. Although the bomber was somewhat underpowered with this powerplant, it provided Swedish bomber pilots a much better mount than their lumbering old Junkers. When the Daimler-Benz DB 605 was installed after the war, the B18B displayed characteristics equal to the bombers of the belligerents. The slower B18As were converted to reconnaissance duties in two wings and redesignated S18As. The deep-jowled T18B torpedo bomber was actually used as an attack plane with a Bofors 57 mm cannon added to its already formidable armament. The Saab bombers never achieved the acclaim they deserved, for they arrived two years behind world progress.

The fighter squadrons flew Saab J21As and North American J26s, two of the finest piston-engined fighters in the world. Designed to produce a concentrated barrage from a heavy battery of nose guns, the J21A had required its engineers to solve several problems unique to pusher aircraft. These included compressed air cooling for the engine, tricycle landing gear, and one of the first ejection seats employed in combat aircraft. The craft had pleasant handling characteristics, with excellent vision for its pilot. However, production delays required the purchase of North American P-51Ds in the Spring of 1945 as a stopgap. The Mustang was generally considered the best fighter of the war, and proved popular with Swedish pilots. Yet, the excellence was in vain, for neighboring air forces were already equipped with faster jet aircraft.

340

Sleek J21As of Flygflottilj 12 Poised at Kalmar

## Swedish Air Force

**1. Flygeskadern** - Göteborg
Flygflottilj 6 - Karlsborg
   **48 Saab B17A-C**
Flygflottilj 7 - Satenås
   **76 Saab B17A-C**
Flygflottilj 14 - Halmstad
   **36 Saab B18B**
Flygflottilj 17 - Ronneby
   **62 Saab T18B**

**Saab T18B**
1945, 17 m span, 572 km/h, 2600 km,
9800 m SC, 1-57 mm, 2-20 mm,
1500 kg T or B

**2. Flygeskadern** - Ängelholm
Flygflottilj 4 - Östersund
   **45 North American J26**
Flygflottilj 9 - Göteborg
   **45 Saab J21A**
Flygflottilj 10 - Ängelholm
   **45 North American J26**
Flygflottilj 12 - Kalmar
   **45 Saab J21A**
Flygflottilj 15 - Söderhamn
   **36 Saab B17A-C**

**Saab J21A, A21A**
1943, 12 m span, 641 km/h,
11000 m SC, 1-20 mm, 2 mgs
(5-10 Bofors rockets or 8 mgs as A)

**3. Flygeskadern** - Stockholm
Flygflottilj 1 - Vasterås
   **36 Saab B18B**
Flygflottilj 3 - Malmslatt
   **45 FFVS J22**
Flygflottilj 8 - Stockholm
   **45 Saab J21A**
Flygflottilj 13 - Norrköping
   **70 De Havilland J28A**
Flygflottilj 16 - Uppsala
   **45 North American J26**
Flygflottilj 18 - Stockholm
   **45 FFVS J22**

**Saab B18B**
1944, 17 m span, 572 km/h, 2600 km,
9800 m SC, 3 mgs, 1500 kg B

**4. Flygeskadern** - Luleå
Flygflottilj 2 - Hagernås (Stockholm)
   **Saab S17BS**
Flygflottilj 11 - Nyköping
   **30 Saab S18A**
Flygflottilj 21 - Luleå
   **30 Saab S18A**

**Saab Sk50 Safir**
1949, 11 m span, 275 km/h, 1100 km,
6250 m SC, 2 mgs, 8 rockets

Flygflottilj 5 (school) - Ljungbyhed
   **Saab Sk50, North American Sk16A (AT-6)**

171

As airpower appeared the arbiter of future warfare, development of indigenous combat aircraft continued at a high level. The J21A was obsolescent by the time it was delivered. Nonplussed, Swedish engineers accomplished the first fully successful conversion of a piston-engined plane to jet power, producing the J21R. Two wings of J21Rs were ordered, but deliveries were reduced to 60 to clear the factory for a more advanced design. After serving briefly from **1950** as interceptors with *Flygflottilj* 10, they were converted to A21R attack planes and transferred to F7. The J/A21R was popular with its pilots, being a stable gun platform and proving adept at ground attack.

**Swedish Air Force**
1. **Flygeskadern** - Göteborg
   Flygflottilj 6 - Karlsborg
   **45 Saab A21A**
   Flygflottilj 7 - Satenås
   **45 Saab A21A**
   **60 Saab A21R** (1951 on)
   Flygflottilj 14 - Halmstad
   **36 Saab B18B**
   Flygflottilj 17 - Ronneby
   **62 Saab T18B**

**Saab J21R, A21R**
1947, 11 m span, 800 km/h (0.69), 720 km,
7/5000 m, 12000 m SC, 1-20 mm, 4 mgs
(5-10 Bofors rockets or 8 mgs as A)

2. **Flygeskadern** - Ängelholm
   Flygflottilj 4 - Östersund
   **45 North American J26**
   Flygflottilj 9 - Göteborg
   **45 De Havilland J28B**
   Flygflottilj 10 - Ängelholm
   **60 Saab J21R**
   Flygflottilj 12 - Kalmar
   **45 Saab J21A**
   Flygflottilj 15 - Söderhamn
   **45 Saab J21A**

**De Havilland J28B**
1949, 12 m span, 855 km/h (0.72), 1175 km,
8700 m SC, 4-20 mm
(De Havilland Vampire F.B.50)

3. **Flygeskadern** - Stockholm
   Flygflottilj 1 - Vasterås
   **60 De Havilland J30**
   Flygflottilj 3 - Malmslatt
   **45 FFVS J22**
   Flygflottilj 8 - Stockholm
   **60 De Havilland J28B**
   Flygflottilj 13 - Norrköping
   **70 De Havilland J28A**
   Flygflottilj 16 - Uppsala
   **45 North American J26**
   Flygflottilj 18 - Stockholm
   **45 FFVS J22**
   **60 De Havilland J28B** (1951 on)

**De Havilland J30**
1941, 16 m span, 576 km/h, 2500 km,
7/4575 m, 10525 m SC, 4-20 mm
(De Havilland Mosquito N.F.XIX)

4. **Flygeskadern** - Luleå
   Flygflottilj 2 - Hagernås (Stockholm)
   Rescue Service - **3 Tp47** (PBY-5A)
   OCU school - **FFVS Sk22, D.H. Sk28A**
   Flygflottilj 11 - Nyköping
   **30 Saab S18A**
   **36 Supermarine S31**
   Flygflottilj 21 - Luleå
   **30 Saab S18A**
   **36 North American S26**

Flygflottilj 5 (school) - Ljungbyhed
**Saab Sk50, N.A. Sk16A**

172

**Supermarine S31**
1944, 11 m span, 721 km/h, 1370 km,
7/6100 m, 13580 m SC
(Supermarine Spitfire P.R.19)

Unfortunately for Sweden, the advent of the jet engine rendered almost the whole Air Force obsolescent. Noting the potency of late war jet fighters, Sweden ordered 70 De Havilland Vampire F.1s from Great Britain in 1946. The little interceptors operated as J28As with F13 at Norrköping in defense of Stockholm and the industrial area south of Lake Malar. Excellent maneuverability rewarded pilots with targets for their four 20 mm cannon. When new Swedish designs became available in 1952, the J28As were retired, some being sold to the Dominican Republic.

Despite prodigious efforts in difficult circumstances, the fruits of the Swedish air industry looked immature and undernourished beside the current products of other nations. Nevertheless, the situation was about to change radically, for Swedish engineers had achieved access to the highly interesting research conducted by German engineers during the war and now had sufficient material resources for production.

Tre Kronor - Sweden's Final Cruiser

The Navy also engaged in introspection. Two modern coast defense battleships had been under development from the early days of the war. However, wartime invasion forces had included land or carrier-based aircraft which invariably initiated amphibious operations by pounding shore bases and their protecting warships. In such a situation, particularly with the proximity of many foreign airbases to the Swedish coast, the largely static armored coast defense ship would not survive for long. Armored ship construction was abandoned. Naval planners returned to a coast defense concept first promulgated in the previous century - the small, fast attack boat. A class of modern motor torpedo boats was purchased, and construction of gun-armed fast attack craft begun. The concept was soon given a boost by the development of potent surface-to-surface missiles that could be carried by small craft, yet have a deadly effect upon approaching surface vessels.

With the need for large armored port-defense vessels gone, the Swedish Navy reconfigured its specifications to provide needed replacements for the old *Sverige* class armored cruisers. *Göta Lejon* and *Tre Kronor* emerged as large, fast light cruisers. When they were commissioned in 1947, they embodied many characteristics of the armored cruisers they replaced. Well protected with up to 13 centimeters of belt armor, they epitomized the modern cruising greyhound-of-the-sea. However, they were rather under-gunned and expensive for their mission. After only 20 years, they were removed from active service. *Göta Lejon* was sold to Chile in 1971, where it became the *Almirante Latorre*.

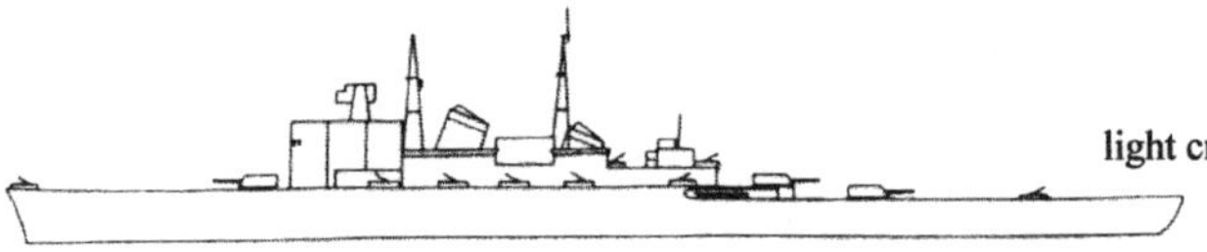

light cruiser

| Göta Lejon | Tre Kronor | 1947, 8,330 tons, 53 km/h,<br>7-15 cm, 15 small AA, 6 TT, 8/13 cm armor,<br>Tre Kronor stricken 1964,<br>Göta Lejon sold to Chile in 1971 |
|---|---|---|

anti-aircraft cruiser

| Gotland | 1934, 4,851 tons, 45 km/h,<br>4-15 cm, 24 small AA, 5 cm armor,<br>refitted in 1944, stricken 1961 |
|---|---|

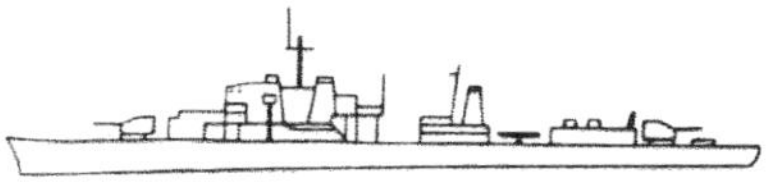

destroyer

| Östergotland<br>Gästrikland | Södermanland<br>Hälsingland | 1955, 2,083 tons, 56 km/h, 3500 km,<br>4-12 cm, 60 mines<br>stricken 1979-82 |
|---|---|---|

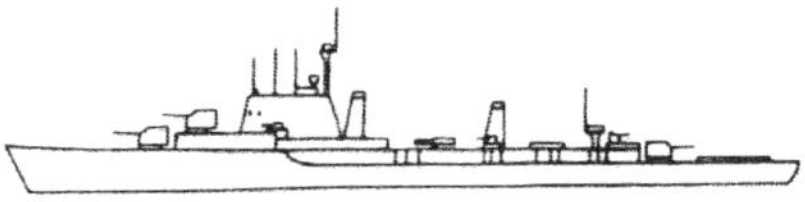

destroyer

| Halland<br>Lappland | Småland<br>Värmland | 1951, 2,774 tons, 56 km/h, 4800 km,<br>4-12 cm, 8 TT, stricken 1982-5<br>Lappland and Värmland canceled |
|---|---|---|

sub

motor torpedo boat

| Aldebaran | Altair | 1950, 170 tons, | Abborren | 1962, 425 tons, 26/17 km/h, |
|---|---|---|---|---|
| Arcturus | Antares | 61 km/h, | Gäddan | 4 TT, rebuilt from U class, |
| Argo | Astrea | 1000 km, 6 TT | Forellen | stricken 1976 |
| Perseus | Plejad | | Laxen | |
| Polaris | Pollux | | Makrillen | |
| Regulus | Rigel | | Siken | |

sub

sub

| Bävern | 1956, 812 tons, 30/37 km/h, | Delfinen | 1960, 781 tons, |
|---|---|---|---|
| Hajen | 4 TT, stricken 1978 | Draken | 37/31 km/h, 4 TT |
| Illern | | Nordkaparen | |
| Sälen | | Gripen | |
| Uttern | | Springaren | |
| Valen | | Vargen | 173 |

344

Probing the Fog, A Stridsvagn 74H Leads a Route Reconnaissance

Communist power was rapidly increasing in Eastern Europe. Sweden's neighbors were being submerged. Eschewing association with NATO, Sweden was forced into considerable expenditures to rebuild her defenses. Swedish ground forces had been neglected while the aerial umbrella was being repaired. Sweden possessed nothing capable of facing the large main battle tanks now deployed by the Warsaw Pact. Moreover, there was some question about the vulnerability of the tank on the modern battlefield. The effective infantry anti-tank weapons developed late in World War II, and the advent of nuclear weapons, had led some to sound the death knell of armor. However, following the success of North Korean tanks in driving through the rugged terrain of the Korean peninsula, the Swedes reconsidered their doctrine. Acquisition of a number of modern armored vehicles resulted.

Sweden began development of a range of specialized vehicles to fulfill various battlefield missions. The 75 mm shell was too weak for modern fire missions so it was decided to replace it in the infantry support vehicles with a 105 mm howitzer. Thirty-six Ikv 72s were thus converted to Ikv 102s in 1954. When 65 more were ordered, they were delivered in 1956 with a different engine and designated Ikv 103s, otherwise being identical to the Ikv 102s. Hampered by light armor, the *Infanterikanonvagn* was not suitable for anti-tank work and was limited to infantry fire-support missions.

Retired Strv m/41s were utilized to produce Pbv 301 armored personnel carriers to supplement the Tgbil m/42 (SKPF, VKPF) armored trucks. Altogether, 116 Strv m/41 SI and 104 Strv m/41 SII were rebuilt during 1962-3. Although an economical use of a vehicle already in Sweden's possession, the Pbv 301 was not an outstanding design. Thus, it was replaced at the same time as the much older Tgbil m/42. It went into reserve in 1969 and was scrapped six years later.

In typical Scandinavian fashion, the peacetime army of **1958** was maintained by brigade staffs in local regimental districts, intended to mobilize quickly in place if hostilities broke out. It was distributed around the country in seven *Militärbefälsstaben* (Military Commands), each divided for training and administration into *Försvarsområdestaben* (Defense Districts).

345

**Swedish Army**
**I. Militärbefälsstaben** - Kristianstad
11. Försvarsområdestaben (FOS)- Malmö
  **7. Pansarbrigad** - Ystad
    7. Infanteriregiment - **48 Strv 81**
14. FOS - Kristianstad
  **8. Pansarbrigad** - Hässleholm
    2. Pansarregiment - **48 Strv 81**
15. FOS - Karlskrona
16./18. FOS - Kalmar
  6.,11.,12. Infanteriregimenten
  2. Kavalleri, 2.,6. Artilleriregimenten
  4. Luftregiment - **Sk 50**

**II. Militärbefälsstaben** - Östersund
22. FOS - Östersund
24. (Naval), 23./25. FOS - Härnösand
  5.,14.,21. Infanteri, 4. Artilleriregimenten
  5. Luftregiment - **Sk 50**

**III. Militärbefälsstaben** - Skövde
33. (Naval) FOS - Göteborg
31./32. FOS - Göteborg
  **5. Pansarbrigad** - Borås
    15. Infanteriregiment - **48 Strv 74**
34. FOS - Uddevalla
35. FOS - Skövde
  **9. Pansarbrigad** - Skövde
    4. Pansarregiment - **48 Strv 81**
16.,17. Infanteriregimenten
  3. Kavalleri, 2. Artilleriregimenten
  1.,6. Luftregimenten - **Sk 50**

**IV. Militärbefälsstaben** - Stockholm
41. FOS - Linköping
43. FOS - Strängnäs
  **10. Pansarbrigad** - Strängnäs
    10. Infanteriregiment - **48 Strv 74**
44. FOS - Stockholm
  **6. Pansarbrigad** - Enköping
    1. Pansarregiment - **48 Strv 81**
46. (Naval) FOS - Vaxholm
47./48. FOS - Uppsala
  4.,8. Infanteriregimenten
  1. Kavalleri, 1. Artilleriregimenten
  2.,3. Luftregimenten - **Sk.50**

**V. Militärbefälsstaben** - Karlstad
51., 52. FOS - Örebro, Karlstad
53. FOS - Falun
  2.,3.,13. Infanteri, 9. Artilleriregimenten

**VI. Militärbefälsstaben** - Boden
61./62., 63. FOS - Umeå, Boden
65./66. FOS - Kiruna
67. FOS - Kalix
  19.,20. Infanteriregimenten
  4. Kavalleri, 8. Artilleriregimenten
  7 Luftregiment - **Sk 50**

**VII. Militärbefälsstaben** - Visby (Gotland)
18. Infanteriregiment
1G. Pansarkompani - **Pvkv 71**
  7. Artilleriregiment

**Stridsvagn 74**
1958, 26 tons, 1-75 mm, 2 mgs,
45 km/h, 80/40 mm, 4 men
150 mm/1000 m P

**Stridsvagn 81**
1948, 50.2 tons, 1-83.4 mm, 1 mg,
34 km/h, 105 km, 152/76/51 mm,
165 mm/1000 m P, 4 men
(Centurion Mk.3, 5)

**Stridsvagn 101, 102**
1963, 50.8 tons, 1-105 mm, 1 mg,
34 km/h, 241 km, 152/76/51 mm,
380 mm/1000 m P, 4 men
(Centurion Mk.10)

**Infanterikanonvagn 73**
1941, 22.8 tons, 1-75 mm, 3 mgs,
45 km/h, 80/40 mm, 4 men
80 mm/1000 m P          174

346

An Element of J29Fs from Flygflottilj 3 Maneuvers Over Eastern Sweden

Quality, and the ingenuity displayed by Swedish aeronautical engineering at the end of World War II, prophesied the plethora of first-rate aircraft to grace *Flygvapnet* runways in succeeding decades. The initial entry was the Saab J29, a winged barrel fully the equal of the contemporary American Sabre and Soviet MiG-15. The J29A appeared in 1951, followed two years later by the improved B model and the photo reconnaissance J29C. The A29B was an attack version of the J29B. Addition of an afterburner doubled the climb rate of the J29B and conversion of the early models began in 1954. The resulting J29F was also produced new, eventually completing replacement of the heterogeneous collection of stopgap fighters equipping the Air Force. Swedish airpower had leapt from mediocre to menacing.

As production of the J29 interceptor was lagging, Sweden went again to Britain for help, acquiring 120 Hawker Hunter Mk.50s in 1954. This export version of the F.4 was used to reequip the two wings flying De Havilland J28Bs, F8 and F18. The J34 was not the only British aircraft acquired as Sweden attempted to purge its inventory of foreign designs. Night defense of Stockholm was in the hands of *Flygflottilj* 1. But its old J30 Mosquitos were incapable of catching the intruders now flooding the squadrons of the Warsaw Pact. While Saab worked feverishly on a new design to solve the problem, an interim purchase was made of 60 De Havilland Venoms, which joined F1 as the J33.

The anticipated new Swedish night fighter appeared initially as an attack plane, the A32. From 1955, it began equipping the ground attack squadrons of the 1. Flygeskadern along the southwestern coast. It was very popular, possessing pleasant flying characteristics and providing a stable gun platform. A more powerful engine gave the night flying J32B version better performance when it was delivered in 1958-9. The 20 mm cannons of the A32 were replaced by superior 30 mm guns. The two night fighter wings were stationed along Sweden's east coast, with a squadron added in 1964 to F21, keeping watch over events in the far north. Maritime reconnaissance S32Cs in 1959 replaced the last piston-engined combat aircraft, the old S18s at Nyköping. The old bombers made sweeps over the Baltic, but were as vulnerable as the Catalina flying boat shot down by Soviet planes in 1952.

347

The Swedish Air Force of 1958 was becoming formidable as the new jet aircraft swelled the rosters of the squadrons. After the reforms of 1953, the *flygflottilj* was increased to 4 *divisioner* (squadrons), styled 1,2,3,4/F17 (for example). Each squadron had a complement of 15 aircraft.

**Swedish Air Force**

**1. Flygeskadern** - Göteborg
Flygflottilj 6 - Karlsborg
   **60 Saab A29B**
Flygflottilj 7 - Satenås
   **60 Saab A32A**
Flygflottilj 14 - Halmstad
   **60 Saab A32A**
Flygflottilj 17 - Ronneby
   **60 Saab A32A**

**2. Flygeskadern** - Ängelholm
Flygflottilj 9 - Göteborg
   **60 Saab J29B**
Flygflottilj 10 - Ängelholm
   **60 Saab J29F**
Flygflottilj 12 - Kalmar
   **60 Saab J29F**

**Saab J29F, A29B, S29C**
1954, 11 m sp, 1060 km/h(0.86), 2700 km
15500 m SC, 4-20 mm, 500 kg

**3. Flygeskadern** - Stockholm
Flygflottilj 1 - Vasterås
   **60 De Havilland J33**
Flygflottilj 3 - Malmslatt
   **60 Saab J29F**
Flygflottilj 8 - Stockholm
   **60 Hawker J34**
Flygflottilj 13 - Norrköping
   **60 Saab J29A**
Flygflottilj 16 - Uppsala
   **60 Saab J29F**
Flygflottilj 18 - Stockholm
   **60 Hawker J34**

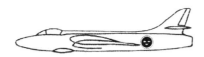

**De Havilland J33**
1951, 13 m sp, 1014 km/h(0.86), 1600 k
4-20 mm, 900 kg W
(De Havilland Venom N.F.51)

**4. Flygeskadern** - Luleå
Flygflottilj 2 - Hagernås (Stockholm)
   school - **Sk50**
   Rescue Service
      **2 Convair Tp47 (PBY-5A)**
      **Noorduyn Tp 78** (Norseman)
Flygflottilj 11 - Nyköping
   **40 Saab S18A**
Flygflottilj 21 - Luleå
   **60 Saab S29C**
Flygflottilj 4 - Östersund
   **60 Saab J29F**
Flygflottilj 15 - Söderhamn
   **60 Saab J29F**

**Hawker J34**
1954, 10 m span, 1079 km/h, (0.92),
1/3660 m, 13725 m SC, 4-30 mm, 4 Fire
(Hawker Hunter F.B.50)

Flygflottilj 20 (OCU school) - Uppsala
   **D.H. Sk28B, Hawker Sk34** (from 1962) [175]

The Air Force had also begun operating helicopters. The first two Sud-Est Hkp2s were delivered to the Rescue Service in January 1959 for use in SAR work. Six Agusta-Bell Hkp3As were added in 1962, as well as 2 Vertol Hkp1s. Fighter training could now be increased over the Baltic, as the new helicopters allowed retrieval of aircraft and crews after training mishaps.

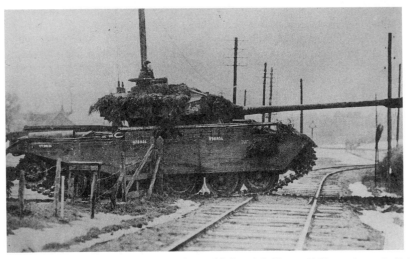

Armored Strike - A Stridsvagn 81 Thrusts Across the Rails

**ARMORED BRIGADE**

HQ - 2 tanks
1 reconnaissance battalion
3 tank battalions
    1 tank company
        HQ - 2 tanks
        3 tank platoons
            **3 Strv 74 or 81**
    2 armored infantry companies
        **11 Tgbl m/42 KP**
    1 mortar company
        3 platoons
            **4 m/29 81 mm mortars**
1 support battalion
    HQ - 2 tanks
    1 tank company
        HQ - 2 tanks
        3 tank platoons
            **3 Strv 74 or 81**
    2 mortar companies
        3 platoons
            **4 m/41 120 mm mortars**
1 artillery battalion
    3 batteries
        **4 Bofors m/39 105 mm howitzers**
1 anti-aircraft company
    4 platoons
        **3 Bofors m/36 40 mm AA guns**

1 engineer company           176

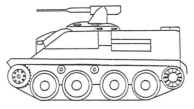

**Pansarbandvagn 301**
1962, 11.5 tons, 1-20 mm,
45 km/h, 300 km, 50/20/15 mm,
20 mm/500 m P, 2 crew, 8 troops

    The most pressing need was for a main battle tank, the British Centurion being adopted to fulfill the role. Eighty Mark 3s were delivered in 1953, followed two years later by 160 Mark 5s. Carrying 83.4 mm main guns, they were designated *Stridsvagn 81*s. Initially, the Mk.3 Centurions reequipped two brigades, the others retaining Strv m/42s until Mk.5s arrived in 1955, completely reequipping four tank battalions.

It was soon obvious that the 83.4 mm gun of the Strv 81 was outranged by the 100-125 mm guns of the Warsaw Pact. Two years after 110 Centurion Mk.10s were delivered in 1960 as the Strv 101, all Strv 81s were fitted with their 105 mm gun, being redesignated Strv 102s. Sweden then had 350 main battle tanks armed with one of the best guns in the world, equipping four armored brigades.

For the secondary vehicles, the Army began converting its large inventory of mechanically new, but tactically obsolescent medium tanks that had been delivered late in the war. The Strv 74 light tank was produced from 1958-60 by mounting a rather ungainly new turret on the chassis of the Strv m/42. Its powerful 75 mm gun gave it a good anti-tank capability, although its rather tall profile hindered concealment. A total of 100 Strv m/42 TVs were converted to Strv 74Vs, and 125 THs became Strv 74Hs. The remaining 57 Strv m/42 EHs, retaining their original turrets and less powerful guns, were relegated to the infantry support role as Ikv 73s.

The 1. Pansarbrigad had been converted to an infantry brigade and was replaced by the 6. Pansarbrigad with a new 1. Armored Regiment. Infantry brigades were reorganized, their specialized support companies being grouped into a support battalion, which was strengthened with the addition of rocket launchers, recoilless rifles and two platoons of mobile assault guns.

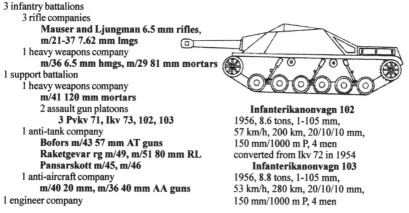

**INFANTRY BRIGADE**
3 infantry battalions
    3 rifle companies
        **Mauser and Ljungman 6.5 mm rifles,**
        **m/21-37 7.62 mm lmgs**
    1 heavy weapons company
        **m/36 6.5 mm hmgs, m/29 81 mm mortars**
1 support battalion
    1 heavy weapons company
        **m/41 120 mm mortars**
    2 assault gun platoons
        **3 Pvkv 71, Ikv 73, 102, 103**
    1 anti-tank company
        **Bofors m/43 57 mm AT guns**
        **Raketgevar rg m/49, m/51 80 mm RL**
        **Pansarskott m/45, m/46**
    1 anti-aircraft company
        **m/40 20 mm, m/36 40 mm AA guns**
1 engineer company

**Infanterikanonvagn 102**
1956, 8.6 tons, 1-105 mm,
57 km/h, 200 km, 20/10/10 mm,
150 mm/1000 m P, 4 men
converted from Ikv 72 in 1954
**Infanterikanonvagn 103**
1956, 8.8 tons, 1-105 mm,
53 km/h, 280 km, 20/10/10 mm,
150 mm/1000 m P, 4 men

With the advent of the powerful armor-piercing guns of the new tanks, the Pvkv m/43s were no longer required in the *pansarbrigaden* and were transferred entirely to the infantry brigades. Redesignated Pvkv 71s in 1953, they remained in use until 1973, the last examples in service on Gotland.

The *Jaeger-korpset* consisted of special service commandos for long-range reconnaissance and guerrilla-type operations in enemy rear areas. Parachute battalions first appeared in 1953, armed with KP m/45 "Carl Gustav" machine pistols. Cavalry continued to include horsed squadrons. Mechanization was deliberately retarded as Sweden's rough terrain and lack of fuel resources dictated more primitive transportation.

**CAVALRY REGIMENT**
1 horse squadron
1 cyclist squadron
1 armored car squadron
    **4 Pb m/40**

The *5. Pansarbrigad* was reorganized as an infantry brigade in 1963, its Strv 74s going to the new *6.* Armored Regiment which became the core of a new *26. Pansarbrigad* at Kristianstad. Having had no experience with large armored formations, and puzzling over conflicting observations of German, Soviet and NATO operations, Sweden experimented with various organizations. From a period of training in 1964, Per Åke Kronbladh recalls maneuvers involving a 1958 type brigade of 48 Strv 74s operating against a brigade of 72 Strv 81s with the new 1963 organization. Possessing more staying power, the 1963 configuration was adopted as standard, remaining largely unchanged to the present day.

After 1965, the armored brigades equipped with Strv 74s were reorganized as infantry brigades, and their tanks distributed by companies to infantry brigades in southern Sweden (those in the north retained Ikv 102s and 103s).

1 tank company
HQ - 2 tanks
3 tank platoons
**3 Strv 74**

The reorganized Army received a new uniform in 1959. The cut remained unchanged, but the color became a dark green. Rank insignia was worn on the shoulder straps of the uniform and also on the left collar patch of the combat uniform (gold branch devices were on the right collar: generals - 3 oak leaves, infantry - crossed rifles, artillery - crossed cannon, armor - crossed swords).

Generals - gold shoulder straps with crossed gold batons at base,
gold 5 ptd. stars and oak leaves
General - 3 stars, 1 oak leaf
General-löjtnant - 2 stars, 2 oak leaves
General-major - 1 star, 3 oak leaves

Field Officers - gold crown above small gold 5 ptd. stars,
gold regimental number at base
Överste, 1 klass - 4 stars (no number)
Överste - 3 stars
Överste-löjtnant - 2 stars
Major - 1 star

Company Officers - small 5 ptd. gold stars above number
Kapten - 3 stars
Löjtnant - 2 stars
Fanrik (ensign) - 1 star

Överste-löjtnant

Senior Non-commissioned Officers - gold button, bearing a
5 ptd. star, above the regimental number
Förvaltare (administrative sergeant) - 3 stars
Fanjunkare (color sergeant) - 2 stars
Sergeant - 1 star

Junior Non-commissioned Officers - short gold bars above
the reginental number
Rustmästre (master sergeant) - 1 thick over 3 thin bars
Överfurir (senior sergeant) - 4 thin bars
Furir (junior sergeant) - 3 thin bars
Korpral - 2 thin bars
Vice-korpral - 1 thin bar
Menig (private) - regimental number          177

Rustmästre

351

The Swedish Navy was administered by the Southern, Eastern, Western, Norrland, Gotland and Öresund naval districts. When the *Flottan* finally received large ocean-going destroyers, the *Öland, Visby, Göteborg, Ehrenskjold, Mode* and *Romulus* classes were rerated as frigates. The new thousand ton *Nacken* and *Sjöormen* submarines were joined by U4-9 rebuilt as the *Abboren* class with a streamlined conning tower.

Baltic Storm Brewing - Halland Breasts a Choppy Sea

Actually, the Navy was the first Swedish service to employ helicopters, contracting with Ostermans Aero AB from 1951-8 to fly Bell 47s and Sikorsky S-55s from naval vessels and bases. In 1958, 4 Vertol 44As were purchased outright as the Hkp1 (Helikopter No.1). Ten more arrived from 1960-4. Thirteen Sud-Est Alouette IIs (Hkp2) were purchased in France between 1959-62. From America came three Hkp4 in 1964. Two helicopter squadrons were organized in 1957 and 1959. By 1966, they possessed:

1. Helikopter Division - Bromma
   **4 Hkp1, 7 Hkp2, 3 Hkp4**
2. Helikopter Division - Göteborg
   **6 Hkp1, 3 Hkp2**

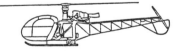

**Sud-Est Hkp2**
1955, 10 m rotor, 175 km/h, 530 km,
4500 m SC, 5 crew
(Sud-Est SE-3130 Alouette II)

By 1965, the *Flygvapnet* was completely equipped with high performance jet aircraft constructed by national firms. The J34s of F8 were used for operational training after the J34s of F18 were retired in favor of J35Bs.

**Swedish Air Force**

**1. Flygeskadern** - Göteborg
Flygflottilj 6 - Karlsborg
**60 Saab A32A**
Flygflottilj 7 - Satenås
**60 Saab A32A**
Flygflottilj 14 - Halmstad
**60 Saab A32A**
Flygflottilj 17 - Ronneby
**60 Saab A32A**

**2. Flygeskadern** - Ängelholm
Flygflottilj 9 - Göteborg
**60 Saab J29F**
Flygflottilj 10 - Ängelholm
**60 Saab J29F**
Flygflottilj 12 - Kalmar
**60 Saab J32B**

**3. Flygeskadern** - Stockholm
Flygflottilj 1 - Vasterås
**60 Saab J32B**
Flygflottilj 3 - Malmslatt
**60 Saab J29F**
Flygflottilj 8 - Stockholm
**60 Hawker J34**
Rescue Service (in F8 from 1962)
**2 Tp47, 2 Hkp1,
3 Hkp2, 6 Hkp3A**
Flygflottilj 13 - Norrköping
**60 Saab J35A,B**
Flygflottilj 16 - Uppsala
**60 Saab J29F**
**60 Saab J35B** (1961 on)
Flygflottilj 18 - Stockholm
**60 Hawker J34**
**60 Saab J35B** (1961 on)

**Saab A32A**
1952, 13 m span, 1127 km/h(0.95),3200km
15000 m SC, 4-20 mm, 1000 kg W
**Saab J32B, S32C**
1957, 13 m span, 1103 km/h (0.93), 3200 km,
1/3600 m, 16000 m SC, 4-30 mm, 2-4 Side

**4. Flygeskadern** - Luleå
Flygflottilj 2 - Hagernås (Stockholm)
school - **Sk50**
Flygflottilj 11 - Nyköping
**60 Saab S32C**
Flygflottilj 21 - Luleå
**60 Saab S29C**
Flygflottilj 4 - Östersund
**60 Saab J29F**
Flygflottilj 15 - Söderhamn
**60 Saab J29F**

Flygflottilj 20 (OCU school) - Uppsala
**Hawker Sk34, Saab Sk29**

Bofors had long had a fine reputation for its artillery, and now also manufactured missiles and armored fighting vehicles. Saab-Scania was rapidly achieving a position near the top of aircraft designers, powered by Volvo's excellent jet engines. Hagglunds produced several light armored vehicles. Small arms came from Forenade Fabriksverken (FFV).

Light aircraft had been used by the Army for liaison duties since the early 1950s. More modern equipment was procured in 1958. Six Fpl51As and 6 Fpl51Bs arrived (the 51As were later replaced by 6 more 51Bs). In 1961, 5 Fpl53s entered service, as did 2 Fpl54s (MFI-10B) in 1965. In addition, the Army began to acquire helicopters. A dozen Hkp2s were the first to arrive, in 1959. Two Hkp5s of 1962 were followed the next year by 12 Hkp3Bs. In combat, the Army aircraft would be deployed in small squads:

light aircraft squad (liaison)
  **Dornier Fpl53**
artillery spotter squad
  **Piper Fpl51B**

light helicopter squad (utility)
  **Sud-Est Hkp2**
medium helicopter squad (transport)
  **Agusta-Bell Hkp3B**

**Agusta-Bell Hkp3B**
1963, 15 m rotor, 237 km/h, 420 km,
5368 m SC, 8-10 troops or 1560 kg C
(Agusta-Bell 204B)

**Piper Fpl51B**
1955, 11 m span, 209 km/h, 600 km,
5790 m SC, no mg, 2 crew
(Piper L-21B)

**Dornier Fpl53**
1955, 12 m span, 227 km/h,
3300 m SC, 2 crew, 4 troops
(Dornier Do.27A-4)

Ironically, the products of Swedish arms manufacturers were winning world-wide respect at the time the United Nations was ineptly trying to quell warfare among its members. Sweden became involved in the warfare she had avoided for so long.

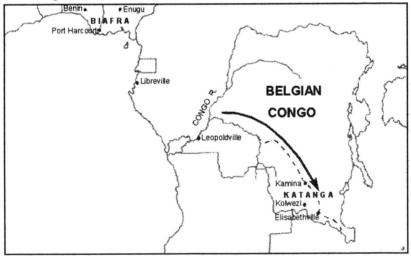

Swedish UN Operations in the Congo

354

The Cold War between the Communist powers and the Western democracies was fought in the underdeveloped countries of the "Third World". Exploiting the rightful grievances of the inhabitants of various colonies, Communist subversives sought to stir the native population into revolt, anticipating the establishment of a Communist government following the revolution.

In Africa, trouble erupted early in the Belgian Congo. Although ruled relatively benignly by the Belgians, the Congo was the source of much wealth for Belgium. The long-standing feuds between Congolese tribes caused factionalization of the revolt, allowing the Belgians to maintain control by playing one side against the other.

On 14 July 1960, the UN Security Council demanded the withdrawal of Belgian troops and authorized its Secretary-General, Dag Hammarskjöld of Sweden, to send military forces to replace them. Within two days, the first men began arriving:

**Force de l'Organisation des Nations Unies au Congo** (ONUC)
3,500 troops of Ethiopia, Ghana, Morocco, Tunisia

Wearing their own national uniforms, the men of the force soon increased to 10,000. As the Congo had a primitive communications network, a number of Swedish volunteers arrived to fly supplies to the UN forces, using DHC Beaver and Otter light transports. However, this show of force did not have the effect upon the warring factions that Hammarskjöld had anticipated. Under the UN charter, the UN commanders had to consult with the Congo government before mounting each operation. The details of the operations had to be arranged by conferring with the governments of each contingent of ONUC. In addition, the Belgians did everything they could to prevent occupation of wealthy Katanga province. The unwillingness, or inability, of the United Nations to forcibly occupy Katanga, caused the president of the Congo, Patrice Lumumba, to turn to the Soviet Union for help.

Swedish airmen manned the UN Helicopter and Light Aircraft Squadron just outside Leopoldville, at Ndolo. Attempting to avoid civil war, a small force of ONUC troops entered Katanga province on **12 August 1960**, displacing Belgian troops and mounting peace-keeping operations. The Swedes supported them with reconnaissance and supply missions. However, Lamumba's government troops, now equipped with Soviet arms, thrust into the province anyway, hoping to oust Maurice Tshombe. They were totally routed. The Congo leaders fell to squabbling and the central government disintegrated. Colonel Joseph Mobutu announced a military takeover.

A Swedish Battalion arrived at Leopoldville in January 1961 riding SKPF APCs. The airmen at Ndolo shifted 20 kilometers away to Ndjili, their unit redesignated Support Squadron. At the same time, an Air Division of transport aircraft was set up to overcome the supply problems caused by the primitive communications system in the Congo. Commanded by Colonel Norstrom, the Air Division became an important part of UN operations.

President Kasavubu succeeded in bringing the Congo factions into a new government under Premier Cyrille Adoula in August 1961. But new dissensions broke out and Adoula resorted to force to regain Katanga. To face him, Maurice Tshombe hired an army of South African, French and Belgian white mercenaries. The ill-trained Congolese Army was unable to make headway against the mercenaries until the United Nations stepped in.

The first UN offensive, Operation Rumpunch in **August 1961**, was followed the next month by Operation Morthor. However, 15,000 Katangese troops faced the 5,000 UN men involved, and the operations were only partially successful. Better results were achieved by another operation in December. The ground troops were now supported by Swedish and Indian combat aircraft. Five Saab J29Bs arrived from Sweden on 4 October as *Flygflottilj 22* at Kamina. Under Captain Everstal, the wing maintained high efficiency. The J29s mainly flew cover for the transport operations, as ground attack was difficult due to the problem of distinguishing friend from foe. They, and the Indian Canberras, were quite effective when used against ground targets, although world attention was brought to their success by an unfortunate rocket attack of a J29 on an unmarked field hospital. Sufficient progress was made to force negotiations upon Tshombe.

For a year, no progress was made in the talks. The UN built up its troop strength during the lull, although the Canberra light bombers returned to India and the never efficient Ethiopian Sabres also went home. The Swedes had been reinforced by four more J29Bs and two S29C reconnaissance planes. The quiet was broken on 28 December when Katangese police fired on UN troops in Elisabethville. The following day, a decisive attack fell on the Kolwezi-Kengere airbase, greatly affecting the ground operations.

**Saab J29B**
1954, 11 m span, 1060 km/h (0.86), 2700 km, 15500 m SC, 4-20 mm, 500 kg W

At dawn, 6 J29Bs left Kamina and dove through low clouds over the Katangese airbase, strafing the length of the field despite taking some 20 mm hits. Photos taken later by the S29Cs revealed that almost all combat aircraft of the Katanga rebels had been destroyed. Free from air attack, Operation Jacaranda made sufficient progress into Katanga to force Tshombe to surrender on **21 January 1963**.

During the four years of conflict, 93,000 men from 35 members of the United Nations had been rotated to the Congo. In an atmosphere of conciliation, Moise Tshombe was asked to lead the Congolese Army against a rebellion in the eastern provinces. From July 1964, the UN backed the Congolese offensive against many fanatical attacks by the Soviet-led Simba rebels. Adding mercenaries to his force, Tshombe opened a bloody campaign early in 1965. The war finally ended in mid-1967.

Even before the conflict ended in the Congo, another broke out far to the west. The Republic of Biafra had declared its independence from Nigeria on 30 May 1967, resulting in an immediate invasion by brutal Nigerian troops.

Swedish Count Karl Gustaf von Rosen made a relief flight into the new country. Appalled by what he saw, he called for United Nations action against the invaders. Five Swedish MFI-9B light planes arrived in Biafra on 14 May 1969, armed with 6 Matra rockets under each wing. Operating from a secret airfield in Gabon, south of Libreville, they began operations against government forces.

**MFI-9B**
1958, 7 m span, 240 km/h, 800 km, 4500 m SC, 6-18 rockets

On 22 May, they flew to a new base north of Uga in Biafra. On the way, they attacked Port Harcourt with rockets, destroying three Nigerian planes and damaging several others. Two days later, four MFI-9Bs destroyed two more Nigerian aircraft on the airfield at Benin. A Nigerian MiG and two Canberras were heavily damaged at Enugu by four of the pesky little planes. A few days later, the Nigerians reacted. The Biafran base was attacked by two MiGs, but suffered no damage. Four little MFIs struck back that same afternoon, putting the Ughelli power station off line for a time. Although four more MFI-9Bs arrived during the summer of 1969, their combat days were over, most of the Swedes going home and the Biafrans taking over their own aerial responsibilities. [178]

Swedish troops continued to be deployed as United Nations peacekeepers in such places as Lebanon and Cyprus. The operational experience thus gained was valuable to a nation that had not engaged in war for nearly two centuries. The irresolution of the United Nations often placed Swedes in the buffer zone of renewed conflict.

### Renewal and Reduction - 1967-1975

Sweden's willingness to engage in combat under the auspices of the United Nations surprised many, as her reputation for non-belligerency was well known. Yet, Sweden possessed one of the world's best-armed military forces by 1970. Through a judicial use of new heavy equipment for vital functions, and light or rebuilt vehicles calculated to be adequate in secondary and specialized roles, Sweden constructed an army with few weaknesses.

To replace the economical equipment converted from earlier types, purpose-built weapons began to enter service during the second half of the 1960s. To provide light anti-tank protection within the *pansarbrigaden*, the Pvpjäs 1110 90 mm recoilless rifle was mounted on the Volvo L.3314 Laplander light truck to produce the Pvpjtgbil 9031 Huggpipan in 1963.

Huggpipans on the Point - Light Anti-tank Support in the Armored Brigade.

357

A Platoon of Low-slung Stridsvagn 103Bs Deploys Behind a Roadbank

A remarkable new tank appeared in 1967. Designed under the concept that a turretless vehicle was just as efficient as a turreted one in Sweden's close country, the 335 *Stridsvagn* 103Bs possessed several unique features. Most salutary was the use of hydraulic movement of the entire vehicle to lay its 105 mm gun. With its resulting low profile, the Strv 103B could be easily concealed, as well as find ramparts in every road ditch from which to fire. However, its unique method of gun-laying was to prove cumbersome in some situations. With nearly 700 main battle tanks now deployed, the Army relegated its Strv 74s to infantry support.

Hagglunds simultaneously produced a new armored personnel carrier. Some 600 *Pansarbandvagn* 302s provided transport for the armored infantry, possessing up-to-date NBC protection and rectifying most of the faults of the earlier makeshift equipment. To provide mobile artillery for the divisions, Bofors developed the *Bandkanon* 1A, a self-propelled 155 mm gun mounted on a chassis utilizing many components of the Strv 103. Thirty entered service from 1966, production ending two years later.

Infantry units also received new weapons, the AK4 assault rifle (the Spanish CETME adopted by NATO) finally replaced the old Ljungmans and the even older Browning light machinegun. The m/ 58 (Belgian FN MAG) became the heavy machinegun. However, the greatest advance was in protection against tanks, the Carl Gustav ATGW and towed 90 mm recoilless rifle being among the best such weapons in the world. However, Sweden still suffered a lack of fuel resources, making full mechanization futile. In the event of war, it was planned to use civilian farm tractors to pull many of the army's towed weapons, including the Pvpjäs 1110 90 mm recoilless rifles.

Although Sweden was purportedly neutral, her armed forces were too small to withstand a determined attack for more than a few weeks, regardless of their efficiency. This evaluation became the basis of the General Staff's instructions for the Army to prepare delaying operations, undoubtedly anticipating that help from NATO would appear should the Warsaw Pact initiate hostilities. Aerial defense remained high on the list of priorities, but the Navy continued to feel the axe, for it was believed that its ships would become mere expensive targets for enemy aircraft. New maritime expenditures were to be limited to submarines and small vessels.

358

Just as the prodigious efforts to strengthen the armed forces reached fruition, the reductions of the 1972 Defense Plan fell like Thor's thunderbolt.

## Swedish Army

**Militärområdet Övre Norrland** - Boden
3 Norrland brigades

**Militärområdet Norra** - Östersund
2 Norrland brigades

**Militärområdet Bergslagen** - Karlstad
3 infantry brigades

**Militärområdet Östra** - Strängnäs
3 infantry brigades
6. **Pansarbrigad** - Enköping
   1. Armored Regiment - Strv 101,102
10. **Pansarbrigad** - Strängnäs
   10. Armored Regiment - Strv 101,102

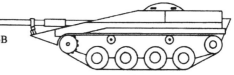

**Pansarvärnspjäspansarbil 9031**
1962, 1.6 tons, 1-90 mm RR,
97 km/h, 330 km, 4 men
380 mm/900 m P   "Huggpipan"

**Militärområdet Västra** - Skövde
3 infantry brigades
9. **Pansarbrigad** - Skövde
   4. Armored Regiment - Strv 103B

**Militärområdet Södra** - Kristianstad
4 infantry brigades
7. **Pansarbrigad** - Ystad
   7. Armored Regiment - Strv 103B
8. **Pansarbrigad** - Hässleholm
   2. Armored Regiment - Strv 103B
26. **Pansarbrigad** - Kristianstad
   6. Armored Regiment - Strv 101,102   179

**Stridsvagn 103B**
1963, 43 tons, 1-105 mm, 3 mgs,
50 km/h, 390 km,
300 mm/1000 m P, 3 men

In the restructuring, the Army fared better than the other services, its strength remaining relatively unchanged.

### INFANTRY BRIGADE

1 reconnaissance company
3 infantry battalions
  3 rifle companies
    **AK4 7.62 mm assault rifles,**
    **m/58 7.62 mm lmgs**
  1 heavy company
    **6 m/29 81 mm mortars,**
    **4 Pvpjäs 1110 towed 90 mm RR**
1 support battalion
  1 light tank company
    HQ - 2 tanks
    3 platoons
    **3 Strv 74**
  1 anti-tank company
    **6 Pvpjäs 1110 towed 90 mm RR**
  2 mortar companies
    **8 m/41 120 mm mortars**
  1 anti-aircraft company
    **18 Bofors Ivakan 20 mm AA guns**
1 artillery battalion
  3 batteries
    **6 m/39, m/40 105 mm howitzers**
2 engineer companies

**Automatkarbin 4**
7.62 mm, 4.5 kg, 787 m/s, 600 rpm

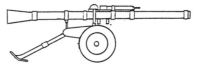

**m/58 lmg**
7.62 mm, 11 kg, 1000 rpm

**Pansarvärnspjäs 1110**
1960, 90 mm, 260 kg, 3.1 kg shell,
900 m, 715 m/s, 6 rpm,
380 mm/900 m P

Most of the population and industry are located in the southern third of Sweden, but the only land invasion route from the east lies in the far north. The Arctic conditions of northern Sweden required troops trained and equipped to fight in a severe environment. As they would be the first to face any Soviet attack, they were specially trained and heavily equipped with over-snow vehicles and anti-tank weapons.

**NORRLAND BRIGADE**
1 reconnaissance company
3 Norrland infantry battalions
    4 rifle companies
      ski troops, towed by:
        **Bolinder Munktell BV 202N**
    1 mortar company
      **6 m/41 120 mm mortars**
1 assault gun company
    **6 Ikv 102, 103**
1 Norrland artillery battalion
    3 batteries
      **6 m/39, m/40 105 mm howitzers**
1 anti-aircraft company
    **18 Bofors Ivakan 20 mm AA guns**
1 Norrland engineer battalion

While the Swedish Army and Air Force were modernized, the Navy was drastically reduced. The advent of powerful long-range aircraft and missiles made the narrow Baltic Sea too dangerous for surface ships during wartime. Accepting the changed situation with regret, the Navy decommissioned its three cruisers, the elderly *Gotland* in 1961 and the *Göta Lejon* and *Tre Kronor* in 1964-8. The destroyers of the World War II era were rerated as frigates from 1961-5, resulting in the scrapping of the older frigates. The only surface ships remaining were six modern destroyers (four *Östergotland*s and two *Halland*s) and twelve old frigates (six *Stockholm*s, two *Öland*s and four *Visby*s). Under the 1972 Defense Act, the *Stockholm* class was stricken in 1971-4, with most of the rest to follow by the end of the decade.

Maritime defenses were to consist of helicopters for anti-submarine warfare, submarines for offensive/defensive actions along lines of communication, and fast missile boats for coastal defense.

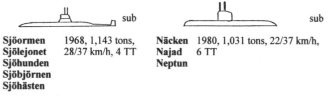

| Sjöormen | 1968, 1,143 tons, | Näcken | 1980, 1,031 tons, 22/37 km/h, |
| Sjölejonet | 28/37 km/h, 4 TT | Najad | 6 TT |
| Sjöhunden | | Neptun | |
| Sjöbjörnen | | | |
| Sjöhästen | | | |

Sweden finally achieved her goal of equipping the Air Force entirely with indigenous combat aircraft. The remarkable Saab company revealed a new fighter plane in October 1955. An excellent design, the double-delta J35 Draken (Dragon) stirred international interest. In some respects it was superior to the French Mirage III. Beginning in 1960, 180 J35As and Bs were delivered, the B model having improved electronics. In the same year, the faster D model appeared, all earlier models (capable of only Mach 1.8) being subsequently converted to the new configuration. In 1963, cameras were added to the D to produce the S35E photo reconnaissance version. However, the greatest production was reserved for the J35F, which replaced the last J29Fs from 1968.

J35F Drakens of F10 Taxi to Takeoff Past an Hkp4 at Ängelholm

Advanced training had been conducted for years with retired fighters originally acquired from Britain. In 1963, a new jet trainer made its first flight. The Saab 105 proved to be a versatile aircraft that attracted orders from both the Swedish and foreign air forces. The first of 130 were delivered to the *Flygvapnet* in December 1965 as the Sk60 trainer. A simple conversion made the trainer into a light strike aircraft, of which 20 were delivered as the A60. All Sk60s could be quickly converted to the strike configuration. Thus, the school squadrons acquired the capability of entering the fray in the event of war.

Ten Boeing Vertol 107-II helicopters provided the *Flygvapnet* with greater training flexibility when the were distributed to several *flygflotti* as the Hkp4B, available for rescuin downed pilots from the Baltic. Th Navy's Sud-Est Hkp2s were now use only for training as they had been replaced by 10 Hkp6Bs Jet Rangers in the liaison role. For anti-submarine and sea-air rescue duties, the Navy acquired 3 Hkp4Bs and 7 Hkp4Cs.

**Agusta-Bell Hkp6B**
1965, 10 m rotor, 270 km/h, 700 km,
6096 m SC, 3 depth bombs or 2 torpedoes
(Agusta-Bell 206A Jet Ranger)

The Swedish Air Force was directed to take over many of the defense responsibilities formerly allotted to the Navy. For decades, the *Flygvapnet* had been organized by mission. The *1. Flygeskadern* was tasked with bombing and ground attack. Air defense was the primary mission of the *2.* and *3. Flygeskadern*. The *4. Flygeskadern* operated principally in the role of maritime surveillance and attack, but also included the air force's flying school. As the capabilities of Soviet aircraft increased, the *4. Flygeskadern* added fighter defense of northern Sweden to its responsibilities.

The *Flygvapnet* now had numerous secondary landing grounds to allow dispersal of its units in the event of war. Underground nuclear-proof hangars were provided for a worse-case scenario.

# Swedish Air Force

**1. Flygeskadern** - Göteborg
Flygflottilj 6 - Karlsborg
**60 Saab A32A**
Flygflottilj 7 - Satenås
**60 Saab A32A**
Flygflottilj 14 - Halmstad
**60 Saab A32A**
Flygflottilj 17 - Ronneby
**60 Saab A32A**

**2. Flygeskadern** - Ängelholm
Flygflottilj 9 - Göteborg
**60 Saab J35F**
Flygflottilj 10 - Ängelholm
**60 Saab J35F**
Flygflottilj 12 - Kalmar
**60 Saab J32B**

**Saab J35D,F, S35E Draken**
1958, 9 m span, 2125 km/h (2.2),
4.5/15250 m, 21350 m SC,
1-30 mm, 2-4 Falcon AAM

**3. Flygeskadern** - Stockholm
Flygflottilj 1 - Vasterås
**60 Saab J32B**
Flygflottilj 3 - Malmslatt
**60 Saab J35F**
Flygflottilj 8 - Stockholm
**60 Saab J35F**
Flygflottilj 13 - Norrköping
**60 Saab J35D**
Flygflottilj 16 - Uppsala
**60 Saab J35D**
Flygflottilj 18 - Stockholm
**60 Saab J35D**

**Boeing Vertol Hkp4**
1958, 16 m rotor, 267 km/h, 385 km,
4265 m SC, 25 troops or 6000 kg C
(Boeing Vertol 107-II)

**4. Flygeskadern** - Luleå
Flygflottilj 2 - Hagernäs (Stockholm)
school
**Saab Sk50, Saab Sk60**
1 light attack division
**20 Saab A60**
Flygflottilj 11 - Nyköping
**60 Saab S32C**
Flygflottilj 21 - Luleå
**15 Saab J32B**
**45 Saab S35E**
Flygflottilj 4 - Östersund
**60 Saab J35F**
Flygflottilj 15 - Söderhamn
**60 Saab J35F**

**Saab Sk 60, A 60**
1963, 10 m span, 805 km/h, 1400 km,
7.5/6000 m, 12700 m SC, 2-30 mm or
2 Saab 305 ASMs or 12 rockets or 750 kg B
(Saab 105)

Flygflottilj 20 (OCU school) - Uppsala
**Hawker Sk34, Saab Sk29**

The A32s of the *1. Flygeskadern* were deployed around the coasts of southern Sweden where they could efficiently aid the movements of the principal Swedish ground forces in the only Swedish terrain favorable to mobile operations. *Drakens* were now the principal interceptors, those of the *2. Flygeskadern* covering the west and south, with the *3. Flygeskadern* guarding the east coast around the capital. A wing of J32B night fighters was present in both of the interceptor *eskadern*. Two wings of J35s screened the industrial heart of the nation from the north, while S35Es kept an eye on things in the Arctic. Maritime surveillance of the Baltic was now in the hands of the S32Cs of F11.

362

# SWEDEN'S PLACE IN THE NEW EUROPE

Although the armed forces were reduced in the wake of the 1972 Defense Program, weaponry was improved. Infantry anti-tank guided weapons now included the man-portable 84 mm Grg m/48 Carl Gustav, the disposable 74 mm Miniman and the wire-guided 110 mm Bantam missile launchers. The new AK4 assault rifle, a version of the Spanish CETME which had also been adopted by NATO via the German G3, added much needed firepower to infantry squads.

Likewise, the mobility of machine-gun fire was much improved with the acquisition of the Belgian MAG in place of the ancient Browning. Mortar support continued to be provided by the venerable wartime m/29 80 mm and m/41 120 mm models. The Army possessed 1,000 m/29s and 600 m/41s in 1980.

Regulations of **1977** created new organizations for the Army's units. To the twelve divisions expected to form upon mobilization were attached both a regiment of 155 mm artillery and a battalion of anti-aircraft guns. Together with reconnaissance and engineer battalions, these formed the only permanent units assigned to the division, which was activated only in wartime and composed of a varying number of brigades and smaller attachments.

**ARMY DIVISION**

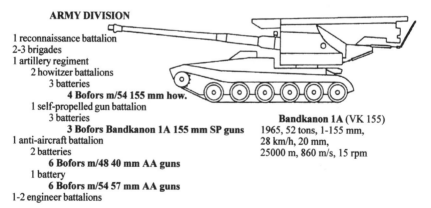

1 reconnaissance battalion
2-3 brigades
1 artillery regiment
  2 howitzer battalions
    3 batteries
      **4 Bofors m/54 155 mm how.**
  1 self-propelled gun battalion
    3 batteries
      **3 Bofors Bandkanon 1A 155 mm SP guns**
1 anti-aircraft battalion
  2 batteries
      **6 Bofors m/48 40 mm AA guns**
  1 battery
      **6 Bofors m/54 57 mm AA guns**
1-2 engineer battalions

**Bandkanon 1A** (VK 155)
1965, 52 tons, 1-155 mm,
28 km/h, 20 mm,
25000 m, 860 m/s, 15 rpm

The principal striking arm was composed of six armored brigades, two of which were actually mechanized brigades. Twenty-one infantry brigades formed most of the Army's strength. For operations in the Arctic, there were also two special Norrland brigades. The large island of Gotland had its own combat group of brigade size. Mobilization would produce 500,000 men.

Mountains and lakes make much of Sweden difficult for mechanized movement. Horses and bicycles were long retained in the Swedish Army to overcome these problems. The modern Army has become more mechanized, although many units still retain non-motorized transport in reserve.

## Swedish Army

**Militärområdet Övre Norrland** - Boden
4. Armored Cavalry Regiment
19., 22., 30. Infantry Regiments
8. Artillery Regiment
7. Air Defense Regiment
3. Engineer Regiment

**Militärområdet Norra** - Östersund
5., 21. Infantry Regiments
4. Artillery Regiment
5. Air Defense Regiment

**Militärområdet Bergslagen** - Karlstad
2., 3., 13. Infantry Regiments
9. Artillery Regiment

**Militärområdet Östra** - Strängnäs
1. Armored Cavalry Regiment
1., 4., 14. Infantry Regiments
1., 7. Artillery Regiments
2., 3. Air Defense Regiments
1. Engineer Regiment

**Militärområdet Västra** - Skövde
2. Armored Cavalry Regiment
9. **Pansarbrigad** - Skövde
4. Armored Regiment - Strv 103B
15., 16., 17. Infantry Regiments
3. Artillery Regiment
6. Air Defense Regiment

**Militärområdet Södra** - Kristianstad
3. Armored Cavalry Regiment
7. **Pansarbrigad** - Ystad
7. Armored Regiment - Strv 103B
8. **Pansarbrigad** - Hässleholm
2. Armored Regiment - Strv 103B
26. **Pansarbrigad** - Kristianstad
6. Armored Regiment - Strv 101, 102
6., 7., 11., 12. Infantry Regiments
2., 6. Artillery Regiments

**Gotland Combat Group**
Pvkv 71, SKPF

Army Aviation Corps
2 battalions
**17 BAe Sk61C Bulldog, 12 Piper Fpl51B**
**15 Agusta-Bell Hkp3B, 19 Agusta-Bell Hkp6B**

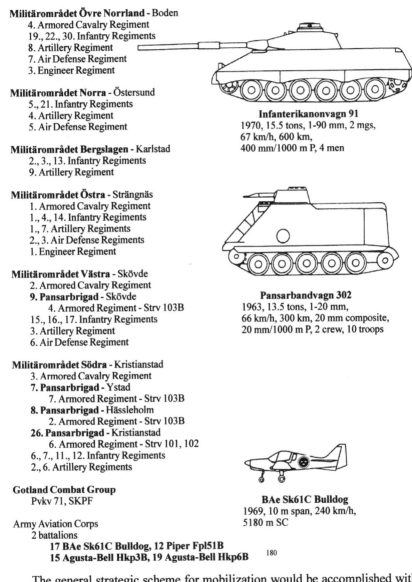

**Infanterikanonvagn 91**
1970, 15.5 tons, 1-90 mm, 2 mgs,
67 km/h, 600 km,
400 mm/1000 m P, 4 men

**Pansarbandvagn 302**
1963, 13.5 tons, 1-20 mm,
66 km/h, 300 km, 20 mm composite,
20 mm/1000 m P, 2 crew, 10 troops

**BAe Sk61C Bulldog**
1969, 10 m span, 240 km/h,
5180 m SC

180

The general strategic scheme for mobilization would be accomplished with each unit forming up in its locale. The bulk of Swedish settlement and industry was in the southern third of the country with the plains of Skåne, in the extreme south, the most likely site of invasion. Thus, 90% of Swedish armor was south of Stockholm. A strong force also blocked the only route through the Arctic.

The armored brigades, of 1963 Type, were now rather well armed, possessing 78 main battle tanks mounting 105 mm guns. Their chief deficiency was a lack of self-propelled artillery.

**ARMORED BRIGADE**

1 armored reconnaissance company
  HQ - **6 Grg m/48 Carl Gustav 84 mm RR**
  2 reconnaissance platoons
    **3 Volvo L.3314 Laplander, 2 motorcycles**
  2 armored infantry platoons
    **3 Pbv 302 APCs**
  1 anti-tank platoon
    **4 Volvo Pvspb 9031 Huggpipan**
2 anti-tank companies
  1 light anti-tank platoon
    **7 Grg m/48 Carl Gustav 84 mm RR**
  2 anti-tank platoons
    **4 Volvo Pvspb 9031 Huggpipan**
  1 anti-tank platoon
    **36 RB 53 Bantam 110 mm ATGW**
3 armored battalions
  HQ company
    3 reconnaissance platoons
      **3 Volvo L.3314 Laplander, 2 motorcycles**
      **9 Bolinder Munktell BV 202** (Norrland)
  2 tank companies
    HQ - 1 tank, **3 Grg m/48 Carl Gustav 84 mm RR**
    4 tank platoons
      **3 Strv 101, 102, 103B**
    1 mechanized infantry platoon
      **3 Pbv 302 APCs**
  2 mechanized infantry companies
    HQ - 1 APC, **3 Grg m/48 Carl Gustav 84 mm RR**
    3 mechanized infantry platoons
      **3 Pbv 302 APCs**
    1 anti-tank platoon
      **4 Volvo Pvspb 9031 Huggpipan**
  1 artillery company
    HQ - **3 Pbv 302, 3 Volvo L.3314 Laplander,**
      **2 Grg m/48 Carl Gustav 84 mm RR**
    **4 towed Bofors 4140 105 mm how**
1 artillery battalion
  2 light artillery batteries (3 to 1980)
    **4 towed Bofors 4140 105 mm how**
  1 medium artillery battery (from 1980)
    **4 towed Bofors m/54 155 mm how**
1 air defense company
  3 platoons
    **6 towed 20 mm AA guns**
    **RB 69 Redeye SAMs**
1 engineer battalion

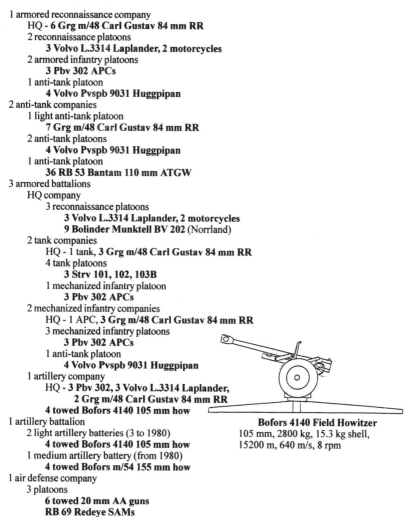

**Bofors 4140 Field Howitzer**
105 mm, 2800 kg, 15.3 kg shell,
15200 m, 640 m/s, 8 rpm

In 1983, the first of 110 Strv 101s and 240 Strv 102s were rebuilt with Continental engines, laser rangefinders, and Lyran illumination.

From 1974, the old assault guns were replaced by Hagglund's lightly-armored Ikv 91, one company in each infantry brigade serving as mobile anti-tank protection. The displaced Pvkv 71s were added to the defenses of Gotland while the Ikv 102s and 103s were again rebuilt in 1982-4 to create 94 Pvrbv 551 anti-tank missile carriers and Lvrbv 701 anti-aircraft missile carriers in independent companies attached to armored brigades and army headquarters.

Tank Killers - A Platoon of Ikv 91s Maneuvers Over the Snow

The advent of the Hagglunds Ikv 91 provided the greatest change in the capability of the 1977 Type infantry brigade. In conception not unlike the American tank destroyer of World War II, the lightly-armored vehicle provided a mobile anti-tank and fire base for the brigade commander, its smooth-bore gun able to penetrate any main battle tank of the time.

### INFANTRY BRIGADE

1 armored reconnaissance company
    HQ - **6 Grg m/48 Carl Gustav 84 mm RR**
    2 platoons
        **3 Volvo L.3314 Laplander, 2 motorcycles**
    2 platoons
        **3 Pbv 302 APCs**
    1 anti-tank platoon
        **4 Volvo Pvspb 9031 Huggpipan**
1 armored anti-tank company
    3 platoons
        **4 Ikv 91**
3 rifle battalions
    HQ - **4 Volvo Pvspb 9031 Huggpipan**
    4 rifle companies
        **AK 4 7.62 mm AR, m/58 7.62 mm mg**
        **6 Grg m/48 Carl Gustav 84 mm RR**
    1 mortar company
        **m/29 80 mm mortars, m/41 120 mm mortars**
1 artillery battalion
    3 batteries
        **6 Bofors 4140 105 mm howitzers**
1 anti-aircraft company
    3 platoons
        **6 Bofors 20 mm AA guns**
2 engineer companies

The Volvo Laplander light truck became the "jeep" of the Swedish Army, serving both in reconnaissance and anti-tank roles (as the Huggpipan). However, 130 old SKPFs remained in service, mainly on the islands.

366

**1. Flygeskadern** - Göteborg
Flygflottilj 6 - Karlsborg
**30 Saab AJ37**
Flygflottilj 7 - Satenås
**45 Saab AJ37**
Flygflottilj 11 - Nyköping
**15 Saab S32C, S35E**
Flygflottilj 15 - Söderhamn
**15 Saab AJ37**

**Militärområdet Övre Norrland** - Luleå
Flygflottilj 21 - Luleå
**15 Saab J35D,F**
**15 Saab SF37**

**Militärområdet Norra** - Östersund
Flygflottilj 2 - Hagernås (Stockholm)
4 light strike (school) divisioner
**Saab Sk60**
1 light strike division
**Saab A60**
Flygflottilj 4 - Östersund
**45 Saab J35D**

**Militärområdet Östra** - Vasterås
Flygflottilj 1 - Vasterås
**30 Saab J35F**
Flygflottilj 13 - Norrköping
**30 Saab J35F**
**15 Saab SH37, SF37**
Flygflottilj 16 - Uppsala
**30 Saab J35F**

**Militärområdet Södra** - Ängelholm
Flygflottilj 10 - Ängelholm
**45 Saab J35F**
Flygflottilj 17 - Ronneby
**30 Saab J35F**
**15 Saab SH37**

1 electronic countermeasures unit
**2 Sud-Est Caravelle**
2 transport divisioner
**3 Lockheed C-130E,H, 6 Douglas C-47**
5 liaison divisioner
**16 Saab Sk60E, 5 Saab Sk61, Sk50**
5 helicopter groups (3-4 aircraft)
**6 Sud-Est Hkp2, 16 Agusta-Bell Hkp3,**
**10 Boeing Vertol Hkp4B**
6 air defense divisioner
**Bloodhound 2 SAMs**

The A32 was outdated and in need of replacement. The *Flygvapnet* required a combat plane capable of short takeoffs and landings from roads throughout Sweden. Other nations had opted for the maintenance complexities of the swing-wing, rejecting the STOL-capable canard configuration because it lacked the necessary maneuverability unless the aircraft was made unstable. Saab was able to take advantage of newly-developed computer technology to control a canard precisely, resulting in a fighter bomber with subsonic maneuverability equal to other designs yet possessing supersonic superiority - the AJ37.

## Swedish Army

**Militärområdet Övre Morrland** - Boden
6. Division
19., 50. Norrland Brigades

**Militärområdet Norra** - Östersund
2. Division
35., 51. Norrland Brigades

**Militärområdet Bergslagen** - Karlstad
3 infantry regiments

**Militärområdet Östra** - Strängnäs
4. Division
   10. **Mechanized Brigade**
   13. Norrland Brigade
   1. Infantry Brigade

**Militärområdet Västra** - Skövde
3. Division
   9. **Pansarbrigad** - Skövde
   4 Armored Regiment - Strv 103C
   45., 46. Infantry Brigades

**Militärområdet Södra** - Kristianstad
13. Armored Division
   7. **Pansarbrigad** - Ystad
   7. Armored Regiment - Strv 103C
   8. **Pansarbrigad** - Hässleholm
   2. Armored Regiment - Strv 103C
   42. Infantry Brigade
14. Division
   2., 4. Infantry Brigades     181

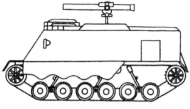

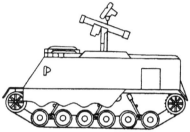

**Pansarvärnsraketebandvagn 551**
1983, 9.7 tons, 1 TOW,
41 km/h, 300 km, 20 mm, 4 men

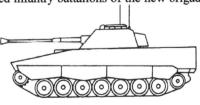

**Luftvärnsraketebandvagn 701**
1983, 9.7 tons, 1 RBS-70 SAM,
41 km/h, 300 km, 20 mm, 4 men

All 335 Strv 103s delivered were developed B models, and from 1992 they were upgraded to C models with Detroit Diesel engines and other improvements. Evaluations have been going on to reequip a brigade each in central and southern Sweden, and two battalions in the north, with new main battle tanks. The German Leopard 2 and the American M1A2 Abrams are the final contenders, with deliveries of 200 to take place in 1996-8. All other brigades will retain their Strv 103Cs.

Currently, some infantry brigades are being converted to mechanized brigades with the delivery of 280 Stridsfordon 90 (Combat Vehicle 90) from November 1993. The principal version is the CV 9040 mechanized infantry combat vehicle. The CV 9040 AAV anti-aircraft vehicle with a 40 mm AA gun is also in service, but carrying no troops. When deliveries end in 1998, the vehicles will equip the main mechanized infantry battalions of the new brigades:

3 mechanized infantry battalions
  4 mechanized rifle companies
    **CV 9040**
  1 mortar company
  1 supply company

**CV 9040 MICV**
1990, 22.4 tons, 1-40 mm, 1 mg,
70 km/h, 300 km, 3 crew, 8 troops
150 mm/2000 m P

368

Göteborg Cleaves the Baltic.

Numerous fast missile boats constitute the main defense of the coasts and harbors of Sweden. The heat-seeking Penguin SSMs of the smaller *Hugin* class possess a range of 27 kilometers, carrying a warhead of 120 kilograms. The older *Norrköping* class employs heavier radar-guided Saab SSMs which deliver a 150 kilogram warhead as far away as 70 kilometers. The six corvettes of the *Göteborg* and *Stockholm* classes act as flotilla leaders for the missile boats.

missile corvette

**Göteborg** 1990, 300 tons, 59 km/h,
**Gävle** 8 Saab RBS 15 SSM, 2 TT
**Sundsvall**
**Kalmar**

missile corvette

**Stockholm** 1985, 314 tons, 59 km/h,
**Malmö** 8 Saab RBS 15 SSM, 2 TT

fast missile attack boat

**Hugin** 1978, 120 tons, 58 km/h,
**Munin** 1-5.7 cm, 6 Penguin Mk.2 SSM
**Magne**
**Mode**
**Vale**
**Vidar**
**Mjölner**
**Mysing**
**Kaparen**
**Väktaren**
**Snapphanen**
**Spejaren**
**Styrbjörn**
**Starkodder**
**Tordön**
**Tirfing**

fast missile attack boat

**Norrköping** 1973, 190 tons, 65 km/h,
**Nynäshamn** 1-5.7 cm, 6 TT, 8 RBS 15 SSM
**Norrtälje**
**Varberg**
**Västerås**
**Västervik**
**Umeå**
**Piteå**
**Luleå**
**Halmstad**
**Strömstad**
**Ystad**

182

369

From 1971, the Saab AJ37 Viggen (Thor's Thunderbolt) began replacing A32s in the 1. Flygeskadern. They were followed by 26 SH37s, which replaced S32Cs in the maritime reconnaissance role from 1975, and were also capable of attack missions. In 1977-80, the photo reconnaissance S35Es gave way to 26 SF37s. The final model to be delivered was the interceptor JA37, 149 of which retired most of the J35s from 1980-90. However, one wing (F10) retained Drakens, which were updated to the J35J configuration until sufficient JAS39s arrive to replace them by the end of the century. F15 received 18 Sk37s to act as an operational conversion unit. From 1991-3, 115 older AJ, SF and SH models were rebuilt with modern equipment, emerging as the all-purpose AJS37.

**Swedish Air Force**

**1. Flygeskadern** - Göteborg
  Flygflottilj 6 - Karlsborg
    **30 Saab AJS37**
  Flygflottilj 7 - Satenås
    **45 Saab AJS37**
  Flygflottilj 15 - Söderhamn (OCU)
    **18 Saab Sk37**
**Militärområdet Övre Norrland** - Luleå
  Flygflottilj 21 - Luleå
    **30 Saab JA37**
    **15 Saab AJS37**
**Militärområdet Norra** - Östersund
  Flygflottilj 2 - Hagernås (Stockholm)
    1 light attack division
      **Saab A60**
    4 light attack (school) divisioner
      **Saab Sk60**
  Flygflottilj 4 - Östersund
    **30 Saab JA37**
**Militärområdet Östra** - Vasterås
  Flygflottilj 1 - Vasterås
    **30 Saab JA37**
  Flygflottilj 13 - Norrköping
    **15 Saab JA37**
    **15 Saab AJS37**
**Militärområdet Södra** - Ängelholm
  Flygflottilj 10 - Ängelholm
    **45 Saab J35J**
  Flygflottilj 17 - Ronneby
    **15 Saab JA37**
    **15 Saab AJS37**

1 electronic countermeasures unit
    **2 Sud-Est SE.210 Caravelle**
2 transport divisioner
    **3 Lockheed C-130E,H,**
    **6 Douglas C-47, 2 Metro III,**
    **3 Beech King Air 200**
5 liaison divisioner
    **16 Saab Sk60E, 5 Saab Sk61, Sk50**
8 SAR helicopter groups (3-4 aircraft)
    **10 Boeing Vertol Hkp4B,**
    **3 M-B-B Hkp9B** (BO105 CBS)
    **10 Super Puma**
2 utility helicopter groups (4 aircraft)
    **6 Agusta-Bell Hkp3, 2 Super Puma**
6 air defense divisioner
    **RB77 SAMs** (Improved Hawk)

**Saab AJ, JA, SF, SH, AJS37 Viggen**
1969, 11 m span, 2125 km/h (2.2), 1000 km,
19000 m SC, 1-2-30 mm,
2 Falcon AAM or other W

**Saab JAS39 Gripen**
1987, 8 m span, km/h ( ), km,
m SC, 1-27 mm,
5 Skyflash or Sidewinder AAM or
Maverick ASM

370

Armament of the new fighter varied with the mission. The initial AJ37 attack plane normally carried Bofors 135 mm rockets or 16 bombs for ground attack, with 2-4 RB24 (Sidewinder) AAMs for encounters with enemy aircraft. However, against large ground targets the RB05A homing or RB75 (Hughes Maverick) television-guided SSMs could be carried. The SF37 reconnaissance plane carried cameras and radar, with 2 RB24 AAMs for defense. The SH37 maritime reconnaissance model had a secondary ship attack mission, carrying RB04E or RB05A homing SSMs. It, too, carried two RB24s for self defense. The JA37 interceptor was a more powerful aircraft and carried the excellent Oerlikon KCA 30 mm cannon, as well as RB24 (Sidewinder), RB28 (Falcon) or BAe Skyflash AAMs. The Saab 37 has proven to be remarkably versatile.

The advent of the all-purpose Viggen permitted a further reduction in the number of *Flygvapnet* wings. Each of the Army's main military areas is protected by wings of interceptors and reconnaissance aircraft. Only the ground attack AJ37s of the 1. Flygeskadern operate in an independent wing.

If all Drakens and Viggens are to be retired by the end of the century, from 340-350 of the new Saab JAS39 Gripens (Griffons) are needed to equip 21-23 surviving *divisioner*. The first thirty were scheduled for delivery in 1993, but were held up by various development problems, including a crash by the only prototype. They are the smallest of the world's fourth-generation fighters, made possible because they will carry no iron bombs, only missiles. Of cropped-delta configuration, they will probably be the last combat aircraft of Swedish design.

The *Svenska Aeroplan Aktiebolaget* has produced aircraft of high quality for decades. However, rapid escalation in electronic complexity and cost of production, together with the use of exotic materials, has pushed the engineering and production requirements for combat aircraft beyond the capabilities of a small nation. Sweden will be forced to either buy future fighters from the large manufacturing nations or, as have several other European nations, join a consortium to develop her future aerial weapons.

371

Västergötland - Creature of the Deep

Sweden's once-powerful Navy has been reduced to a small force of submarines and fast missile boats. The *Halland* alone remains of the numerous destroyers, as the flagship of the fleet. The principal striking force consists of a dozen modern submarines.

sub

**Gotland Uppland** 1996-8, 1270 tons,
**Halland**

sub

sub

**Västergotland** 1987-90, 1087 tons, 20/37 km/h,
**Södermanland** 6 TT, 22 mines
**Hälsingland**
**Östergotland**

**Näcken** 1980, 1031 tons, 22/37 km/h,
**Neptun** 6 TT
**Najad**

Naval aircraft consist mainly of helicopters operating from shore bases with a couple of fixed-wing planes in anti-submarine warfare.

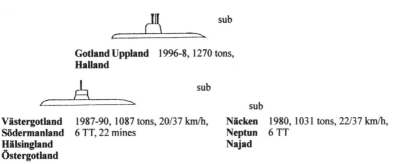

2 ASW helicopter squadrons
   **14 Boeing Vertol Hkp4C**
1 liaison helicopter squadron
   **9 Agusta-Bell Hkp6**
1 ASW flight
   **1-2 C-212 Aviocar**
1 liaison flight
   **2 Piper Navajo**

**C.A.S.A. 212 Aviocar**
1971, 19 m span, 400 km/h, 720 km,
7500 m SC, 21 troops, 2000 kg C

After it was revealed that a number of Soviet submarines were skulking in Swedish territorial waters, the Navy strengthened its anti-submarine defenses. Late in the 1980s, two *amfibiebatalionen* (AMFBAT) were formed to deal with intrusions among the skerries. Four more organized from the obsolete coast artillery units.

AMPHIBIOUS BATTALION - 800 men

1 amphibian company
1 mortar company
2 coastal ranger companies
   3 rifle platoons
   1 recoilless rifle platoon
   1 small arms platoon
1 support company
   1 reconnaissance platoon
   3 diver platoons
   1 supply platoon
35 *Stridsbåt 90*, 13 *Stridsbåt 90E*,
   4 *Trossbåt*, 45 smaller

Sweden's defense problems were greatly eased with the disintegration of the Soviet Union into many smaller states. She is once again surrounded by buffer states. Thus, the fiscally-necessary reduction in the Swedish armed forces fortunately occurred as potential enemies lost their strength.

Northern Europe in 1995

373

| | | |
|---|---|---|
| J1 - 1 D.III, 30 D.II, Phönix | B1,2 - 5, Fiat | Strv m/21-29 - 12 |
| J2 - 10, Nieuport-Delage | B3 - 40, Junkers, 16 licence | Strv m/37 - 48 |
| J3 - 14, Fokker | B4 - 3, Hawker, 42 licence | Strv m/38 - 16 |
| J4 - 6, Heinkel | B5 - 7, Douglas, 102 licence | Strv m/39 - 20 |
| J5 - undeveloped project | B6 - 52, Seversky | Strv m/40 - 100 L, 80 K |
| J6 - 17, ASJA | B7 - 18, Fokker, 77 option | Strv m/41 - 116 SI, 104 SII |
| J7 - 11, Bristol | B8 - redesignated B17 | Strv m/42 - 57 EH, 100 TV, |
| J8 - 55, Gloster | B16 - 82, Caproni | 115 TH |
| J9 - 60, 120 ordered, Seversky | B17 - 55B, 77C, 77A, Saab | Strv 74 - 100 V, 115 H |
| J10 - 144 ordered, Vultee | B18 - 60A, 120B, Saab | Strv 81 - 80 Mk.3, 160 Mk.5 |
| J11 - 72, Fiat | | Strv 101 - 110 Mk.10 |
| J12 - redesignated J20 | S1 - 16, Casper, licence | Strv 102 - 240, conv. Strv 81 |
| J19 - undeveloped project | S2,3,4 - 13, Heinkel | Strv 103 - 335 B |
| J21A - 298, Saab | S5 - 26, Heinkel | |
| J21R - 60, conv, Saab | S6 - 77, Fokker, 35 licence | Ikv 72 - 38 |
| J22 - 202, FFVS | S7 - version of B4 | Ikv 73 - 65, conv Strv m/42 |
| J23, 24 - undeveloped projects | S8 - undeveloped project | Ikv 91 - 200 |
| J26 - 135, North American | S9 - 6, Hawker | Ikv 102 - 38, conv Ikv 72 |
| J27 - undeveloped project | S10 - 12 ordered, Breguet | Ikv 103 - 65 |
| J28 - 70 A, 120 B, De Havilland | S11 - 12 ordered, Dornier | |
| J29 - 60A, 60D, 360 F, Saab | S12 - 12, 27 ord, Heinkel | Sav m/43 - 36, 18 conv m/41 |
| J30 - 60, De Havilland | S13 - version of B7 | Pvkv m/43 - 87 |
| J32 - 135 B, Saab | S14 - 26, Fieseler | Lvkv fm/43 - 17 |
| J33 - 60, De Havilland | S15 - redesignated S17 | Lvrb 701, Pvrbbv 551 - 94 |
| J34 - 120, Hawker | S16 - version of B16 | |
| J35 - 180 A,B, 180 D, 240 F, Saab | S17 - 21 B, 37 BS, Saab | Pb m/31 - 30 |
| JA37 - 110, Saab | S18 - version of B18 | Pb m/39 - 15, confiscated |
| JAS39 - 140 ordered, Saab | S26 - 36, conv J26 | Pb m/40 - 30 |
| | S29C - 60, Saab | |
| A1, E1 - 30-40, Phönix | S31 - 36, conv Supermarine | Tgbl m/42 - 262 SKPF, |
| A21A - 90, Saab | S32 - 60, Saab | ca.250 VKPF |
| A21R - 60, conv J21R, Saab | S35E - 42, Saab | Pbv 301 - 220, conv m/41 |
| A29B - 60, Saab | SF37 - 26, Saab | |
| A32A - 240, Saab | SH37 - 26, Saab | Pbv 302 - 700 |
| AJ37 - 110, Saab | | |
| AJS37 - 115, conv AJ,SF,SH | T1 - 2, Heinkel | |
| A60 - 20, Saab | T2 - 12, Heinkel | |
| | T18B - 62, Saab | |
| Hkp1 - 9, Vertol | | |
| Hkp2 - 22, Sud-Est | Fpl51 - 18, Piper | |
| Hkp3 - 22, Agusta-Bell | Fpl53 - 5, Dornier | |
| Hkp4 - 13, Boeing-Vertol | Fpl54 - 3, MFI | |
| Hkp5 - Hughes | | |
| Hkp6 - 10, Agusta-Bell | Sk16 - North American | |
| Hkp7 - 7, Kawasaki-Vertol | Sk28 - conv De Havilland | |
| Hkp8 - | Sk29 - conv Saab | |
| Hkp9 - 3, M-B-B | Sk34 - conv Saab | |
| | Sk37 - 18, Saab | |
| | Sk50 - 80, Saab | |
| | Sk60 - 130, Saab | |
| | Sk61 - 78, Scottish Aviation | |

The number of Swedish manufacturers was small. Landsverk made armored vehicles. Bofors, in Karlskrona, manufactured artillery, armored vehicles, missiles and ammunition. Volvo produced jet engines and Bolinder Munktell tracked vehicles. Hagglunds, with plants in Mellansel and Ornskoldavik, was the leading manufacturer of armored vehicles after the Second World War. The Forenade Fabriksverken (FFV) made small arms, anti-tank weapons, missiles and ammunition at Eskilstuna. Most aircraft, many missiles, and various ground vehicles were made in Linköping, Jonköping and Sodertälje by Saab-Scania. A.B. Malmö Flygindustri (MFI) at Malmö makes light aircraft. Postwar, the Swedish manufacturers have enjoyed the benefits of cheap nuclear power.

# FINLAND

The origin of the modern inhabitants of Finland differs from that of other Scandinavians, giving some status to arguments against regarding them as true Scandinavians. Regardless, they have often participated in most Scandinavian events and thus warrant inclusion in this discussion.

During the latest major glaciation, Eastern Europe was not covered by ice because of its meagre precipitation. However, the extreme cold limited vegetative growth to such an extent, and the streams and lakes were so greatly reduced, that the area proved uninhabitable. When the climate moderated around **7000 B.C.**, bands of nomads followed herds of reindeer northward across the vast plains stretching westward from the Ural Mountains. Among the tribes leading the advance was a hardy race, short of stature and with greyish eyes set in round heads. Thriving in the harsh environment of northern Europe, they learned to domesticate the reindeer that provided food, tools and clothing. Settling in the tundra and forests adjacent to the Arctic Ocean, they became known to their neighbors as Finns and Ugrians.

Many of the Finno-Ugrian tribes remained nomads but, from the 1st Century A.D., some tribes moved into more stable environments and developed individual civilizations. When the Huns began pressing westward from North Asia, they drove the Slavs before them into East Europe. Around **500 A.D.**, the less organized Finns were forced out of their territory. Two Ugrian-speaking tribes, the Bulgars and Magyars, moved to the banks of the Danube. The Lapps, Finns, Esths, Livs, Karelians and related tribes moved northwestwards to the Baltic and settled into a stable agricultural lifestyle, although the Lapps continued their wanderings along the Arctic coast. [183]

The Finns had the misfortune of settling a homeland between two peoples who later developed into nations desiring empires. As a result, they were often involved in conflicts not of their own choosing. To the west, the Svear tribe had begun to expand eastward along the Baltic waterways to trade through Russia to the Arabs. As traders plied the gulfs, they established settlements along the coasts. Swedish Vikings increased the incursions, eventually resulting in a large element of Swedish descendants among the Finns. Because of their more advanced civilization, the Swedes gained control of the Finnish economy and government. Nevertheless, the two peoples generally lived together peacefully.

As the Finns sought to expand eastward into Karelia, there was conflict with Russia during the 14th-16th Centuries, many Finnish settlements being wiped out by Russian raids. A buffer was finally formed in 1617 when Ingria was ceded to Sweden, excluding Russia from the Baltic.

During the Thirty Years War, Finnish regiments were recruited into the Swedish Army. By 1636, there were:

Wunsch, Wrangel and Ekholt Horse Regiments
Vyborg, Wrangel, Essen, Grass, Horn and Bürtz Infantry Regiments

The campaigns through Germany decimated the Finnish regiments, just as they did the original Swedish regiments that accompanied Gustavus Adolphus across the Baltic. But Finland's fate was now tied inexorably to the ventures of Swedish kings. When Charles XII set out in **1700** to enlarge his empire, Finnish troops marched with him:

Rehbinder Cavalry and Knorring Dragoon Regiments
Tiesenhausen, Lode and Gyllenström Infantry Regiments

Russia desired open water access to the trade of Western Europe, and protection for its "Eye on the West", St. Petersburg (later Leningrad). At the decisive Battle of Poltava, Peter the Great destroyed Charles XII. Again, the Finnish regiments were lost. Finland was overrun in 1713, Russian troops plundering the countryside and thousands of Finns being sent into captivity in Russia. Few ever returned. Finland's prewar population of 400,000 had decreased to 300,000. In addition, her buffer disappeared when Ingria, Estonia and Livonia were ceded to Russia. [184]

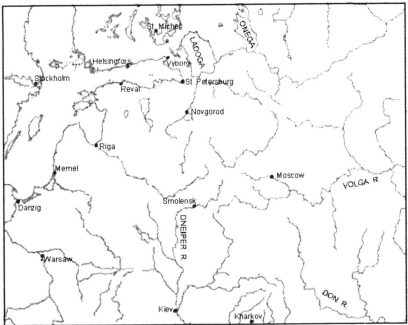

Finland - 18th-19th Centuries

376

Poltava was the watershed between two empires, the Swedish declining, the Russian ascending. Therein lay danger for Finland. Sweden had used Finland as a buffer state between it and the massive Russian Empire. She was about to become the battleground of the two powers. Yielding to greed, Swedish King Gustav III took advantage of Russia's war against Turkey to march on St. Petersburg in **July 1788**. The fiesty Russian czarina, Catherine the Great, moved quickly to block his advance. The war turned into minor naval scraps along the coast. Afraid their country would be partitioned between the two antagonists, some Finnish officers formed the Anjala League to promote separation from Sweden and formation of an independent Finland under Russian protection. Gustav III's execution of some of the officers resulted in his assassination, ending the war.

Although Finland was little affected by Gustav III's war, disaster accompanied that of Gustav IV. When the Russians crossed the Kymene River in **February 1808**, most of the troops available to the Swedish Army were Finnish:

Karelen Dragoon Regiment
Nyland, Savolaks, Österbotten, Björneborg, Tavastehus and
Åbo Infantry Regiments
Tavastehus Jägarebataljon

The Swedish generals were not prepared to face the invasion and General Klingspor ordered the Finnish regiments to withdraw along the coast while the dragoons attempted to hold the swarms of Cossacks at bay. The Swedes concentrated at Tammerfors, under General Adlercreutz. There the Björneborg and Tavastehus Regiments were attacked by the Russian troops of General Bagration and forced back to the coast near Vasa. At St. Michel, General Cronstedt had led the Savolaks Regiment in stopping a flanking movement by General Tuchkov's troops, who were trying to cut off the retirement. In mid-April, a counterattack by the Nylands and Björneborg Regiments stopped the Russian pursuit and they drew back to Kuopio. Klingspor did not pursue and, by the end of August, the Russians were ready to renew the offensive. The Savolaks Regiment, under General Adlercreutz, had been sent ahead as an advance guard and struck the Russians east of Vasa. With the time gained, the Björneborg and Österbotten Regiments prepared the main Swedish position. However, the regiments had been depleted by constant fighting and now had only 5,000 men between them. The Russians overwhelmed the stubborn defenders, who retreated to Vasa. The enemy formed a ring around the city, but Klingspor negotiated a truce on 17 September. After a brief period of renewed fighting, an armistice was agreed upon in November and General Klercker then retired to Tornio, far to the north near the Swedish border. The Finnish troops disbanded to begin guerrilla warfare. [185]

Even before an armistice was signed, on **29 March 1809** Finland was declared part of the Russian Empire as a Grand Duchy. For the first time, the border with Sweden was defined. Her regiments, trained in Swedish traditions, were disbanded. However, the continuing war against Napoleon led the Czar to allow Finnish volunteers to form three regiments of light infantry in 1812.

Throughout the century, the strength of the Finnish armed forces fluctuated with the diplomatic situation. Within the Russian Army, 8 Finnish regiments and 3 jager battalions were maintained. Finnish troops took part in crushing the Polish Uprising in 1830-1 and the Russo-Turkish War of 1877-8. Although the Russian Army was responsible for Finland's defense, a general conscription law passed in 1878 provided a force of 6,000 men for local defense. Rifle battalions were formed in 1881 to carry out the training specified by the new law. Reserves were trained within local companies.

By **1900**, Finland had an army of 8 provincial battalions, a regiment of dragoons, and the Finnish Guard, all commanded by a Governor-General answering to the Czar. Each military province contained 4 reserve companies. The uprisings throughout the Russian Empire after the fiasco of the Russo-Japanese War brought repressive measures from the alarmed Czar. The army of the Grand Duchy of Finland was abolished and a policy of "Russification" initiated to submerge minority traditions within the realm. Finland was still part of Russia, but had independent armed forces:

Finland Division (rifles)
1 independent rifle brigade

An Activist Opposition party had formed in 1904 and, a year later, began running guns to separtists. However, they could not deliver nearly enough arms for a revolt. When the Great War broke out in **August 1914**, the Activists petitioned Sweden for a union between the two states. Determined on neutrality, Sweden refused. Finland then turned to Germany, making arrangements to train cadets near Hamburg. In May 1916, the volunteers were organized into the 27. Royal Prussian Jäger Battalion, which eventually served 2,000 men. Against the original agreement, it was sent to the Eastern Front where it fought as the northernmost unit, on the Gulf of Riga, from June-August 1916. The protesting volunteers were withdrawn to Libau in December, then dismissed to Finland in 1918. Underground units sprang up all over Finland.

## *War of Independence* - 1917-1918

Finland had no military forces when it took advantage of the revolution in Russia to declare independence on **6 December 1917**. There were more than 40,000 Russian troops in the country, and Finns had received no training in modern military operations since their army was disbanded. Despite opposition from leftists, the new Finnish government reestablished an army on 7 January 1918 to prepare for independence. Trained Finns were ready to fill its ranks, for 2,000 volunteers had gone to Germany in 1915, when it appeared that Russia would be defeated in the Great War. In the homeland, the Civic Guards were formed as a home guard. But arms and officers from the jäger battalion did not arrive from Germany until the autumn of 1917, for the Germans had broken their agreement and sent the Finns to the front. General Lieutenant C.G. Mannerheim was appointed commander-in-chief of the Civic Guards on 16 January 1918, and ordered to restore order, then remove the Russian forces from Finland. However, when he began operations against the Russians, the numerous members of the leftist Social Democrat party rose in revolt. The war for independence became a civil war between "Red Guards" and "White Guards", in which the Russian troops took no part. The government invoked the 1878 conscription law to garner enough troops to prosecute the war. The officers and non-commissioned officers of the White Guards came from the Jägers in Germany. Mannerheim formed his general staff with a mixture of officers from the old Finnish army, some returned from the Czarist army, and a few volunteers from the Swedish general staff. A Swedish volunteer brigade also aided the White Guards. German troops did not arrive until April 1918.

Meanwhile, with the aid of Soviet agents, the Bolsheviks had gained control of the Central Revolutionary Council and went into action on 28 January. At the time, the government of Prime Minister P.E. Svinhufvud had no organized army. Although the Volunteer Defense Corps came under his control on 25 January as the *Suojeluskuntajärjestö* (Civic Guards), they were not prepared when the Reds attacked. The Red Guards eventually grew to 100,000 men, supported by Soviet artillery. Mannerheim followed the government to Vasa, which became the provisional capital, and began to organize an army. With the aid of local militia, he launched an offensive into central and northern Finland on **27 January 1918**, overrunning Österbotten within 4 days and capturing 5,000 Red Guards. [186]

The first aircraft reached the Finnish camp late in February 1918. A second that arrived in March displayed a blue swastika as the personal insignia of the pilot. The Finns adopted the insignia along with the aircraft. A number of local air units were formed, possessing 15 aircraft:

Turun lentoasema - Turku
Hermannin lentoasema - Helsinki
Koiviston lentoasema - Koivisto (Primorsk)
Kenttä lentoasema I - Sortavala
Lappeenrannan lentoasema - Lappeenranta
Utin lentoasema - Utti

The *Ilmailuvoimat* appeared on 6 March and Flying Divisions 1 and 2 were formed near Tampere and Viipuri, respectively. Equipment included the Thulin D, Albatros B.II and C.III, DFW C.V, Rumpler C.VIII, together with captured Russian types such as the Nieuport 11, 16, 23 and Spad S.7 fighters and Shchetinin M5, M9, M15 and M16 flying boats. Including trainers, the *Ilmailuvoimat* flew 47 planes. The operational units flew a few bombing and reconnaissance sorties which had little effect on the outcome of the war.

After securing northern Finland, Mannerheim advanced southward with 70,000 men armed with 154,000 rifles, 300 machineguns and 40 light guns, mostly of Russian origin:

12 Civic Guards regiments
2 grenadier regiments
6 light infantry regiments (conscripts)

1 cavalry regiment
1 dragoon regiment

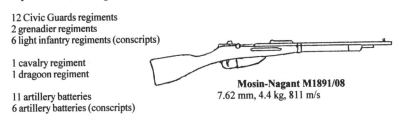

**Mosin-Nagant M1891/08**
7.62 mm, 4.4 kg, 811 m/s

11 artillery batteries
6 artillery batteries (conscripts)

6 signal units

Mannerheim opposed an agreement reached between his government and the German government to send an expeditionary force, believing that he had enough strength to eject the Reds without German help. Nevertheless, 9,500 German troops under General von der Goltz landed at Hanko on 3-5 April, with 2,500 more placed ashore east of Helsinki two days later to cut off the Red troops in the future capital. As the Finns had already won the main battle at Tampere on 6 April, Helsinki was occupied by the Germans a week later against weak opposition, creating a false impression that they had won the war for Finland. The Finns entered Viipuri at the end of the month and the last Red Guards were pushed out of the Karelian Isthmus on 15 May.

Disapproving of the inordinate influence applied by the late-arriving German division on postwar reorganization of the Finnish Army, Mannerheim resigned in May 1918.  German officers proceeded to organize the new army.  In the chaos rapidly sweeping over Europe as the Great War came to a close, the Finns decided they wanted a stable monarchy, in the fashion of other Scandinavian countries, and selected Prince Frederick Karl of Hesse as their king.  However, with the collapse of Germany in November 1918, the prince refused the crown and a republican constitution was adopted in July 1919.  A monarchist, Premier Svinhufvud resigned and General Mannerheim was chosen as "Protector", resuming command of the Army also.

The Germans had left Finland in December and Mannerheim was able to parley his opposition to them into support by the victorious Allies, who also gave diplomatic recognition to the new state in May 1919.  A new legislature was elected in March.  It appointed Kaarlo Ståhlberg as permanent president.

When the new government was formed in 1919, the President became the Commander-in-Chief of the armed forces.  German advisors had trained the airmen until the Great War ended.  A French mission arrived in 1919 to continue the training.  From August-December 1918, the remaining aircraft were reorganized into:

    Lento-osasto 1 - Sortavala
    Lento-osasto 2 - Helsinki
    Lento-osasto 3 - Utti
    Lento-osasto 4 - Koivisto
    Lento-osasto 5 - Turku

Mobilization was a problem as Finland was sparsely settled and considerable time would be required to concentrate the reserves.  With a great power across the border, it was imperative that mobilization occur rapidly.  At first, the plan instituted by the German officers in 1919 was used, whereby 3 standing infantry divisions and a light brigade would be augmented to 6 divisions, 2 brigades and other units.  A defensive stance was adopted in 1919.  However, when it became apparent that the new Soviet state was very weak, militarily, an active operational plan was adopted late in the 1920s.

The Treaty of Dorpat on **14 October 1920** established boundaries with the Soviet Union.  The Civic Guard was separated from the army in 1921 and placed directly under the President.  New conscription laws of 1919 and 1922 required a period of service of one year for conscripts.  Training was gradually standardized and adapted to Finnish conditions.  The Civic Guards were still the largest military force, but a regular army was also organized:

**Field Army** - 36,600 men

3 infantry divisions
    **Mosin-Nagant M1891/08 rifle**
    **Madsen lmg, Maxim M.09 hmg**
    **Putilov M.02 76 mm field gun**
1 independent rifle brigade
1 cavalry brigade
1 technical division
    **32 Renault M.17FT**
    aircraft, engineers, signals, train
**Civic Guards** - 100,000 men

Weapons for the new Finnish Army were mainly those left over from the War of Independence. The Russian Mosin-Nagant M/1891 was the principal rifle. Also originating in Russia was the Maxim M.1909 machinegun, although the Madsen light machinegun was also used. The Russian Putilov M.02 76 mm field gun was a good artillery weapon. Thirty-two surplus Renault M.17 light tanks arrived from France in August to equip the Tank Regiment established on 15 July 1919 at Helsinki. Fourteen were armed with short 37 mm guns, with machineguns mounted in the other 18.

The White Guards had worn whatever they could get their hands on during the Independence War, but continuing efforts were made after the war to obtain uniform clothing. The first decisions were standardized in regulations of 1922. A neat light gray tunic was combined with dark gray trousers tucked into black knee boots. The shape of the dark gray cuff, along with the piping color on the shoulder straps designated branch of service and regiment. Rank was indicated on the shoulder straps.

In an atmosphere of unrest that could spill over into Finland, the Air Force was reorganized on 1 April 1921 (ILs 2 moved to Viipuri on 24 Aug):

Ilmailuosasto 1 - Utti
  **20 Gourdou-Leseurre G.L.21** (from 1923)
  **19 Breguet 14A.2**
Ilmailuosasto 2 - Koivisto
  **19 Breguet 14A.2**
Ilmailuosasto 3 - Sortavala
  **12 Georges Levy Type R** (1919)
  **IVL A.22** (from 1923)

**Breguet 14A.2**
1916, 15 m span, 177 km/h, 2½ hrs, 5800 m SC, 3 mgs, 32 (255) kg B

**Georges Levy Type R**
1919, 19 m span, 142 km/h, 435 km, 22/2000 m, 3500 m SC, 1 mg, 250 kg B

**Gourdou-Leseurre GL.21**
1923, 9 m span, 230 km/h, 480 km, 7500 m SC, 2 mgs

In 1920, the *Ilmailuvoimen Lentokonetehdas* (Aviation Force Aircraft Factory) was established. Initially, it built 120 Hansa-Brandenburg W.33s under licence in 1922 as the IVL A.22. The next year, Finland purchased 20 Gourdou-Leseurre GL 21 fighters, 38 Breguet 14A.2s reconnaissance-bombers and 12 Georges Levy Type R flying boats through the French mission. Another reorganization of 1 March 1924 reflected the mixed equipment of the air units with the designation "eskaaderi":

Hävittäjäeskaaderi - Utti
  Hävittäjädustelulaivue
    **20 Gourdou-Leseurre G.L.21**
  Maatiedustelulaivue
    **19 Breguet 14A.2**
Pommituseskaaderi - Viipuri
    **19 Breguet 14A.2**
Meritiedustelulaivue 2 - Sortavala
    **20 IVL A.22**

381

The Navy of 1924 consisted of vessels left behind by the Russians. The patrol boats *Karjala* and *Turunmaa* were sister vessels of the Polish *Haller* class. *Matti Kurki* and *Klas Horn* were much older vessels of the same type. The torpedo boats *S1, 2* and *5* and the minelayers, *Uusimaa* and *Hameenmaa*, were also Russian. No new vessels were added until the next decade. During 1924, a British mission arrived and recommended reequipping the air force with floatplanes to make use of the country's lakes. Neither Germany nor the Soviet Union possessed appreciable numbers of fighters or bombers at the time. The principal need was for aircraft capable of operating anywhere within a country with undeveloped aerial facilities. The Air Force was reorganized on **1 April 1926** with the new equipment (formation of the 3. EMLLv was delayed until 15 April 1927):

Maalentoeskaaderi - Utti
   **20 Gourdou-Leseurre G.L. 21** (1923)
   **12 Koolhoven FK.31** (1926)
1. Erillinen Merilentolaivue - Viipuri
   **IVL A.22**
2. Erillinen Merilentolaivue - Sortavala
   **IVL A.22**
3. Erillinen Merilentolaivue - Turkinsaari
   **IVL A.22**
4. Erillinen Merilentolaivue - Suur-Merijoki
   **8 Aero A.11** (1927)
   **16 Aero A.32** (1928)

**I.V.L. A.22**
1918, 16 m span, 171 km/h, 4 hrs,
13/1980 m, 2-3 mgs
(licence-built Hansa-Brandenburg W.33)

**Aero A.11**
1923, 13 m span, 214 km/h, 750 km,
7200 m SC, 3 mgs, light B

**Aero A.32**
1928, 13 m span, 225 km/h, 800 km,
5490 m SC, 4 mgs, 120 kg B       187

In 1925, the general staff and army staff were combined in a Command Staff of the Defense Forces. A Defense Council was set up to advise the President. It grew in importance when Mannerheim became its president in 1931, for President Svinhufvud stated he would delegate his position as commander-in-chief to Mannerheim in the event of war. The Civic Guards were attached to the armed forces in 1928. Large-scale maneuvers began in 1928, but the officers gained insufficient experience in handling large units.

During the decade, the political situation deteriorated. The squabbles of the five major political parties produced a new government nearly every year. The Communists were allowed complete freedom until they organized a revolutionary demonstration on 1 August 1929. Continued agitation as the international economic situation worsened led to a ban after the elections of October 1930. Agitation ended when prosperity returned in 1933.

Some Finns who opposed the Communists advocated a government along Fascist lines, but they were never able to garner more than 10% of the vote. Later, some Western media claimed that Finland had fallen under fascism. However, relations were always strained with the Nazi regime, although they had been friendly with the preceding Weimar Republic. It was the Soviet Union that became the target of Finnish antagonism because of its refusal to allow Eastern Karelia, with a strong population of Finns, to join their brethren to the west. Although a non-aggression treaty was signed between them in 1932, and renewed for ten years in 1934, both knew it was a meaningless piece of paper.

The original mobilization scheme had been developed by German officers after the War of Independence and was based on German conditions - dense population and a highly-developed communications net. In Finland, it would have resulted in a slow mobilization with the mobilized units widely scattered and susceptible to enemy attack. The vital Karelian Isthmus would have been left virtually undefended. Because of the small size of Finnish forces, a defensive posture was prescribed.

Instituted on **1 May 1934**, a new regional mobilization plan provided for a standing army (termed the Army Corps) garrisoned in the Isthmus, with each of the thirty military districts (31 from 1938) expected to provide an infantry regiment and an artillery battalion. The units of the four districts on the eastern border would become Frontier Guards while those in the Karelian Isthmus would come immediately under control of the Army Corps. The total mobilized army would contain 315,000 men (9% of the population), 45,000 horses and 4,500 motor vehicles. By 1935, the Finnish Army possessed:

**Finnish Army Corps**

1. Infantry Division - Helsinki
   **1 tank company**
       16 Renault M.17
2. Infantry Division - Viipuri
3. Infantry Division - Mikkeli

1. Cavalry Brigade - Lappeenranta
   **1 armored car squadron**
       2 Fiat M.16
   **1 tank company**
       16 Renault M.17

**Fiat M.16**
1916, 4.2 tons, 3 mgs,
68/6 km/h, 100 km, 6 mm, 6 men

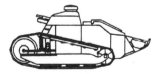

**Renault M.17F.T.**
1917, 6.8 tons, 1-37 mm or 1 mg,
8 km/h, 60 km, 22/15 mm,
15 mm/500 m P, 2 men

Finnish-built weapons finally replaced the old equipment after this reorganization. The M.39 rifle (an improved Mosin-Nagant) and Lahti-Saloranta light machinegun reequipped the infantry companies, along with mortars. Production of artillery in Finnish factories had barely begun when war again broke out in Europe.

## INFANTRY DIVISION

2 cyclist battalions
  3 cyclist companies
  1 machinegun company
3 infantry regiments
  2 infantry battalions
   3 rifle companies
   1 machinegun company
1 field artillery regiment (2 in 1.Div.)
  3 light batteries
1 engineer battalion (3. Div.)
1 anti-aircraft artillery regiment (2. Div.)

## CAVALRY BRIGADE

1 mounted rifle battalion
  3 cyclist companies
  1 machinegun company
2 cavalry regiments (3 in 1920)
  4 saber squadrons
  1 machinegun squadron
1 horse artillery battery
1 engineer company
attached armor      188

In wartime, the army was to be expanded to 3 army corps staffs commanding 9 divisions, 4 independent brigades, 1 cavalry brigade, 38 field artillery battalions, 7 bicycle battalions, 15 independent battalions, and various other companies. The Frontier Guard and the Coast Guard were administered by the Ministry of the Interior for guarding the nation's borders. The Frontier Guard had five units, each of several companies, deployed along the eastern border. The Coast Guard was organized into three districts - Gulf of Finland, Gulf of Bothnia and the Åland Islands.

As more information of Soviet armed forces was gained, it became obvious that they were weak. However, the overwhelming success of the mechanized German forces in Poland forced the Finns to readopt a defensive policy in the face of known heavy Russian mechanization. A counterattack option was rejected and Mannerheim stressed stubborn fighting on the frontiers.

The Finns had taken British advice to equip their air force with seaplanes, well adapted to the sparse communications network in Finland and the abundance of lakes within the tangled forests. IVL also began licence-production of the Blackburn Ripon IIF seaplane in 1931 to replace IVL A.22s. Six Junkers K.43s came the same year. Two army cooperation wings were forming, each with a squadron of fighters and one of army cooperation planes.

The Air Force tested Fokker C.Vs in 1927, resulting in the purchase of 13 C.VEs, along with 8 Aero A.11 reconnaissance-bombers. Although 16 Aero A.32 reconnaissance-bombers arrived in 1928, the Aero aircraft apparently were unsatisfactory, for they were soon replaced by Fokker C.Vs, which proved well adapted to the rigorous Finnish climate.

384

Although slow and clumsy, the Blackburn seaplanes gave good service, being sturdy and reliable. The Junkers was a more potent aircraft, therefore deployed in the Isthmus while the Ripons plied more remote areas.

**Blackburn Ripon IIF**
1926, 14 m span, 217 km/h, 725 km,
4000 m SC, 2 mgs, 500 kg B

**Junkers K-43**
1928, 19 m span, 266 km/h, 900 km,
6300 m SC, 3 mgs, 300 kg B

After evaluation of a pair of Gloster Gamecocks, 15 Gamecock IIs were built under licence from 1929-30. Seventeen Bristol Bulldog IVAs followed in 1934. The Gamecocks were agile little wasps but, being 1925 designs, were outmoded by the time they were delivered to the Finns. They had a lower performance than the Fokker army cooperation planes of the period. The situation was remedied by the high-powered model of Bristol Bulldog delivered four years later. Except for its weaker armament, the Bulldog IVA was comparable to the I-15 of the Soviet Air Force. The Air Force was reorganized on **15 July 1933** into Lentoasema (Flight Stations) and Lentolaivue (Flight Squadrons - LLv):

Lentoasema 1 - Utti
    Lentolaivue 10
        trainers
    Lentolaivue 24
        **17 Gloster Gamecock II** (1929)

**Gloster Gamecock II**
1925, 9 m span, 250 km/h, 590 km,
7/3000 m, 6740 m SC, 2 mgs

Lentoasema 2 - Santahamina
    Lentolaivue 36
        **8 Blackburn Ripon IIF**

Lentoasema 3 - Sortavala
    Lentolaivue 38
        **8 Blackburn Ripon IIF**

Lentoasema 4 - Turkinsaari
    Lentolaivue 34
        **8 Blackburn Ripon IIF**

Lentoasema 5 - Suur-Merijoki
    Lentolaivue 12
        **13 Fokker C.VE**
    Lentolaivue 26
        **17 Bristol Bulldog IVA** (1934)

**Fokker C.VE**
1925, 15 m span, 254 km/h, 1200 km,
7500 m SC, 2 mgs, 50 kg B

Lentoasema 6 - Viipuri (Immola from 16 Nov 1936)
    Lentolaivue 44
        **6 Junkers K-43**

**Bristol Bulldog IVA**
1930, 10 m span, 361 km/h,
10200 m SC, 2 mgs

An expansion programme was approved in 1936 as Europe deteriorated. From Britain came 18 Blenheim Is with 4 Fokker C.Xs and 7 Fokker D.21s arriving from the Netherlands in 1937, with licences to build. The reorganization of **1 January 1938** produced Lentorykmentti (Flight Regiments):

Lentorykmentti 1 - Suur-Merijoki
  Lentolaivue 10
    **Fokker C.X**
  Lentolaivue 12
    **Fokker C.X**
  Lentolaivue 14
    **Fokker C.VE, X**
  Lentolaivue 16
    **Blackburn Ripon IIF,**
    **Junkers K.43**

Lentorykmentti 2 - Utti
  Lentolaivue 24
    **Fokker D.21**
  Lentolaivue 26
    **Bristol Bulldog IVA**

Lentorykmentti 3 - Sortavala
  Lentolaivue 38
    **Blackburn Ripon IIF**

Lentorykmentti 4 - Immola
  Lentolaivue 42
    **Bristol Blenheim I**
  Lentolaivue 44
    **Bristol Blenheim I**
  Lentolaivue 46
    **Bristol Blenheim I**

Lentoasema 2 - Santahamina
  Lentolaivue 36
    **Blackburn Ripon IIF**

Lentoasema 4 - Turkinsaari
  Lentolaivue 34
    **Blackburn Ripon IIF** [189]

The new regiments were largely administrative units with homogeneous aircraft types. The First Regiment was responsible for the training and deployment of the army cooperation squadrons, now largely equipped with the ultimate Fokker - the C.X. The Bulldogs were still used by a squadron of the fighter regiment, LR 2, situated strategically to cover both Viipuri and Helsinki. However, the first modern fighters had arrived in the form of Fokker D.21s, which replaced the old Gamecocks. Equally important, the Fourth Regiment had formed with the first truly up-to-date aircraft of the Finnish Air Force. Three squadrons of Bristol Blenheim Is were deployed fifty kilometers north of Viipuri, in position to intervene in the Karelian Isthmus. Four squadrons of seaplanes were still operating from their remote lakes, but they were becoming increasingly vulnerable to modern fighters.

Thus, unlike its Nordic neighbors to the west, Finland was making realistic strides in creating defenses capable of resisting invaders. Fortunately, the first it was to encounter was a bloated, headless monster.

# THE RUSSO-FINNISH WARS

The Soviets had for some time been worried about the proximity of Finnish territory to Leningrad, and what may happen should it fall into enemy hands. They wanted arrangements allowing Soviet troops to enter the Karelian Isthmus, in the event of war, and establish defensive positions well north of Leningrad. They also wished to deny the Gulf of Finland to a hostile fleet by fortifying Hangö and several islands. The Finns would receive territory in Eastern Karelia in exchange. In the spring of 1938, secret meetings took place between Soviet officials and the government of Prime Minister A.K. Cajander. At first, the Soviet Union displayed remarkable restraint in pressing its desires upon tiny Finland. Yet, when the Finns proved obstinate, their patience ran out. The Soviet ambassador left Finland on 6 April 1939, after the final meetings, hinting darkly that the matter had not been settled to Russia's satisfaction.

Strapped by financial woes, and an industrial base only beginning to grow, Finland's defenses were weak. Infantry divisions lacked heavy support:[190]

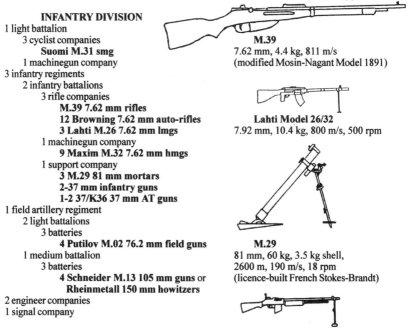

**INFANTRY DIVISION**
1 light battalion
   3 cyclist companies
      **Suomi M.31 smg**
   1 machinegun company
3 infantry regiments
   2 infantry battalions
      3 rifle companies
         **M.39 7.62 mm rifles**
         **12 Browning 7.62 mm auto-rifles**
         **3 Lahti M.26 7.62 mm lmgs**
      1 machinegun company
         **9 Maxim M.32 7.62 mm hmgs**
      1 support company
         **3 M.29 81 mm mortars**
         **2-37 mm infantry guns**
         **1-2 37/K36 37 mm AT guns**
1 field artillery regiment
   2 light battalions
      3 batteries
         **4 Putilov M.02 76.2 mm field guns**
   1 medium battalion
      3 batteries
         **4 Schneider M.13 105 mm guns** or
         **Rheinmetall 150 mm howitzers**
2 engineer companies
1 signal company

**M.39**
7.62 mm, 4.4 kg, 811 m/s
(modified Mosin-Nagant Model 1891)

**Lahti Model 26/32**
7.92 mm, 10.4 kg, 800 m/s, 500 rpm

**M.29**
81 mm, 60 kg, 3.5 kg shell,
2600 m, 190 m/s, 18 rpm
(licence-built French Stokes-Brandt)

**BAR M.1918**
7.92 mm, 9.4 kg, 845 m/s, 500 rpm

**CAVALRY BRIGADE**
1 mounted rifle battalion
2 cavalry regiments
   4 horse squadrons
   1 machinegun squadron
1 horse artillery battery
1 engineer company

**Bofors M35**
37 mm, 388 kg, 0.74 kg shell,
850 m/s, 40 mm/500 m P

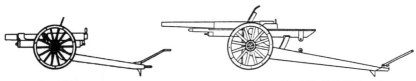

**Putilov M.02**
76.2 mm, 942 kg, 6.5 kg shell,
11040 m, 589 m/s, 10 rpm

**Schneider Mle.1913 105 mm L**
105 mm, 2297 kg, 15.9 kg shell,
11040 m, 545 m/s, 6 rpm

The three peacetime divisions (1.,2.,3.) were broken up to form the nuclei of eight new infantry divisions (4.,5.,6.,8.,10.,11.,12.,13.). The 6.,10. and 11. were later renumbered 2.,3. and 7., respectively. Later, the 1.,9.,21. and 23. Infantry Divisions were added. The eastern frontier was held by 17 para-military Civic Guard battalions and 5 elite Frontier Guard units, all with local personnel accustomed to the terrain and eager to abandon hunting wolves to hunt Russians.

Tanks were organized as the 1.,2.,3. and 4. Independent Tank Companies, totalling 59 Vickers Mk.E and obsolete Renault FT tanks, but only the 4. Company was to see action in the coming Winter War.

As late as 1939, many troops were still wearing the khaki-brown uniform established by the 1927 regulations. In 1936, a new uniform had been authorized and came gradually into use as the campaign went on. It consisted of a light field gray tunic with blue gray trousers. A brown belt was worn, but the boots were black. The gray helmet was originally of the German M.1915 pattern, but by 1944 had been largely replaced by the M.35 model. With the Lapland War of 1944, a new round helmet appeared that persisted into the postwar era.

All ranks displayed their rank insignia on the collar tab, which was red and gold for generals and field officers. For line officers and non-commissioned officers, the tab and piping on the shoulder strap was of branch color (infantry - blue, jägers - gray-green, artillery - crimson, cavalry - yellow, cyclists - orange, armor - black, engineers and signals - purple, air force - bright blue). Officers also displayed gold bars above the cuff and non-commissioned officers duplicated the collar insignia on the shoulder straps.

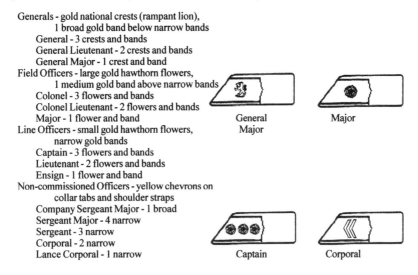

Generals - gold national crests (rampant lion),
　　　1 broad gold band below narrow bands
　General - 3 crests and bands
　General Lieutenant - 2 crests and bands
　General Major - 1 crest and band
Field Officers - large gold hawthorn flowers,
　　　1 medium gold band above narrow bands
　Colonel - 3 flowers and bands
　Colonel Lieutenant - 2 flowers and bands
　Major - 1 flower and band
Line Officers - small gold hawthorn flowers,
　　　narrow gold bands
　Captain - 3 flowers and bands
　Lieutenant - 2 flowers and bands
　Ensign - 1 flower and band
Non-commissioned Officers - yellow chevrons on
　　　collar tabs and shoulder straps
　Company Sergeant Major - 1 broad
　Sergeant Major - 4 narrow
　Sergeant - 3 narrow
　Corporal - 2 narrow
　Lance Corporal - 1 narrow

General
Major

Major

Captain

Corporal

Hitler's invasion of Poland in 1939, and the subsequent declaration of war by the Western Powers, were not thought to be threatening to Finland. However, when the Soviet Union occupied the Baltic States, and Finnish officials were summoned to Moscow for political discussions on 5 October, their trepidations increased. Yet, they persisted in refusing the Soviet demands made during the meetings, which continued from 11 October to 8 November. Although the Finns believed that the Soviet Union would not resort to force, the government mobilized the armed forces.

An Armed Vickers Company Mustered Behind the Firs

Because of the Army's weakness in anti-tank (112 Bofors 37 mm) and anti-aircraft (100 Bofors 40 mm) weapons, Field Marshal Mannerheim decided to eschew offensive operations and urged his soldiers to meet the enemy at the frontiers and fight doggedly. They deployed according to his instructions:

**Finnish Army** (Marshal C.G. Mannerheim) - Mikkeli

**Lapland Group** (Gen.Maj. Wallenius) - Petsamo
    1 infantry battalion
**V. Army Corps** (Gen.Maj. Tuompo) - Salla
    1 infantry battalion - Salla
    2 reserve infantry battalions - Suomussalmi
**IV. Army Corps** (Gen.Maj. Heiskanen, Hagglund shortly) - Joensuu
    12., 13. Infantry Divisions
    Group T (Col. Talvela)

**Army of Karelia** (Gen.Lt. Oesterman) - Viipuri
    **II. Army Corps** (Gen.Lt. Ohquist) - Viipuri
        4., 5., 11. Infantry Divisions
    **III. Army Corps** (Gen.Lt. Heinrichs) - Käkisalmi
        8., 10. Infantry Divisions

**Vickers Mk.E Type B**
1931, 6.9 tons, 1-47 mm, 1 mg,
35 km/h, 161 km/h, 16 mm, 3 men
23 mm/500 m P

General Reserve
    6., 9. Infantry Divisions
    I. Cavalry Brigade (Gen.Maj. Palmroth)
    **I. Tank Battalion**
        1., 2. Tank Companies
            32 Renault M.17 (18 with machineguns)
        3., 4. Tank Companies
            32 Vickers Mk.E Type B (19 with machineguns)

389

The Finns possessed an infantry army. Field Marshal Mannerheim decided to retain his few mobile reserves near Viipuri, behind the Mannerheim Line. Hopelessly obsolete, the Renault tanks were demobilized, with many dug in as machinegun nests in the Mannerheim Line. Thirty-two Vickers Mk.E Type Bs had been ordered, and 16 were received in 1938-9 without armament or optics (16 more were later delivered to the 3. Tank Company). For a parade in 1938, all 37 mm guns had been removed from the Renaults and mounted in 13 of the new tanks. They were still in place when the war began. The rest of the Vickers tanks retained only their machineguns. At full strength, the tank battalion possessed 4 companies, each of 3 platoons of 5 tanks, with an additional tank at company headquarters.

The Finnish air units were dispersed to support various ground units. Only two Finnish fighter and two bomber squadrons were fully operational.

**Finnish Air Force** (Gen.Lt. J.F. Lundqvist)

Lentorykmentti 1 (Col. Opas) - Suur-Merijoki
  Lentolaivue 10 - Lappeenranta
    **12 Fokker C.X** (dive bombers)
  Lentolaivue 12 - Suur-Merijoki (II Corps)
    **13 Fokker C.X**
  Lentolaivue 14 - Laikko (III Corps)
    **7 Fokker C.VE**
    **4 Fokker C.X**
  Lentolaivue 16 - Viipuri (IV Corps)
    **8 Blackburn Ripon IIF** - Värtsilä
    **4 Junkers K.43** - Lahdenpohja
    **3 Fokker C.VD** (Jan. 1940)
Lentorykmentti 2 (Col.Lt. Lorenz) - Utti
  Lentolaivue 24 - Immola
    **36 Fokker D.21**
  Lentolaivue 26 - Raulampi
    **10 Bristol Bulldog IVA**
    **30 Gloster Gladiator II** (Dec. 1939)
    **28 Fiat G.50** (March 1940)
  Lentolaivue 28 (from February 1940) - Sakyla
    **30 Morane-Saulnier M.S.406**
Lentorykmentti 4 (Col.Lt. Somerto) - Immola
  Lentolaivue 42 (from Jan. 1940) - Luonnetjärvi
    **12 Bristol Blenheim I**
  Lentolaivue 44 - Luonnetjärvi
    **8 Bristol Blenheim I**
    **12 Bristol Blenheim IV** (Jan. 1940)
  Lentolaivue 46 - Luonnetjärvi
    **9 Bristol Blenheim I**
    **3 Avro Anson I**

Lentolaivue 36 - Kallvik
  **6 Blackburn Ripon IIF**
  **2 Koolhoven FK-52** (Jan. 1940)
Lentolaivue 39 - Mariehamn, Åland Is.
  **2 Junkers K.43**

**Fokker C.X**
1934, 12 m span, 336 km/h, 840 km,
8100 m SC, 2 mgs, 500 kg B

**Fokker D.21**
1936, 11 m span, 460 km/h, 850 km,
5.9/5000 m, 11000 m SC, 2 mgs, 100 kg B

**Koolhoven F.K.52**

**Gloster Gladiator I,II**
1934, 10 m span, 407 km/h, 692 km,
6/4575 m, 10000 m SC, 4 mgs

**Bristol Blenheim I**
1935, 17 m span, 459 km/h, 1810 km,
8320 m SC, 2 mgs, 454 kg B

**Avro Anson Mk.I**
1935, 17 m span, 303 km/h, 1271 km,
5791 m SC, 2 mgs, 165 kg B

A few old Bristol Bulldog IVAs remained in service, but the principal Finnish fighter at the start of the conflict was the agile, lightly-armed Fokker D.21. Thirty-five Fiat G.50s had been ordered from Italy, but had not yet arrived. The sleek and fast Bristol Blenheim I was the most modern aircraft possessed by the Finns. It became the workhorse of the Winter War, but its weak defensive armament left it progressively more vulnerable as its initial speed advantage was eroded by new Soviet aircraft. One of the leading army cooperation designs of the period, the Fokker C.X had been adapted to Arctic conditions by replacing its standard water-cooled engine with an air-cooled radial. One squadron was trained, and used, as dive bombers. Except for the Fokker dive bombers, which were under GHQ control, the army cooperation aircraft were assigned to specific army corps. In December, four Junkers K.43s were moved to Lake Kemi, the only aircraft in the north. LLv 36 operated in support of the Finnish Navy.

Ominously, Soviet Foreign Minister Molotov declared on 26 November that Finnish artillery had shelled Soviet territory, an obvious ploy to excuse military action. On **30 November 1939**, the Soviets invaded Finland, with the two principal missions of creating a buffer zone around Leningrad and acquiring the vital nickel mines at Petsamo. President Kyösti Kallio immediately relinquished the role of commander-in-chief to Marshal Mannerheim in accordance with prewar plans. The Finns astounded the world by taking on the Russian colossus. Their conviction that they could use their knowledge and expertise within their beloved forests to thwart the invader was not shared by other European military observers. The sheer mass of Soviet armaments was thought to be capable of overcoming their inept command situation. The events of the opening days illustrated their opinions.

Sixteen Finnish cities were bombed in the first few days, but bad weather mercifully restricted full operations by the 800 aircraft initially deployed by the Soviet Air Force. Although they could have struck Finland with similarly daunting numbers of troops, the Soviets advanced on a broad front with forces not much more numerous than their opponents. Apparently they believed that their 2,000 tanks would quickly rout the weakly-armed Finnish infantry army.

Leningrad Military District (Army Commander Meretskov)

Fourteenth Army - on Petsamo
104 Rifle Division
Ninth Army - on Salla and Suomussalmi
44, 54, 122, 163 Rifle Divisions
Eighth Army - on Sortavala
1, 56 Rifle Corps
18, 139, 155, 168 Rifle Divisions
Reserve
56, 75 Rifle Divisions
Seventh Army - into the Karelian Isthmus
19 Rifle Corps - western sector
123, 70, 24 Rifle Divisions
50 Rifle Corps - eastern sector
43, 90, 142 Rifle Divisions
Reserve
10 Tank Corps
13, 20, 50 Tank Brigades
35 Independent Heavy Tank Brigade
40 Independent Medium Tank Brigade
49, 138 Rifle Divisions
1 cavalry division

391

The strongest effort was directed through the Karelian Isthmus between Lake Ladoga and the Gulf of Finland. There, the Finns had built a line of fortifications known as the Mannerheim Line. It was not as formidable as often portrayed, consisting of 140 kilometers of field fortifications with 66 concrete bunkers interspersed, most of which were vulnerable to heavy artillery fire. A zone of lakes and bogs, 20-50 kilometers wide, lay in front of it, channeling the approach of an invader to provide numerous delaying positions and opportunities for vicious crossfire.

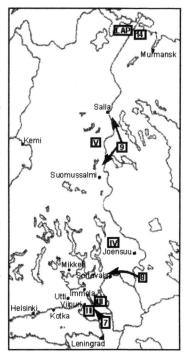

The Fokker C.Vs and C.Xs of LLv 12 and 14 watched the 140,000 men of the Russian 7 Army advance over the border. The Soviet 123 and 138 Rifle Divisions attacked at Summa, the weakest point in the line. Russian tactics revealed the effects of Stalin's purge of most of his senior officers. Attacks were made in clumsy groups of 20-50 tanks. Infantry then moved forward behind the tanks, in successive waves of close-packed battalions of deceptive strength.

During December, fighters of LeR 2 flew cover for the Finnish troops in the Karelian Isthmus, the Fokker D.21s and Bristol Bulldog IVAs shooting down 60 Soviet planes, while losing 9 of their own. As Soviet observation planes were unable to operate, their supporting artillery fire was inaccurate. Soviet tanks tried to crush the concrete anti-tank obstacles of the Mannerheim Line, for Soviet engineers had been unsuccessful in destroying them. Finnish demolition teams disabled and destroyed many stranded tanks with their explosives. Under control of the Finnish high command, the dive bombers of LLv 10 flailed at attractive targets on three occasions. Thousands of Soviet infantrymen died as Finnish bullets cut a swathe through the masses. Not until 18-9 December did fifty tanks succeed in breaking into Summa. The Finns then surrounded the armor, inflicted heavy losses, and forced it to withdraw. The initial Soviet assault on the Mannerheim Line had failed with large losses.

The Russo-Finnish border north of Lake Ladoga is long, but broken by lakes and forests, rendering it defensible by small forces. The defenders were particularly aided by a severe winter. The Soviet 14 Army advanced simultaneously toward Petsamo and around the south shore of Lake Inari to secure the vital nickel mines at Petsamo. It achieved neither objective, being stopped 60 kilometers short of Petsamo and at Ivalo on Inarijärvi.

The Soviet 9 Army pushed two prongs into the waist of Finland to drive to the Gulf of Bothnia and cut off Finland from Swedish aid. The 163 Division halted at Suomussalmi on 7 December, only 30 kilometers beyond the border. General Siilasvuo led an infantry regiment of the 6. Division northward from the general reserve and made a surprise attack on **11 December**, cutting the Russian line of communication. Advancing westward into the rear of the

163 Division, the Finns fought fiercely in Suomussalmi for several days but, without artillery, suffered heavy casualties. Word was also received that the Soviet 44 Motorized Division was approaching from the east. When two Finnish companies blocked a narrow passage between two lakes, the poorly-trained Russians became jumbled on the road, buying time to deal with the situation. Harried crews of LeR 4's Blenheims reconnoitered the Soviet movements. Some cruised as far as the White Sea to bomb the railway to Murmansk. Five battalions of the newly formed 9. Division were rushed northward, with two batteries of artillery and two anti-tank guns. Aided by the bombing and strafing of Blenheims, they destroyed the trapped 163 Division on 27-30 December, despite Soviet air attacks. The victorious Finnish forces then turned on the hapless 44 Motorized Division. With partisans on skis harassing the Russian columns, the Finns used successive shallow envelopments to nibble away at the Soviet division during the first week of **January 1940**. Few Russians escaped. The two Soviet divisions lost 27,500 killed, 1,100 prisoners, 50 tanks and all their artillery. The Finns did not go unscathed, suffering nearly 2,700 casualties. This great victory raised Finnish morale.

The second Soviet prong fared no better. Two divisions quickly occupied Salla and advanced westward. They were routed by four weak Finnish battalions on 18 December and fled to Salla, leaving 10 tanks behind. The main advance toward Kemijärvi made better progress as but two Finnish regiments could be spared for its defense. The only air support came from the 4 old Junkers K.43 floatplanes based on Lake Kemi. Thus they welcomed F19, a unit of volunteer Swedish military airmen, which began operating from Kemi on 12 January 1940. The newcomers immediately attacked Soviet mechanized columns approaching Kemijärvi. Using the same *mottisota* pincer tactics that had worked so well at Suomussalmi, the Finns stopped the advance and forced the invaders onto the defensive. The Swedish Volunteer Brigade moved up from Kemi in mid-February to relieve the Finns, who entrained for Karelia where greater danger threatened.

In Eastern Karelia (northeast of Lake Ladoga), the Soviet 8 Army had forced the Finns back more than 150 kilometers on a broad front between Sortavala and Ilomantsi, threatening to take the Army of Karelia in rear. Advancing through the close terrain of lakes and forest, the Russian columns were incapable of supporting each other. The Finnish IV Corps attacked the central column moving west toward Suojärvi.

Blackburn Ripons of LLv 16 could not safely operate in the fighter-infested skies over Karelia, so the hard pressed Blenheims of LeR 4 flew reconnaissance and bombing missions over the area. Late in the afternoon of 1 December, three Blenheim Is of LLv 46 left Luonnetjärvi and flew east in bad weather. Circling around Suojärvi, they approached from the east at low altitude. Flying at only 100 meters, just below the clouds, they dropped 2,000 kilograms of bombs on a large bivouac of surprised Soviet troops.

As ski troops slashed at the flanks of the Soviet 139 Division near Tolvajärvi, a surprise attack was made on **12 December** by 7 infantry battalions, supported by 4 artillery batteries. The advance was halted, and the division was then destroyed piecemeal by the efficient Finnish pincers. The Soviet 75 Division rushed forward to save it, but was similarly defeated by Group T after a battle lasting several days. The deadly Finns had killed 4,000 Russians and captured 59 tanks, 31 field guns and 220 machineguns. Although the IV Corps had lost a fourth of its men, the crisis ended and the front stabilized at Suojärvi to the end of the war. [192]

By 1940, Blackburn Ripons were still useful over the less fiercely contested seas. Together with a pair of old Junkers K.43s in the Åland Islands, those of LLv 36 flew coastal reconnaissance, anti-submarine, and convoy patrol missions from the Kallvik base near Helsinki in cooperation with the Finnish Navy. From January, they were aided by a couple of Koolhoven FK.52 two-seat fighters that arrived from Sweden. The Navy's submarines also got in a few licks. Between 4-9 December, *Vetehinen* attacked an icebreaker off Liepaja, *Iku-Tursu* loosed torpedoes at Soviet ships off Stockholm, and *Saukko* targeted Soviet warships shelling near Koivisto (Primorsk), but all without success. The *Vesikko* went after Soviet ships off Koivisto again on 14 December. Six days later, *Vesihiisi* laid mines off Paldiski, Estonia. Finnish submarines continued to be active despite large numbers of Soviet aircraft overhead.

The Crew of a Fokker C.X Prepares to Cross Enemy Lines

LLv 10 took its Fokker C.Xs to the Eastern Karelia front and mounted 38 sorties during January against lucrative Russian concentrations. Bombers and army cooperation planes were forced to begin their sorties at dusk, or fly at night. Finnish fighters downed 53 Soviet planes during January, losing only 6 of their own. Even when the Russians increased their strength to 1,500 planes in February (2,000 in March), superior Finnish tactics and dispersal of their units allowed the Finnish Air Force to continue to operate.

On 1 December, the Finnish parliament had elected Risto Ryti as Prime Minister. After capturing the frontier town of Terijoki, the Soviets established a puppet "Democratic Government of Finland" there, with the Finnish Communist, O.W. Kuusinen, as president. Announcing that it had invited the Soviets to "occupy" reactionary Finland, the Terijoki government signed a treaty on 2 December that met all Russian demands.

In January, the Russians brought up their 13 Army to reinforce the units on the Karelian Isthmus, and formed a new front under their best commander.

Northwestern Front (Army Commander Timoshenko)
13 Army
9 rifle divisions
39 Tank Brigade
7 Army
19, 50, 10, 34 Rifle Corps
12 rifle divisions
6 Army - attack across Gulf of Viipuri
28 Corps
3 rifle divisions
34 Tank Brigade
1 cavalry corps

Klimenti E. Voroshilov was placed in overall command of the operations against Finland. Timoshenko spent January feverishly training his inept troops. He gathered five brigades of BT tanks, and brought up independent brigades of the new KV heavy tank. At noon on **1 February 1940**, Soviet tanks rolled forward toward Summa after the artillery had rained many shells on the deafened Finns. Five hundred ground attack planes struck the Finnish positions. Yet, all Russian attacks were repelled by the valiant defenders. A second attack a week later brought the same result.

A third strong attack was launched on **11 February**. One hundred batteries of artillery pounded the eastern sector around Lähde for two and a half hours, destroying numerous trenches and strongpoints. Now the Russians employed more skillful infantry tactics, flanking each position instead of attacking frontally as they had done in December. Soviet artillery fire was also much more accurate, inflicting heavy casualties. The handful of Finnish Blenheims in LeR 4 attacked the new Soviet offensive, but were too few to have much effect. The Soviet tanks and infantry penetrated two kilometers into the Finnish rear areas. Only the last reserves of the II Corps remained to stop them. Yet, it required three more days to break through. As the Summa position was now outflanked, it was abandoned and the Finns formed up in an intermediate position. Believing the Finns finished, the Soviets rashly charged the position without preparation on **18 February**, and were thrown back with heavy losses.

The threat was not lost on Mannerheim, who ordered a retirement to the main defense line guarding Viipuri, extending from Tali to Vuoksi. He reorganized his forces for the final defense:

**Finnish Army** (Marshal Mannerheim)
**Lapland Group** (Gen.Maj. Wallenius) - Petsamo
1 infantry battalion
**V Corps** (Gen.Maj. Tuompo) - Salla
2 reserve infantry regiments
Swedish Volunteer Brigade
**IV Corps** (Gen.Maj. Hagglund) - Joensuu
12., 13. Infantry Divisions
**Army of Karelia** (Gen.Lt. Heinrichs) - Mikkeli
**I Corps** (Gen.Maj. Laatikainen) - Viipuri
2., 3., 9. Infantry Divisions
**II Corps** (Gen.Lt. Ohquist) - Viipuri
1., 4., 5., 7. Infantry Divisions
General Reserve
1. Cavalry Brigade
**I. Tank Battalion**
32 Vickers Mk.E, 32 Renault M.17

395

Often harassed by more than 1,000 Soviet aircraft, the Finnish ground troops retired to the main Mannerheim Line around Viipuri. As the weather improved, Soviet aircraft began switching from bombing cities to attacking Finnish ground forces. However, several cities were still ravished by hundreds of bombers, Viipuri receiving particular attention. In the face of the massive Soviet aerial onslaught, tactical reconnaissance could be conducted only by fighters. For that purpose, the recently acquired Gladiators of LLv 26 were distributed to LLv 12, 14 and 16 at the end of the month when the fighter squadron received new Fiat G.50s. Although initially well-liked by its pilots, the Gladiator had no pilot armor or self-sealing fuel tanks. Thirteen had been lost to Soviet fighters by the end of February.

Machinegun-armed Vickers Mk.Es Advance Along a Forest Road With Guns Ready

Obviously the crucial struggle of the war was at hand. The massive Soviet attacks in the Isthmus required all the resistance the Finns could muster. However, the only modern tanks available to them, the Vickers Mk.Es, were armed with weak 37 mm guns or machineguns. With this inadequate armament the 4. Tank Company was thrown into the battle near Honkeniemi on 26 February, but was decimated by powerful Russian armor.

Finnish fighter capabilities greatly increased by the end of February. The Fokker D.21s of LLv 24, and Fiat G.50s of LLv 26 were joined by Morane-Saulnier M.S.406s in LLv 28, which used them primarily for ground strafing. However, overwhelming Soviet air forces pounded Finnish counterattacks. A fighter sweep by 40 I-153s and I-16s on **29 February** was met by a mere flight of Fokkers from LLv 24 and a flight of Gladiators from LLv 26. Three Gladiators were shot down taking off, and two more fell later, together with one Fokker. Only one I-16 was downed. This was the worst aerial defeat the Finns were to suffer during their five years of conflict with the Russians. Nevertheless, Finnish fighters shot down 71 Russian planes during the last weeks of combat.

Having defeated all Finnish countermeasures, the Russians prepared to capture Viipuri. Ten Soviet raids struck the Finnish fighter bases, destroying 7 aircraft on the ground and shooting 12 Gladiators and 10 other fighters out of the air. On **4 March**, the Soviet 6 Army advanced across the thick ice of the Gulf of Viipuri, with a hundred tanks in the lead. They enveloped the right wing of the Finnish line and reached the coast near Vilaniemi, west of Viipuri, cutting the coastal highway. At the same time, heavy frontal attacks struck the main defenses before Viipuri. Three brigades of Soviet tanks broke through a hole four kilometers wide, but were thrown back. The 37 mm anti-tank guns of II Corps harvested 72 Russian tanks, destroying the Soviet 34 Tank Brigade. While the bombers of LeR 4 attacked Soviet concentrations and supply columns, all Finnish fighters concentrated on strafing the Soviet troops exposed on the open stretches of ice and snow, slowing their progress. During these forays, the Finns downed 20 enemy planes, but lost 8 of their own and had 10 more badly damaged.

An isolated Soviet column advanced over the ice from Hogland Island toward Kotka. Although it was also repelled, the last Finnish reserves had been expended and, on 6 March, a Finnish delegation went to Moscow for peace talks. As they were going on, the Finns sought to improve their position by attacking the Soviet beachhead at Vilaniemi on 12 March, pushing them back onto the ice.

An armistice was declared on **13 March**. The Finns had killed 200,000 Russians and destroyed or captured 1,600 tanks during the war. Finnish planes had downed 207 Soviet aircraft, with 314 more shot down by anti-aircraft gunners. Only 74 Finnish aircraft were destroyed. The fortified frontier post of Salla was annexed by the Soviet Union, which also procured a long-term lease on Hangö, flanking the mouth of both the Gulf of Finland and Gulf of Bothnia. Most painful was the loss of the Karelian Isthmus and Viipuri, where much of Finland's industrial growth had occurred. Finland had lost 23,150 men killed for these results, a bitter price. [193,194]

### *The Middle Peace* - 1940-1941

The heroic resistance of tiny Finland to the invasion by the Soviet Union in 1939 had stirred many nations to sell arms to them. From neighboring Norway came 12 Ehrhardt 75 mm field guns. Sweden supplied 77,000 rifles, 56 Bofors 75 mm field guns, 76 Bofors 40 mm AA guns, and 29 heavy field artillery pieces. From France came 5,000 Chauchat auto-rifles, 40-25 mm AT guns, 24 heavy field artillery pieces, 30 Morane-Saulnier M.S.406 and 6 Caudron C.714 fighters. Great Britain sent 30-84 mm (18 pdr) field guns, 200 BOYS AT rifles, 37 heavy artillery pieces, 30 Gloster Gladiator II and 12 Hawker Hurricane I fighters and 24 Blenheim light bombers. From Italy came 48-20 mm AA guns, and 24 other guns. Thirty-five Fiat G.50 fighters had already been ordered by the Finns before the war began. The United States shipped 200 M1916/1917 75 mm field guns and 44 Brewster 239 fighters. Important anti-aircraft guns came from Hungary (40-40 mm), Denmark (178-20 mm), and Germany (30-20 mm). Belgium sent 700 valuable BAR auto-rifles. South Africa supplied 25 Gloster Gauntlet IIs as fighter trainers.

Most shipments had been delayed in German-controlled territories until Hitler released them in August 1940. Depleted Finnish regiments welcomed the numerous weapons, although the heterogeneous new equipment produced a logistics nightmare for Finnish quartermasters.

The Finnish Army was reorganized in May 1940 to create 16 infantry divisions. Each division had one regiment of regular troops (numbered 1.-16.), which was joined upon mobilization by two reserve regiments (numbered by adding 21 and 42 to the number of the regular regiment). The cavalry brigade was trained to operate as mounted infantry during the summer and as ski troops during the winter. Two jäger brigades had also been formed of infantry carried in trucks or riding bicycles. In addition, with the many functional tanks captured from the Russians during the Winter War, a workshop was established to rebuild tanks for a second battalion.

**INFANTRY DIVISION**
1 reconnaissance brigade
  1 cavalry squadron (horsed)
  1 motorcycle company
  1 submachinegun battalion
    **Suomi M.31 smg**
3 infantry regiments
  2 infantry battalions
    3 rifle companies
      **M.39 7.62 mm rifles**
      **Suomi M.31 SMGs**
      **BAR 7.62 mm auto-rifles**
      **Lahti M.26 7.62 mm lmgs**
    1 machinegun company
      **Maxim M.32 7.62 mm hmgs**
    1 support company
      **81 mm mortars**
      **45 pst K/32 AT guns**
1 field artillery regiment
  2 light battalions
    3 batteries
      **4 Ordnance M1916/1917 75 mm field guns** or
      **Bofors m/02 75 mm field guns** or
      **Ehrhardt M.01 75 mm field guns** or
      **Putilov M.02 76.2 mm field guns** or
      **British 84 mm field guns**
  1 medium battalion
    3 batteries
      **4 Schneider** or **Bofors 105 mm field guns,** or
      **Rheinmetall 150 mm field howitzers,** or
      **Coventry 114 mm field howitzers**
1 engineer battalion
1 signal company

**Suomi M.31 smg**
9mm, 5.1 kg, 400 m/s, 900 rpm

**45 pst K/32**
45 mm, 560 kg, 1.4 kg shell,
4400 m, 820 m/s, 25 rpm
47 mm/1000 m P

**M1A1 (M1916)**
75 mm, 1457 kg, 6.7 kg shell,
11490 m, 580 m/s

**Coventry 4.5" Field Howitzer**
114.3 mm, 1362 kg, 15.9 kg shell,
6440 m, 308 m/s, 8 rpm

Relations with the Soviet Union soon worsened. Russia insisted that the Finns build a railway from Salla to Kemijärvi to link northern Russia to the Gulf of Bothnia, then repeatedly vetoed an exception to the peace treaty to allow Finland to enter a defensive pact with Sweden. Resentment was exacerbated by crude Russian allusions to "uniting all Finnish races", within the Soviet Union, of course.

With Finland now cut off from the West, Germany was the only country still capable of supplying munitions to her. To ensure Germany's support, Finland signed an agreement on 22 September 1940 to allow transit of German troops to the Arctic coast. Finland's irritation with Germany, for having pressured Sweden into neutrality during the Winter War, began to disappear when the Soviet Union started making demands. They wanted permission to run trains over Finnish tracks to Hangö and participate in the production of nickel at Petsamo. Resentment increased when President Kallio died and the Soviets informed the Finns that only certain candidates to replace him would be acceptable to them.

In November 1940, discussions between Molotov and Ribbentrop, the Soviet and German foreign ministers, improved Germany's attitude toward Finland. Molotov insisted that the interests of the Soviet Union in Finland be recognized by Germany. Ribbentrop informed Molotov of Hitler's fears that a Soviet move into Finland would provoke the Western Allies into establishing air bases in Scandinavia for attacks on Germany. Hitler was already planning the betrayal of his pact with Stalin and wanted access to Finland's nickel and timber. On 25 May 1941, the German High Command pressed General Heinrichs to persuade his government to assist Germany if war broke out with Russia. Heinrichs refused to collaborate, unless Finland was attacked. Early in June 1941, Hitler used his agreed right of passage to move a division from Norway, and another from Germany, to northern Finland. The Finns realized that something was afoot.

## *The Continuation War* - 25 June 1941

With both German and Russian troops gathering on his borders, on 17 June President Ryti ordered that a partial mobilization be carried out quietly to avoid provoking Russia. A German liaison officer had arrived in Helsinki, but Field Marshal Mannerheim skillfully avoided any commitments that could be detrimental to Finnish aspirations. He directed the Finnish General Staff in developing a plan designed to keep the coming battleground off of Finnish soil, rather than assisting the Germans in a conquest of Russia. Nevertheless, Finland cultivated a more cordial relationship with Germany than did any other of its allies, although no formal alliance was ever signed.

Hitler's hordes poured into Russia on 21 June 1941, with Army Group North driving on Leningrad. By the end of the month, Russian troops were being withdrawn from the far north to participate in the disasters farther south. Soviet forces remaining along the Finnish borders included:

**Karelian Front**
**14 Army** - Murmansk
14, 52, 54, 88, 104, 122, 133, 186 Rifle Divisions
1 Tank Division
**7 Army** - Petrozavodsk
55, 69, 70, 73 Naval Rifle Divisions
**23 Army** - Vyborg
3 divisions
**Hangö Garrison**
2 rifle brigades

When Germany initiated its invasion, the Finns declared neutrality. However, Soviet air attacks against Finnish territory, and movements along the frontier, convinced the Finns that they could not escape involvement.

399

On **25 June 1941**, the Finnish government announced that a state of war existed, and deployed its troops. Although the Finns protested, the Western Allies declared Finland a satellite of Germany and treated her as such throughout the war. The V. Corps was redesignated the III. Corps and subordinated to the German Army of Norway, along with other Finnish units. As their recruiting districts in East Karelia had been lost during the Winter War, the 9., 13. and 16. Divisions were not formed.

**German Army of Norway** (Gen.Lt. Falkenhorst) - Petsamo

**Mountain Korps Norway** (Gen. Dietl) - Petsamo
   German 2., 3. Mountain Divisions
**XXXVI Army Korps** (Gen. Fiege) - Salla
   German 169. Infantry Division
   German SS Kampfgruppe Nord
   Finnish 6. Infantry Division (detd. from III. Corps)
   **2 German tank battalions**
     Pz.Kw. I, II, III
**Finnish III. Corps** (Gen.Maj. Siilasvuo) - Suomussalmi
   Finnish 3. Infantry Division
   **1 German tank company**
     Pz.Kw. I, II

**Finnish Army** (Field Marshal C.G. Mannerheim) - Mikkeli

14. Infantry Division (Col. Raapana) - Lieksa

**Army of Karelia** (Gen.Lt. Heinrichs)
   Group D
     II. Jäger Brigade (Col. Sundman)
     I. Cavalry Brigade (Col. Oinonen)
   VI. Corps (Gen.Maj. Talvela)
     I. Jäger Brigade (Col. Lagus)
     5., 11. Infantry Divisions
   VII. Corps (Gen.Maj. Hagglund)
     7., 19. Infantry Divisions
   Reserve
     1. Infantry Division

**South-East Army** (Gen.Lt. Oesch)
   II. Corps (Gen.Maj. Laatikainen)
     2., 15., 18. Infantry Divisions
   IV. Corps (Gen.Lt. Oesch)
     4., 8., 10., 12. Infantry Divisions

17. Infantry Division - Hangö
   Swedish Volunteer Battalion

General Reserve
   German 163. Infantry Division - Joensuu
   **I. Tank Battalion**
     4 companies
       32 T-26E, 30 T-26A,B,S,
       7 T-28C

**T-26E**
1940, 7.6 tons, 1-45 mm, 1 mg,
35 km/h, 160 km, 16 mm, 3 men
47 mm/1000 m P

**T-26B**
1932, 9.9 tons, 1-37 mm or 45 mm, 1 mg,
43 km/h, 270 km, 15/15/15 mm, 3 men,
45 mm/500 m P or 47 mm/1000 m P

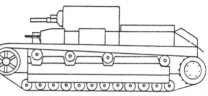

**T-28C**
1937, 32.5 tons, 1-76.2 mm, 3 mgs,
24 km/h, 175 km, 80/80/50 mm,
50 mm/1000 m P, 6 men    [195,196]

400

Munitions captured from the Soviets during the Winter War, and those procured from many other nations, had greatly strengthened the Finnish Army. Heavy artillery and anti-aircraft defenses were particularly enhanced. Many Russian 45 mm anti-tank guns had been captured and these provided the infantry with some possibility of stopping Soviet tanks. Of even greater benefit was the fitting of high velocity Russian 45 mm guns to all Vickers Mk.E tanks. With the new armament they were redesignated T-26Es, for many Russian-built T-26s had been captured during the winter campaign. Many more were soon supplied from the thousands captured by the Germans in the early days of the Barbarossa campaign of 1941. The T-26 remained the principal Finnish tank throughout the war. The crude exterior of the T-28C belied what was a good medium tank of the period. Captured vehicles were refurbished by the Army workshops at Varkaus before being issued to the field units. Many Soviet BT-5 and 7 tanks also had been captured. However, they were not suited to Finnish conditions, having been designed for rapid movement over the steppes of Russia. Varkaus built a huge turret, mounted a 144 mm howitzer *à la* the Soviet KV-2, and delivered them as the BT-42 assault gun. This improvisation was a failure, as it overloaded the BT chassis and proved difficult to conceal in combat. Nevertheless, it soldiered on until replaced by German *sturmgeschutzen* in 1943. To accomodate the new tanks, late in 1941 the II. Tank Battalion was organized. Each battalion received three companies.

Likewise, the Finnish Air Force had profited from the one year martial hiatus. Fighter defenses, especially, had been strengthened. Just as the Winter War ended, 35 Fiat G.50s were released to Finland from Germany, where they had been detained when that war began. They were the least successful of the modern fighters that reequipped the Finnish squadrons, having considerable difficulty with the cold climate and armed too lightly for effective combat in the 1940s. Nevertheless, they remained in service until 1944, possessing fair speed and good maneuverability. They also could carry a number of 1 kilogram anti-personnel or incendiary bombs internally. Another valuable acquisition, from France in February 1940, was 30 Morane-Saulnier M.S.406C.1s. They were augmented by 25 more in 1941 that had been captured and refurbished by Germany. The Moranes were faster and more maneuverable than any Soviet fighters, until the LaGG-3 appeared late in 1940. Their nose cannons proved valuable in attacking ground targets. Also acquired from France, but by way of German refurbishment of captured machines, were 36 Curtiss Hawk 75A-1,2,3s that arrived late in July 1941. In addition, the Germans supplied 8 Hawk 75A-6s they found still in their crates at Oslo. The Curtiss was a delight to fly and capable of absorbing a good deal of combat damage. Most remarkable was the performance of another American aircraft in Finnish hands. The Brewster F2A had never been considered a successful fighter by the United States Navy, which declared 44 F2A-2s as surplus and supplied them to Finland in April 1940 as the Brewster Model 239. Stripped of naval gear, and less lightly loaded than later models, the rotund Brewsters proved highly popular with Finnish pilots, who used them very effectively to the end of the war. Fokker D.21s, standard fighters of the Winter War, were displaced to lesser duties with the start of the Continuation War. Along with a handful of Hurricanes, they equipped LLv 30, which had formed from the disbanded LLv 10 for fighter reconnaissance missions. After repairing aircraft damaged in the Winter War, VL began building new D.21s. Mercury engines were needed for the 15 Blenheims Is they were also constructing, so the Fokker airframe was adapted to take the

401

Pratt and Whitney Twin Wasp Junior. With it, the D.21 had a lower performance, but 50 were built and issued to units flying the Mercury-powered version. Others went to army cooperation squadrons LLv 12 and 14 in August of 1941 for use in tactical reconnaissance and ground attack.

**Finnish Air Force** (Gen.Lt. J.F. Lundqvist) - Helsinki

Lentorykmentti 1 - distributed to ground units
  Lentolaivue 12
    **2 Curtiss Hawk 75A**
    **2 Gloster Gladiator II**
    **10 Fokker D.21** (from August)
    **6 Fokker C.X**
  Lentolaivue 14
    **3 Gloster Gladiator II**
    **15 Fokker D.21** (from August)
    **8 Fokker C.X**
  Lentolaivue 16
    **8 Gloster Gladiator II**
    **8 Fokker C.X**
    **4 Westland Lysander I**

**Hawker Hurricane Mk.I**
1935, 12 m span, 522 km/h, 684 km,
9.8/6100 m, 10431 m SC, 8 mgs

Lentorykmentti 2 (Col.Lt. R. Lorenz) - Viipuri
  Lentolaivue 24
    **33 Brewster 239**
  Lentolaivue 28
    **29 Morane-Saulnier M.S.406C.1**

**Curtiss Hawk 75A-1, 2, 3**
1938, 11 m span, 504 km/h, 1330 km,
4.8/4575 m, 10065 m SC, 4-6 mgs

Lentorykmentti 3 (Col.Lt. E. Nuotio) - Pori
  Lentolaivue 30
    **5 Hawker Hurricane I** (to LLv 32 in July)
    **13 Fokker D.21** (from July 1)
  Lentolaivue 32
    **25 Fokker D.21** (to LLv 12, 14 in Aug.)
    **5 Hawker Hurricane I** (from July 1)
    **7 Curtiss Hawk 75A-1,2,3**
  Lentolaivue 26 (from LeR 2 on Sept. 13)
    **26 Fiat G.50**

**Fiat G.50**
1937, 11 m span, 472 km/h, 676 km,
8/5000 m, 10757 m SC, 2 mgs

Lentorykmentti 4 (Col.Lt. T. Somerto)
  Lentolaivue 42
    **9 Bristol Blenheim I**
  Lentolaivue 44
    **9 Bristol Blenheim I**
  Lentolaivue 46
    **1 Bristol Blenheim I**
    **3 Bristol Blenheim IV**
    **2 Ilyushin DB-3**

**Morane-Saulnier M.S.406C.1**
1935, 11 m span, 486 km/h, 750 km,
7/5000 m, 9400 m SC, 1-20 mm, 2 mgs

Lentolaivue 10 (from August 15)
  **Fokker D.21, C.X** (dive bombers)
Lentolaivue 6 (naval cooperation)
  **6 Tupolev SB-2, SB-2bis**
  **Blackburn Ripon IIF**
Lentolaivue 15 (long-range recco groups)
  **2 Höver MF.11**
  **3 Blackburn Ripon IIF**
  **2 Junkers K-43**
  **1 Heinkel He.115kA-2**
  **2 Beriev MBR-2bis**

**Brewster 239**
1938, 11 m span, 485 km/h, 1554 km,
9913 m SC, 4 mgs, 91 kg B

**Höver MF.11**
1931, 11 m span, 235 km/h, 800 km,
5000 m SC, 3 mgs, 300 kg B

197

402

When Norway fell, a Heinkel He.115A-2, 3 Höver MF.11s and 2 Fokker C.VDs escaped from the Narvik area and were taken into the Finnish Air Force. Finland also ordered 26 Fokker G.IB strike fighters and 5 Fokker T-VIIIL reconnaissance bombers from the Netherlands, but these were seized by the Germans in May 1940.

**Fokker T.VIII-L**
1939, 18 m span, 285 km/h, 2100 km,
6800 m SC, 3 mgs, 590 kg B

The tiny Finnish Navy had been developed to protect Finnish ports and coastal commerce, and interfere with those of the enemy. Most of the vessels were of modern construction, if not conception:

**Finnish Navy** (Gen.Maj. Valve)

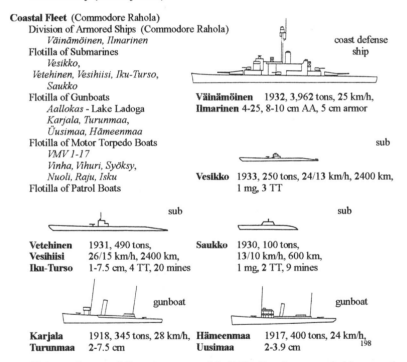

**Coastal Fleet** (Commodore Rahola)
  Division of Armored Ships (Commodore Rahola)
    *Väinämöinen, Ilmarinen*
  Flotilla of Submarines
    *Vesikko,*
    *Vetehinen, Vesihiisi, Iku-Turso,*
    *Saukko*
  Flotilla of Gunboats
    *Aallokas* - Lake Ladoga
    *Karjala, Turunmaa,*
    *Üusimaa, Hämeenmaa*
  Flotilla of Motor Torpedo Boats
    *VMV 1-17*
    *Vinha, Vihuri, Syöksy,*
    *Nuoli, Raju, Isku*
  Flotilla of Patrol Boats

coast defense ship

**Väinämöinen** 1932, 3,962 tons, 25 km/h,
**Ilmarinen** 4-25, 8-10 cm AA, 5 cm armor

sub

**Vesikko** 1933, 250 tons, 24/13 km/h, 2400 km,
1 mg, 3 TT

sub

**Vetehinen** 1931, 490 tons,
**Vesihiisi** 26/15 km/h, 2400 km,
**Iku-Turso** 1-7.5 cm, 4 TT, 20 mines

sub

**Saukko** 1930, 100 tons,
13/10 km/h, 600 km,
1 mg, 2 TT, 9 mines

gunboat

**Karjala** 1918, 345 tons, 28 km/h,
**Turunmaa** 2-7.5 cm

gunboat

**Hämeenmaa** 1917, 400 tons, 24 km/h,
**Uusimaa** 2-3.9 cm

198

*Väinämöinen* and *Ilmarinen* were tidy little diesel-powered ships, mechanically modern but tactically outdated. Conceived as slow-speed protectors of the island-studded Finnish coast, they were used initially for offensive shore bombardment, later as static anti-aircraft defenses in port. All Finnish submarines were of modern construction, the *Vetehinen* class possessing sufficient size and range for effective operations. In the event, the submarines and the small surface craft produced most of the Navy's successes.

Four days after the German invasion of central Russia, Soviet bombers raided the fighter bases of LeR 2. At Joroinen, 6 Fiat G.50s of LLv 26 took off at 1140 amid falling bombs and shot down 13 of the 15 Tupolev SB-2bis bombers roaring over. Brewsters downed 10 more over their base at Vesivehmaa and Fokker D.21s of LLv 32 added two over Hyvinkää. The Russians also bombed the Finnish armored ships and the forts of Turku. On the same day, the Finnish High Command was established at Mikkeli, where it remained for the rest of the war.

General Lundqvist proved adept at organizing the Finnish Air Force for maximum effectiveness, yet with minimum exposure to Soviet attack. Squadrons were broken into flights that moved from airfield to airfield, evading Soviet discovery. There were too few aircraft to intercept all Soviet raiders, but the situation was less desperate than during the Winter War. The Soviets had been busy building many airbases in Karelia since the Winter War, but when Barbarossa began they could spare only a few obsolescent aircraft for the Finnish theatre. The Finns quickly gained a considerable aerial superiority, and the massive air raids that devastated Finnish cities during the Winter War were not repeated. Relieved of the necessity for defending their cities, Finnish fighters were able to concentrate close behind the front lines, from where they could cover Finnish ground operations and escort bombers. The German advance through the Baltic States would soon eliminate the Estonian bases being used by the Soviet bombers, but the airfields in Soviet East Karelia would provide them with bases from which to continue the air campaign.

As the Germans advanced in Russia, they transported the 163. Infantry Division across Sweden from Norway to destroy the menacing Soviet base at Hangö. When the war began, the Finnish 17. Division had sealed off the base on the landward side. German bombers began softening up the fortifications. However, Hitler had more extensive tasks in mind for the Finnish Army and diverted his infantry division to Karelia, east of Lake Ladoga, leaving the reduction of Hangö to the 17. Division and a Swedish battalion that arrived later.

Large Soviet forces had gathered in Karelia to invade Finland, but with the initial German successes they were withdrawn and sent south. Mannerheim proposed advancing sufficiently into East Karelia to overrun the airfields, then apply most of his forces to the recapture of Vyborg and the Karelian Isthmus. The Germans urged the Finns to cooperate in a drive on Leningrad by continuing their advance in East Karelia as far as the Syväri (Svir) River, where they would link up with the German Army Group North crossing the Volkhov River. On 28 June, Mannerheim decided to comply with the German request, forming the Army of Karelia to command the troops as the High Command was too far away at Mikkeli for direct control.

Group D was sent north from Korpiselkä toward Ilomantsi to guard the left flank of the offensive. The reinforced Finnish I. Jäger Brigade (Task Force Lagus) led VI. Corps in the main attack on **10 July 1941**, crossing the frontier north of Lake Jänis. At Tuuslosjoki, the T-26s and T-28s of the I. Tank Battalion assisted the jägers in blasting a hole in the enemy defensive line. Racing southward along the lake shore, they reached Tolvajärvi and Kokkari within two days. A further two days advance placed the jägers on the flank of strong Russian forces holding up the advance of VI Corps at Värtsilä. Curling in behind the Soviets, they forced withdrawal on 14 July.

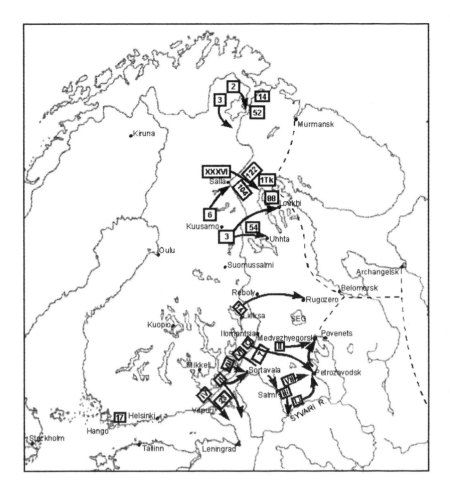

The Advance in Karelia - Summer, 1941

The main body of VI Corps pushed southward through rolling country and the jägers entered Loimola on 15 July, severing communications to the east. But the Russians were still holding up the Finnish advance around Lake Jänis and General Talvela recognized an opportunity to trap them by advancing to Lake Ladoga. With the I. Jäger Brigade leading the way, the corps progressed on a broad front, the 11. Division reaching the Jänis River on **17 July**. The remnants of the Soviet 7 Army streamed back to the isthmus between Lake Jänis and Lake Ladoga. The VII Corps had opened its offensive on 10 July, slowly pushing the Russians back between Lakes Pyhä and Jänis toward Sortavala. A large mass of Soviet troops was now surrounded. To aid in reducing the Sortavala pocket, the 11. Division was moved from VI. Corps to VII Corps.

Mannerheim moved to consolidate the success of the Army of Karelia. The German 163. Infantry Division was given the mission of fighting through to Suojärvi, while the Finnish 17. Division was moved from Hangö to Värtsilä in support. To guard against Russian moves from Petrozavodsk, the 1. Division came out of reserve and moved to Loimola to relieve security forces of VI Corps.

VI Corps drove southward along the eastern shore of Lake Ladoga, but encountered heavy resistance. An emotional scene developed when troops reached the old boundary stones set up by Gustavus Adolphus centuries earlier. General Talvela declared the Russians expelled from Finland. After heavy fighting, VI Corps entered Salmi on **21 July**. Pushing 30 kilometers beyond the old border, the Finns were met by fierce Russian counterattacks, including amphibious landings from Lake Ladoga. Heavy fighting continued into August. However, Soviet opposition in the air decreased as the huge losses farther south forced transfer of many squadrons.

The inexperienced German 163. Infantry Division and the Finnish 17. Division encountered hard fighting as they pushed toward Suojärvi on Lake Suo. The terrain was rugged and stoutly defended by the Russians. The advance stalled at the end of the month. To add a mobile punch to the operation, the German division's general took command of *Kampfgruppe Engelbrecht*, which also included the II. Jäger and Cavalry Brigades recalled from Ilomantsi. The *gruppe* resumed slow progress toward Petrozavodsk.

Many Soviet units were now pinned against the north shore of Lake Ladoga. Reinforced by the 10. Division from IV Corps, South-East Army's II. Corps opened an assault between Imatra and Uukunjemi on the last day of July, initiated by a heavy artillery bombardment. Brewster 239s of LLv 24 downed a number of attacking Soviet planes. By **5 August**, the corps had reached the shore of Lake Ladoga at Hiitola, cutting off the Soviet forces on the north shore. As lake vessels began evacuating two Russian divisions, a gruppe of Junkers Ju.88s from Luftflotte 1 attacked the lucrative targets.

The remnants of the Soviet 7 Army were now isolated at Sortavala, but the Finnish VII. Corps made little progress against it. To conclude the issue, I. Corps took over the 7. and 19. Divisions investing Sortavala. Not until **16 August** was the city occupied, by which time most of the Soviet troops had escaped over Lake Ladoga. The left wing of II. Corps mopped up the north shore of Lake Ladoga as far as Sortavala and its right wing turned south into the Karelian Isthmus on 18 August. Within three days, the eastern half of the isthmus, from the Vuoksi River to Lake Ladoga, had been occupied.

To help prevent Soviet excursions from the islands in the Gulf of Finland, such as had occurred during the Winter War, the Finnish submarines *Vetehinen, Vesihiisi, Iku-Tursu, Vesikko* and *Saukko* had been active during the summer, laying mines off Soviet islands and ports. Communications with Hangö were also attacked. On 4 July, the *Vetehinen, Vesikko* and *Saukko* had stalked and sunk a Russian cargo vessel off Someri.

IV. Corps began an offensive on 22 August against a division of the Soviet 23 Army that had been left to defend Vyborg. By **25 August**, the city was surrounded, and the Soviets surrendered. With the aid of some T-38 amphibious tanks that traversed Lake Uuksu, II. Corps crossed the Vuoksi River at Pakkola. Soviet counterattacks were successfully defeated and the Finns pursued the retiring enemy. Against decreased Soviet aerial strength, Fokker D.21s and Gloster Gladiators operated effectively with Fokker C.Xs in attacking the Soviet columns as they retired toward Leningrad. Koivisto was reached on 2 September. On 24 August, I. Corps had taken over 2 divisions of II. Corps to form a defensive line along the old border, while II. Corps headquarters moved to Eastern Karelia. To protect the troops in the Isthmus from Soviet air attack, Lentorykmentti 3 moved forward to bases just behind the frontier. The Fokker D.21s of LLv 30 and the Hawker Hurricanes and Curtiss Hawk 75As of LLv 32 were joined in September by the Fiat G.50s of LLv 26. [199]

VII. Corps headquarters was shifted to command a quieter section of the front in East Karelia between VI. Corps and Kampfgruppe Engelbrecht, 50 kilometers east of Salmi on the Tulemeyoki River. As Kampfgruppe Engelbrecht continued pushing toward Suojärvi from the northwest, enveloping the Russian positions with its cavalry and jäger brigades, the VII. Corps approached from the southwest on 19 August, forming an anvil for the mobile troops. They quickly routed the Soviets and reached the frontier. Exhausted by constant heavy fighting, the German 163. Division was withdrawn to the reserve.

The Division of Armored Ships Passes a Vetehinen-class Submarine

Estonian airfields were now largely in German hands, but the large islands offshore were still occupied by Soviet troops. On **13-4 September**, Finnish naval units were involved in the capture of the largest - Ösel Island in the mouth of the Gulf of Riga. Groups of small German vessels, designated *Westwind* and *Sudwind* distracted the defenders with feints toward the west and south coasts. The Finnish Division of Armored Ships, screened by the patrol boats *VMV 1, 14, 15* and *16*, formed the *Nordwind* task group. While engaged in bombarding the north coast in preparation for the landing of troops, *Ilmarinen* struck a floating mine and sank, but the island was secured by 5 October.

Finnish naval units continued harassing Soviet bases in the Gulf of Finland. The motor torpedo boats *Vinha* and *Svöksy* sank a minesweeper in the harbor of Suursaari (Hogland Is.) on 22 September. Then, the gunboats *Hämeenmaa* and *Üusimaa*, accompanied by 6 patrol boats, attacked a Soviet convoy evacuating troops from Hangö. They skirmished with the convoy escort of 7 Soviet patrol vessels on 30 November-1 December, but failed to destroy any ships. Hangö was occupied by the Finns on 4 December. [200]

Early in August, the Germans had informed Mannerheim that they intended to renew the advance upon Leningrad on the Sixth of the month and requested a Finnish offensive toward the Svir (Syväri) River. Mannerheim believed the Soviet forces near Lake Suo to be too much of a threat to any advance by his VI. Corps, and delayed until they had been driven away. He brought up Lentorykmentti 2 to support the advance on the Syväri, basing its Brewster, Fiat and Morane-Saulnier fighters in the Salmi area.

407

The final offensive in Eastern Karelia began on **4 September** with a heavy artillery bombardment. VI. Corps moved south (with 163. Division in reserve), the I. Jäger Brigade reaching the Syväri at Lotinapelto (Lodeynoye Pole) within 3 days. At the same time, VII. Corps (reinforced by the 4. Division) had advanced to within fifty kilometers of the capital of Karelia, Petrozavodsk. Blenheim Is were particularly useful in reconnoitering and bombing enemy opposition to the wide-ranging movements. LLv 26 moved its Fiat G.50s back to Immola on 13 September when it was relieved in the interceptor role by the Brewsters of LLv 24. The Moranes of LLv 28 had proven useful in supporting the ground troops, using their nose cannon to good advantage against Russian trains and road columns.

Again the I. Jäger Brigade lead elements of the VI. Corps as it turned east and cleared the north bank of the Syväri. A concentric advance on Petrozavodsk began on 18 September. As the jägers raced northward along the Murmansk Railway, the VII. and II. Corps closed in from the west and northwest. Petrozavodsk fell on **1 October**, and was renamed Äänislinna by the Finns. VI. Corps now got a well-deserved rest as the Syväri front quieted down. Action shifted to the north of the great lakes.

Securing the northern flank of the Karelian operations, the 14. Division had advanced north from Lieksa and encircled a Russian division near Reboly on 6 July. This was a well-travelled division for, when the war began, it was still garrisoning the Åland Islands. Withdrawn to general reserve at Riihimäki, north of Helsinki, it was soon ordered by Mannerheim to join in seizing the Murmansk Railway. Traversing rugged terrain against weak opposition, the division had approached Rugozero at the end of August. There the advance bogged down, the last gains made on **11 September,** and the Murmansk Railway was never reached. In an attempt to disrupt traffic on the railway, the Fokker C.Xs of LLv 10 were brought north in September and flew from Tiiksjärvi airfield, 20 kilometers west of Rugozero. Reinforced by a flight of Fokker D.21s from LLv 30, and one of Hurricanes from LLv 32, the dive bombers flailed at the vital communications link to the Western Allies, with little success. The dive bomber pilots were among the most highly trained in the Air Force, but their mounts were obsolescent and winter was coming on. There were few vital targets, such as large bridges, freight yards and engine terminals, available for attention from the bombers and mere breaks in the roadbed were quickly repaired. With most of its aircraft incapacitated, LLv 10 was disbanded on 1 November. Although the northern forces were unable to stop rail traffic, success was achieved near Lake Onega.

On **15 October**, the II. Corps began a drive eastward from Porajärvi (Porozero) as the mobile troops of the Army of Karelia advanced from Petrozavodsk. They reached the north tip of Lake Onega four days later. Cleverly coordinating their movements, the two columns trapped the Russians aronnd Medvezhyegorsk as a severe winter set in. Exhausted, the Finns paused to regroup on 16 November, deep snow making further progress nearly impossible. A final attack was made on **5 December**, penetrating into the city and reaching the Stalin Canal at Povenets. Two days later, the pocket of miserable Soviet troops south of Medvezhyegorsk was eliminated. Some dominating hills to the east were occupied to protect the defensive lines established along the canal, then the front stabilized. Aerial protection was provided by the Brewster 239s of LLv 24, which moved to a base on the western shore of Lake Onega, 60 kilometers south of Medvezhyegorsk, and by the Moranes of LLv 28 flying from a similar base just north of Petrozavodsk. The Finns settled in to stay. [201]

Meanwhile, an independent war was occurring in the Arctic. The two divisions of Finnish troops of the III. Corps (renamed from V. Corps when the war began) were placed under the German Army of Norway to aid in the defense of far northern regions and the "Waist of Finland" to the south of the Arctic Circle. The operations of the German Army of Norway were designated *Silberfuchs* (Silver Fox), with the mission of stopping Western supplies moving through the White Sea to Murmansk and seizing the mickel mines at Petsamo. Three separate offensives began - toward the mines of Petsamo, and to cut the railway at two points on the White Sea coast.

Operation *Platinfuchs* (Platinum Fox), a drive along the Arctic Coast to Petsamo and Murmansk, began when the German Mountain Korps moved out on **29 June 1941** against the Soviet 14 and 52 Divisons of 14 Army, but was halted short of Petsamo. On 30 July, 18 Fairey Albacores, escorted by 4 Hawker Sea Hurricanes and 6 Fairey Fulmars from the British aircraft carrier *Furious*, attacked German positions near Petsamo. The Germans renewed their advance on 8 September, but again bogged down. A new Army of Lapland, under Gen. Dietl, was formed in November, but no further action took place as the front had lapsed into winter slumber.

Operation *Polarfuchs* (Polar Fox) began on **1 July** with the German 169. Infantry Division and SS Kampfgruppe Nord advancing toward Salla, a rugged hilly area defended by the Soviet 122 Rifle Division and a tank brigade. In addition, the Finnish 6. Division was to move on Salla from a position 70 kilometers to the south. SS Nord, an ad hoc unit of elderly reservists armed with captured Czech weapons, disintegrated after suffering heavy casualties when it encountered an undiscovered Soviet fortification. However, the German 169. Division still succeeded in pushing the Russians out of Salla, destroying 50 Russian tanks by 6 July. The advance, with tanks and cyclists leading, was halted in the lakes east of the city when it encountered the Soviet 104 Rifle Division and 1 Tank Division. A renewed attack on 26 July by 169. Division and the 6. Division failed to make progress. The Finnish 6. Division spearheaded a third attack on **19 August** that nearly accomplished the encirclement of the Soviet troops, who abandoned their heavy equipment and fled. By 27 August, the pursuers were approaching the old border. The 6. Division reached the north tip of Lake Toiwand. However, the Russians were emplaced in strong bunkers along the Wojta River and the Germano-Finnish units had insufficient troops to continue the attack. As it appeared that Russia was about to collapse, the Far Northern operations were halted and preparations were made to return all Finnish troops to Finnish command.

Farther south, from Suomussalmi the Finnish III. Corps had sent its remaining 3. Division against the Soviet 54 Rifle Division on **1 July**, capturing Vuojärvi on 4 July. Within three weeks, it had penetrated 100 kilometers into Russian territory, reaching Uhtua and Kiestinki. While the Blenheims of LLv 46 flew photo reconnaissance missions, those of LLv 42 and 44 bombed traffic on the Russian railways. The Army of Norway ordered the Finnish 3. Division to capture Kiestinki, which it did on 8 August, but only after it had suffered heavy casualties in the ill-advised attack. Indignant Finns rejected German requests for more Finnish troops in the north and demanded that III. Corps be returned to Finnish control. Hitler responded by ordering the transfer before he was faced with a rebellion and by dividing the front into purely German and Finnish zones. [202]

Nevertheless, the delighted Finns had to wait for implementation as reluctant German commanders used every excuse to hang on to their excellent Finnish troops. The Finns had been successful, where the Germans had failed, because of superior tactics. The experienced Finnish forest fighters used short envelopments that trapped Russian groups, whereas the longer German pincers had failed to close through difficult Arctic conditions. The Soviet 88 Rifle Division was rushed up from Archangelsk and the III. Corps also ground to a halt, 80 kilometers short of the vital railway. On **9 September**, the rejuvenated Russians moved forward. Reunited with the 6. Finnish Division, the 3. Division counterattacked on **30 October**, but little progress was made. The two Finnish pincers never met, and the railway continued to carry sustenance to the Soviet armies fighting desperately in the central areas of Russia.

During the first half of January 1942, the Finns were slowly pushed back from the Murmansk Railway, but Finnish units managed to trap and destroy a Russian division. The isolated 14. Division mounted an even more spectacular operation. A strong ski detachment set out eastward on 19 January for a long-range reconnaissance. Meeting no resistance, it penetrated all the way to the railway and disrupted railroad traffic for some time by destroying the supply base at Segesha. The detachment returned to base with little loss.

### *Reorganization of the Finnish Army* - Spring 1942

On 8 January 1942, the Wehrmacht finally released the III. Corps. However, the severe winter had frozen the Baltic, preventing the arrival of the German 7. Mountain Division to replace it. When the 5. Mountain Division was also delayed, it was necessary to leave III. Corps in place. As a result, on 8 February Mannerheim informed the Germans that Finnish forces would make no further attacks on the Murmansk Railway.

The war was already taking its toll on Finland. Nearly a fifth of the population was in the armed forces. By the end of September 1941, Mannerheim began considering the reorganization of Finnish divisions into brigades, then discharging the older men to bolster the flagging home economy. Early in 1942, a lull set in on the Karelian front and Mannerheim decided to use the opportunity to implement his reorganization. Some 111,500 older men were sent home, or posted to reserve battalions. However, after only the 6. and 12. Divisions had been converted into the XII. and III. Brigades, respectively, the reduction program was abandoned on 16 May. The XII. Brigade became part of a new 6. Division in January 1943, so only the III. Brigade, and a new I. Jäger Brigade, remained in the Finnish order of battle for the remainder of the war.

Mannerheim disbanded the Karelian Army on 4 March 1942 and formed three fronts directly under his command:

**Maaselkä Front** (Gen.Brig. Laatikainen) - north of Lake Onega
**Aunus Front** (Gen.Maj. Oehquist) - Syväri (Svir) River
**Isthmus Front** (Gen.Maj. Oesch) - Karelian Isthmus

General Heinrichs was to return to his post of chief of staff. When the plan was later implemented, Generals Oesch and Oehquist exchanged commands. After reforming from the battered 6. Division, the XII. Brigade moved up to reinforce the 14. Division at Rukajärvi.

410

With the recovery in 1941 of the mainland areas ceded to the Russians after the Winter War, the Finns proceeded to occupy the islands in the Gulf of Finland also. On **26 March 1942**, the Finnish 18. Division headed for strategic Suursari (Hogland) Island in mid-gulf and landed safely, securing it the next day. The Curtiss 75As of LLv 32 covered the operation. Two flights of the Hawks were over Suursari on 28 March when three formations of Soviet fighters, totalling 29 Polikarpov I-153s and I-16s were sighted at 1630. A bitter hour-long fight resulted in the destruction of 10 I-153s and 7 I-16s at no loss to the Finns, one of the finest Finnish air actions of the war.

### Soviet Spring Offensive - April 1942

As the severe winter passed, the Finns noted Soviet troop movements along the Karelian Front between Lake Onega and the White Sea. The 14 and 26 Armies were being reinforced with miscellaneous brigades and battalions. Aerial activity also increased, the diminutive Soviet 7 Air Army operating along the Murmansk railway. The Soviet Union was now receiving a great deal of weaponry from the Western Allies and the Karelian units welcomed them.

At 1345 on **6 April**, 8 Brewster 239s of LLv 24 took off from their base on the northwestern shore of Lake Onega. While reconnoitering a suspected area northwest of Rugozero, they encountered a formation of 7 DB-3Fs and Pe-2s escorted by 18 Hurricanes and LaGG-3s. Without loss to themselves, the Finns shot down 2 DB-3Fs and 12 Hurricanes. This amazing, but typical, result was to be repeated many times over the next two years. Although they possessed material of equal or greater efficiency, the Russian pilots were inferior in training and experience to the brave and skillful Finns. However, the sheer number of Soviet fighters was making it difficult for Finnish bombers to operate.

The activity noted to the north was intended to pin Finnish units in place on the Maaselkä Front where strong Finnish forces were holding the railway.

**Maaselkä Front** (Gen.Maj. Laatikainen) - Povenets
14. Division - Rugozero region
    Attd. - XII. Brigade
II. Corps - Povenets
    1., 4. Divisions
Reserve
    8. Division
    III. Brigade
    German 163. Infantry Division

The I. Jäger Brigade had been in almost continuous action at the point of the Finnish advances during the summer and autumn of 1941 and was exhausted. When the 1. Division relieved it, the brigade moved to the west shore of Lake Seg and began a reorganization. Its services were not required in the coming months for the principal Russian objective was to drive the Finns away from the Svir (Syväri) River where the Aunus (Olonets) Front was in position to link up with the Germans and advance on Leningrad.

**Aunus Front** (Gen.Maj. Oesch) - Kolatselkä
VI Corps - west
    5., 11. Divisions
VII Corps - east
    7., 19. Divisions
Reserve
    17. Division

411

When the thaw began on **11 April**, a strong Soviet offensive erupted all along the Syväri River. After penetrating for 10 kilometers through the center of the front, the Soviet spearheads were sealed off and destroyed, with the aid of army cooperation Fokker D.21s from LLv 12 and 14. Forced back across the river, the Russians again lapsed into quiesence by 21 April.

Russian activity progressed northward with the Spring. North of the Maaselkä Front, the German Army of Lapland retained control of operations. There, the Soviet 26 Army attacked the Finnish III. Corps on **24 April**. West of Loukhi, one division pinned the Finns in front, while the main infantry forces struck their northern flank. The Finns gave way and the Army of Lapland rushed up its meagre reserves. Nevertheless, the Finns managed to surround the Soviet columns and annihilate them.

On the Arctic coast, two Soviet divisions hit Mountain Korps Norway on 27 April, while a naval brigade landed on the shore and advanced upon the German flank. Yet, the Germans frustrated the enemy envelopment. When they asked for Finnish help, Mannerheim shrewdly offered to exchange the German 163. Infantry Division for all Finns remaining under German command. Once the ice broke up in the Gulf of Bothnia, the German 5. and 7. Mountain Divisions were able to relieve the Finnish III. Corps troops, which gladly moved south. [203]

Ghosts in the Forest - Finnish Ski Troops Deploy

Yet, not all Finnish fighting men came home. From the frontier settlements were recruited five *Sissi* (raider) battalions, well adapted to the rugged conditions around the White Sea. Sharp attacks on Soviet intruders, followed by skillful encirclements, ended Russian security operations. The Germans successfully requested they stay in place.

After these offensives, a lull developed that lasted until 1944. Although he was now much stronger than the Soviet forces facing him, Mannerheim realized that a further advance into Russia would result in a declaration of war by the United States. He ordered his troops to dig in along the historical borders claimed by Finland. Both sides concentrated on training their troops and improving the field fortifications that now marked the stagnant front lines. In the Karelian Isthmus were four divisions:

**Isthmus Front** (Gen.Maj. Oehquist) - Mikkeli
I Corps - east
15., 18. Divisions
IV Corps - west
2., 10 Divisions

With the development of trench warfare, in May 1942 the Finnish air regiments were reorganized with mixed compositions to support specific parts of the front. Reflecting the alterations, the abbreviation for *lentolaivue* was changed to LeLv. Logistics were further complicated by an infusion of captured Soviet aircraft, purchased from Germany.

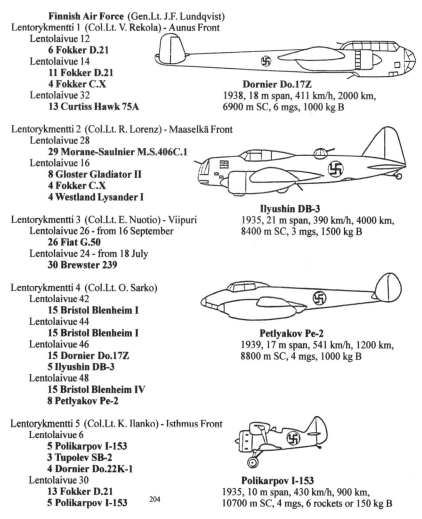

**Finnish Air Force** (Gen.Lt. J.F. Lundqvist)
Lentorykmentti 1 (Col.Lt. V. Rekola) - Aunus Front
  Lentolaivue 12
    **6 Fokker D.21**
  Lentolaivue 14
    **11 Fokker D.21**
    **4 Fokker C.X**
  Lentolaivue 32
    **13 Curtiss Hawk 75A**

**Dornier Do.17Z**
1938, 18 m span, 411 km/h, 2000 km,
6900 m SC, 6 mgs, 1000 kg B

Lentorykmentti 2 (Col.Lt. R. Lorenz) - Maaselkä Front
  Lentolaivue 28
    **29 Morane-Saulnier M.S.406C.1**
  Lentolaivue 16
    **8 Gloster Gladiator II**
    **4 Fokker C.X**
    **4 Westland Lysander I**

**Ilyushin DB-3**
1935, 21 m span, 390 km/h, 4000 km,
8400 m SC, 3 mgs, 1500 kg B

Lentorykmentti 3 (Col.Lt. E. Nuotio) - Viipuri
  Lentolaivue 26 - from 16 September
    **26 Fiat G.50**
  Lentolaivue 24 - from 18 July
    **30 Brewster 239**

Lentorykmentti 4 (Col.Lt. O. Sarko)
  Lentolaivue 42
    **15 Bristol Blenheim I**
  Lentolaivue 44
    **15 Bristol Blenheim I**
  Lentolaivue 46
    **15 Dornier Do.17Z**
    **5 Ilyushin DB-3**
  Lentolaivue 48
    **15 Bristol Blenheim IV**
    **8 Petlyakov Pe-2**

**Petlyakov Pe-2**
1939, 17 m span, 541 km/h, 1200 km,
8800 m SC, 4 mgs, 1000 kg B

Lentorykmentti 5 (Col.Lt. K. Ilanko) - Isthmus Front
  Lentolaivue 6
    **5 Polikarpov I-153**
    **3 Tupolev SB-2**
    **4 Dornier Do.22K-1**
  Lentolaivue 30
    **13 Fokker D.21**
    **5 Polikarpov I-153**   204

**Polikarpov I-153**
1935, 10 m span, 430 km/h, 900 km,
10700 m SC, 4 mgs, 6 rockets or 150 kg B

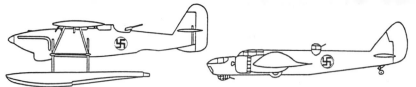

**Dornier Do.22K**
1935, 16 m span, 349 km/h, 2300 km,
8000 m SC, 3 mgs, 800 kg T

**Bristol Blenheim IV**
1938, 17 m span, 428 km/h, 3140 km,
8235 m SC, 5 mgs, 454 kg B

The Air Force was organized according to mission. Only two squadrons of interceptors remained, as intrusions by Soviet bombers were now infrequent, and the Brewsters of LeLv 24 and the Fiats of LeLv 26 were the only fighters capable of catching them. They were stationed in the Karelian Isthmus, forming Lentorykmentti 3. Also on the Isthmus Front was LeR 5 with the ground support Lentolaivue 30 flying Fokker D.21s, covered by captured Polikarpov I-153s, and the naval squadron, LeLv 6, which also had a flight of I-153s for protection of the base of short-range maritime reconnaissance Dornier Do.22K floatplanes and long-range SB-2s. Supporting ground forces on the Syväri River was LeR 1, deploying three squadrons of fighter bombers. A similar task was undertaken on the Maaselkä Front by Lentorykmentti 2, where a few Fokker C.X and Lysander army cooperation planes operated alongside Morane and Gladiator fighter bombers. The bombers of the *Ilmavoimien* (Air Force) were also organized by mission. Two squadrons of Blenheim Is were now capable of no more than reconnaissance and incidental bombing. Serious work was assigned to the Dorniers and Ilyushins of LeLv 46, while the Blenheim IVs and Pe-2s of LeLv 48 drew fast attack missions. Thus, Finnish combat experience had matured the air force.

The principal weakness revealed by the initial aerial clashes was the inadequate control exercised over Finnish fighters in the air. The lull in the fighting allowed General Lundqvist to improve the techniques of his fighter directors, using radio in conjunction with ground observers to vector interceptors toward incoming Soviet raiders. A great deal of tactical training sharpened his fighter pilots, the best of which remained in LeLv 24, the "Lynx squadron".

The Germans were still determined to destroy the Murmansk Railway, along which increasing supplies were passing to the hard-pressed Russians. Although the armored vehicles received from the Allies amounted to only one fifth of those used by the Soviet Union during the war, they arrived at a time when the Soviets had lost almost their entire tank park. By the end of 1942, over 6,200 British and American tanks had arrived. Thirteen hundred Allied aircraft also came by mid-1942, although many of them were flown in from Iran as many shiploads were sunk on the way to Murmansk. The majority were fighter bombers and attack bombers, useful in interdicting the German armored columns. Many of them began to appear on the Karelian Front.

The plan was for the German Twentieth Mountain Army to advance a hundred kilometers eastward from the Finnish border and capture Kandalaksha on the railway at the western tip of the White Sea. At the same time, the Finns were to attack toward the railroad junction at Soroka (Belomorsk) on the west coast of the White Sea and toward Rugozero. Although the west branch of the railway, to Leningrad, had been overrun during the initial offensive in the summer of 1941, the eastern branch passed from Soroka along the south shore of the White Sea to meet the line from icebound Archangel, thence south to Moscow. As long as the eastern branch was in Soviet hands, they would continue to receive vital supplies from the Allies.

After witnessing the successes of the German panzer divisions in Russia, and the inefficiency of Soviet units dispersed in infantry support, the Finnish High Command determined the necessity of organizing their motley tank battalions into a large mobile formation on 23 July 1942:

## PANSAR DIVISION

I. Jäger Brigade
  1 motorcycle company
  3 submachinegun battalions
  1 panzerjäger battalion
    3 companies
      **6 STZ** armored tractors, towing
        45 pst K/32 AT guns
Pansar Brigade
  I., II Tank Battalions
    3 tank companies
    HQ - 1 tank
    3 tank platoons
      **5 T-26, T-28**
Assault Gun Battalion
  3 companies
    3 platoons
      **3 BT-42**
Artillery Regiment
  2 light battalions
    3 batteries
      **4 field guns**
  1 medium battalion
    3 batteries
      **4 field howitzers**
Armored Anti-aircraft Battery
  3 platoons
    **2 ITPSV 40**
Armored Signal Company
  **4 T-37, 38**    <sup>205</sup>

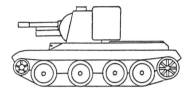

**BT-42**
1942, 14 tons, 1-114 mm howitzer,
60 km/h, 23 mm

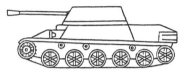

**ITPSV 40**
1937, 10.7 tons, 1-40 mm,
40 km/h, 5 men, 5000 m VR,
50 mm/1000 m P
(Landsverk 10)

**T-37**
1933, 3.5 tons, 1 mg,
64 km/h, 230 km, 6/9/7 mm, 2 men

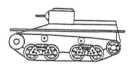

**T-38**
1936, 3.4 tons, 1 mg,
45 km/h, 250 km, 6/9/9 mm, 2 men

Based at Petrozavodsk, the armored division began training exercises along the western shore of Lake Onega. Its principal equipment consisted of 120 T-26s, mostly Soviet material captured in the early weeks of Barbarossa. Seven refurbished T-28Cs also proved valuable. Much less successful were the ungainly BT-42s of the Assault Gun Battalion. There were also five Independent Armored Car Platoons, equipped with captured Soviet T-37 and T-38 amphibious light tanks and BAF armored cars. They were used to spearhead lake and river crossings, and other special operations, and for protecting Finnish supply columns from partisans.

The Germans requested Finnish participation in *Operation Lachsfang* to settle the question. Marshal Mannerheim conveyed his requirement that Leningrad must first be captured to release troops from his southern fronts. He would then move his best divisions, in the Karelian Isthmus, to Medvezhyegorsk and Rukajärvi on the Maaselkä Front as the principal attacking forces in the offensive. The divisions of the II. Corps would support the initial assault. West of Lake Seg, the Finns new mobile division would deploy in position to counterattack Soviet penetrations. The Finnish frontline was now only 100 kilometers from the vital railway. As the principal fighter unit of the Maaselkä Front, LeLv 28 moved to Hirvas, 30 kilometers northwest of Lake Onega, on 3 August 1942. From there, its Moranes made frequent raids on the railway, shooting up trains with cannon and machinegun fire.

The plan would probably have succeeded, but it depended upon the prior reduction of Leningrad in order to free the Finnish divisions in the Karelian Isthmus. When Leningrad continued to hold out, the Germans were forced to cancel *Lachsfang* on 30 August.

To bolster the air effort against Leningrad, the German Luftflotte 5 had moved the units of Fliegerfuhrer Kirkenes southward to Kemijarvi, deploying two bomber groups forward to Utti on 6 April 1942. By June, it mustered 30 Bf.109s, 30 Ju.87s, 103 Ju.88s, 42 He.111s (torpedo bombers), 15 He.115s and 24 reconnaissance planes (Fw.200s, Ju.88s and Bv.138s). Missions were flown mainly toward the birthplace of the Bolshevik Revolution, as Army Group North struggled to subdue the stubborn defenders.

Lively shipping lanes supplied Germany with vital Scandinavian resources and permitted movement of German troops to the Arctic. The Soviets had few naval units with which to interdict the movements. The home base of the Soviet Baltic Fleet was at Kronstadt, at the head of the Gulf of Finland. Although it was surrounded and under frequent bombardment by 1942, the base continued to send submarine packs into the Baltic. The Finns and Germans laid mine barrages around the base to stop them, but the Russians swept channels through which their submarines passed. On the night of **12-3 June 1942** the *Hämeenmaa* and *Üusimaa*, 2 minelayers and 3 MTBs engaged Soviet minesweepers leading Soviet submarines through the mine barrage around Suurisaari (Hogland Is.). One submarine struck a mine and sank, but the rest eventually broke out into the Baltic.

As the Soviets desperately tried to maintain their position at the head of the Gulf of Finland, flotillas of Finnish gunboats harassed small Soviet craft. From 7-11 July 1942, the *Üusimaa*, *Hämeenmaa* and *Turunmaa* were joined by motor torpedo boats in engaging Soviet small craft around the island of Someri. The MTBs *Syoksy*, *Vihuri* and *Vinha* torpedoed and sank the Soviet gunboat *Krasnoe Znamya* in the harbor of Lavansaari during the night of 17-8 November.

416

Finnish submarines were engaged in hunting their Soviet brothers of the deep in the Åland Sea. In those narrow waters at the mouth of the Gulf of Bothnia, the Soviet submariners had found lucrative targets among convoys supplying German troops in northern Finland. Finnish seawolves were sent to stalk their own kind. *Vesihiisi* sank several Soviet submarines near Soderarm on **21 October 1942**. *Iku-Tursu* destroyed the *Shch-305* five days later and *Vetehinen* similarly slew *Shch-306* on 5 November. Finnish seamen were proving as scrappy as their brethren on land. [206]

As both sides built their strength for the decisive battle, the Soviets flailed at Finnish forces in the Karelian Isthmus. Eight SB-2bis bombers, escorted by 15 I-16s and 3 LaGG-3s, approached the base of LeLv 24, south of Viipuri, on **16 August 1942**. Six Brewster 239s rose at 1700 to intercept and shot down 11 I-16s over Seiskari, without loss. Two days later, another flight of 6 Brewsters from the same squadron discovered 60 Russian aircraft over Seivästö. Seven more Brewsters reinforced the first flight, and the largest air combat to date resulted. A single Brewster was destroyed, but 12 I-16s, 1 Hurricane and 2 Pe-2s were lost by the Russians that day.

The Soviets were holding doggedly to Leningrad, suffering horrible privations. When they launched a major offensive against the Germans on the Volkhov, south of Lake Ladoga, they were concerned about a possible advance by the Finnish Aunus Front from the Syväri River to cut the tenuous lifeline maintained eastward from Leningrad. All summer long, the pilots of LeLv 32, based south of Olonets (Aunus) at Nurmoila, had been battling Soviet raiders bent on reducing Finnish strength. Attrition had reduced the number of combat-worthy Curtiss Hawk 75As. They gained a measure of redress on **5 September**, when a pilot of LeLv 32 discovered 40 Soviet aircraft over Lotinanpelto (Lodenoye Pole). Joined by 4 more Hawk 75As, he engaged the Russians. Finns downed 6 LaGG-3s, 4 I-16s, 3 MiG-3s and 1 Pe-2 in fierce combat, without loss.

Unable to witness the reduction of Leningrad, the German bombers of Luftflotte 5 left Utti on 27 October to rejoin their other units at Kemijarvi. When, two days later, the Germans counterattacked on the Volkhov Front, they regained their positions. With winter approaching, an offensive involving Finland was unlikely. The Russians had other ideas.

A counteroffensive erupted south of Lake Ladoga, breaking through to reestablish a land route to Leningrad. The Finns were badly shaken by the news, raising the possibility of eventual German defeat with adverse consequences for Finland. Mannerheim realized the danger to the Karelian Isthmus and dispatched the reconstituted 6. Division to the shore of Lake Onega to relieve the Cavalry Division, placed in reserve east of Viipuri.

The United States delivered a diplomatic note to the Finnish ambassador on 20 March, urging them to make a separate peace with the Soviet Union. However, when queried by German Foreign Minister Ribbentrop, the Finnish government declared its intention to continue the war.

The struggle continued around the Soviet Baltic naval base. The Soviet 13 Air Army of the Leningrad Front also operated over southern Finland. Late in the afternoon of **18 April 1943**, LeLv 24 pilots attacked an enemy ground attack force near Kronstadt. Thirteen Brewster 239s waded into the formation of 8 Il-2s and 40 fighters. They managed to shoot down 8 LaGG-3s, 7 Yak-1s, 3 La-5s and 2 Il-2s, landing again with no casualties. Three days later the same squadron fought 35 Soviet fighters over the same territory. Although they returned without 2 of their own, 17 Brewsters harvested 10 Yak-1s, 5 LaGG-3s and 4 La-5s during a morning of profitable work. [208]

The Pansar Division Advances - a T-26S on the Road

In the spring of 1943, the Russians renewed demonstrations along the Syväri River, although no offensive developed. The new Pansar Division was in reserve of the Aunus Front and some of its units saw their first action. The Assault Gun Battalion confronted Soviet Armor crossing the Syväri River, the BT-42s proving clumsy and ineffective. However, the Russians were forced back over the river, leaving much heavy equipment behind, including 7 T-34s and 2 KV-1s which were taken into the Pansar Division. Three more T-34s were later received from Germany. On 1 June, Mannerheim sent to the Germans a request for 50 captured T-34s to reequip one of the tank battalions, but was informed that none were available. The Germans promised to deliver 30 of their formidable *Stumgeschutz* assault guns, instead. They arrived on 14 December, along with a German team tasked to train the Finnish crews. The Pansar Division now possessed weapons effective against the Soviet T-34.

A number of other changes also had occurred within the Finnish Army during the summer of 1943. The Finnish Volunteer Battalion returned from service with the German SS. For long-range reconnaissance work directly under the High Command, the IV. Independent Battalion formed on 15 July. Three new mixed brigades (XIX, XX, XXI) were organized on 28 October, but by the end of the year their 8 light field howitzer batteries had not arrived. Thus, the Finnish Army slowly gathered strength.

As 1942 faded into autumn, Finnish airmen began to encounter more modern Soviet aircraft. LaGG-3s, Yak-1s and Yak-7s replaced the outdated Polikarpov fighters. In addition, many of the Hurricane II, Kittyhawk and Airacobra fighters received by the Soviet Union via Lend-Lease were deployed to the north, but the capabilities of Soviet pilots still left much to be desired. Despite facing superior new Soviet aircraft, the Finns retained their high morale and maintained their ascendancy in combat. However, overall Finnish aerial superiority began to decline, a trend accelerated by the marked improvement in the quality of the Russian pilots during 1943. Fast and powerful La-5s and Yak-9s began to take a toll of the Finnish fighter units. More modern equipment was imperative, and 16 Messerschmitt Bf.109G-2s reequipped the new LeLv 34, stationed at Utti from where they could intervene over either Viipuri or Helsinki. They were immediately successful when the squadron became operational in May 1943. A few also went to replace the losses of LeLv 30 in the Karelian Isthmus. However, the most numerous fighter of 1943 was the Morane-Saulnier M.S.406, by which time 87 had been received from Germany. LeLv 14 and 28 used the Morane for fighter reconnaissance and ground support on both sides of Lake Ladoga. The harried LeLv 32 welcomed 12 Curtiss Hawk 75A-3s to replace those lost over the Syväri River. They also received 3 LaGG-3s for use in high-speed reconnaissance. Neighboring LeLv 12 received equipment capable of utilizing the large lakes and rivers of the area as bases for reconnaissance - 4 captured Beriev MBR-2 flying boats.

The bomber squadrons of LeR 4 were also strengthened. To replace the battle losses of LeLv 42, VL delivered 30 more Blenheim Is, some of which also brought LeLv 48 to full operational strength. A second medium bomber squadron was gained when the Blenheims of LeLv 44 were replaced in the spring of 1943 by new Junkers Ju.88A-4s from Germany. LeR 4 had concentrated upon short-range tactical bombing close to the battle fronts. Only one strategic operation was carried out during the Continuation War. On **19 September 1943**, 14 Ju.88s of LeLv 44, 6 Do.17Zs and 4 DB-3s of LeLv 46, and 6 Blenheims of LeLv 42 set out to attack Lavansaari Island in the Gulf of Finland. As they progressed southward, the weather deteriorated and many of the bombers became lost, making forced landings on scattered landing grounds in Finland. Only a few reached the target.

This disappointment was somewhat ameliorated by a great victory that occurred four days later when the Finns caught a mixed force of Soviet fighters and *schturmovik* over the Oranienbaum encirclement in northern Estonia. From 1530 to 1630 in the afternoon, 7 Brewsters of LeLv 24 were joined by 4 Messerschmitts of LeLv 34 in shooting down 7 LaGG-3s, 6 La-5s, 1 Yak-1 and an Il-2. All of the Finns returned safely to their base.

Following the German defeat at Stalingrad, the Swedish government had been urging the Finns to withdraw from the war as they were fearful that Finland would eventually be occupied by the Soviet Union, placing Russian troops just a boat ride from Swedish shores. The Americans were also pressuring them to reach an accomodation with the Soviets, threatening to declare war if the Finns mounted new offensives. To quell German anxiety, the government assured Ribbentrop on 3 September that Finland would continue the war. Many Finns feared that the agreement would involve Finland in Germany's schemes, while others were complaining that the Army was dallying when it should be attacking the weak Russian forces trying to hold the Karelian Front. However, Mannerheim now believed that Germany would inevitably lose in the end and did not wish to jeopardize postwar negotiations with the Soviet Union.

The strong Soviet offensive that began on **17 January 1944** did not encourage the Finnish high command. Erupting from Novgorod to Oranienbaum, the attack drove the German Eighteenth Army back to Narva, exposing the Finnish positions both on the Syväri River and in the Karelian Isthmus. Now Finns began to raise the question of a separate peace with Russia. At the end of the month, Mannerheim requested the transfer of the 3. Division from Ukhta to the Finnish reserve and asked for 4,000 German MG42 light machineguns and captured Russian artillery (60-122 mm and 200-152 mm). An envoy met with Soviet representatives in Stockholm but, after lengthy negotiation, the Russian terms were rejected on 18 April.

Russian bombers appeared over Finnish cities again early in 1944. Heavy raids hit Helsinki on 6 and 27 February, causing much destruction and bringing German night fighters to Tallinn and Helsinki. A night raid on 6 March against the naval base at Kotka also did damage. By this time, few Finnish warships were active, the remaining armored ship and patrol vessels being used primarily as static anti-aircraft defenses for the naval base. Concurring with German fears that Soviet vessels may try to break out of the Gulf of Finland to raid supply lines to Finland, on 10 May Mannerheim allowed the German heavy cruiser *Prinz Eugen* to establish a base near the Åland Islands.

Mannerheim began to gather aerial and ground forces to face an expected attack in the Karelian Isthmus. The Cavalry Brigade had been reinforced with the 6. Jäger Battalion in June 1943. After operational training on the Aunus Front for more than a year, the Pansar Division was sent to the Viipuri plateau on 13 February 1944 to form a mobile reserve with the cavalry.

**PANSAR DIVISION**
I. Jäger Brigade
    1 motorcycle company
    3 submachinegun battalions
    1 panzerjäger battalion
        3 companies
            **6 STZ** armored tractors, towing
                45 pst K/32 AT guns
Pansar Brigade
    2 tank battalions
        3 tank companies
            3 tank platoons
                **5 T-26, T-34, KV-1**
Assault Gun Battalion
    3 companies
        3 platoons
            **5 Stu 40**
Independent Assault Gun Company
    3 platoons
        **5 BT-42**
Artillery Regiment
    2 light battalions
        3 batteries
            **4 field guns**
    1 medium battalion
        3 batteries
            **4 field howitzers**
Armored Anti-aircraft Battery
    3 platoons
        **2 ITPSV 40**
Armored Signal Company
    **4 T-37, 38**

New equipment had strengthened the pansar division. The tank battalions were still equipped mainly with T-26s, except for 10 T-34s and 2 KV-1s, but the Pansar Division had gained much firepower with the acquisition of 59 *Sturmgeschutz G.III* assault guns from Germany. Designated Stu 40s, they were well suited to Finnish fighting conditions, where the forests and many lakes channeled Soviet attacks into killing grounds ideal for turretless anti-tank vehicles. However, Hitler ordered curtailment of arms shipments to Finland on 19 April, depriving the Finnish Army of badly needed anti-tank weapons and artillery. The order also delayed delivery of 15 Pz.Kw.IVJ medium tanks to the Pansar Division until it was too late to use them.

Late in the spring, Finnish communication and supply centers began receiving attention from the Soviet 13 Air Army, 1,000 sorties appearing over Helsinki. A formation of 27 Pe-2 bombers, escorted by 15 Yak-9s and La-5s, approached Hamina on **17 May**. Ten Bf.109Gs of HLeLv 34 rose from their base near Kotka at 1030 and intercepted, downing 8 Pe-2s before the escort could come down. When they did descend, they lost 3 Yak-9s while downing 1 Bf.109G. Finnish bombers made successful attacks on the Soviet bomber bases near Leningrad in retaliation.

With the German forces driven completely out of southern and central Russia early in 1944, and Army Group North pushed back a hundred kilometers from Leningrad, the Finns realized it was only a matter of time until the Soviets spared enough troops to reactivate their Karelian Front. Russian rifle divisions were weak and the Soviets relied on overwhelming superiority in tanks, artillery and aircraft. Their forces in the Karelian Isthmus included 800 tanks and assault guns in 4 tank brigades and 4 assault gun regiments:

> Far North
> 14 Army
> 6 divisions, 8 brigades
> **Karelian Front** (Meretskov)
> 7 Army (Krutikov) - Svir River
> 14 divisions
> 32 Army (Gorelenko)
> 3 divisions
> **Leningrad Front** (Gororov) - Karelian Isthmus
> 21 Army (Gusev) - western
> 10 divisions
> 23 Army (Cherepanov) - eastern
> 8 divisions
> 13 Air Army
> 1500 aircraft

Under the changed conditions, Mannerheim had reorganized his fronts on 24 February. On 25 March, he sent the III. Brigade to Kemijärvi as a reserve behind the German units guarding their supply ports at the head of the Gulf of Bothnia. Leaving the Maaselkä Front in the capable hands of General Talvela, General Laatikainen took his management skills to the locus of the most likely Soviet attack in the Karelian Isthmus.

The Finns had improved the fortifications of the Mannerheim Line during the years of inactivity, knowing that the Karelian Isthmus would be the site for the main Soviet offensive. A forward line of emplacements along the frontier was intended to blunt the attack, with the main Second Position somewhat farther back between Vammelsuu and Taipale. The defiles created by the many lakes and forests were pre-registered by the scarce Finnish anti-tank guns and artillery. Finnish fighter bombers were prepared to assist.

The feared Soviet armor would be largely negated if it could be contained in the morainal forests and lakes of the Isthmus. Unfortunately, the Finns had so few armored vehicles that they dared not risk them in the forward areas for fear of being isolated. The Third Position ran from Viipuri to Vuoksi. Here the Finnish armor was held in reserve for counterattacking any penetrations, the final opportunity to halt the enemy. If tanks reached the more open country around Viipuri, there would be no stopping them. Once again, the brave Finns were to fight a much better-equipped enemy.

The Finns had used the long respite to strengthen and reorganize their forces. From Mikkeli, Mannerheim controlled a large mobile reserve, but delegated local command to his three front commanders:

Finnish Army (Field Marshal Mannerheim) - Mikkeli

III. Brigade - Kemijärvi

Maaselkä Front (Gen.Maj. Talvela) - Povenets
14. Division - Rugozero
II Corps (Gen.Maj. Maekinen) - Povenets
1., 4. Divisions

T-26S
1937, 10.5 tons, 1-45 mm, 2 mgs,

Aunus Front (Gen.Maj. Oesch) - Kolatselkä
V Corps (Gen.Maj. Svenson) - east
6., 8. Divisions, XX. Brigade
VI Corps (Gen.Maj. Blick, Martola from July 8) - west
17. Division, XXI. Brigade

31 km/h, 225 km, 25/25/16 mm,
47 mm/1000 m P, 3 men

Isthmus Front (Gen.Maj. Oehquist) - Mikkeli
III Corps (Gen.Maj. Siilasvuo) - east
18., 15. Divisions, XIX. Brigade
IV Corps (Gen.Maj. Laatikainen) - west
10., 2. Divisions

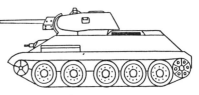

General Reserve
IV. Independent Battalion - Mikkeli
BAF armored cars

T-34C-F
1942, 31.3 tons, 1-76.2 mm, 2 mgs,

Pansar Division (Gen.Maj. Lagus) - Viipuri
142 tanks and assault guns
Cavalry Brigade (Gen.Maj. Melander) - Viipuri

50 km/h, 450 km, 70/47/45 mm,
61 mm/1000 m P, 4 men

3. Infantry Division
200. Estonian Regiment

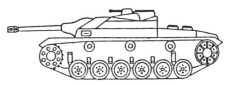

Stu 40
1943, 26 tons, 1-75 mm L48,
40 km/h, 155 km, 80/30 mm,
117 mm/1000 m P, 4 men
(Sturmgeschutz IIIG)                    209,210

The Messerschmitt Bf.109G had become the principal Finnish interceptor, 30 Bf.109G-2s and 132 Bf.109G-6s being received during 1943-4. They arrived armed with three 20 mm cannon to deal with Allied heavy bombers. The Finns removed two of them to enhance their ability to oppose the nimble Soviet fighters. The Morane-Saulnier M.S.406 was the best ground attack plane possessed by the Finns, but it was at a serious disadvantage against the new Soviet fighters. Germany offered to supply quantities of captured Klimov M-105P engines for installation in the remaining Moranes. A developed version of the Hispano-Suiza that powered the French fighters, the more powerful Soviet engine was easily mounted, boosting speed by 60 km/h. As Moranes in service came due for an overhaul, they were fitted with the Klimovs, beginning in the early summer of 1944. However, the critical fighting that erupted in June forced many fighters to operate beyond their maintenance limits, and only about 20 of the "Mörkö-Moranni" had been converted by the Armistice.

The Finnish Air Force continued to face the enemy with a plethora of outdated equipment:

**Finnish Air Force** (Gen.Lt. J.F. Lundqvist) - Helsinki

Lentorykmentti 1 (Col.Lt. V. Rekola) - Aunus Front
   Tiedustelulentolaivue 12
      **13 Fokker D.21**
      **3 Bristol Blenheim I**
      **4 Beriev MBR.2**
      **26 VL Myrsky II** (from August)
   Hävittäjälentolaivue 32
      **12 Curtiss Hawk 75A**
      **3 Lavochin LaGG-3**

**Beriev MBR-2**
1931, 19 m span, 221 km/h, 1500 km,
5000 m SC, 3 mgs,
300 kg B, mines or DC

Lentorykmentti 2 (Col.Lt. J. Harju-Jeanty) - Maaselkä Front
   Tiedustelulentolaivue 16
      **4 Gloster Gladiator II**
      **3 Polikarpov I-153**
      **4 Fokker C.X**
      **4 Westland Lysander**
   Hävittäjälentolaivue 28
      **16 Morane-Saulnier M.S.406**
      **8 Messerschmitt Bf.109G-2**
      **3 Mörkö-Moranni** (by Sept.)
   Hävittäjälentolaivue 26 (from August 8)
      **16 Brewster 239**

**Lavochkin LaGG-3**
1940, 10 m span, 560 km/h, 650 km,
7.1/5000 m, 9000 m SC, 1-20 mm,
1-3 mgs, 6 rockets or 220 kg B

Lentorykmentti 3 (Col.Lt. G. Magnusson) - Isthmus Front
   Hävittäjälentolaivue 24
      **24 Messerschmitt Bf.109G-6**
   Hävittäjälentolaivue 26 (to August 4)
      **16 Brewster 239**
   Hävittäjälentolaivue 34
      **16 Messerschmitt Bf.109G-6**

**Messerschmitt Bf.109G**
1941, 10 m span, 641 km/h, 725 km,
6/5700 m, 11800 m SC, 3-20 mm, 2 mgs

Lentorykmentti 4 (Col.Lt. B. Gabrielsson) - general reserve
   Pommituslentolaivue 42
      **18 Bristol Blenheim I**
   Pommituslentolaivue 44
      **23 Junkers Ju.88A-4**
   Pommituslentolaivue 46
      **9 Dornier Do.17Z-2**
      **5 Ilyushin DB-3F**
      **3 Ilyushin DB-3**
   Pommituslentolaivue 48
      **19 Bristol Blenheim I, IV**
      **3 Petlyakov Pe-2**
      **3 Ilyushin DB-3**

**Junkers Ju.88A**
1938, 20 m span, 470 km/h, 2270 km,
8240 m SC, 6 mgs, 1500 kg B

Lentorykmentti 5 (Col.Lt. K. Ilanko) - Pori
   Tiedustelulentolaivue 6
      **14 Tupolev SB-2, SB-2bis**
      **3 Dornier Do.22K-1**
   Tiedustelulentolaivue 14
      **16 Morane-Saulnier M.S.406**
      **5 Fokker D.21**
   Hävittäjälentolaivue 30
      **16 Messerschmitt Bf.109G**

**Tupolev SB.2**
1934, 20 m span, 410 km/h, 1200 km,
8500 m SC, 4 mgs, 600 kg B

Osasto Jauri (long-range recco groups) -Hirviranta
      **3 Liore et Olivier H-246**
      **2 Heinkel He.115A**
      **2 Arado Ar.196A-3**
      **2 Heinkel He.59C-2**

**Ilyushin DB-3F (Il-4)**
1939, 21 m span, 446 km/h, 3500 km,
9000 m SC, 3 mgs, 2500 kg B

211

423

The *Ilmavoimien* was included in the Army restructuring of 24 February. Army cooperation squadrons were redesignated *Tiedustelulentolaivue* (TLeLv). Fighter squadrons became *Hävittäjälentolaivue* (HLeLv) while the bomber squadrons were called *Pommituslentolaivue* (PLeLv). Thus, the designation reflected the mission of each squadron, of which the most important had received new aircraft during the lull in fighting. Finnish production of obsolete aircraft tapered off during 1944. Since 1942, Valtion Lentokonetehdas had been developing its own fighter design, but had encountered numerous problems. Production finally began in 1944, 46 being delivered as the VL Myrsky II. They began reaching TLeLv 12 in August, too late to see much action before the Armistice. The Myrsky was a disappointment, being two years out of date and lacking the flying qualities of types already in Finnish service.

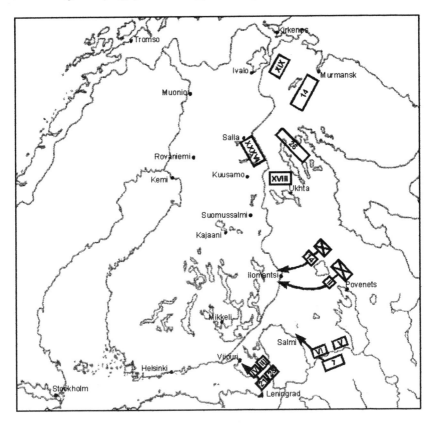

Although an offensive had long been expected in the Karelian Isthmus, the Russians achieved surprise when a thousand aircraft joined massed artillery in pummeling the Finnish lines on **9 June 1944**. The weight of the attack struck the Finnish right wing, which managed to seal off the minor encroachments achieved by the Russian infantry. The tremendous artillery barrage was renewed at 0500 the following morning. Battalions of heavy Soviet assault guns struck the forward Finnish positions while Ilyushin Il-2s lashed at everything in sight from low altitude. By noon, Soviet armor had blasted more than 10 kilometers through the Finnish IV Corps.

Communications were lost to the 10. Division, which held the weakest point in the forward line at Valkeasaari. There was little left with which to communicate, for a swarm of heavy tanks had burst over the division and destroyed the regiment in its path. Mannerheim tried to stop the rampage with his Cavalry Brigade, but it was thrown back along the coast to the Second Line, to which the remnants of the 10. Division were also forced to retreat. The neighboring 2. and 18. Divisions fought to hold the flanks of the penetration, but the Soviets succeeded in enlarging the breach during the afternoon. Although the III. Corps was able to hold the eastern sector of the line against lesser attacks, the magnitude of the western breach threatened the entire Mannerheim Line. The High Command ordered the III. Brigade and the 4. Division to rush southward from the Maaselkä Front.

Supported by the 3. Division, the Estonians, and reserve elements of the frontline divisions, General Lagus was ordered to break the armored spearpoint. With the jägers leading, his Pansar Division confronted the oncoming Soviet tankers on **12 June**, its Stu 40s destroying 29 Russian tanks. All day, the Finnish infantry beat back attacks between Vammelsuu and Siiranmäki. The dangerous thrust faltered. The Finns were given time to complete their withdrawal to the Second Line in good order while the 15. Division and the XIX. Brigade maintained their positions in the First Line.

The Finnish front line was now 80 kilometers long. Even with the 4. Division and the III. Brigade arriving, more help was required, for the Finns had identified 18 Soviet divisions in the assault. Realizing the crisis was at hand, Mannerheim also called in the 17. Division and the XX. Brigade from the Aunus Front. Large scale Russian attacks resumed on **14 June**. A penetration at Sahakylä was restored by a counterattack, but disaster threatened when Soviet armor erupted at Kuuterselkä. A fierce tank battle raged all night, allowing four Soviet infantry divisions to advance 8 kilometers into the Finnish position by morning. III. Corps pulled back to the Second Position to shorten the lines.

Soviet pressure continued. To prevent a further weakening of his defenses, Marshal Mannerheim ordered all units in the Second Position to fall back to the Third Position around Viipuri, reducing frontages and placing his units within supporting distance of each other. He recalled General Oesch from East Karelia to take command of the battle, for it had proven too difficult to control the confused events from Mikkeli. General Svenson was transfered from the Aunus Front to command the troops arriving to defend Viipuri. General Lagus commanded the threatened coastal sector, the Cavalry Brigade at Inonkylae, along the coast, with the 10. Division and III. Brigade holding the line between it and the Pansar Division. Lagus was to conduct a mobile defense while slowly withdrawing toward Viipuri.

Urgent requests for German weapons to stop the Soviet tanks produced an airlift from the Twentieth Mountain Army. Motor torpedo boats also carried 9,000 *panzerfaust* anti-tank recoilless rifles across the Gulf of Finland on 19 June. The new weapons helped the Isthmus troops to stop a strong tank attack west of Kaukjärvi on **17 June**, harvesting 34 Soviet heavy tanks. The Cavalry Brigade was particularly hard hit, General Melander requiring replacement by Colonel Tachtinen. Vicious fighting continued around Summa the following day, as the Finns desperately tried to keep Russian armor from reaching the open country around Viipuri. They were now in a dangerous position forward of the Vuoksi River which was crossed by only one bridge outside of Viipuri. Should the Soviets beat the Finns to the city, which lay south of the river, they would lose all of their heavy equipment. [212,213]

425

Mannerheim intended to mount his final resistance in the Third Position behind the Vuoksi River. As the forces gathered on 19 June, several dozen Russian aircraft raided Viipuri. They were intercepted at 2000 by 8 Bf.109Gs of HLeLv 34 and 10 Bf.109Gs from HLeLv 24 which shot down 6 Pe-2s, 2 DB-3Fs, 2 Il-2s, 2 La-5s and 3 Bell Airacobras without loss.

Numerous combats took place in the Viipuri area on **20 June** as the Soviets entered the city, fighting from house to house. Air action began at daybreak when 10 Bf.109Gs of HLeLv 34 took off from Immola and, with 8 Bf.109Gs of HLeLv 24 from Lapeenranta attacked several dozen Soviet planes, shooting down 2 DB-3Fs, 2 Il-2s, 4 Yak-9s, 2 La-5s and 1 LaGG-3. An hour later 10 other Bf.109Gs of HLeLv 24 and 6 of HLeLv 34 were airborne and spent two hours over Viipuri destroying 5 Bell Airacobras, 1 Pe-2, 1 Il-2, 1 La-5, 4 Yak-9s, 2 LaGG-3s, and 1 MiG-3 without loss. At mid-morning, a third melee occurred over Viipuri when 5 Bf.109Gs from HLeLv 24 and 4 from HLeLv 34 arrived to protect ground forces from the attentions of 8 Soviet ground attack planes, covered by a few dozen fighters. After a spirited combat, 5 Il-2s, 3 La-5s, 1 Airacobra and 1 U-2 were on the ground, with no Finnish casualties. [214]

Despite overwhelming opposition, the Finnish aviators continued to pile up victories. Yet, they were irreplaceable and the strength of the *Ilmavoimien* was waning. In conjunction with Finnish Ju.88s and Blenheims, the Kemi-based units of Luftflotte 5 began flying missions on 21 June to support the last desperate stand being made to prevent egress of the Soviets from the Isthmus. Had the Finns time to complete the Third Position, it would have been formidable. However, the western part of the line, from Viipuri to Vuoksi, lacked fortifications, allowing enemy mechanized forces to operate unhindered by the lakes and forests of the lower Isthmus. The Finnish government began to waver, until Ribbentrop met with them and promised to send an assault gun brigade to aid in stopping the Soviet advance.

On 21 June, Soviet motorized columns broke through Viipuri along the coastal road. The city had to be abandoned, for only behind the streams north of the city would the Finns have any chance of stopping them. East of the city, Russian tanks advanced over increasingly favorable terrain. General Oesch committed all of his new heavy weapons in an attempt to prevent a disastrous breakthrough in good tank country. Finnish tanks entered the fray at Tali on **22 June** and, along with infantry employing the new anti-tank weapons, beat off repeated Soviet attacks. The next day, 20 Il-2s and 8 R-10s, together with 15 fighters, were bombing and strafing Finnish positions at Tali when they were met by 8 Bf.109Gs of HLeLv 24. Without loss to themselves, the Finns shot down 6 Il-2s, 1 Airacobra, 1 Mustang and 3 La-5s. Yet, they harvested only a fraction of a sky full of Soviet raptors.

The Finnish Army was to lose 18,000 men in the heavy fighting through the Isthmus, although 12,000 replacements arrived. Driven to desperation, Mannerheim invoked the new pact with Ribbentrop, accepting massive German assistance in exchange for agreeing to the alliance. Some 5,000 *panzerschreck* anti-tank rocket launchers arrived by air on 22 June. The next day, the German 303. Sturmgeschutz Brigade disembarked and raced to Viipuri where it went straight into battle. The 122. Infantry Division took a more leisurely pace from Helsinki to Viipuri, where it was to relieve the Cavalry Brigade on the west flank of the Finnish line. Of the aerial help requested, Luftflotte 5 could spare only a squadron of Focke-Wulf Fw.190 fighters and one of Junkers Ju.87 dive bombers. A month later, the aircraft were returned to Luftflotte 1.

Because of the crisis in Karelia, Finnish submarines were deployed into the upper Gulf of Finland from 22-8 June. The three large submarines hunted south of Koivisto (Primorsk), and the two small ones near Tiurinsaari, with no success. During the first week of July, the *Vetehinen* and *Vesihiisi* laid mines near Peninsaari and in Koivisto Sound. The 14 refurbished Tupolev SB-2s of LeLv 6 proved their value by sinking several Soviet submarines in the Gulf. German cruisers entered the Gulf to prevent Soviet crossings.

On **25 June**, 10 Russian divisions, supported by SU battalions, assaulted the main Finnish defenses, achieving a deep penetration at Repola. For four days, a fierce battle raged in the air and on the ground. Several dozen Soviet fighters escorted 20 Il-2s and 20 Pe-2s in an attack on Finnish positions at Tali on the morning of 28 June. They were intercepted by 11 Bf.109Gs of HLeLv 24 and, for the expenditure of 1 Messerschmitt, 8 Il-2s, 2 Pe-2s and a fighter were destroyed. Early in the afternoon of the same day, a huge formation of 60-70 Il-2s returned to the same area, strafing and bombing the battered Finnish troops. Eight Bf.109Gs of HLeLv 34 and 8 more from HLeLv 24 slashed through the swarm of 40 Soviet fighters covering the operation. Together, they shot down 6 Il-2s, 2 Yak-9s, 2 Mustangs and 1 Airacobra. Many more enemy aircraft got through.

Although the Finns succeeded in containing the penetration by committing their last reserves, for four days the Soviets persistently enlarged it. The German 303. Sturmgeschutz Brigade went into line at Tali on 27 June. A huge combat took place on 30 June when 7 Bf.109Gs of HLeLv 34 and 7 of HLeLv 24 attacked more than a hundred Russian aircraft just before noon. The Russians lost 3 Pe-2s, 2 DB-3Fs, 1 Il-2, 1 La-5, 9 Yak-9s and 1 Airacobra. But the Russians had many more aircraft, the Finns did not.

The Soviets decided to battle the pesky Finnish hornets at their nest. On 2 July the Soviets succeeded in mounting a night attack with escorted 35 Pe-2s and 40 Il-2s. About 2000, HLeLv 24 sent up 11 Bf.109Gs and HLeLv 34 flew off 8 more to intercept the attackers. Some 11 Il-2s, 4 Pe-2s and 1 Yak-9 were downed, but 2 Bf.109Gs were destroyed on the ground. Operations from the Viipuri airbases soon become impossible.

Captured T-34/85s and KV-1s Were Put to Good Use by the Finns

Direct contact had already been established with Moscow on 16 February, but proposed armistice terms were rejected. The situation was precarious and, through Stockholm, the Soviets had been informed on 22 June that Finland was willing to negotiate. Ribbentrop had arrived in Helsinki the next day and insisted that Finland remain in the war to the end. President Ryti sent a letter to Hitler on 26 June, assuring him of Finland's intention to continue. Shipments of German arms resumed. The alliance between Germany and Finland was announced on 26 June 1944, causing a crisis in the Finnish government. The United States broke off diplomatic relations with Finland, but stopped short of declaring war.

By **3 July**, the Soviet armies had been replenished and a new attack threatened Ihantala. As the Russians tried to cross the Bay of Viipuri, their attack struck the German 122. Infantry Division, which had just relieved the Finnish Cavalry Brigade. Along with German *sturmgeschutzen*, the Finnish T-34s and Stu 40s were employed skillfully. The Russians withdrew without 7 T-34/85s and 2 JSU-152s, which were soon being operated by grateful Finnish tankers. However, the unwieldy BT-42s were largely destroyed, and the Independent Assault Gun Company was disbanded. As motor torpedo boats could not operate in the shallow water, the Russians did gain a foothold on the river delta at Viipuri, but got no farther.

Early in July, the Finns had a respite as the Soviets paused to regroup and replenish their units. They poured more troops into the vital Karelian Isthmus until by 15 July the two armies there had 26 rifle divisions and 12-14 tank brigades. Finnish casualties reached 44,000 by the last week in July, 6,500 of which were dead men. Mannerheim was forced to mobilize reservists as old as 42 years of age.

A crisis developed on the Aunus Front when the Soviets broke through in the direction of Laimola on **11 July**. It was necessary to abandon Petrozavodsk and Salmi to straighten the lines. There were few good defensive positions and the Finnish ground troops were caught in open ground, with the sky full of enemy aircraft. Losses were heavy. The Aunus Front was disbanded on 18 July. Thereafter, General Martola's VI Corps and General Maekinen's II Corps operated east of Lake Ladoga directly under the orders of the High Command.

A curious lull set in. A number of Soviet assault units left for the Narva Front, replaced by poor quality fortress troops. The Germans began to withdraw some of their troops and aircraft. Thus the promised 202. Sturmgeschutz Brigade never appeared. The Finnish 10. Division relieved the German 122. Infantry Division and the 200. Infantry Regiment left for Estonia. To give freedom of action to Finland, President Ryti officially resigned on 1 August, thus abrogating his March 1943 agreement with Ribbentrop. Parliament immediately nominated Marshal Mannerheim to succeed him.

Only the Finnish II Corps on the northeastern flank remained under Russian attack. The Cavalry Brigade and XX. Brigade left Viipuri to reinforce it. XX. Brigade went into line with the 1. Division on the extreme left flank of the corps. Two Russian divisions were enveloped and nearly destroyed near Ilomantsi on **10 August** by the 14. Division, XXI. Brigade and Cavalry Brigade. Then this sector also became quiescent.

On 23 August, the Russians reminded the Finns of their continued presence with numerous air attacks on Finnish settlements. Finnish fighters had enjoyed much success during 1944, downing 550 Soviet planes. However, the Finns had lost 209 aircraft in aerial combat, with 327 more being destroyed on the ground.

Mannerheim took charge of the government on 4 August. His cabinet was formed with the express purpose of getting Finland out of the war. On 17 August, he informed Germany that the agreement with Ribbentrop was no longer binding. The first peace feelers were extended on 25 August, and discussions with the Soviet Union began five days later. A ceasefire was followed by an armistice, signed on **19 September 1944**.

The Germans attempted to seize strategic localities before the armistice went into effect. They planned Operation BIRKE, the withdrawal along the Arctic coast, and Operation TANNE, the occupation of the Åland Islands. The latter operation was later broken into TANNE OST, the occupation of Suursaari (Hogland) Island by troops crossing from Estonia, and TANNE WEST, landings in the Åland Islands by naval parties and paratroops to hold open the supply routes to northern Finland. Hitler canceled TANNE WEST, as he had insufficient forces to carry it through, settling instead for U boats stationed near the islands. The last German vessel left Kemi, at the head of the Gulf of Bothnia, on 21 September. Troops landed on Suursaari on 15 September. However, the Soviet Air Force prevented reinforcement and the Finnish troops on the island were able to drive off the Germans. [215]

*The Lapland War* - September-December 1944

Following the Armistice, the Germans were informed that the Finnish 6. Division would occupy Kajaani while the 15. Division went to Oulu, moves they considered a threat to their Arctic forces. Twentieth Mountain Army in northern Finland and Norway was considered to be Hitler's most powerful army by late 1944, and as such was of great interest to the Allies. Its quarter of a million men were highly trained and retained high morale despite the difficult theatre in which they served. The Western Allies feared that this fine fighting force of 9 divisions would be transferred to Central Europe where its presence would have serious consequences for Allied plans. They deployed the British Navy to block the movement.

Hoping to break Finno-German collaboration, Stalin demanded that the Finns drive the Germans from their country, not merely allow them to leave at their own pace. Yet, he insisted that the Finnish Army be demobilized by 1 December, an action incompatible with an active campaign. The Finns were weary of war, but the alternative to complying with Stalin's wishes was an occupation by Soviet troops to prosecute the campaign. As the Finns were reluctant to attack their former comrades-in-arms, they readily agreed to a secret conference on 11 September with General Rendulic, commander of the German forces. The former allies developed a "campaign" that would involve measured withdrawals by the German forces, with Finnish units given orders to take objectives just short of the German positions, thus purveying evidence to Soviet observers of compliance with Stalin's directive. The German insistence upon destruction of roads and bridges would lend credence to the slow Finnish advance.

Finnish leftists got wind of the collaboration and publicly urged Finnish soldiers to kill their officers. Mannerheim believed strife in Lapland to be an inevitable alternative to incurring Stalin's wrath if Finland was to retain any sovereignty. His plan called for an advance from Pudasjärvi toward the important road junction of Rovaniemi, a move that would cut the best route of withdrawal for the main German forces. Another force would then drive southwestward from Rovaniemi to Kemi, trapping all German troops south of that city. The general staff hoped the campaign would end at that point.

To implement the plan, Mannerheim had gathered some of his weary forces to the waist of Finland and, on 22 September, appointed General Lieutenant Siilasvuo as the commander of "Autumn Maneuvers" as the campaign was called.

**III. Corps** (Gen.Lt. Siilasvuo) - Oulu
  **1. Pansar Division**
    15 Ps IV, 10 T-34, 7 T-34/85, 45 Stu 40, 60 T-26
  3., 6., 11. Infantry Divisions
  XV. Infantry Brigade

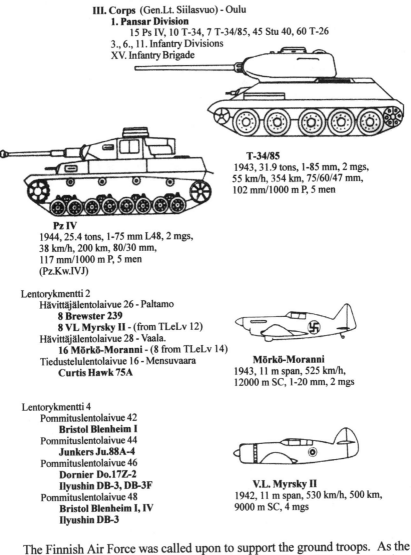

**T-34/85**
1943, 31.9 tons, 1-85 mm, 2 mgs,
55 km/h, 354 km, 75/60/47 mm,
102 mm/1000 m P, 5 men

**Pz IV**
1944, 25.4 tons, 1-75 mm L48, 2 mgs,
38 km/h, 200 km, 80/30 mm,
117 mm/1000 m P, 5 men
(Pz.Kw.IVJ)

Lentorykmentti 2
  Hävittäjälentolaivue 26 - Paltamo
    **8 Brewster 239**
    **8 VL Myrsky II** - (from TLeLv 12)
  Hävittäjälentolaivue 28 - Vaala.
    **16 Mörkö-Moranni** - (8 from TLeLv 14)
  Tiedustelulentolaivue 16 - Mensuvaara
    **Curtis Hawk 75A**

**Mörkö-Moranni**
1943, 11 m span, 525 km/h,
12000 m SC, 1-20 mm, 2 mgs

Lentorykmentti 4
  Pommituslentolaivue 42
    **Bristol Blenheim I**
  Pommituslentolaivue 44
    **Junkers Ju.88A-4**
  Pommituslentolaivue 46
    **Dornier Do.17Z-2**
    **Ilyushin DB-3, DB-3F**
  Pommituslentolaivue 48
    **Bristol Blenheim I, IV**
    **Ilyushin DB-3**

**V.L. Myrsky II**
1942, 11 m span, 530 km/h, 500 km,
9000 m SC, 4 mgs

The Finnish Air Force was called upon to support the ground troops. As the Messerschmitt Bf.109Gs were too short-ranged, and lacked spare parts, they were retained as interceptors in southern Finland while the older fighters of LeR 2 were sent to bases west of Suomussalmi. Attached to the squadrons were two newly-delivered types. The Mörkö-Moranni had been produced by wedding the engine of the Soviet LaGG-3 to the obsolete Morane-Saulnier fuselage, producing a surprisingly efficient fighter superior to the LaGG-3. On the other hand, the VL Myrsky II was not well liked by its pilots, lacking maneuverability and acceleration.

The southernmost German troops on the Finnish mainland prepared to withdraw westward. To keep the Finns from hindering the retirement of the XVIII Mountain Korps, the Nazis formed two Kampfgruppes (West and Ost) from motorized units of XXXVI and XVIII Korps to block the routes leading to their lines of communications. While Divisiongruppe Kräutler (including the Kampfgruppe West) shielded the line of retreat from Finnish forces in the south, and the German 7. Mountain Division held the critical Rovaniemi crossroads, XVIII Korps passed behind XXXVI Korps which then began retiring on 9 September, the Russians following as far as the frontier. More than 120,000 men, 22,000 horses and 20,000 motor vehicles were streaming toward Rovaniemi.

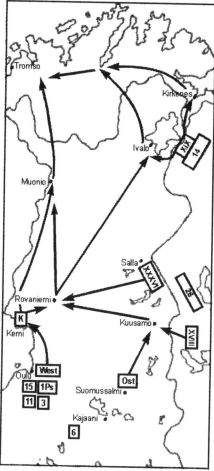

However, the jig was up. Soviet officers had examined Mannerheim's general plan at headquarters and, on 30 September, issued an ultimatum - formulate new orders or risk a Soviet takeover. A new plan was readied, but an anomalous situation developed, for General Siilasvuo was of an independent mind with little respect for several members of the Finnish general staff. He believed that the correct course was to start at Kemi, attack the open western flank of the German deployment, and drive on to Rovaniemi. When his plan was rejected, he persisted in it, secretly. A skirmish had already occurred on 28 September when Siilasvuo's orders did not comply with the Finno-German agreement, causing Finnish troops of the Pansar Division and 3. Division to overrun surprised German units southeast of Pudasjärvi. A similar incident in the same area two days later nearly precipitated open warfare. Two Finnish fighter squadrons had moved up to bases west of Suomussalmi, with Mörkö-Morannis and Myrskys participating in desultory ground attack missions against the retreating German troops. The fortuitous fulfillment of Siilasvuo's aberrant orders convinced the Soviets that Mannerheim was serious about complying with their demands.

On the morning of **1 October 1944**, the 11. Infantry Regiment of the 3. Division left Oulu and landed from 3 transports at Röyottä, near Tornio. Heavy fighting near the beachhead resulted in numerous German and Finnish casualties. The rest of the division, and the XV. Brigade, appeared the following day. There were few German troops between them and Rovaniemi, 150 kilometers to the north.

431

Taken by surprise, General Rendulic announced that he would consider the Finns to be enemies from 2 October unless they ended hostilities. He believed the landing to be in cooperation with the Allies who, after the success of the Normandy invasion, were now deploying the British Navy northward to cut off the powerful Twentieth Mountain Army. Advancing on Kemi and Tornio against fierce opposition, the Finns blocked the escape route into Sweden. From 6 October, the gunboats *Üusimaa* and *Hämeenmaa* supported the troops on shore with shelling and anti-aircraft fire against attacking Soviet aircraft. The two German corps having cleared Rovaniemi, Divisiongruppe Kräutler retreated northward on 10 October, closedly pursued, but not attacked by the Finns. HLeLv 26 and 28 moved up to Kemi on 15 October and continued ground attack missions. The Ju.88A-4s of PLeLv 44 were also used to harass the German forces, but suffered heavy losses to anti-aircraft fire.

Along the Arctic coast, the Germans planned to hold Petsamo. Russian forces attacked on 7 October and threatened to envelop the Germans with a landward advance by a reindeer-borne unit and a seaward landing by marine forces. The XIX Mountain Korps retired to Kirkenes and the Russians pursued to the Norwegian border. By April 1945 the Germans had withdrawn to a defensive position in northern Norway. For Finland, the war was over. [216]

## *Rapprochment with the Soviet Union* - Spring 1945

A Soviet delegation arrived at Helsinki in November 1944 to present armistice conditions to the Finnish government. Finnish Communists took the opportunity to demand a major role and the resulting government was dominated by leftists who elected Paasikivi as chairman in March 1945. From Karelia, 420,000 people were forced to move westward.

The demobilization of the Army had been halted at the end of 1944, with 32,000 men remaining under arms. The Air Force retained more of its strength, as the air war in Lapland continued until 25 April 1945. The new leftist government changed aircraft insignia from the swastika to a roundel on 1 April. The Air Force had been reorganized in December 1944:

**Finnish Air Force**
Lentorykmentti 1 - Pori
Hävittäjälentolaivue 11 (ex-TLeLv 12)
**VL Myrsky II**
Hävittäjälentolaivue 13 (ex-TLeLv 16)
**Curtiss Hawk 75A**
Lentorykmentti 2 - Rissala
Hävittäjälentolaivue 21 (ex-HLeLv 26)
**Brewster 239**
Hävittäjälentolaivue 23 (ex-HLeLv 28)
**Mörkö-Moranni**
Lentorykmentti 3 - Utti
Hävittäjälentolaivue 31 (ex-HLeLv 24)
**Messerschmitt Bf.109G-6**
Hävittäjälentolaivue 33 (ex-HLeLv 34)
**Messerschmitt Bf.109G-6**
Lentorykmentti 4 - Luonetjarvi
Pommituslentolaivue 41 (ex-PLeLv 42)
**Bristol Blenheim I**
Pommituslentolaivue 43 (ex-PLeLv 44)
**Junkers Ju.88A-4**
Pommituslentolaivue 45 (ex-PLeLv 46)
**Dornier Do.17Z-2**

All Russian types were phased out. Replacements were available only for the Messerschmitts. The unpopular Myrsky II was withdrawn in 1946-7. Its deficiencies would have been remedied by the succeeding sleek VL Pyörremyrsky, a Daimler-Benz powered design already under development. When completed and flown after the war, it displayed excellent speed, maneuverability and climb rate, and possessed a potent armament. However, the unfavorable end of the war precluded any production of this outstanding fighter.

The Treaty of Paris of **10 February 1947** limited Finland to an army of 34,400 men (its prewar strength), a navy not exceeding 10,000 tons (with no submarines), and an air force of no more than 60 planes (none of them to carry bombs). During the summer, Finland was invited, along with 20 other nations, to take part in Paris talks for implementing the Marshall Plan of economic assistance proposed by the American government. However, under pressure from the Soviet Union and the Finnish Communists, Finland declined the invitation. She ignored a similar invitation to the Nordic Council.

On **23 February 1948**, Stalin proposed a pact between Finland and the USSR. An "Agreement of Friendship, Cooperation and Mutual Assistance" was concluded on 6 April, to remain in force for a period of ten years. A Communist coup, such as had struck Czechoslovakia, was narrowly averted, and the Communist interior minister was dismissed on 22 April. After the Communists failed to win much of the vote in a July election, they were banned from the government. Nevertheless, the "Agreement" gave the Soviet Union an extensive jurisdiction over the development and use of the Finnish armed forces. Finland relied solely on the validity of Russian promises regarding her internal affairs, a precarious sovereignty.

One armored brigade remained in the Army, equipped principally with the Stu 40s, Ps IVs and T-34s left over from the war. In 1947, 200 war-surplus White M2 and M3 halftracks were purchased to pull the 75 K/40 anti-tank guns equipping the 3 infantry divisions. The uniforms of 1944 were retained until the mid-1960s.

The naval limits practically excluded vessels larger than escorts. The Air Force was converted to a purely defensive arm. PLeLv 43 and 45 were disbanded after their Ju.88s and Do.17s were taken out of service. The worn Brewsters and Morko-Morannis of LeR 2 were relegated to training, although they could still fly combat missions in an emergency. All Hawk 75As were retired. By the autumn of 1948, Finnish air defense was limited to:

**Finnish Air Force**

Lentorykmentti 1
  Hävittäjälentolaivue 11
    **Messerschmitt Bf.109G-6**
  Hävittäjälentolaivue 13
    **Messerschmitt Bf.109G-6**
Lentorykmentti 2
  training
Lentorykmentti 3
  Hävittäjälentolaivue 31
    **Messerschmitt Bf.109G-6**
  Hävittäjälentolaivue 33
    **Messerschmitt Bf.109G-6**
Lentorykmentti 4
  Pommituslentolaivue 41 (reconnaissance)
    **Bristol Blenheim I, IV**

In reality, the heavy-handed Soviet treaties had little practical effect upon either the Finnish nation or its armed forces. They allowed the Soviet Union to take actions that they probably would have taken anyway in the event of war. Finland was prohibited from making military commitments to the West, but maintained control of her armed forces. She was hindered by heavy war reparations, but by 1951 sufficient funds were available to allow some attention to be given to modernizing her defenses.

The Air Force was reorganized during the following year, the flying regiment being redesignated a *Lennosto* (wing). A shadow of its wartime strength, it possessed only one fully operational wing - the 3 Lennosto with the Messerschmitts of HävLv 31 and 33. The 2 Lennosto had been converted to a training unit with the remaining Bf.109Gs of HävLv 11 and 13, while the 1 Lennosto possessed only two weak flights of reconnaissance planes (Bf.109Gs and Blenheims). The Finnish Valmet company began producing a trainer, the Vihuri I, which reequipped the 2 Lennosto. Finland's first jets arrived from Britain in the shape of 6 De Havilland Vampire F.B.52s, which were delivered to HävLv 11 in 1953. They were followed by 9 Vampire T.55s for conversion training. Remaining Bf.109Gs were withdrawn in 1954.

The 1948 "Agreement" was extended for another twenty years on **19 September 1955**. As the "Cold War" between East and West heated up, the Finnish armed forces sought to modernize their weaponry. A dozen Folland Gnat light fighters were ordered from Great Britain in 1956 and assigned to HävLv 21, which was reactivated for the purpose. The following year, the wings were renamed for the provinces in which they were based (1 became Häme, 2 became Satakunta and 3 became Karjala). The Air Force then comprised:

**Finnish Air Force**

Häme Lennosto - Luonetjarvi
  (disbanded in 1958 after
    Blenheims were withdrawn)
Satakunta Lennosto - Pori
  HävLv 11

    **6 De Havilland Vampire F.B.52**
    **9 De Havilland Vampire T.55**
  HävLv 13

**De Havilland Vampire F.B. 52**
1945, 12 m span, 882 km/h (0.78), 1964 km,
4-20 mm, 900 kg W

    **Valmet Vihuri I**
Karjala Lennosto - Utti
  HävLv 21
    **12 Folland Gnat Mk.1**
  1 transport/reconnaissance flight
    **Hunting Pembroke Mk.53**
    **Douglas DC-2**

**Folland Gnat Mk. I**
1955, 7 m span, 1119 km/h (0.98), 1610 km
5/13725 m, 15250 m SC, 2-30 mm, 454 kg W

Training units were now distributed among the remaining squadrons and received their first jets in 1958. Valmet licence-built 40 of 62 Fouga Magisters acquired as trainers which could also be used in the light strike role during wartime. HävLv 13 was disbanded in 1961. At the same time, HävLv 11 and 21 exchanged numbers.

Meanwhile, reorganization of the Army began in 1951. The clumsy infantry divisions retained from World War II were divided into 6 infantry brigades. Thirteen British Charioteer tank destroyers arrived in 1958. The next year, the first battalion of a total of 185 T-54s and T-55s was ordered from the USSR, along with 15 PT-76s. To train the tankers of the Armored Brigade on modern tanks, 41 Comets were aquired from Britain in 1960. B.T.R.50PKs and B.T.R.60PA,PBs provided armored transport for the Finnish mechanized infantry units. At the same time, Soviet small arms were supplied in quantity, although the old artillery was replaced more slowly.

The Navy was far understrength, being a collection of patrol boats. The *Nuoli* class of fast attack boats was the forerunner of a number of examples of the type of effective, yet inexpensive small craft that were becoming popular for coastal defense duties worldwide.

### *The Soviet Embrace Tightens* - 1961

Commercial privileges were extended to Finland by the Nordic Council in July 1961. The Soviet Union sent a note to Finland on 30 October, condemning "imperialism by West Germany, NATO and Sweden". Finland's President Kekkonen and Soviet Premier Nikita Khruschev issued a joint communique on 25 November, pledging Finland to consult with the USSR on military and diplomatic measures to counter the events in Europe. Finland benefitted from the accord. By 1970, she had an army of 31,400 men:

**Finnish Army**

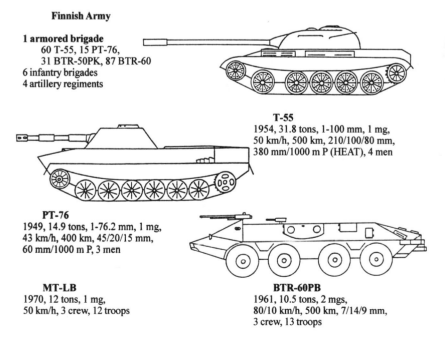

**1 armored brigade**
  60 T-55, 15 PT-76,
  31 BTR-50PK, 87 BTR-60
6 infantry brigades
4 artillery regiments

**T-55**
1954, 31.8 tons, 1-100 mm, 1 mg,
50 km/h, 500 km, 210/100/80 mm,
380 mm/1000 m P (HEAT), 4 men

**PT-76**
1949, 14.9 tons, 1-76.2 mm, 1 mg,
43 km/h, 400 km, 45/20/15 mm,
60 mm/1000 m P, 3 men

**MT-LB**
1970, 12 tons, 1 mg,
50 km/h, 3 crew, 12 troops

**BTR-60PB**
1961, 10.5 tons, 2 mgs,
80/10 km/h, 500 km, 7/14/9 mm,
3 crew, 13 troops

435

The Army maintained a large reserve of trained territorial troops, including an armored brigade equipped with British tanks downgraded to reserve status when the T-55s began arriving for the active brigade.

Reserves
1 armored brigade
   41 Comets, 13 Charioteers
10 infantry brigades

**Charioteer**
1952, 29 tons, 1-83.4 mm, 1 mg,
61 km/h, 242 km/h, 76/57/32 mm,
165 mm/1000 m P, 4 men

**Comet**
1944, 33.9 tons, 1-77 mm, 2 mgs,
61 km/h, 242 km, 79/101/32 mm,
115 mm/1000 m P, 5 men

The troops grey-green garb was retained as the service uniform, but a new field uniform of brown, light-green and dark green camouflage appeared.

The Navy finally received some large surface vessels. A single frigate, the *Matti Kurki*, had been acquired from Britain in 1962 for use as a training ship. Two frigates were purchased from the Soviet Union in 1964, and two corvettes were built in Finnish dockyards three years later. The *Nuoli* type of gun-armed fast attack boats operated coastal patrols.

frigate

corvette

**Hämeenmaa** 1955, 962 tons, 52 km/h, 3200 km,
**Uusimaa**   3-10 cm, 2 small AA, 3 TT, 50 mines,
           Hämeenmaa rerated minelayer in 1979,
           Uusimaa stricken in 1980
           (ex-Soviet Riga class)

**Turunmaa** 1968, 668 tons, 65 km/h,
**Karjala**   1-12 cm, 4 small AA

fast
attack boat

frigate

**Nuoli 1-13**   1961, 40 tons, 74 km/h,
              1-4 cm, 1 small AA

**Matti Kurki**   1946, 1605 tons, 33 km/h, 15300 km,
              4-10 cm, 6 small AA
              (ex-British Parlock Bay, trans. 1962)

The Air Force had tested both the Swedish Saab J35 and the French Dassault Mirage III as replacements for its weak fighter forces, but found the Dassault too expensive and Saab unable to fulfill an order until 1972. Thus, an interim order was placed with the Soviet Union for 19 MiG-21Fs and 2 MiG-21UTI trainers, with deliveries to HävLv 31 beginning in 1963. Some 38 MiGs had arrived by 1967, and the weary Vampires retired, followed by the Gnats, although HävLv 11 was only partly reequipped. It was necessary to alter the treaty with the USSR to allow the MiGs to carry air-to-air missiles. Until 1972, the revamped Air Force deployed:

**Finnish Air Force**

Häme Lennosto - Luonetjarvi
  HävLv 11
    **12 Folland Gnat Mk.1**
    **8 Mikoyan-Gurevich MiG-21F** (1967)
    **12 Fouga Magister**

Karjala Lennosto - Kuopio, Rissala
  HävLv 31
    **15 Mikoyan-Gurevich MiG-21F**
    **12 Fouga Magister**

**Mikoyan-Gurevich MiG-21F**
1955, 7 m span, 2120 km/h (2.0), 1200 km,
4.5/12000 m, 17500 m SC, 2-30 mm,
2 ATOLL AAMs or 38 rockets or 500 kg B

Satakunta Lennosto - Pori
  HävLv 21
    **15 Mikoyan-Gurevich MiG-21F**
    **12 Fouga Magister**

Kuljetuslaivue - Utti
  transport
    **3 Hunting Pembroke C.53**
    **2 Douglas DC-2**
  liaison

    **3 Valmet Viima IIA,**
    **1 De Havilland-Canada DHC-3,**
    **1 Fieseler Fi.156,**
    **1 Focke-Wulf Fw.44**
  helicopter
    **4 SM-1, 6 Mil Mi-4**

**Fouga Magister**
1952, 11 m span, 713 km/h,
12200 m SC, 2 mgs, 4 rockets, 100 kg B

**Mil Mi-4**
1952, 21 m rotor, 185 km/h, 200 km,
5000 m SC, 3 crew, 8-14 troops, 1200 kg C

Another twenty-year extension was given in July 1970 to the pact with Russia. As the Finnish economy improved, more funds became available for strengthening the armed forces. The parliament had been very unstable, socialist and Communist parties generally holding the upper hand. However, the presidency had been a steadying influence. When President Kekkonen became unable to continue in office, Mauno Koivisto succeeded him on **26 January 1982**. In the decade since his election, Koivisto has maintained Finland's consultation with the USSR, but has also involved Finland in the Nordic Council and the European Economic Community.

During the 1970s, the Finnish Army greatly improved the all-weather capabilities of its infantry with the purchase of more than 200 Soviet MT-LB oversnow vehicles. More recently, modern armored vehicles and small arms have been added to the arsenal. The armored brigade received some much-needed modern main battle tanks in **1984** with the arrival of 63 T-72s from the Soviet Union. Mechanized infantry of the armored brigade rode in BTR-50PK, BTR-60PA,PB and BMP-1,2 armored personnel carriers until the first of about 250 SISU XA-180 APCs began arriving in 1985. Armored vehicles are marked with a white-blue-white roundel on the side of the turret (side of hull if the vehicle lacks a turret).

The displaced T-55s were transferred to the two reserve armored brigades, where they retired the long-serving Comets. In 1989, they were upgraded to T-55Ms with improvements to the armament, new electronics, and side skirts over the suspension.

**Finnish Army** - Helsinki

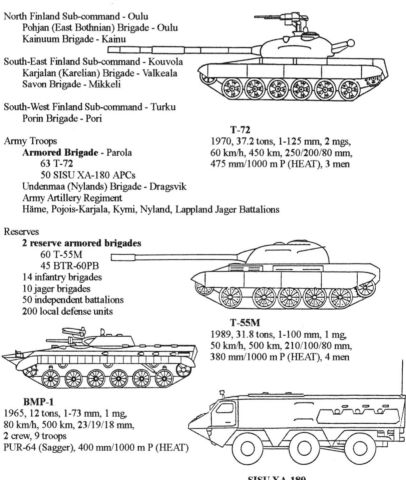

North Finland Sub-command - Oulu
    Pohjan (East Bothnian) Brigade - Oulu
    Kainuum Brigade - Kainu

South-East Finland Sub-command - Kouvola
    Karjalan (Karelian) Brigade - Valkeala
    Savon Brigade - Mikkeli

South-West Finland Sub-command - Turku
    Porin Brigade - Pori

**T-72**

Army Troops
    **Armored Brigade** - Parola
        63 T-72
        50 SISU XA-180 APCs
    Undenmaa (Nylands) Brigade - Dragsvik
    Army Artillery Regiment
    Häme, Pojois-Karjala, Kymi, Nyland, Lappland Jager Battalions

1970, 37.2 tons, 1-125 mm, 2 mgs,
60 km/h, 450 km, 250/200/80 mm,
475 mm/1000 m P (HEAT), 3 men

Reserves
    **2 reserve armored brigades**
        60 T-55M
        45 BTR-60PB
    14 infantry brigades
    10 jager brigades
    50 independent battalions
    200 local defense units

**T-55M**
1989, 31.8 tons, 1-100 mm, 1 mg,
50 km/h, 500 km, 210/100/80 mm,
380 mm/1000 m P (HEAT), 4 men

**BMP-1**
1965, 12 tons, 1-73 mm, 1 mg,
80 km/h, 500 km, 23/19/18 mm,
2 crew, 9 troops
PUR-64 (Sagger), 400 mm/1000 m P (HEAT)

**SISU XA-180**
1983, 15 tons, 1 mg,
100/10 km/h, 800 km, 2 crew, 10 troops

438

The service uniform is grey-green with rank insignia similar to that used during World War II. Since the mid-1960s, field uniforms have been a brown, light green and dark green camouflage overall, with a similarly camouflaged helmet cover. The helmet is the spherical type that came into service in 1944. Black jackboots are worn on the feet. Rank insignia, worn on a hexagonal gray patch on the lower sleeve of the field uniform, differs from the service issue:

Generals - gold bars over a broad band of gold oak leaf lace
    General - 3 bars
    Lieutenant General - 2 bars
    Major General - 1 bar
Field Officers - narrow gold bars over a medium plain gold band
    Colonel - 3 bars
    Lieutenant Colonel - 2 bars
    Major - 1 bar
Line Officers - gold bars
    Captain - 1 very narrow between
        2 narrow bars
    Lieutenant - 2 very narrow over
        1 narrow bar
    Second Lieutenant - 2 narrow bars

Non-commissioned Officers - gold chevrons, point up
    Regimental Sergeant Major - dark blue patch,
        1 very broad, 2 narrow chevrons
    Company Sergeant Major -
        1 broad, 1 narrow chevron
    Staff Sergeant - 1 broad chevron
    Senior Sergeant - 4 narrow chevrons
    Sergeant - 3 narrow chevrons
    Corporal - 2 narrow chevrons
    Lance Corporal - 1 narrow chevron
    Private - no device

The current army is well-equipped with weapons and vehicles, mostly of Soviet derivation. However, the indigeneous SISU company is producing several hundred XA-180 wheeled APCs to reequip motorized infantry units.

**INFANTRY BRIGADE**
3 infantry battalions (2 in peacetime)
   3 rifle companies
      3 rifle platoons
         **MTLB or SISU XA-180 APC** (1985)
         **M-62 or M-62/76 7.62 mm AR**
         **M-62 or M-78 7.62 mm lmg**
      1 support platoon
         **3 M-82 or M-83 ATGW or**
         **M-55 55 mm RR**
   1 support company
      1 anti-tank platoon
         **SM-58-61 95 mm RR**
      1 heavy mortar platoon
         **M-40 120 mm mortar**
1 artillery battalion
   1 field battery
         **H-63 122 mm or M-46 130 mm gun or**
         **M-30 122 mm or ML-30 152 mm howitzer**
   1 air defense battery
         **ZU-23 23 mm AA or**
         **SA-3, 7, 16 or Crotale SAM**
1 engineer company
1 signal company

**M62**
7.62 mm, 4.6 kg, 719 m/s, 650 rpm
(variant of Soviet AK-47)

**JAGER BATTALION**
3 jager companies
   3 jager platoons
   1 support platoon
         **3 M-82 or M-83 ATGW or**
         **M-55 55 mm RR**
1 support company
   1 anti-tank platoon
         **SM-58-61 95 mm RR**
   1 heavy mortar platoon
         **M-40 120 mm mortar**

**M62 lmg**
7.62 mm, 8 kg, 1100 rpm

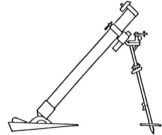

**Tampella m/60**
122 mm, 25 kg shell,
25000 m, 950 m/s, 4 rpm

**ARMORED BRIGADE**
1 armored battalion
   **63 T-72**
1 mechanized infantry battalion
   3 companies
      **SISU XA-180 APC**
1 artillery battalion
1 anti-tank battalion
1 air defense battery

Currently, the Finnish Army possesses 40 BMP-1 and 32 BMP-2 armored infantry fighting vehicles, 250 SISU XA-180, 213 MT-LB, 87 BTR-60 and 31 BTR-50P armored personnel carriers, 276 H-63 122 mm, 252 M-37/61 105 mm, 72 M-38 152 mm and 36 M-74 155 mm artillery pieces, 880-81 mm and 614-120 mm mortars, 100 SM-58-61 95 mm, 75 M-72A3 66 mm and 66 KES 66 mm recoilless rifles. About 20 SISU XA-181s, carrying a Crotale anti-aircraft launcher, were ordered for delivery in 1992-3.

In the Air Force, the MiG-21Fs were transferred to HävLv 21 in 1972 as ground attack aircraft. From 1983, they have been used for reconnaissance. To replace the Fouga Magister in the training/light strike role, 46 BAC Hawk Mk.51s were acquired in 1981.

**Finnish Air Force** - Helsinki
Häme Lennosto - Luonetjarvi
  Tiedustelaivue 21
  **16 MiG-21F**
  **10 BAC Hawk Mk.51**
Lapin Lennosto - Rovaniemi
  HävLv 11
  **21 Saab J-35 F/BS/XS**
  **10 BAC Hawk Mk.51**
Karjalan Lennosto - Rissala
  HävLv 31
  **20 Saab J-35 F/BS/XS**
  **10 BAC Hawk Mk.51**
Kuljetuslaivue - Utti
  transport
  **3 Fokker F.27, 3 Gates Learjet 35**
  1 helicopter/transport squadron
  **2 Hughes 500D, 7 Mil Mi-8**
  liaison
  **9 Piper Cherokee Arrow**
  **6 Piper Chieftain**
  **1 L-90 Redigo**

**BAC Hawk Mk.51**
1975, 9 m span, 1066 km/h (0.88),
7/9150 m, 15250 m SC, 1-30 mm, 2724 kg W

**Saab J35X Draken**
1967, 9 m span, 2125 km/h (2.2),
4.5/15250 m, 2-30 mm, 2 Falcon AAM or
1000 kg W

**Mil Mi-8**
1961, 21 m rotor, 250 km/h, 425 km,
4500 m SC, 2 crew, 28 troops, 4000 kg C

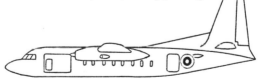

**Fokker F.27M Troopship**
1957, 29 m span, 613 km/h, 1060 km,
8970 m SC, 42 troops, 6810 kg C

441

BAC Hawk at Pori in 1982

For some time, Finland had been walking the fence between East and West, sampling the weapons output of both adversarial groups. The elderly Fouga Magisters were replaced with the BAC Hawk light fighters. Fulfilling the role of proficiency trainer in the fighter squadrons, the Hawks could be called on for ground attack missions in wartime. With the collapse of the Soviet Union as the third renewal of the arms treaty lapsed, Finland took the opportunity to go west for its new air force equipment.

The Swedish Saab J35X had proven an efficient interceptor, well adapted to northern conditions, so it was natural that the same company's JAS 39 was evaluated for the fighter squadrons, along with the MiG-29, F-16 and Mirage 2000. But in April 1992 the American McDonnell Douglas F/A-18C was selected. From late 1995, deliveries of 7 F/A-18D reconnaissance versions, and 57 F/A-18C fighters are to begin from Valmet. Although other aircraft were faster, the F-18 was selected for its long range, and its heavy weapons load, suitable for land and air targets as well as the maritime missions for which it was developed.

**McDonnell Douglas F/A-18C Hornet**
1974, 12 m span, 1912 km/h (1.8), 1480 km,
15240 m SC, 7031 kg W (Sparrow, Sidewinder,
AMR AAMs, Harpoon, Maverick ASMs, bombs)

At a time of chaos and uncertainty within her neighbor's territory, Finland maintains a small, but well-equipped air defense force.

Finland lost her largest naval vessels when the *Matti Kurki* was stricken in 1975, followed by the *Hämeenmaa* class in 1979. Only the small *Turunmaa* class corvettes remain of the escort flotilla. Finland has opted for a coastal defense navy based on missile-armed fast attack craft, a class of vessel becoming very popular in all of the world's navies because of its effectiveness against enemy ships. In 1974, she purchased from the Soviet Union four Osa II class boats, armed with Styx surface-to-surface missiles. Four Finnish-built *Helsinki* class boats followed in 1981-6. They were armed with Swedish Saab RBS 15 SSMs, the same missile used by the succeeding *Rauma* class.

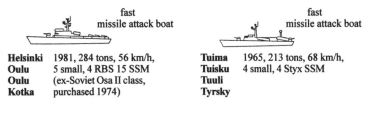

fast
missile attack boat

**Rauma**      1990, 218 tons, 56 km/h,
3 others      3 small, 6 Saab RBS 15 SSM


fast                                          fast
missile attack boat                           missile attack boat

**Helsinki**   1981, 284 tons, 56 km/h,      **Tuima**     1965, 213 tons, 68 km/h,
**Oulu**       5 small, 4 RBS 15 SSM          **Tuisku**    4 small, 4 Styx SSM
**Oulu**       (ex-Soviet Osa II class,      **Tuuli**
**Kotka**      purchased 1974)                **Tyrsky**

As her giant neighbor disintegrated, Finland moved progressively to Western manufacturers for her new military hardware. However, budget slashing will probably occur as in other nations. Renegotiation of treaties with the new eastern republics may permit Finland to acquire offensive weapons banned by the Cold War agreements.

# ÅLAND ISLANDS

The Åland Islands had been ceded by Sweden to Russia, along with Finland, in 1809. As Russia continued increasing her power in the Baltic, the Great Powers became interested in demilitarizing the islands after the Crimean War. In 1856, an international treaty allowed no fortifications or military and naval garrisons to be placed there. However, in 1907 Russia made a secret agreement that allowed Russian military bases. In 1915, with the World War raging on the continent, Russia began building extensive fortifications on the islands. Swedish protests were met by assurances from the Allies that they would be dismantled after the war.

When the Russian Revolution occurred, the local Åland Islands officials were authorized during a meeting in Mariehamn on 20 August 1917 to seek annexation by Sweden, but events in Finland forestalled them. Finland was recognized by Russia as an independent nation on 4 January 1918, and claimed the islands as part of her territory. However, a civil war began the following month and Sweden took the opportunity to send troops to the Åland Islands to "protect life and property". Swedish officers negotiated the end of fighting and brought about the withdrawal of both Finnish and Russian troops.

Sweden favorably received the annexation petition of the Ålanders on 2 February 1918, but Finland protested that, although there were 6,500 islands, the population of 22,000 was too small to qualify for the new League of Nations principle of right of determination. They arrested Julius Sundblom and Carl Björkman, two of the leaders of the separtist movement. The Ålanders presented their proposition to the Paris Peace Conference and the League of Nations the following year. However, on 24 June 1921 the League decided that, as part of a recognition of the new Finnish state, the Åland Islands would be awarded to her in a militarily neutralized condition. Sweden's protests did not avail.

Lest they lose further rights, the Ålanders quickly held elections and, on **9 June 1922**, the first Provincial Council met for the first time in Mariehamn. This day is celebrated as "Åland Independence Day". The League finding had declared the Ålander's right to preserve their Swedish language and unique culture without interference. The Finnish parliament reiterated the unique standing of the Åland Islands in the Autonomy Act of 28 December 1951.

Now a land of 1,500 square kilometers and population of 24,000, the islands have complete control over their internal affairs and are not subject to military service in the Finnish armed forces. Only if the parliament exceeds its authority may the Finns interfere. [218,219]

# BIBLIOGRAPHICAL NOTES

1 Hibben
2 Scandinavia...
3 Hibben
4 Ibid.
5 Magnusson
6 Ibid.
7 Ibid.
8 Ibid.
9 Graham-Campbell
10 Larsen
11 Pendlesonn
12 Scandinavia...
13 Steenstrup
14 Allen
15 Scandinavia...
16 Ibid.
17 Vaupell
18 Ibid.
19 Lisk
20 Örlogsmuseet
21 Rockstroh
22 Lisk
23 Örlogsmuseet
24 Vaupell
25 Dupuy
26 Ibid.
27 Örlogsmuseet
28 Ibid.
29 Hatton
30 Clowes
31 Örlogsmuseet
32 Pivka
33 Holmve
34 Conway's...
35 Scandinavia...
36 Very
37 Sokol
38 Horsetzky
39 Nörgaard
40 Den dansk-tyske Krig
41 Conway's...
42 Kofoed
43 Conway's...
44 Kofoed
45 Ibid.
46 Nörgaard
47 Kofoed
48 Armaments Yearbook
49 Kofoed
50 Ibid.
51 Conway's...
52 Petersen
53 Ziemke
54 Kofoed
55 Scandinavia...
56 Kofoed
57 Statesman's Yearbook
58 Jane's Fighting Ships
59 Kofoed
60 Kofoed
61 Wiener
62 Thomas
63 Isby and Kamp
64 Inter. Defence Review, June, 1979
65 Wiener
66 Jane's Armour and Artillery
67 Vaupell
68 Larsen
69 Cooke
70 Conway's...
71 Ibid.
72 Ibid.
73 RAF Flying Review, June, 1962
74 Derry
75 Armaments Yearbook
76 RAF Flying Review, June, 1962
77 RAF Flying Review, July, 1962
78 Ibid.
79 Lindback-Larsen
80 Ziemke
81 Derry
82 Divine
83 Ibid.
84 Rohwer
85 Derry
86 Haeren etter...
87 RAF Flying Review, July, 1962
88 Haeren etter...

89 RAF Flying Review, July, 1962
90 Jane's Fighting Ships
91 Haeren etter...
92 Inter. Defence Review, June, 1979
93 Jane's Fighting Ships
94 Time, March 8, 1976
95 Scandinavia...
96 Dupuy
97 Scandinavia...
98 Tessin
99 Scandinavian Sea Wars
100 Montross
101 Wagner
102 Tessin
103 Ibid.
104 Montross
105 Gyllengranat
106 Tessin
107 Struggle for Supremacy...
108 Scandinavia...
109 Bäckström
110 Scandinavian Sea Wars
111 Scandinavia...
112 Tessin
113 Wagner
114 Bäckström
115 Hatton
116 Bäckström
117 Hatton
118 Scandinavian Sea Wars
119 Bäckström
120 Hatton
121 Ibid.
122 Gyllengranat
123 Scandinavia...
124 Gyllengranat
125 Ibid.
126 Onacewicz
127 Tessin
128 Björlin
129 Berg
130 Gyllengranat
131 Björlin
132 Very
133 Cooke
134 Yearbook of Sweden
135 Conway's
136 Janes Fighting Ships
137 Ander
138 Svenska Armens Rulla
139 Ander
140 Armaments Yearbook
141 courtesy Lennart Anderson
142 Armaments Yearbook
143 Packard
144 Janes Fighting Ships
145 Furtenbach
146 courtesy Lennart Andersson
147 Bromma landflygplats...
148 Engle and Paananen
149 Salo
150 Furtenbach
151 courtesy Col. Hans Nilsson
152 courtesy Lennart Andersson
153 Widfelt
154 Packard
155 Furtenbach
156 courtesy Col. Hans Nilsson
157 Furtenbach
158 Packard
159 courtesy Col. Hans Nilsson
160 Ibid.
161 courtesy Lennart Andersson
162 courtesy Col. Hans Nilsson
163 Ibid.
164 Ibid.
165 courtesy Lennart Andersson
166 Krigsarkivet
167 courtesy Col. Hans Nilsson
168 courtesy Lennart Andersson
169 Ziemke
170 courtesy Col. Hans Nilsson
171 Green
172 Ibid.
173 Janes Fighting Ships
174 Armens Befäl
175 RAF Flying Review, Oct., 1958,
    Aug., 1965

176 courtesy Col. Hans Nilsson
177 Pivka
178 RAF Flying Review, Nov., 1963
179 courtesy Col. Hans Nilsson
180 Keegan
181 courtesy Col. Hans Nilsson
182 Janes Fighting Ships
183 Coon
184 Wuorinen
185 Björlin
186 Wuorinen
187 Keskinen
188 Vuorenmaa
189 Keskinen
190 Wuorinen
191 Keskinen
192 Engle
193 Ibid.
194 Onaciewicz
195 Erfurth
196 Ziemke
197 Keskinen
198 Conways
199 Erfurth
200 Rohwer
201 Erfurth
202 Ziemke
203 Erfurth
204 Keskinen
205 Pansarmuseet
206 Rohwer
207 Keskinen
208 Ziemke
209 Erfurth
210 Keskinen
211 Ziemke
212 Erfurth
213 Keskinen
214 Erfurth
215 Ahto
216 RAF Flying Review, March, 1962
217 Eriksson
218 Wuorinen

# PHOTOGRAPH CREDITS

# SELECTED BIBLIOGRAPHY

"Action in the North Atlantic", *Time*, March 8, 1976
*Aeroplane, The*, Temple Press, 1939-59
*AFV Profiles*, Doubleday
Ahto, Sampo, "The War in Lapland", *Revue Internationale d'Histoire Militaire*, CISH,
*Air Enthusiast*, Pilot Press, 1970-80
*Aircraft in Profile*, Doubleday
Allen, C.F., *De tre nordiske Rigers Historie, 1497-1536*, 1870
Ander, O. Fritiof, *The Building of Modern Sweden*, Augustana, 1958
Andersson, Lennart, *Svenska Flygplan*, Allt om Hobby, 1990
----, *Svenska Militärflyg.Propellerepoken*, Allt om Hobby, 1992
*Armaments Yearbook*, League of Nations, 1925-35
*Armens Befäl*, iduns Tryckerinktiebolag Esselte A.B., 1959
Ayling, *Combat Aviation*, Military Service Pub., 1943
Barnes, G.M., *Weapons of World War II*, Van Nostrand, 1947
Bäckström, P.O., *Svenska Flottans Historia*, P.A. Norstedt, 1884
Benoist-Mechin, Jacques, *Sixty Days That Shook the West*, Putnam, 1963
Berg, L.O., *Svenska flottans fartyg 1808-1849, skär gårdsfartyg*, 2 vol., Forum Navale No.24, 1968
Bjorkman, Leif, *Sverige infor operation Barbarossa*, Uddevella, 1972
Björlin, Gustaf, *Finska Kriget, 1808 och 1809*, P.A. Norstedt, 1883
Blakeslee, F.G., *Uniforms of the World*, E.P. Dutton, 1929
Bredt, A., *Taschenbuch der Kriegsflotten*, Lehmanns, 1939
Brink, Francis G., *Corps and Army Operations*, War Dept., 1938
*Bromma landflygplats journaler, 1939-45*, Stadsarkivet
Bunkley, J.W., *Military and Naval Recognition Book*, Van Nostrand, 1941
Caiti, Pierangelo, *Modern Armor*, Squadron/Signal, 1978
Carrell, Paul, *Hitler Moves East*, Little, Brown and Co., 1964
----, *Scorched Earth*, Little, Brown and Co., 1966
Chamberlin, Chris and Gander, Terry, *Light and Medium Field Artillery*, Arco, 1975
Chamberlin, P. and Ellis, C., *Allied Combat Tanks*, Arco, 1977
----, *Axis Combat Tanks*, Arco, 1977
----, *British and American Tanks of World War II*, Almark, 1969
----, *British and German Tanks of World War I*, Almark, 1969
----, *Soviet Combat Tanks*, Almark, 1970
----, *Tanks of the World, 1915-45*, Stackpole, 1972
Chinn, George M., *The Machine Gun*, Dept. of the Navy, 1944
Christensen, T.P., "Flyvevaesentsmaterielanskaffelseri 30'eme, 7.og sidste del: 1938-1940", *Flyvehistorisk Tidsskrift*, March, 1983
Clark, Alan, *Barbarossa: The Russian-German Conflict, 1941-5*, William Morrow, 1965
Clowes, William, *The Royal Navy*, 6 vol., Sampson, Low, Marston, 1899
*Conway's All the World's Fighting Ships, 1860-1905*, Conway, 1979
Cooke, Capt. W.S., *The Armed Strength of Sweden and Norway*, HMSO, 1874
Coon, Carleton S., *The Living Races of Man*, Alfred A. Knopf, 1965
Cucari, Attilio, *Sailing Ships*, Rand-McNally, 1976
Darrieus, Capt. Gabriel, *War on the Sea*, Naval Institute, 1908
Daveluy, Cmdr. Rene, *The Genius of Naval Warfare*, 2 vol., Naval Institute Press, 1911
*Den dansk-tyske Krig, 1864*, Generalstaben, 1890
Derry, T.K., *A History of Modern Norway, 1814-1972*, Clarendon, 1973
Disney, P., *Tactical Problems for Armored Units*, War Dept., 1952
Divine, A.D., *Navies in Exile*, E.P. Dutton, 1944
Dolvin, Welborn G., *Tanks in the Infantry Division*, Armor, 1952
Dupuy, R. Ernest and Dupuy, Trevor N., *The Encyclopedia of MilitaryHistory*, Harper and Row, 1970
Dupuy, Trevor N., *The Almanac of World Military Power*, Stackpole, 1970
----, *Military History of WWII*, 19 vols., F. Watts, 1966

*Encyclopedia Britannica*, 24 vols., 1939
Engle, Eloise and Paananen, Lauri, *The Winter War*, Scribners, 1973
Erfurth, Waldemar, *The Last Finnish War*, University Pub., 1979
Erickson, John, *The Road to Stalingrad*, Weidenfeld, 1975
Eriksson, Thorvald, *Åland, An Autonomous Province*, Ålands Landskapsstyrelse, 1972
Ermannsberger, L.R. von, *Mechanized Warfare*, War College, 1935
Evans, J.O., *Flags of the World*, Grosset and Dunlap, 1970
Ewing and Sellers, *Reference Handbook of the Armed Forces of the World*, VanNostrand, 1966
Ezell, Edward C., *Small Arms of the World*, Stackpole, 1983
"Finland's Air Force", *RAF Flying Review*, March, 1962
*Flottans neutralitetsvakt, 1939-1945*
Foss, Christopher, *Tanks and Fighting Vehicles*, Chartwell, 1977
Fuller, Maj.Gen. J.F.C., *Military History of the Western World*, Funk and Wagnalls, 1954
----, *The Second World War, 1939-45*, Duell, Sloan, Pierce, 1949
Furtenbach, Börje, "Sweden During the Second World War", *Revue Internationale d'Histoire Militaire, No.26* Comite Inter. des Sciences Hist., 1967
Gabriel, Richard A., ed., *Fighting Armies: Nonaligned, Third World and Other Ground Armies*, Greenwood, 1983
Gann, L.H., ed., *The Defense of Western Europe*, Auburn House, 1987
*German Tactical Doctrine*, U.S. War Dept., 1942
Goldsmith-Carter, George, *Sailing Ships and Sailing Craft*, Grosset and Dunlap, 1969
Grafstrom, Anders, *The Swedish Army*, Hörsta Förlag, 1954
Graham-Campbell, James, *The Viking World*, Frances Lincoln, 1980
Green, William, *Air Forces of the World*, Hanover House, 1958
----, *Bombers of the Second World War*, Vol. 5-8, McDonald
----, *Fighters of the Second World War*, Vol. 1-4, McDonald
----, *Floatplanes*, McDonald, 1962
----, *Flying Boats*, McDonald, 1962
----, *The World Guide to Combat Planes*, Doubleday, 1970
----, *Warplanes of the Third Reich*, Doubleday, 1970
Guderian, Gen. Heinz, *Panzer Leader*, Michael Joseph, 1952
Gunston, Bill, *Encyclopedia of World Air Power*, Crescent, 1980
Gunther, John, *Inside Europe*, Harpers, 1938
Gyllengranat, C.A., *Sjökrigs Historia*, Ameen, 1840
*Haeren efter annen verdenskrig 1945-90*, Haerstaben, 1990
Hastings, Max, *Overlord*, Simon and Schuster, 1984 *History of the Second World War:*
*Hastings United Kingdom Military Series*, 24 vols., HMSO, 1956-69
Hatton, R.M., *Charles XII of Sweden*, Weybright and Talley, 1968
Heigl, Capt. F., *Taschenbuch der Tanks*, J.F. Lehmanns, 1935-8
Hewish, Sweetman, Wheeler, Gunston, *Air Forces of the World*, Simon and Schuster, 1979
Hibben, Frank C., *Prehistoric Man in Europe*, U.of Oklahoma, 1958
Holmve, P.E., *Danmark-Norges Historie, 1720-1814*, 1892
Horsetzky, Gen. A. von, *A Short History of the Chief Campaigns in Europe Since 1792*, John Murray, 1909
Hutchinson, Lt.Col. G.S., *Machine Guns. Their History and Tactical Employment*, 1938
Icks, R., *Tanks and Armored Vehicles*, Duell, Sloan, Pearce, 1945
*Identification*, U.S. War Dept., 1943
Isby, D. C., *Weapons and Tactics of the Soviet Army*, Janes, 1981
Isby and Kamp, *Armies of NATOs Central Front*, 1985
*Jane's All the World's Aircraft*, Jane's Pub. Co., 1912-1990
*Jane's Armour and Artillery*, Jane's Pub. Co., 1979-1988
*Jane's Fighting Ships*, Jane's Pub. Co., 1908, 1914-90
*Jane's Weapons Systems*, Jane's Pub. Co., 1969-70
Jones, G., *History of the Vikings*, Oxford, 1973

Jones, R.E., Rarey, G.H. and Icks, R.J., *The Fighting Tank Since 1916*, National Service Pub. Co., 1933

Kafka, Roger and Pepperburg, Roy, *Warships of the World*, Cornell Maritime Press, 1944

Kannik, Preben, *Military Uniforms in Color*, Macmillan, 1968

Keegan, John, *World Armies*, Gale Research Co., 1983

Keskinen, K., *Finnish Fighter Aces*, Tietoteos

Keskinen, K., *Suomen Ilmavoimien Lentokoneet, 1918-1938*, Tietoteos, 1973

Keskinen, K., *Suomen Ilmavoimien Lentokoneet, 1939-1972*, Tietoteos, 1973

Knotel, Richard, Knotel, Herbert and Sieg, Herbert, *Uniforms of the World*, Scribners, 1979

Kofoed, Hans, "Denmark's Defenders", *Flying Review*, Jan., 1962

Lamberton, W.M. *Fighter Aircraft of the 1914-1918 War*, Harleyford, 1960

Landstrom, Bjorn, *Sailing Ships*, Doubleday, 1978

Larsen, Karen, *A History of Norway*, Princeton U., 1948

Lemmel, C.F. *Främmande flyg över Sverige under andra världskriget*

Lewis, William J., *The Warsaw Pact: Arms, Doctrine and Strategy*, McGraw-Hill, 1982

Liddell-Hart, B.H., *History of the Second World War*, Putnam, 1970

Lindback-Larsen, Gen.Maj. Odd, *Krigen I Norge 1940*, Gyldendal Norsk Forlag, 1965

Lisk, Jill, *The Struggle for Supremacy in the Baltic, 1600-1725*, Funk and Wagnalls, 1967

Mackintosh, Malcolm, *Juggernaut*, Macmillan, 1967

Magnusson, Magnus, *Viking-Hammer of the North*, Orbis, 1976

Mahan, A.T., *Naval Strategy*, Little, Brown, 1911

*Military Balance, The*, Inter. Inst. for Strategic Studies, 1965-79

Montross, Lynn, *War Through the Ages*, Harper, 1944

Mordal, J., *Twenty-five Centuries of Sea Warfare*, Bramhall, 1969

Mueller-Hillebrand, Burkhart, *Das Heer, 1933-45*, Mittler, 1956

Munson, Kenneth, *Pocket Encyclopedia of World Aircraft in Color*, Macmillan, 1968

*Norwegian Defence - Facts and Figures*, Ministry of Defence, 1992

Nörgaard, F., *Danmark fra 1864 til Genforeningen med Sonderjylland*, 1920

Ogorkiewicz, Richard M. *Armor*, Praeger, 1970

---, *The Design and Development of Fighting Vehicles*, Doubleday, 1973

Onacewicz, Col. Wlodzimierz, *Empires By Conquest*, Hero, 1985

Packard, Jerrold M., *Neither Friend Nor Foe*, Scribners, 1992

Pendlesonn, K.R.G., *The Vikings*, Windward, 1980

Petersen, C., *Luftkrig over Danmark, Bind I September, 1939-1940*, Bollerup Boghandels Forlag, 1985

Pivka, Otto von, *Armies of Europe Today*, David and Charles, 1974

---, *Navies of the Napoleonic Era*, David and Charles, 1980

*Popular Aviation*, Ziff-Davis, 1940

*RAF Flying Review*, Mercury House, 1956-70

Richards, Denis and Saunders, Hilary St.G., *Royal Air Force, 1939-45*, 3 vol., HMSO, 1953

Roberts, A., *Nations in Arms*, Praeger, 1976

Robertson, Bruce, *Aircraft Camouflage and Markings, 1907-1954*, Harleyford, 1954

Robison, S.S., *A History of Naval Tactics*, U.S. Naval Inst., 1940

Rockstroh, K.C., *Udviklingen af den Nationale Haer i Danmark i det 17. og 18. Aarhundrede*, 1909

Rohwer, *Chronology of the War at Sea, 1939-1945*, Praeger, 1958

Rosignoli, Guido, *Army Badges and Insignia of WW 2*, 2 vol., Macmillan, 1975

Rottman, Gordon L., *Warsaw Pact Ground Forces*, Osprey, 1987

Salo, Mauno A., "Arctic Air War", *RAF Flying Review*, April, 1962

*Scandinavia Past and Present*, 3 vol., Arnkrone, 1959

*Scandinavian Sea Wars*

*Schweden, 1941*, Dietrich Reimer, 1941

Seaton, Albert, *The German Army, 1933-45*, Praeger, 1971

---, *The Russo-German War, 1941-45*, Praeger, 1971

Senger und Etterlin, FM F. von, *Die Kampfpanzer, 1916-66*, 1966

Shores, Christopher F., *Finnish Air Force, 1918-1968*, Arco, 1969

Simmons, Jacques, *Warships*, Grosset and Dunlap, 1971

*Small Air Forces Observer*, Small Air Forces Clearing House

Smith, Whitney, *Flags Through the Ages and Across the World*, McGraw-Hill, 1975

Sokol, Anthony, *The Imperial and Royal Austro-Hungarian Navy*, U.S. Naval Institute, 1968

*Statesman's Year-Book*, St. Martins, 1864-1988

Steenstrup, J.J.S., *Danmarks Riges Historie*, 1897

"Strategic Situation in Northern Europe, The", *International Defense Review*, June, 1979

*Svenska Armens Rulla*, P.A. Norstedt, 1919

*Tank Data*, U.S. Army Ordnance School, 1958

Taylor, T., *The March of Conquest*, Simon and Schuster, 1958

Tessin, G., *Truppen und Verbande der Deutschen Wehrmacht und Waffen SS, 1939-1945*

Thetford, Owen, *Aircraft of the Royal Air Force Since 1918*, 1962

Thetford, O.G. and Riding, E.J., *Aircraft of the 1914-1918 War*, Harleyford, 1954

---, *British Naval Aircraft Since 1912*, 1962

Thomas, Nigel, *NATO Armies Today*, 1987

Thornton, J.M., *Warships, 1860-70*, Arco, 1973

Uhlin, Åke, *Febrvarikrisen, 1942*, 1972

Upton, Emory, *Armies of Asia and Europe*, Appleton, 1878

Vaupell, Otto, *Den Dansk Haers Historie til Nutiden Og Den Norske Haers Historie indtil 1814*, 2 vol., 1872

Very, Lt. Edward W., *Navies of the World*, 1880

Vuorenmaa, Anssi, "Finland's Defence Forces: The Years of Construction 1918-1939", *Revue Internationale d'Histoire Militaire*, No.62, CISH, 1985

Wagner, Arthur, *Organization and Tactics*, Westerman, 1894

Weal, Weal and Barker, *Combat Aircraft of World War II*, Macmillan, 1976

White, B.T., *Tanks and Other AFVs of the Blitzkrieg Era*, Macmillan, 1972

Widfelt, Bo, *The Luftwaffe in Sweden, 1939-1945*

Wiener, F., *Armies of NATO Nations*, Herald, 1987

Wiener, F. and Lewis, W., *Warsaw Pact Armies*, Herald, 1977

Wilson, D.M. and Foote, P.G., *Viking Achievement*, Praeger, 1970

Wintringham, Thomas H., *The Story of Weapons and Tactics from Troy to Stalingrad*, Books for Libraries Press, 1971

Wise, Terence, *Medieval Warfare*, Hastings House, 1976

Worley, M. L., *A Digest of New Developments in Army Weapons, Tactics, Organization and Equipment*, Stackpole, 1976

Wuorinen, John H., *A History of Finland*, Columbia U., 1965

*Yearbook of Sweden*

Ziemke, Earl F., *the German Northern Theatre of Operations, 1940-5*, Army Dept. No. 20-271, 1959

# GENERAL INDEX

# NAVAL VESSELS

# Sweden

# MILITARY UNITS

# SPECIFICATIONS

## Rifles, Assault Rifles

AG 3, 171
Automatkarbin 4, 359
G3A3 assault rifle, 98
Grindreng Breechloading Rifle, 51
Krag-Jorgensen M.1889/10, 58, 116
Larsen rifle, 114
Lee-Enfield No.1 Mk.3, 160
Ljungman AG42B, 324
M1 Garand, 89, 164
M62 AR, 440
Mauser M.96, 271
Mauser M.1906, 278
Mauser m/38, 302
Mauser m/94, 301
Mosin-Nagant M1891/08, 379
Musket, 111, 199, 216, 256
M.39 rifle, 387
Remington carbine, 58
Remington M.1867, 266

## Machineguns

BAR M.1918 lmg, 387
BREN, 160
Colt M.29 hmg, 136
Hotchkiss Mle.1900, 276
KK62 lmg, 440
Lahti Model 26/32 lmg, 387
M2 hmg, 89
Madsen M.14 lmg, 120
Madsen M1923, 278
Madsen M.1919-1939 lmg, 69, 72
MG 3, 171
MG 62 (MG 42) 7.62 mm lmg, 98
m/21 lmg, 302
m/36 hmg, 302
m/37 lmg, 323
m/39 lmg, 324
m/58 lmg, 359
STEN, 160
Suomi M.31 SMG, 398

## Mortars

Hovea m/49, 98
M30, 166
MW 50 120 mm, 99
M-40, 440
M.29, 387
M.32 120 mm, 137
M.35 81 mm, 136
M125 SP 120 mm, 98
m/29, 301
m/41, 324
Rheinmetall 81 mm, 72
Tampella m/60, 440

## Anti-tank weapons

LAW, 172
M18 RR, 164
M2 "Carl Gustav", 171
M20 3.5" Bazooka, 89, 166
M56 106 mm RR, 99
M65 "Carl Gustav", 97
M-82, 440
Pansarvärnspjäs 1110, 359
P.I.A.T., 160
RB 53 Bantam, 365
SM-58-61 RR, 440
SS-11, 166
TOW BGM-71C, 98, 171

## Artillery

4 pdr minion, 199
6 pdr Field Gun, 111
12 pdr Field Gun, 44, 52, 216, 256
3 tom field gun, 114
4.5" Field Howitzer, 398
Bandkanon 1A (VK 155), 363
Bofors 4140 Field Howitzer, 365
Bofors Ivakan m/40, 360
Bofors M/1915 field gun, 120
Bofors m/39 howitzer, 302
Cockerill-Nordenfeldt M/1904 field gun, 120
Ehrhardt M.02 field gun, 58, 120
Krupp 15.5 cm howitzer, 66
Krupp field gun, 266
Krupp M/1887 84 mm field gun, 116
Krupp M.98/09 105 mm howitzer, 58
Krupp M.02 field gun, 271
Krupp M.07 field howitzer, 276
Krupp M.13 howitzer, 72
M1A1 (M1916) field gun , 398
M2A1 howitzer, 164
M.27 75 mm field gun, 137
M101 105 mm field howitzer, 99
M109 155 mm SP howitzer, 98, 171
M114 155 mm field howitzer, 88, 98
M115 203 mm heavy field howitzer, 93, 100
Putilov M.02 field gun, 388
Schneider Mle.1913 105 mm L, 388

45 pst K/32 AT, 398
Bofors M35 AT, 387
Bofors m/35 AT, 301
Bohler M35 AT, 72
Madsen M35 37 mm AT, 72
m/39 AT, 302
M/40 6 pdr AT, 160
m/43 AT, 323
Solothurn 20 mm AT, 72

Bofors m/36 AA, 99, 160, 311
Madsen 23 mm AA, 72

Honest John SSM, 93

Hamlet SAM (Redeye), 100
Hawk SAM, 94
Nike SAM, 94

## Armored Fighting Vehicles

Fiat M.16, 383
Humber Mk.II, 84
Humber Mk.IV, 84
Jeep, 164
LandRover, 171
Landsverk Lynx, 73
Landsverk L.120, 128
Landsverk L.181, 73
Landsverk L.185, 69, 128
Mercedes-Benz 230G, 172
Pansarbil m/31, 304
Pansarbil m/39-40 Lynx, 313
Staghound Mk.III, 84

Centurion Mk.3, 88
Centurion Mk.5, 5/2, 93, 97

## Sailing Warships

Knorr, Viking, 8
Longship, Varangian, 15
Longship, Viking, 19
Sloop, Baltic, 46
War Boat, Inguaeone, 3
War Boat, Norse, 6
Warship, Danish, 24

FRIGATE 18 guns, 207
GALLEON 34 guns, 207

FIRST RATE 126 gun ship of line, 212
FIRST RATE 110 gun ship of line, 36
FIRST RATE 110 gun ship of line, 217
FIRST RATE 96 gun ship of line, 32
FIRST RATE 92 gun ship of line, 235

SECOND RATE 86 gun ship of line, 212
SECOND RATE 84 gun ship of line, 45
SECOND RATE 84 gun ship of line, 49
SECOND RATE 80 gun ship of line, 218

THIRD RATE 78 gun ship of line, 36
THIRD RATE 74 gun ship of line, 45
THIRD RATE 74 gun ship of line, 263
THIRD RATE 72 gun ship of line, 212
THIRD RATE 70 gun ship of line, 237
THIRD RATE 64 gun ship of line, 238
THIRD RATE 62 gun ship of line, 218

FOURTH RATE 60 gun ship of line, 32
FOURTH RATE 52 gun ship of line, 36
FOURTH RATE 56 gun ship not line, 218
FOURTH RATE 48 gun ship not line, 212
FOURTH RATE 46 gun frigate, 49
FOURTH RATE 44 gun frigate, 113

FIFTH RATE 44 gun frigate, 238
FIFTH RATE 40 gun frigate, 218
FIFTH RATE 36 gun frigate, 45, 236
FIFTH RATE 32 gun frigate, 32
FIFTH RATE 32 gun frigate, 213, 238

SIXTH RATE 26 gun frigate, 36, 236
SIXTH RATE 22 gun frigate, 218
SIXTH RATE 18 gun frigate, 32

SLOOP 24 gun corvette, 45
SLOOP 20 gun corvette, 49
SLOOP 18 gun corvette, 263
SLOOP 16 gun corvette, 113

SLOOP 18 gun snow, 46
SLOOP 16 gun snow, 238
SLOOP 12 gun brig, 37

SLOOP 12 gun jakt, 238
SLOOP 8 gun sloop, 46
SLOOP 6 gun jagt, 46

BOMB 8 gun ketch, 238

HEMMEMA 34 guns, 250
POJAMA 14 guns, 251
TURUMA 30 guns, 250
UDEMA 13 guns, 250

GALLEY 12 guns, 251
GUNSLOOP 6 guns, 251
GUNYAWL 1 gun, 46, 251
MORTAR VESSEL 1 gun, 251

REVENUE CUTTER 10 gun, 49

MERCHANT East Indiaman, 244
MERCHANT galeas, 50
MERCHANT kof, 247
MERCHANT krayer, 234
MERCHANT packet, 245
MERCHANT West Coast galeas, 258
MERCHANT West Coast koster, 254